Of
Plymouth
Plantation

And first of the occasion, and inducements thereunto;
the which that I may truly unfold, I must begin at the
very root, and rise of the same. The which I shall
endeavor to manifest in a plain style; with singular
regard unto the simple truth in all things, at least as
near as my slender judgment can attain the same.

From the handwritten manuscript of
William Bradford

To which is added the complete text of:
*A Relation or Journal of the Beginning and Proceedings of the English
Plantation Settled at Plymouth in New England* (London, 1622).

Of Plymouth Plantation

Along with the full text of
the Pilgrims' journals for
their first year at Plymouth.

Edited by
Caleb H. Johnson

To order additional copies of this book, contact:
Xlibris Corporation
1-888-795-4274
www.Xlibris.com
Orders@Xlibris.com
32564

To Athena

Preface

This is a brand new edition of Governor William Bradford's classic history, *Of Plymouth Plantation*. The original handwritten manuscript is owned by the Massachusetts State Library in Boston. It was held by the Old South Church library in Boston for most of the 18th century, but the manuscript disappeared around the time of the Revolutionary War. It was rediscovered in 1855 in the Bishop of London's Library at Fulham Palace, and the first published edition was made the following year. After much ado, the manuscript was eventually returned to the United States in 1897. The previous year, a limited edition facsimile of the handwritten manuscript was published in Boston by Ward and Downey, Ltd., with an introduction by John Doyle. In 1912, the Massachusetts Historical Society published the first scholarly edition, a two-volume set edited by Worthington C. Ford. The first popular edition of the work, with modernized spelling and grammar, was edited by Samuel Eliot Morison and published in 1952.

One might ask why a new edition of Bradford is needed. The reason is quite simple: an enormous amount of historical information on the Pilgrims and early Plymouth has been discovered in the past half-century, since the last edition of Bradford's history was published. The popular Morison edition is oddly organized, taking Bradford's letters out of their context within the *History* and relegating them to inconvenient appendices. And there are also known transcription errors in the edition, which are here fixed for the first time.

This is also the first edition of William Bradford's history to also include the complete text of the Pilgrims' journals of their first year at Plymouth, first published in London in 1622 under the title, *A Relation or Journal of the Beginning and Proceedings of the English Plantation Settled at Plymouth in New England*. The journal contains an enormous amount of day-to-day detail that is left out by Bradford because, as he notes, "Many other smaller matters I omit, sundry of them having been already published in a journal made by one of the company; and some other passages of journeys and relations already published to which I refer those that are willing to know them more particularly."

In this edition, I have chosen to update the spelling to modern standards. So, for example, when Bradford writes "But aboute midnight they heard a hideous, & great crie, and their sentinel caled arme arme . . .," I have changed this to "But about midnight, they heard a hideous, and great cry, and their sentinel called 'Arm, arm,' . . ." Unlike Morison, I have avoided making significant changes to punctuation and paragraphing, and I have not taken any of Bradford's material out of order; instead, I have chosen to present Bradford's history in the order that he wrote it. The appendices that I have included herein consist of supplementary material not included by Bradford.

I used the 1896 facsimile edition of Bradford's handwritten manuscript to create my original draft, and then compared it against the Massachusetts Historical Society edition of 1912 to detect any mistakes or transcriptional discrepancies. My wife Anna then compared it to the 1952 Morison edition as a third check. In the case of any dispute, the facsimile of the handwritten manuscript was consulted again. I then went through and added footnotes. The edition that resulted was first printed in my self-published and now out-of-print 1173-page reference work, *The Complete Works of the Mayflower Pilgrims* (Vancouver, 2002). Since that time, I have reviewed the text yet again, made a few typographical corrections, updated and expanded the footnotes, and thus arrived at the present edition.

As an introduction to Bradford's history, I have chosen to use Cotton Mather's short biography of William Bradford, which he published in his 1702 book, *Magnalia Christi Americana*. It is the earliest biography of Bradford, written less than fifty years after his death. Following Bradford's History, I have chosen to include the complete text of the journals written by the Pilgrims during their first year at Plymouth. These journals were compiled together and published in London in 1622 under the title, *A Relation or Journal of the Beginning and Proceedings of the English Plantation Settled at Plymouth in New England*. They provide a day-by-day accounting of events during the first year at Plymouth. Whereas Bradford in his history focuses more on the larger and more notable events of business, politics and religion, the journals read more like a travel log, and go into everything from mundane weather observations to more significant detailed descriptions of voyages, trading explorations, and interactions with the Indians.

I have also included two appendices. The first is simply a selection of supplementary documents that relate to material discussed in Bradford's history. And the second appendix is a brief modern-day overview of what is known about each of the *Mayflower* passengers: home towns, ages, occupations, and any other brief tidbits that may be known about them. Those interested in more detailed biographies of the individual passengers should consult my book, *The Mayflower and Her Passengers*.

Acknowledgments

I would like to especially thank my wife Anna, who not only allowed me to steal a lot of time from her to work on this large project, but who also contributed greatly by helping me check and edit the material, and assisting with photography and image editing: all while pregnant with our daughter Athena.

Special thanks is due to artist Mike Haywood, who graciously allowed the use of his beautiful painting of the *Mayflower*, entitled "Prosperous Wind," to be used on the cover.

Thanks is due also to Peggy Baker of the Pilgrim Hall Museum, for assisting me in locating many valuable photographs from the museum's collections. These are the photos noted throughout the text as being from the Pilgrim Hall Museum in Plymouth, Massachusetts.

Contents

Of Plymouth Plantation: Book I

Of Plymouth Plantation: Book II

A Relation or Journal of the Beginnings and Proceedings of the English Plantation Settled at Plymouth in New England (London, 1622)

Appendix I: Supplementary Documents

Appendix II: The *Mayflower* Passengers

Illustrations

Introduction

"The life of William Bradford, Esq., Governor of Plymouth Colony."
Excerpt from *Magnalia Christi Americana*
By Cotton Mather (1702)

It has been a matter of some observation, that although Yorkshire be one of the largest shires in England; yet, for all the fires of martyrdom which were kindled in the days of Queen Mary, it afforded no more fuel than one poor Leaf, John Leaf, an apprentice, who suffered for the doctrine of the Reformation at the same time and stake with the famous John Bradford. But when the reign of Queen Elizabeth would not admit the Reformation of worship to proceed unto those degrees, which were proposed and pursued by no small number of the faithful in those days, Yorkshire was not the least of the shires in England that afforded suffering witnesses thereunto. The Churches there gathered were quickly molested with such a raging persecution, that if the spirit of separation in them did carry them unto a further extreme than it should have done, one blamable cause thereof will be found in the extremity of that persecution. Their troubles made that cold country too hot for them, so that they were under a necessity to seek a retreat in the Low Countries; and yet the watchful malice and fury of their adversaries rendered it almost impossible for them to find what they sought. For them to leave their native soil, their lands and their friends, and go into a strange place, where they must hear foreign language, and live meanly and hardly, and in other employments than that of husbandry, wherein they had been educated, these must needs have been such discouragements as could have been conquered by none, save those who "sought first the kingdom of God, and the righteousness thereof." But that which would have made these discouragements the more unconquerable unto an ordinary faith, was the terrible zeal of their enemies to guard all ports, and search all ships, that none of them should be carried off. I will not relate the sad things of this kind then seen and felt by this people God; but only exemplify those

15

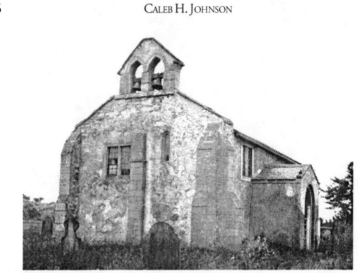

St. Helen's Church in Austerfield, co. York, from a late 19th century photograph.
The church has since been restored. William Bradford was baptized in this church
on 19 March 1589/90.

John Leaf and John Bradford about to be burned at the stake.
Woodcut from John Foxe's *Acts and Monuments* (London, 1576).

trials with one short story. Divers of this people having hired a Dutchman, then lying at Hull, to carry them over to Holland, he promised faithfully to take them in between Grimsby and Hull; but they coming to the place a day or two too soon, the appearance of such a multitude alarmed the officers of the town adjoining, who came with a great body of soldiers to seize upon them. Now it happened that one boat full of men had been carried abroad, while the women were yet in a bark that lay aground in a creek at low water. The Dutchman perceiving the storm that was thus beginning ashore, swore by the sacrament that he would stay no longer for any of them; and so taking the advantage of a fair wind then blowing, he put out to sea for Zealand. The women thus left near Grimly-common, bereaved of their husbands, who had been hurried from them, and forsaken of their neighbors, of whom none durst in this fright stay with them, were a very rueful spectacle; some crying for fear, some shaking for cold, all dragged by troops of armed and angry men from one Justice to another, till not knowing what to do with them, they even dismissed them to shift as well as they could for themselves. But by their singular afflictions, and by their Christian behaviors, the cause for which they exposed themselves did gain considerably. In the mean time, the men at sea found reason to be glad that their families were not with them, for they were surprised with an horrible tempest, which held them for fourteen days together, in seven whereof they saw not sun, moon or star, but were driven upon the coast of Norway. The mariners often despaired of life, and once with doleful shrieks gave over all, as thinking the vessel was foundered: but the vessel rose again, and when the mariners with sunk hearts often cried out, "We sink! We sink!" the passengers, without such distraction of mind, even while the water was running into their mouth and ears, would carefully shout, "Yet, Lord, thou canst save! Yet, Lord, thou canst save!" And the Lord accordingly brought them at last safe unto their desired haven: and not long after helped their distressed relations thither after them, where indeed they found upon almost all accounts a new world, but a world in which they found that they must live like strangers and pilgrims.

Among those devout people was our William Bradford, who was born Anno. 1588[1], in an obscure village called Austerfield, where the people were as unacquainted with the Bible, as the Jews do seem to have been with part of it in the days of Josiah; a most ignorant and licentious people, and like unto their priest. Here, and in some places, he had a comfortable inheritance

---

[1]   William Bradford was baptized at Austerfield on 19 March 1589/90.

left of his honest parents, who died while he was yet a child[2], and cast him on the education, first of his grandparents, and then if his uncles, who devoted him, like his ancestors, unto the affairs of husbandry. Soon a long sickness kept him, as he would afterwards thankfully say, from the vanities of youth, and made him the fitter for what he was afterwards to undergo. When he was about a dozen year old, the reading of the Scriptures began to cause great impression upon him; and those impressions were assisted and improved, when he came to enjoy Mr. Richard Clyfton's illuminating ministry, not far from his abode; he was then also further befriended, by being brought into the company and fellowship of such as were then called professors; though the young man that brought him into it did after become a profane and wicked apostate. Nor could the wrath of his uncles, nor the scoff of his neighbors, now turned upon him, as one of the Puritans, divert him from his pious inclinations.

At last, beholding how fearfully the evangelical and apostolical church from whereinto the churches of the primitive times were cast by the good spirit of God, had been deformed by the apostasy of the succeeding times; and what little progress the Reformation had yet made in many parts of Christendom towards its recovery, he set himself by reading, by discourse, by prayer, to learn whether it was not his duty to withdraw from the communion of the parish-assemblies, and engage with some society of the faithful, that should keep close unto the written word of God, as the rule of their worship. And after many distresses of mind concerning it, he took up a very deliberate and understanding resolution, of doing so; which resolution he cheerfully prosecuted, although the provoked rage of his friends tried all the ways imaginable to reclaim him from it, unto all whom his answer was:

> Were I like to endanger my life, or consume my estate by any
> ungodly courses, your counsels to me were very seasonable; but
> you know that I have been diligent and provident in my calling,
> and not only desirous to augment what I have, but also to enjoy
> it in your company; to part from which will be as great a cross as
> can befall me, Nevertheless. To keep a good conscience, and walk
> in such a way as God has prescribed in his Word, is a thing which
> I must prefer before you all, and above life it self. Wherefore,

---

[2]   Bradford's father died when he was one year old, and his mother died when he
       was seven.

since 'tis for a good cause that I am like to suffer the disasters
which you lay before me, you have no cause to be either angry
with me, or sorry for me; yes, I am not only willing to part with
everything that is dear to me in this world for this cause, but I am
also thankful that God has given me an heart to do, and will
accept me so to suffer for him.

Some lamented him, some derided him, all dissuaded him: nevertheless,
the more they did it, the more fixed he was in his purpose to seek the
ordinances of the gospel, where they should be dispensed with most of the
commanded purity; and the sudden deaths of the chief relations which thus
lay at him, quickly after convinced him what a folly it had been to have
quitted his profession, in expectation of any satisfaction from them. So to
Holland he attempted a removal.

Having with a great company of Christians hired a ship to transport
them for Holland, the master perfidiously betrayed them into the hands of
those persecutors, who rifled and ransacked their goods, and clapped their
persons into prison at Boston, where they lay for a month together. But Mr.
Bradford being a young man of about eighteen, was dismissed sooner than
the rest, so that within a while he had opportunity with some others to get
over to Zealand, through perils, both by land and sea not inconsiderable;
where he was not long ashore ere a viper seized on his hand (that is, an
officer) who carried him unto the magistrates, unto whom an envious
passenger had accused him as having fled out of England. When the
magistrates understood the true cause of his coming thither, they were well
satisfied with him; and so he repaired joyfully unto his brethren at
Amsterdam, where the difficulties to which he afterwards stooped in learning
and serving a Frenchman at the working of silks, were abundantly
compensated by the delight wherewith he sat under the shadow of our
Lord, in his purely dispensed ordinances. At the end of two years, he did,
being of age to do it, convert his estate in England into money; but setting
up for himself, he found some of his designs by the providence of God
frowned upon, which he judged a correction bestowed by God upon him
for certain decays of internal piety, whereinto he had fallen; the consumption
of his estate he thought came to prevent a consumption in his virtue. But
after he had resided in Holland about half a score years, he was one of those
who bore a part in that hazardous and generous enterprise of removing into
New England, with part of the English church at Leiden, where, at their first
landing, his dearest consort accidentally falling overboard, was drowned in

the harbor; and the rest of his days were spent in the services, and the temptation, of that American wilderness.

Here was Mr. Bradford, in the year 1621, unanimously chosen the governor of the plantation: the difficulties whereof were such, that if he had not been a person of more than ordinary piety, wisdom and courage, he must have sunk under them. He had, with a laudable industry, been laying up a treasure of experiences, and he had now occasion to use it: indeed, nothing but an experienced man could have been suitable to the necessities of the people. The potent nations of the Indians, into whose country they were come, would have cut them off, if the blessing of God upon his conduct had not quelled them; and if his prudence, justice and moderation had not over-ruled them, they had been ruined by their own distempers. One specimen of his demeanor is to this day particularly spoken of. A company of young fellows that were newly arrived, were very unwilling to comply with the governor's order for working abroad on the public account; and therefore on Christmas-day, when he had called upon them, they excused themselves, with a pretence that it was against their conscience to work such a day. The governor gave them no answer, only that he would spare them till they were better informed; but by and by found them all at play in the street, sporting themselves with various diversions; whereupon commanding the instruments of their games to be taken from them, he effectually gave them to understand, that it was against his conscience that they should play whilst other were at work: and this gentle reproof put a final stop to all such disorders for the future.

For two years together after the beginning of the colony, whereof he was now governor, the poor people had a great experiment of "man's not living by bread alone;" for when they were left all together without one morsel of bread for many months one after another, still the good providence of God relieved them, and supplied them, and this for the most part out of the sea. In this low condition of affairs, there was no little exercise for the prudence and patience of the governor, who cheerfully bore his part in all: and, that industry might not flag, he quickly set himself to settle propriety among the new-planters; foreseeing that while the whole country labored upon a common stock, the husbandry and business of the plantation could not flourish, as Plato and others long since dreamed that it would, if a community were established. Certainly, if the spirit which dwelt in the old puritans, had not inspired these new-planters, they had sunk under the burden of these difficulties; but our Bradford had a double portion of that spirit.

The plantation was quickly thrown into a storm that almost overwhelmed it, by the unhappy action of a minister sent over from England by the adventures concerned for the plantation; but by the blessing of Heaven on the conduct of the governor, they weathered out that storm. Only the adventures hereupon breaking to pieces, threw up all their concernments with the infant-colony; whereof they gave this as one reason, "That the planters dissembled with His Majesty and their friends in their petition, wherein they declared for a church-discipline, agreeing with the French and others of the reforming churches in Europe." Whereas 'twas now urged, that they had admitted into their communion a person who at his admission utterly renounced the Churches of England, (which person, by the way, was that very man who had made the complaints against them,) and therefore, though they denied the name of Brownists, yet they were the thing. In answer hereunto, the very words written by the governor were these:

> Whereas you tax us with dissembling about the French discipline, you do us wrong, for we both hold and practice the discipline of the French and other Reformed Churches (as they have published the same in the Harmony of Confessions) according to our means, in effect and substance. But whereas would tie up to the French discipline in every circumstance, you derogate from the liberty in Christ Jesus. The Apostle Paul would have none follow him in anything, but wherein he follows Christ; much less ought any Christian or church in the world to do it. The French may err, and other churches may err, and doubtless do it many circumstances. That honor therefore belongs only to the infallible word of God, and pure Testament of Christ, to be propounded and followed as the only rule and pattern for direction herein to all churches and Christians. And it is too great arrogancy for any man or church to think that he or they have so sounded the World of God unto the bottom, as precisely to set down the church's discipline without error in substance or circumstance, that no other without blame may digress or differ in anything from the same. And it is not difficult to show that Reformed Churches differ in many circumstances among themselves.

By which words it appears how far he was free from that rigid spirit of separation, which broke to pieces the Separatists themselves in the Low Countries, unto the great scandal of the reforming churches. He was indeed a person of a well-tempered spirit, or else it had been scarce possible for him to have kept the affairs of Plymouth in so good a temper for thirty-seven years together; in every one of which he was chosen their governor, except the three years wherein Mr. Winslow, and the two years wherein Mr. Prince, at the choice of the people, took a turn with him.

The leader of a people in a wildness had need be a Moses; and if a Moses had not led the people of Plymouth Colony, when this worthy person was their governor, the people had never with so much unanimity and importunity still called to lead them. Among many instances thereof, let this one piece of self-denial be told for a memorial; of him, wheresoever this History shall be considered: The Patent of the Colony was taken in his name, running in these terms: "To William Bradford, his heirs, associates, and assigns." But when the number of the freemen was much increased, and many new townships erected, the General Court there desired of Mr. Bradford, that he would make a surrender of the same into their hands, which he willingly and presently assented unto, and confirmed it according to their desire by his hand and seal, reserving no more for himself than was his proportion, with others, by agreement. But as he found the providence of Heaven many ways recompensing his many acts of self-denial, so he gave this testimony to the faithfulness of the divine promises: "That he had forsaken friends, houses and lands for the sake of the gospel, and the Lord gave them him again." Here he prospered in his estate; and besides a worthy son which he had by a former wife, he had also two sons and a daughter by another, whom he married in this land.

He was a person for study as well as action: and hence, notwithstanding the difficulties through which he passed in his youth, he attained unto a notable skill in languages: the Dutch tongue he could also manage; the Latin and the Greek he had mastered; but the Hebrew he most of all studied, "Because," he said, "He would see with his own eyes the ancient oracles of God in their native beauty." He was also well skilled in History, in Antiquity, and in Philosophy; and for Theology he became so versed in it, that he was an irrefragable disputant against the errors, especially those of Anabaptism, which with trouble he saw rising in his colony; wherefore he wrote some significant things for the confutation of those errors. But the crown of all was his holy, prayerful, watchful, and fruitful walk with God, wherein he was very exemplary.

At length he fell into an indisposition of body, which rendered him unhealthy for a whole winter; and as the spring advanced, his health yet more declined; yet he felt himself not what he could counted sick, till one day; in the night after which, the God of heaven so filled his mind with ineffable consolations, that he seemed little short of Paul, rapt up unto the unutterable entertainments of Paradise. The next morning he told his friends, "That the good Spirit of God had given him a pledge of his happiness in another world, and the first-fruit of his eternal glory;" and on the day following he died, May 9, 1657, in the 69th year of his age, lamented by all the colonies of New England, as common blessing and father to them all.

Of Plymouth Plantation
Book 1

Of plimoth plantation

And first of y occasion, and Indusments ther vnto; the which
that y may truly vnfould, y must begine at y very roote & rise
of y same. The which y shall endevor to manefest in a plaine
Stile; with singuler regard vnto y simple trueth in all things,
at least as near as my slender Judgmente can attaine
the same.

·1· Chapter

It is well known unto the godly, and judicious, how ever since the first breaking out of the light of the gospel, in our honorable nation of England (which was the first of nations, whom the Lord adorned therewith, after the gross darkness of popery which had covered and overspread the Christian world) what wars, and oppositions ever since Satan hath raised, maintained, and continued against the saints, from time, to time, in one sort, or other. Sometimes by bloody death and cruel torments, other whiles imprisonments, banishments, and other hard usages: as being loath his kingdom should go down, the truth prevail; and the churches of God revert to their ancient purity; and recover their primitive order, liberty, and beauty. But when he could not prevail by these means, against the main truths of the gospel, but that they began to take rooting in many places; being watered with the blood of the martyrs and blessed from Heaven with a gracious increase. He then began to take him to his ancient stratagems, used of old against the first Christians: that when by the bloody, and barbarous persecutions of the heathen emperors, he could not stop, and subvert the course of the gospel; but that it speedily overspread, with a wonderful celerity, the then best known parts of the world. He then began to sow errors, heresies, and wonderful dissensions amongst the professors themselves (working upon their pride, and ambition, with other corrupt passions, incident to all mortal men; yea to

27

Though I am growne aged, yet I haue had a longing
desire, to see with my owne eyes, something of that most
ancient Language, and holy tongue, in which the Law,
and oracles of God were write; and in which God,
and angels spake to the holy patriarks, of old
time; and what names were giuen to things,
from the creation. And though I canot
attaine to much herein, yet I am refreshed, to haue seen some glimpse hereof;
(as moyses saw thᵉ Land of ca=
nan afarr of) my aime and
desire is, to see how the words,
and phrases lye in the
holy texte; and to
discerne somewhat
of the same,
for my owne
contente.

חֶסֶד יְהוָה מָלְאָה הָאָרֶץ The earth is full of ye mercie of yehouah.	שָׁם פָּחֲדוּ פָחַד לֹא הָיָה פָחַד Ther they feared a fear, wher no fear was
וַיַּרְא אֱלֹהִים כִּי טוֹב And God saw that it was good.	הוֹן יוֹסִיף רֵעִים רַבִּים Riches gather many friends
לֹא טוֹב הֱיוֹת הָאָדָם לְבַדּוֹ It is not good that man should be alone.	רַע רַע יֹאמַר הַקּוֹנֶה It is naught, it is naught, saith the buyer.
כַּבֵּד אֶת־אָבִיךָ וְאֶת אִמֶּךָ honour thy father, and thy mother	מָצָא אִשָּׁה מָצָא טוֹב he that findeth a wife findeth good
וּשְׂמַח מֵאֵשֶׁת נְעוּרֶיךָ And rejoyce with the wife of thy youth	וַאֲנִי בְּרֹב חַסְדְּךָ אָבוֹא בֵיתֶךָ But I in multitude of thy mercies, will come into thy house.
זְנוּת וְיַיִן וְתִירוֹשׁ יִקַּח־לֵב whordome, and wine, a new wine take away the harte	וְהָיָה כְּעֵץ שָׁתוּל עַל־פַּלְגֵי מָיִם And he shall be as a tree planted by the brooks of waters.
קוֹל דְּמֵי אָחִיךָ צֹעֲקִים אֵלַי The voyce of thy brothers blood crieth unto me.	חַכְמוֹת נָשִׁים בָּנְתָה בֵיתָהּ A wise woman buildeth her house
…y Iudge the דָּן דִּין עָנִי	נְקִי כַפַּיִם וּבַר לֵבָב Innocente in hands, & pure in hart

William Bradford practicing his Hebrew on a preliminary page of his *History*.

the saints themselves in some measure) by which woeful effects followed; as not only bitter contentions, and heartburnings, schisms, with other horrible confusions: but Satan took occasion and advantage thereby to foist in a number of vile ceremonies, with many unprofitable canons, and decrees which have since been as snares, to many poor, and peaceable souls, even to this day. So as in the ancient times, the persecutions by the heathen, and their emperors, was not greater than of the Christians one against other.[3] The Arians, and other their complices, against the orthodox and true Christians. As witnesseth Socrates in his second book.[4] His words are these:

> The violence truly (saith he) was no less than that of old, practiced towards the Christians when they were compelled and drawn to sacrifice to idols; for many endured sundry kinds of torment, often rackings, and dismembering of their joints; confiscating of their goods; some bereaved of their native soil; others departed this life under the hands of the tormentor, and some died in banishment, and never saw their country again, etc.

The like method Satan hath seemed to hold in these later times, since the truth began to spring and spread after the great defection made by Antichrist that man of sin. For to let pass the infinite examples in sundry nations, and several places of the world, and instance in our own: when as that old serpent could not prevail by those fiery flames, and other his cruel tragedies which he (by his instruments) put in ure, everywhere in the days of

---

[3]   For a more detailed account of early church history, and of the differences between the various religious denominations, as seen by Bradford, see Bradford's *A Dialogue, Or The Sum of a Conference Between Some Young Men Born in New England, and Sundry Ancient Men That Came Out of Holland and Old England* (1648) and his *A Dialogue Or Third Conference, Between Some Young Men Born in New England, and some Ancient Men, Which came out of Holland and Old England, Concerning the Church* (n.d., cir. 1652).

[4]   Lib: 2, Chap. 22. (Bradford). Socrates Scholasticus (379-440 AD), Greek ecclesiastical historian. The quote is taken from Meredith Hanmer, editor and translator, *The Ancient Ecclesiastical Histories of the First Six Hundred Years After Christ* (London, 1577).

Queen Mary[5], and before. He then began another kind of war, and went more closely to work, not only to oppugn, but even to ruinate and destroy the kingdom of Christ, by more secret and subtle means: by kindling the flames of contention, and sowing the seeds of discord, and bitter enmity amongst the professors (and seeming reformed) themselves. For when he could not prevail (by the former means) against the principal doctrines of faith, he bent his force against the holy discipline, and outward regiment of the kingdom of Christ, by which those holy doctrines should be conserved, and true piety maintained amongst the saints, and people of God.

Mr. Foxe recordeth[6], how that besides those worthy martyrs and confessors which were burned in Queen Mary's days and otherwise tormented "many (both students, and others) fled out of the land to the number of 800. And became several congregations: at Wesel, Frankfort, Basel, Emden, Markpurge, Strasbourg, and Geneva, etc." Amongst whom (but especially those at Frankfort) began that bitter war of contention, and persecution about the ceremonies[7], and service-book[8], and other popish and antichristian

---

[5]   Queen Mary I (1516-1558). Her reign began in 1553 at the death of Edward VI. She returned England to the Catholic church and heavily persecuted the Protestants, executing about 300 and earning the nickname "Bloody Mary." She died in 1558 and was succeeded by Queen Elizabeth I.

[6]   Acts, & Mon: Pag. 1587, Edition 2. (Bradford). John Foxe (1516-1587), *The Second Volume of the Ecclesiastical History, Containing the Acts and Monuments of the Martyrs* (London, 1576), page 1587.

[7]   Bradford lists some of the offensive ceremonies in his *Third Conference*: ". . . they stood stiffly to maintain a company of vain ceremonies, profitable for nothing (except to maintain their courts, and fill their catch-poll purses) such as the cross in baptism, kneeling at the Lord's Supper, wearing the surplice, keeping of Holy Days, bishoping or confirming of children, etc."

[8]   The *Book of Common Prayer*. Edward Winslow added in his *New England's Salamander* (London, 1645): "I often said the laws of England, to take the body of them, are too unwieldy for our weak condition: besides, there were some things supported by them which we came from thence to avoid, as the hierarchy, the cross in baptism, the holy days, the *Book of Common Prayer*, etc." Thomas Morton noted in his *New English Canaan* (Amsterdam, 1637) that the Pilgrims believed "[t]hat the *Book of Common Prayer* is an idol, and all that use it, idolaters."

Archbishop Thomas Cranmer being burned at the stake at Oxford, on 21 March 1556, during the reign of Queen Mary. His grandnephew, George Cranmer, was a co-worker of *Mayflower* passenger William Brewster when they worked for Secretary of State William Davison under Queen Elizabeth I. Woodcut from John Foxe's *Acts and Monuments* (London, 1576).

stuff: the plague of England to this day, (which are like the high places in Israel, which the prophets cried out against, and were their ruin). Which the better part sought (according to the purity of the gospel) to root out, and utterly to abandon. And the other part (under veiled pretences) for their own ends, and advancements, sought as stiffly, to continue, maintain, and defend: as appeareth by the discourse thereof published in print, Anno. 1575: (a book that deserves better to be known, and considered).[9]

The one side labored to have the right worship of God, and discipline of Christ, established in the church, according to the simplicity of the gospel: without the mixture of men's inventions; and to have and to be ruled by the laws of God's Word, dispensed in those offices, and by those officers of Pastors, Teachers, and Elders, etc. according to the Scriptures.[10] The other party (though under many colors, and pretences) endeavored to have the Episcopal dignity (after the popish manner) with their large power, and jurisdiction still retained; with all those courts, canons, and ceremonies, together with all such livings, revenues, and subordinate officers, with other such means, as formerly upheld their antichristian greatness, and enabled them with lordly, and tyrannous power, to persecute the poor servants of God. This contention was so great, as neither the honor of God, the common persecution; nor the mediation of Mr. Calvin[11], and other worthies of the Lord, in those places could prevail with those thus Episcopally-minded; but they proceeded by all means to disturb the peace of this poor persecuted church: even so far as to charge (very unjustly, and ungodlily; yet prelate-like) some of their chief opposers, with rebellion, and high treason against the Emperor, and other such crimes.

---

9   William Whittingham, *A Brief Discourse of the Troubles Begun at Frankfort in Germany, anno Domini 1554* (Zurich, 1575).

10   Thomas Morton, in his *New English Canaan* (Amsterdam 1637) recorded his observations of the Pilgrim's church structure: "The Church of the Separatists, is governed by pastors, elders, and deacons . . . These are all public preachers. There is amongst these people a deaconess made of the sisters, that uses her gifts at home in an assembly of her sex, by way of repetition, or exhortation . . ."

11   John Calvin (1509-1564), one of the primary religious figures of the Protestant reformation. The Pilgrims frequently reference his writings, and owned many of his works.

And this contention died not with Queen Mary, nor was left beyond the seas, but at her death these people returning into England under gracious Queen Elizabeth[12], many of them being preferred to bishoprics, and other promotions, according to their aims, and desires: that inveterate hatred against the holy discipline of Christ in His church hath continued to this day: insomuch that for fear it should prevail, all plots, and devices have been used to keep it out, incensing the Queen, and State against it as dangerous for the commonwealth; and that it was most needful that the fundamental points of religion should be preached in those ignorant, and superstitious times; and to win the weak and ignorant they might retain divers harmless ceremonies, and though it were to be wished that divers things were reformed, yet this was not a season for it. And many the like to stop the mouths of the more godly, to bring them on to yield to one ceremony after another, and one corruption after another; by these wiles beguiling some, and corrupting others till at length they began to persecute all the zealous professors in the land (though they knew little what this discipline meant) both by word, and deed, if they would not submit to their ceremonies, and become slaves to them, and their popish trash, which have no ground in the Word of God, but are relics of that man of sin. And the more the light of the gospel grew, the more they urged their subscriptions to these corruptions. So as (notwithstanding all their former pretences, and fair colors) they whose eyes God had not justly blinded, might easily see whereto these things tended. And to cast contempt the more upon the sincere servants of God, they opprobriously, and most injuriously, gave unto, and imposed upon them, that name of Puritans; which is said the Novatians (out of pride) did assume and take unto themselves[13]: and lamentable it is to see the effects which have followed; religion hath been disgraced, the godly grieved, afflicted, persecuted, and many exiled, sundry have lost their lives in prisons, and other ways. On the other hand, sin hath been countenanced; ignorance, profaneness, and atheism increased, and the papists encouraged to hope again for a day.

---

[12]   Queen Elizabeth I (1533-1603). Her reign began in 1558; she returned the country to the Church of England and away from the Catholic church, and did not heavily persecute Protestants. The "gracious" Queen Elizabeth died in 1603, and was succeeded by King James I, who was much less tolerant of Protestantism.

[13]   Eus: lib: 6. Chap. 42 (Bradford). Eusibius (260-340 AD), from Meredith Hanmer, editor and translator, *The Ancient Ecclesiastical Histories of the First Six Hundred Years After Christ* (London, 1577).

A late observation, as it were
by the way, worthy to be
noted

Full little did I think, that the downfall of the Bishops, with their courts, cannons, and ceremonies, etc., had been so near, when I first began these scribbled writings (which was about the year 1630), and so pieced up at times of leisure afterward, or that I should have lived, to have seen, or heard of the same; but it is the Lord's doing, and ought to be marvelous in our eyes! Every plant which mine Heavenly Father hath not planted, (saith our Savior) shall be rooted up. Mat. 15:13. I have snared thee, and thou art taken, O Babel [Bishops] and thou wast not aware; thou art found, and also caught, because thou hast striven against the Lord. Jer. 50:24. But will they needs strive? against the truth, against the servants of god, what, and against the Lord Himself? Do they provoke the Lord to anger? Are they stronger than he? 1 Cor: 10:22. No, no, they have met with their match. Behold, I come unto thee, O proud man, saith the Lord God of Hosts; for thy day is come, even the time that I will visit thee. Jer. 50:31. May not the people of God now say, (and these poor people among the rest), the Lord, hath brought forth our righteousness; come let us declare in Zion the work of the Lord our God. Jer. 51:10. Let all flesh be still before the Lord; for he is raised up out of His Holy place. Zach. 2:13.

In this case, these poor people may say (among the thousands of Israel), "When the Lord brought against the captivity of Zion, we were like them in that dream." Psalms 126:1. "The Lord hath done great things for us, whereof we rejoice." v.3 "They that sow in tears, shall reap in joy. They went weeping, and carried precious seed, but they shall return with joy, and bring their sheaves." v.5-6.

Do you not now see the fruits of your labors, O all ye servants of the Lord? that have suffered for His truth, and have been faithful witnesses of the same, and ye little handful amongst the rest, the least amongst the thousands of Israel? You have not only had a seed time, but many of you have seen the joyful harvest. Should you not then rejoice? Yea, and again rejoice, and say Halleluiah, salvation, and glory, and honor, and power, be to the Lord our God; for true, and righteous are His judgments. Rev. 19:1,2.

But thou wilt ask what is the matter, what is done? Why, art thou a stranger, in Israel, that thou shouldest not know what is done? Are not those Jebusites overcome, that have vexed the people of Israel so long, even holding Jerusalem till David's days, and been as thorns in their sides, so many ages; and now began to scorn that any David should meddle with them; they began to fortify their tower, as that of the old Babylonians; but those proud Anakimes are thrown down, and their glory laid in the dust. The tyrannous bishops are ejected, their courts dissolved, their cannons forceless, their service cashiered, their ceremonies useless and despised; their plots for popery prevented, and all their superstitions discarded, and returned to Rome from whence they came, and the monuments of idolatry rooted out of the land. And the proud and profane supporters, and cruel defenders of these (as bloody papists and wicked Athiests, and their malignant consorts) marvelously overthrown. And are not these great things? Who can deny it?

But who hath done it? Who, even he that sitteth on the white horse, who is called faithful, and true, and judgeth, and fighteth righteously. Rev. 19:11. Whose garments are dipped in blood, and his name was called the Word of God. v.13. For he shall rule them with a rod of iron; for it is he that treadeth the winepress of the fierceness, and wrath of God Almighty! And he hath upon his garment, and upon his thigh, a name written, The King of Kings, and Lord of Lords. v.15,16.

Halleluiah. Anno Dom: 1646.

This made that holy man Mr. Perkins[14] cry out in his exhortation to repentance, upon Zeph. 2: Religion (saith he) hath been amongst us this 35 years; but the more it is published, the more it is contemned, and reproached of many, etc.: thus not profaneness, nor wickedness, but religion itself is a byword, a mockingstock; and a matter of reproach; so that in England at this day, the man, or woman that begins to profess religion, and to serve God, must resolve with himself to sustain mocks, and injuries even as though he lived amongst the enemies of religion. And this common experience hath confirmed, and made too apparent.

But that I may come more near my intendment: when as by the travail, and diligence of some godly, and zealous preachers, and God's blessing on their labors; as in other places of the land, so in the North parts, many became enlightened by the Word of God; and had their ignorance and sins discovered unto them, and began by His grace to reform their lives, and make conscience of their ways. The work of God was no sooner manifest in them; but presently they were both scoffed, and scorned by the profane multitude, and the ministers urged with the yoke of subscription, or else must be silenced: and the poor people were so vexed with apparitors, and pursuants, and the commissary courts, as truly their affliction was not small[15]; which notwithstanding they bore sundry years with much patience, till they were occasioned (by the continuance, and increase of these

---

[14] Page 421. (Bradford). William Perkins (1558-1602) from *Godly and Learned Exposition of Christ's Sermon on the Mount* (Cambridge, 1618). See also Perkins' *A Faithful and Plain Exposition Upon the First Two Verses of the Second Chapter of Zephaniah* (London, 1606). William Perkins was a popular and frequently referenced author amongst the Pilgrims.

[15] A number of records have been found in ecclesiastical and court records relating to *Mayflower* passengers. For court records relating to William Brewster, see Henry Dexter, *England and Holland of the Pilgrims* (London 1906), pg. 401-402. For records on Christopher Martin and Solomon Prower, see R.J. Carpenter, *Christopher Martin, Great Burstead and the Mayflower* (Chelmsford, 1993), pg. 4-8. For records on Mrs. James Chilton, and Moses Fletcher, see Michael Paulick, "The 1609-1610 Excommunications of *Mayflower* Pilgrims Mrs. Chilton and Moses Fletcher," *New England Historical and Genealogical Register*, 153(October 1999): 407-412. See also Michael Paulick, "Richard Masterson, John Ellis, Christopher Verrall and the Sandwich Separatists 1603-1620," *New England Historical and Genealogical Register* 154 (July 2000):353-369.

troubles, and other means which the Lord raised up in those days) to see further into things by the light of the Word of God. How not only these base and beggarly ceremonies were unlawful; but also that the lordly, and tyrannous power of the prelates, ought not to be submitted unto; which thus (contrary to the freedom of the gospel) would load and burden men's consciences; and by their compulsive power make a profane mixture of persons, and things in the worship of God. And that their office, and callings; courts, and canons, etc. were unlawful, and antichristian; being such as have no warrant in the Word of God; but the same that were used in popery, and still retained. Of which a famous author thus writeth in his Dutch commentaries[16]:

> At the coming of King James[17] into England: the new king (saith he) found there established the reformed religion, according to the reformed religion of King Edward the 6, retaining, or keeping still the spiritual state of the bishops, etc.: after the old manner, much varying, and differing from the reformed churches, in Scotland, France, and the Netherlands, Emden, Geneva, etc., whose reformation is cut, or shapen much nearer the first Christian churches, as it was used in the Apostles' times.[18]

So many therefore (of these professors) as saw the evil of these things (in these parts) and whose hearts the Lord had touched with heavenly zeal for His truth; they shook off this yoke of antichristian bondage: and as the Lord's free people, joined themselves (by a covenant of the Lord) into a church estate, in the fellowship of the gospel to walk in all His ways, made known, or to be made known unto them (according to their best endeavors) whatsoever it should cost them, the Lord assisting them: and that it cost them something this ensuing history will declare.

---

[16]   Em: meter: lib: 25. fol. 119 (Bradford). Emanuel van Meteren, *General History of the Netherlands* (1608), lib.25, fol. 119.

[17]   King James I (1556-1625). He reigned from the death of Queen Elizabeth I in 1603, until his death in 1625. He was succeeded by Charles I.

[18]   The reformed church shapen much nearer the primitive pattern than England, for they cashered the Bishops with all their courts, cannons, and ceremonies, at the first; and left them amongst the popish trash to which they pertained. (Bradford).

These people became 2 distinct bodies, or churches; and in regard of distance of place did congregate severally; for they were of sundry towns and villages, some in Nottinghamshire, some of Lincolnshire and some of Yorkshire, where they border nearest together. In one of these churches (besides others of note) was Mr. John Smith[19], a man of able gifts, and a good preacher; who afterwards was chosen their pastor. But these afterwards falling into some errors in the Low Countries, there (for the most part) buried themselves, and their names.

But in this other church (which must be the subject of our discourse) besides other worthy men, was Mr. Richard Clyfton[20] a grave and

---

[19] John Smith of Christ's College, Cambridge. He preached in Lincoln before removing to Gainsborough about 1605, where he began a Separatist congregation. Bradford, in his *First Conference*, noted that John Smith was: "an eminent man in his time, and a good preacher and of other good parts; but his inconstancy, and unstable judgment, and being so suddenly carried away with things did soon overthrow him . . . . He was some time pastor to a company of honest and godly men which came with him out of England, and pitched at Amsterdam. He first fell into some errors about the Scriptures, and so into some opposition with Mr. [Francis] Johnson, who had been his tutor, and the church there. But he was convinced of them by the pains and faithfulness of Mr. Johnson and Mr. [Henry] Ainsworth, and revoked them; but afterwards was drawn away by some of the Dutch Anabaptists, who finding him to be a good scholar and unsettled, they easily misled the most of his people, and other of them scattered away. He lived not many years after, but died there of a consumption, to which he was inclined before he came out of England. His and his people's condition may be an object of pity for after times." See also Henry Dexter, *The True Story of John Smyth, the Se-Baptist, As Told By Himself and His Contemporaries* (Boston: Lee and Shepard, 1881).

[20] Richard Clyfton, Rector of Babworth. Bradford, in his *First Conference*, reports that Richard Clyfton "[w]as a grave and fatherly old man when he came first into Holland, having a great white beard; and pity it was that such a reverend old man should be forced to leave his country, and at those years to go into exile. But it was his lot; and he bore it patiently. Much good had he done in the country where he lived, and converted many to God by his faithful and painful ministry, both in preaching and catechizing. Sound and orthodox he always was, and so continued to his end. He belonged to the church at Leiden; but being settled at Amsterdam, and thus aged, he was loath to remove any more; and so when they removed, he was dismissed to them there, and there remained until he died." Richard Clyfton, shortly after the Pilgrims removed to Leiden,

reverend preacher; who by his pains and diligence had done much good, and under God had been a means of the conversion of many: and also that famous and worthy man Mr. John Robinson[21], who afterwards was their pastor for many years, till the Lord took him away by death. Also Mr. William Brewster[22] a reverend man, who afterwards was chosen an elder of the church and lived with them till old age.

But after these things they could not long continue in any peaceable condition; but were hunted, and persecuted on every side, so as their former

---

authored a book entitled *The Plea for Infants and Elder People, Concerning their Baptism, Or, A Process of Passages Betwixt M. John Smyth and Richard Clyfton, wherein, first is proved, that the baptizing of infants of believers, is an ordinance of God, secondly, that the re-baptizing of such, as have been formerly baptized in the apostate churches of Christians, is utterly unlawful, also, the reasons and objects to the contrary, answered.* (Amsterdam: Gyles Thorp, 1610).

21   John Robinson was the pastor of the Pilgrims' church while they were in Leiden, Holland. Bradford, in his *First Conference*, reports that Robinson "[w]as pastor of that famous church of Leiden, in Holland; a man not easily paralleled for all things, . . . [H]e was a man learned and of solid judgment, and of a quick and sharp wit, so was he also of a tender conscience, and very sincere in all his ways, a hater of hypocrisy and dissimulation, and would be very plain with his best friends. He was very courteous, affable, and sociable in his conversation, and towards his own people especially. He was an acute and expert disputant, very quick and ready, and had much bickering with the Arminians, who stood more in fear of him than any of the University [of Leiden]. He was never satisfied in himself until he had searched any cause or argument he had to deal in thoroughly and to the bottom; and we have heard him sometimes say to his familiars that many times, both in writing and disputation, he knew he had sufficiently answered others, but many times not himself; and was ever desirous of any light, and the more able, learned, and holy the persons were, the more he desired to confer and reason with them. He was very profitable in his ministry and comfortable to his people. He was much beloved of them, and as loving was he unto them, and entirely sought their good for soul and body. In a word, he was much esteemed and reverenced of all that knew him, and his abilities both of friends and strangers." John Robinson wrote many books and pamphlets, most of which are found in Robert Ashton, editor, *The Works of John Robinson: Pastor of the Pilgrims* (Boston: Doctrinal Tract and Book Society, 1851).

22   Bradford's own short biography of William Brewster can be found later in this work, in the chapter for the year 1643.

Scrooby Manor, as it appeared in the late 19th century. This is where the Separatist congregation held many of their secret meetings in 1606 and 1607. William Brewster was receiver, bailiff, and postmaster of Scrooby Manor, which then belonged to the Archbishop of York.

afflictions were but as flea-bitings in comparison of these which now came upon them: for some were taken, and clapped up in prison, others had their houses beset and watched night and day, and hardly escaped their hands; and the most were fain to flee, and leave their houses and habitations, and the means of their livelihood. Yet these and many other sharper things which afterward befell them, were no other than they looked for, and therefore were the better prepared to bear them by the assistance of God's Grace and Spirit: yet seeing themselves thus molested, and that there was no hope of their continuance there, by a joint consent they resolved to go into the Low Countries where they heard was freedom of religion for all men; as also how sundry from London, and other parts of the land had been exiled, and persecuted for the same cause, and were gone thither, and lived at Amsterdam, and in other places of the land. So after they had continued together about a year, and kept their meetings every Sabbath, in one place, or other, exercising the worship of God amongst themselves, notwithstanding all the diligence and malice of their adversaries; they seeing they could no longer continue in that condition, they resolved to get over into Holland as they could; which was in the year 1607 and 1608: of which more at large in the next chapter.

William Bradford's personal copy of Pastor John Robinson's *A Justification of Separation from the Church of England* (1610). Photo courtesy of the Pilgrim Hall Museum, Plymouth, Massachusetts.

2 Chap.

Of their departure into Holland
and their troubls ther abouto;
with some of ye many diffi=
culties they found and
mek withall

An⁰ 1608.

Being thus constrained to leave their native soil and country, their lands and livings, and all their friends, and familiar acquaintance, it was much; and thought marvelous by many: but to go into a country they knew not (but by hearsay) where they must learn a new language, and get their livings they knew not how, it being a dear place, and subject to the miseries of war, it was by many thought an adventure almost desperate, a case intolerable, and a misery worse than death. Especially seeing they were not acquainted with trades, nor traffic (by which that country doth subsist) but had only been used to a plain country life, and the innocent trade of husbandry. But these things did not dismay them (though they did sometimes trouble them) for their desires were set on the ways of God, and to enjoy His ordinances, but they rested on His providence, and knew whom they had believed. Yet this was not all, for though they could not stay, yet were they not suffered to go, but the ports and havens were shut against them; so as they were fain to seek secret means of conveyance, and to bribe, and fee the mariners, and give extraordinary rates for their passages. And yet were they oftentimes betrayed (many of them) and both they, and their goods intercepted and surprised, and thereby put to great trouble, and charge, of which I will give an instance, or two, and omit the rest.

There was a large company of them purposed to get passage at Boston in Lincolnshire, and for that end, had hired a ship wholly to themselves; and made agreement with the master to be ready at a certain day, and take them, and their goods in, at a convenient place, where they accordingly would all attend in readiness: so after long waiting, and large expenses (though he kept not day with them) yet he came at length, and took them in, in the night. But when he had them, and their goods aboard; he betrayed them having beforehand complotted with the searchers and other officers so to do; who took them, and put them into open boats, and there rifled and ransacked them, searching them to their shirts for money, yea even the women further than became modesty; and then carried them back into the town, and made them a spectacle, and wonder to the multitude; which came flocking on all sides to behold them. Being thus first, by these catchpoll officers, rifled and stripped of their money, books, and much other goods, they were presented to the magistrates and messengers sent to inform the Lords of the Council of them; and so they were committed to ward. Indeed the magistrates used them courteously, and showed them what favor they could; but could not deliver them, till order came from the Council table. But the issue was that after a month's imprisonment, the greatest part were dismissed, and sent to the places from whence they came, but 7 of the principal were still kept in prison, and bound over to the assizes.

The next spring after, there was another attempt made by some of these and others, to get over at another place. And it so fell out, that they light of a Dutchman at Hull, having a ship of his own belonging to Zealand; they made agreement with him, and acquainted him with their condition, hoping to find more faithfulness in him, than in the former of their own nation; he bade them not fear, for he would do well enough. He was (by appointment) to take them in between Grimsby, and Hull, where was a large common a good way distant from any town; now against the prefixed time, the women, and children, with the goods, were sent to the place in a small bark, which they had hired for that end; and the men were to meet them by land. But it so fell out that they were there a day before the ship came, and the sea being rough, and the women very sick prevailed with the seamen to put into a creek hard by, where they lay on ground at low water. The next morning the ship came, but they were fast, and could not stir until about noon; in the meantime (the shipmaster, perceiving how the matter was) sent his boat, to be getting the men aboard whom he saw ready, walking about the shore. But after the first boatful was got aboard, and she was ready to go for more, the master espied a great company (both horse and foot), with bills, and guns, and other weapons (for the country was raised to take them). The Dutchman seeing that, swore (his country's oath) sacrament; and having the wind fair weighed his anchor, hoisted sails and away. But the poor men which were got aboard, were in great distress for their wives, and children, which they saw thus to be taken, and were left destitute of their helps; and themselves also, not having a cloth to shift them with, more than they had on their backs, and

The jail cells and kitchen in Boston, co. Lincolnshire, as they appear in a late 19th century photograph. This is where some of the Pilgrims were likely held following their arrest in 1608.

some scarce a penny about them, all they had being aboard the bark. It drew tears from their eyes, and anything they had, they would have given to have been ashore again; but all in vain, there was no remedy, they must thus sadly part. And afterward endured a fearful storm at sea, being 14 days or more before they arrived at their port; in 7 whereof they neither saw sun, moon nor stars, and were driven near the coast of Norway; the mariners themselves often despairing of life; and once with shrieks and cries, gave over all, as if the ship had been foundered in the sea, and they sinking without recovery. But when man's hope, and help wholly failed, the Lord's power, and mercy appeared in their recovery; for the ship rose again, and gave the mariners courage again to manage her. And if modesty would suffer me, I might declare with what fervent prayers they cried unto the Lord in this great distress (especially some of them) even without any great distraction when the water ran into their mouths, and ears; and the mariners cried out, "We sink, we sink" they cried (if not with miraculous, yet with a great height or degree of divine faith), yet Lord thou canst save; yet Lord thou canst save; with such other expressions as I will forbear. Upon which the ship did not only recover, but shortly after the violence of the storm began to abate; and the Lord filled their afflicted minds with such comforts as everyone cannot understand. And in the end brought them to their desired haven, where the people came flocking admiring their deliverance; the storm having been so long, and sore in which much hurt had been done, as the master's friends related unto him in their congratulations.

But to return to the others where we left; the rest of the men that were in greatest danger, made shift to escape away before the troop could surprise them; those only staying that best might be assistant unto the women. But pitiful it was to see the heavy case of these poor women in this distress; what weeping, and crying on every side, some for their husbands, that were carried away in the ship as is before related; others not knowing what should become of them, and their little ones; others again melted in tears, seeing their poor little ones hanging about them, crying for fear, and quaking with cold. Being thus apprehended, they were hurried from one place to another, and from one justice to another; till in the end they knew not what to do with them: for to imprison so many women and innocent children, for no other cause (many of them) but that they must go with their husbands; seemed to be unreasonable and all would cry out of them; and to send them home again was as difficult, for they alleged (as the truth was) they had no homes to go to, for they had either sold or otherwise disposed of their houses, and livings. To be short, after they had been thus turmoiled a good while; and conveyed from one constable to another, they were glad to be rid of them in the end upon any terms; for all were wearied, and tired with them. Though in the meantime they, (poor souls) endured misery enough; and thus in the end necessity forced a way for them.

But that I be not tedious in these things, I will omit the rest, though I might relate many other notable passages, and troubles which they endured, and underwent in these their wanderings, and travels both at land, and sea[23]; but I haste to other things: yet I may not omit the fruit that came hereby, for by these so public troubles, in so many eminent places, their cause became famous, and occasioned many to look into the same; and their godly carriage and Christian behavior was such, as left a deep impression in the minds of many. And though some few shrunk at these first conflicts, and sharp beginnings (as it was no marvel) yet many more came on with fresh courage, and greatly animated others. And in the end notwithstanding all these storms of opposition, they all got over at length, some at one time, and some at another; and some in one place, and some in another. And met together again according to their desires, with no small rejoicing.

---

[23] One incident that Bradford left out involved himself, and was reported by Cotton Mather in his *Magnalia Christi Americana* (Boston, 1702): "But Mr. Bradford being a young man of about eighteen, was dismissed sooner than the rest, so that within a while he had opportunity with some others to get over to Zealand [Holland], through perils, both by land and sea not inconsiderable; where he was not long ashore ere a viper seized on his hand (that is, an officer) who carried him unto the magistrates, unto whom an envious passenger had accused him as having fled out of England. When the magistrates understood the true cause of his coming thither, they were well satisfied with him; and so he repaired joyfully unto his brethren at Amsterdam, . . ."

The · 3 · Chap

Of their setling in Holand, &
their maner of living, and
entertainmente ther

2

Being now come into the Low Countries, they saw many goodly and fortified cities, strongly walled, and guarded with troops of armed men; also they heard a strange, and uncouth language, and beheld the different manners, and customs of the people, with their strange fashions, and attires; all so far differing from that of their plain country villages (wherein they were bred, and had so long lived) as it seemed they were come into a new world. But these were not the things, they much looked on, or long took up their thoughts; for they had other work in hand, and another kind of war to wage, and maintain: for though they saw fair, and beautiful cities, flowing with abundance of all sorts of wealth, and riches, yet it was not long before they saw the grim, and grisly face of poverty coming upon them like an armed man; with whom they must buckle; and encounter; and from whom they could not fly; but they were armed with faith, and patience against him, and all his encounters; and though they were sometimes foiled, yet by God's assistance they prevailed, and got the victory.

Now when Mr. Robinson, Mr. Brewster and other principal members were come over (for they were of the last and stayed to help the weakest over before them) such things were thought on as were necessary for their settling, and best ordering of the church affairs. And when they had lived at Amsterdam about a year, Mr. Robinson (their pastor) and some others of best discerning, seeing how Mr. John Smith and his company, was already fallen into contention with the church that was there before them; and no means they could use would do any good to cure the same, and also that the flames of contention were like to break out in that ancient church itself (as afterwards lamentably came to pass) which things they prudently foreseeing, thought it was best to remove; before they were any way engaged with the same. Though they well

47

knew it would be much to the prejudice of their outward estates; both at present, and in likelihood in the future; as indeed it proved to be.

For these and some other reasons they removed to Leiden[24], a fair, and beautiful city, and of a sweet situation, but made more famous by the university wherewith it is adorned, in which (of late) had been so many learned men; but wanting that traffic by sea which Amsterdam enjoys, it was not so beneficial for their outward means of living, and estates. But being now here pitched they fell to such trades, and employments as they best could; valuing peace, and their spiritual comfort above any other riches whatsoever. And at length they came to raise a competent, and comfortable living, but with hard and continual labor.

Being thus settled (after many difficulties) they continued many years, in a comfortable condition; enjoying much sweet, and delightful society, and spiritual comfort together in the ways of God; under the able ministry, and prudent government of Mr. John Robinson, and Mr. William Brewster who was an assistant unto him in the place of an Elder, unto which he was now called, and chosen by the church. So as they grew in knowledge, and other gifts, and graces of the Spirit of God; and lived together in peace, and love, and holiness; and many came unto them, from divers parts of England, so as they grew a great congregation.[25] And if at any time any differences arose, or offenses broke out (as it cannot be, but some time there will, even amongst the best of men) they were ever so met with, and nipped in the head betimes; or otherwise so well composed, as still love, peace, and communion was continued. Or else the church purged off those that were incurable, and incorrigible; when after much patience used no other means would serve, which seldom came to pass.

Yea such was the mutual love, and reciprocal respect that this worthy man had to his flock, and his flock to him; that it might be said of them, as it once was of that famous Emperor Marcus Aurelius, and the people of Rome[26]: that it was hard to judge whether he delighted more in having such

---

[24] Pastor John Robinson filed a petition with the Leiden burgomasters and court of the city of Leiden, requesting permission to move his church to their city. This petition is shown on the page opposite. Leiden Archives 363/SA51 Gfo./12-2-1609 Residence Permit.

[25] Most of the later members of the Leiden congregation referred to here came from Sandwich and Canterbury, co. Kent; Norwich and Yarmouth, co. Norfolk; Colchester, co. Essex, and the London-Middlesex area.

[26] Golden Book, etc. (Bradford). Antonio de Guevara, *The Golden Book of Marcus Aurelius.*

John Robinson's petition of February 1609: "To the Honorable, the Burgomasters and Court of the City of Leiden. With due submission and respect, John Robinson, minister of the Divine Word, and some of the members of the Christian Reformed religion, born in the kingdom of Great Britain, to the number of one hundred persons or thereabouts, men and women, represent that they are desirous of coming to live in this city, by the first day of May next . . ." The Burgomasters responded they "refuse no honest persons free ingress to come and have their residence in this city . . ." Image courtesy of the Leiden Archives.

a people, or they in having such a pastor. His love was great towards them, and his care was always bent for their best good both for soul and body; for besides his singular abilities in divine things (wherein he excelled) he was also very able to give directions in civil affairs, and to foresee dangers, and inconveniences; by which means he was very helpful to their outward estates, and so was every way as a common father unto them.

And none did more offend him, than those that were close, and cleaving to themselves, and retired from the common good; as also such as would be stiff, and rigid in matters of outward order, and inveigh against the evils of others, and yet be remiss in themselves, and not so careful to express a virtuous conversation. They in like manner had ever a reverent regard unto him, and had him in precious estimation as his worth and wisdom did deserve; and though they esteemed him highly whilst he lived, and labored amongst them; yet much more after his death when they came to feel the want of his help, and saw (by woeful experience) what a treasure they had lost; to the grief of their hearts and wounding of their souls; yea such a loss (as they saw) could not be repaired; for it was as hard for them to find such another leader and feeder (in all respects) as for the Taborites to find another Ziska[27]. And though they did not call themselves orphans (as the other did) after his death: yet they had cause as much; to lament (in another regard) their present condition, and after usage. But to return: I know not but it may be spoken, to the honor of God, and without prejudice to any: that such was the true piety, the humble zeal, and fervent love, of this people (whilst they thus lived together) towards God and His ways, and the single-heartedness, and sincere affection one towards another, that they came as near the primitive pattern of the first churches, as any other church of these later times have done, according to their rank, and quality.

But seeing it is not my purpose to treat of the several passages that befell this people whilst they thus lived in the Low Countries (which might worthily require a large treatise of itself)[28] but to make way to show the beginning of

---

27   John Ziska (1376-1424), a Taborite (Hussite) general.

28   For more on the Pilgrims in Holland, see Henry Dexter, *The England and Holland of the Pilgrims* (London, 1906), and Daniel Plooij, *The Pilgrim Fathers from a Dutch Point of View* (New York: New York University Press, 1932). See also Johanna Tammel, *The Pilgrims and Other People from the British Isles in Leiden, 1576-1640* (Isle of Man:Mansk-Svenska, 1989); Jeremy D. Bangs, *The Pilgrims in the Netherlands: Recent Research* (Leiden: Leiden Municipal Archives, 1985); and Jeremy D. Bangs, *Pilgrim Life in Leiden: Text and Images from the Leiden American Pilgrim Museum* (Leiden, 1997).

this plantation, which is that I aim at yet because some of their adversaries, did (upon the rumor of their removal) cast out slanders against them, as if that state had been weary of them, and had rather driven them out (as the heathen historians did feign of Moses and the Israelites when they went out of Egypt) than that it was their own free choice and motion. I will therefore mention a particular or two, to show the contrary, and the good acceptation they had in the place where they lived. And first though many of them were poor, yet there was none so poor but if they were known to be of that congregation, the Dutch (either bakers or others) would trust them in any reasonable matter when they wanted money because they had found by experience how careful they were to keep their word, and saw them so painful, and diligent in their callings yea they would strive to get their custom, and to employ them above others in their work, for their honesty and diligence.

Again the magistrates of the city, about the time of their coming away, or a little before in the public place of justice, gave this commendable testimony of them (in the reproof of the Walloons who were of the French church in that city[29]): these English, said they, have lived amongst us now these 12 years and yet we never had any suit, or accusation come against any of them; but your strifes, and quarrels are continual, etc. In these times also were the great troubles raised by the Arminians[30], who as they greatly molested the whole state, so this city in particular (in which was the chief university) so as there were daily and hot disputes in the schools thereabout, and as the students and other learned were divided in their opinions herein, so were the

---

[29] Edward Winslow in his *Hypocrisy Unmasked* (London, 1646) noted that "And for the French churches: that we held, and do hold communion with them; take notice of our practice at Leiden, viz. that one Samuel Terry was received from the French church there, into communion with us; also the wife of Francis Cooke being a Walloon, holds communion with the Church at Plymouth; and after upon his removal of habitation to Duxbury where Mr. Ralph Partridge is pastor of the church; . . . For the truth is, the Dutch and French churches either of them being a people distinct from the world, and gathered into an holy communion, and not national churches, nay, so far from it, . . . the difference is so small (if moderately pondered, between them and us) as we dare not for the world deny communion with them."

[30] Jacobus Arminius (1560-1609) was a professor of theology at the University of Leiden. Arminius opposed the Pilgrims' views on predestination, arguing election was dependant upon faith. For additional information see D. Plooij, *The Pilgrim Fathers from a Dutch Point of View* (New York, 1932), pg. 52-53.

2 professors, or divinity readers themselves the one daily teaching for it, the other against it. Which grew to that pass, that few of the disciples, of the one, would hear the other teach. But Mr. Robinson (though he taught thrice a week himself, and wrote sundry books besides his manifold pains otherwise) yet he went constantly to hear their readings, and heard the one as well as the other; by which means he was so well grounded in the controversy, and saw the force of all their arguments, and knew the shifts of the adversary; and being himself very able; none was fitter to buckle with them than himself. As appeared by sundry disputes, so as he began to be terrible to the Arminians; which made Episcopius (the Arminian professor) to put forth his best strength, and set forth sundry theses, which by public dispute he would defend against all men. Now Polyander the other professor, and the chief preacher of the city, desired Mr. Robinson to dispute against him; but he was loath, being a stranger; yet the other did importune him: and told him, that such was the ability and nimbleness of the adversary; that the truth would suffer, if he did not help them. So as he condescended, and prepared himself against the time; and when the day came, the Lord did so help him to defend the truth, and foil this adversary; as he put him to an apparent nonplus, in this great and public audience. And the like he did a 2 or 3 time, upon such like occasions. The which as it caused many to praise God, that the truth had so famous victory. So it procured him much honor, and respect from those learned men, and others which loved the truth. Yea so far were they from being weary of him, and his people, or desiring their absence; as it was said by some (of no mean note) that were it not for giving offense to the state of England; they would have preferred him otherwise if he would, and allowed them some public favor. Yea when there was speech of their removal into these parts, sundry of note, and eminency of that nation, would have had them come under them, and for that end made them large offers. Now though I might allege many other particulars, and examples of the like kind, to show the untruth, and unlikelihood of this slander, yet these shall suffice; seeing it was believed of few; being only raised by the malice of some, who labored their disgrace.

The 4. Chap
showing y reasons, & causes of their
remooucall.

After they had lived in this city about some 11 or 12 years (which is the
more observable being the whole time of that famous truce between that state
and the Spaniards[31]) and sundry of them were taken away by death; and many
others began to be well stricken in years (the grave mistress of Experience
having taught them many things): those prudent governors, with sundry of the
sagest members began both deeply to apprehend their present dangers, and
wisely to foresee the future; and think of timely remedy. In the agitation of
their thoughts, and much discourse of things hereabout; at length they began
to incline to this conclusion, of removal to some other place: not out of any
newfangledness, or other such like giddy humor, by which men are oftentimes
transported to their great hurt, and danger. But for sundry weighty, and solid
reasons; some of the chief of which, I will here briefly touch.[32] And first they

---

[31] The twelve year truce between Spain and the Netherlands was signed in Antwerp
on 30 March 1609 and was due to expire in 1621.

[32] Edward Winslow also gives a list of some reasons why they decided to remove to
America, in his *Hypocrisy Unmasked* (London, 1646): "[O]ur Reverend Mr. John
Robinson of late memory, and our grave Elder Mr. William Brewster, (now both at rest
with the Lord) considering amongst many other inconveniences, how hard the country
was where we lived, how many spent their estate in it, and were forced to return for
England; how grievous to live from under protection of the State of England; how like
we were to lose our language, and our name of English; how little good we did, or were
like to do to the Dutch in reforming the Sabbath; how unable there to give such
education to our children, as we ourselves had received, etc . . . . Hereby in their grave
wisdoms they thought we might more glorify God, do more good to our Country,
better provide for our posterity, and live to be more refreshed by our labors, than ever we
could do in Holland where we were."

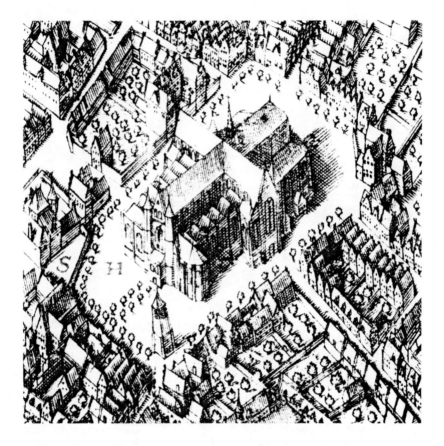

Part of a detailed map of Leiden, made by Peiter Bast in 1600. At the center is St.
Peter's Cathedral. At the lower end of the Cathedral is a separate clock-tower. The
house the Pilgrim church would purchase in 1611, in the names of John Robinson,
William Jepson, Henry Wood and Randall Thickens, is located right across from the
clock-tower—the half-acre lot consisting of a house and a large backyard. The house
was torn down in 1683, and a new house (still extant) was built on the site.

saw, and found by experience, the hardness of the place, and country to be such; as few in comparison would come to them; and fewer that would bide it out, and continue with them; for many that came to them, and many more that desired to be with them, could not endure that great labor, and hard fare, with other inconveniences, which they underwent, and were contented with. But though they loved their persons, approved their cause, and honored their sufferings; yet they left them, as it were weeping, as Orpah did her mother-in-law Naomi; or as those Romans did Cato in Utica, who desired to be excused, and borne with, though they could not all be Catos; for many, though they desired to enjoy the ordinances of God in their purity, and the liberty of the gospel with them, yet (alas) they admitted of bondage, with danger of conscience; rather than to endure these hardships, yea some preferred and chose the prisons in England, rather than this liberty in Holland, with these afflictions. But it was thought that if a better, and easier place of living could be had; it would draw many, and take away these discouragements; yea their pastor would often say, that many of those who both wrote, and preached now against them, if they were in a place, where they might have liberty, and live comfortably, they would then practice as they did.[33]

2ly they saw, that though the people generally, bore all these difficulties very cheerfully, and with a resolute courage, being in the best, and strength of their years; yet old age began to steal on many of them (and their great and continual labors, with other crosses, and sorrows, hastened it before the time) so as it was not only probably thought, but apparently seen, that within a few years more, they would be in danger to scatter (by necessities pressing them)

---

[33] Edward Winslow in his *Hypocrisy Unmasked* (London, 1646) noted: "Tis true, that that poor persecuted flock of Christ, by the malice and power of the late hierarchy were driven to Leiden in Holland, there to bear witness in their practice to the Kingly Office of Christ Jesus in his Church: and there lived together ten years under the United States, with much peace and liberty: but our Reverend Mr. John Robinson of late memory, and our grave Elder Mr. William Brewster, (now both at rest with the Lord) considering amongst many other inconveniences, how hard the country was where we lived, how many spent their estate in it, and were forced to return for England; how grievous to live from under protection of the State of England; how like we were to lose our language, and our name of English; how little good we did, or were like to do to the Dutch in reforming the Sabbath; how unable there to give such education to our children, as we ourselves had received, etc."

or sink under their burdens, or both. And therefore according to the divine proverb, that a wise man seeth the plague when it cometh, and hideth himself, Proverbs 22:3, so they like skillful and beaten soldiers were fearful, either to be entrapped, or surrounded by their enemies; so as they should neither be able to fight, nor fly. And therefore thought it better to dislodge betimes, to some place of better advantage, and less danger, if any such could be found.

Thirdly, as necessity was a taskmaster over them, so they were forced to be such, not only to their servants, (but in a sort) to their dearest children; the which as it did not a little wound the tender hearts of many a loving father, and mother; so it produced likewise sundry sad and sorrowful effects: for many of their children, that were of best dispositions, and gracious inclinations (having learned to bear the yoke in their youth) and willing to bear part of their parents' burden, were (oftentimes) so oppressed with their heavy labors; that though their minds were free and willing, yet their bodies bowed under the weight of the same, and became decrepit in their early youth; the vigor of nature being consumed in the very bud as it were. But that which was more lamentable, and of all sorrows most heavy to be borne, was that many of their children, by these occasions (and the great licentiousness of youth in that country) and the manifold temptations of the place, were drawn away by evil examples into extravagant, and dangerous courses, getting the reins off their necks, and departing from their parents. Some became soldiers, others took upon them far voyages by sea; and others some worse courses, tending to dissoluteness, and the danger of their souls; to the great grief of their parents, and dishonor of God. So that they saw their posterity would be in danger to degenerate and be corrupted.

Lastly (and which was not least) a great hope, and inward zeal they had of laying some good foundation (or at least to make some way thereunto) for the propagating and advancing the gospel of the kingdom of Christ in those remote parts of the world; yea though they should be but even as stepping-stones, unto others for the performing of so great a work.

These, and some other like reasons, moved them to undertake this resolution of their removal; the which they afterward prosecuted with so great difficulties, as by the sequel will appear.

The place they had thoughts on, was some of those vast, and unpeopled countries of America, which are fruitful, and fit for habitation; being devoid of all civil inhabitants; where there are only savage, and brutish men, which range up, and down, little otherwise than the wild beasts of the same. This proposition being made public, and coming to the scanning of all; it raised many variable opinions amongst men, and caused many fears, and doubts amongst themselves. Some from their reasons, and hopes conceived; labored to stir up and encourage the rest to undertake, and prosecute the same; others again out of their fears, objected against it, and sought to divert from it; alleging many things, and those neither unreasonable, nor unprobable. As that it was a great design, and subject to many unconceivable perils, and dangers; as besides the casualties of the seas (which none can be freed from) the length of the voyage was such, as the weak bodies of women[34], and other persons worn out with age, and travail (as many of them were) could never be able to endure. And yet if they should, the miseries of the land, which they should be exposed unto, would be too hard to be borne; and likely some, or all of them together, to consume, and utterly to ruinate them; for there they should be liable to famine, and nakedness, and the want in a manner of all things. The change of air, diet, and drinking of water, would infect their bodies with sore sicknesses, and grievous diseases. And also those which should escape, or overcome these difficulties, should yet be in continual danger of the savage people: who are cruel, barbarous, and most treacherous, being most furious in their rage, and merciless where they overcome; not being content only to kill, and take away life, but delight to torment men in the most bloody manner that may be; flaying some alive with the shells of fishes, cutting off the members, and joints of others by piecemeal; and broiling on the coals eat the collops of their flesh in their sight whilst they live, with other cruelties horrible to be related.[35] And surely it could not

---

[34]   Very few English women had, at this point in time, made the voyage across the Atlantic to North America. Seventeen women had come as a part of Sir Walter Raleigh's second colony in 1587; but the Roanoke colony of 17 women (and 100 men and boys) had disappeared by 1590, leaving only the word "Croatoan" carved in a tree as a clue. The Jamestown Colony, founded in 1607, also had relatively few women prior to 1618.

[35]   This is probably a reference to Englishman George Cassan, whose killing in November 1607 at Jamestown, Virginia, at the hands of the Chickahominy, is described by David A. Price in his *Love and Hate in Jamestown: John Smith, Pocahontas, and the Heart of a Nation* (New York: Alfred A. Knopf, 2003): "The natives prepared a large fire behind his bound and naked body. Then a man grasped his hands and used mussel shells to cut off joint after joint, making his way through Cassen's fingers, tossing the pieces into the flames. That accomplished, the man used shells and reeds to detach the skin from Cassen's face and the rest of his head. Cassen's belly was next, as the man sliced it open, pulled out his bowels, and cast those onto the fire. Finally the natives burned Cassen at the stake through to his bones."

be thought but the very hearing of these things, could not but move the very bowels of men to grate within them, and make the weak to quake and tremble. It was further objected, that it would require greater sums of money to furnish such a voyage (and to fit them with necessaries) than their consumed estates would amount to; and yet they must as well look to be seconded with supplies, as presently to be transported. Also many precedents of ill success, and lamentable miseries befallen others, in the like designs, were easy to be found, and not forgotten to be alleged. Besides their own experience, in their former troubles, and hardships, in their removal into Holland; and how hard a thing it was for them to live in that strange place, though it was a neighbor country, and a civil and rich commonwealth.

It was answered, that all great, and honorable actions, are accompanied with great difficulties; and must be both enterprised, and overcome with answerable courages. It was granted the dangers were great, but not desperate: the difficulties were many, but not invincible. For though there were many of them likely, yet they were not certain; it might be sundry of the things feared, might never befall; others by provident care and the use of good means might in a great measure be prevented; and all of them (through the help of God) by fortitude, and patience, might either be borne, or overcome. True it was at such attempts were no to be made, and undertaken without good ground, and reason; not rashly, or lightly as many have done for curiosity, or hope of gain, etc. But their condition was not ordinary; their ends were good and honorable; their calling lawful, and urgent; and therefore they might expect the blessing of God in their proceeding. Yea though they should lose their lives in this action, yet might they have comfort in the same, and their endeavors would be honorable. They lived here but as men in exile, and in a poor condition; and as great miseries might possibly befall them in this place; for the 12 years of truce were now out, and there was nothing but beating of drums and preparing for war, the events whereof are always uncertain; the Spaniard might prove as cruel, as the savages of America, and the famine, and pestilence, as sore here as there; and their liberty less to look out for remedy. After many other particular things answered, and alleged on both sides, it was fully concluded by the major part, to put this design in execution; and to prosecute it by the best means they could.

The 5. Chap.
shewing what means they used for preparation to this wayghtie viedg.

And first, after their humble prayers unto God, for His direction and assistance; and a general conference held hereabout, they consulted what particular place to pitch upon, and prepare for. Some (and none of the meanest) had thoughts, and were earnest for Guiana[36], or some of those fertile places in those hot climates; others were for some parts of Virginia[37], where the English had already made entrance, and beginning. Those for Guiana alleged that the country was rich, fruitful, and blessed with a perpetual spring and a flourishing greenness; where vigorous nature brought forth all things in abundance, and plenty without any great labor; or art of man. So as it must needs make the inhabitants rich; seeing less provisions of clothing and other things, would serve; than in more colder, and less fruitful countries

---

[36]   The Pilgrims likely read about Guiana in Walter Raleigh's *Discovery of the Large, Rich and Beautiful Empire of Guiana* (London, 1596), and Robert Harcourt's *Relation of a Voyage to Guiana* (London, 1613). Edward Winslow was an apprentice to John Beale, the publisher of Harcourt's *Relation*, so he might have been quite familiar with this work.

[37]   William Brewster is known to have owned a copy of Richard Hakluyt's *Principal Navigations, Voyages and Discoveries of the English Nation*, which contained a large number of first-hand accounts of voyages and travels to the New World, including an account of the failed Raleigh colony at Roanoke. Ralph Hamor's *True Discovery of the Present Estate of Virginia* was published in 1615. Captain John Smith had also published several works on Virginia by this time, including *A True Relation of Such Occurrences and Accidents of Note as Hath Happened in Virginia Since the First Planting* (London, 1608), and *A Map of Virginia, With a Description of the Country* (London, 1612).

must be had. As also that the Spaniards (having much more than they could possess) had not yet planted there, nor anywhere, very near the same. But to this it was answered, that out of question, the country was both fruitful and pleasant; and might yield riches, and maintenance to the possessors, more easily than the other; yet other things considered, it would not be so fit for them. And first that such hot countries, are subject to grievous diseases, and many noisome impediments, which other more temperate places, are freer from, and would not so well agree with our English bodies. Again if they should there live, and do well, the jealous Spaniard would never suffer them long; but would displant, or overthrow them; as he did the French in Florida, who were seated further from his richest countries; and the sooner because they should have none to protect them; and their own strength, would be too small to resist so potent an enemy, and so near a neighbor.

On the other hand for Virginia it was objected: that if they lived among the English which were there planted, or so near them, as to be under their government, they should be in as great danger to be troubled and persecuted for the cause of religion, as if they lived in England; and it might be worse. And if they lived too far off, they should neither have succor, nor defense from them.

But at length the conclusion was, to live as a distinct body by themselves, under the general Government of Virginia; and by their friends to sue to His Majesty that he would be pleased to grant them freedom of religion; and that this might be obtained they were put in good hope (by some great persons of good rank and quality) that were made their friends.[38] Whereupon 2 were chosen and sent into England (at the charge of the rest) to solicit this matter; who found the Virginia Company very desirous to have them go thither. And willing to grant them a patent, with as ample privileges, as they had, or could grant to any, and to give them the best furtherance they could. And some of the chief of that Company doubted not to obtain their suit of the King for liberty in religion and to have it confirmed under the King's broad seal, according to their desires. But it proved a harder piece of work than they took it for; for though many means were used to bring it about, yet it could not be effected; for there were divers of good worth labored with the King to obtain it (amongst whom was one of his chief

---

[38]   William Brewster's landlord at Scrooby Manor was Samuel Sandys, whose brother Sir Edwin Sandys became the treasurer of the Virginia Company of London in 1619.

secretaries[39]) and some others wrought with the archbishop to give way thereunto, but it proved all in vain. Yet thus far they prevailed in sounding His Majesty's mind, that he would connive at them, and not molest them (provided they carried themselves peaceably). But to allow, or tolerate them by his public authority, under his seal, they found it would not be. And this was all (the chief of the Virginia Company) or any other of their best friends could do in the case. Yet they persuaded them to go on, for they presumed they should not be troubled. And with this answer the messengers returned and signified what diligence had been used and to what issue things were come.

But this made a damp in the business, and caused some distraction, for many were afraid that if they should unsettle themselves and put off their estates, and go upon these hopes, it might prove dangerous and prove but a sandy foundation; yea it **was** thought they might better have presumed hereupon, without making any suit at all, than having made it, to be thus rejected. But some of the chiefest, thought otherwise; and that they might well proceed hereupon, and that the King's Majesty was willing enough to suffer them without molestation; though for other reasons he would not confirm it by any public act. And furthermore if there was no security in this promise intimated, there would be no great certainty, in a further confirmation of the same; for if afterwards there should be a purpose, or desire to wrong them, though they had a seal as broad as the house floor, it would not serve the turn; for there would be means anew found to recall, or reverse it. And seeing therefore the course was probable,

---

[39]   Sir Robert Naunton (Bradford). Robert Naunton (1563-1635) became Secretary of State in 1617/18. Edward Winslow reported in *Hypocrisy Unmasked* (London, 1646) that "His Majesty said was a good and honest motion, and asking what profit might arise in the part we intended (for our eye was upon the most northern parts of Virginia): twas answered 'Fishing.' To which he replied with his ordinary asserveration, 'So God have my soul, 'tis an honest trade, 'twas the Apostles own calling," etc. But afterwards he told Sir Robert Naunton, (who took all occasions to further it) that we should confer to the Bishops of Canterbury and London, etc. Whereupon we were advised to persist upon his first approbation, and not to entangle ourselves with them, which caused our agents to repair to the Virginia Company, who in the court demanded our ends of going; which being related, they said the thing was of God, and granted a large patent, and one of them lent us £300 gratis for three years, which was repaid."

they must rest herein on God's providence, as they had done in other things.

Upon this resolution, other messengers were dispatched, to end with the Virginia Company as well as they could. And to procure a patent with as good, and ample conditions as they might by any good means obtain. As also to treat and conclude with such merchants, and other friends, as had manifested their forwardness to provoke to, and adventure in this voyage; for which end they had instructions given them, upon what conditions they should proceed with them, or else to conclude nothing without further advice. And here it will be requisite to insert a letter, or two that may give light to these proceedings.

A Copy of Letter from Sir Edwin Sandys directed to Mr. John Robinson, and Mr. William Brewster

After my hearty salutations. The agents of your congregation, Robert Cushman[40], and John Carver, have been in communication, with divers select gentlemen of His Majesty's Council for Virginia; and by the writing of 7 articles[41] subscribed with your names, have given them that good degree of satisfaction, which hath carried them on with a resolution, to set forward your desire, in the best sort that may be, for your own and the public good. Divers particulars whereof we leave to their faithful report, having carried themselves here, with that good discretion; as is both to their own, and their credit, from whence they came. And whereas being to treat for a multitude of people, they have requested further time to confer with them that are to be interested in this action about the several particularities which in the prosecution thereof will fall out considerable; it hath been very willingly assented to. And so they do now return unto you; if therefore it may please God so to direct your desires, as that on your parts there fall out no just impediments, I trust by the same direction, it shall likewise appear, that on our part all forwardness, to set you forward shall be found, in the best sort, which with reason may be expected. And so I betake you, with this design (which I hope verily is the work of God) to the gracious protection, and blessing of the Highest.

Your very loving friend,
Edwin Sandys

London, November 12
Anno: 1617

---

[40]   Robert Cushman (1577-1625) was a prominent member of the Leiden congregation. He is the author of the sermon *Sin and Danger of Self Love* (London, 1622), which he preached to the Plymouth church in December 1621, having arrived at Plymouth on the ship *Fortune* the previous month.

[41]   The "Seven Articles" are printed in Appendix I.

Their answer was as followeth.

Right Worshipful:

Our humble duties remembered, in our own, our messengers, and our church's name; with all thankful acknowledgment of your singular love, expressing itself as otherwise, so more specially in your great care, and earnest endeavor of our good in this weighty business about Virginia; which the less able we are to requite; we shall think ourselves the more bound to commend in our prayers unto God, for recompense; whom as for the present you rightly behold in our endeavors, so shall we not be wanting on our parts (the same God assisting us) to return all answerable fruit, and respect unto the labor of your love, bestowed upon us. We have (with the best speed, and consideration withal, that we could) set down our requests in writing, subscribed (as you willed) with the hands of the greatest part of our congregation, and have sent the same unto the Council, by our agent, and a deacon of our church John Carver, unto whom we have also requested a gentleman of our company to adjoin himself; to the care, and discretion of which two we do refer the prosecuting of the business. Now we persuade ourselves Right Worshipful that we need not provoke your godly, and loving mind to any further; or more tender care of us, since you have pleased so far to interest us in yourself; that under God above all persons, and things in the world, we rely upon you, expecting the care of your love, counsel of your wisdom, and the help and countenance of your authority. Notwithstanding for your encouragement in the work, so far as probabilities may lead we will not forbear to mention these instances of inducement.

1   We verily believe and trust the Lord is with us, unto whom, and whose service we have given ourselves in many trials; and that He will graciously prosper our endeavors according to the simplicity of our hearts therein.

2   We are well weaned from the delicate milk of our mother country and inured to the difficulties of a strange and hard land; which yet in a great part we have by patience overcome.

3   The people, are for the body of them, industrious, and frugal (we think we may safely say) as any company of people in the world.

4   We are knit together, as a body, in a most strict, and sacred bond and covenant of the Lord; of the violation whereof we make great conscience, and by virtue whereof, we do hold ourselves straightly tied, to all care of each other's good, and of the whole by every one and so mutually.

5   Lastly, it is not with us, as with other men, whom small things, can
     discourage, or small discontentments, cause to wish themselves at
     home again, we know our entertainment in England, and in Holland.
     We shall much prejudice, both our arts, and means by removal; who
     (if we should be driven to return) we should not hope to recover our
     present helps, and comforts; neither indeed look ever (for ourselves)
     to attain unto the like in any other place, during our lives, which are
     now drawing towards their periods.[42]

These motives we have been bold, to tender unto you, which you in
your wisdom may also impart to any other our worshipful friends of the
Council with you; of all whose godly disposition and loving towards our
despised persons, we are most glad, and shall not fail by all good means to
continue, and increase the same. We will not be further troublesome, but do
with the renewed remembrance of our humble duties to your Worship and
(so far as in modesty we may be bold) to any other of our well-willers of the
Council with you; we take our, leaves committing your persons, and counsels,
to the guidance, and direction of the Almighty.

Yours much bounden in all duty,
John Robinson
William Brewster

Leiden, December 15, Anno: 1617

---

[42]   Bradford adds, somewhat later, the following commentary on the blank page
       opposite: "O sacred bond, whilst inviolably preserved! How sweet, and precious
       were the fruits, that flowed from the same? But when this fidelity decayed; then
       their ruin approached. O that these ancient members had not died, or been
       dissipated. If it had been the will of God, or else that this holy care, and constant
       faithfulness had still lived, and remained with those that survived and were in
       times afterwards added unto them. But (alas) that subtle serpent hath slyly wound
       in himself, under fair pretences of necessity, and the like; to untwist those sacred
       bonds, and ties, and as it were insensibly by degrees to dissolve (or in a great
       measure) to weaken the same. I have been happy, in my first times, to see, and
       with much comfort to enjoy, the blessed fruits of this sweet communion, but it is
       now a part of my misery, in old age to find, and feel the decay, and want thereof
       (in a great measure) and with grief, and sorrow of heart to lament, and bewail the
       same. And for others' warning, and admonition (and my own humiliation) do I
       here note the same."

For further light in these proceedings see some other letters and notes as followeth.

The copy of a letter sent to Sir
John Wolstenholme[43]

Right Worshipful: with due acknowledgment of our thankfulness for your singular care, and pains, in the business of Virginia; for our, and (we hope) the common good. We do remember our humble duties unto you, and have sent enclosed (as is required) a further explanation of our judgments in the 3 points specified by some of His Majesty's Honorable Privy Council; and though it be grievous unto us, that such unjust insinuations are made against us; yet we are most glad of the occasion of making our just purgation, unto so honorable personages. The declarations we have sent enclosed, the one more brief, and general, which we think the fitter to be presented; the other something more large, and in which we express some small accidental differences, which if it seem good unto you, and other of our worshipful friends, you may send instead of the former. Our prayers unto God is, that your Worship may see the fruit of your worthy endeavors, which on our parts we shall not fail to further, by all good means in us. And so praying that you would please with the convenientest speed that may be; to give us knowledge of the success of the business with His Majesty's Privy Council; and accordingly what your further pleasure is, either for our direction, or furtherance in the same, so we rest

Your Worship in all duty,
John Robinson
William Brewster

Leiden, January 27 Anno 1617. Old Style

---

43   Sir John Wolstenholme (1562-1639), a member of the council of the Virginia Company.

The first brief note was this:

Touching the ecclesiastical ministry; namely of pastors for teaching, elders for ruling, and deacons for distributing the church's contribution: as also for the two sacraments, baptism and the Lord's Supper, we do wholly, and in all points agree with the French Reformed Churches, according to their public confession of faith.

The oath of supremacy we shall willingly take, if it be required of us; and that convenient satisfaction be not given by our taking the oath of allegiance.

John Robinson
William Brewster

The 2 was this:

Touching the ecclesiastical ministry, etc. as in the former, we agree in all things with the French Reformed Churches, according to their public confession of faith; though some small differences be to be found in our practices, not at all in the substance of the things; but only in some accidental circumstances.[44]

1   As first, their ministers do pray with their heads covered; ours uncovered.
2   We choose none for Governing Elders, but such as are able to teach; which ability they do not require.
3   Their Elders, and deacons are annual, or at most for 2 or 3 years; ours perpetual.
4   Our elders do administer their office, in admonitions, and excommunications for public scandals, publicly and before the congregation; theirs more privately, and in their consistories.
5   We do administer baptism only to such infants as whereof the one parent at the least, is of some church; which some of their churches do not observe; though in it our practice accords with their public confession, and the judgment of the most learned amongst them.

Other differences worthy mentioning we know none in these points. Then about the oath, as in the former.

Subscribed
John R.
W. B..

---

[44]   Bradford goes into much more detail on the differences between the various church denominations in his *Third Conference*.

London Feb. 14
1617

Part of another letter from him
that delivered these.

Your letter to Sir John Worstenholme, I delivered almost as soon as I had it, to his own hands; and stayed with him the opening and reading; there were 2 papers enclosed, he read them to himself, as also the letter, and in the reading he spake to me (and said) "Who shall make them?" viz. the ministers; I answered his Worship that the power of making was in the Church, to be ordained by the imposition of hands, by the fittest instruments they had. It must either be in the Church, or from the Pope, and the Pope is Antichrist.[45] "Ho:" said Sir John, "what the Pope holds good (as in the Trinity) that we do well to assent to; but," said he, "we will not enter into dispute now." And as for your letters he would not show them at any hand, lest he should spoil all; he expected you should have been of the Archbishop's mind for the calling of ministers, but it seems you differed. I could have wished to have known the contents of your two enclosed, at which he stuck so much, especially the larger. I asked his Worship what good news he had for me to write tomorrow. He told me very good news, for both the King's Majesty, and the bishops have consented. He said he would go to Mr. Chancellor, Sir Fulke Greville, as this day, and next week I should know more. I met Sir Edwin Sandys on Wednesday night, he wished me to be at the Virginia Court the next Wednesday, where I purpose to be. Thus loath to be troublesome at present, I hope to have somewhat next week of certainty concerning you. I commit you to the Lord.

Yours,

S[abine] S[taresmore][46]

---

[45]   The Pilgrims believed the pope fit the Biblical description of antichrist, because the Roman Catholics placed the pope higher than the angels, believed in papal infallibility, believed he was "more than a man," and was "above all laws, above all decrees, canons and counsels, and may be contrary unto them." Bradford in his *Third Conference*, citing Mornaeus de Plessis, asked "Would ever any have believed such things . . . if the spirit of God had not foretold as much of antichrist?"

[46]   Thomas Prince, probably before 1736, added the following note to the manuscript: "In Gov. Bradford's *Collection of Letters*, this letter is more large, and subscribed Sabine Staresmore." This portion of Bradford's letterbook was lost during the late 18th century. Sabine Staresmore was originally a member of the Independent church at Southwark, founded by Henry Jacob in 1616. He later became acquainted

These things, being long in agitation, and messengers passing to and again about them, after all their hopes they were long delayed, by many rubs that fell in the way; for at the return of these messengers into England they found things far otherwise than they expected. For the Virginia Council was now so disturbed with factions, and quarrels amongst themselves, as no business could well go forward: the which may the better appear in one of the messenger's letters as followeth:

To his loving friends etc.

I had thought long since to have writ unto you, but could not effect that which I aimed at, neither can yet set things as I wished; yet notwithstanding I doubt not but Mr. B.[47] hath written to Mr. Robinson. But I think myself bound also to do something, lest I be thought to neglect you. The main hindrance of our proceedings in the Virginia business, is the dissensions, and factions (as they term it) amongst the Council, and Company of Virginia, which are such, as that ever I since we came up, no business could by them be dispatched. The occasion of this trouble amongst them is, for that a while since, Sir Thomas Smith, repining at his many offices, and troubles; wished the Company of Virginia to ease him of his office in being Treasurer, and Governor of the Virginia Company. Whereupon the Company took occasion to dismiss him; and chose Sir Edwin Sandys Treasurer, and Governor of the Company, he having 60 voices, Sir John Worstenholme 16 voices, and Alderman Johnson 24. But Sir Thomas Smith when he saw some part of his honor lost; was very angry, and raised a faction, to cavil, and contend about the election; and sought to tax Sir Edwin with many things; that might both disgrace him, and also put him by his office of Governor. In which contentions they yet stick, and are not fit, nor ready to intermeddle in any business; and what issue things will come to, we are not yet certain. It is most like Sir Edwin will carry it away, and if he do things will go well in Virginia, if

---

with John Robinson's Leiden congregation, as well as Henry Ainsworth's congregation in Amsterdam. He wrote a short book, published in 1619, entitled *The Unlawfulness of Reading in Prayer.*

[47]   A reference to William Brewster. Because Brewster was at the time being hunted by English and Dutch authorities for illegally printing and distributing prohibited religious works, members of the Leiden congregation had to be careful what they wrote about him, in case their letters were intercepted and his whereabouts exposed.

otherwise they will go ill enough. Always we hope in some 2 or 3 Courts' days things will settle. Mean space I think to go down into Kent, and come up again about 14 days, or 3 weeks hence; except either by these aforesaid contentions; or by the ill tidings from Virginia we be wholly discouraged, of which tidings I am now to speak.

Captain Argall[48] is come home this week (he upon notice of the intent of the Council came away before Sir George Yeardley came there; and so there is no small dissension); but his tidings are ill, though his person be welcome. He saith Mr. Blackwell's ship came not there till March, but going towards winter, they had still northwest winds, which carried them to the southward beyond their course. And the master of the ship, and some six of the mariners dying, it seemed they could not find the bay, till after long seeking and beating about. Mr. Blackwell is dead, and Mr. Maggner the Captain; yea there are dead he saith 130 persons one, and other in that ship; it is said there was in all an 180 persons in the ship, so as they were packed together like herrings; they had amongst them the flux, and also want of fresh water; so as it is here rather wondered at that so many are alive, than that so many are dead. The merchants here say it was Mr. Blackwell's fault to pack so many in the ship; yea and there were great mutterings, and repinings amongst them, and upbraiding of Mr. Blackwell, for his dealing, and disposing of them; when they saw how he had disposed of them, and how he insulted over them; yea the streets at Gravesend rung of their extreme quarrellings, crying out one of another, "Thou hast brought me to this," and "I may thank thee for this." Heavy news it is, and I would be glad to hear how far it will discourage; I see none here discouraged much, but rather desire to learn to beware by other men's harms, and to amend that wherein they have failed. As we desire to serve one another in love, so take heed of being enthralled, by any imperious person, especially if they be discerned to have an eye to themselves. It doth often trouble me to think that in this business, we are all to learn and none to teach, but better so, than to depend upon such teachers, as Mr. Blackwell was. Such a stratagem, he once made for Mr. Johnson, and his people at Emden, which was their subversion. But though he there cleanly (yet unhonestly) plucked his neck

---

[48]   Sir Samuel Argall made a number of voyages to Virginia. In 1617 he went to Virginia as deputy governor and returned home in April 1619 to be replaced by Sir George Yeardley. Several of Samuel Argall's voyage accounts and letters can be found in Samuel Purchas, *Hakluytus Posthumus or Purchas His Pilgrimes* (London, 1625).

out of the collar, yet at last his foot is caught. Here are no letters come; the ship Captain Argall came in, is yet in the west parts, all that we hear is but his reports, it seemeth he came away secretly; the ship that Mr. Blackwell went in will be here shortly. It is as Mr. Robinson once said: he thought we should hear no good of them.

Mr. B. is not well at this time; whether he will come back to you or go into the north, I yet know not; for myself I hope to see an end of this business ere I come, though I am sorry to be thus from you; if things had gone roundly forward I should have been with you within these 14 days. I pray God direct us, and give us that spirit which is fitting for such a business. Thus having summarily pointed at things which Mr. Brewster (I think) hath more largely writ of to Mr. Robinson. I leave you to the Lord's protection.

Yours in all readiness, etc.

Robert Cushman

London, May 8
Anno. 1619.

A word or two by way of digression touching this Mr. Blackwell, he was an elder of the church at Amsterdam, a man well known of most of them. He declined from the truth with Mr. Johnson[49] and the rest, and went with him when they parted asunder, in that woeful manner which brought so great dishonor to God, scandal to the truth; and outward ruin to themselves in this world. But I hope notwithstanding (through the mercies of the Lord) their souls are now at rest with him in the heavens, and that they are arrived in the haven of happiness; though some of their bodies were thus buried in the terrible seas, and others sunk under the burthen of bitter afflictions. He with some others had prepared for to go to Virginia. And he (with sundry godly citizens) being at a private meeting

---

[49]   Bradford described Francis Johnson in his *First Conference* as follows: "[He] was pastor of the church of God at Amsterdam. A very grave man he was, and an able teacher, and was the most solemn in all his administrations that we have seen any, and especially in dispensing the seals of the covenant, both baptism and the Lord's Supper. And a good disputant he was . . . . He, by reason of many dissensions that fell out in the church, and the subtlety of one of the elders of the same, came after many years to alter his judgment about the government of the church, and his practice thereupon, which caused a division among them. But he lived not many years after, and died at Amsterdam after his return from Emden."

(I take it a fast) in London, being discovered many of them were apprehended whereof Mr. Blackwell was one; but he so glossed with the bishops and either dissembled or flatly denied the truth which formerly he had maintained. And not only so, but very unworthily betrayed, and accused another godly man (who had escaped) that so he might slip his own neck out of the collar, and to obtain his own freedom, brought others into bonds. Whereupon he so won the bishops' favor (but lost the Lord's) as he was not only dismissed but in open court, the archbishop gave him great applause, and his solemn blessing to proceed in his voyage. But if such events follow the bishops' blessing, happy are they that miss the same. It is much better to keep a good conscience, and have the Lord's blessing whether in life or death.

> But see how the man thus apprehended by Mr.
> Blackwell's means, writes to a friend of his

Right dear friend, and Christian brother, Mr. Carver:
    I salute you and yours in the Lord, etc. As for my own present condition, I doubt not but you well understand it ere this, by our brother Masterson[50]; who should have tasted of the same cup, had his place of residence, and his person, been as well known as myself, somewhat I have written to Mr. Cushman how the matter still continues. I have petitioned twice to Mr. Sherives, and once to my Lord Cooke; and have used such reasons to move them to pity, that if they were not overruled by some others, I suppose I should soon gain my liberty; as that I was a young man living by my credit, indebted to divers in our city, living at more than ordinary charges, in a close, and tedious prison, besides great rents abroad; all my business lying still, my only servant lying lame in the country, my wife being also great with child. And yet no answer till the lords of His Majesty's Council gave consent. Howbeit, Mr. Blackwell, a man as deep in this action as I, was delivered at a cheaper rate, with a great deal less ado; yea with an addition of the Archbishop's blessing. I am sorry for Mr. Blackwell's weakness, I wish it may prove no worse. But yet he, and some others of them, before their going, were not sorry; but thought it was for the best that I was nominated, not because the

---

50   Richard Masterson (c1590-1633) was a member of the Pilgrims' church in Leiden.
      He, his wife Mary (Goodall), and two children, Nathaniel and Sarah, came to
      Plymouth about 1629 or 1630. He died at Plymouth in the general sickness that
      occurred in the autumn of 1633.

Lord sanctifies evil, to good: but that the action was good, yea for the best. One reason I well remember he used was, because this trouble would increase the Virginia Plantation, in that now people began to be more generally inclined to go; and if he had not nominated some such as I, he had not been free; being it was known, that divers citizens, besides themselves were there. I expect an answer shortly, what they intend concerning me; I purpose to write to some others of you, by whom you shall know the certainty. Thus not having further at present to acquaint you withal, commending myself to your prayers, I cease, and commit you, and us all to the Lord:

from my chamber in Wodstreet Compter[51]:

Your friend, and brother in bonds,

Sabine Staresmore

September 4, Anno. 1618.

But at last, after all these things (and their long attendance) they had a patent granted them, and confirmed under the Company's seal; but these divisions and distractions, had shaken off many of their pretended friends; and disappointed them of much of their hoped for, and proffered means. By the advice of some friends this patent was not taken in the name of any of their own; but in the name of Mr. John Wincop (a religious gentleman then belonging to the Countess of Lincoln) who intended to go with them; but God so disposed that he never went, nor they ever made use of this patent, which had cost them so much labor, and charge; as by the sequel will appear. This Patent being sent over for them to view, and consider; as also the passages about the propositions, between them, and such merchants, and friends as should either go, or adventure with them; and especially with those on whom they did chiefly depend for shipping and means[52], whose proffers had been large; they were requested to fit and prepare themselves with all speed. A right emblem it may be of the uncertain things of this world; that when men have toiled themselves for them, they vanish into smoke.

---

[51] A prison in London.

[52] Mr. Tho: Weston, etc. (Bradford).

The 6 Chap.

*Concerning ye agreements and articles betwoon
them, and such marchants & others as aduentured
moneys: with other things, falling out abouts
making their provisions.*

Upon the receipt of these things by one of their messengers, they had a solemn meeting and a day of humiliation to seek the Lord for His direction; and their pastor took this text: 1 Samuel 23:3,4: "And David's men said unto him, see, we be afraid here in Judah, how much more if we come to Keilah against the host of the Philistines? Then David asked counsel of the Lord again," etc. From which text he taught many things very aptly, and befitting their present occasion, and condition, strengthening them against their fears, and perplexities, and encouraging them in their resolutions.

After which they concluded both what number, and what persons should prepare themselves to go with the first; for all that were willing to have gone, could not get ready, for their other affairs in so short a time; neither if all could have been ready, had there been means, to have transported them all together. Those that stayed being the greater number, required the pastor to stay with them; and indeed for other reasons, he could not then well go, and so it was the more easily yielded unto. The other then desired the Elder Mr. Brewster to go with them, which was also condescended unto. [53] It was also

---

[53]   Edward Winslow, in *Hypocrisy Unmasked* (London, 1646) added "Our agents returning, we further sought the Lord by a public and solemn fast, for his gracious guidance. And hereupon we came to this resolution, that it was best for one part of the Church to go at first, and the other to stay, viz. the youngest and strongest part to go. Secondly, they that went should freely offer themselves. Thirdly, if the major part went, the pastor to go with them; if not, the Elder only. Fourthly, if the Lord should frown upon our proceedings, then those that went to return, and the brethren that remained

agreed on by mutual consent, and covenant that those that went should be an absolute church of themselves, as well as those that stayed; seeing in such a dangerous voyage, and a removal to such a distance, it might come to pass, they should (for the body of them) never meet again in this world, yet with this proviso, that as any of the rest came over to them, or of the other returned upon occasion; they should be reputed as members without any further dismission, or testimonial. It was also promised to those that went first by the body of the rest; that if the Lord gave them life, and means, and opportunity, they would come to them, as soon as they could.

About this time, whilst they were perplexed with the proceedings of the Virginia Company, and the ill news from thence about Mr. Blackwell, and his company; and making inquiry about the hiring, and buying of shipping for their voyage; some Dutchmen made them fair offers about going with them.[54] Also one Mr. Thomas Weston[55] a merchant of London came to Leiden about the same time (who was well acquainted with some of them, and a furtherer of them in their former proceedings), having much conference with Mr. Robinson and others of the chief of them, persuaded them to go on (as it seems) and not to meddle with the Dutch, or too much to depend on the Virginia Company, for if that failed, if they came to resolution, he, and such merchants as were his friends (together with their own means) would set them forth; and they should make ready, and neither fear want of shipping, nor money; for what they wanted should be provided. And (not so much for himself) as for the satisfying of such friends as he should procure to adventure

---

still there, to assist and be helpful to them, but if God should be pleased to favor them that went, then they also should endeavor to help over such as were poor and ancient, and willing to come."

[54] Edward Winslow briefly comments on the Dutch offer in his *Hypocrisy Unmasked* (London, 1646) as well: "And truly what I have written, is far short of what it was, omitting for brevity sake many circumstances, as the large offers the Dutch offered us, either to have removed into Zealand, and there lived with them: or if we would go on such adventures, to go under them to Hudson's River (where they have since a great plantation, etc.) and how they would freely have transported us, and furnished every family with cattle, etc."

[55] For a good, concise biography of Thomas Weston, see Peter Wilson Coldham, "Thomas Weston, Ironmonger of London and America, 1609-1647," *National Genealogical Society Quarterly* 62 (September 1974):163-172.

in this business, they were to draw such articles of agreement, and make such propositions, as might the better induce his friends to venture. Upon which (after the former conclusion) articles were drawn, and agreed unto, and were shown unto him, and approved by him. And afterwards by their messenger, (Mr. John Carver) sent into England, who together with Robert Cushman were to receive the moneys and make provision, both for shipping, and other things for the voyage; with this charge, not to exceed their commission, but to proceed according to the former articles. Also some were chosen to do the like, for such things, as were to be prepared there; so those that were to go, prepared themselves with all speed, and sold off their estates[56], and (such as were able) put in their moneys into the common stock; which was disposed by those appointed, for the making of general provisions. About this time also they had heard, both by Mr. Weston, and others, that sundry Honorable Lords had obtained a large grant from the King; for the more northerly parts of that country, derived out of the Virginia patent, and wholly secluded from their Government; and to be called by another name, viz., New England. Unto which Mr. Weston, and the chief of them, began to incline it was best for them to go, as for other reasons, so chiefly for the hope of present profit to be made by the fishing that was found in that country.

But as in all businesses the acting part is most difficult, especially where the work of many agents must concur; so was it found in this: for some of those that should have gone in England, fell off and would not go; other merchants, and friends that had offered to adventure their moneys withdrew, and pretended many excuses: some disliking they went not to Guiana; others again would adventure nothing, except they went to Virginia. Some again (and those that were most relied on) fell in utter dislike with Virginia, and would do nothing if they went thither. In the midst of these distractions, they of Leiden, who had put off their estates, and laid out their moneys were brought into a great strait, fearing what issue these

---

[56]   Several of these house sales are recorded in Leiden records. On 19 April 1619, William Bradford sold his house on the north side of the *Achtergracht* between the *Paradijssteeg* and the *Bouwenlouwensteeg* in Leiden to Jan des Obrys for 1120 guilders (Leiden Archives 163/RA67VVfo. 195/19-4-1619). In September 1619, Robert Cushman sold his house on the *Nonnensteeg* to John de Later for 180 guilders, and Roger and Sarah (Minter) Simmons sold their house to Jacob Cornelis de Haas for 746 guilders. And on 1 April 1620, Thomas Rogers sold his house on *Barbarasteeg* for 300 guilders to Mordecai Cohen.

things would come to, but at length the generality was swayed to this latter opinion.

But now another difficulty arose, for Mr. Weston, and some other that were for this course, either for their better advantage or rather for the drawing on of others, as they pretended; would have some of those conditions altered that were first agreed on at Leiden. To which the 2 agents sent from Leiden (or at least one of them[57], who is most charged with it) did consent; seeing else that all was like to be dashed; and the opportunity lost, and that they which had put off their estates, and paid in their moneys were in hazard to be undone. They presumed to conclude with the merchants on those terms, in some things contrary to their order, and commission; and without giving them notice of the same; yea it was concealed lest it should make any further delay; which was the cause afterward of much trouble and contention.

It will be meet I here insert
these conditions, which are as
followeth.

Anno: 1620. July 1.

1. The adventurers[58], and planters do agree, that every person that goeth being aged 16 years, and upward; be rated at $10^£$, and ten pounds to be accounted a single share.
2. That he that goeth in person, and furnisheth himself out with $10^£$ either in money, or other provisions; be accounted as having $20^£$ in stock, and in the division shall receive a double share.
3. The persons transported, and the adventurers shall continue their joint stock, and partnership together, the space of 7 years (except some unexpected impediment, do cause the whole company to agree otherwise) during which time, all profits, and benefits, that are got by trade, traffic, trucking, working, fishing, or any other means of any person, or persons; remain still in the common stock until the division.
4. That at their coming there, they choose out such a number of fit persons, as may furnish their ships and boats for fishing upon the sea; employing the rest in their several faculties upon the land, as

---

[57] Robert Cushman is the man referred to here.

[58] The investors in the Pilgrims' joint stock company were referred to as "adventurers," i.e. those who adventured their money.

building houses, tilling, and planting the ground, and making such commodities as shall be most useful for the colony.

5. That at the end of the 7 years, the capital and profits; viz. the houses, lands, goods and chattels, be equally divided betwixt the adventurers, and planters; which done every man shall be free, from other of them of any debt, or detriment concerning this adventure.

6. Whosoever cometh to the colony hereafter or putteth any into the stock, shall at the end of the 7 years, be allowed proportionably to the time of his so doing.

7. He that shall carry his wife, and children, or servants shall be allowed for every person now aged 16 years, and upward; a single share in the division, or if he provide them necessaries a double share, or if they be between 10 year old and 16 then 2 of them to be reckoned for a person, both in transportation and division.

8. That such children as now go, and are under the age of ten years, have no other share in the division, but 50 acres of unmanured land.

9. That such persons as die before the 7 years be expired, their executors to have their part or share, at the division, proportionably to the time of their life in the colony.

10. That all such persons as are of this colony, are to have their meat, drink, apparel, and all provisions out of the common stock and goods of the said colony.

The chief and principal differences between these, and the former conditions, stood in those 2 points: that the houses, and lands improved, especially gardens, and home lots should remain undivided wholly to the planters at the 7 years' end. 2^{ly} that they should have had 2 days in a week for their own private employment, for the more comfort of themselves, and their families; especially such as had families. But because letters, are by some wise men counted the best parts of histories; I shall show their grievances hereabout by their own letters, in which the passages of things will be more truly discerned.

A Letter of Mr. Robinson's
to John Carver. June
14, 1620. New Style.

My dear friend, and brother, whom with yours I always remember in my best affection; and whose welfare I shall never cease to commend to

God by my best and most earnest prayers: you do thoroughly understand by our general letters the estate of things here, which indeed is very pitiful; especially by want of shipping, and not seeing means likely, much less certain of having it provided; though withal there be great want of money, and means to do needful things. Mr. Pickering[59], you know before this, will not defray a penny here; though Robert Cushman, presumed of I know not how many 100£ from him, and I know not whom; yet it seems strange that we should be put to him to receive, both his and his partner's adventure, and yet Mr. Weston write unto him, that in regard of it, he hath drawn upon him 100£ more. But there is in this some mystery, as indeed it seems there is in the whole course. Besides whereas divers are to pay in some parts of their moneys yet behind, they refuse to do it; till they see shipping provided, or a course taken for it. Neither do I think is there a man here would pay anything, if he had again his money in his purse. You know right well we depended on Mr. Weston alone, and upon such means, as he would procure for this common business; and when we had in hand another course with the Dutchmen, broke it off at his motion, and upon the conditions by him shortly after propounded. He did this in his love I know, but things appear not answerable from him hitherto. That he should have first have put in his moneys, is thought by many to have been but fit. But that, I can well excuse, he being a merchant, and having use of it to his benefit, whereas others, if it had been in their hands would have consumed it. But that he should not but have had either shipping ready before this time, or at least certain means, and course, and the same known to us for it; or have taken other order otherwise, cannot in my conscience be excused. I have heard, that when he hath been moved in the business, he hath put it off from himself, and referred it to the others, and would come to George

---

[59]   Edward Pickering was a long-time member of the Leiden congregation. In his 1612 Leiden marriage record to Mary Stubbs, he is called a merchant of London. He was for a time an agent for London merchant Thomas Weston, and it was probably through him that the Pilgrims and Weston became acquainted. He and Weston got into an unrelated monetary dispute in 1619, which is probably why Pickering refused to contribute his expected investment. See Peter Wilson Coldham, "Thomas Weston, Ironmonger of London and America, 1609-1647," *National Genealogical Society Quarterly* 62 (September 1974):163-172.

Morton[60], and enquire news of him about things as if he had scarce been some accessory unto it. Whether he hath failed of some helps from others, which he expected; and so be not well able to go through with things, or whether he hath feared lest you should be ready too soon, and so increase the charge of shipping above that is meet; or whether he have thought by withholding to put us upon straits, thinking that thereby Mr. Brewer[61], and Mr. Pickering would be drawn by importunity to do more; or what other mystery is in it we know not; but sure we are that things are not answerable to such an occasion. Mr. Weston makes himself merry with our endeavors about buying a ship, but we have done nothing in this but with good reason (as I am persuaded) nor yet that I know in anything else; save in those two, the one, that we employed Robert Cushman, who is known (though a good man and of special abilities in his kind, yet) most unfit to deal for other men by reason of his singularity, and too great indifferency for any conditions, and for (to speak truly) that we have had nothing from him but terms, and presumptions. The other that we have so much relied (by implicit faith, as it were) upon generalities, without seeing the particular course, and means, for so weighty an affair set down unto us: for shipping Mr. Weston (it should seem) is set upon hiring, which yet I wish he may presently effect, but I see little hope of help from hence if so it be. Of Mr. Brewer you know what to expect; I do not think Mr. Pickering will engage, except in the course of buying, in former letters specified. About the conditions, you have our reasons

---

60   George Morton was a member of the Leiden congregation, and came to Plymouth in 1623 on the ship *Anne*; he died about a year later in June 1624. He is generally thought to have been the "G. Mourt" who published *A Relation or Journal of the Beginning and Proceedings of the English Plantation Settled at Plymouth* (London, 1622). His son Nathaniel authored *New England's Memorial* (Cambridge, 1669).

61   Thomas Brewer was an associate of the Leiden congregation who, with William Brewster and others, helped print a number of illegal religious pamphlets for distribution in England, for which he was arrested and imprisoned in Leiden in 1619. Most of the documents relating to this incident are reprinted in Edward Arber's *The Story of the Pilgrim Fathers: As Told By Themselves, Their Friends, and Their Enemies* (Boston: Houghton Mifflon, 1897). Thomas Brewer also wrote a book, published after his death, *Gospel Public Worship: Or the Translation, Metaphrase, Analysis and Exposition of Romans 12 from Verse 1 to 8.* (London, 1656).

for our judgments of what is agreed. And let this specially be borne in mind, that the greatest part of the colony is like to be employed constantly, not upon dressing their particular land, and building houses, but upon fishing, trading, etc. So as the land, and house will be but a trifle for advantage to the adventurers, and yet the division of it, a great discouragement to the planters; who would with singular care make it comfortable, with borrowed hours from their sleep. The same consideration of common employment constantly by the most, is a good reason not to have the two days in a week denied the few planters for private use, which yet is subordinate to common good. Consider also how much unfit, that you and your likes, must serve a new apprenticeship of 7 years, and not a day's freedom from task. Send me word what persons are to go, who of useful faculties, and how many, and particularly of everything; I know you want not a mind: I am sorry you have not been at London all this while, but the provisions could not want you. Time will suffer me to write no more; fare you, and yours well always in the Lord, in Whom I rest.

Yours to use,
John Robinson

Another letter from sundry of them
at the same time

To their loving friends John Carver
and Robert Cushman these etc.

Good brethren after salutations, etc. We received divers letters, at the coming of Mr. Nash[62], and our pilot, which is a great encouragement unto us; and for whom we hope after times will minister occasion of praising God; and indeed had you not sent him many would have been ready to faint and go back partly in respect of the new conditions, which have been taken up by you (which all men are against) and partly in regard of our own inability to do any one of those many weighty businesses you refer to us here. For the former whereof, whereas Robert Cushman desires reasons for our dislike; promising thereupon to alter the same, or else saying we should think he hath no brains; we desire him to exercise

---

[62] Thomas Nash, born c1565, was another member of the Leiden congregation. He remained in Leiden for more than thirty years after the *Mayflower* sailed.

them therein, referring him to our pastor's former reasons, and them to the censure of the godly wise. But our desires are, that you will not entangle yourselves, and us, in any such unreasonable courses as those are, viz. that the merchants should have the half of men's houses, and lands, at the dividend; and that persons should be deprived of the 2 days in a week agreed upon, yea every moment of time for their own particular; by reason whereof we cannot conceive why any should carry servants, for their own help, and comfort; for that we can require no more of them, than all men one of another. This we have only by relation from Mr. Nash, and not from any writing of your own, and therefore hope you have not proceeded far in so great a thing without us. But requiring you not to exceed the bounds of your commission, which was to proceed upon the things, or conditions agreed upon, and expressed in writing (at your going over about it) we leave it; not without marveling, that yourself (as you write) knowing how small a thing troubleth our consultations, and how few, as you fear understands the business aright, should trouble us with such matters, as these are, etc.

Salute Mr. Weston from us, in whom we hope we are not deceived; we pray you make known our estate unto him, and if you think good show him our letters, at least tell him (that under God) we much rely upon him, and put our confidence in him; and as yourselves well know, that if he had not been an adventurer with us, we had not taken it in hand; presuming that if he had not seen means to accomplish it, he would not have begun it; so we hope in our extremity he will so far help us as our expectation be no way made frustrate concerning him. Since therefore good brethren we have plainly opened the state of things with us in this matter you will, etc. Thus beseeching the Almighty, who is all sufficient to raise us out of this depth of difficulties, to assist us herein; raising such means by His providence, and fatherly care for us, His poor children, and servants, as we may with comfort behold the hand of our God, for good towards us in this our business; which we undertake in His name, and fear. We take leave and remain

Your perplexed yet hopeful brethren,
S.F. E.W. W.B. I.A.[63]

---

[63] Thomas Prince made the following note at this point in Bradford's manuscript: "In Gov. Bradford's *Collection of Letters*, these subscribers were thus wrote out at length: Samuel Fuller, William Bradford, Isaac Allerton, Ed. Winslow."

June 10 New Style
Anno: 1620

A letter of Robert Cushman's to them

Brethren, I understand by letters, and passages that have come to me, that there are great discontents, and dislikes of my proceedings amongst you; sorry I am to hear it, yet content to bear it, as not doubting but that partly by writing, and more principally by word when we shall come together, I shall satisfy any reasonable man. I have been persuaded by some, especially this bearer, to come and clear things unto you: but as things now stand I cannot be absent one day, except I should hazard all the voyage. Neither conceive I any great good would come of it. Take then (brethren) this as a step to give you content. First for your dislike of the alteration of one clause in the conditions, if you conceive it right, there can be no blame lie on me at all; for the articles first brought over by John Carver, were never seen of any of the adventurers here, except Mr. Weston; neither did any of them like them because of that clause; nor Mr. Weston himself after he had well considered it. But as at the first there was £500 withdrawn by Sir George Ferrar and his brother, upon that dislike; so all the rest would have withdrawn (Mr. Weston excepted,) if we had not altered that clause. Now whilst we at Leiden conclude upon points, as we did, we reckoned without our host, which was not my fault. Besides I showed you by a letter the equity of that condition, and our inconveniences; which might be set against all Mr. Robinson's inconveniences; that without the alteration of that clause, we could neither have means to get thither, nor supply whereby to subsist when we were there; yet notwithstanding all those reasons, which were not mine, but other men's wiser than myself, without answer to any one of them; here cometh over many querimonies, and complaints against me, of lording it over my brethren, and making conditions, fitter for thieves and bond-slaves, than honest men, and that of my own head I did what I list. And at last a paper of reasons, framed against that clause in the conditions; which as they were delivered me open, so my answer is open to you all. And first as they are no other but inconveniences, such as a man might frame 20 as great on the other side, and yet prove, nor disprove nothing by them; so they miss, and mistake both the very ground of the article; and nature of the project.

1. For, first it is said, that if there had been no division of houses, and lands, it had been better for the poor. True, and that showeth the inequality

of the conditions we should more respect him, that ventureth, both his money, and his person: than him that ventureth but his person only.

2. Consider whereabout we are; not giving alms, but furnishing a storehouse, no one shall be poorer than another for 7 years, and if any be rich, none can be poor. At the least we must not in such business, cry "poor, poor; mercy, mercy." Charity hath its life in wrecks, not in ventures, you are by this most in a hopeful pity of making; therefore complain not before you have need.

3. This will hinder the building of good, and fair houses, contrary to the advice of politics. A[nswer]: So we would have it, our purpose is to build for the present, such houses as, if need be, we may with little grief set afire, and run away by the light. Our riches shall not be in pomp but in strength, if God send us riches, we will employ them to provide more men, ships, munition, etc. You may see it amongst the best politics, that a commonwealth is readier to ebb, than to flow, when once fine houses, and gay clothes come up.

4. The Government may prevent excess in building. A[nswer]: But if it be on all men beforehand resolved on, to build mean houses, the Governor's labor is spared.

5. All men are not of one condition. A[nswer]: If by condition, you mean wealth, you are mistaken; if you mean by condition qualities; then I say he that is not content his neighbor shall have as good a house, fare, means, etc. as himself, is not of a good quality. 2ly such retired persons, as have an eye only to themselves, are fitter to come where catching is, than closing; and are fitter to live alone, than in any society, either civil, or religious.

6. It will be of little value, scarce worth £5. A[nswer]: True it may be not worth half £5. If then so small a thing will content them, why strive we thus about it, and give them occasion to suspect us to be worldly, and covetous, I will not say what I have heard since these complaints came first over.

7. Our friends with us that adventure, mind not their own profit, as did the old adventurers. A[nswer]: Then they are better than we, who for a little matter of profit are ready to draw back, and it is more apparent. Brethren look to it, that make profit your main end, repent of this, else go not lest you be like a Jonas to Tarshish; 2ly, though some of them mind not their profit, yet others do mind it; and why not, as well as we; ventures are made by all sorts of men, and we must labor to give them all content, if we can.

8. It will break the course of community, as may be showed by many reasons; A[nswer]: That is but said, and I say again it will best foster communion, as may be showed by many reasons.

9. Great profit is like to be made by trucking, fishing, etc. A[nswer]: as it is better for them, so for us; for half is ours, besides our living still upon it, and if such profit in that way come, our labor shall be the less on the land, and our houses, and lands, must and will be of less value.

10. Our hazard is greater than theirs. A[nswer]: True, but do they put us upon it; do they urge or egg us? Hath not the motion, and resolution been always in ourselves; do they any more than in seeing us resolute if we had means, help us to means upon equal terms, and conditions; if we will not go, they are content to keep their moneys. Thus I have pointed at a way to loose those knots; which I hope you will consider seriously, and let me have no more stir about them.

Now further I hear a noise of slavish conditions by me made; but surely this is all that I have altered, and reasons I have sent you; if you mean it of the 2 days in a week, for particular, as some insinuate; you are deceived, you may have 3 days in a week for me if you will; and when I have spoken to the adventurers of times of working, they have said they hope we are men of discretion, and conscience, and so fit to be trusted ourselves with that. But indeed the ground of our proceedings at Leiden was mistaken, and so here is nothing but tottering every day, etc.

As for them of Amsterdam I had thought they would as soon have gone to Rome as with us; for our liberty is to them as rat's bane, and their rigor as bad to us, as the Spanish Inquisition; if any practice of mine discourage them, let them yet draw back, I will undertake they shall have their money again presently paid here. Or if the company think me to be the Jonas, let them cast me off before we go, I shall be content to stay with good will, having but the clothes on my back; only let us have quietness, and no more of these clamors, full little did I expect these things which now are come to pass, etc.

Yours, R. Cushman.

But whether this letter of his ever came to their hands at Leiden, I well know not; I rather think it was stayed by Mr. Carver and kept by him, forgiving offense. But this which follows was there received; both which I thought pertinent to recite.

Another of his to the foresaid, June 11, 1620

Salutations, etc. I received your letter yesterday, by John Turner[64];
with another the same day from Amsterdam by Mr. W. savoring of the
place whence it came. And indeed the many discouragements I find here
together with the demurs, and retirings there; had made me to say, I would
give up my accounts to John Carver, and at his coming acquaint him fully
with all courses, and so leave it quit, with only the poor clothes on my
back. But gathering up myself, by further consideration I resolved yet to
make one trial more. And to acquaint Mr. Weston with the fainted state of
our business; and though he hath been much discontented at some thing
amongst us of late; which hath made him often say, that save for his promise,
he would not meddle at all with the business any more; yet considering
how far we were plunged into matters; and how it stood both on our credits,
and undoing; at the last he gathered up himself a little more, and coming to
me 2 hours after, he told me he would not yet leave it. And so advising
together, we resolved to hire a ship, and have took liking of one till Monday,
about 60 last[65], for a greater we cannot get except it be too great, but a fine
ship it is. And seeing our near friends there, are so straight-laced, we hope
to assure her without troubling them any further; and if the ship fall too
small, it fitteth well that such as stumble at straws already, may rest them
there awhile, lest worse blocks come in the way, ere 7 years be ended. If
you had beaten this business so thoroughly, a month ago; and write to us as
now you do; we could thus have done much more conveniently. But it is, as
it is; I hope our friends there, if they be quitted of the ship hire, will be

---

[64] John Turner was an eventual *Mayflower* passenger; he and his two sons died the
    first winter at Plymouth in 1621.

[65] Sixty lasts is approximately 120 tons, although there is no exact conversion
    factor. Bradford, later in this history, indicates the *Mayflower* was 180 tons. This
    has led some editors to suspect the ship referred to here is not the *Mayflower*,
    and that the Pilgrims must have found the *Mayflower* subsequent to this letter.
    However, it may be worth noting that the *Mayflower* was recorded as 120 tons
    in "A Note of the Shipping Provided for Virginia," in the Duke of Manchester's
    Papers, No. 121 (J.R. Hutchinson, "The *Mayflower*: Her Identity and Tonnage,"
    NEHGR October 1916, p. 341). That the *Mayflower* was truly larger than 120
    tons seems clear, however, because the Customs Books of the Exchequer for the
    Port of London show the *Mayflower* unloading, on several occasion, more than
    180 tons of wine.

induced to venture the more. All that I now require is that salt, and nets[66], may there be bought, and for all the rest we will here provide it; yet if that will not be, let them but stand for it a month, or two, and we will take order to pay it all. Let Mr. Reynolds[67] tarry there, and bring the ship to Southampton. We have hired another pilot here, one Mr. Clark[68], who went last year to Virginia with a ship of kine. You shall hear distinctly by John Turner, who I think shall come hence on Tuesday night; I had thought to have come with him, to have answered to my complaints, but I shall learn to pass little for their censures; and if I had more mind to go, and dispute, and expostulate with them, than I have care of this weighty business, I were like them who live by clamors, and jangling. But neither my mind, nor my body, is at liberty to do much, for I am fettered with business; and had rather study to be quiet, than to make answer to their exceptions; if men be set on it, let them beat the air; I hope such as are my sincere friends, will not think but I can give some reason of my actions. But of your mistaking about the matter, and other things tending to this business, I shall next inform you more distinctly; mean space entreat our friends, not to be too busy in answering matters, before they know them. If I do such things as I cannot give reasons for, it is like you have set a fool about your business, and so turn the reproof to yourselves, and send another, and let me come again to my combs.[69] But setting aside my natural infirmities, I refuse not to have my cause judged, both of God, and all indifferent men; and when we come together I shall give account of my actions here; the Lord who judgeth justly without respect of persons, see into the equity of my cause; and give us quiet,

---

[66] Salt and nets—a further indication the Pilgrims hope to make money by fishing.

[67] Reynolds was the master of the *Speedwell*, the ship that brought the Pilgrims from Delftshaven to Southampton, and which was to have accompanied the *Mayflower* to America. A William Reynolds was master of the ship *Charity* that Thomas Weston sent out in 1622, and is likely the same man. (*Acts of the Privy Council, Colonial Series, 1613-1680*, p. 50-51).

[68] John Clark, master's mate of the *Mayflower*. He had been to Virginia on several occasions, including once in 1611 when he was captured by the Spanish and held for more than 5 years. The interrogations, recorded by his Spanish captors, were reprinted by Irene A. Wright, "Documents: Spanish Policy towards Virginia," *American Historical Review* 25(April 1920):448-479. Clark made another trip to Jamestown in 1618, and moved there permanently in 1623, but died shortly thereafter.

[69] While in Leiden, Cushman was occupied as a wool-comber.

peaceable, and patient minds in all these turmoils, and sanctify unto us all crosses whatsoever. And so I take my leave of you all, in all love, and affection.

I hope we shall get all here ready in 14 days.

Your poor brother,

Robert Cushman

June 11, 1620

Besides these things, there fell out a difference among those 3 that received the moneys and made the provisions in England; for besides these two formerly mentioned sent from Leiden for this end, viz., Mr. Carver, and Robert Cushman, there was one chosen in England, to be joined with them to make the provisions for the voyage; his name was Mr. Martin[70] he came from Billericay in Essex, from which parts came sundry others to go with them, as also from London and other places; and therefore it was thought meet and convenient by them in Holland that these strangers that were to go with them, should appoint one thus to be joined with them, not so much for any great need of their help, as to avoid all suspicion, or jealousy of any partiality; and indeed their care for giving offense, both in this and other things afterward, turned to great inconvenience unto them, as in the sequel will appear; but however it showed their equal, and honest minds. The provisions were for the most part, made at Southampton contrary to Mr. Weston's, and Robert Cushman's, mind (whose counsels did most concur in all things). A touch of which things I shall give in a letter of his to Mr. Carver, and more will appear afterward.

To his loving friend Mr. John Carver

these, etc.

Loving friend I have received from you some letters, full of affection and complaints, and what it is you would have of me I know not; for your crying out, "Negligence, negligence, negligence;" I marvel why so negligent a man was used in the business. Yet know you, that all I have power to do here, shall not be one hour behind I warrant you. You have reference to Mr. Weston to help us with money, more than his adventure; when he protesteth but for his promise, he would not have done anything. He saith we take a heady course, and is offended, that our provisions are made so far off; as also that he was not made acquainted with our quantity of things; and saith that in now being in 3

---

[70]   For information on Christopher Martin, see R.J. Carpenter, *Christopher Martin, Great Burstead and the Mayflower* (Chelmsford, 1993).

places so far remote; we will with going up, and down, and wrangling, and expostulating pass over the summer before we will go. And to speak the truth there is fallen already amongst us a flat schism; and we are readier to go to dispute, than to set forward a voyage. I have received from Leiden since you went, 3 or 4 letters directed to you, though they only concern me, I will not trouble you with them. I always feared the event of the Amsterdams striking in with us[71], I trow you must excommunicate me, or else you must go without their company, or we shall want no quarreling, but let them pass. We have reckoned it should seem without our host; and counting upon a 150 persons, there cannot be found above £1200 and odd moneys of all the ventures you can reckon; besides some cloth, stockings, and shoes which are not counted, so we shall come short at least 3 or £400. I would have had something shortened at first, of beer, and other provisions, in hope of other adventures; and now we could have both in Amsterdam; and Kent have beer enough to serve our turn, but now we cannot accept it without prejudice. You fear we have begun to build and shall not be able to make an end. Indeed our courses, were never established by counsel; we may therefore justly fear their standing. Yea there was a schism amongst us three at the first. You wrote to Mr. Martin, to prevent the making of the provisions in Kent; which he did, and set down his resolution, how much he would have of everything, without respect to any counsel, or exception. Surely he that is in a society, and yet regards not counsel, may better be a king, than a consort. To be short, if there be not some other disposition settled unto than yet is, we that should be partners of humility and peace shall be examples of jangling and insulting; yet your money which you there must have; we will get provided for you instantly, £500 you say will serve; for the rest which here, and in Holland is to be used, we may go scratch for it. For Mr. Crabe[72] of whom you write, he hath promised to go with us, yet I tell you I shall not be without fear till I see him shipped, for he is much opposed,

---

[71] Some of the Separatists from the church at Amsterdam, which the Pilgrims had moved to Leiden to get away from in 1609, now wanted to join the voyage.

[72] He was a minister (Bradford). Cushman's suspicions were well-founded—Mr. Crabe would not make the voyage. But it appears this man might have been the person who hooked up the Pilgrims with the ship *Mayflower*. The *Mayflower* was primarily a wine-trading ship, and in May 1620 it had just come into London with a cargo of French wines from either Bordeaux or Rochelle. The Customs Books of the Exchequer indicate that John Crabbe purchased 19 tons of Cognac wine on May 15 from Master Christopher Jones. Crabbe returned four days later to purchase an additional hogshead of wine. (PRO E190/24/3).

yet, I hope he will not fail. Think the best of all, and bear with patience what is wanting; and the Lord guide us all.

Your loving friend,
Robert Cushman

London, June 10
Anno 1620

I have been the larger in these things; and so shall crave leave in some like passages following, (though in other things I shall labor to be more contract) that their children may see with what difficulties their fathers wrestled in going through these things, in their first beginnings; and how God brought them along notwithstanding all their weaknesses, and infirmities. As also that some use may be made hereof in after times by others in such like weighty employments, and herewith I will end this chapter.

The · 7 · Chap ·
Of their departure from Leyden, and other things
ther abuts; with their arivall at Southhamton
wore they all mete togeather; and looks in ther
provisions ·

At length after much travail, and these debates; all things were got ready, and provided; a small ship[73] was bought and fitted in Holland, which was intended as to serve to help to transport them, so to stay in the country, and attend upon fishing, and such other affairs as might be for the good, and benefit of the colony when they came there. Another was hired at London, of burthen about 9 score[74]; and all other things got in readiness. So being ready to depart, they had a day of solemn humiliation, their pastor taking his text from Ezra 8:21: "And there at the river, by Ahava, I proclaimed a fast, that we might humble ourselves before our God, and seek of him a right way for us, and for our children, and for all our substance." Upon which he spent a good part of the day very profitably, and suitable to their present occasion; the rest of the time was spent in pouring out prayers to the Lord, with great fervency, mixed with abundance of tears. And the time being come that they must depart, they were accompanied with most of their brethren out of the city, unto a town sundry miles off called Delftshaven where the ship lay ready to receive them. So they left that goodly, and pleasant city, which had been their resting place, near 12 years; but they knew they were

---

[73] Of some 60 ton. (Bradford). The ship's name was the *Speedwell.*

[74] Nine score is 180 tons. This was the *Mayflower.* William Bradford, oddly, never mentions the name of the ship in his *History.* The ship's name was mentioned in the 1623 Division of Land (*Plymouth Colony Records* 12:4-6, also reprinted in Appendix I), and in Nathaniel Morton's history of Plymouth, *New England's Memorial* (Cambridge, 1669).

pilgrims[75], and looked not much on those things; but lift up their eyes
to the heavens, their dearest country; and quieted their spirits. When
they came to the place they found the ship and all things ready, and
such of their friends as could not come with them followed after them,
and sundry also came from Amsterdam to see them shipped and to take
their leave of them. That night was spent with little sleep by the most but
with friendly entertainment, and Christian discourse and other real
expressions of true Christian love. The next day (the wind being fair) they
went aboard, and their friends with them, where truly: doleful was the
sight of that sad, and mournful parting, to see what sighs and sobs and
prayers did sound amongst them, what tears did gush from every eye, and
pithy speeches pierced each heart; that sundry of the Dutch strangers that
stood on the quay as spectators could not refrain from tears[76]; yet

---

[75]   Hebrews 11 (Bradford). This is one of the earliest uses of the term "pilgrims" to
describe the *Mayflower* passengers. The use of the term "pilgrims" in Hebrews
11:13 (Geneva version) is as a sojourner or traveler to foreign lands; this is the
same connotation used by Robert Cushman in his *Sin and Danger of Self Love*,
when he wrote "but now we are all in all places strangers and pilgrims, travelers
and sojourners, most properly, having no dwelling but in this earthen
tabernacle . . ." Bradford used the term again in his poem "*Epitaphium Meum*,"
when he wrote "In this wilderness he did me guide / And in strange lands for me
provide. / In fears and wants, through weal and woe, / A pilgrim, passed I to and
fro." Cotton Mather also used the term in his short biography of William Bradford,
which is reprinted in the Introduction.

[76]   Edward Winslow in his *Hypocrisy Unmasked* (London, 1646) described the
scene as well: "And when the ship was ready to carry us away, the brethren that
stayed having again solemnly sought the Lord with us, and for us, and we
further engaging ourselves mutually as before; they, I say, that stayed at Leiden
feasted us that were to go at our pastor's house being large, where we refreshed
ourselves after our tears, with signing of Psalms, making joyful melody in our
hearts, as well as with the voice, there being many of the congregation very
expert in music; and indeed it was the sweetest melody that ever mine ears
heard. After this they accompanied us to Delftshaven, where we were to embark,
and there feasted us again; and after prayer performed by our pastor, where a
flood of tears was poured out, they accompanied us to the ship, but were not
able to speak one to another for the abundance of sorrow to part: but we only
going aboard (the ship lying at the quay and ready to set sail, the wind being

comfortable, and sweet it was to see such lively, and true expressions of dear, and unfeigned love. But the tide (which stays for no man) calling them away, that were thus loath to depart, their reverend pastor falling down on his knees (and they all with him) with watery cheeks, commended them with most fervent prayers to the Lord, and His blessing. And then with mutual embraces and many tears they took their leaves one, of another; which proved to be the last leave to many of them.

Thus hoisting sail[77], with a prosperous wind they came in short time to Southampton, where they found the bigger ship come from London lying ready, with all the rest of their company. After a joyful welcome, and mutual congratulations, with other friendly entertainments, they fell to parley about their business, how to dispatch with the best expedition. As also with their agents, about the alteration of the conditions, Mr. Carver pleaded he was employed here at Hampton, and knew not well what the other had done at London; Mr. Cushman answered he had done nothing but what he was urged to, partly by the grounds of equity, and more especially by necessity otherwise all had been dashed and many undone. And in the beginning he acquainted his fellow agents herewith, who consented unto him, and left it to him to execute, and to receive the money at London and send it down to them at Hampton, where they made the provisions; the which he accordingly did, though it was against his mind and some of the merchants, that they were there made. And for giving them notice at Leiden of this change, he could not well in regard of the shortness of the time; again he knew it would trouble them and hinder the business, which was already delayed overlong in regard of the season of the year which he feared they would find to their cost. But these things gave not content at present.[78] Mr. Weston likewise, came up from London to see them dispatched and to have the conditions confirmed, but they refused, and answered him that he knew right well that these were not according to the first agreement, neither could they yield to

---

fair) we gave them a volley of small shot, and three pieces of ordnance, and so lifting up our hands to each other, and our hearts for each other to the Lord our God, we departed, . . ."

[77] This was about 22 of July. (Bradford).

[78] This sentence was erroneously omitted from Samuel Eliot Morison's edition of this work. (Random House, 1952).

them, without the consent of the rest that were behind. And indeed they
had special charge when they came away from the chief of those that were
behind not to do it. At which he was much offended and told them, they
must then look to stand on their own legs, so he returned in displeasure, and
this was the first ground of discontent between them. And whereas there
wanted well near £100 to clear things at their going away he would not take
order to disburse a penny but let them shift as they could, so they were
forced to sell off some of their provisions to stop this gap, which was some 3
or 4 score firkins[79] of butter, which commodity they might best spare having
provided too large a quantity of that kind. Then they write a letter to the
merchants, and adventurers about the differences concerning the conditions;
as followeth:

Aug. 3 Anno. 1620[80]

Beloved friends, sorry we are that there should be occasion of writing at
all unto you, partly because we ever expected to see the most of you here; but
especially because there should any difference at all be conceived between
us. But seeing it falleth out that we cannot confer together, we think it meet
(though briefly) to show you the just cause and reason of our differing from
those articles last made by Robert Cushman without our commission, or
knowledge; and though he might propound good ends to himself, yet it no
way justifies his doing it. Our main difference is in the 5 and 9 article,
concerning the dividing, or holding of house, and lands. The enjoying whereof
some of yourselves well know, was one special motive, amongst many other,
to provoke us to go; this was thought so reasonable, that when the greatest of
you in adventure, (whom we have much cause to respect) when he propounded
conditions to us freely of his own accord, he set this down for one. A copy
whereof we have sent unto you, with some additions then added by us,
which being liked, on both sides, and a day set for the payment of moneys;
those of Holland paid in theirs. After that Robert Cushman, Mr. Peirce[81],
and Mr. Martin, brought them into a better form, and write them in a book

---

[79]   One firkin of butter is 56 pounds.

[80]   Thomas Prince made the following note in Bradford's manuscript: "In Gov.
       Bradford's *Collection of Letters*, this letter is dated at Southampton."

[81]   John Pierce, a London merchant and clothier, was an associate of Thomas Weston;
       he became the treasurer of the Pilgrims' joint-stock company.

now extant; and upon Robert's showing them, and delivering Mr. Mullins[82] a copy thereof under his hand (which we have) he paid in his money. And we of Holland had never seen other, before our coming to Hampton, but only as one got for himself a private copy of them. Upon sight whereof we manifested utter dislike, but had put off our estates, and were ready to come, and therefore was too late to reject the voyage. Judge therefore we beseech you indifferently of things, and if a fault have been committed, lay it where it is, and not upon us; who have more cause to stand for the one, than you have for the other. We never gave Robert Cushman commission to make any one article for us, but only sent him, to receive moneys upon articles, before agreed on, and to further the provisions, till John Carver came, and to assist him in it. Yet since you conceive yourselves wronged, as well as we, we thought meet to add a branch to the end of our 9 article, as will almost heal that wound of itself, which you conceive to be in it. But that it may appear to all men, that we are not lovers of ourselves only; but desire also the good, and enriching of our friends, who have adventured your moneys, with our persons; we have added our last article to the rest, promising you again by letters in the behalf of the whole company; that if large profits should not arise within the 7 years, that we will continue together longer with you; if the Lord give a blessing.[83] This we hope is sufficient to satisfy any in this case, especially friends; since we are assured, that if the whole charge was divided into 4 parts, 3 of them will not stand upon it, neither do regard it, etc. We are in such a strait at present, as we are forced to sell away £60 worth of our provisions, to clear the haven, and withal to put ourselves upon great extremities, scarce having any butter, no oil, not a sole to mend a shoe nor every man a sword to his side, wanting many muskets, much armor, etc. And yet we are willing to expose ourselves to such eminent dangers, as are like to ensue, and trust to the good providence of God; rather than His name, and truth should be evil spoken of, for us. Thus saluting all of you in

---

[82] William Mullins, a shoe and boot dealer from Dorking, co. Surrey, came on the *Mayflower* with wife Alice and two of his children, Joseph and Priscilla. He and his whole family died the first winter, except Priscilla, who married the *Mayflower's* cooper, John Alden.

[83] It was well for them, that this was not accepted. (Bradford). The company was still in significant debt after the seven years were up, and the debt continued to build for many years thereafter due to mismanagement and needless engagements in risky side ventures.

love, and beseeching the Lord to give a blessing to our endeavor, and keep all our hearts in the bonds of peace, and love; we take leave and rest,

Yours, etc.

Aug. 3, 1620[84]

It was subscribed with many names of the chiefest of the company.

At their parting Mr. Robinson writ a letter
to the whole company, which though it hath already
been printed[85], yet I thought good here likewise
to insert it, as also a brief letter writ at the
same time to Mr. Carver, in which
the tender love, and godly care of
a true pastor appears.

My dear brother[86], I received enclosed in your last letter the note of information, which I shall carefully keep, and make use of as there shall be occasion. I have a true feeling of your perplexity of mind, and toil of body; but I hope that you who have always been able so plentifully to administer comfort unto others, in their trials, are so well furnished for yourself; as that far greater difficulties, than you have yet undergone (though I conceive them to have been great enough) cannot oppress you, though they press you, as the Apostle speaks. The spirit of a man (sustained by the Spirit of God) will sustain his infirmity; I doubt not so will yours. And the better much when you shall enjoy, the presence, and help of so many godly, and

---

[84] Thomas Prince made a note in the Bradford manuscript at this point, stating this letter was dated at Southampton. Thomas Prince, writing in the early 18th century, had access to William Bradford's *Letterbook*, part of which was lost during the Revolutionary War.

[85] John Robinson's letter to the departing Pilgrims was first published in *A Relation or Journal of the Beginning and Proceedings of the English Plantation Settled at Plymouth in New England* (London, 1622).

[86] Pastor John Robinson refers to John Carver as his brother because their wives' were sisters. John Robinson married Bridget White, and John Carver married Katherine White, both daughters of Alexander White of Sturton-le-Steeple, Nottinghamshire. See Robert S. Wakefield, "The Family of Alexander White of Sturton le Steeple," *Mayflower Descendant* 43:182-185. See also the statement later in the letter, "what shall I say, or write unto you, and your goodwife my loving sister?"

wise brethren, for the bearing of part of your burthen; who also will not admit into their hearts, the least thought of suspicion, of any the least negligence, at least presumption to have been in you, whatsoever they think in others. Now what shall I say, or write unto you, and your goodwife my loving sister? Even only this, I desire (and always shall) unto you from the Lord, as unto my own soul. And assure yourself that my heart is with you, and that I will not fore-slow my bodily coming, at the first opportunity. I have written a large letter to the whole, and am sorry, I shall not rather speak than write to them; and the more considering, the want of a preacher; which I shall also make some spur, to my hastening after you. I do ever commend my best affection unto you, which if I thought you made any doubt of, I would express in more, and the same more ample, and full words. And the Lord in whom you trust, and whom you serve, ever in this business, and journey, guide you with His hand, protect you with His wings, and show you, and us, His salvation in the end, and bring us in the meanwhile together in the place desired; if such be His good will, for His Christ's sake. Amen.

Yours, Jo: R

July 27, 1620.

This was the last letter, that Mr. Carver lived to see from him.[87]

The other follows.[88]

Loving and Christian friends, I do heartily and in the Lord salute you all, as being they with whom I am present in my best affection, and most earnest longings after you, though I be constrained for a while to be bodily absent from you, I say constrained; God knowing how willingly, and much rather than otherwise, I would have borne my part with you in this first brunt, were I not by strong necessity held back for the present. Make account of me in the meanwhile, as of a man divided in myself with great pain, and as (natural bonds set aside) having my better part with you.

And though I doubt not but in your godly wisdoms, you both foresee and resolve upon that which concerneth your present state and condition

---

[87] John Carver died in April 1621.

[88] "This letter is omitted in Governor Bradford's *Collection of Letters.*" This note was inserted into the manuscript by Thomas Prince, probably before 1736. Since this portion of Bradford's *Letterbook* is lost, these notes by Thomas Prince are the only clues we have to what was, and was not, in that missing portion.

both severally and jointly, yet have I thought it but my duty to add some further spur of provocation unto them, who run already, if not because you need it, yet because I owe it in love and duty. And first, as we are daily to renew our repentance with our God, especially for our sins known, and generally, for our unknown trespasses; so doth the Lord call us in a singular manner upon occasions of such difficulty and danger as lieth upon you, to a both more narrow search, and careful reformation of your ways in His sight; lest He calling to remembrance our sins forgotten by us or unrepented of, take advantage against us, and in judgment leave us for the same to be swallowed up in one danger or other; whereas on the contrary, sin being taken away by earnest repentance and the pardon thereof from the Lord, sealed up unto a man's conscience by His Spirit, great shall be his security and peace in all dangers, sweet his comforts in all distresses, with happy deliverance from all evil, whether in life or in death.

Now next after this heavenly peace with God and our own consciences, we are carefully to provide for peace with all men what in us lieth, especially with our associates, and for that watchfulness must be had, that we neither at all in ourselves do give, no nor easily take offense being given by others. Woe be unto the world for offenses, for though it be necessary (considering the malice of Satan and man's corruption) that offenses come, yet woe unto the man or woman either by whom the offense cometh, saith Christ, Matthew 18:7. And if offenses in the unseasonable use of things in themselves indifferent, be more to be feared than death itself, as the Apostle teacheth, 1 Corinthians 9:15, how much more in things simply evil, in which neither honor of God nor love of man is thought worthy to be regarded. Neither yet is it sufficient that we keep ourselves, by the grace of God from giving offense, except withal we be armed against the taking of them when they be given by others; for how unperfect and lame is the work of grace in that person, who wants charity to cover a multitude of offenses, as the Scriptures speaks. Neither are you to be exhorted to this grace only upon the common grounds of Christianity, which are, that persons ready to take offense, either want charity, to cover offenses, or wisdom duly to weigh human frailty; or lastly are gross, though close hypocrites, as Christ our Lord teacheth, Matthew 7:1,2,3, as indeed in my own experience, few or none have been found which sooner give offense, than such as easily take it; neither have they ever proved sound and profitable members in societies, which have nourished this touchy humor. But besides these, there are divers motives provoking you above others to great care and conscience this way: as first, you are many of you strangers, as to the persons, so to the infirmities one of another, and so stand in need of more watchfulness this way, lest when such things fall out in men and women as you suspected not, you be inordinately affected with them; which doth require at your hands much wisdom and charity for the covering and preventing of incident offenses that way. And, lastly, your intended course of civil community will minister continual occasion of offense, and will be as fuel for that fire, except you diligently quench it with brotherly forbearance. And if taking of offense causelessly or easily at men's doings be so carefully to be avoided, how much more heed is to be taken, that we take not offense at God Himself, which yet we certainly do so oft as we do murmur at His providence in our crosses, or bear impatiently such afflictions as wherewith He pleaseth to visit us. Store up therefore patience against that evil day, without which we take offense at the Lord Himself in His holy and just works.

A 4 thing there is carefully to be provided for, to wit; that with your common employments you join common affections truly bent upon the general good, avoiding as a deadly plague of your both common and special comfort all retiredness of mind for proper advantage, and all singularly affected any manner of way; let every man repress in himself and the whole body in each person, as so many rebels against the common good, all private respects of men's selves, not sorting with the general conveniency. And as men are careful not to have a new house shaken with any violence before it be well settled and the parts firmly knit, so be you, I beseech you brethren, much more careful, that the house of God which you are, and are to be, be not shaken with unnecessary novelties or other oppositions at the first settling thereof.

Lastly, whereas you are become a body politic, using amongst yourselves civil government[89], and are not furnished with any persons of special eminency above the rest, to be chosen by you into office of government: let your wisdom and godliness appear, not only in choosing such persons as do entirely love, and will promote the common good, but also in yielding unto them all due honor, and obedience in their lawful administrations; not beholding in them the ordinariness of their persons, but God's ordinance for your good; not being like the foolish multitude who more honor the gay coat, than either the virtuous mind of the man, or glorious ordinance of the Lord. But you know better things, and that the image of the Lord's power and authority which the magistrate beareth, is honorable, in how mean persons soever.

---

[89] This paragraph from Robinson's letter appears to have influenced the wording of the "Mayflower Compact."

And this duty you both may the more willingly, and ought the more conscionably to perform because you are at least for the present to have only them for your ordinary governors, which yourselves shall make choice of for that work.

Sundry other things of importance I could put you in mind of, and of those before mentioned in more words, but I will not so far wrong your godly minds, as to think you heedless of these things, there being also divers among you so well able to admonish both themselves and others of what concerneth them. These few things therefore, and the same in few words I do earnestly commend unto your care, and conscience, joining therewith my daily incessant prayers unto the Lord, that He who hath made the heavens and the earth, the sea and all rivers of waters, and whose providence is over all His works, especially over all His dear children for good, would so guide and guard you in your ways, as inwardly by His Spirit, so outwardly by the hand of His power, as that both you and we also, for and with you may have after matter of praising His name all the days of your and our lives. Fare you well in Him in whom you trust, and in whom I rest.

An unfeigned well-willer of your happy success in this hopeful voyage,

John Robinson

This letter though large, yet being so fruitful in itself, and suitable to their occasion; I thought meet to insert in this place.

All things being now ready and every business dispatched; the company was called together and this letter read amongst them, which had good acceptation with all, and after fruit with many; then they ordered and distributed their company for either ship, as they conceived for the best; and chose a Governor and 2 or 3 assistants for each ship, to order the people by the way, and see to the disposing of their provisions, and such like affairs. All which was not only with the liking of the masters of the ships, but according to their desires; which being done, they set sail from thence about the 5 of August; but what befell them further upon the coast of England will appear in the next chapter.

The · 8 · chap ·

Of the troubls that befea them on the coaste and at sea. being forced, after much trouble to leaue one of their ships,& some of their companie behind them ·

Being thus put to sea they had not gone far, but Mr. Reynolds the master of the lesser ship[90] complained that he found his ship so leaky as he durst not put further to sea till she was mended: so the master of the bigger ship (called Mr. Jones[91]) being consulted with, they both resolved to put into Dartmouth and have her there searched and mended which accordingly was done to their great charge and loss of time and a fair wind; she was here thoroughly searched from stem, to stern, some leaks were found and mended, and now it was conceived by the workmen and all, that she was sufficient, and they might proceed without either fear, or danger. So with good hopes from hence, they put to sea again[92],

---

[90] The *Speedwell.*

[91] The *Mayflower* was mastered by Christopher Jones of Rotherhithe, co. Surrey, formerly of Harwich, co. Essex. See Winifred Cooper, *Harwich, the Mayflower and Christopher Jones* (London, 1970) for a good history of Christopher Jones, and J.W. Horrocks, "The Mayflower," *The Mariner's Mirror* 8(1922):1-9,81-88,140-147, 237-245,354-362 for a good history of the *Mayflower* ship as shown from the records found in the Customs Books of the Exchequer. See Caleb Johnson, *The Mayflower and Her Passengers* (Xlibris: Philadelphia, 2005), for a biography of the ship that utilizes many records from the High Court of Admiralty.

[92] This occurred on August 23 according to Captain John Smith, in his *New England's Trials* (London, 1622). He wrote: "Upon these inducements some few well-disposed gentlemen and merchants of London and other places provided two ships, the one of 160 tons, the other of 70; they left the coast of England the 23 of August, with about 120 persons: but the next day the lesser ship sprung a leak, that forced their return to Plymouth: where discharging her and 20 passengers, with the great ship and a hundred persons besides sailors, they set sail again the sixth of September, and the ninth of November fell with Cape James [i.e. Cape Cod]."

conceiving they should go comfortably on, not looking for any more lets of this kind; but it fell out otherwise, for after they were gone to sea again above 100 leagues without the Lands End, holding company together all this while; the master of the small ship complained his ship was so leaky as he must bear up or sink at sea, for they could scarce free her with much pumping. So they came to consultation again, and resolved both ships to bear up back again, and put into Plymouth, which accordingly was done. But no special leak could be found, but it was judged to be the general weakness of the ship, and that she would not prove sufficient for the voyage. Upon which it was resolved, to dismiss her, and part of the company, and proceed with the other ship; the which (though it was grievous and caused great discouragement) was put into execution. So after they had took out such provision as the other ship could well stow; and concluded both what number, and what persons to send back[93], they made another sad parting, the one ship going back for London; and the other was to proceed on her voyage. Those that went back were for the most part such as were willing so to do, either out of some discontent, or fear they conceived of the ill success of the voyage; seeing so many crosses befall, and the year time so far spent; but others in regard of their own weakness, and charge of many young children, were thought least useful, and most unfit to bear the brunt of this hard adventure; unto which work of God, and judgment of their brethren, they were contented to submit. And thus like Gideon's army this small number was divided; as if the Lord by this work of His providence, thought these few, too many, for the great work He had to do. But here by the way let me show, how afterward it was found, that the leakiness of this ship, was partly, by being over-masted, and too much pressed with sails, for after she was sold and put into her old trim, she made many voyages, and performed her service very sufficiently, to the great profit of her owners. But more especially, by the cunning and deceit of the master and his company (who were hired to stay a whole year in the country) and now fancying dislike, and fearing want of victuals, they plotted this stratagem to free

---

[93]   According to Captain John Smith (see previous footnote) twenty passengers disembarked at this point. Of the twenty who quit the voyage, only a few names are known with certainty: Robert Cushman and William Ring, and the family members that were with them, along with Thomas Blossom and one of his sons. It is also likely that Roger and Sarah (Minter) Simmons were passengers, since they had sold off their house in Leiden in 1619, presumably in preparation for the voyage.

themselves; as afterwards was known and by some of them confessed; for they apprehended that the greater ship (being of force and in whom most of the provisions were stowed) she would retain enough for herself, whatsoever became of them or the passengers. And indeed such speeches had been cast out by some of them; and yet besides other encouragements the chief of them that came from Leiden went in this ship to give the master content; but so strong was self love and his fears, as he forgot all duty and former kindnesses, and dealt thus falsely with them, though he pretended otherwise. Amongst those that returned was Mr. Cushman and his family, whose heart and courage was gone from them before (as it seems) though his body was with them till now he departed; as may appear by a passionate letter he write to a friend in London from Dartmouth whilst the ship lay there a-mending; the which besides the expressions of his own fears, it shows much of the providence of God working for their good beyond man's expectation; and other things concerning their condition in these straits. I will here relate it. And though it discover some infirmities in him (as who under temptation is free) yet after this, he continued to be a special instrument for their good, and to do the offices of a loving friend, and faithful brother unto them, and partaker of much comfort with them.

The letter is as followeth.

To his loving friend
Ed: S.[94] at Heneage House in the Duke's place, these etc.

Dartmouth Aug. 17
Anno: 1620

Loving friend my most kind remembrance to you, and your wife; with loving E. M. etc., whom in this world I never look to see again; for besides the eminent dangers of this voyage, which are no less than deadly; an infirmity of body hath seized me, which will not in all likelihood leave me till death; what to call it I know not, but it is a bundle of lead, as it were crushing my heart more, and more, these 14 days, as that although I do the

---

[94] "In Gov. Bradford's *Collection of Letters*, this is Edward Southworth." This note was added to Bradford's manuscript by Thomas Prince, probably before 1736. This portion of Bradford's *Letterbook* no longer exists. In 1623, William Bradford married Alice, the widow of Edward Southworth—which likely explains how Bradford got access to this letter.

actions of a living man, yet I am but as dead, but the will of God be done. Our pinnace will not cease leaking, else I think we had been halfway at Virginia; our voyage hither hath been as full of crosses, as ourselves have been of crookedness. We put in here to trim her, and I think, as others also, if we had stayed at sea, but 3 or 4 hours more, she would have sunk right down. And though she was twice trimmed at Hampton, yet now she is as open, and leaky as a sieve; and there was a board a man might have pulled off with his fingers 2 foot long, where the water came in, as at a mole hole; we lay at Hampton 7 days in fair weather waiting for her, and now we lie here waiting for her in as fair a wind as can blow and so have done these 4 days, and are like to lie 4 more, and by that time the wind will happily turn as it did at Hampton. Our victuals will be half eaten up I think before we go from the coast of England, and if our voyage last long, we shall not have a month's victuals when we come in the country. Near £700 hath been bestowed at Hampton, upon what I know not, Mr. Martin[95] saith he neither can, nor will give any account of it; and if he be called upon for accounts, he crieth out of unthankfulness for his pains and care, that we are suspicious of him, and flings away, and will end nothing. Also he so insulteth over our poor people, with such scorn and contempt as if they were not good enough to wipe his shoes. It would break your heart to see his dealing, and the mourning of our people, they complain to me, and alas I can do nothing for them; if I speak to him, he flies in my face, as mutinous and saith no complaints shall be heard, or received but by himself, and saith they are forward, and waspish discontented people, and I do ill to hear them. There are others that would lose all they have put in, or make satisfaction for what they have had, that they might depart, but he will not hear them, nor suffer them to go ashore lest they should run away. The sailors also are so offended at his ignorant boldness, in meddling and controlling, in things he knows not what belongs to; as that some threaten to mischief him, others say they will leave the ship, and go their way; but at the best this cometh of it, that he makes himself a scorn and laughing stock unto them.

As for Mr. Weston, except grace do greatly sway with him, he will hate us, ten times more than ever he loved us, for not confirming the conditions; but now since some pinches have taken them, they begin to revile the truth, and say Mr. Robinson was in the fault who charged them never to consent to those conditions, nor choose me into office, but indeed

---

[95]   He was governor in the bigger ship and Mr. Cushman assistant. (Bradford).

appointed them to choose them they did choose.[96] But he and they will rue too late, they may now see, and all be ashamed when it is too late, that they were so ignorant, yea and so inordinate in their courses. I am sure as they were resolved not to seal those conditions, I was not so resolute at Hampton to have left the whole business, except they would seal them; and better the voyage to have been broken off then, than to have brought such misery to ourselves, dishonor to God, and detriment to our loving friends, as now it is like to do. 4 or 5 of the chief of them which came from Leiden, came resolved never to go on those conditions; and Mr. Martin, he said he never received no money on those conditions, he was not beholden to the merchants for a pin, they were bloodsuckers, and I know not what; simple man, he indeed never made any conditions with the merchants, nor ever spake with them; but did all that money fly to Hampton, or was it his own? Who will go and lay out money so rashly, and lavishly as he did, and never know how he comes by it, or on what conditions. 2ly, I told him of the alteration long ago, and he was content; but now he domineers, and said I had betrayed them into the hands of slaves; he is not beholden to them, he can set out 2 ships himself to a voyage; when good man? He hath but £50 in, and if he should give up his accounts he would not have a penny left him, as I am persuaded, etc.[97] Friend if ever we make a plantation God works a miracle; especially considering how scant we shall be of victuals, and most of all ununited amongst ourselves, and devoid of good tutors, and regiment. Violence will break all, where is the meek and humble spirit, of Moses? And of Nehemiah who re-edified the walls of Jerusalem, and the state of Israel; is not the sound of Rehoboam's brags daily here amongst us. Have not the philosophers and all wise men observed that even in settled commonwealths, violent governors, bring either themselves, or people, or both to ruin; how much more in the raising of commonwealths, when the mortar is yet scarce tempered that should bind the walls. If I should write to you of all things which promiscuously forerun our ruin, I should overcharge my weak head, and grieve your tender heart; only this I pray you prepare for evil tidings of us every day; but pray for us instantly, it may be the Lord will be yet entreated one way or other to make for us. I see not in reason how we shall escape, even the gasping of hunger-starved persons, but God can do much, and His will be done. It is better for me to die, than now for me to bear it, which I do daily, and expect it hourly; having

---

[96] I think he was deceived in these things. (Bradford).

[97] This was found true afterward. (Bradford).

received the sentence of death, both within me and without me. Poor William Ring[98], and myself do strive who shall be meat first for the fishes; but we look for a glorious resurrection, knowing Christ Jesus after the flesh no more, but looking unto the joy that is before us, we will endure all these things, and account them light, in comparison of that joy we hope for. Remember me in all love to our friends, as if I named them, whose prayers I desire earnestly, and wish again to see, but not till I can with more comfort look them in the face; the Lord give us that true comfort which none can take from us. I had a desire to make a brief relation of our estate to some friend, I doubt not but your wisdom will teach you seasonably to utter things, as hereafter you shall be called to it. That which I have written is true, and many things more which I have forborne; I write it as upon my life, and last confession in England; what is of use to be spoken of presently, you may speak of it, and what is fit to conceal, conceal. Pass by my weak manner, for my head is weak, and my body feeble; the Lord make me strong in Him; and keep both you and yours.

Your loving friend
Robert Cushman

Dartmouth, Aug. 17, 1620.

These being his conceptions and fears at Dartmouth, they must needs be much stronger, now at Plymouth.

---

[98]   William Ring was one of the members of the Leiden congregation. In Leiden, he took up the occupation of say-weaver. He died sometime before his wife Mary came to Plymouth in 1629 or 1630. Mary died in 1631 at Plymouth. She left behind the earliest will and estate inventory on record for a woman at Plymouth Colony.

The ·9· Chap:

Of their vioage, & how they passed ƴ sea;
and of their safe arriuall at
Cape Codd · v· v· v

September 6. These troubles being blown over, and now all being compact together in one ship, they put to sea again with a prosperous wind, which continued divers days together, which was some encouragement unto them; yet according to the usual manner many were afflicted with seasickness. And I may not omit here a special work of God's providence: there was a proud and very profane young man, one of the seamen, of a lusty able body, which made him the more haughty; he would always be contemning the poor people in their sickness, and cursing them daily with grievous execrations; and did not let to tell them, that he hoped to help to cast half of them overboard before they came to their journey's end, and to make merry with what they had; and if he were by any gently reproved, he would curse and swear most bitterly. But it pleased God before they came half seas over, to smite this young man with a grievous disease, of which he died in a desperate manner; and so was himself the first that was thrown overboard; thus his curses light on his own head; and it was an astonishment to all his fellows, for they noted it to be the just hand of God upon him.[99]

---

[99]   Francis Higginson recorded a similar experience in his voyage to New England in 1629 on the *Talbot*: "[A] notorious wicked fellow, that was given to swearing and boasting of his former wickedness, bragged that he had got a wench with child before he came this voyage, and mocked at our days of fast, railing and jesting against Puritans; this fellow fell sick of the pox, and died." Alexander Young, *Chronicles of the First Planters of the Colony of the Massachusetts Bay* (Boston: Charles C. Little and James Brown, 1846), p. 230.

After they had enjoyed fair winds, and weather for a season, they were encountered many times with cross winds, and met with many fierce storms, with which the ship was shroudly shaken, and her upper works made very leaky; and one of the main beams in the midships was bowed and cracked, which put them in some fear, that the ship could not be able to perform the voyage. So some of the chief of the company (perceiving the mariners to fear the sufficiency of the ship, as appeared by their mutterings) they entered into serious consultation with the master, and other officers of the ship, to consider in time of the danger; and rather to return, than to cast themselves into a desperate, and inevitable peril. And truly there was great distraction, and difference of opinion amongst the mariners themselves; fain would they do what could be done for their wages' sake (being now near half the seas over) and on the other hand they were loath to hazard their lives too desperately. But in examining of all opinions, the master and others affirmed they knew the ship to be strong, and firm under water[100], and for the buckling of the main beam, there was a great iron screw[101] the passengers brought out of Holland, which would raise the beam into his place; the which being done, the carpenter, and master affirmed that with a post put under it, set firm in the lower deck, and other ways bound he would make it sufficient. And as for the decks and upper works they would caulk them as well as they could, and though with the working of the ship they would not long keep staunch,

---

[100]   The *Mayflower* had been in a much worse North Sea storm in 1609, on a return voyage from Norway, when Christopher Jones and the *Mayflower* "met with such tempestuous and foul weather" that to lighten the ship he had thrown overboard "a cable and hawser, an iron pot, a pair of mustard querns of the ship's provision and about fourscore or one hundred deals [boards of pine] of the merchant's to save ship and goods and men's lives." P.R.O. High Court of Admiralty, Deposition of John Cowbridge in Christopher Jones vs. Andrew Pawling, 13/42 folio 45-45d.

[101]   J. Rendel Harris speculated in 1920 in the introduction to *The Pilgrim Press*, that the great iron screw was part of a printing press brought by the Pilgrims. This is almost certainly not the case. There is no evidence for any printing presses in early New England, and the Pilgrims' printing press and types had been confiscated in 1618. Jeremy D. Bangs showed that, in fact, great screws were standard carpentry tools used with levers and pulleys to raise a roof. See more in Jeremy D. Bangs, *Pilgrim Edward Winslow: New England's First International Diplomat* (Boston: New England Historic Genealogical Society, 2004), pp. 9-10.

yet there would otherwise be no great danger, if they did not overpress her with sails; so they committed themselves to the will of God, and resolved to proceed. In sundry of these storms the winds were so fierce, and the seas so high, as they could not bear a knot of sail, but were forced to hull, for divers days together; and in one of them as they thus lay at hull in a mighty storm, a lusty young man (called John Howland) coming upon some occasion above the gratings, was with a seele of the ship, thrown into sea; but it pleased God, that he caught hold of the topsail halyards, which hung overboard, and ran out at length, yet he held his hold (though he was sundry fathoms under water) till he was hauled up by the same rope to the brim of the water; and then with a boat hook, and other means got into the ship again and his life saved; and though he was something ill with it, yet he lived many years after, and became a profitable member, both in church and commonwealth: in all this voyage there died but one of the passengers, which was (William Butten[102]) a youth, servant to Samuel Fuller, when they drew near the coast. But to omit other things (that I may be brief) after long beating at sea[103], they fell with that land which is called Cape Cod; the which being made, and certainly known to be it they were not a little joyful. After some deliberation had amongst themselves, and with the master of the ship; they tacked about, and resolved to stand for the southward (the wind and weather being fair) to find some place, about Hudson's River for their habitation.[104] But after they had sailed that course about half the day, they fell amongst dangerous shoals, and roaring breakers, and they were so far entangled therewith; as they conceived themselves in great danger; and the wind shrinking upon them withal, they

---

[102] William Butten died on November 6, just three days before Cape Cod was sighted.

[103] John Smith noted in his *New England's Trials* (London, 1622) that "being pestered nine weeks in this leaking unwholesome ship, lying wet in their cabins, most of them grew very weak, and weary of the sea; then for want of experience, ranging to and again, six weeks before they found a place they liked to dwell on, forced to lie on the bare ground without coverture in the extremity of winter; forty of them died: and 60 were left in very weak estate at the ship's coming away, . . ."

[104] The Hudson's River, near present-day Long Island, New York, was the intended destination of the *Mayflower* and her passengers. At the time, this area was right on the border between Virginia and New England. John Pory, a representative of the Virginia Company, wrote a letter in January 1622/3, in which he reported to the treasurer of the Virginia Company: "For whereas your Lordship knows, their voyage was intended for Virginia, being by letters from Sir Edwin Sandys

resolved to bear up again for the Cape; and thought themselves happy to get out of those dangers, before night overtook them, as by God's good providence they did; and the next day they got into the Cape Harbor[105] where they rid in safety. A word or two by the way of this cape, it was thus first named by Captain Gosnold[106], and his company; Anno 1602. And after by Captain Smith was called Cape James, but it retains the former name amongst seamen.

Also that point which first showed those dangerous shoals unto them, they called Point Care, and Tucker's Terror; but the French, and Dutch to this day call it Malabar, by reason of those perilous shoals, and the losses they have suffered there.

Being thus arrived in a good harbor, and brought safe to land, they fell upon their knees and blessed the God of Heaven, who had brought them over the vast, and furious ocean, and delivered them from all the perils, and miseries thereof; again to set their feet on the firm and stable earth, their proper element. And no marvel if they were thus joyful, seeing wise Seneca was so affected with sailing a few miles on the coast of his own Italy; as he affirmed, that he had rather remain twenty years on his way by land, than pass by sea to any place in a short time; so tedious and dreadful was the same unto him.[107]

But here I cannot but stay, and make a pause, and stand half amazed at this poor people's present condition; and so I think will the reader too, when

---

and Mr. Deputy Ferrar recommended to Sir Yeardley, then governor, that he should give them the best advice he could for trading in Hudson's River." This letter is reprinted in Sydney V. James, ed., *Three Visitors to Early Plymouth* (Plymouth: Plimoth Plantation, 1963). Edward Winslow in his *Hypocrisy Unmasked* (London, 1646) reported that the Dutch had asked the Pilgrims to plant a colony at the Hudson River under their government, offering transportation and supplies, but the Pilgrims turned down the offer, because they still considered themselves English.

[105]   Provincetown Harbor

[106]   Because they took much of that fish there. (Bradford). A first-hand account of Gosnold's voyage was made by John Brereton, *A Brief and True Relation of the Discovery of the North Part of Virginia* (London, 1602). Also Gabriel Archer, "Relation of Captain Gosnold's Voyage," *Purchas His Pilgrims* 4(1625):1648.

[107]   Epistle 53 (Bradford). William Brewster's copy of *Works of Lucius Annaeus Seneca, Both Moral and Natural* (London, 1614) is currently in the collections of the Pilgrim Hall Museum in Plymouth, Massachusetts. A photo of it can be seen later in this work.

John Smith's map of New England, made in 1614. The Pilgrims used this map, and had access to Smith's other books and maps. Cape Cod is located at the bottom left of the map (and is shown enlarged). It is labeled "Cape James" on the map—a name which did not stick. One place name applied by Smith did stick: "Plimouth."

he well considers the same. Being thus passed the vast ocean, and a sea of troubles before in their preparation (as may be remembered by that which went before) they had now no friends to welcome them, nor inns to entertain, or refresh their weather-beaten bodies, no houses, or much less towns to repair to, to seek for succor; it is recorded in Scripture[108] as a mercy to the Apostle and his shipwrecked company, that the barbarians showed them no small kindness in refreshing them, but these savage barbarians, when they met with them (as after will appear) were readier to fill their sides full of arrows than otherwise. And for the season it was winter, and they that know the winters of that country, know them to be sharp and violent, and subject to cruel and fierce storms, dangerous to travel to known places, much more to search an unknown coast. Besides what could they see, but a hideous and desolate wilderness, full of wild beasts, and wild men, and what multitudes there might be of them they knew not; neither could they (as it were) go up to the top of Pisgah, to view from this wilderness, a more goodly country to feed their hopes; for which way soever they turned their eyes (save upward to the heavens) they could have little solace or content, in respect of any outward objects, for summer being done, all things stand upon them with a weather-beaten face; and the whole country (full of woods and thickets) represented a wild and savage hue; if they looked behind them, there was the mighty ocean which they had passed, and was now as a main bar, and gulf, to separate them from all the civil parts of the world. If it be said they had a ship to succor them, it is true; but what heard they daily from the master and company? But that with speed they should look out a place (with their shallop) where they would be, at some near distance; for the season was such, as he would not stir from thence, till a safe harbor was discovered by them, where they would be, and he might go without danger; and that victuals consumed apace, but he must and would keep sufficient for themselves, and their return; yea it was muttered by some, that if they got not a place in time, they would turn them, and their goods ashore, and leave them. Let it be also considered what weak hopes of supply, and succor, they left behind them; that might bear up their minds in this sad condition, and trials they were under; and they could not but be very small; it is true, indeed, the affections and love of their brethren at Leiden was cordial and entire towards them, but they had little power to help them, or themselves; and how the case stood between them, and the merchants, at their coming away hath already been declared. What could now sustain them, but the Spirit of God and His grace? May not, and ought not the children of these

---

[108]   Acts 28 (Bradford).

fathers rightly say, "Our fathers were Englishmen which came over this great ocean, and were ready to perish in this wilderness, but they cried unto the Lord, and He heard their voice, and looked on their adversity, etc.[109] Let them therefore praise the Lord, because He is good; and His mercies endure forever. Yea, let them which have been redeemed of the Lord, show how He hath delivered them, from the hand of the oppressor. When they wandered in the desert wilderness out of the way, and found no city to dwell in; both hungry, and thirsty, their soul was overwhelmed in them. Let them confess before the Lord His loving kindness, and His wonderful works before the sons of men.[110]"

---

[109] Deuteronomy 26:5, 7 (Bradford).

[110] Psalms 107:1, 2, 4, 5, 8 (Bradford).

ϷSALM CVII.

Sing this as the 1**8**. *Pfalm.*

1 COnfeſſe ye to Jehovah thankfully,
   for *he is* good: for ever his mercy.
2 Let the redeemed of Jehovah ſay :
   whom he from foes hand hath redeemd-away.
3 And gather them out of the lands did hee ;
   from eaſt from weſt ; from north & frō the ſea.

4 They in the wildernes in deſert way
   wandred : no dwelling city find-did they.
5 Hungry and thirſty eke: *that* them within
   their ſoul, hath faynting-overwhelmed hin.
6 Ard to the LORD they cryde in their diſtreſſe:
   he freely-rid them from their anguiſhes.

7 And in a right way he did make them goe:
   a dwelling citie for to come untó.
8 Confeſſe they to Jehovah his mercy:
   his marvels eke, to ſonns of man-earthly.
9 For he the thirſty ſoul hath ſatiated:
   and hungry ſoul with good repleniſhed.

Psalm 107, from Henry Ainsworth's *Book of Psalms: Englished in both Metre and Prose* (Amsterdam, 1612). This was the psalm book used by the early Plymouth church.

The · 10 · Chap.

showing how they sought out a place of
    habitation; and what befell them ther-
            abouts

Being thus arrived at Cape Cod the 11 of November[111], and necessity calling them to look out a place for habitation (as well as the master's and mariners' importunity), they having brought a large shallop with them out of England, stowed in quarters in the ship, they now got her out, and set their carpenters to work to trim her up; but being much bruised and shattered in the ship with foul weather, they saw she would be long in mending. Whereupon a few of them tendered themselves, to go by land and discover those nearest places, whilst the shallop was in mending, and the rather because as they went into that harbor there seemed to be an opening some 2 or 3 leagues off, which the master judged to be a river. It was conceived there might be some danger in the attempt, yet seeing them resolute they were permitted to go; being 16 of them well armed under the conduct of Captain Standish[112], having such instructions given them as was thought meet. They set forth the 15 of November and when they had marched about the space of a mile by the seaside they espied 5 or 6 persons with a dog coming towards them who were savages, but they fled from them, and ran up into the woods, and the English followed them, partly to see if they could speak with them, and partly

---

[111] The events summarized in this chapter are covered in much greater detail in the Pilgrims' day-by-day journals compiled and published as *A Relation or Journal of the Beginning and Proceedings of the English Plantation Settled at Plymouth* (London, 1622).

[112] Myles Standish was hired by the Pilgrims to be their militia captain. He was therefore in charge of many of the early explorations, and in charge of organizing the colony's defense.

to discover if there might not be more of them lying in ambush; but the Indians seeing themselves thus followed, they again forsook the woods, and ran away on the sands as hard as they could, so as they could not come near them, but followed them by the track of their feet sundry miles, and saw that they had come the same way. So night coming on they made their rendezvous and set out their sentinels, and rested in quiet that night, and the next morning followed their track till they had headed a great creek and so left the sands, and turned another way into the woods, but they still followed them by guess, hoping to find their dwellings, but they soon lost both them, and themselves; falling into such thickets as were ready to tear their clothes, and armor in pieces; but were most distressed for want of drink; but at length they found water and refreshed themselves, being the first New England water they drunk of, and was now in great thirst as pleasant unto them as wine, or beer, had been in foretimes. Afterwards they directed their course to come to the other shore for they knew it was a neck of land they were to cross over, and so at length got to the sea side; and marched to this supposed river, and by the way found a pond of clear fresh water, and shortly after a good quantity of clear ground, where the Indians had formerly set corn; and some of their graves; and proceeding further they saw new stubble where corn had been set the same year, also they found where lately a house had been where some planks and a great kettle was remaining, and heaps of sand newly paddled with their hands, which they digging up, found in them divers fair Indian baskets filled with corn, and some in ears, fair and good of divers colors, which seemed to them a very goodly sight, (having never seen any such before); this was near the place of that supposed river they came to seek; unto which they went, and found it to open itself into 2 arms with a high cliff of sand in the entrance, but more like to be creeks of salt water than any fresh for aught they saw; and that there was good harborage for their shallop, leaving it further to be discovered by their shallop when she was ready. So their time limited them being expired, they returned to the ship, lest they should be in fear of their safety; and took with them part of the corn, and buried up the rest, and so like the men from Eshcol carried with them of the fruits of the land, and showed their brethren; of which, and their return they were marvelously glad, and their hearts encouraged.

After this the shallop being got ready they set out again, for the better discovery of this place, and the master of the ship desired to go himself, so there went some 30 men, but found it to be no harbor for ships but only for boats; there was also found 2 of their houses covered with mats, and sundry of their implements in them, but the people were run away, and could not be

Corn Hill, with the Pamet River in the foreground. This is the area where the Pilgrim explorers first dug up baskets of Indian corn that had been buried by the Nauset to preserve the seed for the next planting time.

seen; also there was found more of their corn, and of their beans of various colors; the corn, and beans they brought away, purposing to give them full satisfaction when they should meet with any of them (as about some 6 months afterward they did, to their good content). And here is to be noted a special providence of God, and a great mercy to this poor people, that here they got seed to plant them corn the next year; or else they might have starved, for they had none, nor any likelihood to get any till the season had been past (as the sequel did manifest); neither is it likely they had, had this, if the first voyage had not been made, for the ground was now all covered with snow, and hard frozen; but the Lord is never wanting unto His in their greatest needs, let His holy name have all the praise.

The month of November being spent in these affairs, and much foul weather falling in; the 6 of December they sent out their shallop again with 10 of their principal men, and some seamen, upon further discovery intending to circulate that deep bay of Cape Cod; the weather was very cold, and it froze so hard as the spray of the sea lighting on their coats, they were as if they had been glazed, yet that night betimes they got down into the bottom of the bay, and as they drew near the shore they saw some 10 or 12 Indians very busy about something; they landed about a league or 2 from them, and had much ado to put ashore anywhere it lay so full of flats; being landed it grew late, and they made themselves a barricade with logs and boughs as well as they could in the time, and set out their sentinel and betook them to rest, and saw the smoke of the fire the savages made that night. When morning was come they divided their company, some to coast along the shore in the boat, and the rest marched through the woods to see the land if any fit place might be for their dwelling; they came also to the place where they saw the Indians the night before, and found they had been cutting up a great fish like a grampus being some 2 inches thick of fat like a hog, some pieces whereof they had left by the way; and the shallop found 2 more of these fishes dead on the sands, a thing usual after storms in that place by reason of the great flats of sand that lie off. So they ranged up and down all that day, but found no people, nor any place they liked; when the sun grew low, they hasted out of the woods to meet with their shallop, to whom they made signs to come to them into a creek hard by, the which they did at high water; of which they were very glad, for they had not seen each other all that day, since the morning. So they made them a barricade (as usually they did every night) with logs, stakes, and thick pine boughs the height of a man, leaving it open to leeward, partly to shelter them from the cold, and wind (making their fire in the middle, and lying round about it) and partly to defend them from any sudden assaults of the savages, if they should surround them; so being very weary they betook them to rest. But about midnight, they heard a hideous, and great cry, and their sentinel called "Arm, arm," so they bestirred them and stood to their arms, and shot off a couple of muskets and then the noise ceased; they concluded it was a company of wolves, or such like wild beasts; for one of the seamen told them he had often heard such a noise in Newfoundland. So they rested till about 5 of the clock in the morning, for the tide and their purpose to go from thence, made them be stirring betimes. So after prayer they prepared for breakfast, and it being day dawning it was thought best to be carrying things down to the boat; but some said it was not best to carry the arms down, others said they would be the readier, for they had lapped them up in their coats from the dew; but some 3 or 4 would not carry theirs till they went themselves, yet as it fell out the water being not high enough, they laid them down on the bank side, and came up to breakfast. But presently all on the sudden they heard a great and strange cry, which they knew to be the same voices, they heard in the night, though they varied their notes, and one of their company being abroad came running in, and cried, "Men, Indians, Indians;" and withal their arrows came flying amongst them; their men ran with all speed to recover their arms, as by the good providence of God they did. In the meantime, of those that were there ready, two muskets were discharged at them, and 2 more stood ready in the entrance of their rendezvous but were commanded not to shoot till they could take full aim at them, and the other 2 charged again with all speed, for there were only 4 had arms there, and defended the barricade which was first assaulted; the cry of the Indians was dreadful, especially when they saw their men run out of the rendezvous, toward the shallop to recover their arms, the Indians wheeling about upon them, but some running out with coats of mail on, and cutlasses in their hands, they soon got their arms and let fly amongst them, and quickly stopped their violence. Yet there was a lusty man, and no less valiant, stood behind a tree within half a musket shot, and let his arrows fly at them, he was seen to shoot 3 arrows which were all avoided; he stood 3 shots of a musket till one taking full aim at him, and made the bark or splinters of the tree fly about his ears, after which he gave an extraordinary shriek; and away they went all of them; they left some to keep the shallop, and followed them about a quarter of a mile and shouted once or twice, and shot off 2 or 3 pieces, and so returned; this they did, that they might conceive that they were not afraid of them or any way discouraged. Thus it pleased God to vanquish their enemies, and give them deliverance; and by His special providence so to dispose that not any one of them, were either hurt, or hit, though their arrows came close by them, and on every side them, and sundry of their coats, which hung up in the barricade, were shot through, and through.

Afterwards they gave God solemn thanks, and praise, for their deliverance, and gathered up a bundle of their arrows, and sent them into England afterward by the master of the ship, and called that place the First Encounter. From hence they departed, and coasted all along, but discerned no place likely for harbor; and therefore hasted to a place, that their pilot, (one Mr. Coppin[113] who had been in the country before) did assure them was a good harbor which he had been in, and they might fetch it before night; of which they were glad, for it began to be foul weather.

After some hours' sailing it began to snow, and rain, and about the middle of the afternoon, the wind increased; and the sea became very rough; and they broke their rudder, and it was as much as 2 men could do to steer her with a couple of oars. But their pilot bade them be of good cheer for he saw the harbor, but the storm increasing, and night drawing on, they bore what sail they could to get in, while they could see; but herewith they broke their mast in 3 pieces and their sail fell overboard, in a very grown sea, so as they had like to have been cast away; yet by God's mercy they recovered themselves, and having the flood with them struck into the harbor. But when it came to, the pilot was deceived in the place, and said the Lord be merciful unto them, for his eyes never saw that place before; and he, and the master's mate would have run her ashore, in a cove full of breakers before the wind but a lusty seaman which steered, bade those which rowed if they were men, about with her, or else they were all cast away; the which they did with speed, so he bid them be of good cheer, and row lustily for there was a fair sound before them and he doubted not, but they should find one place or other, where they might ride in safety. And though it was very dark, and rained

---

[113]   Robert Coppin, a master's mate on the *Mayflower* and shallop pilot, who had been to the Cape Cod region on a previous voyage. He may be the same man, or related to, the Robert Coppin who is listed as a shareholder in the Second Virginia Charter (23 May 1609). John Pory, in a letter from January 1622/3, related "arriving first at that stately harbor called Cape Cod, called by Indians Pamet, from whence in shallop the pilot (a more forward undertaker than performer) promised to bring them to be seated in a pleasant and fertile place called Angawam, situated within Cape Anne about 40 leagues from Plymouth. After some dangerous and almost incurable errors and mistakings, he stumbled by accident upon the harbor of Plymouth, . . ." Pory's letter is reprinted in Sydney V. James, ed., *Three Visitors to Early Plymouth* (Plymouth: Plimoth Plantation, 1963).

sore; yet in the end they got under the lee of a small island and remained there all that night in safety. But they knew not this to be an island till morning, but were divided in their minds, some would keep the boat for fear they might be amongst the Indians; others were so wet and cold, they could not endure, but got ashore, and with much ado got fire (all things being so wet) and the rest were glad to come to them, for after midnight the wind shifted to the northwest, and it froze hard. But though this had been a day, and night of much trouble, and danger unto them; yet God gave them a morning of comfort and refreshing (as usually He doth to His children) for the next day was a fair sunshining day, and they found themselves to be on an island secure from the Indians, where they might dry their stuff, fix their pieces, and rest themselves, and gave God thanks for His mercies, in their manifold deliverances. And this being the last day of the week, they prepared there to keep the Sabbath; on Monday they sounded the harbor, and found it fit for shipping; and marched into the land, and found divers cornfields, and little running brooks, a place (as they supposed) fit for situation, at least it was the best they could find; and the season, and their present necessity made them glad to accept of it. So they returned to their ship again with this news to the rest of their people, which did much comfort their hearts.

On the 15 of December they weighed anchor to go to the place they had discovered, and came within 2 leagues of it, but were fain to bear up again; but the 16 day the wind came fair, and they arrived safe in this harbor. And afterwards took better view of the place, and resolved where to pitch their dwelling; and the 25 day began to erect the first house, for common use to receive them, and their goods.

Of Plymouth Plantation
Book 2

The 11 Chap̃ . ᵗ̃. Jhe · 2 · Booke ·

Jhe rest of this history (Jf god giue me Life, & opportunitie) Jf
Jhall (for breuitis sake, handle by may of annals, noteing only
the heads of principall things, and passages as they fell in or=
der of time, And may seeme to be profitable to know, or to
make vse of. And this may be as Jᵉ 2 · Books ·

Jhe remainder of Añ: 1620, e̲——————

I shall a little return back, and begin with a combination made by them before they came ashore; being the first foundation of their government in this place. Occasioned partly by the discontented, and mutinous speeches that some of the strangers amongst them, had let fall from them in the ship: that when they came ashore they would use their own liberty; for none had power to command them, the patent they had being for Virginia, and not for New England, which belonged to another government with which the Virginia Company had nothing to do. And partly that such an act by them done (this their condition considered) might be as firm as any patent; and in some respects more sure.

The form was as followeth[114]:

---

[114] This document has come to be known as the "Mayflower Compact." The original no longer exists. It was first published in *A Relation or Journal of the Beginning and Proceedings of the English Plantation Settled at Plymouth* (London, 1622). The names of the signers of the Compact were first published by Nathaniel Morton in his *New England's Memorial* (Cambridge, 1669). The signers were: John Carver, William Bradford, Edward Winslow, William Brewster, Isaac Allerton, Myles Standish, John Alden, Samuel Fuller, Christopher Martin, William Mullins, William White, Richard Warren, John Howland, Stephen Hopkins, Edward Tilley, John Tilley, Francis Cooke, Thomas Rogers, Thomas Tinker, John Rigsdale, Edward Fuller, John Turner, Francis Eaton, James Chilton, John Crackston, John Billington, Moses Fletcher, John Goodman, Degory Priest, Thomas Williams, Gilbert Winslow, Edmund Margesson, Peter Browne, Richard Britteridge, George Soule, Richard Clarke, Richard Gardinar, John Allerton, Thomas English, Edward Doty, and Edward Leister.

In y name of god Amen· we whose names are vnderwriten,
the loyall subiects of our dread soueraigne Lord king Iames
by y grace of god, of great Britaine, franc, & Ireland king
defendor of y faith, &c

Haueing vndertaken, for y glorie- of god, and aduancement
of y christian faith, and honour of our king & countrie, a voyage to
plant y first Colonie in y Northerne parts of Virginia· doe
by these presents solemnly & mutualy in y presence of god, and
one of another, Couenant, & combine our selues togeather into a
Ciuill body politick; for our beter ordering, & preseruation & fur=
therance- of y ends aforesaid; and by vertue hearof to enacte,
constitute, and frame shuch just & equall Lawes, ordinances,
Acts, constitutions, & offices, from time to time, as shall be thought
most meete & conuenient for y generall good of y Colonie: vnto
which we promise all due submission and obedience· In witnes
wherof we haue here vnder subscribed our names at Cap=
Codd y ·11· of Nouember, in y year of y raigne of our soueraigne
Lord king James of England, franc, & Ireland y eighteenth
and of scotland, y fiftie- fourth. An: Dom·1620·]

The "Mayflower Compact," as it is found hand written in William Bradford's
manuscript. The original Mayflower Compact is lost.

In the name of God Amen. We whose names are underwritten, the loyal subjects of our dread Sovereign Lord King James by the Grace of God, of Great Britain, France, and Ireland King, Defender of the Faith, etc.

Having undertaken, for the glory of God, and advancement of the Christian faith and honor of our King and Country, a voyage to plant the first colony in the northern parts of Virginia, do by these presents solemnly and mutually in the presence of God, and one of another, covenant, and combine ourselves together into a civil body politic; for our better ordering, and preservation and furtherance of the ends aforesaid; and by virtue hereof to enact, constitute, and frame such just and equal laws, ordinances, acts, constitutions, and offices, from time to time, as shall be thought most meet and convenient for the general good of the Colony: unto which we promise all due submission and obedience. In witness whereof we have hereunder subscribed our names at Cape Cod, the 11 of November, in the year of the reign of our Sovereign Lord King James of England, France, and Ireland the eighteenth and of Scotland the fifty-fourth. Anno Domini 1620.

After this they chose, or rather confirmed Mr. John Carver (a man godly and well approved amongst them) their governor for that year. And after they had provided a place for their goods, or common store, (which were long in unlading for want of boats, foulness of the winter weather, and sickness of divers) and begun some small cottages for their habitation; as time would admit they met and consulted of laws, and orders, both for their civil, and military government, as the necessity of their condition did require, still adding thereunto as urgent occasion in several times, and as cases did require.

In these hard and difficult beginnings they found some discontents and murmurings arise amongst some, and mutinous speeches and carriages in other[115]; but they were soon quelled, and overcome by the wisdom, patience,

---

[115] In 1736, Thomas Prince, quoting from a now lost register of William Bradford, noted the first two offenses at Plymouth: "[March 1621] The first offense since our arrival is of John Billington who came on board at London, and is this month convened before the whole company for his contempt of the captain's lawful command with opprobrious speeches, for which he is adjudged to have his neck and heels tied together; but upon humbling himself and craving pardon, and it being the first offense, he is forgiven . . . . June 18. The second offense is the first duel fought in New England, upon a challenge of single combat with sword and

and just and equal carriage of things, by the Governor and better part which clave faithfully together in the main.

But that which was most sad, and lamentable, was that in 2 or 3 months' time half of their company died, especially in January and February[116], being the depth of winter, and wanting houses and other comforts; being infected with the scurvy and other diseases, which this long voyage and their inaccommodate condition had brought upon them; so as there died some times 2 or 3 of a day, in the foresaid time; that of 100 and odd persons scarce fifty remained[117]: and of these in the time of most distress there was but 6 or 7 sound persons; who to their great commendations, be it spoken, spared no pains, night nor day, but with abundance of toil and hazard of their own health, fetched them wood, made them fires, dressed them meat,

---

dagger between Edward Doty and Edward Leister, servants of Stephen Hopkins; both being wounded, the one in the hand, the other in the thigh, they are adjudged by the whole company to have their head and feet tied together, and so to lie for twenty-four hours, without meat or drink, which is begun to be inflicted, but within an hour, because of their great pains, at their own and their master's humble request, upon promise of better carriage, they are released by the governor." *Chronological History of New England in the Form of Annals* (Boston, 1736).

[116]   Thomas Prince, using a now-lost register of William Bradford, noted in more detail some of the deaths of the first winter. He reports that one died on the voyage (William Butten); six died in December (Edward Thompson, Jasper More, Dorothy Bradford, James Chilton, Richard Britteridge, and Solomon Prower); eight died in January (including Degory Priest, Christopher Martin, and Rose Standish); seventeen died in February (including William White, William Mullins, and Mary Allerton); and thirteen died in March (including Elizabeth Winslow). *Chronological History of New England in the Form of Annals* (Boston, 1736).

[117]   Phineas Pratt, who arrived at Plymouth in 1622 with Thomas Weston's colonists, recalled in a 1662 court deposition what he had been told about the first winter at Plymouth: "Their second ship [the *Fortune*] was returned for England before we came to them. We asked them where the rest of our friends were that came in the first ship [the *Mayflower*]. They said that God had taken them away by death, and that before the second ship came, they were so distressed with sickness that they, fearing the savages should know it, had set up their sick men with their muskets upon their rests and their backs leaning against trees." The full deposition can be found in the *Collections of the Massachusetts Historical Society*, 4th Series 4(1858):474-491.

The will of William Mullins. This will was made aboard the *Mayflower* in
February 1621, and is the only surviving will of a *Mayflower* passenger who
died the first winter. It was signed by Governor John Carver, *Mayflower*
master Christopher Jones, and *Mayflower* surgeon Giles Heale.

made their beds, washed their loathsome clothes, clothed and unclothed them. In a word did all the homely, and necessary offices for them, which dainty and queasy stomachs cannot endure to hear named; and all this willingly and cheerfully, without any grudging in the least, showing herein their true love unto their friends and brethren; a rare example and worthy to be remembered. Two of these 7 were Mr. William Brewster their reverend Elder, and Myles Standish their captain and military commander, (unto whom myself, and many others were much beholden in our low, and sick condition) and yet the Lord so upheld these persons, as in this general calamity they were not at all infected either with sickness, or lameness. And what I have said of these, I may say of many others who died in this general visitation, and others yet living: that whilst they had health, yea or any strength continuing, they were not wanting to any that had need of them; and I doubt not but their recompense is with the Lord.

But I may not here pass by, another remarkable passage not to be forgotten. As this calamity fell among the passengers that were to be left here to plant; and were hasted ashore and made to drink water, that the seamen might have the more beer[118], and one in his sickness[119] desiring but a small can of beer, it was answered that if he were their own father he should have none; the disease began to fall amongst them also, so as almost half of their company died before they went away, and many of their officers and lustiest men: as the boatswain, gunner, 3 quartermasters, the cook and others. At which the Master was something stricken and sent to the sick ashore and told the Governor he should send for beer for them that had need of it, though he drunk water homeward bound; but now amongst his company there was far another kind of carriage in this misery, than amongst the passengers, for they that before had been boon companions in drinking, and jollity in the time of their health and welfare, began now to desert one another in this calamity, saying they would not hazard their lives for them, they should be infected by coming to help them in their cabins, and so after they came to lie by it; would do little or nothing for them, but if they died let them die. But such of the passengers

---

[118]   Beer was the primary drinking beverage during this time period; water was a last resort, because it was often contaminated with bacteria and parasites that made people sick. The brewing process killed most parasites, making beer and other alcoholic drinks safer than water.

[119]   Which was this author himself. (Bradford).

as were yet aboard showed them what mercy they could; which made some of their hearts relent, as the boatswain (and some others) who was a proud young man, and would often curse, and scoff at the passengers; but when he grew weak they had compassion on him and helped him, then he confessed he did not deserve it at their hands, he had abused them in word and deed; "O" (saith he) "you, I now see, show your love like Christians indeed one to another, but we let one another lie, and die like dogs." Another lay cursing his wife, saying if it had not been for her he had never come this unlucky voyage, and anon cursing his fellows, saying he had done this, and that for some of them, he had spent so much, and so much, amongst them, and they were now weary of him, and did not help him having need; another gave his companion all he had if he died, to help him in his weakness; he went and got a little spice and made him a mess of meat once, or twice; and because he died not so soon as he expected, he went amongst his fellows, and swore the rogue would cozen[120] him, he would see him choked before he made him any more meat; and yet the poor fellow died before morning.

All this while the Indians came skulking about them, and would sometimes show themselves aloof off, but when any approached near them, they would run away; and once they stole away their tools where they had been at work and were gone to dinner. But about the 16 of March a certain Indian came boldly amongst them, and spoke to them in broken English which they could well understand, but marveled at it; at length they understood by discourse with him, that he was not of these parts, but belonged to the eastern parts where some English ships came to fish, with whom he was acquainted and could name sundry of them by their names, amongst whom he had got his language.[121] He became profitable to them in acquainting them with many things concerning the state of the country in the east parts where he lived which was afterwards profitable unto them; as also of the people here, of their names, number and strength, of their situation and distance from this place, and who was chief amongst them. His name was Samoset; he told them also of another Indian whose name was Squanto, a native of this place, who had been in England and could speak better English than himself.

---

[120] To mislead by trick, or to obtain by deceit.

[121] This is described in more detail in *A Journal or Relation of the Beginning and Proceedings of the English Plantation Settled at Plymouth* (London, 1622).

Men working with various tools in an orchard. Woodcut from Gervase Markham's *A New Orchard* (London, 1631).

Seventeenth-century tools. A hammer, saw, and saw case. Photo courtesy of the Pilgrim Hall Museum, Plymouth, Massachusetts.

Being after some time of entertainment, and gifts dismissed, a while after he came again, and 5 more with him, and they brought again all the tools that were stolen away before, and made way for the coming of their great Sachem, called Massasoit. Who about 4 or 5 days after came with the chief of his friends, and other attendance with the aforesaid Squanto. With whom after friendly entertainment, and some gifts given him, they made a peace with him (which hath now continued this 24 years) in these terms:

1. That neither he nor any of his, should injure or do hurt, to any of their people.
2. That if any of his, did hurt to any of theirs; he should send the offender, that they might punish him.
3. That if anything were taken away from any of theirs, he should cause it to be restored; and they should do the like to his.
4. If any did unjustly war against him, they would aid him; if any did war against them, he should aid them.
5. He should send to his neighbors confederates, to certify them of this, that they might not wrong them, but might be likewise comprised in the conditions of peace.
6. That when their men came to them, they should leave their bows and arrows behind them.

After these things he returned to his place called Sowams, some 40 miles from this place, but Squanto continued with them, and was their interpreter, and was a special instrument, sent of God for their good beyond their expectation; he directed them how to set their corn, where to take fish, and to procure other commodities, and was also their pilot to bring them to unknown places for their profit, and never left them till he died. He was a native of this place, and scarce any left alive besides himself. He was carried away with divers others by one Hunt a master of a ship, who thought to sell them for slaves in Spain, but he got away for England and was entertained by a merchant in London and employed to Newfoundland and other parts, and lastly brought hither into these parts, by one Mr. Dermer, a gentleman employed by Sir Ferdinando Gorges and others, for discovery, and other designs in these parts[122]; of whom I shall say something;

---

[122] Tisquantum, or "Squanto" as Bradford nicknamed him, was one of twenty-four Indians taken captive by Captain Thomas Hunt in 1614. The Nauset and Patuxet

because it is mentioned in a book set forth Anno 1622 by the President and Council for New England, that he made the peace between the savages of these parts; and the English, of which this plantation, (as it is intimated had the benefit) but what a peace it was may appear by what befell him and his men.

This Mr. Dermer was here the same year that these people came, as appears by a relation written by him, and given me by a friend, bearing date June 30, Anno 1620. And they came in November following, so there was but 4 months difference. In which relation to his honored friend, he hath these passages of this very place:

> I will first begin (saith he) with that place from whence Squanto, or Tisquantum, was taken away; which in Captain Smith's map is called Plymouth; and I would that Plymouth had the like commodities. I would that the first plantation might here be seated, if there come to the number of 50 persons, or upward. Otherwise, Charlton, because there the savages are less to be feared. The Pokanokets which live to the west of Plymouth, bear an inveterate malice to the English, and are of more strength than all the savages from thence to Penobscot. Their desire of revenge was occasioned by an Englishman, who having many of them on board, made a greater slaughter with their murderers, and small shot; when as (they say) they offered no injury on their parts. Whether they were English or no, it may be doubted; yet they believe they were, for the French have so possessed them; for which cause Squanto cannot deny but they would have killed me, when I was at Nemasket, had he not entreated hard for me. The soil of the borders of this great

---

Indians were taken to Malaga, Spain to be sold as slaves, but Sir Ferdinando Gorges reported that some Spanish friars took custody of them and "so disappointed this unworthy fellow of the hopes of gain he conceived to make by this new and devilish project." Tisquantum then made it to England, where he stayed for a time with John Slaney, treasurer of the Newfoundland Company, and picked up some English, before being sent to Newfoundland. In Newfoundland, he assisted Captain John Mason, and later Captain Thomas Dermer, in exploring the New England coastline. Dermer returned Tisquantum to his home in 1619, but they found the Patuxet had been completely decimated by a plague the previous year, so he went further inland to Pokanoket to take up residence near Massasoit.

bay, may be compared to most of the plantations which I have seen
in Virginia; the land is of divers sorts for Patuxet is a hardy but
strong soil, Nauset and Satucket are for the most part a blackish,
and deep mould much like that where groweth the best tobacco in
Virginia. In the bottom of that great bay is store of cod, and bass,
or mullet, etc.

But above all he commends Pokanoket for the richest soil, and much
open ground fit for English grain, etc. Massachusetts is about 9 leagues
from Plymouth, (and situated in the midst between both) is full of islands
and peninsulas very fertile for the most part, with sundry such relations
which I forbear to transcribe, being now better known than they were to
him.

He was taken prisoner by the Indians at Manamoyick (a place not far
from hence now well known) he gave them what they demanded for his
liberty, but when they had got what they desired they kept him still, and
endeavored to kill his men, but he was freed by seizing on some of them, and
kept them bound till they gave him a canoe's load of corn; of which, see
Purchas, lib. 9, fol.1778.[123] But this was Anno 1619.

After the writing of the former relation, he came to the Isle of
Capawack[124] (which lies south of this place in the way to Virginia) and the
aforesaid Squanto with him, where he going ashore amongst the Indians to
trade as he used to do, was betrayed and assaulted by them, and all his men
slain, but one that kept the boat, but himself got aboard very sore wounded,
and they had cut off his head upon the cuddy of his boat, had not the man
rescued him with a sword and so they got away, and made shift to get into
Virginia, where he died whether of his wounds or the diseases of the country,
or both together is uncertain. By all which it may appear how far these
people were from peace, and with what danger this plantation was begun,
save as the powerful hand of the Lord did protect them. These things were
partly the reason why they kept aloof and were so long before they came to
the English; another reason (as after themselves made known) was how about
3 years before a French ship was cast away at Cape Cod but the men got
ashore, and saved their lives, and much of their victuals, and other goods;
but after the Indians heard of it they gathered together from these parts, and
never left watching, and dogging them till they got advantage, and killed

---

[123] Samuel Purchas, *Purchas His Pilgrims* (London, 1625).

[124] Martha's Vineyard

them all but 3 or 4 which they kept, and sent from one sachem to another to make sport with, and used them worse than slaves; (of which the aforesaid Mr. Dermer redeemed 2 of them), and they conceived this ship was now come to revenge it.[125]

Also (as after was made known) before they came to the English to make friendship they got all the Powahs of the country, for 3 days together, in a horrid and devilish manner, to curse and execrate them with their conjurations, which assembly, and service they held in a dark and dismal swamp.

But to return; the spring now approaching, it pleased God the mortality began to cease amongst them; and the sick and lame recovered apace, which put as were new life into them; though they had borne their sad affliction with much patience and contentedness, as I think any people could do, but it was the Lord which upheld them, and had beforehand prepared them; many having long borne the yoke, yea from their youth. Many other smaller matters I omit, sundry of them having been already

---

[125]   Phineas Pratt related more details of this story in his 1662 deposition: "Then he said, 'you say Frenchmen do not love you, but I will tell you what we have done to them. There was a ship broken by a storm. They saved most of their goods and hid it in the ground. We made them tell us where it was. Then we made them our servants. They wept much. When we parted them, we gave them such meat as our dogs eat. One of them had a book he would often read in. We asked him what his book said. He answered 'It saith, there will a people, like Frenchmen, come into this country and drive you all away, and now we think you are they.' We took away their clothes. They lived but a little while. One of them lived longer than the rest, for he had a good master and gave him a wife. He is now dead, but hath a son alive. And another ship came into the bay with much goods to truck, then I said to the Sachem, I will tell you how you shall have all for nothing. Bring all our canoes and all our beaver and a great many men, but no bow nor arrow, clubs nor hatchets, but knives under the skins about our loins. Throw up much beaver upon their deck; sell it very cheap and when I give the word, thrust your knives in the Frenchmen's bellies. Thus we killed them all. But Monsieur Finch, master of their ship, being wounded, leapt into the hold. We bid him come up, but he would not. Then we cut their cable and the ship went ashore and lay upon her side and slept there. Finch came up and we killed him.'" Phineas Pratt's full deposition is found reprinted in the *Collections of the Massachusetts Historical Society*, 4th Series 4(1858):474-491.

published in a journal made by one of the company[126]; and some other passages of journeys and relations already published to which I refer those that are willing to know them more particularly. And being now come to the 25 of March I shall begin the year 1621.

---

[126] This is a reference to the Pilgrims' journals, published in London in 1622 under the title *A Relation or Journal of the Beginning and Proceedings of the English Settled at Plymouth*.

Anno · 1621 ·

They now began to dispatch the ship away which brought them over, which lay till about this time, or the beginning of April.[127] The reason on their parts why she stayed so long, was the necessity, and danger that lay upon them; for it was well towards the end of December before she could land anything here; or they able to receive anything ashore; afterwards the 14 of January the house which they had made for a general rendezvous by casualty fell afire, and some were fain to retire aboard for shelter; then the sickness began to fall sore amongst them, and the weather so bad as they could not make much sooner any dispatch; again the Governor and chief of them, seeing so many die, and fall down sick daily, thought it no wisdom to send away the ship, their condition considered, and the danger they stood in from the Indians, till they could procure some shelter; and therefore thought it better, to draw some more charge upon themselves, and friends, than hazard all. The master and seamen likewise, though before they hasted the passengers ashore to be gone, now many of their men being dead, and of the ablest of them (as is before noted) and of the rest many lay sick and weak, the master durst not put to sea, till he saw his men begin to recover, and the heart of winter over.

Afterwards they (as many as were able) began to plant their corn, in which service Squanto stood them in great stead, showing them both the manner how to set it, and after how to dress and tend it; also he told them, except they got fish, and set with it (in these old grounds) it would come to nothing, and he showed them that in the middle of April, they should have store enough, come up the brook, by which they began to build, and taught them how to take it; and where to get other provisions necessary for them;

---

[127] According to Captain John Smith in his *New England's Trials* (London, 1622), the *Mayflower* left Plymouth "about the fifth of April following, and arrived in England the sixth of May."

all which they found true by trial, and experience. Some English seed they sowed, as wheat, and peas, but it came not to good; either by the badness of the seed, or lateness, of the season, or both; or some other defect.

In this month of April whilst they were busy about their seed; their Governor (Mr. John Carver) came out of the field very sick, it being a hot day, he complained greatly of his head, and lay down, and within a few hours his senses failed, so as he never spoke more till he died, which was within a few days after; whose death was much lamented, and caused great heaviness amongst them, as there was cause.[128] He was buried in the best manner they could, with some volleys of shot by all that bore arms; and his wife[129] being a weak woman, died within 5 or 6 weeks after him.

Shortly after William Bradford was chosen Governor in his stead and being not recovered of his illness, in which he had been near the point of death; Isaac Allerton was chosen to be an assistant unto him, who by renewed election every year, continued sundry years together, which I here note once for all.

May 12 was the first marriage in this place[130]; which according to the laudable custom of the Low Countries, in which they had lived, was thought most requisite to be performed, by the magistrate, as being a civil thing,

---

[128] Nathaniel Morton, in the Plymouth Church Records (*Collections of the Colonial Society of Massachusetts* 22(1920):51-52), adds this: "Before I pass on I may not omit to take notice of the sad loss the church and infant commonwealth sustained by the death of Mr. John Carver who was one of the deacons of the Church in Leiden but now had been and was their first Governor: this worthy gentleman was one of singular piety and rare for humility which appeared (as otherwise) so by his great condescendancy when as this miserable people were in great sickness he shunned not to do very mean services for them, yea the meanest of them; he bore a share likewise of their labor in his own person; according as their great necessity required; who being one also of a considerable estate spent the main part of it, in this enterprise and from first to last approved himself, not only as their agent in the first transacting of things, but also all along to the period of his life; to be a pious, faithful and very beneficial instrument; he deceased in the month of April in the year 1621, and now is reaping the fruit of his labor with the Lord."

[129] Katherine (White) Carver, daughter of Alexander White of Sturton le Steeple, Nottinghamshire.

[130] Thomas Prince, in his *Chronological History of New England* (Boston, 1736), quoted from a now-lost register belonging to William Bradford: "May 12. The first marriage in this place, is of Mr. Edward Winslow to Mrs. Susanna White, widow of Mr. William White."

upon which many questions about inheritances do depend, with other things most proper to their cognizance; and most consonant to the Scriptures, Ruth 4; and nowhere found in the Gospel to be laid on the ministers as a part of their office.[131] This decree or law about marriage was published by the States of the Low Countries Anno 1590, "That those of any religion (after lawful, and open publication) coming before the magistrates, in the town, or statehouse, were to be orderly (by them) married one, to another." Petit's History, folio 1029.[132] And this practice hath continued amongst, not only them, but hath been followed by all the famous churches of Christ in these parts to this time. Anno 1646.

Having in some sort ordered their business at home; it was thought meet to send some abroad to see their new friend Massasoit, and to bestow upon him some gratuity to bind him the faster unto them; as also that hereby they might view the country, and see in what manner he lived, what strength he had about him, and how the ways were to his place; if at any time they should have occasion. So the 2 of July they sent Mr. Edward Winslow, and Mr. Hopkins, with the foresaid Squanto for their guide; who gave him a suit of clothes, and a horseman's coat, with some other small things, which were kindly accepted; but they found but short commons, and came both weary, and hungry home[133]; for the Indians used then, to

---

[131]   Thomas Morton, in his *New English Canaan* (Amsterdam, 1637), noted that the Pilgrims' believed it was "a relic of popery to make use of a ring in marriage: and that it is a diabolical circle for the Devil to dance in." The Pilgrims' pastor John Robinson included a chapter "On Marriage," in his *Observations Divine and Moral* (London, 1628), in which he argues that marriage should be between one man and one woman; and that women are not a "necessary evil" but were rather created by God to be a companion for man. He argues that marriage is "of God," and therefore good, in opposition to the papists who believe that lifelong virginity is more holy. Robinson argues that general goodness and compatibility (in age, social status, financial status, and personality) are the primary conditions necessary for a successful marriage. He argues the man should have "love and wisdom" towards his wife, and his wife should be subject to her husband "in all lawful things."

[132]   Edward Grimstone, J.F. Petit, et.al., *A General History of the Netherlands* (London, 1608).

[133]   The travel to Massasoit is chronicled in much further detail in a chapter of *A Relation or Journal of the Beginning and Proceedings of the Plantation Settled at Plymouth* (London, 1622).

have nothing so much corn, as they have since the English have stored them with their hoes, and seen their industry in breaking up new grounds therewith. They found his place to be 40 miles from hence, the soil good, and the people not many, being dead and abundantly wasted in the late great mortality, which fell in all these parts, about three years before the coming of the English; wherein thousands of them died, they not being able to bury one another, their skulls, and bones were found in many places lying still above ground, where their houses and dwellings had been, a very sad spectacle to behold. But they brought word that the Narragansetts, lived but on the other side of that great bay, and were a strong people, and many in number living compact together, and had not been at all touched with this wasting plague.

About the latter end of this month, one John Billington lost himself in the woods, and wandered up and down some 5 days living on berries, and what he could find; at length he light on an Indian plantation, 20 miles south of this place called Manomet, they conveyed him further off, to Nauset, among those people that had before set upon the English when they were coasting whilst the ship lay at the Cape, as is before noted. But the Governor caused him to be inquired for among the Indians, and at length Massasoit sent word where he was, and the Governor sent a shallop for him, and had him delivered. Those people also came and made their peace; and they gave full satisfaction, to those whose corn they had found, and taken when they were at Cape Cod.[134]

Thus their peace, and acquaintance was pretty well established with the natives about them; and there was another Indian called, Hobomok, come to live amongst them, a proper lusty man, and a man of account for his valor and parts amongst the Indians; and continued very faithful and constant to the English till he died. He and Squanto being gone upon business among the Indians, at their return (whether it was out of envy to them, or malice to the English) there was a sachem called Corbitant, allied to Massasoit, but never any good friend to the English to this day, met with them at an Indian town called Nemasket 14 miles to the west of

---

[134] The voyage to find and recover young John Billington is chronicled in detail in the chapter of *A Relation or Journal of the Beginning and Proceedings of the Plantation Settled at Plymouth* (London, 1622) titled "A Voyage made by ten of our men to the Kingdom of Nauset, to seek a boy that had lost himself in the woods."

this place, and began to quarrel with them and offered to stab Hobomok, but being a lusty man, he cleared himself of him, and came running away all sweating and told the Governor what had befallen him, and he feared they had killed Squanto, for they threatened them both, and for no other cause, but because they were friends to the English, and serviceable unto them. Upon this the Governor taking counsel, it was conceived not fit to be borne, for if they should suffer their friends, and messengers thus to be wronged, they should have none would cleave to them, or give them any intelligence, or do them service afterwards; but next they would fall upon themselves. Whereupon it was resolved to send the Captain, and 14 men well armed, and to go, and fall upon them in the night; and if they found that Squanto was killed, to cut off Corbitant's head; but not to hurt any but those that had a hand in it. Hobomok was asked if he would go, and be their guide, and bring them there before day; he said he would, and bring them to the house where the man lay, and show them which was he. So they set forth the 14 of August, and beset the house round, the Captain giving charge to let none pass out, entered the house to search for him; but he was gone away that day, so they missed him; but understood that Squanto was alive, and that he had only threatened to kill him, and made an offer to stab him but did not; so they withheld and did no more hurt, and the people came trembling, and brought them the best provisions they had, after they were acquainted, by Hobomok what was only intended. There was 3 sore wounded which broke out of the house, and assayed to pass through the guard, these they brought home with them, and they had their wounds dressed, and cured, and sent home.[135] After this they had many gratulations from divers sachems, and much firmer peace; yea those of the Isles of Capawack sent to make friendship; and this Corbitant himself, used the mediation of Massasoit to make his peace, but was shy to come near them a long while after.

After this the 18 of September they sent out their shallop to the Massachusetts, with 10 men, and Squanto for their guide, and interpreter,

---

[135]   For more detail, see the chapter titled "A Journey to the Kingdom of Nemasket . . . to revenge the supposed death of our interpreter Tisquantum," in *A Relation or Journal of the Beginning and Proceedings of the Plantation Settled at Plymouth* (London, 1622).

to discover, and view that bay, and trade with the natives; the which they performed, and found kind entertainment[136]; the people were much afraid of the Tarrantines a people to the eastward which used to come in harvest time, and take away their corn, and many times kill their persons.[137] They returned in safety, and brought home a good quantity of beaver, and made report of the place, wishing they had been there seated, (but it seems the Lord, who assigns to all men the bounds of their habitations, had appointed it for another use). And thus they found the Lord to be with them in all their ways; and to bless their outgoings, and incomings; for which let His holy name have the praise forever, to all posterity.

They began now to gather in the small harvest they had; and to fit up their houses and dwellings, against winter, being all well recovered in health and strength; and had all things in good plenty, for as some were thus employed in affairs abroad; others were exercised in fishing, about cod, and bass, and other fish of which they took good store, of which every family had their portion; all the summer there was no want; and now began to come in store of fowl, as winter approached, of which this place did abound when they came first, (but afterward decreased by degrees) and besides waterfowl, there was great store of wild turkeys[138], of which they took many, besides venison etc. Besides they had about a peck a meal a week to a person, or now since harvest, Indian corn to that proportion. Which made many afterwards write so largely of their plenty

---

[136] They also had the Indians of the Massachusetts Bay sign a treaty in which they acknowledged themselves the subjects of King James. This document is preserved in Nathaniel Morton's *New England's Memorial*. It read "Know all men by these presents, that we, whose names are underwritten, do acknowledge ourselves to be the royal subjects of King James, King of Great Britain, France, Ireland, defender of the faith, etc. In witness whereof, and as a testimonial of the same, we have subscribed our names or marks, as followeth . . ." It was signed by Ohquamehud, Cawnacome, Obbatinnua, Nattawahunt, Caunbatant, Cheekatawback, Quadequina, Huttmoiden, and Appannow.

[137] For a detailed account of this voyage, see the chapter titled "A Relation of our Voyage to the Massachusetts," in *A Relation or Journal of the Beginning and Proceedings of the Plantation Settled at Plymouth* (London, 1622).

[138] This is the only historical basis for the "Thanksgiving turkey" tradition.

here to their friends in England, which were not feigned, but true reports.[139]

In November about that time twelvemonth, that themselves came: there came in a small ship[140] to them unexpected or looked for[141]; in which came Mr. Cushman[142] (so much spoken of before) and with him 35 persons to remain and live in the plantation which did not a little rejoice them; and they when they came ashore and found all well, and saw plenty of victuals in every

---

[139]   Likely a reference to Edward Winslow's letter, which was published in *A Relation or Journal of the Beginning and Proceedings of the Plantation Settled at Plymouth* (London, 1622).

[140]   Edward Winslow in his *Good News from New England* (London, 1624), reported: "The Good Ship called the *Fortune*, which the month of November 1621 (blessed be God) brought us a new supply of 35 persons, . . ." According to Captain John Smith in his *New England Trials* (London, 1624): "Immediately after her [the Mayflower's] arrival, from London they sent another of 55 tons [the Fortune] to supply them, with 37 persons. They set sail in the beginning of July, but being crossed by westerly winds, it was the end of August ere they could pass Plymouth [England], and arrived at New Plymouth, in New England, the eleventh of November, where they found all the people they left in April, as is said, lusty and in good health, except six that died." Although there is no passenger list for the ship *Fortune*, the majority of the passengers are identifiable by their entry in the 1623 Division of Land at Plymouth, *Plymouth Colony Records* 12:5 (also reprinted in Appendix I).

[141]   She came the 9th to the Cape. (Bradford).

[142]   While at Plymouth, Robert Cushman gave a sermon entitled *The Sin and Danger of Self Love*, which was published in London in 1624. The sermon focused on 1 Corinthians 10:24, "Let no man seek his own: but every man another's wealth." Cushman argued that the Plymouth settlers needed to work collectively for the benefit of the whole community, rather than individually for their private gain. Some in Plymouth objected to this because "many are idle and slothful, and eat up other's labors, and therefore it is best to part, and then every man may do his pleasure," but Cushman countered this with four answers, namely (1) that if they changed the laws and rules just because of some inconvenience, then they would be changing laws every day; (2) that hard work by some would be a good example to those who are slothful; (3) all men "have not strength, skill, faculty, spirit, and courage to work alike," and lastly he argued that any truly slothful people could be dealt with by the governors and courts.

house, were no less glad; for most of them were lusty young men, and many of them wild enough, who little considered whither, or about what they went till they came into the harbor at Cape Cod, and there saw nothing but a naked and barren place; they then began to think what should become of them, if the people here were dead, or cut off by the Indians; they began to consult, (upon some speeches that some of the seamen had cast out) to take the sails from the yard lest the ship should get away and leave them there, but the master, hearing of it, gave them good words; and told them, if anything but well should have befallen the people here, he hoped he had victuals[143] enough to carry them to Virginia, and whilst he had a bit they should have their part; which gave them good satisfaction. So they were all landed, but there was not so much as biscuit cake or any other victuals for them, neither had they any bedding, but some sorry things they had in their cabins, nor pot, or pan to dress any meat in; nor over-many clothes, for many of them had brushed away their coats, and cloaks at Plymouth as they came; but there was sent over some Birching Lane suits in the ship, out of which they were supplied; the plantation was glad of this addition of strength, but could have wished, that many of them, had been of better condition; and all of them better furnished with provisions. But that could not now be helped.[144]

---

[143] Nay they were fain to spare the ship some to carry her home. (Bradford).

[144] Bradford's summary of what the *Fortune* passengers found upon arrival differs somewhat from the account of actual *Fortune* passenger William Hilton, who shortly after arrival wrote a letter back to his cousin: "At our arrival at New Plymouth in New England, we found all our friends and planters in good health, though they were left sick and weak with very little means; the Indians round about us peaceable and friendly, the country very pleasant and temperate, yielding naturally of itself great store of fruits, as vines of divers sorts, in great abundance. There is likewise walnuts, chestnuts, small nuts and plums, with much variety of flowers, roots, and herbs, no less pleasant than wholesome and profitable: no place hath more gooseberries or strawberries, nor better. Timber of all sorts you have in England, doth cover the land, that affords beasts of divers sorts, and great flocks of turkeys, quails, pigeons, and partridges: many great lakes abounding with fish, fowl, beavers and otters. The sea affords us great plenty of all excellent sorts of sea-fish, as the rivers and isles doth variety of wild fowl of most useful sorts . . . . I desire your friendly care to send my wife and children to me, where I wish all the friends I have in England, and so I rest, your loving kinsman, William Hilton." This letter was first published by John Smith in his *New England's Trials* (London, 1624).

In this ship Mr. Weston sent a large letter, to Mr. Carver, the late governor, now deceased; full of complaints and expostulations about former passages, at Hampton; and the keeping the ship, so long in the country, and returning her without lading, etc., which for brevity I omit; the rest is as followeth:

Part of Mr. Weston's letter

I durst never acquaint the adventurers, with the alterations of the conditions first agreed on between us; which I have since been very glad of, for I am well assured had they known as much as I do, they would not have adventured a halfpenny, of what was necessary for this ship. That you sent no lading in the ship, is wonderful, and worthily distasted; I know your weakness was the cause of it, and I believe more weakness of judgment, than weakness of hands; a quarter of the time you spent in discoursing, arguing, and consulting, would have done much more; but that is past, etc. If you mean, bona fide, to perform the conditions agreed upon; do us the favor to copy them out fair and subscribe them with the principal of your names. And likewise give us account as particularly as you can, how our moneys were laid out. And then I shall be able to give them some satisfaction whom I am now forced with good words to shift off. And consider that the life of the business depends on the lading of this ship; which if you do to any good purpose, that I may be freed from the great sums I have disbursed for the former; and must do for the latter. I promise you, I will never quit the business, though all the other adventurers should.

We have procured you a charter[145], the best we could, which is better than your former, and with less limitation. For anything that is else worth writing Mr. Cushman can inform you; I pray write instantly for Mr. Robinson to come to you. And so praying God to bless you with all graces necessary, both for this life and that to come, I rest

Your very loving friend
Thomas Weston

London July 6, 1621

This ship (called the *Fortune*) was speedily dispatched away, being laden with good clapboard as full as she could stow, and 2 hogsheads of beaver, and otter skins, which they got with a few trifling commodities brought with them at first, being altogether unprovided for trade; neither was there any amongst them that ever saw a beaver skin till they came here, and were

---

[145]   The Pierce Patent. The full text can be found in Appendix I.

informed by Squanto. The freight was estimated to be worth near £500. Mr. Cushman returned back also with this ship, for so Mr. Weston and the rest had appointed him, for their better information. And he doubted not, nor themselves neither, but they should have a speedy supply; considering also how by Mr. Cushman's persuasion, and letters received from Leiden, wherein they willed them so to do, they yielded to the aforesaid conditions, and subscribed them with their hands. But it proved otherwise, for Mr. Weston who had made that large promise in his letter (as is before noted) that if all the rest should fall off, yet he would never quit the business but stick to them; if they yielded to the conditions, and sent some lading in the ship; and of this Mr. Cushman was confident, and confirmed the same from his mouth, and serious protestations to himself before he came. But all proved but wind, for he was the first, and only man that forsook them; and that before he so much as heard of the return of this ship, or knew what was done. (So vain is the confidence in man) but of this more in its place.

A letter in answer to his write to Mr. Carver; was sent to him from the Governor of which, so much as is pertinent to the thing in hand, I shall here insert:

Sir: Your large letter written to Mr. Carver, and dated the 6 of July 1621, I have received the 10 of November, wherein (after the apology made for yourself) you lay many heavy imputations upon him, and us all. Touching him, he is departed this life, and now is at rest in the Lord, from all those troubles, and encumbrances with which we are yet to strive. He needs not my apology; for his care and pains was so great for the common good, both ours, and yours; as that therewith (it is thought) he oppressed himself, and shortened his days; of whose loss we cannot sufficiently complain. At great charges in this adventure, I confess you have been, and many losses may sustain; but the loss of his, and many other honest and industrious men's lives, cannot be valued at any price; of the one, there may be hope of recovery; but the other no recompense can make good. But I will not insist in generals, but come more particularly to the things themselves. You greatly blame us for keeping the ship so long in the country, and then to send her away empty. She lay 5 weeks at Cape Cod; whilst with many a weary step (after a long journey) and the endurance of many a hard brunt, we sought out (in the foul winter) a place of habitation. Then we went in so tedious a time to make provision to shelter us, and our goods, about which labor, many of our arms, and legs can tell us to this day, we were not negligent. But it pleased God to visit us then, with death daily, and with so general a disease; that the living were scarce able to bury the dead; and the well not in any measure sufficient to tend the sick. And now to be so greatly blamed, for not freighting the ship, doth indeed go near us, and much discourage us. But you say, you know we will pretend weakness, and do you think we had not cause? Yes, you tell us you believe it; but it was more weakness of judgment than of hands. Our weakness herein is great we confess, therefore we will bear this check patiently amongst the rest till God send us wiser men. But they which told you we spent so much time in discoursing, and consulting, etc., their hearts can tell their tongues, they lie. They cared not, so they might salve their own sores, how they wounded others. Indeed, it is our calamity, that we are (beyond expectation) yoked with some ill-conditioned people who will never do good, but corrupt and abuse others, etc.

The rest of the letter declared how they had subscribed those conditions according to his desire, and sent him the former accounts very particularly; also how the ship was laden, and in what condition their affairs stood; that the coming of these people would bring famine upon them unavoidably; if they had not supply in time (as Mr. Cushman could more fully inform him and the rest of the adventurers). Also that seeing he was now satisfied in all his demands, that offenses would be forgotten, and he remember his promise, etc.

After the departure of this ship (which stayed not above 14 days[146]) the Governor and his assistant having disposed these late comers into several

---

[146]   John Smith in *New England's Trials* (London, 1624) reports the *Fortune* departed on 13 December 1621, which means the ship did stay longer than Bradford indicates. This is confirmed by a letter of Robert Cushman's, reprinted in his *Sin and Danger of Self Love* (London, 1624), which he dated 12 December 1621 from "Plymouth in New England." John Smith wrote that "Within a month they returned here for England, laded with clapboard, wainscot and walnut; with about three hogsheads of beaver skins and some sassafras, the 13 of December; and drawing near our coast, was taken by a Frenchman, set out by the Marquis of Cera, Governor of Ile D'Yeu on the coast of Poitu: where they kept the ship, imprisoned the master and company, took from them to the value of about 500 pounds; and after 14 days sent them home with a poor supply of victual, their own being devoured by the Marquis and his hungry servants. They arrived at London the 14 of February, leaving all them they found and carried to New England well and in health, with victual and corn sufficient till next harvest."

families, as they best could; took an exact account of all their provisions in store, and proportioned the same to the number of persons; and found that it would not hold out above 6 months, at half allowance, and hardly that; and they could not well give less this winter time till fish came in again. So they were presently put to half allowance, one as well as another, which began to be hard, but they bore it patiently under hope of supply.

Soon after this ship's departure, that great people of the Narragansetts in a braving manner, sent a messenger unto them with a bundle of arrows tied about with a great snakeskin; which their interpreters told them, was a threatening, and a challenge; upon which the Governor, with the advice of others, sent them a round answer, that if they had rather have war, than peace, they might begin when they would; they had done them no wrong, neither did they fear them, or should they find them unprovided. And by another messenger sent the snakeskin back with bullets in it, but they would not receive it but sent it back again. But these things I do but mention, because they are more at large already put forth in print, by Mr. Winslow at the request of some friends.[147] And it is like the reason was their own ambition, (who since the death of so many of the Indians,) thought to domineer and lord it over the rest, and conceived the English would be a bar in their way, and saw that Massasoit took shelter already under their wings.

But this made them the more carefully to look to themselves so as they agreed to enclose their dwellings with a good strong pale, and make flankers in convenient places with gates to shut which were every night locked; and a watch kept, and when need required there was also warding on the daytime. And the company was by the Captain's and the Governor's advice, divided into 4 squadrons, and everyone had their quarter appointed them, unto which they were to repair upon any sudden alarm. And if there should be any cry of fire, a company were appointed for a guard, with muskets, whilst others quenched the same, to prevent Indian treachery. This was accomplished very cheerfully, and the town impaled round by the beginning of March, in which every family had a pretty garden plot secured. And herewith I shall end this year.[148] Only I shall remember one passage more, rather of mirth,

---

[147]   Bradford refers to Edward Winslow's book *Good News from New England* (London, 1624), where the incident is described in much greater detail.

[148]   The Julian calendar, in use in England and her American colonies during this time period, began the new year on March 25. The Gregorian calendar, in which the year begins on January 1, was not officially instituted by the American colonies until 1752.

than of weight. On the day called Christmas Day, the Governor called them out to work, (as was used) but the most of this new company excused themselves, and said it went against their consciences to work on that day. So the Governor told them that if they made it matter of conscience, he would spare them, till they were better informed[149]; so he led away the rest and left them; but when they came home at noon, from their work, he found them in the street at play openly; some pitching the bar, and some at stool-ball, and such like sports.[150] So he went to them, and took away their implements, and told them, that was against his conscience, that they should play, and others work; if they made the keeping of it matter of devotion, let them keep their houses, but there should be no gaming, or reveling in the streets. Since which time nothing hath been attempted that way, at least openly.

---

[149]   The Puritans and Separatists did not celebrate religious holidays such as Christmas or Easter, because the holidays themselves were inventions of man (or inventions of the Catholic church), and therefore nothing was holy about them. Henry Ainsworth, a leading member of the Separatist church in Amsterdam (and author of the Pilgrims' psalmbook), called Christmas one of the "pagan festivities" in his *Arrow Against Idolatry*.

[150]   Stoolball was an ancestor to both baseball and cricket, and appears to have been played by women as well as men. Today, the predominantly female sport is still played in Sussex and surrounding counties, though it has evolved a more cricket-like play since the 17th century.

Anno · 1622 ·

At the spring of the year they had appointed the Massachusetts to come again and trade with them; and began now to prepare for that voyage about the latter end of March; but upon some rumors heard, Hobomok their Indian told them upon some jealousies he had, he feared they were joined with the Narragansetts and might betray them if they were not careful; he intimated also some jealousy of Squanto, by what he gathered from some private whisperings between him and other Indians. But they resolved to proceed and sent out their shallop with 10 of their chief men about the beginning of April, and both Squanto and Hobomok with them, in regard of the jealousy between them. But they had not been gone long, but an Indian, belonging to Squanto's family came running in seeming great fear, and told them that many of the Narragansetts, with Corbitant, and he thought also Massasoit were coming against them; and he got away to tell them, not without danger; and being examined by the Governor he made as if they were at hand, and would still be looking back, as if they were at his heels. At which the Governor caused them to take arms, and stand on their guard and supposing the boat to be still within hearing (by reason it was calm) caused a warning piece or 2 to be shot off; the which they heard and came in. But no Indians appeared, watch was kept all night, but nothing was seen; Hobomok was confident for Massasoit, and thought all was false; yet the Governor caused him to send his wife privately, to see what she could observe (pretending other occasions) but there was nothing found, but all was quiet. After this they proceeded on their voyage to the Massachusetts, and had good trade and returned in safety, blessed be God.[151]

---

[151] A more detailed journal of this voyage can be found in Edward Winslow's *Good News from New England* (London, 1624).

But by the former passages, and other things of like nature they began to see that Squanto sought his own ends, and played his own game, by putting the Indians in fear, and drawing gifts from them; to enrich himself, making them believe he could stir up war against whom he would, and make peace for whom he would; yea he made them believe they kept the plague buried in the ground, and could send it amongst whom they would; which did much terrify the Indians, and made them depend more on him, and seek more to him than to Massasoit. Which procured him envy, and had like to have cost him his life; for after the discovery of his practices Massasoit sought it both privately and openly; which caused him to stick close to the English, and never durst go from them till he died. They also made good use of the emulation that grew between Hobomok and him, which made them carry more squarely; and the Governor seemed to countenance the one, and the Captain the other, by which they had better intelligence, and made them both more diligent.

Now in a manner their provisions were wholly spent, and they looked hard for supply but none came. But about the latter end of May, they spied a boat at sea (which at first they thought had been some Frenchman) but it proved a shallop which came from a ship which Mr. Weston, and another, had set out a-fishing, at a place called Damariscove 40 leagues to the eastward of them; where were that year many more ships come a-fishing. This boat brought 7 passengers; and some letters, but no victuals nor any hope of any. Some part of which I shall set down.

Mr. Carver, in my last letters by the *Fortune,* in whom Mr. Cushman went, and who I hope is with you, for we daily expect the ship back again: she departed hence, the beginning of July, with 35 persons, though not over-well provided with necessaries, by reason of the parsimony of the adventurers. I have solicited them to send you a supply of men, and provisions before she come; they all answer they will do great matters, when they hear good news; nothing before, so faithful, constant and careful of your good are your old and honest friends; that if they hear not from you, they are like to send you no supply, etc. I am now to relate the occasion of sending this ship, hoping if you give credit to my words, you will have a more favorable opinion of it, than some here, whereof (Pickering is one) who taxed me to mind my own ends, which is in part true, etc. Mr. Beauchamp[152] and myself, bought this

---

[152] John Beauchamp was one of the adventurers, or investors, in the Pilgrims' joint-stock company.

little ship, and have set her out, partly if it may be, to uphold the plantation[153] as well as to do others good as ourselves; and partly to get up what we are formerly out; though we are otherwise censured, etc. This is the occasion we have sent this ship, and these passengers on our own account. Whom we desire you will friendly entertain, and supply with such necessaries as you can spare, and they want, etc. And among other things, we pray you lend, or sell them some seed corn, and if you have the salt remaining of the last year, that you will let them have it for their present use, and we will either pay you for it, or give you more when we have set our saltpan to work; which we desire may be set up in one of the little islands in your bay, etc. And because we intend if God please, (and the generality do it not) to send within a month another ship who having discharged her passengers; shall go to Virginia, etc. And it may he we shall send a small ship to abide with you on the coast which I conceive may be a great help to the plantation. To the end our desire may be effected, which I assure myself will be also for your good we pray you give them entertainment in your houses the time they shall be with you; that they may lose no time, but may presently go in hand to fell trees, and cleave them, to the end lading may be ready and our ship stay not.

Some of the adventurers have sent you herewith all some directions for your furtherance in the common business; who are like those St. James speaks of, that bid their brother, eat, and warm him, but give him nothing; so they bid you make salt, and uphold the plantation, but send you no means wherewithal to do it, etc.

By the next we purpose to send more people on our own account, and to take a patent; that if your people should be as unhuman as some of the adventurers, not to admit us to dwell with them, which were extreme barbarism; and which will never enter into my head, to think you have any such Pickerings, amongst you. Yet to satisfy our passengers I must of force do it; and for some other reasons not necessary to be written, etc.

I find the general so backward; and your friends at Leiden so cold, that I fear you must stand on your legs, and trust (as they say) to God and yourselves.

Subscribed

Your loving friend
Tho: Weston

Jan. 12, 1621
Sundry other things I pass over, being tedious and impertinent.

---

[153] I know not which way. (Bradford).

All this was but cold comfort to fill their hungry bellies; and a slender performance of his former late promise; and as little did it either fill, or warm them, as those the Apostle James spoke of, by him before mentioned. And well might it make them remember what the Psalmist saith, Psalm 118:8, "It is better to trust in the Lord; than to have confidence in man." And Psalm 146, "Put not your trust in princes," (much less in merchants) "nor in the son of man, for there is no help in them." v. 5. "Blessed is he that hath the God of Jacob for his help, whose hope is in the Lord his God." And as they were now failed of supply, by him and others, in this their greatest need; and wants, which was caused by him and the rest, who put so great a company of men upon them, as the former company were, without any food and came at such a time, as they must live almost a whole year before any could be raised, except they had sent some: so upon the point they never had any supply of victuals more afterwards; (but what the Lord gave them otherwise) for all the company sent at any time, was always too short for those people that came with it.

There came also by the same ship other letters but of later date; one from Mr. Weston, another from a part of the adventurers as followeth:

Mr. Carver since my last; to the end we might the more readily proceed to help the general: at a meeting of some of the principal adventurers, a proposition was put forth, and allowed, by all present (save Pickering) to adventure each man the third part of what he formerly had done, and there are some other that follow his example, and will adventure no further. In regard whereof the greater part of the adventurers being willing to uphold the business, finding it no reason that those that are willing should uphold the business of those that are unwilling, whose backwardness doth discourage those that are forward, and hinder other new adventurers from coming in: we having well considered thereof, have resolved according to an article in the agreement ("that it may be lawful by a general consent of the adventurers, and planters, upon just occasion, to break off their joint stock") to break it off; and do pray you to ratify, and confirm the same on your parts; which being done we shall the more willingly go forward for the upholding of you with all things necessary. But in any case you must agree to the articles, and send it by the first under your hands and seals. So I end

Your loving friend,
Tho: Weston

Jan. 17, 1621.

Another letter was write from part of the company of the adventurers to the same purpose and subscribed with 9 of their names, whereof Mr. Weston's and

Mr. Beauchamp's were two. These things seemed strange unto them, seeing this unconstancy and shuffling; it made them to think there was some mystery in the matter. And therefore the Governor concealed these letters from the public, only imparted them to some trusty friends for advice, who concluded with him, that this tended to disband and scatter them (in regard of their straits) and if Mr. Weston, and others, who seemed to run in a particular way, should come over with shipping so provided as his letters did intimate, the most would fall to him, to the prejudice of themselves, and the rest of the adventurers, their friends; from whom as yet they heard nothing. And it was doubted whether he had not sent over such a company in the former ship, for such an end; yet they took compassion of those 7 men which this ship (which fished to the eastward) had kept till planting time was over, and so could set no corn. And also wanting vitals, (for they turned them off without any) and indeed wanted for themselves, neither was their saltpan come, so as they could not perform any of those things which Mr. Weston had appointed; and might have starved if the plantation had not succored them, who in their wants, gave them as good as any of their own. The ship went to Virginia, where they sold both ship, and fish, of which (it was conceived) Mr. Weston had a very slender account.

After this came another of his ships[154], and brought letters dated the 10 of April; from Mr. Weston, as followeth:

Mr. Bradford these etc. The *Fortune* is arrived, of whose good news touching your estate and proceedings, I am very glad to hear. And howsoever he was robbed on the way by the Frenchmen; yet I hope your loss will not be great, for the conceit of so great a return doth much animate the adventurers, so that I hope some matter of importance will be done by them, etc. As for myself I have sold my adventure, and debts unto them. So as I am quit of you[155], and you of me, for that matter, etc. Now though I have nothing to pretend as an adventurer amongst you, yet I will advise you a little for your good, if you can apprehend it. I perceive, and know as well as another, the dispositions of your adventurers, whom the hope of gain hath drawn on to this they have done; and yet I fear that hope will not draw them much

---

[154]   The *Charity*. Edward Winslow notes in his *Good News from New England* (London, 1624) that: "In the end of June, or beginning of July, came into our harbor two ships of Master Weston's aforesaid, the one called the *Charity*, the other the *Swan*, having in them some fifty or sixty men sent over at his own charge to plant for him."

[155]   See, how his promise is fulfilled. (Bradford).

further. Besides most of them, are against the sending of them of Leiden, for whose cause this business was first begun, and some of the most religious (as Mr. Greene by name) excepts against them. So that my advice is (you may follow it if you please) that you forthwith break off your joint stock; which you have warrant to do, both in law, and conscience, for the most part of the adventurers have given way unto it by a former letter. And the means you have there, which I hope will be to some purpose by the trade of this spring; may with the help of some friends here, bear the charge of transporting those of Leiden, and when they are with you I make no question; but by God's help you will be able to subsist of yourselves; but I shall leave you to your discretion.

I desired divers of the adventurers, as Mr. Peirce, Mr. Greene and others, if they had anything to send you either victuals, or letters to send them by these ships, and marveling they sent not so much as a letter, I asked our passengers what letters they had, and with some difficulty one of them told me he had one, which was delivered to him with great charge of secrecy, and for more security to buy a pair of new shoes, and sew it between the soles for fear of intercepting. I taking the letter, wondering what mystery might be in it, broke it open; and found this treacherous letter subscribed by the hands of Mr. Pickering, and Mr. Greene: which letter had it come to your hands, without answer, might have caused the hurt, if not the ruin of us all. For assuredly if you had followed their instructions, and showed us that unkindness which they advise you unto, to hold us in distrust as enemies, etc., it might have been an occasion to have set us together by the ears, to the destruction of us all; for I do believe that in such a case, they, knowing what business hath been between us, not only my brother, but others also would have been violent, and heady against you, etc. I meant to have settled the people I before, and now send, with, or near you, as well for their, as your more security and defense, as help on all occasions. But I find the adventurers so jealous and suspicious, that I have altered my resolution, and given order to my brother, and those with him, to do as they, and himself shall find fit. Thus etc.

Your loving friend
Tho: Weston

April 10, 1621.

Some part of Mr. Pickering's letter before mentioned

To Mr. Bradford and Mr. Brewster, etc.

My dear love remembered unto you all, etc. The company hath bought out Mr. Weston, and are very glad they are freed of him, he being judged a man that thought himself above the general, and not expressing, so much the fear of God as was meet in a man, to whom such trust should have been reposed in a matter of so great importance, I am sparing to be so plain as indeed is clear against him; but a few words to the wise.

Mr. Weston will not permit letters to be sent in his ships, nor anything for your good, or ours, of which there is some reason in respect of himself, etc. His brother Andrew whom he doth send as principal in one of these ships, is a heady young man, and violent, and set against you there, and the company here; plotting with Mr. Weston, their own ends, which tend to your, and our undoing in respect of our estates there, and prevention of our good ends; for by credible testimony we are informed his purpose is to come to your colony, pretending he comes, for, and from the adventurers, and will seek to get what you have in readiness into his ships, as if they came from the company, and possessing all will be so much profit to himself. And further to inform themselves, what special places, or things you have discovered, to the end that they may suppress and deprive you, etc.

The Lord, who is the watchman of Israel, and sleepeth not, preserve you and deliver you from unreasonable men. I am sorry that there is cause to admonish you of these things concerning this man; so I leave you to God, who bless and multiply you into thousands, to the advancement of the glorious gospel of our Lord Jesus, Amen.

Farewell.

I pray conceal both the writing and delivery of this letter, but make the best use of it. We hope to set forth a ship ourselves within this month.

Your loving friends,
Edward Pickering
William Greene

The heads of his answer

Mr. Bradford, this is the letter, that I wrote unto you of; which to answer in every particular is needless, and tedious, my own conscience, and all our people can and I think will testify that my end in sending the ship *Sparrow* was your good, etc. Now I will not deny but there are many of our people rude fellows, as these men term them; yet I presume they will be governed, by such as I set over them; and I hope not only to be able to reclaim them from that profaneness that may scandalize the voyage, but by degrees to draw them to God, etc. I am so far from sending rude fellows, to deprive you either by fraud, or violence of what is yours; as I have charged the master of the ship *Sparrow*, not only to leave with you 2000 of bread, but also a good quantity of fish, etc.[156] But I will leave it to you to consider what evil this letter would, or might have done, had it come to your hands, and taken the effect the other desired.

Now if you be of the mind that these men are, deal plainly with us, and we will seek our residence elsewhere; if you are as friendly as we have thought you to be, give us the entertainment of friends; and we will take nothing from you, neither meat, drink, nor lodging, but what we will in one kind or other, pay you for, etc. I shall leave in the country a little ship (if God send her safe thither) with mariners, and fishermen to stay there. Who shall coast, and trade with the savages, and the old plantation; it may be we shall be as helpful to you, as you will be to us. I think I shall see you the next spring; and so I commend you to the protection of God, who ever keep you.

Your loving friend,
Tho: Weston

Thus all their hopes in regard of Mr. Weston were laid in the dust; and all his promised help, turned into an empty advice, which they apprehended was neither lawful, nor profitable for them to follow. And they were not only thus left destitute of help in their extreme wants, having neither victuals nor anything to trade with; but others prepared and ready to glean up, what the country might have afforded for their relief.

As for those harsh censures, and suspicions intimated in the former, and following letters; they desired to judge as charitably, and wisely of them as they could, weighing them in the balance of love, and reason; and though they (in part) came from godly, and loving friends, yet they conceived, many things might arise from over-deep jealousy, and fear, together with unmeet provocations. Though they well saw Mr. Weston pursued his own ends, and was embittered in spirit. For after the receipt of the former letters the Governor received one from Mr. Cushman (who went home in the ship) and was always intimate with Mr. Weston, (as former passages declare) and it was much marveled that nothing was heard from him, all this while. But it should seem it was the difficulty of sending, for this letter was directed as the letter of a wife to her husband, who was here, and brought by him to the Governor. It was as followeth:

Beloved Sir: I heartily salute you, with trust of your health, and many thanks for your love. By God's providence we got well home the 17 of February being robbed by the Frenchmen by the way, and carried by them into France, and were

---

[156]   But he left not his own men a bite of bread. (Bradford).

kept there 15 days[157]; and lost all that we had, that was worth taking, but thanks be to God, we escaped with our lives and ship. I see not that it worketh any discouragement here; I purpose by God's grace to see you shortly, I hope in June next, or before. In the mean space know these things, and I pray you be advertised a little. Mr. Weston hath quite broken off from our company, through some discontents that arose betwixt him and some of our adventurers, and hath sold all his adventures, and hath now sent 3 small ships for his particular plantation. The greatest whereof, being 100 tons, Mr. Reynolds[158] goeth master, and he with the rest purposeth to come himself, for what end I know not.

The people which they carry, are no men for us, wherefore I pray you entertain them not, neither exchange man, for man, with them, except it be some of your worst. He hath taken a patent for himself; if they offer to buy anything of you, let it be such as you can spare, and let them give the worth of it. If they borrow anything of you, let them leave a good pawn, etc. It is like he will plant to the southward of the Cape, for William Trevore hath lavishly told but what he knew, or imagined of Capawack, Mohegan, and the Narragansetts; I fear these people will hardly deal so well with the savages as they should; I pray you therefore signify to Squanto, that they are a distinct body from us; and we have nothing to do with them, neither must be blamed for their faults, much less can warrant their fidelity. We are about to recover our losses in France; our friends at Leiden are well, and will come to you as many as can this time. I hope all will turn to the best, wherefore I pray you be not discouraged, but gather up yourself, to go through these difficulties, cheerfully, and with courage in that place wherein God hath set you, until the day of refreshing come. And the Lord God of sea, and land bring us comfortably together again, if it may stand with His glory.

Yours, Robert Cushman

On the other side of the leaf, in the same letter,
came these few lines,
from Mr. John Peirce in whose name
the patent was taken,
and of whom more will
follow to be spoken in its place.

---

[157] A legal deposition relating to the pirating of the ship *Fortune* is recorded in the Public Records Office, State Papers Colonial, Vol. 5, No. 112, and is reprinted in Appendix I.

[158] Likely the same Mr. Reynolds who was the master of the *Speedwell*.

Worthy Sir: I desire you to take into consideration that which is written on the other side, and not any way to damnify your own colony, whose strength is but weakness, and may thereby be more enfeebled. And for the letters of association, by the next ship we send I hope you shall receive satisfaction. In the meantime whom you admit I will approve. But as for Mr. Weston's company, I think them so base in condition (for the most part) as in all appearance, not fit for an honest man's company; I wish they prove otherwise; my purpose is not to enlarge myself, but cease in these few lines, and so rest

Your loving friend,
John Peirce.

All these things they pondered, and well considered; yet concluded to give his men friendly entertainment; partly in regard of Mr. Weston himself, considering what he had been unto them, and done for them, and to some more especially; and partly in compassion to the people, who were now come into a wilderness (as themselves were) and were by the ship to be presently put ashore (for she was to carry other passengers to Virginia, who lay at great charge) and they were altogether unacquainted, and knew not what to do; so as they had received his former company of 7 men and victualed them as their own hitherto, so they also received these (being about 60 lusty men) and gave housing for themselves, and their goods, and many being sick they had the best means the place could afford them; they stayed here the most part of the summer till the ship came back again from Virginia. Then by his direction, or those whom he set over them, they removed into the Massachusetts Bay, he having got a patent for some part there, (by light of their former discovery in letters sent home). Yet they left all their sick folk here till they were settled, and housed; but of their victuals they had not any, though they were in great want, nor anything else in recompense of any courtesy done them; neither did they desire it, for they saw they were an unruly company, and had no good government over them, and by disorder would soon fall into wants if Mr. Weston came not the sooner amongst them; and therefore to prevent all after occasion would have nothing of them.

Amidst these straits, and the desertion of those from whom they had hoped for supply, and when famine began now to pinch them sore, they not knowing what to do, the Lord, (who never fails His) presents them with an occasion, beyond all expectation; this boat which came from the eastward brought them a letter, from a stranger of whose name they had never heard before (being a captain of a ship come there a-fishing). This letter was as followeth, being thus inscribed:

To all his good friends at Plymouth
these, etc.

Friends, countrymen, and neighbors, I salute you, and wish you all health, and happiness in the Lord. I make bold with these few lines to trouble you, because unless I were unhuman, I can do no less. Bad news doth spread itself too far, yet I will so far inform you that myself, with many good friends in the south colony of Virginia, have received such a blow, that 400 persons large will not make good our losses. Therefore I do entreat you (although not knowing you) that the old rule which I learned when I went to school, may be sufficient: that is "happy is he whom other men's harms doth make to beware." And now again, and again, wishing all those that willingly would serve the Lord, all health, and happiness in this world, and everlasting peace in the world to come. And so I rest,

Yours,
John Huddleston[159]

By this boat the Governor returned a thankful answer as was meet, and sent a boat of their own with them, which was piloted by them, in which Mr. Winslow was sent to procure what provisions he could of the ships; who was kindly received by the foresaid gentleman; who not only spared what he could, but writ to others to do the like. By which means he got some good quantity and returned in safety, by which the plantation had a double benefit, first a present refreshing by the food brought and, secondly they knew the way to those parts for their benefit hereafter. But what was got, and this small boat brought, being divided among so many came but to a little; yet by God's blessing it upheld them till harvest; it arose but to a quarter of a pound of bread a day to each person; and the Governor caused it to be daily given them; otherwise had it been in their own custody they would have ate it up, and then starved; but thus, with what else they could get they made pretty shift till corn was ripe.

This summer they built a fort with good timber both strong and comely, which was of good defense, made with a flat roof and battlements

---

[159]   Master of a 200-ton ship called the *Bona Nova*.

on which their ordnance were mounted, and where they kept constant watch, especially in time of danger.[160] It served them also for a meetinghouse, and was fitted accordingly for that use. It was a great work for them in this weakness, and time of wants, but the danger of the time required it and both the continual rumors of the fears from the Indians here, especially the Narragansetts; and also the hearing of that great massacre in Virginia[161] made all hands willing to dispatch the same.

---

[160] Edward Winslow in *Good News from New England*, reported on the fort: "In the time of these straits . . . the Indians began again to cast forth many insulting speeches, glorying in our weakness, and giving out how easy it would be ere long to cut us off. Now also Massasoit seemed to frown on us, and neither came or sent to us as formerly. These things occasioned further thoughts of fortification: And whereas we have a hill called the Mount, enclose[d] within our pale, under which our town is seated, we resolved to erect a fort thereon, from whence a few might easily secure the town from any assault the Indians can make, whilest the rest might be employed as occasion served. This work was begun with great eagerness . . . [a]nd though it took the greatest part of our strength from dressing our corn, yet (life being continued) we hoped God would raise some means instead thereof for our further preservation." Winslow added later, "Now was our fort made fit for service and some ordnance mounted; and through it may seem long work it being ten months since it begun, yet we must note, that where so great a work is begun with such small means, a little time cannot bring to perfection: . . ."

Emmanuel Altham, in a letter to his brother Sir Edward Altham in September 1623, wrote about Plymouth and its fort: "In this plantation is about twenty houses, four or five of which are very fair and pleasant, and the rest (as time will serve) shall be made better. And this town is in such manner that it makes a great street between the houses, and at the upper end of the town there is a strong fort, both by nature and art, with six pieces of reasonable good artillery mounted thereon; in which fort is continual watch, so that no Indian can come near thereabouts but he is presently seen. This town is paled round abut with pale of eight foot long, or thereabouts, and in the pale are three great gates." Altham's letter is reprinted in full in Sydney V. James, ed., *Three Visitors to Early Plymouth* (Plymouth: Plimoth Plantation, 1963).

[161] The Indians in Virginia had massacred 347 English colonists at Jamestown on 22 March 1622.

Now the welcome time of harvest approached, in which all had their hungry bellies filled. But it arose but to a little, in comparison of a full year's supply; partly because they were not yet well acquainted with the manner of Indian corn (and they had no other) also their many other employments, but chiefly their weakness for want of food, to tend it as they should have done; also much was stolen both by night and day, before it became scarce eatable, and much more afterward; and though many were well whipped (when they were taken) for a few ears of corn; yet hunger made others, (whom conscience did not restrain) to venture. So as it well appeared that famine must still ensue, the next year also if not some way prevented, or supply should fail to which they durst not trust. Markets there was none to go to, but only the Indians, and they had no trading commodities; behold now another providence of God, a ship comes into the harbor, one Captain Jones[162], being chief therein; they were set out by some merchants, to discover all the harbors between this and Virginia, and the shoals of Cape Cod, and to trade along the coast where they could. This ship had store of English beads (which were then good trade) and some knives; but would sell none but at dear rates, and also a good quantity together; yet they were glad of the occasion and fain to buy at any rate; they were fain to give after the rate of cento, per cento, if not more, and yet pay away coat-beaver, at 3s per £ which in a few years after yielded 20s. By this means they were fitted again to trade for beaver, and other things; and intended to buy what corn they could.

But I will here take liberty to make a little digression; there was in this ship a gentleman by name Mr. John Pory, he had been secretary in Virginia, and was now going home passenger in this ship. After his departure he write a letter to the Governor in the postscript whereof he hath these lines:

To yourself and Mr. Brewster, I must acknowledge myself many ways indebted; whose books I would have you think very well bestowed on him, who esteemeth them such jewels. My haste would not suffer me to remember

---

[162] Thomas Jones, a some-time pirate and slave trader, who in 1618 took some cattle in the ship *Falcon* to Virginia. Many 19th century histories of the *Mayflower* and the Pilgrims incorrectly state that Thomas Jones was the master of the *Mayflower*, but it has since been conclusively proven that the *Mayflower*'s master was Christopher Jones of Harwich, co. Essex, England.

(much less to beg) Mr. Ainsworth's elaborate work upon the 5 books of Moses.[163] Both his, and Mr. Robinson's do highly commend the authors; as being most conversant in the Scriptures of all others: and what good (who knows) it may please God to work by them, through my hands, (though most unworthy) who finds such high content in them. God have you all in his keeping.

Your unfeigned, and firm friend,
John Pory[164]

August 28, 1622

These things I here insert for honor sake, of the author's memory which this gentleman doth thus ingeniously acknowledge; and himself after his return did this poor plantation much credit, amongst those of no mean rank. But to return.

Shortly after harvest Mr. Weston's people who were now seated at the Massachusetts, and by disorder (as it seems) had made havoc of their provisions began now to perceive that want would come upon them. And hearing that they here had bought trading commodities, and intended to trade for corn, they write to the Governor and desired they might join with them, and they would employ their small ship in the service; and further requested either to lend or sell them so much of their trading commodities as their part might come to, and they would undertake to make payment when Mr. Weston, or their supply should come. The Governor condescended upon equal terms of agreement, thinking to go about the Cape to the southward with the ship, where some store of corn might be got. All things being provided Captain Standish was appointed to go with them, and Squanto for a guide and interpreter, about the latter end of September, but

---

[163] Henry Ainsworth's *Annotations Upon the Five Books of Moses* was one of the more popular books in early the Plymouth Colony. All, or portions of, his *Five Books* are known to have been owned by Plymouth Colony residents Richard Lanckford, Samuel Fuller, Sarah Jenny, William and Love Brewster, John Hazel, William and Alice Bradford, William Carpenter, William Bassett, and Thomas Willet. The most popular books in early Plymouth were Pastor John Robinson's *Observations Divine and Moral*, and John Dod's *Plain and Familiar Exposition Upon the Ten Commandments*.

[164] Several of John Pory's letters relating to his 1622 visit to Plymouth have survived, and are reprinted in Sydney V. James, ed., *Three Visitors to Early Plymouth* (Plymouth: Plimoth Plantation, 1963).

the winds put them in again, and putting out the 2 time he fell sick of a fever, so the Governor went himself; but they could not get about the shoals of Cape Cod for flats, and breakers neither could Squanto direct them better, nor the master durst venture any further, so they put into Manamoyick Bay and got with they could there. In this place Squanto fell sick of an Indian fever, bleeding much at the nose (which the Indians take for a symptom of death[165]) and within a few days died there, desiring the Governor to pray for him, that he might go to the Englishmen's God in Heaven; and bequeathed sundry of his things to sundry of his English friends as remembrances of his love; of whom they had a great loss. They got in this voyage in one place, and other about 26 or 28 hogsheads of corn, and beans, which was more than the Indians could well spare in these parts, for they set but a little till they got English hoes. And so were fain to return, being sorry they could not get about the Cape, to have been better laden. Afterward the Governor took a few men and went to the inland places, to get what he could, and to fetch it home at the spring, which did help them something.

After these things, in February a messenger came from John Sanders, who was left chief over Mr. Weston's men in the Bay of Massachusetts, who brought a letter showing the great wants they were fallen into; and he would have borrowed a hogshead of corn of the Indians but they would lend him none. He desired advice whether he might not take it from them by force to succor his men till he came from the eastward whither he was going. The Governor and rest dissuaded him by all means from it, for it might so exasperate the Indians as might endanger their safety; and all of us might smart for it; for they had already heard how they had so wronged the Indians by stealing their corn, etc. as they were much incensed

---

[165] This statement has intrigued some modern medical researchers: could this be evidence that hemorrhagic fevers played a part in the early plagues? Or perhaps it is a manifestation of one of the rarer symptoms of the Bubonic plague? Edward Winslow in *Good News from New England*, reported that after Tisquantum died they traveled to the Massachusetts Indians, where they "found a great sickness to be amongst the Indians, not unlike the plague, if not the same." Symptoms of the plague are painfully swollen lymph nodes, high fever, "ring around the rosy" (the rash described in the children's nursery rhyme about the plague—before everyone falls down and dies), and occasionally bleeding from body openings. Demetres Velendzas, MD, et.al., "Plague," *eMedicine Journal* 2-10(16 October 2001).

against them; yea so base were some of their own company as they went, and told the Indians that their Governor was purposed to come and take their corn by force. The which with other things made them enter into a conspiracy against the English, of which more in the next. Herewith I end this year.[166]

---

[166]   This incident is described in more detail by Edward Winslow in his *Good News from New England* (London, 1624).

Anno Dom: 1623 •

It may be thought strange that these people should fall to these extremities in so short a time; being left competently provided when the ship left them, and had an ambition by that moiety of corn that was got by trade, besides much they got of the Indians where they lived by one means and other. It must needs be their great disorder, for they spent excessively whilst they had, or could get it; and it may be wasted part away among the Indians (for he that was their chief was taxed by some amongst them, for keeping Indian women) how truly I know not. And after they began to come into wants, many sold away their clothes, and bed coverings; others (so base were they) became servants to the Indians, and would cut them wood, and fetch them water, for a capful of corn; others fell to plain stealing, both night and day from the Indians, of which they grievously complained. In the end they came to that misery, that some starved and died with cold and hunger; one in gathering shellfish was so weak as he stuck fast in the mud, and was found dead in the place.[167] At last most of them left their dwellings; and scattered up, and down in the woods, and by the watersides, where they could find ground nuts and clams, here 6 and there ten: by which their carriages they became contemned and scorn of the Indians; and they began greatly to insult over them, in a most insolent manner. Insomuch that many times as they lay thus scattered abroad,

---

[167] Phineas Pratt of the Wessagussett Colony made a deposition in 1662 that provides many historical details on this colony. The full deposition can be found in the *Collections of the Massachusetts Historical Society*, 4th Series 4(1858):474-491. Thomas Morton also describes events at Wessagussett in some detail in his *New English Canaan* (Amsterdam, 1637), primarily in chapters 2 through 5 of his "Third Book."

and had set on a pot with ground nuts, or shellfish, when it was ready the Indians would come and eat it up; and when night came, whereas some of them had a sorry blanket, or such like, to lap themselves in, the Indians would take it, and let the other lie all night in the cold; so as their condition was very lamentable. Yea in the end they were fain to hang one of their men, whom they could not reclaim from stealing, to give the Indians content.

Whilst things went in this manner with them; the Governor and people here had notice that Massasoit their friend was sick, and near unto death; they sent to visit him, and withal sent him such comfortable things as gave him great content, and was a means of his recovery[168]; upon which occasion he discovers the conspiracy of these Indians how they were resolved to cut off Mr. Weston's people, for the continual injuries they did them, and would now take opportunity of their weakness to do it; and for that end had conspired with other Indians their neighbors thereabout; and thinking the people here would revenge their death, they therefore thought to do the like by them, and had solicited him to join with them; he advised them therefore to prevent it, and that speedily by taking of some of the chief of them, before it was too late, for he assured them of the truth hereof.

This did much trouble them, and they took it into serious deliberation and found upon examination, other evidence to give light hereunto, too long here to relate. In the meantime, came one of them from the Massachusetts with a small pack at his back, and though he knew not a foot of the way yet he got safe hither, but lost his way, which was well for him for he was pursued, and so was missed.[169] He told them here, how all things stood amongst them, and that he durst stay no longer, he apprehended they (by what he observed) would be all knocked in the head shortly. This

---

[168]   This visit to Massasoit is described at length in Winslow's *Good News from New England* (London, 1624). Winslow visited Massasoit in his sickness and provided medical care and chicken broth that actually helped Massasoit return to health.

[169]   This was Phineas Pratt. He details his amazing ordeal in his 1662 deposition. He reported: "But when we understood that their plot was to kill all English people in one day when the store was gone, I would have sent a man to Plymouth, but none were willing to go. Then I said if Plymouth men know not of this treacherous plot, they and we are all dead men; therefore if God willing, tomorrow I will go. That night a young man, wanting wit, told Pecksuot early in the morning. . . . [They] were careless of their watch near two hours on the morning.

made them make the more haste, and dispatched a boat away with Captain Standish, and some men, who found them in a miserable condition, out of which he rescued them, and helped them to some relief cut off some few of the chief conspirators. And according to his order, offered to bring them all hither if they thought good, and they should fare no worse than themselves, till Mr. Weston, or some supply came to them. Or if any other course liked them better, he was to do them any helpfulness he could. They thanked him, and the rest; but most of them desired he would help them with some corn, and they would go with their small ship to the eastward, where haply they might hear of Mr. Weston, or some supply from him, seeing the time of the year was for fishing ships to be in the land; if not they would work among the fishermen for their living and get their passage into England, if they heard nothing from Mr. Weston in time. So they shipped what they had of any worth, and he got them all the corn he could (scarce leaving to bring him home) and saw them well out of the bay, under sail at sea, and so came home, not taking the worth of a penny of anything that was theirs. I have but touched these things briefly because they have already been published in print more at large.[170]

Then said I to our company, 'now it is time to run to Plymouth . . .' I run southward till 3 of the clock, but the snow being in many places, I was the more distressed because of my footsteps. The sun being beclouded, I wandered, not knowing my way; but at the going down of the sun, it appeared red; then hearing a great howling of wolves, I came to a river; the water being deep and cold and many rocks, I passed through with much ado. Then was I in great distress for want of food, weary with running, fearing to make a fire because of them that pursued me . . . . The day following I began to travel but being unable, I went back to the fire; the day following the sun shined and about three of the clock I came to that part of Plymouth Bay where there is a town of later time called Duxbury . . . . I kept running in the path; then passing through James River I said in my thoughts, now am I as a deer chased by wolves. If I perish, what will be the condition of distressed Englishmen." Pratt eventually met up with Mr. John Hamden, a visitor to Plymouth, and made it to Plymouth to notify the English settlers there of the plot. The Plymouth men had already heard of the plot from Massasoit, however. Pratt's deposition is found in the *Collections of the Massachusetts Historical Society*, 4th Series 4(1858):474-491.

[170]   Bradford refers to the more detailed description of events found in Edward Winslow's *Good News from New England* (London, 1624).

This was the end of these, that some time boasted of their strength, (being all able lusty men) and what they would do and bring to pass; in comparison of the people here, who had many women and children and weak ones amongst them. And said at their first arrival, when they saw the wants here, that they would take another course, and not to fall into such a condition, as this simple people were come to. But a man's way is not in his own power, God can make the weak to stand; let him also that standeth take heed lest he fall.

Shortly after Mr. Weston came over with some of the fishermen, under another name, and the disguise of a blacksmith; where he heard of the ruin and dissolution of his colony; he got a boat and with a man or 2 came to see how things were. But by the way, for want of skill, in a storm he cast away his shallop in the bottom of the bay between Merrimack River and Piscataqua, and hardly escaped with life. And afterwards fell into the hands of the Indians, who pillaged him of all he saved from the sea, and stripped him out of all his clothes to his shirt. At last he got to Piscataqua, and borrowed a suit of clothes, and got means to come to Plymouth. A strange alteration there was in him, to such as had seen, and known him, in his former flourishing condition; so uncertain are the mutable things of this unstable world, and yet men set their hearts upon them though they daily see the vanity thereof.

After many passages, and much discourse (former things boiling in his mind, but bit in as was discerned) so he desired to borrow some beaver of them; and told them he had hope of a ship, and good supply to come to him, and then they should have anything for it they stood in need of. They gave little credit to his supply, but pitied his case, and remembered former courtesies; they told him he saw their wants, and they knew not when they should have any supply, also how the case stood between them and their adventurers, he well knew; they had not much beaver, and if they should let him have it, it were enough to make a mutiny among the people; seeing there was no other means to procure them food which they so much wanted, and clothes also. Yet they told him they would help him, considering his necessity, but must do it secretly for the former reasons. So they let him have 100 beaver skins, which weighed 170-odd pounds.

Thus they helped him when all the world failed him; and with this means he went again to the ships, and stayed his small ship, and some of his men, and bought provisions and fitted himself; and it was the only foundation of his after course. But he requited them ill, for he proved after a bitter enemy unto them upon all occasions; and never repaid them anything for it, to this day but reproaches and evil words. Yea he divulged it to some, that were none of their best friends, whilst he yet had the beaver in his boat; that he could now set them altogether by the ears, because they had done more than they could answer in letting him have this beaver; and he did not spare to do what he could, but his malice could not prevail.

All this while no supply was heard of, neither knew they when they might expect any. So they began to think how they might raise as much corn as they could, and obtain a better crop than they had done; that they might not still thus languish in misery. At length after much debate of things, the Governor (with the advice of the chiefest amongst them) gave way that they should set corn every man for his own particular, and in that regard trust to themselves; in all other things to go on in the general way as before. And so assigned to every family a parcel of land, according to the proportion of their number, for that end, only for present use (but made no division for inheritance) and ranged all boys, and youth under some family.[171] This had very good success; for it made all hands very industrious, so as much more corn was planted, than otherwise would have been; by any means the Governor or any other could use, and saved him a great deal of trouble, and gave far better content; the women now went willingly into the field, and took their little ones with them to set corn; which before would allege weakness and inability; whom to have compelled would have been thought great tyranny, and oppression.

The experience that was had in this common course, and condition, tried sundry years, and that amongst godly, and sober men, may well evince, the vanity of that conceit, of Plato's, and other ancients, applauded by some of later times: that the taking away of property, and bringing in community, into, a commonwealth; would make them happy, and flourishing; as if they were wiser than God. For this community, (so far as it was) was found to breed much confusion, and discontent, and retard much employment, that would have been to their benefit, and comfort; for the young men that were most able and fit for labor and service, did repine that they should spend their time, and strength to work for other men's wives, and children, without

---

[171] The full 1623 Division of Land is found in the *Plymouth Colony Records* 12:4-6, and is also reprinted in Appendix I. This document is useful to historians and genealogists because it lists the head of every family, what ship they came on (*Mayflower, Fortune,* or *Anne*), and the number of acres assigned to each family. Since each person in the family received an acre, it is possible to determine how many people were in each family.

any recompense.[172] The strong, or man of parts, had no more in division of victuals, and clothes, than he that was weak, and not able to do a quarter the other could, this was thought injustice. The aged and graver men to be ranked, and equalized, in labors, and victuals, clothes etc., with the meaner, and younger sort, thought it some indignity, and disrespect unto them. And for men's wives to be commanded, to do service for other men, as dressing their meat, washing their clothes, etc., they deemed it a kind of slavery, neither could many husbands well brook it. Upon the point all being to have alike, and all to do alike, they thought themselves in the like condition, and one as good as another; and so if it did not cut off, those relations, that God hath set amongst men; yet it did at least much diminish, and take off, the mutual respects that should be preserved amongst them. And would have been worse if they had been men of another condition. Let none object this is men's corruption; and nothing to the course itself; I answer seeing all men have this corruption in them, God in His wisdom saw another course fitter for them.

But to return, after this course settled; and by that their corn was planted all their victuals were spent; and they were only to rest on God's providence; at night, not many times knowing where to have a bit of anything the next day. And so as one well observed, had need to pray that God would give them their daily bread, above all people in the world. Yet they bore these wants with great patience, and alacrity of spirit; and that for so long a time as for the most part of 2 years. Which makes me remember what Peter Martyr writes[173] (in magnifying the Spaniards) in his 5 decade page 208. "They" (saith he) "led a miserable life for 5 days together, with the parched grain of maize only, and that not to saturity"; and then concludes, "that such pains, such labors, and such hunger, he thought none living, which is not a Spaniard could have endured."

But alas these, when they had maize (that is Indian corn) they thought it as good as a feast, and wanted not only for 5 days together, but some time 2 or 3 months together, and neither had bread, nor any kind of corn. Indeed in

---

[172] The Jamestown Colony's experiment with the communal property met with a similar result. Ralph Hamor wrote that "When our people were fed out of the common store, and labored jointly together, glad was he who could slip from his labor or slumber over his task he cared not how, nay, the most honest among them would hardly take so much pains in a week, as now they themselves will do in a day." *Purchas His Pilgrims* 4:1766.

[173] Peter Martyr, *De Novo Orbe, or The History of the West Indies* (London, 1612).

another place, in his 2 decade, page 94 he mentions how others of them were worse put to it; where they were fain to eat dogs, toads, and dead men; and so died almost all from these extremities, the Lord in His goodness, kept these His people; and in their great wants, preserved both their lives and healths; let His name have the praise. Yet let me here make use of his conclusion; which in some sort may be applied to this people: "That with their miseries they opened a way to these new lands; and after these storms, with what ease other men came to inhabit in them; in respect of the calamities these men suffered; so as they seem to go to a bride feast where all things are provided for them."

They having but one boat left, and she not over well fitted, they were divided into several companies, 6 or 7 to a gang, or company, and so went out (with a net they had bought) to take bass and such like fish, by course, every company knowing their turn; no sooner was the boat discharged of what she brought, but the next company took her, and went out with her.[174] Neither did they return, till they had caught something; though it were 5 or 6 days before, for they knew there was nothing at home, and to go home empty would be a great discouragement to the rest; yea they strive who should do best; if she stayed long, or got little, then all went to seeking of shellfish, which at low water they digged out of the sands. And this was their living in the summer time, till God sent them better; and in winter they were helped with ground nuts, and fowl; also in the summer they got now, and then a deer; for one, or 2 of the fittest was appointed to range the woods for that end, and what was got that way, was divided amongst them.

At length they received some letters from the adventurers, too long and tedious here to record; by which they heard of their further crosses and frustrations. Beginning in this manner.[175]

Loving friends, as your sorrows, and afflictions, have been great; so our crosses, and interceptions in our proceedings here, have not been small. For

---

[174] Isaac de Rasieres, a Dutch official who visited Plymouth in 1628, reported "The bay is very full of fish, of cod, so that the Governor before named [Bradford] has told me that when the people have a desire for fish they send out two or three persons in a sloop, whom they remunerate for their trouble, and who bring them in three or four hours time as much fish as the whole community require for a whole day: and they muster about fifty families."

[175] These letters were dated Dec. 21, 1622. (Bradford).

after we had with much trouble, and charge sent the *Paragon* away to sea, and thought all the pain past; within 14 days after she came again hither, being dangerously leaked, and bruised with tempestuous storms; so as she was fain to be had into the dock, and an £100 bestowed upon her. All the passengers lying upon our charge for 6 or 7 weeks, and much discontent, and distemper, was occasioned hereby, so as some dangerous event had like to ensued. But we trust all shall be well, and work for the best, and your benefit; if yet with patience you can wait, and but have strength to hold in life. Whilst these things were doing, Mr. Weston's ship came and brought divers letters from you, etc. It rejoiceth us much, to hear of those good reports that divers have brought home from you, etc. So far of this letter.

This ship was bought by Mr. John Peirce, and set out at his own charge, upon hope of great matters; these passengers, and the goods the company sent in her, he took in for freight, for which they agreed with him to be delivered here. This was he in whose name their first patent was taken, by reason of acquaintance, and some alliance that some of their friends had with him. But his name was only used in trust; but when he saw they were here hopefully thus seated, and by the success God gave them, had obtained, the favor of the Council of New England, he goes and sues to them for another patent of much larger extent (in their names), which was easily obtained. But he meant to keep it to himself, and allow them what he pleased, to hold of him as tenants, and sue to his courts as chief lord. As will appear by that which follows. But the Lord marvelously crossed him; for after this first return, and the charge above mentioned; when she was again fitted, he pesters himself and takes in more passengers, and those not very good to help to bear his losses, and sets out the 2 time. But what the event was will appear from another letter from one of the chief of the company, dated the 9 of April 1623, writ to the Governor here, as followeth:

Loving friend when I writ my last letter, I hoped to have received one from you well-nigh by this time. But when I writ in December I little thought to have seen Mr. John Peirce till he had brought some good tidings from you. But it pleased God, he brought us the woeful tidings of his return when he was half way over, by extreme tempest. Wherein the goodness, and mercy of God appeared in sparing their lives, being 109 souls. The loss is so great to Mr. Peirce, etc., and the company put upon so great charge as verily, etc.

Now with great trouble, and loss, we have got Mr. John Peirce to assign over the grand patent to the company, which he had taken in his own name, and made quite void our former grant. I am sorry to write how many here, think that the hand of God was justly against him, both the first and 2 time of his return; in regard he, whom you, and we so confidently trusted, but only to use his name for the company; should aspire to be lord over us all. And so make you, and us, tenants at his will, and pleasure; our assurance, or patent being quite void, and disannulled by his means. I desire to judge charitably of him. But his unwillingness to part with his royal lordship, and the high rate he set it at, which was £500 which cost him but £50; makes many speak and judge hardly of him. The company are out, for goods in his ship, with charge about the passengers £640, etc.

We have agreed with 2 merchants for a ship of 140 tuns called the *Anne* which is to be ready the last of this month to bring 60 passengers, and 60 tun of goods, etc. This was dated April 9, 1623.

These were their own words, and judgment of this man's dealing, and proceedings; for I thought it more meet to render them in theirs, than my own words. And yet though there was never got, other recompense than, the resignation of this patent, and the shares he had in adventure, for all the former great sums, he was never quiet, but sued them in most of the chief courts in England, and when he was still cast, brought it to the Parliament. But he is now dead and I will leave him to the Lord.

This ship suffered the greatest extremity at sea, at her 2 return, that one shall lightly hear of, to be saved; as I have been informed by Mr. William Peirce who was then master of her, and many others that were passengers in her. It was about the middle of February; the storm was for the most part of 14 days, but for 2 or 3 days and nights together in most violent extremity. After they had cut down their mast, the storm beat off their round house, and all their upper works; 3 men had work enough at the helm, and he that conned the ship before the sea was fain to be bound fast for washing away; the seas did so over-rake them, as many times, those upon the deck knew not, whether they were within board, or without; and once she was so foundered in the sea as they all thought she would never rise again. But yet the Lord preserved them, and brought them at last safe to Portsmouth, to the wonder of all men that saw in what a case she was in, and heard what they had endured.

About the latter end of June came in a ship[176]; with Captain Francis West, who had a commission to be Admiral of New England; to restrain

---

[176] The *Plantation*.

interlopers; and such fishing ships, as came to fish and trade without a license from the Council of New England, for which they should pay a round sum of money; but he could do no good of them, for they were too strong for him, and he found the fishermen to be stubborn fellows. And their owners upon complaint made to the Parliament, procured an order that fishing should be free. He told the Governor they spoke with a ship at sea, and were aboard her, that was coming for this Plantation, in which were sundry passengers, and they marveled she was not arrived, fearing some miscarriage, for they lost her, in a storm that fell shortly after they had been aboard; which relation filled them full of fear, yet mixed with hope. The master of this ship had some 2 hogsheads of peas to sell; but seeing their wants, held them at £9 sterling a hogshead, and under £8 he would not take, and yet would have beaver at an under rate. But they told him they had lived so long without, and would do still, rather than give so unreasonably. They went from hence to Virginia.

About 14 days after came in this ship, called the *Anne*, whereof Mr. William Peirce was master, and about a week or 10 days after came in the pinnace which in foul weather they lost at sea, a fine new vessel of about 44 tun, which the company had built to stay in the country[177]. They brought about 60 persons for the general[178], some of them being very useful persons, and became good members to the body, and some were the wives and children of such as were here already. And some were so bad; as they were fain to be at charge to send them home again the next year. Also besides these there came a company, that did not belong to the general body; but came on their particular, and were to have lands assigned them, and be for themselves, yet to be subject to the general government, which caused some difference, and disturbance amongst them, as will after appear. I shall here again take liberty to insert a few things out of such letters as came in this ship, desiring rather to manifest things in their words, and apprehensions, than in my own, as much as may be, without tediousness.

Beloved friends I kindly salute you all, with trust of your healths, and welfare; being right sorry that no supply hath been made to you all this while; for defense whereof, I must refer you to our general letters. Neither indeed have we now sent you many things, which we should,

---

[177] The *Little James*

[178] Most of the names of the *Anne*'s passengers can be picked out from the 1623 Division of Land, *Plymouth Colony Records* 12:4-6, reprinted in Appendix I.

and would, for want of money. But persons, more than enough, (though not all we should) for people come flying in upon us, but moneys come creeping in to us. Some few of your old friends are come as, etc. So they come dropping to you, and by degrees, I hope ere long you shall enjoy them all. And because people press so hard upon us to go, and often such as are none of the fittest; I pray you write earnestly to the treasurer, and direct what persons should be sent; it grieveth me to see, so weak a company sent you; and yet had not been here they had been weaker. You must still call upon the company here to see that honest men be sent you, and threaten to send them back if any other come, etc. We are not any way, so much in danger, as by corrupt, and naughty persons. Such, and such, came without my consent; but the importunity of their friends, got promise of our treasurer in my absence; neither is there need we should take any lewd men, for we may have honest men anew, etc.

Your assured friend,
R[obert] C[ushman]

This following was from the general.

Loving friends we most heartily salute you, in all love and hearty affection. Being yet in hope that the same God which hath hitherto, preserved you in a marvelous manner; doth yet continue, your lives, and health, to His own praise, and all our comforts. Being right sorry that you have not been sent unto all this time, etc. We have in this ship sent such women, as were willing, and ready to go to their husbands, and friends, with their children, etc. We would not have you discontent, because we have not sent you more of your old friends; and in special him, on whom you most depend; far be it from us to neglect you, or contemn him. But as the intent was at first, so the event at last shall show it, that we will deal fairly, and squarely answer your expectations to the full. There are also come unto you, some honest men to plant upon their own particulars besides you. A thing which if we should not give way unto, we should wrong, both them, and you: them by putting them on things more inconvenient; and you, for that being honest men, they will be a strengthening to the place; and good neighbors unto you. Two things we would advise you of, which we have likewise signified to them here. First the trade for skins to be retained for the general till the dividend; 2ly that their settling by you, be with such distance of place, as is neither inconvenient for the lying of your lands, nor hurtful to your speedy and easy assembling together.

We have sent you divers fishermen with salt, etc. Divers other provisions we have sent you as will appear in your bill of lading, and though we have not sent all we would (because our cash is small) yet it is that we could, etc.

And although it seemeth you have discovered many more rivers, and fertile grounds than that where you are; yet seeing by God's providence, that place fell to your lot, let it be accounted as your portion; and rather fix your eyes upon that which may be done there than languish in hopes, after things elsewhere. If your place be not the best, it is better; you shall be the less envied, and encroached upon; and such as are earthly minded, will not settle too near your border.[179] If the land afford you bread, and the sea yield you fish, rest you a while contented; God will one day afford you better fare. And all men shall know, you are neither fugitives, nor discontents; but can if God so order it, take the worst to yourselves, with content; and leave the best to your neighbors with cheerfulness.

Let it not be grievous unto you, that you have been instruments, to break the ice for others, who come after with less difficulty; the our shall be yours to the world's end, etc.

We bear you always in our breasts, and our hearty affection is towards you all; as are the hearts of hundreds more, which never saw your faces; who doubtless pray for your safety as their own; as we ourselves, both do, and ever shall, that the same God, which hath so marvelously preserved you, from seas, foes, and famine, will still preserve you from all future dangers; and make you honorable amongst men and glorious in bliss at the last day. And so the Lord be with you all, and send us joyful news from you; and enable us with one shoulder, so to accomplish and perfect this work; as much glory may come to Him, that confoundeth the mighty, by the weak, and maketh small things great. To whose greatness, be all glory forever, and ever.

This letter was subscribed with
13 of their names.

These passengers when they saw their low, and poor condition ashore, were much daunted, and dismayed; and according to their divers humors

---

[179] This proved rather, a prophecy, than advice. (Bradford)

were, diversely affected; some wished themselves in England again; others fell a-weeping, fancying their own misery, in what they saw now in others; other some pitying the distress they saw their friends had been long in, and still were under; in a word all were full of sadness. Only some of their old friends rejoiced, to see them; and that it was no worse with them, for they could not expect it should be better; and now hoped they should enjoy better days together. And truly it was no marvel they should be thus affected, for they were in a very low condition, many were ragged in apparel, and some little better than half naked; though some that were well stored before, were well enough in this regard. But for food they were all alike (save some that had got a few peas of the ship that was last here). The best dish they could present their friends with was a lobster, or a piece of fish, without bread or anything else, but a cup of fair spring water. And the long continuance of this diet, and their labors abroad; had something abated the freshness of their former complexion, but God gave them health and strength in a good measure. And showed them by experience the truth of that word, Deuteronomy 8:3 "That man liveth not by bread only, but by every word that proceedeth out of the mouth of the Lord doth a man live."

When I think how sadly the Scripture, speaks, of the famine in Jacob's time, when he said to his sons, "Go buy us food, that we may live, and not die," Genesis 42:2 and 43:1, that the famine was great, or heavy in the land. And yet they had such great herds and store of cattle of sundry kinds; which besides flesh, must needs produce other food as milk, butter and cheese, etc. And yet it was counted a sore affliction. Theirs here must needs be very great therefore; who not only wanted, the staff of bread, but all these things, and had no Egypt to go to. But God fed them out of the sea for the most part; so wonderful is His providence over His, in all ages; for His mercy endureth forever.

I may not here omit, how notwithstanding all their great pains and industry, and the great hopes of a large crop; the Lord seemed to blast, and take away the same, and to threaten further, and more sore famine unto them. By a great drought which continued from the 3 week in May till about the middle of July, without any rain, and with great heat (for the most part) insomuch as the corn began to wither away though it was set with fish, the moisture whereof helped it much: yet at length it began to languish sore, and some of the drier grounds were parched like withered hay, part whereof was never recovered. Upon which they set apart a solemn day of humiliation; to seek the Lord by humble and fervent prayer, in this great distress. And He was pleased to give them a gracious, and speedy answer; both to their own, and the Indians' admiration, that lived amongst them. For all the morning, and greatest part of the day, it was clear weather and very hot, and not a cloud, or any sign of rain to be seen; yet toward evening it began to overcast, and shortly after to rain, with such sweet and gentle showers, as gave them cause of rejoicing, and blessing God; it came without either wind, or thunder, or any violence, and by degrees in that abundance, as that the earth was thoroughly wet and soaked therewith. Which did so apparently revive, and quicken the decayed corn, and other fruits, as was wonderful to see, and made the Indians astonished to behold[180]; and afterwards the Lord sent them

---

[180]   *New England's First Fruits* (Anonymous; London 1643), the first of 11 pamphlets known as the "Eliot Tracts," also noted this event: "Many years since at Plymouth Plantation, when the Church did fast and pray for rain in extreme drought; it being a very hot and clear sunshine day, all the former part thereof; an Indian of good quality, being present, and seeing what they were about, fell a-wondering at them for praying for rain in a day so unlikely, when all sun and no clouds appeared; and thought that their God was not able to give rain at such a time as that: but this poor wretch seeing them still continue in their prayers, and beholding that at last the clouds began to rise, and by that time they had ended their duty, the rain fell in a most sweet, constant, soaking shower, fell into wonderment at the power that the English had with their God, and the greatness and goodness of that God whom they served, and was smitten with terror that he had abused them and their God by his former hard thoughts of them; and resolved from that day not to rest till he did know this great good God, and for that end to forsake the Indians, and cleave to the English, which he presently did, and labored by all public and private means to suck in more and more of the knowledge of God, and his ways. And as he increased in knowledge so in affection, and also in his practice, reforming and confirming himself accordingly: and (though he was much tempted by inducements, scoffs and scorns from the Indians) yet, could he never be gotten from the English, nor from seeking after their God, but died amongst them, leaving some good hopes in their hearts, that his soul went to rest."

Edward Winslow, in his *Good News from New England* (London, 1624) also mentions this: "For though in the morning when we assembled together, the heavens were as clear and the drought as like to continue as ever it was: yet (our exercise continuing some eight or nine hours) before our departure the weather was over-cast, the clouds gathered together on all sides, and on the next morning distilled such soft, sweet, and moderate showers of rain, continuing some fourteen days, and mixed with such seasonable weather, as it was hard to say whether our

such seasonable showers, with interchange of fair warm weather, as through (His blessing) caused a fruitful, and liberal harvest, to their no small comfort, and rejoicing; for which mercy (in time convenient) they also set apart a day of thanksgiving. This being over-slipped in its place I thought meet here to insert the same.

On the other hand, the old planters were afraid that their corn when it was ripe should be imparted to the newcomers; whose provisions which they brought with them, they feared would fall short, before the year went about, (as indeed it did). They came to the Governor and besought him that as it was before agreed, that they should set corn for their particular, and accordingly they had taken extraordinary pains thereabout; that they might freely enjoy the same; and they would not have a bit of the victuals now come, but wait till harvest for their own; and let the newcomers enjoy what they had brought; they would have none of it, except they could purchase any of it of them by bargain, or exchange. Their request was granted them; for it gave both sides good content; for the newcomers were as much afraid that the hungry planters, would have ate up the provisions brought, and they should have fallen into the like condition.

This ship was in a short time laden with clapboard, by the help of many hands; also they sent in her all the beaver, and other furs they had; and Mr. Winslow was sent over with her to inform of all things, and procure such things, as were thought needful for their present condition.[181] By this time harvest was come; and instead of famine, now God gave them plenty,

---

withered corn or drooping affections were most quickened or revived. Such was the bounty and goodness of our God. Of this the Indians by means of Hobomok took notice: who being then in the town, and this exercise in the midst of the week, said, it was but three days since Sunday, and therefore demanded of a boy what was the reason thereof? Which when he knew and saw what effects followed thereupon, he and all of them admired the goodness of our God towards us, that wrought so great a change in so short a time, showing the difference between their conjuration, and our invocation on the name of God for rain; theirs being mixed with such storms and tempests, as sometimes instead of doing them good, it layeth the corn flat on the ground, to their prejudice: but ours in so gentle and seasonable a manner, as they never observed the like."

[181] Bradford and Allerton wrote a letter dated 8 September 1623, that ended up as evidence in the High Court of Admiralty lawsuit, Stevens and Fell vs. *Little James*. This letter sheds additional light on the business involving the *Anne* and *Little James*. It is reprinted in Appendix I.

and the face of things was changed, to the rejoicing of the hearts of many; for which they blessed God. And the effect of their particular planting was well seen, for all had one way, and other, pretty well to bring the year about; and some of the abler sort, and more industrious had to spare, and sell to others; so as any general want or famine hath not been amongst them, since to this day.

Those that came on their particular, looked for greater matters than they found, or could attain unto, about building great houses, and such pleasant situations for them, as themselves had fancied; as if they would be great men and rich all of a sudden. But they proved castles in the air. These were the conditions agreed on between the Colony and them.

1. First, that the Governor in the name, and with the consent of the company; doth in all love and friendship, receive and embrace them; and is to allot them competent places for habitations, within the town. And promiseth to show them all such other courtesies, as shall be reasonable for them to desire, or us to perform.
2. That they on their parts, be subject to all such laws and orders as are already made; or hereafter shall be for the public good.
3. That they be freed, and exempt from the general employments of the said company (which their present condition of community requireth) except common defense, and such other employments, as tend to the perpetual good of the Colony.
4. 4ly. Towards the maintenance of government and public officers of the said Colony, every male above the age of 16 years; shall pay a bushel of Indian wheat, or the worth of it, into the common store.
5. 5ly. That (according to the agreement the merchants made with them before they came) they are to be wholly debarred from all trade with the Indians, for all sorts of furs, and such like commodities; till the time of the communality be ended.

About the middle of September arrived Captain Robert Gorges in the Bay of the Massachusetts, with sundry passengers, and families; intending there to begin a plantation; and pitched upon the place, Mr. Weston's people had forsaken. He had a commission from the Council of New England, to be general governor of the country; and they appointed for his counsel, and assistance, Captain Francis West the aforesaid admiral, Christopher Levitt Esquire, and the Governor of Plymouth for the time being, etc. Also they gave him authority, to choose such other as he should find fit; also they gave (by their commission) full power to him, and his assistants or any 3 of them, whereof himself was all way to be one; to do and execute what to them should seem good; in all cases, capital, criminal, and civil, etc., with divers other instructions. Of which, and his commission, it pleased him to suffer the Governor here to take a copy.

He gave them notice of his arrival by letter, but before they could visit him, he went to the eastward with the ship he came in: but a storm arising (and they wanting a good pilot to harbor them in those parts) they bore up for this harbor. He and his men were here kindly entertained; he stayed here 14 days. In the meantime came in Mr. Weston with his small ship, which he had now recovered. Captain Gorges took hold of the opportunity, and acquainted the Governor here, that one occasion, of his going to the eastward was to meet with Mr. Weston, and call him to account for some abuses he had to lay to his charge. Whereupon he called him before him, and some other of his assistants, with the Governor of this place; and charged him first, with the ill carriage of his men, at the Massachusetts; by which means the peace of the country was disturbed, and himself, and the people which he had brought over to plant in that bay, were thereby much prejudiced. To this Mr. Weston easily answered, that what was that way done, was in his absence, and might have befallen any man; he left them sufficiently provided, and conceived they would have been well governed, and for any error committed, he had sufficiently smarted. This particular was passed by; a second was, for an abuse done to his father Sir Ferdinando Gorges, and to the State. The thing was this, he used him and others of the Council of New England, to procure him a license for the transporting of many pieces of great ordnance, for New England, pretending great fortification here in the country, and I know not what shipping. The which when he had obtained, he went and sold them beyond seas for his private profit[182]; for which (he said) the State was much offended, and his father suffered a shrewd check, and he had order to apprehend him for it. Mr. Weston excused it as well as he could, but could not deny it; it being one main thing (as was said) for which he withdrew himself. But after many passages, by the mediation of the Governor and some other friends here, he was inclined to gentleness (though he apprehended

---

[182]   For further details on Thomas Weston's legal troubles following his illegal sale of arms to the Turks, see Peter Coldham, "Thomas Weston: Iremonger of London and America, 1609-1647" *National Genealogical Society Quarterly* 62(1974):163-172.

the abuse of his father deeply) which when Mr. Weston saw he grew more presumptuous and gave such provoking, and cutting speeches, as made him rise up in great indignation, and distemper, and vowed that he would either curb him, or send him home for England; at which Mr. Weston was something daunted; and came privately to the Governor here to know whether they would suffer Captain Gorges to apprehend him. He was told they could not hinder him; but much blamed him, that after they had pacified things, he should thus break out, by his own folly, and rashness, to bring trouble upon himself, and them too. He confessed it was his passion, and prayed the Governor to entreat for him, and pacify him if he could. The which at last he did, with much ado; so he was called again, and the Governor was content to take his own bond, to be ready to make further answer, when either he, or the Lords should send for him, and at last he took only his word and there was a friendly parting on all hands.

But after he was gone, Mr. Weston in lieu of thanks to the Governor and his friends here, gave them this quip (behind their backs) for all their pain: that though they were but young justices; yet they were good beggars. Thus they parted at this time, and shortly after the Governor took his leave and went to the Massachusetts by land, being very thankful for his kind entertainment. The ship stayed here, and fitted herself to go for Virginia, having some passengers there to deliver, and with her returned sundry of those from hence, which came over on their particular, some out of discontent, and dislike of the country; others by reason of a fire that broke out, and burned the houses they lived in and all their provisions so as they were necessitated thereunto. This fire was occasioned by some of the seamen, that were roistering in a house where it first began, making a great fire in very cold weather, which broke out of the chimney into the thatch, and burned, down 3 or 4 houses, and consumed all the goods and provisions in them. The house in which it began, was right against their storehouse which they had much ado to save, in which were their common store and all their provisions, the which if it had been lost, the plantation had been over thrown. But through God's mercy it was saved, by the great diligence of the people, and care of the Governor and some about him, some would have had the goods thrown out, but if they had, there would much have been stolen, by the rude company that belonged to these 2 ships, which were almost all ashore. But a trusty company was placed within, as well as those that with wet cloths and other means kept off the fire without; that if necessity required they might have them out with all speed, for they suspected some malicious dealing, if not plain treachery, and whether it was only suspicion or no, God knows; but this is certain, that when the tumult was greatest, there was a voice heard (but from whom it was not known) that bid them look well about them, for all were not friends that were near them; and shortly after, when the vehemency of the fire was over, smoke was seen to arise within a shed that was joined to the end of the storehouse, which was wattled up with boughs, in the withered leaves whereof, the fire was kindled; which some running to quench, found a long firebrand of an ell long, lying under the wale on the inside, which could not possibly come there by casualty, but must be laid there by some hand, in the judgment of all that saw it. But God kept them from this danger, whatever was intended.

Shortly after Captain Gorges, the general Governor, was come home to the Massachusetts, he sends a warrant to arrest Mr. Weston, and his ship; and sends a master to bring her away thither, and one Captain Hanson (that belonged to him) to conduct him along. The Governor and others here, were very sorry to see him take this course, and took exception at the warrant, as not legal, nor sufficient; and withal write to him, to dissuade him from this course, showing him that he would but entangle, and burden himself in doing this; for he could not do Mr. Weston a better turn, (as things stood with him); for he had a great many men that belonged to him in this bark, and was deeply engaged to them for wages, and was in a manner out of victuals (and now winter) all which would light upon him, if he did arrest his bark. In the meantime, Mr. Weston had notice, to shift for himself; but it was conceived, he either knew not whither to go, or how to mend himself, but was rather glad of the occasion, and so stirred not. But the Governor would not be persuaded, but sent a very formal warrant, under his hand and seal, with strict charge as they would answer it to the State; he also write that he had better considered of things since he was here, and he could not answer it to let him go so; besides other things that were come to his knowledge since, which he must answer to. So he was suffered to proceed, but he found in the end that to be true that was told him; for when an inventory was taken of what was in the ship, there was not victuals found for above 14 days, at a poor allowance, and not much else of any great worth; and the men did so cry out of him for wages, and diet in the meantime, as made him soon weary. So as in conclusion it turned to his loss, and the expense of his own provisions; and towards the spring they came to agreement (after they had been to the eastward) and the Governor restored him his vessel again; and made him satisfaction, in biscuit, meal, and such like provisions, for what he had made use of that was his, or what his men had any way wasted or consumed.

So Mr. Weston came hither again; and afterward shaped his course for Virginia, and so for present I shall leave him.[183]

The Governor and some that depended upon him returned for England having scarcely saluted the country in his government; not finding the state of things here to answer his quality, and condition. The people dispersed themselves, some went for England, others for Virginia, some few remained, and were helped with supplies from hence. The Governor brought over a minister with him, one Mr. Morrell[184], who about a year after the Governor returned took shipping from hence; he had I know not what power, and authority of superintendency over other churches granted him; and sundry instructions for that end; but he never showed it, or made any use of it, (it should seem he saw it was in vain) he only spoke of it to some here at his going away. This was in effect the end of a 2 plantation in that place.

There were also, this year some scattering beginnings made in other places, as at Piscataqua by Mr. David Thompson, at Mohegan, and some other places, by sundry others.

It rests now that I speak a word about the pinnace spoken of before, which was sent by the adventurers to be employed in the country. She was a fine vessel and with her flags, and streamers, pendants, and waistcloths, etc., bravely set out, (and I fear the adventurers did over-pride themselves in her) for she had ill success. However they erred grossly in two things about her: first though she had a sufficient master, yet she was rudely manned, and all her men were upon shares, and none was to have any wages but the master. 2ly whereas they mainly looked at trade, they had sent, nothing of any value to trade with. When the men came here, and met with ill counsel, from Mr. Weston and his crew, with others of the same stamp; neither master, nor Governor could scarce rule them, for they exclaimed, that they were abused, and deceived, for they were told they should go for a man of war, and take I know not whom, French, and Spaniards, etc. They would neither trade, nor fish, except they had wages; in fine they would obey no command of the masters; so as it was apprehended they would either run away with the vessel, or get away with the ships and leave her. So as Mr. Peirce, and others of their friends persuaded, the Governor to change their condition, and give them

---

[183] He died afterwards at Bristol, in the time of the wars, of the sickness in the place. (Bradford).

[184] While in the Massachusetts Bay, William Morrell penned a poem, found in the *Collections of the Massachusetts Historical Society*, 1st Series 1:125.

wages; which was accordingly done.[185] And she was sent about the Cape to the Narragansetts to trade, but they made but a poor voyage of it; some corn, and beaver they got; but the Dutch used to furnish them with cloth, and better commodities, they having only a few beads, and knives, which were not there much esteemed. Also in her return home, at the very entrance into their own harbor, she had like to have been cast away, in a storm, and was forced to cut her mainmast by the board; to save herself from driving on the flats that lie without, called Brown's Islands, the force of the wind being so great as made her anchors give way and she drove right upon them; but her mast and tackling being gone, they held her till the wind shifted.

---

[185] The 1623-1624 letters of Emmanuel Altham provide more detail on the problems with the *Little James*. His letters are reprinted in Sydney V. James, ed., *Three Visitors to Early Plymouth* (Plymouth: Plimoth Plantation, 1963).

Anno Dom: 1624 •

The time of new election of their officers, for this year being come; and the number of their people increased; and their troubles and occasions therewith. The Governor desired them to change the persons, as well as renew the election, and also to add more Assistants to the Governor for help and counsel, and the better carrying on of affairs. Showing that it was necessary it should be so; if it was any honor, or benefit, it was fit others should be made partakers of it; if it was a burthen (as doubtless it was) it was but equal others should help to bear it; and that this was the end of annual elections. The issue was, that as before there was but one Assistant, they now chose 5, giving the Governor a double voice; and afterwards they increased them to 7, which course hath continued to this day.[186]

They having with some trouble and charge new-masted, and rigged their pinnace; in the beginning of March they sent her well victualed to the eastward

---

[186] Captain John Smith, in his *General History of Virginia, New England and the Summer Isles* (London, 1624), wrote a brief status report on the present estate of Plymouth in 1624: "At New Plymouth there is about 180 persons, some cattle and goats, but many swine and poultry; 32 dwelling houses, whereof 7 were burnt the last winter, and the value of five hundred pounds in other goods; the town is impaled about half a mile compass. In the town upon a high mount they have a fort well built with wood, loam, and stone, where is planted their ordnance: also a fair watchtower, partly framed, for the sentinel . . . . The Governor is one Master William Bradford; their Captain Myles Standish, a bred soldier in Holland; the chief men for their assistance is Master Isaac Allerton, and divers others as occasion serveth; their preachers are Master William Brewster and Master John Lyford."

on fishing; she arrived safely at a place near Damariscove, and was there well harbored, in a place where ships used to ride, there being also some ships already arrived out of England. But shortly after there arose such a violent, and extraordinary storm, as the seas broke over such places in the harbor as was never seen before; and drove her against great rocks, which beat such a hole in her bilge, as a horse, and cart, might have gone in, and after drove her into deep water where she lay sunk; the master was drowned, the rest of the men, all save one, saved their lives, with much ado; all her provision, salt, and what else was in her was lost. And here I must leave her to lie till afterward.

Some of those that still remained here on their particular, began privately to nourish a faction, and being privy to a strong faction, that was among the adventurers in England, on whom sundry of them did depend. By their private whispering, they drew some of the weaker sort of the company to their side, and so filled them with discontent; as nothing would satisfy them, except they might be suffered to be in their particular also; and made great offers, so they might be freed from the general. The Governor consulting with the ablest of the general body what was best to be done herein; it was resolved to permit them so to do upon equal conditions. The conditions were the same in effect with the former before related; only some more added, as that they should be bound here to remain till the general partnership was ended. And also that they should pay into the store, the one half of all such goods and commodities as they should any wise raise above their food, in consideration of what charge had been laid out for them, with some such like things. This liberty granted, soon stopped this gap; for there was but a few that undertook this course, when it came to; and they were as soon weary of it; for the other had persuaded them, and (Mr. Weston together) that there would never come more supply to the general body; but the particulars had such friends as would carry all, and do for them I know not what.

Shortly after Mr. Winslow came over, and brought a pretty good supply, and the ship came on fishing, (a thing fatal to this plantation). He brought 3 heifers and a bull, the first beginning of any cattle of that kind in the land; with some clothing, and other necessaries, as will further appear; but withal the report of a strong faction amongst the adventurers against them, and especially against the coming of the rest from Leiden; and with what difficulty this supply was procured, and how, by their strong, and long opposition business was so retarded; as not only they were now fallen too late for the fishing season; but the best men were taken up of the fishermen in the West Country, and he was forced to take such a master, and company for that employment, as he could procure upon the present. Some letters from them shall better declare these things; being as followeth.

Most worthy, and loving friends, your kind and loving letters I have received and render you many thanks, etc. It hath pleased God to stir up the hearts of our adventurers, to raise a new stock, for the setting forth of this ship called the *Charity* with men and necessaries, both for the plantation, and the fishing, though accomplished with very great difficulty. In regard we have some amongst us, which undoubtedly aim more at their own private ends, and the thwarting, and opposing of some here; and other worthy instruments[187] of God's glory elsewhere; than at the general good, and furtherance of this noble, and laudable action. Yet again we have many other, and I hope the greatest part very honest Christian men; which I am persuaded their ends and intents are wholly for the glory of our Lord Jesus Christ, in the propagation of His gospel, and hope of gaining those poor savages to the knowledge of God. But as we have a proverb one scabbed sheep may mar a whole flock; so these malcontented persons, and turbulent spirits, do what in them lieth, to withdraw men's hearts, from you, and your friends; yea even from the general business, and yet under show and pretence of godliness, and furtherance of the plantation. Whereas the quite contrary doth plainly appear; as some of the honester hearted men (though of late of their faction) did make manifest, at our late meeting. But what should I trouble you, or myself, with these restless opposers of all goodness; and I doubt will be continual disturbers of our friendly meetings, and love. On Thursday, the 8 of January we had a meeting about the articles, between you, and us; where they would reject that, which we in our late letters pressed you to grant (an addition to the time of our joint stock). And their reason which they would make known to us; was it troubled their conscience to exact longer time of you, than was agreed upon at the first. But that night they were so followed, and crossed of their perverse courses, as they were even wearied; and offered to sell their adventures; and some were willing to buy. But I doubting they would raise more, scandal and false reports; and so divers ways do us more hurt, by going off in such a fury; than they could, or can by continuing adventurers amongst us, would not suffer them.

But on the 12 of January we had another meeting, but in the interim divers of us had talked with most of them privately, and had great combats,

---

[187] He means Mr. Robinson. (Bradford).

and reasoning, pro, and con. But at night when we met to read the general letter, we had the lovingest, and friendliest meeting, that ever I knew[188], and our greatest enemies, offered to lend us £50. So I sent for a pottle of wine[189] (I would you could do the like) which we drank friendly together. Thus God can turn the hearts of men, when it pleaseth Him, etc. Thus loving friends I heartily salute you all in the Lord, hoping ever to rest,

Yours to my power
James Sherley

January 25, 1623.

Another Letter

Beloved Sir, etc. We have now sent you, we hope men and means, to settle these 3 things viz. fishing, salt making, and boat making; if you can bring them to pass to some perfection, your wants may be supplied. I pray you bend yourself what you can to settle these businesses; let the ship be fraught away as soon as you can; and sent to Bilbao. You must send some discreet man for factor whom once more, you must also authorize, to confirm the conditions, if Mr. Winslow could be spared, I could wish he came again.

This ship carpenter is thought to be the fittest man for you in the land, and will no doubt do you much good; let him have an absolute command over his servants, and such as you put to him. Let him build you 2 ketches, a lighter and some 6 or 7 shallops, as soon as you can. The salt man is a skillful, and industrious man, put some to him, that may quickly apprehend the mystery of it. The preacher we have sent, is (we hope) an honest plain man, though none of the most eminent, and rare; about choosing him into office, use your own liberty, and discretion; he knows he is no officer

---

[188] But this lasted not long; they had now provided Lyford and others to send over. (Bradford).

[189] It is worthy to be observed, how the Lord doth change times, and things; for what is now more plentiful than wine? and that of the best, coming from Malaga and Canaries, and other places, sundry ships lading in a year. So as there is now more cause to complain of the excess, and the abuse of wine (though men's corruption) even to drunkenness; than of any defect, or want of the same. Witness this year 1646. The good Lord lay not the sins, and unthankfulness, of men to their charge in this particular. (Bradford). A pottle is a half gallon.

amongst you, though perhaps custom, and universality may make him forget himself. Mr. Winslow, and myself, gave way to his going, to give content, to some here, and we see no hurt in it, but only his great charge of children.

We have took a patent for Cape Anne[190], etc. I am sorry there is no more discretion used by some, in their letters hither, some say you are starved in body, and soul; others that you eat pigs, and dogs that die alone; others that the things here spoken of the goodness of the country, are gross, and palpable lies; that there is scarce a fowl to be seen or a fish to be taken, and many such like.[191] I would such discontented men were here again, for it is a misery when the whole state of a plantation, shall be thus exposed, to the passionate humors of some discontented men. And for myself I shall hinder, for hereafter some that would go, and have not better composed their affections; mean space it is all our crosses, and we must bear them.

I am sorry we have not sent you more, and other things; but in truth we have run into so much charge, to victual the ship, provide salt, and other fishing implements, etc., as we could not provide other comfortable things, as butter, sugar, etc. I hope the return of this ship, and the *James*, will put us in cash again. The Lord make you full of courage, in this troublesome business, which now must be stuck unto, till God give us rest from our labors. Farewell in all hearty affection.

Your assured friend,
R.C.

January 24, 1623

With the former letter write by Mr. Sherley, there were sent sundry objections concerning which he thus writeth: "These are the chief objections which they that are now returned make against you, and the country; I pray you consider them, and answer them by the first conveniency." These objections were made by some of those that came over on their particular and were returned home, as is before mentioned and were of the same suit with those that this other letter mentions.

I shall here set them down, with the answers then made unto them, and sent over at the return of this ship: which did so confound the objectors, as some confessed their fault, and others denied what they had said, and eat their words; and some others of them, have since come over again, and here

---

[190] The patent for Cape Anne is reprinted in Appendix I.

[191] This was John Oldham and his like. (Bradford).

lived to convince themselves sufficiently, both in their own and other men's judgments.

1   objection: was diversity about religion.
     Answer: We know no such matter, for here was never any controversy, or opposition, either public, or private (to our knowledge) since we came.

2   objection: Neglect of family duties, on the Lord's Day.
     Answer: We allow no such thing, but blame it in ourselves and others; and they that thus report it, should have showed their Christian love, the more if they had in love, told the offenders of it; rather than thus to reproach them behind their backs. But (to say no more) we wish themselves had given better example.

3   objection: Want of both the sacraments.
     Answer: The more is our grief, that our pastor is kept from us, by whom we might enjoy them; for we used to have the Lord's Supper, every Sabbath, and baptism as often as there was occasion, of children to baptize.

4   objection: Children not catechized, nor taught to read.
     Answer: Neither is true; for divers take pains with their own as they can, indeed we have no common school for want of a fit person, or hitherto means to maintain one; though we desire now to begin.

5   objection: Many of the particular members of the plantation, will not work for the General.
     Answer: This also is not wholly true; for though some do it not willingly, and others not honestly, yet all do it; and he that doth worst gets his own food, and something besides. But we will not excuse them, but labor to reform them the best we can; or else to quit the plantation of them.

6   objection: The water is not wholesome.
     Answer: If they mean, not so wholesome as the good beer, and wine in London (which they so dearly love) we will not dispute with them, but else for water it is as good as any in the world (for aught we know) and it is wholesome enough to us, that can be content therewith.

7   objection: The ground is barren, and doth bear no grass.
     Answer: It is here (as in all places) some better, and some worse; and if they well consider their woods in England, they shall not find such grass in them, as in their fields, and meadows. The cattle find grass for they are as fat as need be; we wish we had but one for every hundred, that here is grass to keep. Indeed this objection (as

some other) are ridiculous to all here which see, and know the contrary.

8   objection: The fish will not take salt to keep sweet.
Answer: This is as true, as that which was written, that there is scarce a fowl to be seen, or a fish to be taken. Things likely to be true in a country where so many sail of ships come yearly a-fishing; they might as well say, there can no ale, or beer in London, be kept from souring.

9   objection: Many of them are thievish, and steal one from another.
Answer: Would London had been free from that crime, then we should not have been troubled with these here; it is well known sundry have smarted well for it, and so are the rest like to do, if they be taken.

10   objection: The country is annoyed with foxes, and wolves.
Answer: So are many other good countries too; but poison, traps, and other such means will help to destroy them.

11   objection: The Dutch are planted near Hudson's Bay[192] and are likely to overthrow the trade.
Answer: They will come and plant in these parts, also, if we, and others do not but go home and leave it to them. We rather commend them, than condemn them for it.

12   objection: The people are much annoyed with mosquitoes.
Answer: They are too delicate, and unfit to begin new plantations, and colonies that cannot endure the biting of a mosquito; we would wish such to keep at home, till at least they be mosquito-proof. Yet this place is as free as any; and experience teacheth that the more the land is tilled, and the woods cut down, the fewer there will be, and in the end scarce any at all.

Having thus dispatched these things, that I may handle things together, I shall here insert 2 other letters from Mr. Robinson, their pastor, the one to the Governor, the other to Mr. Brewster their Elder; which will give much light to the former things; and express the tender love, and care of a true pastor over them.

His letter to the Governor:

My loving and much beloved friend, whom God hath hitherto preserved, preserve, and keep you still to His glory, and the good of

---

[192]   This is the Hudson River in modern-day New York, not Hudson's Bay in Canada.

many; that His blessing may make your godly, and wise endeavors answerable to the valuation which they there have, and set upon the same. Of your love to, and care for us here we never doubted, so are we glad to take knowledge of it, in that fullness we do; our love and care to, and for you, is mutual; though our hopes of coming unto you be small, and weaker than ever. But of this at large in Mr. Brewster's letter, with whom you, and he with you mutually, I know communicate your letters, as I desire you may do these, etc.

Concerning the killing of those poor Indians, of which we heard at first by report, and since by more certain relation. Oh, how happy a thing had it been, if you had converted some, before you had killed any; besides where blood is once begun to be shed, it is seldom staunched of a long time after. You will say they deserved it, I grant it; but upon what provocations, and invitements, by those heathenish Christians? Besides you being no magistrates over them, were to consider, not what they deserved, but what you were by necessity constrained to inflict. Necessity of this, especially of killing so many (and many more it seems they would, if they could) I see not. Methinks, one or two principals should have been full enough, according to that approved rule: the punishment to a few, and the fear to many. Upon this occasion, let me be bold to exhort you, seriously to consider of the disposition of your Captain, whom I love; and am persuaded, the Lord in great mercy and for much good, hath sent you him, if you use him aright. He is a man humble, and meek amongst you, and towards all in ordinary course. But now if this be merely from an human spirit, there is cause to fear that by occasion, especially of provocation, there may be wanting that tenderness of the life of man (made after God's image) which is meet. It is also a thing more glorious, in men's eyes, than pleasing in God's, or convenient for Christians, to be a terror to poor barbarous people; and indeed I am afraid lest by these occasions, others should be drawn to affect a kind of ruffling course in the world. I doubt not but you will take in good part these things which I write, and as there is cause make use of them. It were to us more comfortable, and convenient, that we communicated our mutual helps in presence; but seeing that cannot be done, we shall always long after you, and love you, and wait God's appointed time. The adventurers it seems have neither money, nor any great mind of us, for the most part; they deny it to be any part of the covenants betwixt us, that they should transport us, neither do I look for any further help from them, till means come from you. We here are strangers in effect to the whole course, and so both we, and you (save as your own wisdoms, and worths, have interested you further) of principals intended in this business are scarce accessories, etc. My wife with me, resalutes you, and yours. Unto Him who is the same to His in all places; and near to them, which are far, from one another, I commend you and all with you, resting,

Yours truly loving,
John Robinson

Leiden, December 19, 1623

His to Mr. Brewster

Loving and dear friend, and brother; that which I most desired of God in regard of you, namely the continuance of your life, and health, and the safe coming of these sent unto you; that I most gladly hear of, and praise God for the same. And I hope Mrs. Brewster's weak, and decayed state of body, will have some repairing, by the coming of her daughters, and the provisions in this and former ships, I hear is made for you. Which makes us with more patience bear our languishing state, and the deferring of our desired transportation which I call desired, rather than hoped for; whatsoever you are borne in hand by any others. For first there is no hope at all, that I know, or can conceive of, of any new stock to be raised for that end; so that all must depend upon returns from you, in which are so many uncertainties, as that nothing with any certainty can thence be concluded: besides, howsoever for the present the adventurers allege nothing but want of money, which is an invincible difficulty; yet if that be taken away by you, others without doubt will be found for the better clearing of this; we must dispose the adventurers into 3 parts; and of them some 5 or 6 (as I conceive) are absolutely bent for us, above any others; other 5 or 6 are our bitter professed adversaries; the rest being the body, I conceive to be honestly minded, and lovingly also toward us. Yet such as have others (namely the forward preachers) nearer unto them, than us; and whose course so far as there is any difference, they would rather advance than ours. Now what a hanck these men have over the professors you know. And I persuade myself, that for me, they of all others, are unwilling I should be transported, especially such of them, as have an eye that way themselves, as thinking if I come there, their market will be marred, in many regards. And for these adversaries: if they have but half the wit, to their malice, they will stop my course, when they see it intended, for which this delaying serveth them very opportunely. And as one resty jade can hinder, by hanging back, more than two or 3 can (or will at least, if they be not very free) draw forward, so will it be in this case. A notable experiment of this, they gave in your messenger's presence, constraining the company to promise, that none of the money now gathered, should be expended, or employed to the help of any of us towards you. Now touching the question propounded by you, I judge it not lawful for you, being a ruling Elder, as Romans 12:7, 8, and 1 Timothy 5:17 opposed to the Elders, that teach, and exhort, and labor in the Word and doctrine, to which the sacraments are annexed, to administer them, nor convenient, if it were lawful. Whether any learned man will come unto you, or not, I know not; if any do, you must *consilium capere in arena.* Be you most heartily saluted, and your wife with you, both from me, and mine. Your God, and ours, and the God of all His, bring us together if it be His will, and keep us in the meanwhile, and always to His glory, and make us serviceable to His Majesty, and faithful to the end. Amen.

Your very loving brother,
John Robinson

Leiden December 20, 1623

These things premised, I shall now prosecute the proceedings and affairs here, and before I come to other things, I must speak a word of their planting this year; they having found the benefit of their last year's harvest and setting corn for their particular, having thereby with a great deal of patience overcome hunger and famine. Which makes me remember a saying of Seneca's Epistle 123: "That a great part of liberty, is a well governed belly; and to be patient in all wants." They began now highly to prize corn, as more precious than silver, and those that had some to spare, began to trade one with another, for small things, by the quart, pottle, and peck, etc.; (for money they had none) and if any had, corn was preferred before it. That they might therefore increase their tillage to better advantage: they made suit to the Governor to have some portion of land given them for continuance; and not by yearly lot; for by that means, that which the more industrious had brought into good culture (by much pains) one year; came to leave it the next, and often another might enjoy it; so as the dressing of their lands were the more slighted over, and to less profit. Which being well considered, their request was granted. And to every person was given only one acre of land, to them and theirs, as near the town as might be; and they had no more till the 7 years were expired. The reason was, that they might be kept close together, both for more safety and defense, and the better improvement of the general employments. Which condition of theirs, did make me often think, of what I had read in Pliny[193], of the Romans' first beginnings in Romulus' time. How every man contented himself with 2 acres

---

[193]   Pliny, Library 18, Chapter 2 (Bradford).

Elder William Brewster's personal copy of *Works of Lucius Annaeus Seneca, Both Moral and Natural (London, 1614)*, which he bought from master William Peirce. The original is in the collections of the Pilgrim Hall Museum. Photo courtesy of the Pilgrim Hall Museum, Plymouth, Massachusetts.

of land, and had no more assigned them. And Chapter 3, "It was thought a great reward, to receive at the hands of the people of Rome, a pint of corn." And long after, the greatest present given to a Captain, that had got a victory over their enemies, was as much ground as they could till in one day. And he was not counted a good, but a dangerous man; that would not content himself with 7 acres of land. As also how they did pound their corn in mortars, as these people were forced to do many years before they could get a mill.

The ship which brought this supply was speedily discharged, and with her master and company sent to Cape Anne (of which place they had got a patent, as before is showed) on fishing, and because the season was so far spent some of the planters were sent to help to build their stage, to their own hindrance. But partly by the lateness of the year, and more especially by the baseness of the master, one Baker, they made a poor voyage of it; he proved a very drunken beast, and did nothing (in a manner) but drink, and guzzle, and consume away the time and his victuals, and most of his company followed his example; and though Mr. William Peirce was to oversee the business, and to be master of the ship home; yet he could do no good amongst them; so as the loss was great; and would have been more to them, but that they kept on a-trading there, which in those times got some store of skins, which was some help unto them.

The ship carpenter that was sent them, was an honest, and very industrious man, and followed his labor very diligently, and made all that were employed with him do the like; he quickly built them 2 very good and strong shallops (which after did them great service), and a great, and strong lighter, and had hewn timber for two ketches; but that was lost, for he fell into a fever, in the hot season of the year, and though he had the best means the place could afford, yet he died; of whom they had a very great loss, and were very sorry for his death. But he whom they sent to make salt, was an ignorant, foolish, self-willed fellow; he bore them in hand, he could do great matters, in making salt-works; so he was sent to seek out fit ground for his purpose, and after some search, he told the Governor that he had found a sufficient place, with a good bottom, to hold water, and otherwise very convenient, which he doubted not, but in a short time to bring to good perfection; and to yield them great profit, but he must have 8 or ten men to be constantly employed. He was wished to be sure that the ground was good, and other things answerable, and that he could bring it to perfection; otherwise he would bring upon them a great charge by employing himself and so many men. But he was after some trial, so confident as he caused them to send carpenters to rear a great frame for a large house, to receive the salt, and such other uses.

But in the end all proved vain; then he laid fault of the ground in which he was deceived; but if he might have the lighter to carry clay, he was sure then he could do it. Now though the Governor and some other foresaw that this would come to little, yet they had so many malignant spirits amongst them, that would have laid it upon them in their letters of complaint to the adventurers; as to be their fault that would not suffer him to go on, to bring his work to perfection: for as he by his bold confidence, and large promises, deceived them in England that sent him; so had he wound himself into these men's high esteem here, so as they were fain to let him go on till all men saw his vanity. For he could not do anything but boil salt in pans, and yet would make them, that were joined with him believe, there was so great a mystery in it, as was not easy to be attained, and made them do many unnecessary things to blind their eyes till they discerned his subtlety. The next year he was sent to Cape Anne, and the pans were set up there, where the fishing was; but before summer was out he burnt the house, and the fire was so vehement, as it spoiled the pans, at least some of them, and this was the end of that chargeable business.

The 3d eminent person (which the letters before mention) was the minister which they sent over; by name Mr. John Lyford, of whom, and whose doing I must be more large, though I shall abridge things as much as I can. When this man first came ashore, he saluted them with that reverence, and humility, as is seldom to be seen, and indeed made them ashamed, he so bowed, and cringed unto them, and would have kissed their hands, if they would have suffered him[194]; yea he wept and shed many tears, blessing God that had brought him to see their faces; and admiring the things they had done in their wants, etc., as if he had been made all of love, and the humblest person in the world.

And all the while (if we may judge by his after carriages) he was but like him mentioned in Psalm 10:10, "That croucheth, and boweth, that heaps of poor, may fall by his might." Or like to that dissembling Ishmael,[195] who when he had slain Gedaliah, went out weeping and met them that were coming to offer incense in the house of the Lord: saying "Come to Gedaliah" when he meant to slay them.

They gave him the best entertainment they could (in all simplicity) and a larger allowance of food out of the store, than any other had, and as the Governor had used, in all weighty affairs, to consult with their Elder, Mr.

---

[194]   Of which were many witnesses. (Bradford).

[195]   Jeremiah 41:6 (Bradford).

Brewster, (together with his Assistants) so now he called Mr. Lyford also to counsel with them in their weightiest businesses. After some short time he desired to join himself a member to the church here, and was accordingly received. He made a large confession of his faith; and an acknowledgment of his former disorderly walking, and his being entangled with many corruptions, which had been a burthen to his conscience; and blessed God for this opportunity, of freedom and liberty, to enjoy the ordinances of God in purity among His People, with many more such like expressions. I must here speak a word also of Mr. John Oldham (who was a copartner with him, in his after courses) he had been a chief stickler in the former faction among the particulars, and an intelligencer to those in England. But now since the coming of this ship and he saw the supply that came, he took occasion, to open his mind to some of the chief amongst them here, and confessed he had done them wrong both by word, and deed, and writing into England; but he now saw the eminent hand of God to be with them, and His blessing upon them, which made his heart smite him; neither should those in England ever use him as an instrument any longer against them in anything; he also desired former things might be forgotten and that they would look upon him, as one that desired to close with them in all things, with such like expressions. Now whether this was in hypocrisy, or out of some sudden pang of conviction (which I rather think) God only knows; upon it they show all readiness to embrace his love, and carry towards him in all friendliness, and called him to counsel with them in all chief affairs, as the other, without any distrust at all.

Thus all things seemed to go very comfortably, and smoothly on amongst them; at which they did much rejoice; but this lasted not long: for both Oldham, and he, grew very perverse, and showed a spirit of great malignancy, drawing as many into faction as they could; were they never so vile, or profane, they did nourish and back them in all their doings: so they would but cleave to them, and speak against the church here; so as there was nothing but private meetings and whisperings amongst them; they feeding themselves, and others, with what they should bring to pass in England by the faction of their friends there, which brought others as well as themselves into a fool's paradise. Yet they could not carry so closely but much of both their doings and sayings were discovered; yet outwardly they still set a fair face of things.

At length when the ship was ready to go, it was observed Lyford was long in writing and sent many letters; and could not for bear to communicate to his intimates, such things, as made them laugh in their sleeves, and thought he had done their errand sufficiently. The Governor and some other of his friends knowing how things stood in England, and what hurt these things might do: took a shallop and went out with the ship, a league or 2 to sea; and called for all Lyford's and Oldham's letters. Mr. William Peirce being master of the ship (and knew well their evil dealing both in England, and here) afforded him all the assistance he could. He found above 20 of Lyford's letters; many of them large, and full of slanders, and false accusations, tending not only to their prejudice, but to their ruin and utter subversion; most of the letters they let pass, only took copies of them; but some of the most material they sent true copies of them, and kept the originals lest he should deny them; and that they might produce his own hand against him. Amongst his letters they found the copies of two letters, which he sent enclosed in a letter of his, to Mr. John Pemberton, a minister and a great opposite of theirs. These 2 letters of which he took the copies, were one of them writ by a gentleman in England to Mr. Brewster here, the other by Mr. Winslow to Mr. Robinson, in Holland, at his coming away, as the ship lay at Gravesend. They lying sealed in the great cabin (whilst Mr. Winslow was busy about the affairs of the ship) this sly merchant takes, and opens them, takes these copies, and seals them up again; and not only sends the copies of them thus to his friend, and their adversary, but adds thereto in the margin many scurrilous, and flouting annotations.

This ship went out towards evening, and in the night the Governor returned. They were somewhat blank at it; but after some weeks, when they heard nothing, they then were as brisk as ever, thinking nothing had been known but all was gone current, and that the Governor went but to dispatch his own letters. The reason why the Governor and rest concealed these things the longer, was to let things ripen that they might better discover their intents, and see who were their adherents. And the rather because amongst the rest they found a letter, of one of their confederates; in which was written that Mr. Oldham, and Mr. Lyford intended a reformation, in church and commonwealth; and as soon as the ship was gone, they intended to join together, and have the sacraments, etc.

For Oldham few of his letters were found (for he was so bad a scribe, as his hand was scarce legible) yet he was as deep in the mischief as the other. And thinking they were now strong enough, they began to pick quarrels at everything; Oldham being called to watch (according to order) refused to come, fell out with the Captain, called him rascal, and beggarly rascal, and resisted him, drew his knife at him; though he offered him no wrong, nor gave him no ill terms, but with all fairness required him to do his duty. The Governor hearing the tumult, sent to quiet it, but he ramped more like a furious beast than a man, and called them all traitors, and rebels, and other such foul language as I am ashamed to remember. But after he was clapped up a while, he came to himself, and with some slight punishment, was let go upon his behavior for further censure.

But to cut things short, at length it grew to this issue, that Lyford with his complices, without ever speaking one word, either to the Governor, Church, or Elder, withdrew themselves, and set up a public meeting apart, on the Lord's Day, with sundry such insolent carriages, too long here to relate, beginning now publicly to act, what privately they had been long plotting.[196]

It was now thought high time (to prevent further mischief) to call them to account; so the Governor called a court, and summoned the whole company to appear. And then charged Lyford, and Oldham with such things as they were guilty of, but they were stiff, and stood resolutely upon the denial of most things, and required proof; they first alleged what was write to them out of England, compared with their doings, and practices here, that it was evident they joined in plotting against them, and disturbing their peace, both in respect of their civil, and church state, which was most injurious; for both they, and all the world knew, they came hither to enjoy the liberty of their conscience, and the free use of God's Ordinances, and for that end had ventured their lives, and passed through so much hardship hitherto, and they and their friends had borne the charge of these beginnings which was not small. And that Lyford for his part was sent over on this charge, and that both he and his great family was maintained on the

---

[196] Thomas Morton provides his own version of the Oldham and Lyford controversies in his *New English Canaan* (Amsterdam, 1637): "Master Lyford was at the merchants' charge sent to Plymouth plantation to be their pastor. But the Brethren, before they would allow of it, would have him first renounce his calling, to the office of the ministry, received in England, as heretical and Papistical, (so he confessed) and then to receive a new calling from them, after their fantastical invention, which he refused, alleging and maintaining, that his calling as it stood was lawful, and that he would not renounce it; and so John Oldham his opinion was on the affirmative, and both together did maintain the Church of England, to be a true Church, although in some particulars (they said) defective . . . and by this means cancelled their good opinion amongst the number of the Separatists, that stay they must not, lest they should be spies . . . therefore against Master Lyford they had found out some scandal to be laid on his former course of life, to blemish that, and so to conclude he was a spotted beast, and not to be allowed . . ."

same, and also was joined to the church, and a member of them; and for
him to plot against them, and seek their ruin, was most unjust and perfidious.
And for Oldham, or any other, that came over at their own charge, and
were on their particular: seeing they were received in courtesy, by the
plantation, when they came only to seek shelter, and protection under their
wings, not being able to stand alone; that they (according to the fable) like
the hedgehog whom the coney in a stormy day (in pity) received into her
burrow, would not be content to take part with her; but in the end with her
sharp pricks forced the poor coney to forsake her own burrow. So these
men with the like injustice, endeavored to do the same to those that
entertained them.

Lyford denied, that he had anything to do with them in England, or
knew of their courses; and made other things as strange, that he was charged
with. Then his letters were produced, and some of them read, at which he
was struck mute; but Oldham began to rage furiously, because they had
intercepted, and opened his letters, threatening them in very high language,
and in a most audacious, and mutinous manner, stood up and called upon
the people; saying "My masters where is your hearts? Now show your
courage, you have oft complained to me so, and so; now is the time, if you
will do anything I will stand by you," etc. Thinking that everyone (knowing
his humor) that had soothed, and flattered him, or otherwise in their
discontent uttered anything unto him; would now side with him in open
rebellion. But he was deceived, for not a man opened his mouth, but all
were silent, being strucken with the injustice of the thing. Then the Governor
turned his speech to Mr. Lyford and asked him if he thought, they had
done evil to open his letters; but he was silent, and would not say a word,
well knowing what they might reply. Then the Governor showed the people
he did it as a magistrate, and was bound to it by his place, to prevent the
mischief, and ruin, that this conspiracy, and plots of theirs, would bring on
this poor Colony.

But he, besides his evil dealing here, had dealt treacherously with his
friends that trusted him, and stole their letters, and opened them, and
sent copies of them, with disgraceful annotations, to his friends in
England. And then the Governor produced them, and his other letters,
under his own hand (which he could not deny) and caused them to be
read before all the people; at which all his friends were blank, and had
not a word to say.

It would be too long and tedious here to insert his letters (which would
almost fill a volume) though I have them by me; I shall only note a few of the

chief things collected out of them, with the answers to them, as they were then given: and but a few, of those many, only for instance by which the rest may be judged of.

1. First he saith, the church would have none to live here but themselves; 2ly, neither are any willing so to do, if they had company to live elsewhere.

    Answer: Their answer was, that this was false, in both the parts of it; for they were willing and desirous, that any honest men may live with them, that will carry themselves peaceably, and seek the common good, or at least do them no hurt. And again there are many, that will not live elsewhere, so long as they may live with them.

2. That if there come over any honest men that are not of the Separation, they will quickly distaste them, etc.

    Answer: Their answer was as before, that it was a false calumniation, for they had many amongst them, that they liked well of, and were glad of their company; and should be of any such like that should come amongst them.[197]

3. That they excepted against him for these 2 doctrines; raised from 2 Samuel 12:7. First, that ministers must sometimes particularly, apply their doctrine to special persons; 2ly, that great men, may be reproved, as well as meaner.

---

[197] For more on this controversy, see the letter Bradford received from James Sherley, William Collier, Thomas Fletcher and Robert Holland, dated 18 December 1624, which is found in William Bradford's *Letterbook*, reprinted in *Collections of the Massachusetts Historical Society* 3(1794):27-76. Those investors inform Bradford and those of Plymouth that a rift has developed amongst the various investors because "you are (as they affirm) Brownists, condemning all other churches, and persons but yourselves and those in your way; and you are contentious, cruel and hard-hearted, among your neighbors, and towards such as in all points both civil and religious, jump not with you." Edward Winslow's responded to the controversy in his *Hypocrisy Unmasked* (London, 1646), claiming "[T]he church of Leiden differed in some particulars, yet made no schism or separation from the reformed churches, but held communion with them occasionally . . ." and then goes on to mention occasions in which the church had communion with the reformed churches of the Netherlands, France, and Scotland.

Answer: Their answer was, that both these; were without either truth or color of the same (as was proved to his face) and that they had taught, and believed these things, long before they knew Mr. Lyford.

4. That they utterly sought the ruin of the particulars; as appeareth by this: that they would not suffer, any of the general, either to buy, or sell with them; or to exchange one commodity, for another.

Answer: This was a most malicious slander, and void of all truth (as was evidently proved to him before all men) for any of them, did both buy, sell, or exchange with them, as of ten as they had any occasion; yea and also, both lend, and give to them when they wanted; and this the particular persons, themselves, could not deny, but freely confessed in open court. But the ground from whence this arose made it much worse for he was in council with them; when one was called before them, and questioned, for receiving powder, and biscuit from the gunner of the small ship, which was the Company's, and had it put in at his window in the night; and also for buying salt of one that had no right to it. He not only stood to back him (being one of these particulars) by excusing, and extenuating his fault, as long as he could; but upon this, builds this mischievous, and most false slander; that because they would not suffer them to buy stolen goods, ergo they sought their utter ruin. Bad logic for a divine.

5. Next he writes, that he choked them with this: that they turned men into their particular, and then sought to starve them, and deprive them of all means of subsistence.

Answer: To this was answered, he did them manifest wrong; for they turned none into their particular; it was their own importunity, and earnest desire, that moved them, yea constrained them to do it. And they appealed to the persons themselves, for the truth hereof. And they testified the same against him, before all present, as also that they had no cause to complain of any either hard, or unkind usage.

6. He accuseth them with unjust distribution, and writeth: that it was a strange difference, that some have been allowed $16^£$ of meal by the week, and others but $4^£$; and then (floutingly) saith, it seems some men's mouths and bellies, are very little and slender over others.

Answer: This might seem strange indeed, to those to whom he write his letters in England, which knew not the reason of it; but to him, and others here, it could not be strange, who knew how things stood. For the first comers had none at all but lived on their corn. Those which came in the *Anne*, the August before, and were to live 13 months of the provisions they brought, had as good allowance in meal, and peas as it would extend to, the most part of the year; but a little before harvest, when they had not only fish, but other fruits began to come in, they had but 4$^£$ having their liberty to make their own provisions. But some of these which came last, as the ship carpenter, and sawyers, the salt men, and others that were to follow constant employments, and had not an hour's time, from their hard labors, to look for anything above their allowance; they had at first, 16$^£$ allowed them, and afterwards as fish, and other food could be got, they had abatement, to 14 and 12; yea some of them to 8 as the times, and occasions did vary. And yet those which followed planting, and their own occasions, and had but 4$^£$ of meal a week, lived better than the other (as was well known to all). And yet it must be remembered that Lyford and his, had always the highest allowance.

Many other things (in his letters) he accused them of, with many aggravations; as that he saw exceeding great waste of tools, and vessels; and this when it came to be examined, all the instance he could give was, that he had seen an old hogshead or two fallen to pieces, and a broken hoe or two, left carelessly in the fields by some. Though he also knew that a godly honest man was appointed to look to these things; but these things, and such like, was write of by him, to cast disgrace, and prejudice upon them; as thinking what came from a minister would pass for current. Then he tells them that Winslow should say, that there was not above 7 of the adventurers, that sought the good of the colony. That Mr. Oldham, and himself, had had much to do with them; and that the faction here, might match the Jesuits for policy with many the like grievous complaints, and accusations.

Then in the next place, he comes to give his friends counsel, and direction. And first, that the Leiden company (Mr. Robinson, and the rest) must still be kept back, or else all will be spoiled. And lest any of them should be taken in privately somewhere on the coast of England (as it was feared might be done) they must change the master of the ship (Mr. William Peirce) and put another also, in Winslow's stead for merchant, or else it would not be prevented.

2. Then he would have such a number provided as might over-sway them here. And that the particulars should have voices in all courts and elections, and be free to bear any office. And that every particular, should come over as an adventurer; if he be but a servant, some other venturing 10$^£$ the bill may be taken out in the servant's name, and then assigned to the party whose money it was, and good covenants drawn between them for the

clearing of the matter; and this (saith he) would be a means to strengthen this side the more.

3. Then he tells them, that if that Captain they spoke of, should come over hither as a general; he was persuaded he would be chosen Captain; for this Captain Standish looks like a silly boy, and is in utter contempt.

4. Then he shows that if by the forementioned means, they cannot be strengthened to carry, and overbear things; it will be best for them, to plant elsewhere by themselves; and would have it articled by them, that they might make choice of any place, that they liked best within 3 or 4 miles' distance, showing there were far better places for plantation than this.

5. And lastly he concludes that if some number came not over to bear them up here; then there would be no abiding for them, but by joining with these here. Then he adds, "Since I began to write, there are letters come from your company; wherein they would give sole authority, in divers things unto the Governor here; which if it take place, then *vae nobis*. But I hope you will be more vigilant hereafter, that nothing may pass in such a manner. I suppose" (saith he) "Mr. Oldham will write to you further of these things. I pray you conceal me in the discovery of these things," etc.

Thus I have briefly touched some chief things in his letters; and shall now return to their proceeding with him. After the reading of his letters before the whole company; he was demanded what he could say to these things. But all the answer he made, was that Billington, and some others, had informed him, of many things, and made sundry complaints, which they now denied. He was again asked if that was a sufficient ground for him, thus to accuse, and traduce them by his letters; and never say word to them, considering the many bonds between them. And so they went on from point to point. And wished him, or any of his friends, and confederates, not to spare them in anything; if he or they had any proof, or witness of any corrupt, or evil dealing of theirs; his or their evidence must needs be there present, for there was the whole company, and sundry strangers. He said he had been abused by others, in their informations (as he now well saw) and so had abused them. And this was all the answer they could have, for none would take his part in anything, but Billington, and any whom he named denied the things and protested he wronged them; and would have drawn them to such, and such things, which they could not consent to, though they were sometimes drawn to his meetings. Then they dealt with him about his dissembling with them about the church, and that he professed to concur with them in all things, and what a large confession he made, at his admittance, and that he held not himself a minister, till he had a new calling, etc. And yet now he contested against them, and drew a company apart, and sequestered himself, and would go minister the sacraments (by his Episcopal calling) without ever speaking a word, unto them, either as magistrates, or brethren.

In conclusion he was fully convicted; and burst out into tears, and confessed, he feared he was a reprobate, his sins were so great that he doubted God would not pardon them, he was unsavory salt, etc. And that he had so wronged them, as he could never make them amends, confessing all he had write against them was false, and naught, both for matter, and manner. And all this he did, with as much fullness, as words, and tears could express.

After their trial, and conviction, the court censured them to be expelled the place; Oldham presently, though his wife and family, had liberty to stay all winter, or longer, till he could make provision to remove them comfortably. Lyford had liberty to stay 6 months; it was indeed, with some eye to his release, if he carried himself well in the meantime, and that his repentance proved sound. Lyford acknowledged his censure was far less than he deserved.

Afterwards he confessed his sin publicly in the church with tears more largely than before, I shall here put it down as I find it recorded by some, who took it from his own words, as himself uttered them. Acknowledging:

> That he had done very evil, and slanderously abused them; and thinking most of the people would take part with him, he thought to carry all by violence, and strong hand against them. And that God might justly lay innocent blood to his charge, for he knew not what hurt might have come of these his writings, and blessed God they were stayed. And that he spared not to take knowledge from any, of any evil that was spoken, but shut his eyes, and ears against all the good; and if God should make him a vagabond in the earth, as was Cain, it was but just, for he had sinned in envy, and malice against his brethren as he did. And he confessed 3 things to be the ground, and causes of these his doings: pride, vainglory, and self-love. Amplifying these heads with many other sad expressions, in the particulars of them.

So as they began again to conceive good thoughts of him, upon this his repentance, and admitted him to teach amongst them as before, and Samuel Fuller (a deacon amongst them) and some other tenderhearted men amongst them, were so taken with his signs of sorrow, and repentance, as they professed they would fall upon their knees to have his censure released.

But that which made them all stand amazed in the end, and may do all others that shall come to hear the same (for a rarer precedent can scarce be shown) was, that after a month or 2, notwithstanding all his former confessions, convictions, and public acknowledgments, both in the face of the church, and whole company, with so many tears and sad censures of himself, before God and men, he should go again to justify what he had done.

For secretly he writ a 2^d letter to the adventurers in England, in which he justified all his former writings (save in some things which tended to their damage); the which because it is briefer than the former I shall here insert.

Worthy Sirs, though the filth of mine own doings, may justly be cast in my face, and with blushing cause my perpetual silence; yet that the truth may not hereby be injured, yourselves any longer deluded, nor injurious dealing carried out still, with bold out facings; I have adventured once more, to write unto you. First I do freely confess, I dealt very indiscreetly in some of my particular letters which I wrote to private friends, for the courses in coming hither, and the like, which I do in no sort seek to justify, though stirred up thereunto in the beholding, the indirect courses held by others, both here, and there with you for effecting their designs. But am heartily sorry for it, and do to the glory of God, and mine own shame acknowledge it. Which letters being intercepted by the Governor I have for the same undergone the censure of banishment. And had it not been for the respect I have unto you, and some other matters of private regard, I had returned again at this time by the pinnace for England for here I purpose not to abide, unless I receive better encouragement from you; than from the church (as they call themselves) here I do receive. I purposed before I came to undergo hardness; therefore I shall, I hope cheerfully bear the conditions of the place though very mean, and they have changed my wages ten times already. I suppose my letters, or at least copies of them, are come to your hands, for so they here report; which, if it be so: I pray you take notice of this, that I have written nothing but what is certainly true; and I could make so appear plainly to any indifferent men, whatsoever colors be cast to darken the truth, and some there are very audacious this way; besides many other matters which are far out of order here. My mind was not to enlarge myself any further, but in respect of divers poor souls here, the care of whom in part belongs to you, being here destitute of the means of salvation. For howsoever the church are provided for, to their content, who are the smallest number in the colony, and do so appropriate the ministry to themselves, holding this principle, that the Lord hath not appointed, any ordinary ministry for the conversion of those that are without. So that some of the poor souls have with tears complained of this to me, and I was taxed for preaching to all in general. Though in truth they have had no ministry here since they came, but such as may be performed by any of you, by their own position, whatsoever great pretences they make, but herein they equivocate, as in many other things they do. But I exceed the bounds I set myself, therefore resting thus, until I hear further from you, so it be within the time limited me. I rest, etc.

Remaining yours ever
John Lyford exile

dated August 22, Anno. 1624.

They made a brief answer to some things in this letter, but referred chiefly to their former. The effect was to this purpose: that if God in His providence had not brought these things to their hands (both the former and latter) they might have been thus abused, traduced, and calumniated; overthrown, and undone; and never have known, by whom, nor for what. They desired but this equal favor, that they would be pleased to hear their just defense; as well as his accusations, and weigh them in the balance of justice, and reason, and then censure as they pleased. They had write briefly to the heads of things before, and should be ready to give further answer as any occasion should require, craving leave to add a word or two to this last.

1. And first they desire to examine what filth that was, that he acknowledgeth might justly be thrown in his face; and might cause blushing, and perpetual silence, some great matter sure? But if it be looked into, it amounts to no more, than a point of indiscretion, and that's all; and yet he licks off that too, with this excuse, that he was stirred up thereunto by beholding the indirect course here. But this point never troubled him here, it was counted a light matter, both by him and his friends; and put off with this, that any man might do so, to advise his private friends, to come over for their best advantage. All his sorrow, and tears here, was for the wrong and hurt he had done us, and not at all for this he pretends to be done to you, it was not counted so much as indiscretion.

2. Having thus paid you full satisfaction; he thinks he may lay load off us here. And first complains that we have changed his wages ten

times. We never agreed with him for any wages, nor made any bargain at all with him, neither know of any that you have made; you sent him over to teach amongst us, and desired he might be kindly used, and more than this we know not. That he hath been kindly used (and far better than he deserves from us) he shall be judged first of his own mouth. If you please to look upon that writing of his, that was sent you amongst his letters, which he calls a general relation; in which though he doth otherwise traduce us, yet in this he himself clears us; in the latter end thereof he hath these words: "I speak not this," saith he, "out of any ill affection to the men, for I have found them very kind and loving to me." You may there see these to be his own words, under his own hand. 2ly, it will appear by this, that he hath ever had a larger allowance of food out of the store for him and his than any, and clothing as his need hath required; a dwelling in one of our best houses, and a man wholly at his own command to tend his private affairs. What cause he hath, therefore, to complain judge ye; and what he means in his speech we know not, except he alludes to that of Jacob and Laban; if you have promised him more or otherwise, you may do it when you please.

3. Then with an impudent face; he would have you take notice, that (in his letters) he hath write nothing but what is certainly true; yea and he could make it so appear plainly to any indifferent men. This indeed doth astonish us, and causeth us to tremble at the deceitfulness and desperate wickedness of man's heart. This is to devour holy things, and after vows to inquire. It is admirable that after such public confession, and acknowledgment in court, in church, before God, and men, with such sad expressions, as he used and with such melting into tears, that after all this, he should now justify all again. If things had been done in a corner, it had been something to deny them, but being done in the open view of the country, and before all men, it is more than strange; now to avow to make them plainly appear to any indifferent men, and here where things were done, and all the evidence that could be were present, and yet could make nothing appear, but even his friends condemned him and gave their voice to his censure; so gross were they; we leave yourselves to judge herein. Yet lest this man should triumph in his wickedness, we shall be ready to answer him, when, or where you will, to anything he shall lay to our charge, though we have done it sufficiently already.

4. Then he saith he would not enlarge, but for some poor souls here who are destitute of the means of salvation, etc. But all his soothing is but that you would use means, that his censure might be released that he might here continue, and under you (at least) be sheltered till he sees what his friends (on whom he depends) can bring about, and effect. For such men pretend much for poor souls, but they will look to their wages, and conditions, if that be not to their content, let poor souls do what they will, they will shift for themselves, and seek poor souls somewhere else, among richer bodies.

5. Next he falls upon the church, that indeed is the burthensome stone that troubles him; first he saith they hold this principle, that the Lord hath not appointed, any ordinary ministry for the conversion of those without. The church needs not be ashamed of what she holds in this, having God's Word for her warrant; that ordinary officers are bound chiefly to their flocks, Acts 20:28, and are not to be extravagants, to go, come and leave them at their pleasures, to shift for themselves, or to be devoured of wolves. But he perverts the truth in this as in other things, for the Lord hath as well appointed them to convert, as to feed in their several charges; and he wrongs the church to say otherwise. Again, he saith he was taxed for preaching to all in general, this is a mere untruth, for this dissembler knows that every Lord's Day some are appointed, to visit suspected places and if any be found idling, and neglect the hearing of the Word (through idleness or profaneness) they are punished for the same; now to procure all to come to hear, and then to blame him for preaching to all, were to play the mad men.

6. Next (he saith) they have had no ministry since they came, whatsoever pretenses they make, etc. We answer the more is our wrong, that our pastor is kept from us, by these men's means, and then reproach us for it when they have done; yet have we not been wholly destitute of the means of salvation as this man would make the world believe. For our reverend Elder hath labored diligently in dispensing the Word of God to us, before he came; and since, hath taken equal pains with himself, in preaching the same; and be it spoken without ostentations he is not inferior, to Mr. Lyford (and some of his betters) either in gifts, or learning, though he would never be persuaded to take higher office upon him. Nor ever was more pretended in this matter; for equivocating he may take it to himself, what the church holds, they have manifested to the world, in all plainness, both in open confession, doctrine, and writing.

This was the sum of their answer; and here I will let them rest for the present. I have been longer in these things than I desired, and yet not so long as the things might require; for I pass many things in silence, and many more deserve to have been more largely handled. But I will return to other things; and leave the rest to its place.

The pinnace that was left sunk and cast away near Damariscove, as is before showed; some of the fishing masters said, it was a pity so fine a vessel should be lost; and sent them word, that if they would be at the cost, they would both direct them how to weigh her; and let them have their carpenters to mend her. They thanked them, and sent men about it, and beaver to defray the charge, (without which all had been in vain). So they got coopers to trim, I know not how many ton of cask, and being made tight and fastened to her at low water, they buoyed her up; and then with many hands hauled her on shore, in a convenient place, where she might be wrought upon; and then hired sundry carpenters to work upon her, and other to saw planks, and at last fitted her, and got her home. But she cost a great deal of money, in thus recovering her, and buying rigging, and sails for her, both now and when before she lost her mast; so as she proved a chargeable vessel to the poor plantation; so they sent her home, and with her Lyford sent his last letter in great secrecy, but the party entrusted with it, gave it the Governor.

The winter was passed over in their ordinary affairs, without any special matter worth noting; saving that many who before stood something off from the church; now seeing Lyford's unrighteous dealing, and malignity against the church; now tendered themselves to the church, and were joined to the same; professing that it was not out of the dislike of anything, that they had stood off so long, but a desire to fit themselves better for such a state, and they saw now the Lord called for their help.

And so these troubles produced a quite contrary effect, in sundry here; than these adversaries hoped for. Which was looked at as a great work of God, to draw on men by unlikely means; and that in reason which might rather have set them further off. And thus I shall end this year.

Anno Dom: 1625

At the spring of the year, about the time of their Election Court, Oldham came again amongst them; and though it was a part of his censure for his former mutiny and miscarriage not to return without leave first obtained, yet in his daring spirit he presumed without any leave at all; being also set on and hardened by the ill counsel of others; and not only so, but suffered his unruly passion to run beyond the limits of all reason, and modesty; insomuch that some strangers which came with him, were ashamed of his outrage, and rebuked him, but all reproofs were but as oil to the fire, and made the flame of his choler greater; he called them all to naught, in this his mad fury, and a hundred rebels, and traitors, and I know not what. But in conclusion they committed him, till he was tamer, and then appointed a guard of musketeers which he was to pass through, and every one was ordered to give him a thump on the breech, with the butt end of his musket, and then was conveyed to the waterside, where a boat was ready to carry him away; then they bid him go, and mend his manners.[198]

---

[198] Thomas Morton, in his *New English Canaan* (Amsterdam, 1637), recalled this incident: "[A]s for John Oldham, they could see he would be passionate, and moody; and prove himself a Mad Jack in his mood, and as soon moved to be moody, and this impatience would minister advantage to them to be rid of him . . . . They enjoin him to come to their needless watch house in person, and for refusing give him a cracked crown . . . and make the blood run down about his ears . . . and for his further behavior in the case, proceed to sentence him with banishment, which was performed after a solemn invention in this manner: a lane of musketeers was made, and he compelled in scorn to pass along between, and to receive a bob upon the bum by every musketeer, and then aboard a shallop, and so conveyed to Wessagussett shore . . ."

Whilst this was in doing; Mr. William Peirce, and Mr. Winslow, came up from the waterside, being come from England; but they were so busy with Oldham, as they never saw them, till they came thus upon them; they bid them not spare, either him or Lyford, for they had played the villains with them. But that I may here make an end with him, I shall here once for all, relate what befell concerning him in the future and that briefly. After the removal of his family from hence, he fell into some straits, (as some others did) and about, a year or more afterwards towards winter he intended a voyage for Virginia; but it so pleased God that the bark that carried him, and many other passengers was in that danger; as they despaired of life, so as many of them, as they fell to prayer, so also did they begin to examine their consciences and confess such sins as did most burthen them; and Mr. Oldham, did make a free and large confession of the wrongs, and hurt he had done to the people and church here, in many particulars, that as he had sought their ruin, so God had now met with him, and might destroy him; yea he feared, they all fared the worse for his sake; he prayed God to forgive him; and made vows that if the Lord spared his life, he would become otherwise, and the like. This I had from some of good credit, yet living in the Bay, and were themselves partners in the same dangers on the shoals of Cape Cod, and heard it from his own mouth. It pleased God to spare their lives, though they lost their voyage; and in time afterwards, Oldham carried himself fairly towards them; and acknowledged the hand of God to be with them, and seemed to have an honorable respect of them; and so far made his peace with them, as he in after time had liberty to go and come, and converse with them at his pleasure. He went after this to Virginia, and had there a great sickness, but recovered and came back again, to his family in the Bay, and there lived till some store of people came over; at length going a trading in a small vessel among the Indians, and being weakly manned, upon some quarrel they knocked him on the head with a hatchet, so as he fell down dead, and never spoke word more; 2 little boys that were his kinsmen were saved, but had some hurt; and the vessel was strangely recovered from the Indians, by another that belonged to the Bay of Massachusetts; and this his death, was one ground of the Pequot War, which followed.[199]

---

[199] For a more detailed account of the Pequot War, see John Mason, *A Brief History of the Pequot War: Especially of the memorable taking of their Fort at Mystic in Connecticut in 1637*, edited by Thomas Prince and published in Boston, 1736.

I am now come to Mr. Lyford; his time being now expired his censure was to take place, he was so far from answering their hopes, by amendment in the time; as he had doubled his evil as is before noted. But first behold the hand of God concerning him, wherein that of the Psalmist is verified, Psalm 7:15: "He hath made a pit, and digged it, and is fallen into the pit, he made." He thought to bring shame, and disgrace upon them; but instead thereof, opens his own to all the world; for when he was dealt withal about his second letter, his wife was so affected with his doings, as she could no longer conceal, her grief, and sorrow of mind; but opens the same to one of their deacons, and some other of her friends, and after uttered the same to Mr. Peirce upon his arrival. Which was to this purpose, that she feared some great judgment of God would fall upon them; and upon her, for her husband's cause, now that they were to remove, she feared to fall into the Indians' hands, and to be defiled by them, as he had defiled other women; or some such like judgment, as God had threatened, David, 2 Samuel 12:11, "I will raise up evil against thee, and will take thy wives and give them," etc.

And upon it showed how he had wronged her, as first he had a bastard by another before they were married, and she having some inkling of some ill carriage that way, when he was a suitor to her, she told him what she heard, and denied him, but she not certainly knowing the thing, otherwise than by some dark and secret mutterings, he not only stiffly denied it, but to satisfy her, took a solemn oath there was no such matter, upon which she gave consent, and married with him, but afterwards it was found true, and the bastard brought home to them. She then charged him with his oath, but he prayed pardon and said he should else not have had her. And yet afterwards she could keep no maids but he would be meddling with them, and some time she hath taken him in the manner, as they lay at their beds' feet, with such other circumstances as I am ashamed to relate; the woman being a grave matron, and of good carriage all the while she was here, and spoke these things out of the sorrow of her heart, sparingly, and yet with some further intimations. And that which did most seem to affect her (as they conceived) was, to see his former carriage in his repentance not only here with the church but formerly about these things; shedding tears, and using great, and sad expressions, and yet eftsoons fall into the like things.

Another thing of the same nature did strangely concur herewith; when Mr. Winslow, and Mr. Peirce, were come over; Mr. Winslow informed them that they had, had the like bickering with Lyford's friends in England, as they had with himself and his friends here, about his

letters, and accusations in them. And many meetings, and much clamor
was made by his friends thereabout; crying out, a minister, a man so
godly, to be so esteemed and taxed; they held a great scandal, and
threatened to prosecute law against them for it. But things being referred
to a further meeting of most of the adventurers, to hear the case, and
decide the matters; they agreed to choose 2 eminent men for moderators,
in the business; Lyford's faction chose Mr. White, a counselor at law, the
other part chose Reverend Mr. Hooker the minister, and many friends
on both sides were brought in, so as there was a great assembly. In the
meantime, God in His providence, had detected Lyford's evil carriage in
Ireland, to some friends amongst the company who made it known to
Mr. Winslow and directed him to 2 godly and grave witnesses; who would
testify the same, (if called thereunto) upon their oath. The thing was this:
he being got into Ireland, had wound himself into the esteem of sundry
godly, and zealous professors in those parts, who having been burdened
with the ceremonies in England, found there some more liberty to their
consciences, amongst whom were these 2 men; which gave this evidence.
Amongst the rest of his hearers, there was a godly young man that intended
to marry, and cast his affection on a maid which lived thereabout, but
desiring to choose in the Lord, and preferred the fear of God before all
other things; before he suffered his affection to run too far he resolved to
take Mr. Lyford's advice, and judgment, of this maid (being the minister
of the place) and so broke the matter unto him; and he promised faithfully
to inform him, but would first take better knowledge of her, and have
private conference with her; and so had sundry times; and in conclusion
commended her highly to the young man as a very fit wife for him; so
they were married together. But some time after marriage, the woman
was much troubled in mind, and afflicted in conscience; and did nothing
but weep and mourn, and long it was before her husband could get of her
what was the cause; but at length she discovered the thing. And prayed
him to forgive her, for Lyford had overcome her, and defiled her body,
before marriage, after he had commended him unto her for a husband,
and she resolved to have him; when he came to her in that private way.
The circumstances I forbear, for they would offend chaste ears to hear
them related (for though he satisfied his lust on her, yet he endeavored to
hinder conception.) These things being thus discovered, the woman's
husband took some godly friends with him to deal with Lyford for this
evil; at length he confessed it, with a great deal of seeming sorrow and
repentance, but was forced to leave Ireland upon it, partly for shame and

partly for fear of further punishment, for the godly withdrew themselves from him upon it; and so coming into England, unhappily he was lit upon and sent hither.

But in this great assembly, and before the moderators, in handling the former matters about the letters, upon provocation in some heat of reply, to some of Lyford's defenders, Mr. Winslow let fall these words, that he had dealt knavishly; upon which, one of his friends took hold, and called for witnesses that he called a minister of the gospel "knave," and would prosecute law upon it, which made a great tumult. Upon which (to be short) this matter broke out, and the witnesses were produced, whose persons were so grave, and evidence so plain, and the fact so foul, yet delivered in such modest, and chaste terms, and with such circumstances, as struck all his friends mute, and made them all ashamed; insomuch as the moderators with great gravity declared, that the former matters gave them cause enough to refuse him, and to deal with him as they had done; but these made him unmeet forever to bear ministry any more, what repentance soever he should pretend; with much more to like effect, and so wished his friends to rest quiet, thus was this matter ended.

From hence Lyford went to Nantasket in the Bay of the Massachusetts, with some other of his friends with him, where Oldham also lived; from thence he removed to Naumkeag, since called Salem; but after there came some people over, whether for hope of greater profit, or what ends else I know not, he left his friends that followed him and went from thence to Virginia; where he shortly after died; and so I leave him to the Lord. His wife afterwards returned again to this country, and thus much of this matter.

This storm being thus blown over, yet sundry sad effects followed the same; for the company of adventurers broke in pieces hereupon, and the greatest part wholly deserted the colony in regard of any further supply, or care of their subsistence; and not only so, but some of Lyford's, and Oldham's friends, and their adherents, set out a ship on fishing on their own account, and getting the start of the ships that came to the plantation, they took away their stage, and other necessary provisions that they had made for fishing at Cape Anne the year before; at their great charge; and would not restore the same, except they would fight for it. But the Governor sent some of the planters to help the fishermen to build a new one, and so let them keep it; this ship also brought them some small supply, of little value; but they made so poor a business of their fishing (neither could these men make them any return for the supply sent) so as after this year, they never looked more after them.[200]

Also by this ship, they some of them sent (in the name of the rest) certain reasons of their breaking off from the plantation; and some tenders (upon certain conditions of reuniting again). The which because they are long, and tedious, (and most of them about the former things already touched) I shall omit them only giving an instance in one, or two; 1 reason, they charged them for dissembling with His Majesty in their petition, and with the adventurers about the French discipline, etc. 2ly

---

[200] William Hubbard, writing in his *General History of New England* (17th century manuscript first published in 1815), gave some more details on this incident: "In one of the fishing voyages about the year 1625, under the charge and command of one Mr. Hewes, employed by some of the west country merchants, there arose a sharp contest between the said Hewes and the people of New Plymouth, about a fishing stage, built the year before about Cape Anne by Plymouth men, but was now, in the absence of the builders made use of by Mr. Hewes his company; which the other, under the conduct of Capt. Standish very eagerly and peremptorily demanded. For the Company of New Plymouth, having themselves obtained a useless patent for Cape Anne about the year 1623, sent some of the ships, which their Adventurers employed to transport over to them, to make fish there; for which end they had built a stage there in the year 1624. The dispute grew to be very hot, and high words passed between them; which might have ended in blows, if not in blood and slaughter, had not the prudence and moderation of Mr. Roger Conant, at that time there present, and Mr. [William] Peirce's interposition, that lay just by with his ship, timely preserved. For Mr. Hewes had barricaded his company with hogsheads on the stage-head, while the demandants stood upon the land, and might easily have been cut off. But the ship's crew, by advice, promising to help them build another, the difference was thereby ended. Capt. Standish had been bred a soldier in the Low Countries, and never entered the school of our Savior Christ, or of John Baptist, his harbinger; or, if he was ever there, had forgot his first lessons, to offer violence to no man, and to part with the cloak rather than needlessly contend for the coat, though taken away without order. A little chimney is soon fired; so was the Plymouth captain, a man of very little stature [i.e. short], yet of a very hot and angry temper. The fire of his passion soon kindled, and blown up into a flame by hot words, might easily have consumed all, had it not been seasonably quenched."

for receiving a man[201] into their church, that in his confession renounced all universal, national, and diocesan churches, etc., by which (say they) it appears, that though they deny the name of Brownists, yet they practice the same, etc. And therefore they should sin against God in building up such a people.

Then, they add, our dislikes thus laid down, that we may go on in trade with better content, and credit, our desires are as followeth:

1. First that as we are partners in trade; so we may be in government there, as the patent doth give us power, etc.
2. That the French discipline may be practiced in the plantation, as well in the circumstances thereof, as in the substance; whereby the scandalous name of the Brownists, and other church differences may be taken away.
3. Lastly that Mr. Robinson, and his company may not go over, to our plantation, unless he, and they will reconcile themselves, to our church by a recantation under their hands, etc.

Their answer in part to these things was then as followeth. Whereas you tax us for dissembling with His Majesty, and the adventurers about the French discipline, you do us wrong, for we both hold, and practice the discipline of the French, and other reformed churches, (as they have published the same in the Harmony of Confessions[202]) according to our means in effect, and substance. But whereas you would tie us to the French discipline in every circumstance, you derogate from the liberty we have in Christ Jesus. The Apostle Paul would have none to follow him in anything, but wherein he follows Christ, much less ought any Christian, or church in the world to do it; the French may err, we may err, and other churches may err, and doubtless do in many circumstances; that honor therefore belongs only to the infallible Word of God, and pure Testament of Christ, to be propounded, and followed, as the only rule, and pattern, for direction herein to all churches, and Christians. And it is too great arrogancy for any man, or church to think that he, or they, have so sounded the Word of God to the bottom, as precisely to set down the church's discipline, without error in substance, or circumstance,

---

[201]   This was Lyford himself. (Bradford).

[202]   *An Harmony of the Confessions of the Faith of the Christian and Reformed Churches* (London, 1586).

as that no other, without blame may digress, or differ in anything from the same. And it is not difficult to show, that the reformed churches differ in many circumstances amongst themselves. The rest I omit, for brevity's sake, and so leave to prosecute these men or their doings any further; but shall return to the rest, of their friends of the company which stuck to them. And I shall first insert some part of their letters as followeth, for I think it best to render their minds in their own words.[203]

To our loving friends, etc.

Though the thing we feared be come upon us, and the evil we strove against have overtaken us; yet we cannot forget you, nor our friendship, and fellowship which together we have had some years; wherein though our expressions have been small, yet our hearty affections towards you (unknown by face) have been no less, than to our nearest friends, yea to our own selves. And though this your friend Mr. Winslow can tell you the state of things here, yet lest we should seem to neglect you, to whom by a wonderful providence of God, we are so nearly united; we have thought good once more to write unto you, to let you know what is here befallen, and the reasons of it; as also our purposes, and desires toward you for hereafter.

The former course, for the generality here, is wholly dissolved, from what it was; and whereas you, and we, were formerly sharers, and partners in all voyages, and dealings, this way is now no more; but you, and we, are left to bethink ourselves, what course to take in the future, that your lives, and our moneys be not lost.

The reasons, and causes of this alteration have been these. First and mainly, the many losses, and crosses at sea, and abuses of seamen, which have caused us to run into so much charge, debts, and engagements as our estates, and means were not able, to go on without impoverishing ourselves; except our estates had been greater, and our associates cloven better unto us. 2ly, as here hath been a faction, and siding amongst us now more than 2 years; so now there is an utter breach, and sequestration amongst us; and in two parts of us, a full desertion, and forsaking of you, without any intent, or purpose of meddling more with you. And though we are persuaded, the main cause, of this their doing is want of money (for need whereof men use

---

[203]   This abbreviated letter is found in full in William Bradford's *Letterbook*, which is reprinted in *Collections of the Massachusetts Historical Society* 3(1794):27-76.

to make many excuses) yet other things are pretended, as that you are Brownists, etc.

Now what use you, or we ought to make of these things, it remaineth to be considered, for we know the hand of God to be in all these things, and no doubt He would admonish something thereby; and to look what is amiss. And although it be now too late for us, or you, to prevent, and stay these things; yet is it not too late to exercise patience, wisdom, and conscience in bearing them; and in carrying ourselves in, and under them, for the time to come.

And as we ourselves stand ready to embrace all occasions, that may tend to the furtherance of so hopeful a work; rather admiring of what is, than grudging, for what is not, so it must rest in you to make all good again. And if in nothing else you can be approved; yet let your honesty, and conscience, be still approved, and lose not one jot of your innocency, amidst your crosses, and afflictions. And surely if you upon this alteration behave yourselves wisely, and go on fairly, as men whose hope is not in this life; you shall need no other weapon to wound your adversaries; for when your righteousness is revealed as the light, they shall cover their faces with shame; that causelessly, have sought your overthrow.

Now we think it but reason, that all such things as there appertain to the general, be kept, and preserved together, and rather increased daily, than any way be dispersed, or embezzled away for any private ends, or intents whatsoever. And after your necessities, are served you gather, together such commodities as the country yields, and send them over to pay debts, and clear engagements here, which are not less than 1400£. And we hope you will do your best to free our engagements, etc. Let us all endeavor to keep a fair and honest course, and see what time will bring forth, and how God in His providence will work for us. We still are persuaded, you are the people that must make a plantation, in those remote places when all others fail and return. And your experience of God's providence, and preservation of you is such, as we hope your hearts will not fail you, though your friends should forsake you (which we ourselves shall not do whilst we live, so long as your honesty so well appeareth). Yet surely help would arise from some other place whilst you wait on God, with uprightness, though we should leave you also.

And lastly be you all entreated to walk circumspectly, and carry yourselves so uprightly in all your ways, as that no man may make just exceptions against you. And more especially that the favor, and countenance of God may be so toward you; as that you may find abundant joy, and peace even amidst tribulations, that you may say with David, though my father, and mother should forsake me, yet the Lord would take me up.

We have sent you here some cattle, cloth, hose, shoes, leather, etc. but in another nature than formerly, as it stood us in hand to do; we have committed them to the charge, and custody of Mr. Allerton, and Mr. Winslow, as our factors; at whose discretion they are to be sold, and commodities to be taken for them, as is fitting. And by how much the more they will be chargeable unto you, the better they had need to be husbanded, etc. Go on good friends comfortably, pluck up your spirits, and quit yourselves like men in all your difficulties; that notwithstanding all displeasure, and threats of men, yet the work may go on you are about, and not be neglected. Which is so much for the glory of God, and the furtherance of our countrymen; as that a man may with more comfort spend his life in it, than live the life of Methuselah, in wasting the plenty of a tilled land, or eating the fruit of a grown tree. Thus with hearty salutations to you all, and hearty prayers for you all, we lovingly take our leaves, this 18 of December 1624.

Your assured friends to our powers,

J.S. W.C. T.F. R.H.[204] etc.

By this letter it appears in what state the affairs of the plantation stood at this time. These goods they bought, but they were at dear rates, for they put 40 in the hundred upon them, for profit and adventure, outward bound; and because of the venture of the payment homeward, they would have 30$^£$ in the 100 more[205], which was in all 70 per cent: a thing thought unreasonable by some, and too great an oppression upon the poor people, as their case stood; the cattle were the best goods, for the other being ventured ware, were neither of the best (some of them) nor at the best prices; sundry of their friends disliked these high rates, but coming from many hands, they could not help it.

They sent over also 2 ships on fishing on their own account; the one was the pinnace that was cast away the last year here in the country, and recovered by the planters, (as was before related) who after she came home, was attached by one of the company, for his particular debt; and now sent again on this account; the other was a great ship, who was well fitted with an experienced master, and company of fishermen, to make a voyage, and to go to Bilbao, or Sebastians with her fish; the lesser her order was to load with cor-fish, and to bring the beaver home for England, that should be received for the goods

---

[204]   Initials are for James Sherley, William Collier, Thomas Fletcher, and Robert Holland.

[205]   If I mistake not, it was not much less. (Bradford).

sold to the plantation. This bigger ship made a great voyage of good dry fish, the which (if they had gone to a market with) would have yielded them (as such fish was sold that season) 1800£ which would have enriched them; but because there was a bruit of war with France, the master neglected (through timorousness) his order, and put first into Plymouth, and after into Portsmouth, and so lost their opportunity, and came by the loss. The lesser ship had as ill success, though she was as hopeful as the other, for the merchant's profit, for they had filled her with goodly cor-fish taken upon the bank, as full as she could swim, and besides she had some 800£ weight of beaver, besides other, furs to a good value from the plantation. The master seeing so much goods come, put it aboard the bigger ship, for more safety; but Mr. Winslow (their factor in this business) was bound in a bond of £500 to send it to London in the small ship; there was some contending between the master and him about it. But he told the master he would follow his order about it, if he would take it out afterward it should be at his peril; so it went in the small ship, and he sent bills of lading in both; the master was so careful, being both so well laden, as they went joyfully home together; for he towed the lesser ship at his stern all the way over bound, and they had such fair weather, as he never cast her off till they were shot deep into the English Channel, almost within the sight of Plymouth; and yet there she was unhaply taken by a Turks man of war, and carried into Sallee, where the master, and men were made slaves, and many of the beaver skins were sold for 4d apiece.

Thus was all their hopes dashed and the joyful news, they meant to carry home turned to heavy tidings; some thought this a hand of God for their too great exaction of the poor plantation, but God's judgments are unsearchable, neither dare I be bold therewith, but however it shows us the uncertainty of all human things, and what little cause there is of joying in them, or trusting to them.

In the bigger of these ships was sent over Captain Standish from the plantation, with letters, and instructions, both to their friends of the company which still clave to them; and also to the Honorable Council of New England; to the company to desire that, seeing that they meant only to let them have goods upon sale; that they might have them upon easier terms, for they should never be able to bear such high interest, or to allow so much per cent: also that what they would do in that way that it might be disbursed in money, or such goods as were fit and needful for them, and bought at best hand; and to acquaint them with the contents of his letters to the Council (abovesaid) which was to this purpose, to desire their favor, and help; that such of the adventurers as had thus forsaken and deserted them, might be brought to

Portrait of Captain Myles Standish, from a painting made in 1625. The whereabouts of the original are unknown. This drawing, based on the now lost original, was done for Justin Winsor's *Memorial History of Boston* (1881).

some order and not to keep them bound, and themselves be free. But that they might either stand to their former covenants, or else come to some fair end, by dividend, or composition. But he came in a very bad time for the State was full of trouble, and the plague very hot in London, so as no business could be done; yet he spoke with some of the Honored Council, who promised all helpfulness to the plantation which lay in them. And sundry of their friends the adventurers, were so weakened with their losses the last year, by the loss of the ship taken by the Turks, and the loss of their fish, which by reason of the wars, they were forced to land at Portsmouth, and so came to little. So as, though their wills were good, yet their power was little; and there died such multitudes weekly of the plague, as all trade was dead, and little money stirring. Yet with much ado he took up 150$^£$ (and spent a good deal of it in expenses) at 50 per cent, which he bestowed in trading goods, and such other most needful commodities, as he knew requisite for their use; and so returned passenger in a fishing ship; having prepared a good way for the composition that was afterward made.

In the meantime it pleased the Lord to give the plantation peace, and health, and contented minds; and so to bless their labors, as they had corn sufficient (and some to spare to others,) with other food; neither ever had they any supply of food but what they first brought with them. After harvest this year, they sent out a boat's load of corn 40 or 50 leagues to the eastward (up a river called Kennebec) it being one of those 2 shallops which their carpenter had built them the year before; for bigger vessel had they none. They had laid a little deck over her midships to keep the corn dry, but the men were fain to stand it out all weathers without shelter, and that time of the year begins to grow tempestuous. But God preserved them, and gave them good success, for they brought home 700$^£$ of beaver, besides some other furs, having little, or nothing else but this corn, which themselves had raised out of the earth. This voyage was made by Mr. Winslow, and some of the old standers; for seamen they had none.

Anno Dom: 1626

About the beginning of April they heard of Captain Standish his arrival, and sent a boat to fetch him home, and the things he had brought; welcome he was, but the news he brought was sad in many regards; not only in regard of the former losses (before related) which their friends had suffered, by which some in a manner were undone, others much disabled from doing any further help, and some dead of the plague. But also that Mr. Robinson their pastor was dead, which struck them with much sorrow, and sadness, as they had cause; his, and their adversaries, had been long, and continually plotting how they might hinder his coming hither, but the Lord had appointed him a better place[206]; concerning whose death, and the manner thereof, it will appear by these few lines write to the Governor and Mr. Brewster.

---

[206] An anonymous poem on the death of Pastor John Robinson is found in the Plymouth Church Records; it is thought that Bradford may have written it: "Blessed Robinson hath run his race / From earth to heaven is gone / To be with Christ in heavenly place / The blessed saints among. / A burning and a shining light / Was he whiles he was here / A preacher of the Gospel bright / Whom we did love most dear. / What tho' he died his works alive / And live will to all age / The comfort of them pleasant is / To living saints each day. / Oh blessed Holy Savior / The fountain of all Grace / From whom such blessed instruments / Are sent and run their race. / To lead us to and guide us in / The ways to happiness / That so oh Lord we may always / For evermore confess. / That whosoever Gospel preacher be / Or waterer of the same / We may always most constantly / Give Glory to Thy Name."

NEVV
ESSAYES
OR
OBSERVATIONS
DIVINE and MORALL.

Collected out of the holy Scriptures, Ancient and Moderne Writers, both Diuine
and Humane.

As alſo out of the great volume of Mens manners.

Tending to the furtherance of Knowledge and Vertue.

By IOHN ROBINSON.

PROV. 9. 9.
*Giue inſtruction to a wiſe man, and he will be yet wiſer: teach a iuſt man,
and he will increaſe in learning.*

Experientia docet, aut nocet.

Printed, *Anno* M DC XXVIII.

Title page of Pastor John Robinson's *New Essays, Or Observations Divine and Moral*
(London, 1628). This, along with John Dod's *Exposition Upon the Ten Commandments*,
were the most popularly-owned books in early Plymouth Colony.

Loving and kind friends, etc. I know not whether this will ever come to your hands, or miscarry, as other my letters have done; yet in regard of the Lord's dealing with us here, I have had a great desire to write unto you. Knowing your desire to bear a part with us, both in our joys, and sorrows; as we do with you; these are therefore to give you to understand, that it hath pleased the Lord to take out of this vale of tears, your, and our loving, and faithful pastor, and my dear, and Reverend brother, Mr. John Robinson, who was sick some 8 days. He began to be sick on Saturday in the morning, yet the next day (being the Lord's Day) he taught us twice. And so the week after grew weaker, every day more than other; yet he felt no pain, but weakness all the time of his sickness. The physic he took, wrought kindly in man's judgment, but he grew weaker every day, feeling little, or no pain and sensible to the very last. He fell sick the 22 of February and departed this life the 1 of March. He had a continual inward ague, but free from infection, so that all his friends came freely to him. And if either prayers, tears, or means would have saved his life, he had not gone hence. But he having faithfully finished his course, and performed his work which the Lord had appointed him here to do, he now resteth with the Lord in eternal happiness. We wanting him and all church governors yet we still (by the mercy of God) continue, and hold close together, in peace, and quietness, and so hope we shall do though we be very weak. Wishing (if such were the will of God) that you, and we, were again united together in one, either there, or here; but seeing it is the will of the Lord thus to dispose of things, we must labor with patience to rest contented, till it please the Lord otherwise to dispose. For news here is not much; only as in England we have lost our old King James, who departed this life, about a month ago, so here they have lost the old prince, Grave Maurice[207]. Who both departed this life since my brother Robinson, and as in England we have a new King Charles, of whom there is great hope; so here they have made Prince Hendrick general in his brother's place, etc. Thus with my love remembered, I take leave and rest

Your assured loving friend,
Roger White

Leiden, April 28, Anno. 1625

---

[207]   King James I died 27 March 1625 and was succeeded by his son, King Charles I. Maurice, from the House of Orange, son of William the Silent, died 23 April 1625, and was succeeded by his brother Frederick Hendrick.

Thus these two great princes, and their pastor left this world near about one time. Death makes no difference.

He further brought them notice of the death of their ancient friend Mr. Cushman, whom the Lord took away also this year, and about this time; who was as their right hand, with their friends the adventurers, and for divers years had done, and agitated all their business with them, to their great advantage. He had write to the Governor but some few months before, of the sore sickness of Mr. James Sherley (who was a chief friend to the plantation) and lay at the point of death, declaring his love and helpfulness, in all things; and much bemoaned the loss, they should have of him, if God should now take him away, as being the stay, and life of the whole business. As also his own purpose, this year to come over, and spend his days with them. But he that thus write of another's sickness, knew not that his own death was so near; it shows also that a man's ways, are not in his own power, but in His hands, who hath the issues of life and, death. Man may purpose, but God doth dispose.

Their other friends from Leiden writ many letters to them full of sad laments for their heavy loss; and though their wills were good to come to them, yet they saw no probability of means, how it might be effected; but concluded (as it were) that all their hopes were cut off. And many being aged began to drop away by death.

All which things (before related) being well weighed, and laid together it could not but strike them, with great perplexity; and to look humanly on the state of things as they presented themselves, at this time, it is a marvel it did not wholly discourage them, and sink them. But they gathered up their spirits, and the Lord so helped them; whose work they had in hand; as now when they were at lowest note they began to rise again, and being stripped (in a manner) of all human helps, and hopes, He brought things about otherwise, in His divine providence; as they were not only upheld and sustained, but their proceedings both honored, and imitated by others; as by the sequel will more appear, if the Lord spare me life, and time to declare the same.

Having now no fishing business, or other things to intend, but only their trading, and planting, they set themselves to follow the same, with the best industry they could, the planters finding their corn (what they could spare from their necessities) to be a commodity, (for they sold it at 6s a bushel) used great diligence in planting the same. And the Governor and such as were designed to manage the trade (for it was retained for the general good, and none were to trade in particular) they followed it to the best advantage they could. And wanting trading goods, they understood that a plantation which was at Mohegan, and belonged to some merchants of Plymouth, was to break up, and divers useful goods was there to be sold; the Governor and Mr. Winslow took a boat and some hands and went thither; but Mr. David Thompson, who lived at Piscataqua, understanding their purpose, took opportunity to go with them, which was some hindrance to them both, for they perceiving their joint desires to buy, held their goods at higher rates, and not only so, but would not sell a parcel of their trading goods, except they sold all; so lest they should further prejudice one another, they agreed to buy all and divide them equally between them. They bought also a parcel of goats, which they distributed at home as they saw need and occasion, and took corn for them, of the people, which gave them good content; their moiety of the goods came to above 400$^£$ sterling.

There was also that spring a French ship cast away at Sagadahoc, in which were many Biscay rugs and other commodities, which were fallen into these men's hands, and some other fishermen at Damariscove; which were also bought in partnership, and made their part arise to above 500$^£$. This they made shift to pay for, for the most part, with the beaver and commodities they had got the winter before, and what they had gathered up that summer; Mr. Thompson having something overcharged himself, de-sired they would take some of his; but they refused except he would let them have his French goods only; and the merchant (who was one of Bristol) would take their bill for to be paid the next year; they were both willing, so they became engaged for them, and took them. By which means, they became very well furnished for trade, and took off thereby some other engagements which lay upon them, as the money taken up by Captain Standish, and the remains of former debts. With these goods, and their corn after harvest, they got good store of trade, so as they were enabled to pay their engagements against the time, and to get some clothing for the people, and had some commodities beforehand; but now they began to be envied, and others went and filled the Indians with corn, and beat down the price, giving them twice as much as they had done, and undertraded them in other commodities also.

This year they sent Mr. Allerton into England; and gave him order to make a composition with the adventurers, upon as good terms as he could, (unto which some way had been made the year before by Captain Standish) but yet enjoined him not to conclude absolutely, till they knew the terms and had well considered of them, but to drive it to as good an issue as he could, and refer the conclusion to them. Also they gave him a commission[208] under their hands, and seals to take up some money, provided it exceeded not such a sum specified, for which they engaged themselves; and gave him order how to lay out the same for the use of the plantation.

And finding they ran a great hazard, to go so long voyages in a small open boat, especially the winter season; they began to think how they might get a small pinnace, as for the reason aforesaid; so also because others had raised the price with the Indians above the half, of what they had formerly given, so as in such a boat they could not carry a quantity sufficient to answer their ends. They had no ship carpenter amongst them, neither knew how to get one at present; but they having an ingenious man, that was a house carpenter[209], who also had wrought with the ship carpenter (that was dead) when he built their boats; at their request he put forth himself to make a trial that way of his skill; and took one of the biggest of their shallops, and sawed her in the middle, and so lengthened her some 5

---

[208] Allerton's commission is found in Bradford's *Letterbook*, reprinted in *Collections of the Massachusetts Historical Society* 3(1794):27-76. Bradford comments in his *Letterbook*, "This next year being Anno. 1626, we sent Mr. Allerton into England, partly to make some supply for us, and to see if he could make any reasonable composition with the adventurers; and because we well knew that nothing can be done without money, we gave him an order to procure some, binding ourselves to make payment thereof, . . . Upon this order, he got two hundred pounds, but it was at thirty in the hundred interest [i.e. 30% interest], by which appears in what straits we were; and yet this was upon better therms than the goods which were sent us the year before, being at forty-five percent, so that it was God's marvelous providence, that we were ever able to wade through things, as will better appear, if God give me life and opportunity to handle them more particularly, in another treatise more at large, as I desire and purpose (if God permit) with many other things, in better order. Besides the obtaining of this money, he with much ado made a composition and agreement with the body of the adventurers. Mr. [Robert] Alden (something softened by my letter before mentioned) who was one of our powerfullest opposers, did not only yield thereunto, but was a furtherer of the same."

[209] *Mayflower* passenger Francis Eaton was a house carpenter, so might be the man referred to here. See Neil D. Thompson, "The Origin and Parentage of Francis Eaton of the *Mayflower*," *The American Genealogist* 72(1997):301-304.

or 6 foot, and strengthened her with timbers, and so built her up, and laid a deck on her; and so made her a convenient, and wholesome vessel, very fit and comfortable for their use, which did them service 7 years after; and they got her finished, and fitted with sails and anchors the ensuing year. And thus passed the affairs of this year.

Anno Dom: 1627 ·

At the usual season of the coming of ships, Mr. Allerton returned, and brought some useful goods with him, according to the order given him. For upon his commission he took up 200$^£$ which he now got at 30 per cent. The which goods they got safely home, and well conditioned, which was much to the comfort, and content of the plantation. He declared unto them also, how with much ado, and no small trouble, he had made a composition with the adventurers, by the help of sundry of their faithful friends there who had also took much pains thereabout. The agreement or bargain he had brought a draft of, with a list of their names thereto annexed, drawn by the best counsel of law they could get, to make it firm. The heads whereof I shall here insert.

To all Christian people greeting, etc. Whereas at a meeting the 26 of October last past, divers, and sundry persons, whose names to the one part of these presents, are subscribed in a schedule hereunto annexed, adventurers to New Plymouth in New England in America, were contented and agreed, in consideration of the sum of one thousand and eight hundred pounds sterling to be paid, (in manner, and form following) to sell, and make sale of all, and every the stocks, shares, lands, merchandise and chattels, whatsoever to the said adventurers, and other their fellow adventurers, to New Plymouth aforesaid, any way accruing, or belonging to the generality of the said adventurers aforesaid, as well by reason of any sum or sums of money, or merchandise, at any time heretofore adventured, or disbursed by them, or otherwise howsoever. For the better expression, and setting forth of which said agreement, the parties to these presents subscribing, do for themselves severally, and as much as in them is grant, bargain, alien, sell, and transfer all and every the said shares, goods, lands, merchandise, and chattels to them belonging as aforesaid; unto Isaac Allerton, one of the Planters resident at Plymouth aforesaid, assigned, and sent over, as agent for the rest of the planters there. And to such other planters at Plymouth aforesaid as the said Isaac his heirs, or assigns, at his, or their arrival, shall by writing, or otherwise think fit to join or partake in the premises, their heirs, and assigns, in as large, ample, and beneficial manner, and form to all intents, and purposes, as the said subscribing adventurers here, could or may do, or perform. All which stocks, shares, lands, etc. to the said adventurers in severality allotted, apportioned or any way belonging, the said Adventurers do warrant, and defend unto the said Isaac Allerton his heirs and assigns; against them, their heirs and assigns, by these presents. And therefore the said Isaac Allerton doth, for him his heirs and assigns covenant, promise, and grant to and with the adventurers whose names are hereunto subscribed, their heirs, etc. well and truly to pay, or cause to be paid unto the said adventurers, or 5 of them which were at that meeting aforesaid nominated, and deputed; viz. John Pocock, John Beauchamp, Robert Keane, Edward Bass, and James Sherley, merchants, their heirs, etc. to and for the use of the generality of them; the sum of 1800$^£$ of lawful money of England, at the place appointed for the receipts of money, on the west side of the Royal Exchange in London; by 200$^£$ yearly, and every year, on the feast of St. Michael, the first payment to be made Anno 1628, etc. Also the said Isaac is to endeavor to procure and obtain from the planters of New Plymouth aforesaid security, by several obligations, or writings obligatory, to make payment of the said sum of 1800$^£$ in form aforesaid, according to the true meaning of these presents. In testimony whereof to this part of these presents, remaining with the said Isaac Allerton, the said subscribing adventurers have set to their names, etc. And to the other part remaining with the said adventurers, the said Isaac Allerton hath subscribed his name, the 15 November Anno 1626 in the 2 year of His Majesty's reign.[210]

---

[210]   Bradford's *Letterbook*, reprinted in *Collections of the Massachusetts Historical Society* 3(1794):27-76, provides a list of the signers to this document. They were: John White, John Pocock, Robert Kean, Edward Bass, William Hobsen, William Pennington, William Quarles, Daniel Pointon, Richard Andrews, Newman Rookes, Henry Browning, Richard Wright, John Ling, Thomas Goffe, Samuel Sharp, Robert Holland, James Sherley, Thomas Mott, Thomas Fletcher, Timothy Hatherley, Thomas Brewer, John Thornhill, Myles Knowles, William Collier, John Revell, Peter Gudburn, Emmanuel Altham, John Beauchamp, Thomas Hudson, Thomas Andrews, Thomas Ward, Fria. Newbald, Thomas Heath, Joseph

This agreement was very well liked of and approved by all the plantation, and consented unto; though they knew not well how to raise the payment, and discharge their other engagements; and supply the yearly wants of the plantation seeing they were forced for their necessities to take up money, or goods at so high interests. Yet they undertook it, and 7 or 8 of the chief of the place became jointly bound for the payment of this 1800$^£$ (in the behalf of the rest) at the several days. In which they ran a great adventure, as their present state stood, having many other heavy burdens already upon them; and all things in an uncertain condition amongst them. So the next return it was absolutely confirmed on both sides, and the bargain fairly engrossed in parchment and in many things put into better form, by the advice of the learnedest counsel they could get, and lest any forfeiture should fall on the whole for none payment at any of the days: it ran thus to forfeit 30s a week if they missed the time; and was concluded under their hands and seals; as may be seen at large by the deed itself.

Now though they had some untoward persons, mixed amongst them from the first, which came out of England, and more afterwards by some of the adventurers, as friendship or other affections led them; though sundry were gone, some for Virginia, and some to other places, yet divers were still mingled amongst them; about whom the Governor and Council with other of their chief friends had serious consideration, how to settle things in regard of this new bargain, or purchase made; in respect of the distribution of things both for the present, and future. For the present, except peace and union were preserved, they should be able to do nothing, but endanger to overthrow all, now that other ties and bonds were taken away. Therefore they resolved, for sundry reasons, to take in all amongst them that were either heads of families, or single young men, that were of ability, and free; (and able to govern themselves with meet discretion and their affairs, so as to be helpful in the commonwealth) into this partnership, or purchase. First they considered that they had need of men, and strength both for defense, and carrying on of businesses. 2ly most of them had borne their parts in former miseries, and wants with them, and therefore (in some sort) but equal to partake in a better condition if the Lord be pleased to give it. But chiefly they saw not how peace would be preserved without so doing, but danger, and great disturbance might grow to their great hurt, and prejudice otherwise. Yet they resolved to keep such a mean

---

Tilden, William Penrin, Eliza Knight, Thomas Coventry, Robert Alden, Laurence Anthony, John Knight, Matthew Thornhill, and Thomas Millsop.

in distribution of lands, and other courses, as should not hinder their growth in others coming to them.

So they called the company together and conferred with them; and came to this conclusion, that the trade should be managed as before to help to pay the debts; and all such persons as were above named should be reputed and enrolled for purchasers; single free men to have a single share, and every father of a family to be allowed to purchase so many shares as he had persons in his family, that is to say, one for himself, and one for his wife, and for every child that he had living with him one. As for servants they had none, but what either their masters should give them out of theirs, or their deservings should obtain from the company afterwards. Thus all were to be cast into single shares according to the order abovesaid; and so every one was to pay his part according to his proportion towards the purchase, and all other debts, what the profit of the trade would not reach to, viz. a single man, for a single share, a master of a family for so many as he had. This gave all good content. And first accordingly the few cattle which they had were divided; which arose to this proportion: a cow to 6 persons or shares, and 2 goats to the same, which were first equalized for age, and goodness and then lotted for; single persons consorting with others, as they thought good, and smaller families likewise; and swine though more in number, yet by the same rule.[211] Then they agreed that every person or share should have 20 acres of land divided unto them, besides the single acres they had already; and they appointed were to begin first on the one side of the town, and how far to go; and then on the other side in like manner, and so to divide it by lot, and appointed sundry by name to do it, and tied them to certain rules to proceed by; as that they should only lay out settable or tillable land, at least such of it as should butt on the waterside, (as the most they were to lay out did) and pass by the rest, as refuse, and common; and what they judged fit should be so taken. And they were first to agree of the goodness and fitness of it before the lot was drawn, and so it might as well prove some of their own as another man's; and this course they were to hold throughout. But yet seeking to keep the people together as much as might be they also agreed upon this order, by mutual consent, before any lots were cast, that whose lots soever should fall next the town, or most convenient for nearness, they should take to them a

---

[211] The 1627 Division of Cattle is found in the *Plymouth Colony Records* 12:9-13, and is also reprinted in Appendix I. It is a valuable document because it contains the names of all persons (men, women, and children) then living in Plymouth.

neighbor, or two, whom they best liked, and should suffer them to plant corn with them for 4 years, and afterwards they might use as much of theirs for as long time, if they would. Also every share or 20 acres was to be laid out five acres in breadth by the waterside, and four acres in length (excepting nooks and corners) which were to be measured, as they would bear to best advantage. But no meadows were to be laid out at all; nor were not of many years after, because they were but strait of meadow grounds, and if they had been now given out, it would have hindered all addition to them afterwards. But every season all were appointed where they should mow, according to the proportion of cattle they had. This distribution gave generally good content and settled men's minds. Also they gave the Governor and 4 or 5 of the special men amongst them the houses they lived in, the rest were valued, and equalized at an indifferent rate, and so every man kept his own, and he that had a better allowed something to him that had a worse, as the valuation went.[212]

There is one thing that fell out in the beginning of the winter before, which I have referred to this place, that I may handle the whole matter together. There was a ship[213], with many passengers in her and sundry goods, bound for Virginia. They had lost themselves at sea, either by the insufficiency of the master or his illness for he was sick and lame of the scurvy; so that he could but lie in the cabin door and give direction, and it should seen was badly assisted either with mate, or mariners, or else the fear and unruliness of the passengers were such as they made then steer a course between the southwest, and the northwest, that they might fall with some land whatsoever it was they caret not. For they had been 6 weeks at sea, and had no water, nor beer, nor any wood left, but had burnt up all their empty cask; only one of the company had a hogshead of wine or 2 which was also almost spent, so as they feared they should be starved at sea or consumed with diseases, which made them run this desperate course.

But it pleased God that though they came so near the shoals of Cape Cod or else ran stumbling over them in the night, they knew not how; they came right before a small blind harbor that lies about the middle of Manamoyick Bay to the southward of Cape Cod, with a small gale of wind, and about high water touched upon a bar of sand that lies before it, but had

---

[212] The rules for the January 1627/8 Division of Land are found in *Plymouth Colony Records* 11:4-5. The earliest records relating to the sale of the land and cattle received during these divisions can be found in the *Plymouth Colony Records*, volume 12, beginning on page 15.

[213] The "*Sparrow-Hawk.*"

Remnants of the 1626 shipwreck nicknamed the *Sparrow Hawk*. The wreck remained embedded in sand and mud until it was uncovered in a storm in 1862. It became a traveling exhibit until 1889 when it was given to the Pilgrim Hall Museum. The vessel was approximately 36 tons and measured about 40 feet in length. She was carrying about 25 passengers from England at the time of her wreck. Photo courtesy of the Pilgrim Hall Museum, Plymouth, Massachusetts.

no hurt, the sea being smooth; so they laid out an anchor. But towards the evening the wind sprung up at sea, and was so rough, as broke their cable and beat them over the bar, into the harbor; where they saved their lives, and goods, though much were hurt with salt water, for with beating they had sprung the butt end of a plank or two, and beat out their oakum; but they were soon over and ran on a dry flat within the harbor, close by a beach; so at low water they got out their goods on dry shore, and dried those that were wet, and saved most of their things without any great loss; neither was the ship much hurt, but she might be mended, and made serviceable again. But though they were not a little glad that they had thus saved their lives; yet when they had a little refreshed themselves; and began to think on their condition, not knowing where they were, nor what they should do, they began to be strucken with sadness. But shortly after they saw some Indians come to them in canoes, which made them stand upon their guard; but when they heard some of the Indians speak English unto them, they were not a little revived, especially when they heard them demand if they were the Governor of Plymouth's men, or friends; and that they would bring them to the English houses, or carry their letters.

They feasted these Indians, and gave them many gifts. And sent 2 men and a letter with them to the Governor and did entreat him to send a boat unto them; with some pitch, and oakum, and spikes, with divers other necessaries for the mending of their ship (which was recoverable). Also they besought him to help them with some corn and sundry other things they wanted, to enable them to make their voyage to Virginia. And they should be much bound to him; and would make satisfaction for anything they had, in any commodities they had aboard. After the Governor was well informed by the messengers of their condition, he caused a boat to be made ready, and such things to be provided as they write for; and because others were abroad upon trading, and such other affairs, as had been fit to send unto them, he went himself, and also carried some trading commodities, to buy them corn of the Indians. It was no season of the year to go without the Cape, but understanding where the ship lay, he went into the bottom of the bay on the inside, and put into a creek called Namskaket, where it is not much above 2 mile over land to the bay where they were, where he had the Indians ready to carry over anything to them. Of his arrival they were very glad, and received the things to mend their ship, and other necessaries. Also he bought them as much corn as they would have; and whereas some of their seamen were run away among the Indians he procured their return to the ship, and so left them well furnished and contented, being very thankful for the courtesies they received. But after the Governor thus left them, he went into some other harbors thereabout and loaded his boat with corn which he traded; and so went home. But he had not been at home many days, but he had notice from them, that by the violence of a great storm, and the bad mooring of their ship (after she was mended) she was put ashore, and so beaten, and shaken as she was now wholly unfit to go to sea; and so their request was that they might have leave to repair to them, and sojourn with them; till they could have means to convey themselves to Virginia; and that they might have means to transport their goods and they would pay for the same, or anything else wherewith the plantation should relieve them. Considering their distress, their requests were granted, and all helpfulness done unto them; their goods transported, and themselves, and goods sheltered in their houses as well as they could.

The chief amongst these people was one, Mr. Fells, and Mr. Sibsey, which had many servants belonging unto them, many of them being Irish. Some others there were that had a servant or 2 apiece, but the most were servants, and such as were engaged to the former persons, who also had the most goods. After they were hither come, and something settled; the masters desired some ground to employ their servants upon. (Seeing it was like to be the latter end of the year, before they could have passage for Virginia) and they had now the winter before them, they might clear some ground, and plant a crop, (seeing they had tools and necessaries for the same) to help to bear their charge, and keep their servants in employment; and if they had opportunity to depart before the same was ripe, they would sell it on the ground. So they had ground appointed them in convenient places; and Fells and some other of them raised a great deal of corn; which they sold at their departure. This Fells, amongst his other servants, had a maidservant, which kept his house, and did his household affairs, and by the intimation of some that belonged unto him, he was suspected to keep her as his concubine; and both of them were examined thereupon, but nothing could be proved, and they stood upon their justification, so with admonition they were dismissed; but afterward it appeared she was with child, so he got a small boat, and ran away with her, for fear of punishment; first he went to Cape Anne, and after into the Bay of the Massachusetts, but could get no passage, and had like to have been cast away; and was forced to come again and submit himself; but they packed him away, and those that belonged unto him, by the first opportunity; and dismissed all the rest as soon as could, being many untoward people amongst them; though there were also some that carried themselves very orderly all the time they stayed. And the plantation had some benefit by them; in selling them corn, and other provisions of food; for clothing; for they had of divers kinds, as cloth, perpetuanes, and other stuffs, besides hose and shoes and such like commodities as the planters stood in need of. So they both did good, and received good one from another. And a couple of barks carried them away at the latter end of summer. And sundry of them have acknowledged their thankfulness since from Virginia.

That they might better take all convenient opportunity to follow their trade, both to maintain themselves; and to disengage them of those great sums which they stood charged with, and bound for, they resolved to build a small pinnace at Manomet, a place 20 miles from the plantation[214]; standing on the sea to southward of them, unto which by another creek on this side, they could carry their goods, within 4 or 5 miles, and then transport them overland, to their vessel. And so avoid the compassing of Cape Cod, and those dangerous shoals; and so make any voyage to the southward in much shorter time, and with far less danger. Also for the safety of their vessel, and goods, they built a house there, and kept some servants, who also planted corn, and rear some swine; and were always ready to go out with the bark when there was occasion. All which took good effect and turned their profit.

They now sent (with the return of the ships) Mr. Allerton again into England, giving him full power (under their hands and seal) to conclude the former bargain with the adventurers; and sent their bonds for the payment of the money. Also they sent what beaver they could spare to pay some of their engagements, and to defray his charges, (for those deep interests still kept them low). Also he had order to procure a patent for a fit trading place in the river of Kennebec, for being emulated both by the planters, at Piscataqua,

---

[214]   On the Manomet river which enters into Buzzard's Bay. It is now located within the modern-day city of Bourne. Dutchman Isaac de Rasieres, writing in a letter in 1628, describes this trading post briefly in his report: "Coming out of the river Nassau, you sail east-and-by-north about fourteen leagues, along the coast, a half league from the shore, and you then come to Frenchman's Point at a small river where those of Patuxet [Plymouth] have a house made of hewn oak planks, called Aptucxet, where they keep two men, winter and summer, in order to maintain the trade and possession. Here also they have built a shallop, in order to go and look after the trade in sewan, in Sloup's Bay and thereabouts, . . . From Aptucxet the English can come in six hours, through the woods, passing several little rivulets of fresh water, to New Plymouth, the principal place in the district Patuxet, so called in their patent from His Majesty in England." Rasieres' letters are reprinted in Sydney V. James, ed., *Three Visitors to Early Plymouth* (Plymouth: Plimoth Plantation 1963).

and other places to the eastward of them; and also by the fishing ships (which used to draw much profit from the Indians of those parts) they threatened, to procure a grant and shut them out from thence, especially after they saw them so well furnished with commodities, as to carry the trade from them. They thought it but needful to prevent such a thing, at least that they might not be excluded from free trade there, where themselves had first begun, and discovered the same, and brought it to so good effect.

This year also they had letters, and messengers from the Dutch plantation sent unto them from the Governor there; written, both in Dutch, and French. The Dutch had traded in these southern parts, divers years before they came; but they began no plantation here, till 4 or 5 years after their coming, and here beginning. Their letters were as followeth. It being their manner to be full of complimental titles.

Eedele, Eerenfeste Wyse Voorsinnige Heeren, den Goveerneur, ende Raeden in Nieu-Pliemuen Residerende; onse seer Goede Vrinden. Den directeur ende Raed van Nieu-Nederlande, wensen vue Ede: eerenfesten, ende wijse voorsinnige gelukzaligheid, in Christi Jesu onsen Heere; met geode voorspoet, ende gesonthijt, near siele, ende lichaem.[215] Amen.

The rest I shall render in English, leaving out the repetition of superfluous titles.

We have often before this wished for an opportunity, or an occasion, to congratulate you, and your prosperous and praiseworthy undertakings; and government of your colony there. And the more, in that we also have made a good beginning to pitch the foundation of a colony here; and seeing our native country lies not far from yours; and our forefathers (divers hundred years ago) have made, and held friendship, and alliance with your ancestors; as sufficiently appears by the old contracts, and intercourses, confirmed under the hands of kings, and princes, in the point of war, and traffic; as may be seen, and read by all the world in the old chronicles. The which are not only, by the King now reigning confirmed; but it hath pleased His Majesty, upon mature deliberation, to make a new covenant, (and to take up arms)

---

[215] Translation: Noble, worshipful, wise, and prudent lords, the Governor and Councilors residing in New Plymouth, our very dear friends, the Director and Council of New Netherlands wish to your Lordships, worshipful, wise and prudent, happiness in Christ Jesus our Lord, with prosperity and health, in soul and body.

with the States General of our dear native country; against our common enemy the Spaniards, who seek nothing else but to usurp, and overcome other Christian kings' and princes' lands; that so he might obtain, and possess his pretended monarchy, over all Christendom; and so to rule, and command, after his own pleasure; over the consciences of so many hundred thousand souls, which God forbid.

And also seeing it hath, some time since, been reported unto us, by some of our people, that by occasion, came so far northward with their shallop; and met with sundry of the Indians, who told them, that they were within half a day's journey of your plantation, and offered their service, to carry letters unto you; therefore we could not forbear to salute you with these few lines, with presentation of our good will, and service unto you, in all friendly kindness, and neighborhood. And if it so fall out, that any goods that come to our hands, from our native country, may be serviceable unto you; we shall take ourselves bound to help, and accommodate you therewith; either for beaver, or any other wares, or merchandise, that you should be pleased to deal for. And if in case we have no commodity at present that may give you content; if you please to sell us any beaver, or otter, or such like commodities as may be useful for us, for ready money; and let us understand thereof by this bearer in writing (whom we have appointed to stay three or four days for your answer). When we understand your minds therein; we shall depute one to deal with you, at such place as you shall appoint. In the meantime we pray the Lord, to take you, our honored good friends, and neighbors, into His holy protection.

From the Manhattas, by the appointment of the Governor and council, etc.

In the fort Amsterdam,

Isaack de Rasieres, Secretary

March 9, Anno. 1627.

To this they returned answer as followeth on the other side.

To the Honored, etc.[216]

The Governor and Council of New Plymouth wisheth, etc. We have received your letters, etc. wherein appeareth your good wills, and friendship towards us, but is expressed with over high titles, more than belongs to us; or is meet for us to receive. But for your good will, and congratulations of our prosperity in these small beginnings of our poor colony, we are much bound unto you, and with

---

[216] The full version of this letter can be found in William Bradford's *Letterbook*, reprinted in *Collections of the Massachusetts Historical Society* 3(1794):27-76.

many thanks do acknowledge the same; taking it both for a great honor done unto us, and for a certain testimony, of your love, and good neighborhood.

Now these are further to give your Worships to understand, that it is to us no small joy, to hear, that His Majesty hath not only, been pleased to confirm that ancient amity, alliance, and friendship, and other contracts, formerly made, and ratified, by his predecessors of famous memory; but hath himself (as you say) strengthened the same with a new union, the better to resist the pride of that common enemy the Spaniard; from whose cruelty the Lord keep us both, and our native countries. Now forasmuch as this is sufficient to unite us together in love, and good neighborhood, in all our dealings; yet are many of us further obliged, by the good and courteous entreaty we have found in your country; having lived there many years, with freedom, and good content; as also many of our friends, do to this day. For which we, and our children after us, are bound to be thankful to your nation; and shall never forget the same, but shall heartily desire your good, and prosperity, as our own forever.

Likewise for your friendly tender, and offer to accommodate, and help us with any commodities, or merchandise you have; or shall come to you, either for beaver, otters or other wares, it is to us very acceptable, and we doubt not but in short time, we may have profitable commerce and trade together. But for this year we are fully supplied with all necessaries, both for clothing, and other things, but hereafter it is like we shall deal with you, if your rates be reasonable. And therefore when you please to send to us again by any of yours, we desire to know how you will take beaver, by the pound, and otters by the skin; and how you will deal per cent for other commodities, and what you can furnish us with. As likewise what other commodities from us may be acceptable unto you, as tobacco, fish, corn or other things, and what prices you will give, etc.

Thus hoping that you will pardon, and excuse us for our rude and imperfect writing in your language, and take it in good part because for want of use we cannot so well express that we understand; nor happily understand everything so fully as we should. And so we humbly pray the Lord for His mercy sake that He will take both us, and you into His keeping, and gracious protection.

Your Worships' very good friends, and neighbors, etc.

By the Governor and Council of New Plymouth

New Plymouth: March 19

After this there was many passages, between them both by letters, and other intercourse; and they had some profitable commerce together for divers years; till other occasions interrupted the same, as may happily appear afterwards, more at large.

Before they sent Mr. Allerton away for England this year, the Governor and some of their chief friends had serious consideration, not only how they might discharge those great engagements which lay, so heavily upon them, as is afore mentioned. But also how they might (if possibly they could) devise means to help some of their friends, and brethren of Leiden, over unto them; who desired so much to come to them, and they desired as much their company. To effect which, they resolved to run a high course, and of great adventure; not knowing otherwise how to bring it about. Which was to hire the trade of the company for certain years; and in that time to undertake to pay that 1800$^£$ and all the rest of the debts that then lay upon the plantation, which was about some 600$^£$ more; and so to set them free, and return the trade to the generality again at the end of the term. Upon which resolution they, called the company together, and made it clearly appear unto all, what their debts were, and upon what terms, they would undertake to pay them all, in such a time, and set them clear. But their other ends they were fain to keep secret, having only privately acquainted some of their trusty friends therewith, which were glad of the same; but doubted how they would be able to perform it. So after some agitation of the thing with the company, it was yielded unto; and the agreement made upon the conditions following:

Articles of agreement between the Colony of New Plymouth
of the one party; and William Bradford, Captain Myles
Standish, Isaac Allerton, etc. on the other party,
and such others as they shall think good to take
as partners, and undertakers with them
concerning the trade for beaver and other
furs and commodities, etc. Made July 1627[217]

First it is agreed, and covenanted betwixt the said parties; that the aforesaid William Bradford, Captain Myles Standish, and Isaac Allerton, etc. have

---

[217] The full version of this letter can be found in William Bradford's *Letterbook*, reprinted in *Collections of the Massachusetts Historical Society* 3(1794):27-76. It was signed by William Brewster, Stephen Hopkins, Francis Eaton, Jonathan Brewster, Manassas Kempton, Thomas Prence, Anthony Annable, John Shaw, William Bassett, Godbert Godbertson, John Adams, Phineas Pratt, Stephen Tracey, Edward Doty, Joshua Pratt, Stephen Dean, William Wright, Francis Cooke, William Palmer, Experience Mitchell, Edward Bangs, Samuel Fuller, Robert Hicks, John Howland, John Billington, Peter Browne, and John Faunce.

undertaken, and do by these presents, covenant and agree to pay, discharge
and acquit the said Colony of all the debts both due for the purchase, or any
other belonging to them, at the day of the date of these presents.

Secondly the abovesaid parties, are to have; and freely enjoy the pinnace
lately built, the boat at Manomet, and the shallop called the bass boat, with
all other implements to them belonging, that is in the store of the said
Company. With all the whole stock of furs, fells, beads, corn, wampampeag,
hatchets, knives, etc. that is now in the store; or any way due unto the same
upon account.

3ly that the above said parties have the whole trade to themselves, their
heirs, and assigns; with all the privileges thereof, as the said Colony doth now or
may use the same, for 6 full years, to begin the last of September next ensuing.

4ly in further consideration of the discharge of the said debts; every
several purchaser doth promise, and covenant yearly to pay, or cause to be
paid, to the abovesaid parties, during the full term, of the said 6 years, 3
bushels of corn or 6$^£$ of tobacco, at the undertakers' choice.

5ly the said undertakers shall during the aforesaid term bestow 50$^£$ per
annum in hose and shoes, to be brought over for the Colony's use, to be sold
unto them for corn at 6s per bushel.

6ly that at the end of the said term of 6 years the whole trade shall return
to the use, and benefit of the said Colony, as before.

Lastly, if the aforesaid undertakers, after they have acquainted their
friends in England with these covenants; do (upon the first return) resolve to
perform them, and undertake to discharge the debts of the said Colony,
according to the true meaning, and intent of these presents; then they are
(upon such notice given) to stand in full force; otherwise all things to remain,
as formerly they were, and a true account to be given to the said Colony, of
the disposing of things according to the former order.

Mr. Allerton carried a copy of this agreement with him in England; and
amongst other his instructions, had order given him to deal with some of
their special friends, to join with them this trade upon the above recited
conditions, as also to impart their further ends that moved them to take this
course, namely the helping over of some of their friends from Leiden as the
should be able, in which if any of them would join with them they should
thankfully accept of their love, and partnership herein. And withal (by their
letters) gave them some grounds of their hopes of the accomplishment of
these things; with some advantage.

After Mr. Allerton's arrival in England, he acquainted them with his commission and full power, to conclude the forementioned bargain, and purchase; upon the view whereof, and the delivery of the bonds for the payment of the money yearly (as is before mentioned) it was fully concluded, and a deed[218] fairly engrossed in parchment was delivered him, under their hands, and seals confirming the same. Moreover he dealt with them about other things according to his instructions, as to admit some of these their good friends into this purchase if they pleased, and to deal with them for moneys at better rates, etc. Touching which I shall here insert a letter of Mr. Sherley's, giving light to what followed thereof; writ to the Governor as followeth.

Sir, I have received yours of the 26 of May, by Mr. Gibbs, and Mr. Goffe[219], with the barrel of otter skins according to the contents, for which I got a bill of store, and so took them up and sold them together at 78ᶠ 12s sterling and since Mr. Allerton hath received the money, as will appear by the account. It is true (as you writ) that your engagements are great, not only the purchase, but you are yet necessitated to take up the stock you work upon, and that not at 6 or 8 percent as it is here let out, but at 30, 40, yea and some at 50 percent. Which were not your gains great, and God's blessing on your honest endeavors, more than ordinary; it could not be that you should long subsist, in the maintaining of and upholding of your worldly affairs. And this

---

[218]   Nov. 6, 1627, Page 238. (Bradford).

[219]   John Gibbs, master of the ship *Marmaduke* which carried Allerton to England; and Thomas Goffe, an investor in the Plymouth Colony.

your honest, and discreet agent Mr. Allerton hath seriously considered, and deeply laid to mind, how to ease you of it. He told me, you were contented to accept of me and some few others, to join with you in the purchase, as partners; for which I kindly thank you and all the rest, and do willingly accept of it. And though absent, shall willingly be at such charge, as you, and the rest shall think meet, and this year am contented to forbear my former 50$^£$ and two years increase for the venture both which now makes it 80$^£$ without any bargain, or condition for the profit; you (I mean) the generality, stand to the adventure, outward and homeward. I have persuaded Mr. Andrews, and Mr. Beauchamp to do the like, so as you are eased of the high rate, you were at the other 2 years. I say we leave it freely to yourselves, to allow us what you please, and as God shall bless. What course I run Mr. Beauchamp desireth to do the same, and though he have been or seemed somewhat harsh heretofore, yet now you shall find he is new molded. I also see by your letter, you desire I should be your agent, or factor here; I have ever found you so faithful, honest, and upright men, as I have even resolved with myself (God assisting me) to do you all the good lieth in my power, and therefore if you please to make choice of so weak a man, both for abilities, and body, to perform your business, I promise (the Lord enabling me) to do the best I can according to those abilities he hath given me; and wherein I fail, blame yourselves, that you made no better choice. Now because I am sickly, and we are all mortal, I have advised Mr. Allerton to join Mr. Beauchamp with me in your deputation, which I conceive to be very necessary and good for you; your charge shall be no more, for it is not your salary makes me undertake your business. Thus commending you, and yours, and all God's people, unto the guidance and protection of the Almighty, I ever rest,

Your faithful loving friend,
James Sherley

London, November 17, 1628

Another letter of his; that should have
been placed before.[220]

We cannot but take notice, how the Lord hath been pleased to cross our proceedings, and caused many disasters, to befall us therein. I conceive the only reason to be, we or many of us, aimed at other ends, than God's glory; but now I hope that cause is taken away. The bargain being fully concluded,

---

[220] This letter is also found in Bradford's *Letterbook*.

as far as our powers will reach, and confirmed under our hands and seals, to Mr. Allerton and the rest of his, and your copartners. But for my own part, I confess as I was loath to hinder the full confirming of it, being the first propounder thereof at our meeting; so on the other side, I was as unwilling to set my hand to the sale; being the receiver of most part of the adventures, and a second causer of much of the engagements. And one more threatened, being most envied, and aimed at (if they could find any step, to ground their malice on) than any other whosoever. I profess I know no just cause they ever had, or have so to do; neither shall it ever be proved, that I have wronged them, or any of the adventurers, wittingly, or willingly, one penny in the disbursing of so many pounds, in those 2 years' trouble. No the sole cause why they malign me (as I and others conceived) was that I would not side with them against you, and the going over of the Leiden people; but as I then cared not, so now I little fear what they can do, yet charge, and trouble, I know they may cause me to be at. And for these reasons, I would gladly have persuaded, the other 4 to have sealed to this bargain, and left me out, but they would not; so rather than it should fail, Mr. Allerton having taken so much pains, I have sealed with the rest; with this proviso, and promise of his, that if any trouble arise here, you are to bear half the charge. Wherefore now I doubt not, but you will give your generality good content, and settle peace amongst yourselves, and peace with the natives; and then no doubt, but the God of Peace, will bless your going out, and your returning, and cause all that you set your hands unto to prosper; the which I shall ever pray the Lord to grant if it be His blessed will. Assuredly unless the Lord be merciful to us, and the whole land in general, our estate, and condition is far worse, than yours. Wherefore if the Lord should send persecution, or trouble here (which is much to be feared) and so should put into our minds, to fly for refuge, I know no place safer than to come to you (for all Europe is at variance one with another, but chiefly with us). Not doubting but to find such friendly entertainment, as shall be honest, and conscionable, notwithstanding what hath lately passed. For I profess in the word of an honest man, had it not been to procure your peace, and quiet from some turbulent spirits here; I would not have sealed to this last deed; though you would have given me all my adventure, and debt ready down. Thus desiring the Lord to bless, and prosper you; I cease ever resting,

Your faithful, and loving friend to my power,

James Sherley

December 27

With this letter they sent a draft of a formal deputation to be here sealed and sent back unto them, to authorize them as their agents, according to what is mentioned in the abovesaid letter, and because some inconvenience grew thereby afterward, I shall here insert it.

To all to whom these presents shall come greeting, know ye that we William Bradford, Governor of Plymouth in New England in America, Isaac Allerton, Myles Standish, William Brewster, and Edward Winslow of Plymouth aforesaid, merchants, do by these presents for us and in our names make, substitute, and appoint James Sherley, goldsmith, and John Beauchamp, salter, citizens of London, our true and lawful agents, factors, substitutes, and assigns. As well to take, and receive, all such goods, wares, and merchandise whatsoever as to our said substitutes, or either of them, or to the City of London, or other place of the Realm of England shall be sent, transported, or come from us or any of us, as also to vend, sell, barter, or exchange the said goods, wares, and merchandise so from time to time to be sent; to such person, or persons upon credit, or otherwise in such manner as to our said agents and factors jointly, or to either of them severally, shall seem meet. And further we do make and ordain our said substitutes and assigns jointly and severally for us, and to our uses, and accounts, to buy, and consign for and to us into New England aforesaid, such goods and merchandise to be provided here and to be returned hence; as by our said assigns, or either of them, shall be thought fit. And to recover, receive, and demand, for us, and in our names all such debts, and sums of money, as now are, or hereafter shall be due incident accruing, or belonging to us, or any of us, by any ways or means; and to acquit, discharge, or compound for any debt, or sum of money, which now, or hereafter shall be due, or owing by any persons or persons to us, or any of us. And generally for us, and in our names to do, perform and execute every act, and thing which to our said assigns, or either of them shall seem meet to be done in or about the premises, as fully, and effectually to all intents, and purposes, as if we, or any of us, were in person present. And whatsoever our said agents, and factors jointly or severally, shall do, or cause to be done, in or about the premises, we will and do and every of us doth ratify, allow, and confirm, by these presents. In witness whereof we have hereunto put our hands and seals. Dated 18 November 1628.

This was accordingly confirmed, by the above named, and 4 more of the chief of them under their hands and seals, and delivered unto them. Also Mr.

Allerton formerly had authority under their hands, and seals for the transacting of the former business, and taking up of moneys, etc., which still he retained whilst he was employed in these affairs; they mistrusting neither him, nor any of their friends faithfulness, which made them more remiss, in looking to such acts as had passed under their hands, as necessary for the time; but letting them run on too long unminded, or recalled, it turned to their harm afterwards, as will appear in its place.

Mr. Allerton having settled all things thus in a good, and hopeful way; he made haste to return in the first of the spring to be here, with their supply for trade, (for the fishermen with whom he came used to set forth in winter, and be here betimes). He brought a reasonable supply of goods for the plantation, and without those great interests as before is noted; and brought an account of the beaver sold, and how the money was disposed for goods, and the payment, of other debts; having paid all debts abroad to others, save to Mr. Sherley, Mr. Beauchamp, and Mr. Andrews; from whom likewise he brought an account which to them all amounted not to above 400$^£$ for which he had passed bonds[221]; also he had paid, the first payment for the purchase, being due for this year, viz. 200$^£$ and brought them the bond for the same canceled; so as they now had no more foreign debts but the abovesaid 400$^£$ and odd pounds, and the rest of the yearly purchase money, some other debts they had in the country, but they were without any interest, and they had wherewith to discharge them, when they were due. To this pass the Lord had brought things for them. Also he brought them further notice that their friends the above named, and some others that would join with them in the trade, and purchase; did intend for to send over to Leiden for a competent number, of them, to be here the next year without fail, if the Lord pleased to bless their journey. He also brought them a patent for Kennebec; but it was so strait, and ill bounded, as they were fain to renew, and enlarge it the next year, as also that which they had at home, to their great charge as will after appear. Hitherto Mr. Allerton did them good and faithful service; and well had it been, if he had so continued, or else they had now ceased for employing him any longer thus into England, but of this more afterwards.

Having procured a patent (as is above said) for Kennebec, they now erected a house up above in the river in the most convenientest place for trade (as they conceived) and furnished the same with commodities for that end, both winter, and summer not only with corn; but also with such other

---

[221]   James Sherley's 1628 accounting is reprinted in Appendix I.

commodities as the fishermen had traded with them, as coats, shirts, rugs, and blankets, biscuit, peas, prunes, etc. and what they could not have out of England, they bought of the fishing ships, and so carried on their business, as well as they could.

This year the Dutch sent again unto them from their plantation, both kind letters, and also divers commodities, as sugar, linen cloth, Holland finer, and coarser, stuffs, etc. They came up with their bark to Manomet, to their house there, in which came their Secretary Rasieres[222], who was accompanied with a noise of trumpeters, and some other attendants, and desired that they would send a boat for him, for he could not travel so far overland. So they sent a boat to Manonscusset, and brought him to the plantation, with the chief of his company. And after some few days entertainment, he returned to his bark, and some of them went with him, and bought sundry of his goods: after which beginning thus made, they sent oftentimes to the same place, and had intercourse together for divers years;

---

[222] Isaac de Rasieres reported on his visit to Plymouth in a letter to Samuel Blommaert in 1628, reprinted in Sydney V. James, *Three Visitors to Early Plymouth* (Plymouth: Plimoth Plantation, 1963). Rasieres' description of Plymouth, in part: "New Plymouth lies in a large bay to the north of Cape Cod, . . . which can be easily seen in clear weather. Directly before the commenced town lies a sandbank, about twenty paces broad, whereon the sea breaks violently with an easterly and east-northeasterly wind . . . . At the south side of the town there flows down a small river of fresh water, very rapid, but shallow, which takes its rise from several lakes in the land above, and there empties into the sea; where in April and the beginning of May, there come so many shad from the sea which want to ascend that river, that it is quite surprising . . . . New Plymouth lies on the slope of a hill stretching east towards the sea coast, with a broad street about a cannon shot of 800 feet long, leading down the hill; with a crossing in the middle, . . . The houses are constructed of clapboards, with gardens also enclosed behind and at the sides with clapboards, so that their houses and courtyards are arranged in very good order, with a stockade against sudden attack; and at the ends of the streets there are three wooden gates. In the center, on the cross street, stands the Governor's house, before which is a square stockade upon which four patereros are mounded, so as to enfilade the streets. Upon the hill they have a large square house, with a flat roof, built of thick sawn planks stayed with oak beams, upon the top of which they have six cannon, which shoot iron balls of four and five pounds, and command the surrounding country. The lower part they use for their church, where they preach on Sundays . . ."

and amongst other commodities, they vended much tobacco for linen cloth, stuffs, etc., which was a good benefit to the people; till the Virginians found out their plantation. But that which turned most to their profit, in time was an entrance into the trade of wampampeag; for they now bough about $50^£$ worth of it of them; and they told them, how vendible it was at their fort Orange, and did persuade them they would find it so at Kennebec; and so it came to pass, in time, though at first it stuck, and it was 2 years before they could put off this small quantity, till the inland people knew of it, and afterwards they could scarce ever get enough for them, for many years together. And so this with their other provisions, cut off their trade quite from the fishermen; and in great part from other of the straggling planters. And strange it was to see the great alteration it made, in a few years among the Indians themselves, for all the Indians of these parts, and the Massachusetts, had none or very little of it[223], but the sachems, and some special persons, that wore a little of it for ornament. Only it was made, and kept among the Narragansetts, and Pequots, which grew rich, and potent by it, and these people were poor, and beggarly, and had no use of it. Neither did the English of this plantation, or any other in the land; till now that they had knowledge of it from the Dutch, so much as know what it was, much less that it was a commodity of that worth, and value. But after it grew thus to be a commodity in these parts, these Indians fell into it also, and to learn how to make it; for the Narragansetts do gather the shells of which they make it from their shores. And it hath now continued a current commodity about this 20 years; and it may prove a drug

---

[223]   Peag. (Bradford). Wampampeag were polished beads made from quahog seashells. Wampum was used extensively in trade, and also to manufacture sacred and cultural artifacts. Roger Williams, in his *Key into the Language of America* (London, 1643) reported "The Indians' [money] is of two sorts: one white, which they make of the stem or stock of the Periwincle, which they call *Meteauhock*, when all the shell is broken off: and of this sort six of their small beads (which they make with holes to string the bracelets) are currant with the English for a penny. The second is black, inclining to blue, which is made of the shell of a fish, which some English call Hens, *Poquauhock*, and of this sort three make an English penny . . . . Their white they call *Wampum* (which signifies white): their black *Suckauhock* (*Sucki* signifying black) . . . . They hang these strings of money about their necks and wrists; as also upon the necks and wriests of their wives and children . . . . Yea, the princes make rich caps and aprons (or small breeches) of these beads thus curiously strung into many forms and figures: their black and white finely mixed together."

in time; in the meantime it makes the Indians of these parts rich, and powerful and also proud thereby; and fills them with pieces, powder and shot; which no laws can restrain, by reason of the baseness of sundry unworthy persons; both English, Dutch and French; which may turn to the ruin of many. Hitherto the Indians of these parts, had no pieces, nor other arms, but their bows, and arrows, nor of many years after; neither durst they scarce handle a gun, so much were they afraid of them and the very sight of one (though out of kilter) was a terror unto them. But those Indians to the east parts, which had commerce with the French, got pieces of them, and they in the end made a common trade of it. And in time our English fishermen led with the like covetousness followed their example, for their own gain; but upon complaint against them, it pleased the King's Majesty to prohibit the same by a strict proclamation, commanding that no sort of arms, or munition, should by any of his subjects be traded with them.

About some 3 or 4 years before this time there came over one Captain Wollaston (a man of pretty parts) and with him 3 or 4 more of some eminency, who brought with them, a great many servants, with provisions, and other implements for to begin a plantation. And pitched themselves in a place within the Massachusetts, which they called after their Captain's name, Mount Wollaston. Amongst whom was one Mr. Morton[224], who it should seem, had some small adventure (of his own or other men's) amongst them. But had little respect amongst them, and was slighted by the meanest servants. Having continued there some time, and not finding things to answer their expectations, nor profit to arise as they looked for, Captain Wollaston takes a great part of the servants, and transports them to Virginia, where he puts them off at good rates, selling their time to other men; and writes back to one Mr. Rasdall (one of his chief partners, and accounted their merchant) to bring another part of them to Virginia likewise, intending to put them off there as he had done the rest. And he (with the consent of the said Rasdall) appointed one Fitcher to be his lieutenant and govern the remains of the plantation, till he or Rasdall returned to take further order thereabout. But this Morton abovesaid, having more craft, than honesty, (who had been a kind of pettifogger, of Furnival's Inn) in the others' absence, watches an opportunity (commons being but hard amongst them) and got some strong drink and other junkets, and made them a feast; and after they were merry,

---

[224] This was Thomas Morton, who later wrote the book *New English Canaan* (Amsterdam, 1637) to discourse on the country and attack the Separatist and Puritan governments of New England.

he began to tell them, he would give them good counsel; you see (saith he) that many of your fellows are carried to Virginia; and if you stay till this Rasdall return, you will also be carried away and sold for slaves with the rest. Therefore I would advise you, to thrust out this Lieutenant Fitcher; and I having a part in the plantation, will receive you as my partners, and consociates; so may you be free from service, and we will converse, plant, trade, and live together as equals, and support, and protect one another, or to like effect.

This counsel was easily received, so they took opportunity, and thrust Lieutenant Fitcher out a doors, and would suffer him to come no more amongst them; but forced him to seek bread to eat, and other relief from his neighbors, till he could get passage for England. After this they fell to great licentiousness, and led a dissolute life, pouring out themselves into all profaneness; and Morton became lord of misrule and maintained (as it were) a School of Atheism. And after they had got some goods into their hands, and got much by trading with the Indians; they spent it as vainly, in quaffing, and drinking, both wine, and strong waters in great excess, (and, as some reported) $10^{£}$ worth in a morning. They also set up a maypole, drinking and dancing about it many days together inviting the Indian women, for their consorts, dancing and frisking together (like so many fairies, or furies, rather,) and worse practices. As if they had anew revived and celebrated the feasts of the Roman goddess Flora; or the beastly practices of the mad Bacchanalians; Morton likewise (to show his poetry) composed sundry rhymes, and verses, some tending to lasciviousness, and others to the detraction, and scandal of some persons, which he affixed to this idle, or idol maypole.[225] They changed also the name of their place, and instead of calling it Mount Wollaston they call it Merrymount, as if this jollity

---

[225] These verses were published by Morton in his *New English Canaan* (Amsterdam, 1637). One such verse went: "Drink and be merry, merry, merry boys, / Let all your delight be in Hymen's joys, / Io to Hymen now the day is come / About the merry maypole take a room. / Make green garlands, bring bottles out; / And fill sweet nectar freely about, / Uncover thy head, and fear no harm, / For hers good liquor to keep it warm. / . . . Nectar is a thing assigned, / By the deity's own mind, / To cure the heart oppressed with grief, / And of good liquors is the chief, / . . . Give to the melancholy man, / A cup or two of it now and then; / This physic will soon revive his blood, / And make him be of a merrier mood. / . . . Give to the Nymph that's free from scorn, / No Irish stuff nor Scotch over worn, / Lasses in beaver coats come away, / Ye shall be welcome to us night and day . . . ."

would have lasted ever. But this continued not long, for after Morton was sent for England (as follows to be declared) shortly after came over that worthy gentleman Mr. John Endecott, who brought over a patent under the broad seal, for the government of the Massachusetts, who visiting those parts caused that maypole to be cut down, and rebuked them for their profaneness, and admonished them, to look there should be better walking. So they or others now changed the name of their place again, and called it Mount Dagon.

Now to maintain this riotous prodigality, and profuse excess; Morton (thinking himself lawless) and hearing what gain the French, and fishermen, made by trading of pieces, powder, and shot to the Indians; he as the head of this consortship, began the practice of the same in these parts; and first he taught them how to use them, to charge, and discharge, and what proportion, of powder, to give the piece, according to the size, or bigness of the same; and what shot to use for fowl, and what for deer. And having thus instructed them, he employed some of them, to hunt, and fowl for him so as they became far more active, in that employment, than any of the English; by reason of their swiftness of foot, and nimbleness of body, being also quick-sighted, and by continual exercise well knowing the haunts of all sorts of game. So as when they saw the execution that a piece would do, and the benefit that might come by the same; they became mad (as it were) after them, and would not stick to give any price (they could attain to) for them; accounting their bows and arrows but baubles in comparison of them.

And here I may take occasion to bewail the mischief that this wicked man began in these parts; and which since base covetousness, prevailing in men that should know better, has now at length got the upper hand, and made this thing common (notwithstanding any laws to the contrary) so as the Indians are full of pieces all over, both fowling pieces, muskets, pistols, etc. They have also their molds to make shot, of all sorts, as musket bullets, pistol bullets, swan and goose shot, and of smaller sorts; yea some have seen them have their screw-plates to make screw-pins themselves when they want them, with sundry other implements, wherewith they are ordinarily better, fitted, and furnished than the English themselves. Yea it is well known that they will have powder, and shot, when the English want it, nor cannot get it; and that in a time of war, or danger; as experience hath manifested, that when lead hath been scarce, and men for their own defense, would gladly have given, a groat a £; which is dear enough, yet hath it been bought up, and sent to other places, and sold to such as trade it with the

Indians, at 12 pence the £. And it is like they give 3 or 4s the pound, for they will have it at any rate. And these things have been done in the same times, when some of their neighbors, and friends, are daily killed by the Indians, or are in danger thereof and live but at the Indians' mercy. Yea some (as they have acquainted them with all other things) have told them how gunpowder is made, and all the materials in it, and that they are to be had in their own land; and I am confident could they attain to make saltpeter, they would teach them to make powder. O the horribleness of this villainy! How many both Dutch, and English, have been lately slain by those Indians, thus furnished; and no remedy provided, nay the evil more increased, and the blood of their brethren sold for gain (as is to be feared) and in what danger all these colonies are in is too well known. Oh that princes and parliaments would take some timely order to prevent this mischief, and at length to suppress it; by some exemplary punishment upon some of these gain-thirsty murderers, for they deserve no better title; before their colonies in these parts be overthrown by these barbarous savages, thus armed with their own weapons, by these evil instruments; and traitors to their neighbors; and country. But I have forgot myself, and have been too long in this digression; but now to return.

This Morton having thus taught them the use of pieces, he sold them all he could spare, and he and his consorts determined to send for many out of England, and had by some of the ships sent for above a score. The which being known; and his neighbors meeting the Indians in the woods armed with guns in this sort, it was a terror unto them, who lived stragglingly, and were of no strength in any place. And other places (though more remote) saw this mischief would quickly spread over all, if not prevented. Besides they saw, they should keep no servants, for Morton would entertain any, how vile soever, and all the scum of the country, or any discontents would flock to him from all places, if this nest was not broken; and they should stand in more fear of their lives, and goods, (in short time) from this wicked, and debased crew, than from the savages themselves.

So sundry of the chief of the straggling plantations meeting together, agreed, by mutual consent, to solicit those, of Plymouth (who were then of more strength than them all) to join with them, to prevent the further growth of this mischief; and suppress Morton, and his consorts before they grew to further head and strength. Those that joined in this action, (and after contributed to the charge of sending him for England) were from Piscataqua, Naumkeag, Winnisimmet, Wessagussett, Nantasket, and other places where any English were seated.[226] Those of Plymouth being thus sought to by their messengers and letters, and weighing both their reasons, and the common danger, were willing to afford them their help; though themselves had least cause of fear, or hurt. So to be short, they first resolved, jointly to write to him, and in a friendly, and neighborly way to admonish him, to forbear those courses, and sent a messenger with their letters to bring his answer. But he was so high as he scorned all advice, and asked who had to do with him; he had and would trade pieces with the Indians, in despite of all, with many other scurrilous terms full of disdain. They sent to him a second time, and bade him be better advised, and more temperate in his terms, for the country could not bear the injury he did. It was against their common safety; and against the King's proclamation; he answered in high terms as before and that the King's proclamation, was no law, demanding what penalty was upon it; it was answered, more than he could bear, His Majesty's displeasure: but insolently he persisted, and said the King was dead and his displeasure with him, and many the like things. And threatened withal that if any came to molest him, let them look to themselves for he would prepare for them. Upon which they saw there was no way but to take him by force, and having so far proceeded, now to give over would make him far more haughty, and insolent; so they mutually resolved to proceed, and obtained of the Governor of Plymouth, to send Captain Standish, and some other aid with him, to take Morton by force. The which accordingly was done, but they found him to stand stiffly in his defense, having made fast his doors, armed his consorts, set divers dishes of powder, and bullets ready on the table; and if they had not been over-armed with drink, more hurt might have been done. They summoned him to yield, but he kept his house, and they could get nothing but scoffs, and scorns from him. But at length fearing they would do some violence to the house, he and some of his crew came out, but not to yield, but to shoot; but they were so steeled with drink, as their pieces were too heavy for them; himself with a carbine (overcharged, and almost half filled, with powder and shot, as was after found) had thought to have shot Captain Standish: but he stepped to him, and put by his piece, and took him; neither was there any hurt done, to any of either side; save that one was so drunk,

---

[226]   The exact charges to each Plantation are enumerated in Bradford's *Letterbook*. Plymouth and Piscataqua both contributed £2, 10s, Mr. Jeffrey and Mr. Burslem contributed £2, Naumkeag and Nantasket contributed £1, 10s., Edward Hilton contributed £1, Mr. Blackston contributed 12s., and Mrs. Thompson contributed 1s.

that he ran his own nose upon the point of a sword that one held before him, as he entered the house; but he lost but a little of his hot blood.[227] Morton

---

[227] Morton's account of his arrest by "Captain Shrimp" is, of course, quite different: "The Separatists envying the prosperity, and hope of the plantation at Merrymount . . . conspired together against Mine Host especially, . . . and made up a party against him; and mustered up what aid they could, accounting of him, as of a great monster. Many threatening speeches were given out both against his person, and his habitation, . . . They set upon my honest host at a place called Wessagussett, where (by accident) they found him . . . . Surprise Mine Host, (who was there all alone) and they charged him, because they would seem to have some reasonable cause against him . . . with criminal things . . . Much rejoicing was made that they had gotten their capital enemy (as they concluded him) whom they propsed to hamper in such a sort . . . The conspirators sported themselves at my honest host, that meant them no hurt; and were so jocund that they feasted their bodies, and fell to tippling [drinking], as if they had obtained a great prize; like the Trojans when they had the custody of Hippeus' pine tree horse. Mine Host fained grief: and could not be persuaded either to eat, or drink, because he knew emptiness would be a means to make him as watchful as the geese kept in the Roman capitol . . . Six persons of the conspiracy were set to watch him at Wessagussett: but he kept waking, and in the dead of night . . . up gets Mine Host, and got to the second door that he was to pass which, notwithstanding the lock, he got open: and shut it after him with such violence, that it affrighted some of the conspirators. The word which was given with alarm was, 'O he's gone, He's gone, What shall we do, He's gone?' The rest (half asleep) start up in a maze, and like rams, ran their heads one at another full but in the dark. Their grand leader Captain Shrimp took on most furiously, and tore his clothes for anger, to see the empty nest, and their bird gone. The rest were eager to have torn their hair from their heads, but it was so short, that it would give them no hold; now Captain Shrimp thought in the loss of this prize (which he accounted his masterpiece), all his honor would be lost forever. In the meantime Mine Host was got home to Merrymount through the woods, eight miles, . . . finding his way by the help of the lightning . . . and there prepared powder three pounds dried, for his present employment, and four good guns for him, and the two assistants left at his house, with bullets fo several sizes three hundred, or thereabouts, to be used if the conspirators should pursue him hither . . . Now Captain Shrimp, the first captain in the land (as he supposed) must do some new act to repair this loss, and to vindicate his reputation, . . . He takes eight persons more to him, and

they brought away to Plymouth where he was kept, till a ship went from the Isle of Shoals for England with which he was sent, to the Council of New England; and letters written to give them information of his course, and carriage; and also one was sent, at their common charge, to inform their Honors more particularly, and to prosecute against him. But he fooled of the messenger, after he was gone from hence, and though he went for England yet nothing was done to him, not so much as rebuked, for aught was heard; but returned the next year. Some of the worst of the company were dispersed, and some of the more modest kept the house, till he should be heard from. But I have been too long about so unworthy a person, and bad a cause.

This year Mr. Allerton brought over a young man for a minister to the people here, whether upon his own head or at the motion of some friends there I well know not. But it was without the church's sending (for they had been so bitten by Mr. Lyford, as they desired to know the person well, whom they should invite amongst them). His name was Mr. Rogers; but they

---

(like the nine Worthies of New Canaan) they embark with preparation against Merrymount, where this monster of a man (as their phrase was) had his den . . . . Now the nine Worthies are approached; and Mine Host prepared: having intelligence by a savage, that hastened in love from Wessagussett, to give him notice of their intent . . . . The nine Worthies coming before the den of this supposed moster, . . . began like Don Quixote against the windmill to beat a party, and to offer quarter (if Mine Host would yield) for they resolved to send him for England, and bade him lay by his arms. But he . . . having taken up arms in his just defense, replied, that he would not lay by those arms, because they were so needful at sea, if he should be sent over. Yet (to save the effusing of so much worthy blood, as would have issued out of the veins of these 9 Worthies of New Canaan, if Mine Host should have played upon them out at his port holes (for they came within danger like a flock of wild geese, as if they had been tailed one to another, as colts to be sold at a fair) Mine Host was content to yield upon quarter, and did capitulate with them . . . . But Mine Host no sooner had set open the door and issued out, but instantly Captain Shrimp, and the rest of the Worthies stepped to him, laid hold of his arms, and had him down, and so eagerly was every man bent against him . . . that they fell upon him, asi f they would have eaten him . . . . Captain Shrimp and the rest of the nine Worthies made themselves (by this outrageous riot) masters of Mine Host of Merrymount, and disposed of what he had at his plantation." *New English Canaan* (Amsterdam, 1637).

perceived upon some trial, that he was, crazed in his brain, so they were fain to be at further charge to send him back again the next year, and lose all the charge that was expended in his hither bringing, which was not small by Mr. Allerton's account, in provisions, apparel, bedding, etc. After his return he grew quite distracted, and Mr. Allerton was much blamed that he would bring such a man over, they having charge enough otherwise.

Mr. Allerton in the years before, had brought over some small quantity of goods, upon his own particular, and sold them for his own private benefit; which was more than any man had yet hitherto attempted. But because he had otherwise done them good service; and also he sold them among the people at the plantation, by which their wants were supplied, and he alleged it was the love of Mr. Sherley, and some other friends that would needs trust him with some goods conceiving it might do him some good, and none hurt; it was not much looked at but passed over. But this year he brought over a greater quantity, and they were so intermixed with the goods of the general, as they knew not which were theirs, and which was his, being packed up together, so as they well saw that if any casualty had befallen at sea, he might have laid the whole on them, if he would; for there was no distinction. Also what was most vendible, and would yield present pay, usually that was his; and he now began also to sell abroad to others of foreign places. Which (considering their common course) they began to dislike. Yet because love thinks no evil, nor is suspicious; they took his fair words for excuse, and resolved to send him again this year for England; considering how well he had done the former business, and what good acceptation he had with their friends there; as also seeing sundry of their friends from Leiden were sent for, which would, or might be much furthered by his means. Again seeing the patent for Kennebec must be enlarged (by reason of the former mistakes in the bounding of it) and it was conceived (in a manner) the same charge would serve to enlarge this at home with it; and he that had begun the former the last year, would be the fittest to effect this. So they gave him instructions and sent him for England this year again. And in his instructions bound him to bring over no goods on their account; but 50$^£$ in hose and shoes and some linen cloth (as they were bound by covenant when they took the trade) also some trading goods to such a value; and in no case to exceed his instructions, nor run them into any further charge; he well knowing how their state stood. Also that he should so provide that their trading goods came over betimes; and whatsoever was sent on their account should be packed up by itself, marked with their mark, and no other goods to be mixed with theirs. For so he prayed them to give him such instructions as they saw good, and he would follow them; to prevent any jealousy, or further offense; upon the former, forementioned dislikes. And thus they conceived they had well provided for all things.

Mr. Allerton safely arriving in England, and delivering his letters, to their friends there and acquainting them with his instructions; found good acceptation with them, and they were very forward and willing, to join with them in the partnership of trade, and in the charge to send over the Leiden people; a company whereof, were already come out of Holland, and prepared to come over, and so were sent away, before Mr. Allerton could be ready to come. They had passage with the ships that came to Salem, that brought over many godly persons, to begin the plantations, and churches of Christ there, and in the Bay of the Massachusetts[228]; so their long stay, and keeping back was recompensed, by the Lord, to their friends here with a double blessing; in that they not only enjoyed them, now beyond their late expectation (when all their hopes seemed to be cut off) but with them, many more godly friends and Christian brethren, as the beginning of a larger harvest unto the Lord; in the increase of His churches, and people in these parts, to the admiration of many, and almost wonder of the world; that of so small beginnings so great things should ensue, as time after manifested, and that here should be a resting place, for so many of the Lord's people; when so sharp a scourge came upon their own nation, but it was the Lord's doing, and it ought to be marvelous in our eyes.

But I shall here insert some of their friends' letters, which do best express their own minds in these their proceedings.

---

[228] Five ships were sent out by the Massachusetts Bay company, upon which a number of the Leiden church were transported over. Rev. Francis Higginson wrote a journal of his voyage on one of these ships, the *Talbot*, which has survived and is reprinted in Alexander Young's *The First Planters of the Colony of the Massachusetts Bay* (Boston, 1846).

A letter of Mr. Sherley's to the Governor: May 25, 1629[229]

Sir, etc. Here are now many of your and our friends from Leiden coming over (who though for the most part, be but a weak company, yet herein, is a good part of that end obtained, which was aimed at, and which hath been so strongly opposed, by some of our former adventurers. But God hath His working in these things, which man cannot frustrate. With them we have also sent some servants in the ship called the *Talbot* that went hence lately; but these come in the *Mayflower*.[230] Mr. Beauchamp, and myself, with Mr. Andrews, and Mr. Hatherley; are with your love and liking joined partners with you, etc. Your deputation we have received, and the goods have been taken up, and sold by your friend, and agent Mr. Allerton; myself having been near 3 months in Holland at Amsterdam and other parts in the Low Countries.

I see further the agreement, you have made with the generality; in which I cannot understand, but you have done very well, both for them, and you, and also for your friends at Leiden. Mr. Beauchamp, Mr. Andrews, Mr. Hatherley and myself, do so like and approve of it as we are willing to join with you, and God directing, and enabling us, will be assisting, and helpful to you, the best that possibly we can. Nay had you not taken this course, I do not see, how you should accomplish the end you first aimed at, and some others endeavored these years past. We know it must keep us from the profit, which otherwise by the blessing of God, and your endeavors might be gained. For most of those that come in May, and these now sent, though I hope honest and good people; yet not like to be helpful to raise profit, but rather, nay certain, must some while be chargeable to you, and us; at which it is likely, had not this wise, and discreet course been taken, many of your generality would have grudged. Again you say well in your letter, and I make no doubt, but you will perform it; that now being but a few, on whom the burthen must be, you will both manage it the better, and set to it more cheerfully, having no discontents, nor contradiction, but so lovingly to join together, in affection and counsel, as God no doubt will bless, and prosper your honest labors, and endeavors. And therefore in all respects I do not see, but you have done marvelously discreetly, and advisedly; and no doubt but it gives all parties good content; I mean that

---

229 This letter is also found in Bradford's *Letterbook*.

230 This was not the same ship that brought the Pilgrims to America in 1620, but simply another ship of the same name.

are reasonable, and honest men, such as make conscience of giving the best satisfaction they be able, for their debts; and that regard not their own particular so much, as the accomplishing of that good end, for which this business was first intended, etc. Thus desiring the Lord to bless, and prosper you, and all yours, and all our honest endeavors; I rest

Your unfeigned, and ever loving friend
James Sherley

March 8, 1629

That I may handle things together, I have put these 2 companies that came from Leiden, in this place; though they came, at 2 several times, yet they both came out of England this year. The former company (being 35 persons) were shipped in May, and arrived here about August. The latter were shipped in the beginning of March, and arrived here the latter end of May 1630. Mr. Sherley's 2 letters, the effect whereof I have before related (as much of them as is pertinent) mentions both. Their charge as Mr. Allerton, brought it in afterwards on account; came to above 550$^£$ besides[231] their fetching hither from Salem, and the Bay where they and their goods were landed, viz., their transportation from Holland to England, and their charges lying there, and passages hither, with clothing provided for them. For I find by account for the one company 125 yards of kersey, 127 ells[232] of linen cloth, shoes 66 pair with many other particulars. The charge of the other company is reckoned on the several families: some 50$^£$, some, 40$^£$, and some 30$^£$, and so more or less, as their number, and expenses were. And besides all this charge their friends and brethren here were, to provide corn and other provisions for them, till they could reap, a crop which was long before; those that came in May, were thus maintained, upward of 16 or 18 months, before they had any harvest of their own, and the other by proportion. And all they could do in the meantime, was to get them some housing, and prepare them grounds to plant on, against the season. And this charge of maintaining them all this while, was little less than the former sum. These things I note more particularly, for sundry regards. First to show a rare example herein of brotherly love, and Christian care in performing their promises, and covenants to their brethren, to, and in a sort beyond their power; that they should

---

[231] The Samuel E. Morison edition of Bradford's *Of Plymouth Plantation* erroneously gives the value as £500.

[232] An ell is 45 inches.

venture so desperately to engage themselves to accomplish this thing, and bear it so cheerfully; for they never demanded, much less had any repayment, of all these great sums thus disbursed. 2ly it must needs be, that there was more than of man, in these achievements; that should thus readily stir up the hearts of such able friends, to join in partnership with them, in such a case, and cleave so faithfully to them as these did, in so great adventures; and the more because the most of them never saw their faces to this day; there being neither kindred, alliance, or other acquaintance, or relations between any of them; than hath been before mentioned; it must needs be, therefore the special work and hand of God. 3ly that these poor people, here in a wilderness, should notwithstanding, be enabled in time, to repay all these engagements, and many more unjustly brought upon them, through the unfaithfulness of some, and many other great losses, which they sustained. Which will be made manifest, if the Lord be pleased, to give life and time. In the meantime I cannot but admire His ways, and works, towards His servants, and humbly desire to bless His holy name for His great mercies hitherto.

The Leiden people being thus come over, and sundry of the generality seeing, and hearing how great the charge was like to be, that was that way to be expended, they began to murmur, and repine at it; notwithstanding the burthen lay on other men's shoulders; especially at the paying of the 3 bushels of corn a year according to the former agreement, when the trade was let for the 6 years aforesaid. But to give them content herein also; it was promised them, that if they could do it in the time, without it; they would never demand it of them, which gave them good content. And indeed it never was paid as will appear by the sequel.

Concerning Mr. Allerton's proceedings about the enlarging, and confirming of their patent, both that at home, and Kennebec; will best appear by another letter of Mr. Sherley's, for though much time, and money was expended about it, yet he left it unaccomplished this year, and came without it.

Most worthy and loving friends, etc.

Some of your letters I received in July, and some since by Mr. Peirce, but till our main business the patent was granted, I could not settle my mind, nor pen to writing. Mr. Allerton was so turmoiled about it, as verily I would not, nor could not have undergone it, if I might have had a thousand pounds; but the Lord so blessed his labors (even beyond expectation in these evil days) as he obtained the love and favor of great men in repute, and place. He got granted from the Earl of Warwick and Sir Ferdinando Gorges, all that Mr. Winslow desired in his letters, to me, and more also, which I leave to him to relate.[233] Then he sued to the King, to confirm their grant, and to make you a corporation; and so to enable you to make, and execute laws, in such large, and ample manner, as the Massachusetts Plantation hath it. Which the King graciously granted; referring it to the Lord Keeper, to give order to the solicitor to draw it up, if there were a precedent for it. So the Lord Keeper furthered it all he could, and also the solicitor (but as Festus said to Paul, with no small sum of money obtained I this freedom) for by the way many riddles must be resolved, and many locks must be opened with the silver, nay the golden key. Then it was to come to the Lord Treasurer, to have his warrant, for freeing the custom for a certain time; but he would not do it, but referred it to the Council table. And there Mr. Allerton attended day by day, when they sat, but could not get his petition read. And by reason of Mr. Peirce his staying, with all the passengers at Bristol; he was forced to leave the further prosecuting of it, to a solicitor.

But there is no fear, nor doubt but it will be granted, for he hath the chief of them to friend. Yet it will be marvelously needful for him to return by the first ship that comes from thence; for if you had this confirmed, then were you complete, and might bear such sway, and government, as were fit for your rank, and place that God hath called you unto. And stop the mouths, of base and scurrilous fellows, that are ready to question, and threaten you in every action you do. And besides if you have the custom free for 7 years inward, and 21 outward, the charge of the patent will be soon recovered, and there is no fear of recovering it. But such things must work by degrees, men cannot hasten it as they would. Therefore we (I write in the behalf of all our partners here) desire you to be earnest with Mr. Allerton to come, and his wife to spare him, this one year more; to finish this great, and weighty business, which we conceive will be much for your good, and I hope for your posterity, and for many generations to come.

Thus much of this letter. It was dated the March 19, 1629.

By which it appears what progress was made herein, and in part what charge it was, and how left unfinished, and some reason of the same; but in truth (as was afterwards apprehended) the main reason was Mr. Allerton's policy, to have an opportunity to be sent over again, for other regards, and for that end procured them thus to write; for it might then well enough have been finished (if not with that clause about the customs, which was Mr.

---

[233] This was the Bradford Patent of 1629/30, which can be found reprinted in Appendix I.

Allerton's, and Mr. Sherley's, device, and not at all thought on by the colony here, nor much regarded) yet it might have been done without it, without all question, having passed the King's hand; nay it was conceived it might then have been done with it, if he had pleased. But covetousness never brings aught home, as the proverb is; for this opportunity being lost, it was never accomplished, but a great deal of money vainly, and lavishly cast away about it, as doth appear upon their accounts. But of this more in its place.

Mr. Allerton gave them great, and just offense in this, (which I had omitted, and almost forgotten) in bringing over this year (for base gain) that unworthy man, and instrument of mischief, Morton, who was sent home but the year before, for his misdemeanors. He not only brought him over, but to the town (as it were to nose them) and lodged him at his own house, and for a while used him as a scribe to do his business; till he was caused to pack him away; so he went to his old nest in the Massachusetts, where it was not long, but by his miscarriage he gave them just occasion to lay hands on him[234]; and he was by them again sent prisoner into England, where he lay a good while in Exeter gaol. For besides his miscarriage here, he was vehemently suspected for the murder of a man, that had adventured moneys with him when he came first into New England. And a warrant was sent from the Lord Chief Justice to apprehend him, by virtue whereof he was by the Governor of the Massachusetts sent into England; and for other his misdemeanors amongst them, they demolished his house, that it might be no longer a roost for such unclean birds to nestle in. Yet he got free again, and write an infamous, and scurrilous book against many godly, and chief men of the country; full of lies, and slanders, and fraught with profane calumnies against their names, and persons[235]; and the ways of God. After sundry years, when the wars were hot in England he came again into the country, and was imprisoned at Boston, for this book, and other things, being grown old in wickedness.[236]

Concerning the rest of Mr. Allerton's instructions, in which they strictly enjoined him, not to exceed above that 50$^£$ in the goods before mentioned,

---

[234] Morton, in *New English Canaan* (Amsterdam, 1637), noted that he was "shipped again for the parts of New Canaan, was put in at Plymouth in the very faces of them, to their terrible amazement to see him at liberty . . ."

[235] This is a reference to Thomas Morton's *New English Canaan* (Amsterdam, 1637).

[236] Morton was allowed to over-winter in Plymouth in 1643. Edward Winslow in a letter to Governor Winthrop in 1643 wrote "Concerning Morton, our Governor gave way that he should winter here, but be gone as soon as winter breaks up. Captain Standish takes great offense thereat, especially that he is so near him as

not to bring any but trading commodities; he followed them not at all but did the quite contrary; bringing over many other sorts, of retail goods (selling what he could by the way, on his own account) and delivering the rest which he said to be theirs into the store; and for trading goods brought but little in comparison, excusing the matter they had laid out much about the Leiden people and patent, etc.; and for other goods they had much of them of their own dealings, without present disbursement and to like effect. And as for passing his bounds and instructions, he laid it on Mr. Sherley, etc., who he said, they might see his mind in his letters. Also that they had set out Ashley at great charge, but next year they should have what trading goods they would send for; if things were now settled, etc. And thus were they put off; indeed Mr. Sherley writ things tending this way, but it is like he was overruled by Mr. Allerton, and hearkened more to him, than to their letters from hence.

Thus he further writes in the former letter:

I see what you write in your letters concerning the overcoming and paying of our debts, which I confess are great, and had need to be carefully look unto; yet no doubt but we joining in love, may soon overcome them; but we must follow it roundly, and to purpose. For if we peddle out the time of our trade, others will step in, and nose us. But we know that you have that acquaintance, and experience in the country, as none have the like; wherefore friends, and partners be no way discouraged with the greatness of the debt, etc. but let us not fulfill the proverb, to bestow 12d on a purse, and put 6d in it. But as you, and we have been at great charge, and undergone much, for settling you there, and to gain experience; so as God shall enable us let us make use of it. And think not with 50$^£$ a year sent you over, to raise such means, as to pay our debts. We see a possibility, of good if you be well supplied, and fully furnished and chiefly if you lovingly agree. I know I write to godly, and wise men, such as have learned to bear one another's infirmities, and rejoice at anyone's prosperities. And if I were able, I would press this the more, because it is hoped by some of your enemies, that you will fall out one, with another, and so overthrow your hopeful business. Nay I have heard it credibly reported, that some have said, that till you be disjointed, by

---

Duxbury, and goeth sometimes a-fowling in his ground. He cannot procure the least respect amongst our people, liveth meanly at 4s. per week and content to drink water, so he may diet at that price." Winslow's letters to John Winthrop are reprinted in *Collections of the Massachusetts Historical Society*, 4th Series 6(1863):162-183.

discontents, and fractions amongst yourselves, it boots not any to go over, in hope of getting, or doing good in those parts. But we hope better things of you; and that you will not only bear one with another; but banish such thoughts, and not suffer them to lodge in your breasts. God grant you may disappoint the hopes of your foes, and procure the hearty desire of yourselves, and friends in this particular.

By this it appears that there was a kind of concurrence between Mr. Allerton and them in these things, and that they gave more regard, to his way, and course in these things, than to the advice from hence, which made him bold to presume above his instructions, and to run on in the course he did, to their greater hurt afterwards, as will appear. These things did much trouble them here, but they well knew not how to help it, being loath to make any breach, or contention hereabout being so premonished as before in the letter above recited. Another more secret cause was herewith concurrent, Mr. Allerton had married the daughter of their Reverend Elder Mr. Brewster (a man beloved, and honored amongst them, and who took great pains in teaching, and dispensing the Word of God unto them), whom they were loath to grieve, or any way offend, so as they bore with much in that respect. And withal Mr. Allerton carried so fair with him, and procured such letters from Mr. Sherley to him, with such applause of Mr. Allerton's wisdom, care, and faithfulness, in the business, and as things stood, none were so fit to send about them as he, and if any should suggest otherwise, it was rather out of envy; or some other sinister respect than otherwise. Besides though private gain I do persuade myself, was some cause to lead Mr. Allerton aside in these beginnings; yet I think, or at least charity carries me to hope that he intended to deal faithfully with them in the main. And had such an opinion of his own ability, and some experience of the benefit that he had made in this singular way, as he conceived he might both raise himself an estate; and also be a means to bring in such profit to Mr. Sherley, (and it may be the rest) as might be as likely to bring in their moneys again with advantage, and it may be sooner than from the general way; or at least it was looked upon by some of them to be a good help thereunto. And that neither he, nor any other did intend to charge the general account with anything that ran in particular: or that Mr. Sherley or any other did purpose but that the genera should be first, and fully supplied. I say charity makes me thus conceive, though things fell out otherwise, and they missed of their aims, and the general suffered abundantly hereby, as will afterwards appear.

Together herewith sorted another business, contrived by Mr. Allerton, and them there, without any knowledge of the partners: and so far proceeded in as they were constrained to allow thereof, and join in the same, though they had no great liking of it, but feared what might be the event of the same. I shall relate it in further part of Mr. Sherley's letter as followeth[237]:

I am to acquaint you that we have thought good to join with one Edward Ashley (a man I think that some of you know) but it is only of that place whereof he hath a patent in Mr. Beauchamp's name. And to that end have furnished him with large provisions, etc. Now if you please to be partners with us in this, we are willing you shall. For after we heard how forward Bristol men, (and as I hear some able men of his own kindred) have been, to stock, and supply him hoping of profit, we thought it fitter for us to lay hold of such an opportunity, and to keep a kind of running plantation, than others who have not borne the burthen of settling a plantation, as we have done. And he on the other side, like an understanding young man, thought it better to join with those, that had means by a plantation, to supply, and back him there, rather than strangers, that look but only after profit. Now it is not known that you, are partners with him; but only we 4, Mr. Andrews, Mr. Beauchamp, myself, and Mr. Hatherley, who desired to have the patent in consideration of our great loss, we have already sustained in settling the first plantation there, so we agreed together to take it in our names. And now as I said before, if you please to join with us, we are willing you should; Mr. Allerton had no power from you to make this new contract, neither was he willing to do anything therein, without your consent, and approbation. Mr. William Peirce is joined with us in this, for we thought it very convenient, because of landing Ashley and his goods there, if God please, and he will bend his course accordingly.

He hath a new boat with him, and boards to make another, with 4 or 5 lusty fellows, whereof one is a carpenter. Now in case you are not willing in this particular to join with us; fearing the charge and doubting the success, yet thus much we entreat of you, to afford him, all the help you can, either by men, commodities, or boats; yet not but that we will pay you for anything he hath; and we desire you to keep the accounts, apart though you join with us; because there is (as you see other partners in this than the other). So for all men's wages, boats' hire, or commodities, which we shall have of you, make

---

[237] This letter is found in full in Bradford's *Letterbook*.

him debtor for it; and what you shall have of him, make the plantation, or yourselves debtor for it to him, and so there will need no mingling of the accounts.

And now loving friends, and partners, if you join in Ashley's patent, and business, though we have laid out, the money, and taken up much to stock this business, and the other; yet I think it conscionable, and reasonable, that you should bear your shares, and proportion of the stock. If not by present money, yet by securing us for so much as it shall come to; for it is not barely the interest that is to be allowed, and considered of, but also the adventure. Though I hope in God, by His blessing, and your honest endeavors, it may soon be paid; yet the years that this partnership holds is not long, nor many; let all therefore lay it to heart, and make the best use of the time that possibly we can, and let every man put to his shoulder, and the burthen will be the lighter; I know you are so honest, and conscionable men, as you will consider hereof and return such an answer as may give good satisfaction. There is none of us that would venture as we have done, were it not to strengthen and settle you, more than our own particular profit.

There is no likelihood of doing any good in buying the debt for the purchase, I know some will not abate the interest, and therefore let it run its course; they are to be paid yearly, and so I hope they shall according to agreement. The Lord grant that our loves, and affections, may still be united, and knit together. And so we rest your ever loving friends,

James Sherley
Timothy Hatherley

Bristol, March 19, 1629

This matter of the buying the debts of the purchase was part of Mr. Allerton's instructions, and in many of them, it might hay been done to good profit for ready pay (as some were), but M Sherley had no mind to it. But this business about Ashley did not a little trouble them; for though he had wit, and ability enough manage the business, yet some of them knew him to be a very profane young man; and he had for some time lived among the Indians as a savage, and went naked amongst them, and used their manners (in which time he got their language). So they feared might still run into evil courses (though he promised better) and God would not prosper his ways.

As soon as he was landed at the place intended, called Penobscot, some 4 score leagues from this place, he write (and afterwards came) for to desire to be supplied with wampampeag, corn against winter, and other things. They considered these were their chief commodities, and would be continually needed by him, and it would much prejudice their own trade at Kennebec if they did not join with him in the ordering of things, if I they should supply him. And on the other hand, if they refused to join with him, and also to afford any supply unto him, they should greatly offend their abovenamed friends, and might haply lose them hereby, and he and Mr. Allerton laying their crafty wits together might get supplies of things elsewhere. Besides they considered that if they joined not in the business, they knew Mr. Allerton would be with them in it, and so would swim (as it were) between both to the prejudice of both, but of themselves especially. For they had reason to think this business, was chiefly of his contriving, and Ashley was a man fit for his turn, and dealings. So they to prevent a worse mischief resolved to join in the business; and gave him supplies, in what they could, and overlooked his proceedings as well as they could; the which they did the better by joining an honest young man[238] (that came from Leiden with him as his fellow in some sort and not merely as a servant), which young man being discreet, and one whom they could trust, they so instructed, as kept Ashley in some good measure within bounds. And so they returned their answer to their friends in England that they accepted of their motion and joined with them in Ashley's business, and yet withal told them what their fears were concerning him.

But when they came to have full notice of all the goods brought them that year, they saw they fell very short of trading goods, and Ashley far better supplied than themselves, so as they were forced to buy of the fishermen to furnish themselves; yea, and cottons, and kerseys, and other such like cloth (for want of trading cloth) of Mr. Allerton himself, and so to put away a great part of their beaver, (at under rate in the country) which they should have sent home, to help to discharge their great engagements, which was to their great vexation, but Mr. Allerton prayed them to be content, and the next year they might have what they would write for. And their engagements of this year were great indeed when they came to know them (which was not wholly till 2 years after) and that which made them the more, Mr. Allerton had taken up some large sums at Bristol at 50$^£$ per cent again; which he excused, that he was forced to it: because otherwise he could (at the spring of year get no goods transported) such were their envy against their trade; but whether this was any more than an excuse, some of them doubted, but however the burden did lie on their backs and they must bear it as they did many heavy loads more in the end.

---

[238] Thomas Willet. (Bradford). For a brief biography of Willet, see the *New England Historic and Genealogical Register* 61:157-164.

This paying of 50$^£$ per cent and difficulty of having their goods transported by the fishing ships at the first of the year, (as was believed) which was the chief season for trade, put them upon another project. Mr. Allerton after the fishing season was over, light of a bargain of salt, at a good fishing place, and bought it, which came to about 113$^£$ and shortly after he might have had 30$^£$ clear profit for it, without any more trouble about it. But Mr. Winslow coming that way from Kennebec, and some of their partners with him in the bark, they met with Mr. Allerton and falling into discourse with him, they stayed him from selling the salt; and resolved, if it might please the rest, to keep it for themselves, and to hire a ship in the west country to come on fishing for them on shares according to the custom; and seeing she might have her salt here ready, and a stage ready built and fitted where the salt lay safely landed and housed instead of bringing salt they might stow her full of trading goods, as bread, peas, cloth, etc. and so they might have a full supply of goods, without paying freight, and in due season, which might turn greatly to their advantage. Coming home this was propounded, and considered on, and approved by all, but the Governor who had no mind to it, seeing they had always lost by fishing; but the rest were so earnest, as thinking that they might gain well by the fishing in this way; and if they should but save, yea or lose something by it, the other benefit would be advantage enough. So seeing their earnestness he gave way and it was referred to their friends in England to allow, or disallow it. Of which more in its place.

Upon the consideration of the business, about the patent, and in what state it was left, as is before remembered, and Mr. Sherley's earnest pressing to have Mr. Allerton to come over again to finish it, and perfect the accounts, etc. It was concluded to send him over this year again, though it was with some fear and jealousy, yet he gave them fair words and promises of well performing all their businesses according to their directions, and to mend his former errors. So he was accordingly sent with full instructions for all things, with large letters to Mr. Sherley and the rest, both about Ashley's business and their own supply with trading commodities, and how much it did concern them to be furnished therewith, and what they had suffered for want thereof; and of what little use other goods were in comparison thereof; and so likewise about this fishing ship, to be thus hired; and fraught with trading goods; which might both supply them, and Ashley, and the benefit thereof; which was left to their consideration, to hire, and set her out, or not; but in no case not to send any, except she was thus freighted with trading goods. But what these things came to will appear in the next year's passages.

I had like to have omitted another passage that fell out the beginning of this year. There was one Mr. Ralph Smith, and his wife, and family, that came over into the Bay of the Massachusetts, and sojourned at present, with some straggling people, that lived at Nantasket, here being a boat of this place, putting in there on some occasion; he earnestly desired that they would give him and his passage for Plymouth, and some such things as they could well carry; having before heard that there was likelihood he might procure house room for some time, till he should resolve to settle there if he might, or elsewhere as God should dispose, for he was weary of being in that uncouth place, and in a poor house that would neither keep him nor his goods dry. So seeing him to be a grave man, and understood he had been a minister, though they had no order for any such thing; yet they presumed and brought him, he was here accordingly kindly entertained, and housed, and had the rest of his goods and servants sent for, and exercised his gifts amongst them, and afterwards was chosen into the ministry and so remained for sundry years.

It was before noted that sundry of those that came from Leiden, came over in the ships that came to Salem, where Mr. Endecott had chief command; and by infection that grew among the passengers at sea, it spread also among them ashore, of which many died, some of the scurvy, other of an infectious fever, which continued some time amongst them, though our people through God's goodness, escaped it. Upon which occasion he write hither for some help, understanding here was one that had some skill that way, and had cured divers of the scurvy, and others of other diseases by letting blood, and other means. Upon which his request the Governor here sent him unto them, and also write to him from whom he received an answer; the which, because it is brief, and shows the beginning of their acquaintance, and closing in the truth, and ways of God, I thought it not unmeet, nor without use, here to insert it, and another showing the beginning of their fellowship, and church estate there.

Being as followeth.

Right Worthy Sir

It is a thing not usual, that servants to one master, and of the same household should be strangers; I assure you I desire it not, nay to speak more plainly I cannot be so to you. God's People are all marked with one, and the same mark, and sealed with one and the same seal; and have for the main, one and the same heart, guided by one and same spirit of truth; and where this is, there can be no discord, nay here must needs be sweet harmony. And the same request (with you) I make unto the Lord, that we may as Christian brethren be united, by a heavenly and unfeigned love; bending all our hearts and forces, in furthering a work beyond our strength, with reverence and fear, fastening our eyes always on Him: that only is able to direct, and prosper all our ways. I acknowledge myself much bound to you, for your kind love, and care, in sending Mr. Fuller, among us; and rejoice much that I am by him satisfied touching your judgments of the outward form of God's worship. It is as far as I can gather, no other than is warranted by the evidence of truth. And the same which I have professed, and maintained, ever since the Lord in mercy revealed Himself unto me. Being far from the common report that hath been spread of you touching that particular; but God's children must not look for less here below, and it is the great mercy of God, that He strengthens them, to go through with it. I shall not need at this time to be tedious unto you, for God willing I purpose to see your face shortly. In the meantime, I humbly take my leave of you, committing you to the Lord's blessed protection, and rest

Your assured loving friend
John Endecott

Naumkeag, May 11, Anno 1629

> This second letter showeth their proceedings in their church affairs
> at Salem, which was the 2 church erected in these parts; and
> afterwards the Lord established many more in sundry places.[239]

Sir, I make bold to trouble you with a few lines, for to certify you how it hath pleased God to deal with us, since you heard from us. How notwithstanding all opposition that hath been here, and elsewhere; it hath pleased God to lay a foundation, the which I hope is agreeable to His Word in everything. The 20 of July, it pleased the Lord to move the heart of our Governor to set it apart for a solemn day of humiliation, for the choice of a pastor, and teacher. The former part of the day being spent, in prayer and teaching; the latter part about the election, which was after this manner. The persons thought on (who had been ministers in England) were demanded concerning their callings. They acknowledged there was a twofold calling, the one an inward calling, when the Lord moved the heart of a man to take that calling upon him, and fitted him with gifts for the same; the second was an

---

[239]   This letter is found in full in Bradford's *Letterbook*.

outward calling which was from the people, when a company of believers are joined together in covenant, to walk together in all the ways of God. And every member (being men) are to have a free voice in the choice of their officers, etc. Now we being persuaded that these 2 men, were so qualified, as the Apostle speaks to Timothy, where he saith a bishop must be blameless, sober, apt to teach, etc., I think I may say, as the eunuch said unto Philip, what should let from being baptized, seeing there was water and he believed? So these 2 servants of God, clearing all things, by their answers (and being thus fitted) we saw no reason but we might freely give our voices for their election, after this trial. So Mr. Skelton was chosen pastor, and Mr. Higginson to be teacher; and they accepting the choice, Mr. Higginson with 3 or 4 of the gravest members of the church laid their hands, on Mr. Skelton, using prayer therewith. This being done, there was imposition of hands on Mr. Higginson also. And since that time, Thursday (being as I take it the 6 of August) is appointed for another day of humiliation, for the choice of elders, and deacons, and ordaining of them.

And now good Sir I hope that you, and the rest of God's people (who are acquainted with the ways of God) with you; will say that here was a right foundation laid, and that these 2 blessed servants of the Lord, came in at the door, and not at the window. Thus I have made bold to trouble you with these few lines; desiring you to remember us, etc. And so rest

At your service in what I may,
Charles Gott
Salem, July 30, 1629

Ashley being well supplied had quickly gathered a good parcel of beaver, and like a crafty pate, he sent it all home; and would not pay for the goods he had, had of the plantation here, but let them stand still on the score, and took up still more; now though they well enough knew his aim, yet they let him go on, and writ of it into England; but partly the beaver they received, and sold (of which they were sensible) and partly by Mr. Allerton's extolling of him; they cast more how to supply him than the plantation, and something to upbraid them with it. They were forced to buy him a bark also, and to furnish her with a master, and men, to transport his corn, and provisions (of which he had put off much; for the Indians of those parts have no corn growing) and at harvest after corn is ready the weather grows foul, and the seas dangerous, so as he could do little good with his shallop for that purpose.

They looked earnestly for a timely supply this spring, by the fishing ship which they expected, (and had been at charge to keep a stage for her) but none came; nor any supply heard of for them; at length they heard some supply was sent to Ashley by a fishing ship. At which they something marveled, and the more that they had no letters either from Mr. Allerton or Mr. Sherley; so they went on in their business as well as they could. At last they heard of Mr. Peirce his arrival in the Bay of the Massachusetts (who brought passengers, and goods thither). They presently sent, a shallop, conceiving, they should have something by him. But he told them he had none; and a ship was set out on fishing, but after 11 week beating at sea, she met with such foul weather as she was forced back again for England, and the season being over, gave off the voyage. Neither did he hear of much goods in her for the plantation, or that she did belong to them, for he had heard something from Mr. Allerton tending that way. But Mr. Allerton had bought another ship, and was to come in her, and was to fish for bass to the eastward, and to bring goods, etc.

These things did much trouble them, and half astonish them; Mr. Winslow having been to the eastward, brought news of the like things, with some more particulars, and that it was like Mr. Allerton would be late before he came. At length they having an opportunity, resolved to send Mr. Winslow (with what beaver they had ready into England) to see how the squares went, being very jealous of these things, and Mr. Allerton's courses; and writ such letters, and gave him such instructions, as they thought meet, and if he found things not well, to discharge Mr. Allerton for being any longer agent for them, or to deal any more in the business, and to see how the accounts stood, etc.

About the middle of summer arrives Mr. Hatherley in the Bay of the Massachusetts (being one of the partners) and came over in the same ship, that was set out on fishing (called the *Friendship*). They presently sent to him; making no question; but now they had goods come, and should know how, all things stood. But they found the former news true, how this ship had been so long at sea, and spent and spoiled her provisions, and overthrown the voyage. And he being sent over by the rest of the partners, to see how things went here, being at Bristol with Mr. Allerton in the ship bought (called the *White Angel*) ready to set sail; overnight came a messenger from Barnstaple to Mr. Allerton, and told him of the return of the ship, and what had befallen. And he not knowing what to do having a great charge under hand, the ship lying at his rates, and now ready to set sail: got him to go and discharge the ship, and take order for the goods. To be short they found Mr. Hatherley something reserved, and troubled in himself (Mr. Allerton not being there) not knowing how to dispose of the goods till he came. But he heard he was arrived with the other ship to the eastward and expected his coming. But he told them there was not much for them in this ship, only 2 packs of Barnstaple rugs and 2 hogsheads of metheglin[240], drawn out in wooden flackets (but when these flackets, came to be received, there was left but 6 gallons of the 2 hogsheads, it being drunk up under the name leakage, and so lost. But the ship was filled with goods for sundry gentlemen, and others that were come to plant in the Massachusetts, for which they paid freight by the tun. And this was all the satisfaction they could have at present. So they brought this small parcel of goods and returned with this news, and a letter as obscure; which made them much to marvel thereat. The letter was as followeth:

Gentlemen, partners, and loving friends, etc.

---

[240] Spiced mead, an alcoholic liquor made from honey and water with spices added; typically used as a medicated drink.

Briefly thus, we have this year, set forth a fishing ship, and a trading ship, which latter we have bought; and so have disbursed a great deal of money, as may, and will appear by the accounts. And because this ship (called the *White Angel)* is to act 2 parts (as I may say) fishing for bass, and trading; and that while Mr. Allerton was employed about the trading, the fishing might suffer, by carelessness, or neglect of the sailors. We have entreated your and our loving friend, Mr. Hatherley, to go over with him, knowing he will be a comfort to Mr. Allerton, a joy to you, to see a careful, and loving friend; and a great stay to the business; and so great content to us, that if it should please God the one should fail (as God forbid) yet the other would keep both reckonings, and things upright. For we are now out great sums of money, as they will acquaint you withal, etc. When we were out but 4 or 5 hundred pounds apiece, we looked not much after it, but left it to you and your agent, (who without flattery, deserveth infinite thanks, and commendations both of you, and us for his pains, etc.). But now we are out double, nay treble apiece some of us, etc. Which makes us both write and send over, our friend (Mr. Hatherley) whom we pray you to entertain kindly (of which we doubt not of). The main end of sending him, is to see the state, and account, of all the business; of all which, we pray you inform him fully, though the ship, and business wait for it, and him. For we should take it very unkindly, that we should entreat him, to take such a journey, and that when it pleaseth God he returns, he could not give us content, and satisfaction, in this particular, through default of any of you. But we hope you will so order business, as neither he, nor we shall have cause to complain, but to do, as we have ever done, think well of you all, etc. I will not promise, but shall endeavor, and hope to effect the full desire, and grant of your patent, and that ere it be long: I would not have you take anything unkindly. I have not writ out of jealousy of any unjust dealing. Be you all kindly saluted in the Lord, so I rest,

Yours in what I may
James Sherley

March 25, 1630

It needs not be thought strange that these things should amaze and trouble them; first that this fishing ship should be set out, and fraught with other men's goods, and scarce any of theirs; seeing their main end was (as is before remembered) to bring them a full supply, and their special order not to set out any except this was done. And now a ship to come on their account, clean contrary to their both end, and order, was a mystery they could not understand, and so much the worse, seeing she had such ill success, as to lose both her voyage, and provisions. The 2 thing, that another ship should be bought and sent out on new designs, a thing not so much as once thought on by any here, much less not a word intimated or spoken of by any either by word, or letter. Neither could they imagine why this should be. Bass fishing was never looked at by them, but as soon as ever they heard on it, they looked at it as a vain thing, that would certainly turn to loss. And for Mr. Allerton to follow any trade for them, it was never in their thoughts. And 3ly, that their friends should complain of disbursements, and yet run into such great things, and charge of shipping, and new projects, of their own heads, not only without, but against all order, and advice: was to them very strange; and 4ly that all these matters of so great charge, and employments, should be thus wrapped up in a brief and obscure letter, they knew not what to make of it. But amidst all their doubts they must have patience till Mr. Allerton, and Mr. Hatherley should come. In the meantime, Mr. Winslow was gone for England; and others of them were forced to follow their employments with the best means they had, till they could hear of better.

At length Mr. Hatherley, and Mr. Allerton came unto them (after they had delivered their goods) and finding them stricken with some sadness about these things, Mr. Allerton told them that the ship *White Angel* did not belong to them, nor their account, neither need they have anything to do with her, except they would. And Mr. Hatherley confirmed the same, and said that they would have had him to have had a part, but he refused, but he made question whether they would not turn her upon the general account, if there came loss (as he now saw was like) seeing Mr. Allerton laid down this course, and put them on this project; but for the fishing ship, he told them they need not be so much troubled for he had her accounts here, and showed them that her first setting out, came not much to exceed 600$^£$, as they might see by the account, which he showed them; and for this later voyage, it would arise to profit, by the freight of the goods, and the sale of some cattle which he shipped and had already sold, and was to be paid for partly here and partly by bills into England, so as they should not have this put on their account at all, except they would. And for the former, he had sold so much goods out of her in England, and employed the money in this 2 voyage, as it together with such goods, and implements as Mr. Allerton must need about his fishing, would rise to a good part of the money; for he must have the salt, and nets, also spikes, nails, etc. All which would rise to near 400$^£$. So with the bearing of their parts of the rest of the losses (which would not be much above 200$^£$) they would clear them of this whole account. Of which motion they were glad, not being willing to have any accounts lie upon them, but about their trade; which made them willing to hearken thereunto, and demand of Mr. Hatherley, how he could make this good if they should agree thereunto; he told them he was sent over as their agent, and had this order from them that whatsoever he, and Mr. Allerton did together, they would stand to it, but they would not allow of what Mr. Allerton did alone, except they liked it, but if he did it alone they would not gainsay it. Upon which they sold to him, and Mr. Allerton all the rest of the goods, and gave them present possession of them, and a writing was made, and confirmed under both Mr. Hatherley's, and Mr. Allerton's hands, to the effect aforesaid. And Mr. Allerton being best acquainted with the people, sold away presently, all such goods as he had no need of for the fishing, as 9 shallop sails, made of good new canvas, and the rodes[241] for them being all new with sundry such useful goods, for ready beaver by Mr. Hatherley's allowance. And thus they thought they had well provided for themselves. Yet they rebuked Mr. Allerton very much for running into these courses, fearing the success of them.

Mr. Allerton, and Mr. Hatherley brought to the town with them, after he had sold what he could abroad, a great quantity of other goods besides trading commodities as linen cloth, bedticks, stockings, tape, pins, rugs, etc.; and told them they were to have them if they would. But they told Mr. Allerton that they had forbid him before, for bringing any such on their account; it would hinder their trade and returns. But he and Mr. Hatherley said if they would not have them they would sell them themselves, and take corn for what they could not otherwise sell. They told them they might if they had order for it. The goods of one sort, and other came to upward of 500£.

After these things Mr. Allerton went to the ship about his bass fishing, and Mr. Hatherley (according to his order) after he took knowledge how things stood at the plantation, (of all which they informed him fully) he then desired a boat of them to go and visit the trading houses, both Kennebec, and Ashley at Penobscot, for so they in England had enjoined him. They accordingly furnished him with a boat and men for the voyage, and acquainted him plainly, and thoroughly with all things, by which he had good content, and satisfaction, and saw plainly that Mr. Allerton played his own game, and ran a course not only to the great wrong, and detriment of the plantation (who employed, and trusted him) but abused them in England also, in possessing them with prejudice against the plantation: as that they would never be able to repay their moneys (in regard of their great charge). But if they would follow his advice, and projects, he, and Ashley (being well supplied) would quickly bring in their moneys with good advantage. Mr. Hatherley

---

[241]   An anchor cable or rope.

disclosed also, a further project about the setting out of this ship, the *White Angel*, how she being well fitted with good ordnance, and known to have made a great fight at sea (when she belonged to Bristol) and carried away the victory; they had agreed (by Mr. Allerton's means) that after she had brought a freight of goods here into the country, and fraught herself with fish, she should go from hence, to Port of Port[242]; and there be sold, both ship, goods, and ordnance, and had for this end had speech with a factor of those parts, beforehand, to whom she should have been consigned. But this was prevented at this time (after it was known) partly by the contrary advice given, by their friends here, to Mr. Allerton, and Mr. Hatherley, showing how it might ensnare their friends in England (being men of estate) if it should come to be known; and for the plantation they did, and would disallow it and protest against it. And partly by their bad voyage, for they both came too late, to do any good for fishing, and also had such a wicked and drunken company, as neither Mr. Allerton, nor any else could rule, as Mr. Hatherley to his great grief, and shame, saw, and beheld, and all others that came near them.

Ashley likewise was taken in a trap, (before Mr. Hatherley returned) for trading powder, and shot, with the Indians; and was seized upon by some in authority, who also would have confiscated above, a thousand weight of beaver, but the goods were freed, for the Governor here made it appear, by a bond under Ashley's hand, wherein he was bound to them, in 500$^£$ not to trade any munition with the Indians, or otherwise to abuse himself. It was also manifest against him that he had committed uncleanness with Indian women, (things that they feared at his first employment, which made them take this strict course with him in the beginning). So to be short they got their goods freed, but he was sent home prisoner. And that I may make an end concerning him, after some time of imprisonment in the Fleet, by the means of friends he was set at liberty; and intended to come over again. But the Lord prevented it; for he had a motion made to him, by some merchants to go into Russia, because he had such good skill in the beaver trade; the which he accepted of, and in his return home was cast away at sea, this was his end.

Mr. Hatherley fully understanding the state of all things, had good satisfaction; and could well inform them how all things stood between Mr. Allerton and the plantation. Yea he found that Mr. Allerton had got within him, and got all the goods into his own hands, for which Mr. Hatherley stood jointly engaged to them here, about the ship *Friendship*, as also most of the freight money, besides some of his own particular estate; about which

---

[242]   Oporto, Portugal.

more will appear hereafter. So he returned to England, and they sent a good quantity of beaver with him to the rest of the partners; so both he, and it was very welcome unto them.

Mr. Allerton followed his affairs, and returned with his *White Angel*, being no more employed by the plantation, but these businesses, were not ended till many years after; nor well understood of a long time, but folded up in obscurity, and kept in the clouds; to the great loss, and vexation of the plantation, who in the end were, (for peace sake) forced to bear the unjust burthen of them, to their almost undoing. As will appear if God give life to finish this history.

They sent their letters also by Mr. Hatherley to the partners there, to show them how Mr. Hatherley, and Mr. Allerton had discharged them, of the *Friendship's* account; and that they both affirmed, that the *White Angel* did not at all belong to them, and therefore desired that their account might not be charged therewith. Also they write to Mr. Winslow their agent, that he in like manner should (in their names) protest against it, if any such thing should be intended; for they would never yield to the same. As also to signify to them, that they renounced Mr. Allerton wholly, for being their agent or to have anything to do in any of their business.

This year John Billington the elder (one that came over with the first) was arraigned; and both by grand, and petty jury found guilty of willful murder; by plain and notorious evidence. And was for the same accordingly executed.[243] This as it was the first execution amongst them, so was it a

---

[243]   William Hubbard, in his *General History of New England* (17th century manuscript, first published in 1815) provides the most detailed extant account of this murder: "About September 1630, was one Billington executed at Plymouth for murder. When the world was first peopled, and but one family to do that, there was yet too many to live peaceably together; so when this wilderness began first to be peopled by the English, when there was but one poor town, another Cain was found therein, who maliciously slew his neighbor in the field, as he accidentally met him, as himself was going to shoot deer. The poor fellow perceiving the intent of this Billington, his mortal enemy, sheltered himself behind trees as well as he could for awhile; but the other not being so ill a marksman as to miss his aim, made a shot at him, and struck him on the shoulder, with which he died soon after. The murderer expected that either for want of powder to execute for capital offenses, or for want of people to increase the plantation, he should have his life spared; but justice otherwise determined, and rewarded him, the first murderer of his neighbor there, with the deserved punishment of death, for a warning to others."

matter of great sadness unto them; they used all due means about his trial, and took the advice of Mr. Winthrop, and other the ablest gentlemen in Bay of the Massachusetts, that were then newly come over, who concurred with them that he ought to die, and the land to be purged from blood. He and some of his, had been often punished for miscarriages before, being one of the profanest families amongst them; they came from London, and I know not by what friends shuffled into their company. His fact was, that he waylaid a young man, one John Newcomen[244] (about a former quarrel) and shot him with a gun, whereof he died.

Having by a providence a letter, or two that came to my hands concerning the proceedings of their reverend friends in the Bay of the Massachusetts, who were lately come over, I thought it not amiss here to insert them, (so far as is pertinent and may be useful for after times) before I conclude this year.[245]

Sir, being at Salem the 25 of July, being the Sabbath, after the evening exercise, Mr. Johnson received a letter from the Governor Mr. John Winthrop, manifesting the hand of God to be upon them; and against them at Charlestown, in visiting them with sickness, and taking divers from amongst them, not sparing the righteous, but partaking with the wicked in these bodily judgments. It was therefore, by his desire, taken into the godly consideration of the best here, what was to be done to pacify the Lord's wrath, etc. Where it was concluded, that the Lord was to be sought in righteousness, and to that end the 6 day (being Friday) of this present week, is set apart, that they may humble themselves, before God, and seek Him in His ordinances; and that then also such godly persons that are amongst them, and known each to other, may publicly at the end of their exercise, make known their godly desire, and practice the same; viz. solemnly to enter into covenant with the Lord to walk in His ways. And since they are so disposed of in their outward estates, as to live in three distinct places; each having men of ability amongst

---

[244] Thomas Morton makes a brief mention of John Billington in his *New English Canaan* (Amsterdam, 1637), giving him the nickname "Old Woodman": "There is a very useful stone in the land, and as yet there is found out but one place where they may be had, in the whole country. Old Woodman (that was choked at Plymouth after he had played the unhappy marksman when he was pursued by a careless fellow that was new come into the land) they say labored to get a patent of it to himself."

[245] The following letters were written by Edward Winslow and Samuel Fuller, and are found in full in Bradford's *Letterbook*.

them, there to observe the day, and become 3 distinct bodies. Not then intending rashly to proceed to the choice of officers, or the admitting of any other to their society than a few, to wit, such as are well known unto them; promising after to receive in such by confession of faith, as shall appear to be fitly qualified for that estate. They do earnestly entreat, that the Church of Plymouth would set apart the same day, for the same ends, beseeching the Lord, as to withdraw His hand of correction from them, so as also to establish, and direct them in His ways. And though the time be short, we pray you be provoked to this godly work, seeing the causes are so urgent, wherein God will be honored, and they, and we undoubtedly have sweet comfort.

Be you all kindly saluted, etc.

Your brethren in Christ, etc.

Salem, July 26, 1630

Sir, etc. The sad news here is, that many are sick, and many are dead, the Lord in mercy look upon them.[246] Some are here entered into church covenant, the first were 4 namely the Governor Mr. John Winthrop, Mr. Johnson, Mr. Dudley, and Mr. Wilson; since that 5 more are joined unto

---

[246] Doctor Samuel Fuller, author of this letter, had been sent by Plymouth to assist the newly-arrived colonists, many of whom were quite sick. Thomas Morton, in his *New English Canaan* (Amsterdam, 1637), reported much more cynically on Fuller's visit: "[H]e was bred a butcher [Doctor Samuel Fuller's father was a butcher]. He wears a long beard, and a garment like the Greek that begged in Paul's Church. This new made doctor comes to Salem to congratulate: where he finds some are newly come from sea, and ill at ease. He takes the patient, and the urinal: views the state there: finds the *Crasis Syptomes*, and the *attomi natantes*: and tells the patient that his disease was wind, which he had taken by gaping, feasting, overboard at sea, but he would quickly ease him of that grief, and quite expel the wind. And this he did perform, with his gifts he had: and then he handled the patient so handsomely, that he eased him of all the wind, he had in an instant. [i.e. he killed the patient]. And yet I hope this man may be forgiven, if he were made a fitting plant for heaven. How he went to work with his gifts is a question: yet he did a great cure for Captain Littleworth, he cured him of a disease called a wife: and yet I hope this man may be forgiven, if she were made a fitting plant for heaven. By this means he was allowed 4 p. a month, and the surgeon's chest, and made physician general of Salem: where he exercised his gifts so well, that of full 42 that there he took to cure, there is not one has more cause to complain, or can say black's his eye. This saved Captain Littleworth's credit, that

them, and others, it is like, will add themselves to them daily; the Lord increase them, both in number, and in holiness for His mercy's sake. Here is a gentleman one Mr. Coddington (a Boston man) who told me, that Mr. Cotton's charge at Hampton was, that they should take advice of them at Plymouth, and should do nothing to offend them. Here are divers honest Christians, that are desirous to see us, some out of love which they bear to us, and the good persuasion they have of us, others to see whether we be so ill, as they have heard of us. We have a name of holiness, and love to God, and His saints, the Lord make us more and more answerable, and that it may be more than a name, or else it will do us no good; be you lovingly saluted, and all the rest of our friends. The Lord Jesus bless us, and the whole Israel of God. Amen.

Your loving brother, etc.

Charlestown

August 12, 1630

Thus out of small beginnings greater things have been produced, by His hand that made all things of nothing, and gives being to all things that are; and as one small candle may light a thousand; so the light here kindled hath shone unto many, yea in some sort to our whole nation; let the glorious name of Jehovah have all the praise.

---

had trucked away the vittles: though it brought forth a scandal on the country by it, and then I hope this man may be forgiven, if they were all made fitting plants for heaven. But in mine opinion, he deserves to be set upon a palfrey, and led up and down in triumph through New Canaan, with a collar of Jurdans about his neck, as was one of like dessert in Richard the Second's time through the streets of London, that men might know where to find a quacksalver."

Ashley being thus by the hand of God taken away; and Mr. Allerton discharged of his employment for them; their business began again to run in one channel, and themselves better able to guide the same; Penobscot being wholly now at their disposing, and though Mr. William Peirce, had a part there as is before noted, yet now as things stood, he was glad to have his money repaid him, and stand out. Mr. Winslow whom they had sent over, sent them over some supply as soon as he could; and afterwards when he came (which was somewhat long by reason of business) he brought a large supply, of suitable goods with him, by which their trading was well carried on. But by no means either he, or the letters they write, could take off Mr. Sherley, and the rest from putting both the *Friendship* and *White Angel* on the general account; which caused continual contention between them as will more appear.

I shall insert a letter of Mr. Winslow's about these things, being as followeth:

Sir,

It fell out by God's providence, that I received, and brought your letters per Mr. Allerton from Bristol, to London, and do much fear what will be the event of things. Mr. Allerton intended to prepare the ship again, to set forth upon fishing. Mr. Sherley, Mr. Beauchamp, and Mr. Andrews, they renounce all particulars; protesting but for us they would never have adventured one penny into those parts; Mr. Hatherley stands inclinable to either. And whereas you write that he, and Mr. Allerton, have taken the *White Angel* upon them, for their partners here, they profess they neither gave any such order, nor will make it good. If themselves will clear the account and do it, all shall be well; what the event of these things will be I know not. The Lord so direct and assist us, as He may not be dishonored by our divisions. I hear (per a friend) that I was much blamed for speaking what I heard in the spring of the year, concerning the buying and setting forth of the ship[247]; sure if I should not have told you, what I heard so peremptorily reported (which report I offered now to prove at Bristol) I should have been unworthy my employment. And concerning the commission so long since given to Mr. Allerton; the truth is, the thing we feared is come upon us; for Mr. Sherley, and the rest have it, and will not deliver it, that being the ground of our agents' credit to procure such great sums. But I look for bitter words, hard thoughts, and sour looks, from sundry, as well for writing this, as reporting the former. I would I had a more thankful employment; but I hope a good conscience shall make it comfortable, etc. Thus far he dated November 16, 1631

The commission abovesaid was given by them under their hand and seal when Mr. Allerton was first employed by them, and redemanded of him in the year 1629 when they began to suspect his course; he told them it was amongst his papers, but he would seek it out and give it them before he went; but he being ready to go it was demanded again; he said he could not find it, but it was amongst his papers, which he must take with him, and he would send it by the boat from the eastward; but there it could not be had neither, but he would seek it up at sea. But whether Mr. Sherley had it before or after, it is not certain; but having it he would not let it go but keeps it to this day. Wherefore even amongst friends men had need be careful whom they trust, and not let things of this nature lie long unrecalled.

Some parts of Mr. Sherley's letter about
those things in which the truth
is best manifested

Sir: Yours I have received, by our loving friends, Mr. Allerton, and Mr. Hatherley, who blessed be God after a long and dangerous passage with the ship *Angel*, are safely come to Bristol. Mr. Hatherley is come up, but Mr. Allerton I have not yet seen; we thank you, and are very glad you have dissuaded him from his Spanish voyage, and that he did not go on in these designs he intended, for we did all utterly dislike of that course, as also of the fishing that the *Friendship* should have performed; for we wished him to sell the salt and were unwilling to have him undertake so much business, partly for the ill success we formerly had in those affairs, and

---

[247] This was about the selling the ship in Spain. (Bradford).

partly being loath to disburse so much money. But he persuaded us, this must be one way, that must repay us; for the plantation would be long in doing of it. Nay to my remembrance, he doubted you could not be able with the trade there, to maintain your charge, and pay us. And for this very cause he brought us on that business with Ed Ashley for he was a stranger to us, etc.

For the fishing ship we are sorry it proves so heavy, and will be willing to bear our parts. What Mr. Hatherley, and Mr. Allerton have done, no doubt but themselves will make good, we gave them no order to make any composition, to separate you, and us, in this or any other. And I think you have no cause to forsake us, for we put you upon no new thing, but what your agent persuaded us to, and you by your letters desired. If he exceed your order, I hope you will not blame us, much less cast us off, when our moneys be laid out, etc. But I fear neither you nor we have been well dealt withal for sure as you write, half 4000$^£$ nay a quarter in fitting commodities, and in seasonable time would have furnished you better than you were. And yet for all this, and much more I might write, I dare not but think him honest, and that his desire, and intent was good; but the wisest may fail. Well now that it hath pleased God to give us hope of meeting, doubt not but we will all endeavor to perfect these accounts just, and right as soon as possibly we can. And I suppose you sent over Mr. Winslow, and we Mr. Hatherley, to certify each other how the state of things stood; we have received some content upon Mr. Hatherley's return, and I hope you will receive good content upon Mr. Winslow's return.

Now I should come to answer more particularly your letter, but herein I shall be very brief. The coming of the *White Angel* on your account, could not be more strange to you, than the buying of her was to us; for you gave him commission[248] that what he did you would stand to. We gave him none, and yet for his credit, and your sakes paid what bills he charged on us, etc. For that I write she was to act two parts, fishing and trade; believe me, I never so much as thought of any particular trade, nor will side with any that doth, if I conceive it may wrong you; for I ever was against it; using these words "they will eat up and destroy the general." Other things I omit as tedious, and not very pertinent. This was dated November 19, 1631.

---

[248] This commission is abused; he never had any for such end as they well know, neither had they any to pay this money, nor would have paid a penny, if they had not pleased for some other respect. (Bradford)

They were too short, in resting on Mr. Hatherley's honest word; for his order to discharge them from the *Friendship* account when he and Mr. Allerton made the bargain with them; and they delivered them the rest of the goods; and thereby gave them opportunity, also to recover all the freight of both voyages; without seeing an order (to have such power) under their hands in writing, which they never doubted of, seeing he affirmed he had power; and they both knew his honesty, and that he was specially employed for their agent at this time. And he was as short in resting on a verbal order from them, which was now denied, when it came to a particular of loss, but he still affirmed the same. But they were both now taught how to deal in the world, especially with merchants, in such cases. But in the end his light upon those here also, for Mr. Allerton had got all into his own hand, and Mr. Hatherley was not able to pay it, except they would have utterly undone him, as the sequel will manifest.

In another letter bearing date the 24 of this month, being an answer to the general letter, he hath these words:

For the *White Angel,* against which you write so earnestly, and say we thrust her upon you, contrary to the intent of the buyer; herein we say you forget yourselves and do us wrong; we will not take upon us to divine, what the thoughts, or intents of the buyer was; but what he spoke we heard, and that we will affirm, and make good against any that oppose it. Which is, that unless she were bought and such a course taken, Ashley could not be supplied; and again if he were not supplied, we could not be satisfied, what we were out for you. And further, you were not able to do it; and he gave some if reasons, which we spare to relate, unless by your unreasonable refusal, you will force us, and so hasten that fire, which is a-kindling too fast already, etc.

Out of another of his bearing dated
January 2, 1631

We purpose to keep the *Friendship* and the *White Angel* for the last year voyages, on the general account; hoping together they will rather produce profit, than loss; and breed less confusion in our accounts, and less disturbance in our affections. As for the *White Angel* though we laid out the money, and took bills of sale in our own names, yet none of us had so much as a thought (I dare say) of dividing from you in anything, this year, because we would not have the world (I may say Bristol) take notice of any breach betwixt Mr.

Allerton, and you, and he, and us; and so disgrace him in his proceedings, on in his intended voyage. We have now let him the ship at 30$^£$ per month by charter-party, and bound him in a bond of 1000$^£$ to perform covenants, and bring her to London (if God please). And what he brings in her, for you shall be marked with your mark, and bills of lading taken, and sent in Mr. Winslow's letter, who is this day riding to Bristol about it. So in this voyage, we deal, and are with him as strangers; he hath brought in 3 books of accounts, one for the company, another for Ashley's business, and the third for the *White Angel* and *Friendship*. The books, or copies we purpose to send you, for you may discover the errors in them better than we. We can make it appear how much money he hath had of us; and you can charge him with all the beaver he hath had of you. The total sum, as he hath put it is 7103-17-1; of this he hath expended, and given to Mr. Vines, and others, about 543$^£$ odd money, and then by your books you will find, whether you had such, and so much goods, as he chargeth you withal; and this is all that I can say at present concerning these accounts; he thought to dispatch them in a few hours, but he, and Straton, and Fogg were above a month about them; but he could not stay till we had examined them, for losing his fishing voyage, which I fear he hath already done, etc.

We bless God who put both you, and us in mind to send each to other, for verily had he run on, in that desperate, and chargeable course one year more, we had not been able, to support him. Nay both he, and we must have lain in the ditch, and sunk under the burthen, etc. Had there been an orderly course taken, and your business better managed, assuredly (by the blessing of God) you had been the ablest plantation, that as we think, or know, hath been undertaken by Englishmen, etc.

Thus far of these letters, of Mr. Sherley.

A few observations, from the former letters; and then I shall set down the simple truth of the things (thus in controversy between them) at least as far as by any good evidence it could be made to appear. And so labor to be brief, in so tedious and intricate a business; which hung in expostulation, between them many years before the same was ended. That though there will be often occasion, to touch these things about other passages, yet I shall not need to be large therein; doing it here once for all.

1. First it seems to appear clearly that Ashley's business, and the buying of this ship, and the courses framed thereupon, were first contrived,

and proposed by Mr. Allerton. As also that the pleas, and pretences which he made, of the inability of the plantation to repay their moneys, etc., and the hopes he gave them of doing it with profit; was more believed and rested on by them (at least some of them) than anything the plantation did, or said.

2. It is like though Mr. Allerton might think not to wrong the plantation in the main, yet his own gain, and private ends led him aside in these things; for it came to be known, (and I have it in a letter under Mr. Sherley's hand) that in the first 2 or 3 years of his employment, he had cleaned up 400£ and put it into a brewhouse of Mr. Collier's[249] in London, at first under Mr. Sherley's name, etc. besides what he might have otherwise. Again Mr. Sherley and he had particular dealings in some things; for he bought up the beaver, that seamen and other passengers brought over to Bristol, and at other places; and charged the bills to London which Mr. Sherley paid; and they got sometimes 50£ apiece in a bargain; as was made known by Mr. Hatherley and others, besides what might be otherwise. Which might make Mr. Sherley hearken unto him in many things, and yet I believe, as he is in his forementioned letter write; he never would side in any particular trade which he conceived would wrong the plantation, and eat up and destroy the general.

3. 3ly it may be perceived that seeing they had done so much, for the plantation, both in former adventures, and late disbursements; and also that Mr. Allerton was the first occasioner of bringing them upon these new designs, (which at first seemed fair, and profitable unto them) and unto which they agreed; but now seeing them to turn to loss, and decline to greater entanglements, they thought it more meet for the plantation, to bear them, than themselves, (who had borne much in other things already). And so took advantage of such commission, and power as Mr. Allerton had formerly had as their agent, to devolve these things upon them.

4. 4ly with pity and compassion; (touching Mr. Allerton) I may say, with the Apostle to Timothy, 1 Timothy 6:9: "They that will be rich, fall into many temptations, and snares," etc., "and pierce themselves through, with many sorrows," etc., "for the love of money is the root of all evil," verse 10. God give him to see the evil in his failings, that

---

[249] Probably William Collier, who settled in Plymouth about 1633 and later moved to Duxbury.

he may find mercy by repentance; for the wrongs he hath done to any, and this poor plantation in special. They that do such things, do not only bring themselves snares, and sorrows, but many with them (though in another kind) as lamentable experience shows; and is too manifest in this business.

Now about these ships, and their setting forth; the truth (as far as could be learned) is this. The motion about setting forth the fishing ship (called the *Friendship*) came first from the plantation, and the reasons of it (as is before remembered) but wholly left to themselves to do, or not to do as they saw cause. But when it fell into consideration, and the design was held to be profitable, and hopeful; it was propounded by some of them why might not they do it of themselves; seeing they must disburse all the money, and what need they have any reference to the plantation in it, they might take the profit themselves, towards other losses, and need not let the plantation share therein; and if their ends were otherwise answered for their supplies to come to them in time, it would be well enough. So they hired her, and set her out, and freighted her as full as she could carry with passengers' goods that belonged to the Massachusetts, which rose to a good sum of money; intending to send the plantation's supply in the other ship. The effect of this Mr. Hatherley not only declared afterward upon occasion; but affirmed upon oath, taken before the Governor and Deputy Governor of the Massachusetts, Mr. Winthrop, and Mr. Dudley: that this ship *Friendship* was not set out, nor intended for the joint partnership of the plantations, but for the particular account of Mr. James Sherley, Mr. Beauchamp, Mr. Andrews, Mr. Allerton, and himself. This deposition was taken at Boston the 29 of August 1639 as is to be seen under their hands; besides some other concurrent testimonies, declared at several times to sundry of them.

About the *White Angel* though she was first bought, or at least the price beaten by Mr. Allerton (at Bristol) yet that had been nothing if Mr. Sherley had not liked it, and disbursed the money. And that she was not intended for the plantation appears by sundry evidences as first the bills of sale, or charter-parties were taken in their own names, without any mention, or reference to the plantation at all, viz. Mr. Sherley, Mr. Beauchamp, Mr. Andrews, Mr. Denison[250], and Mr. Allerton for Mr. Hatherley fell off and would not join with them in this. That she was not bought for their account,

---

[250]	William Denison (1571-1653) came to the Massachusetts Bay in 1631 and took up residence in Roxbury.

Mr. Hatherley took his oath before the parties aforesaid, the day and year above written.

About the *White Angel* they all met at a certain tavern in London, where they had a dinner prepared, and had conference with a factor about selling of her in Spain, or at Port a Porte, as hath been before mentioned, as Mr. Hatherley manifested and Mr. Allerton could not deny.

Mr. Allerton took his oath, to like effect concerning this ship, the *White Angel* before the Governor and Deputy, the 7 of September 1639, and likewise deposed the same time, that Mr. Hatherley, and himself, did in the behalf of themselves, and the said Mr. Sherley, Mr. Andrews, and Mr. Beauchamp, agree and undertake to discharge, and save harmless, all the rest of the partners and purchasers, of and from the said losses of *Friendship* for 200$^£$ which was to be discounted thereupon. As by their depositions (which are in writing) may appear more at large, and some other depositions, and other testimonies by Mr. Winslow, etc. But I suppose these may be sufficient to evince the truth in these things against all pretences to the contrary. And yet the burthen lay still upon the plantation; or to speak more truly, and rightly, upon those few that were engaged for all, for they were fain to wade through these things without, any help from any.

Mr. Winslow deposed the same time before the Governor aforesaid, etc., that when he came into England, and the partners inquired of the success of the *White Angel* which should have been laden with bass and so sent for Port, of Portugal, and their ship, and goods to be sold; having informed them that they were like to fail in their lading of bass; that then, Mr. James Sherley used these terms: Feck, we must make one account of all; and thereupon pressed him as agent for the partners in New England, to accept the said ship, *White Angel* and her account into the joint partnership, which he refused, for many reasons; and after received instructions from New England to refuse her if she should be offered, which instructions he showed them; and whereas he was often pressed to accept her, he ever refused her, etc.

Concerning Mr. Allerton's accounts they were so large, and intricate, as they could not well understand them, much less examine, and correct them without a great deal of time, and help; and his own presence, which was now hard to get amongst them, and it was 2 or 3 years before they could bring them to any good pass, but never make them perfect. I know not how it came to pass, or what mystery was in it, for he took upon him to make up all accounts till this time, though Mr. Sherley was their agent to buy, and sell their goods, and did more than he therein; yet he passed in accounts, in a manner for all disbursements, both concerning goods bought, which he never saw, but were done when he was here in the country, or at sea; and all the expenses of the Leiden people, done by others in his absence, the charges about the patent, etc. In all which he made them debtor to him above 300$^£$ and demanded payment of it. But when things came to scanning he was found above 2000$^£$ debtor to them, (this wherein Mr. Hatherley, and he being jointly engaged [which he only had] being included) besides I know not how much, that could never be cleared; and interest moneys which ate them up, which he never accounted; also they were fain to allow such large bills of charges as were intolerable, the charges of the patent came to above 500$^£$ and yet nothing done in it, but what was done at first without any confirmation; 30$^£$ given at a clap, and 50$^£$ spent in a journey. No marvel therefore if Mr. Sherley said in his letter, if their business had been better managed they might have been the richest plantation of any English at that time. Yea he screwed up his poor old father-in-law's account[251] to above 200$^£$ and brought it on the general account, and to befriend him made most of it to arise out of those goods taken up by him at Bristol, at 50$^£$ per cent: because he knew, they would never let it lie on the old man; when alas he poor man, never dreamt of any such thing, nor that what he had could arise near that value, but thought that many of them had been freely bestowed on him, and his children, by Mr. Allerton. Neither in truth did they come near that value in worth, but that sum was blown up by interest, and high prices, which the company did for the most part bear (he deserving far more) being most sorry, that he should have a name to have much, when he had in effect little.

This year also Mr. Sherley sent over an account, which was in a manner but a cash account, what Mr. Allerton had, had of them, and disbursed, for which he referred to his accounts; besides an account of beaver sold which Mr. Winslow, and some others had carried over, and a large supply of goods which Mr. Winslow had, sent, and brought over; all which was comprised in that account, and all the disbursements about the *Friendship* and *White Angel,* and what concerned their accounts from first, to last, or anything else he could charge the partners with. So they were made debtor in the foot of that account 4770$^£$-19-2, besides 1000$^£$ still due for the purchase yet unpaid. Notwithstanding all the beaver, and returns that both Ashley, and they had made, which were not small.

---

[251]   Isaac Allerton was married to William Brewster's daughter Fear.

So as a while before whereas their great care was how to pay the purchase, and those other few debts which were upon them; now it was with them, as it was some times with Saul's father, who left caring for the asses, and sorrowed for his son, 1 Samuel 10:2; so that which before they looked at as a heavy burden, they now esteem but a small thing and a light matter, in comparison of what was now upon them. And thus the Lord oftentimes deals with His people to teach them, and humble them; that He may do them good in the latter end.

In these accounts of Mr. Sherley's some things were obscure, and some things twice charged, as a 100 of Barnstaple rugs which came in the *Friendship,* and cost 75$^£$ charged before by Mr. Allerton, and now by him again, with other particulars of like nature doubtful to be twice, or thrice charged; as also a sum of 600$^£$ which Mr. Allerton denied and they could never understand for what it was. They sent a note of these, and such like things afterward to Mr. Sherley by Mr. Winslow, but I know not how it came to pass could never have them explained.

Into these deep sums, had Mr. Allerton run them in two years, for in the latter end of the year 1628 all their debts did not amount to much above 400$^£$ as was then noted. And now come to so many thousands, and whereas in the year 1629 Mr. Sherley and Mr. Hatherley being at Bristol, and writ a large letter from thence, in which they had given an account of the debts, and what sums were then disbursed; Mr. Allerton never left begging, and entreating of them till they had put it out. So they blotted out 2 lines in that letter in which the sums were contained, and write upon it so as not a word could be perceived, as since by them was confessed, and by the letters may be seen. And thus were they kept hoodwinked, till now they were so deeply engaged. And whereas Mr. Sherley did so earnestly press that Mr. Allerton might be sent over to finish the great business about the patent, as may be seen in his letter write 1629, as is before recorded, and that they should be earnest with his wife to suffer him to go, etc. He hath since confessed by a letter under my hands, that it was Mr. Allerton's own doings and not his, and he made him write his words, and not his own. The patent was but a pretence and not the thing; thus were they abused in their simplicity, and no better than bought, and sold, as it may seem.

And to mend the matter, Mr. Allerton doth in a sort wholly now desert them; having brought them into the briars, he leaves them to get out as they can; but God crossed him mightily, for he having hired the ship of Mr. Sherley at 30$^£$ a month, he set forth again with a most wicked and drunken crew; and for covetousness' sake did so overlade her not only filling her hold but so stuffed her between decks as she was walte and could not bear sail;

and they had like to have been cast away at sea; and were forced to put for Milford Haven, and new stow her, and put some of their ordnance, and more heavy goods in the bottom. Which lost them time, and made them come late into the country, lose their season, and made a worse voyage than the year before. But being come into the country, he sells trading commodities to any that will buy, to the great prejudice of the plantation here; but that which is worse what he could not sell, he trusts; and sets up a company of base fellows and makes them traders, to run into every hole and into the river of Kennebec, to glean away the trade from the house there; about the patent, and privilege whereof he had dashed away so much money of theirs here. And now what in him lay, went about to take away the benefit thereof, and to overthrow them. Yea not only this but he furnishes a company, and joins with some consorts (being now deprived of Ashley at Penobscot) and sets up a trading house beyond Penobscot, to cut off the trade from thence also. But the French perceiving that that would be greatly to their damage also, they came in their beginning before they were well settled, and displanted them, slew 2 of their men and took all their goods to a good value, the loss being most (if not all Mr. Allerton's) for though some of them should have been his partners, yet he trusted them for their parts, the rest of the men were sent into France, and this was the end of that project.[252] The rest of those he trusted, being loose and drunken fellows, did for the most part but cozen, and cheat him of all they got into their hands, that howsoever he did his friends some hurt hereby for the present yet he got little good, but went by the loss by God's just hand. After in time, when he came to Plymouth, the church called him to account for these, and other his gross miscarriages; he confessed his fault; and promised better walking; and that he would wind himself out of these courses so soon as he could, etc.

This year also Mr. Sherley would needs send them over a new accountant; he had made mention of such a thing the year before; but they write him word, that their charge was great already, and they need not increase it, as this would; but if they were well dealt with, and had their goods well sent over, they could keep their accounts here themselves. Yet he now sent one, which they did not refuse being a younger brother

---

[252] Governor John Winthrop in his *History* wrote "Mr. Allerton of Plymouth, and some others, had set up a trading wigwam there, and left it in five men and store of commodities. La Tour, governor of the French in those parts, making claim to the place, came to displant them, and finding resistance, killed two of the men, and carried away the other three, and the goods."

of Mr. Winslow's; whom they had been at charge to instruct at London before he came. He came over in the *White Angel* with Mr. Allerton, and there began his first employment; for though Mr. Sherley had so far befriended Mr. Allerton, as to cause Mr. Winslow to ship the supply sent to the partners here in his ship, and give him 4$^£$ per tun whereas others carried for 3 and he made them pay their freight ready down, before the ship went out of the harbor, whereas others paid upon certificate of the goods being delivered, and their freight came to upward of 6 score pounds; yet they had much ado to have their goods delivered, for some of them were changed as bread, and peas; then were forced to take worse for better neither could they ever get all. And if Josias Winslow[253] had not been there it had been worse, for he had the invoice, and order to send them to the trading houses.

This year their house at Penobscot was robbed by the French; and all their goods of any worth, they carried away, to the value of 400$^£$ or 500 worth as they cost first penny; in beaver 300$^£$ weight, and the rest in trading goods, as coats, rugs, blanket, biscuit, etc. It was in this manner: the master of the house and part of the company with him, were come with their vessel to the westward to fetch a supply of goods which was brought over for them. In the meantime comes a small French ship into the harbor (and amongst the company was a false Scot). They pretended they were newly come from the sea, and knew not where they were, and that their vessel was very leaky, and desired they might haul her ashore and stop their leaks. And many French compliments they used; and congees they made; and in the end seeing but 3 or 4 simple men, that were servants, and by this Scotchman understanding, that the master and the rest of the company were gone from home, they fell of commending their guns, and muskets, that lay upon racks by the wall side, and took them down to look on them, asking if they were charged; and when they were possessed of them, one presents a piece ready charged, against the servants, and another a pistol; and bid them not stir: but quietly deliver them their goods, and carries some of the men aboard, and made the other help to carry away the goods; and when they had took, what they pleased, they set them at liberty, and went their way, with this mock, bidding them tell

---

[253]   Josias Winslow (1606-1674) was the brother of *Mayflower* passengers Edward and Gilbert Winslow. Another brother, John Winslow, married *Mayflower* passenger Mary Chilton, and yet another brother, Kenelm, married *Anne* passenger Ellen Newton, widow of *Fortune* passenger John Adams.

their master when he came, that some of the Isle of Rey gentlemen had been there.

This year, one Sir Christopher Gardiner, being as himself said descended of that house that the Bishop of Winchester came of (who was so great a persecutor of God's saints in Queen Mary's days); and being a great traveler received his first honor of knighthood, at Jerusalem; being made Knight of the Sepulcher there. He came into these parts, under pretence of forsaking the world, and to live a private life, in a godly course, not unwilling to put himself upon any mean employments, and take any pains for his living; and some time offered himself to join the churches in sundry places; he brought over with him a servant or 2 and a comely young woman, whom he called his cousin (but it was suspected, she [after the Italian manner] was his concubine); living at the Massachusetts, for some miscarriages which he should have answered he fled away from authority, and got among the Indians of these parts; they sent after him, but could not get him, and promised some reward to those that should find him. The Indians came to the Governor here and told where he was, and asked if they might kill him; he told them no by no means, but if they could take him, and bring him hither, they should be paid for their pains; they said he had a gun, and a rapier, and he would kill them if they went about it; and the Massachusetts Indians said they might kill him; but the Governor told them no they should not kill him, but watch their opportunity, and take him. And so they did, for when they light of him by a river side, he got into a canoe to get from them, and when they came near him, whilst he presented his piece at them to keep them off, the stream carried the canoe against a rock and tumbled both him, and his piece, and rapier into the water; yet he got out and having a little dagger by his side, they durst not close with him; but getting long poles they soon beat his dagger out of his hand, so he was glad to yield, and they brought him to the Governor. But his hands and arms were swollen, and very sore with the blows they had given him. So he used him kindly, and sent him to a lodging where his arms were bathed and anointed, and he was quickly well again and blamed the Indians for beating him so much; they said, that they did but a little whip him with sticks. In his lodging house those that made his bed, found a little notebook that by accident had slipped out of his pocket, or some private place, in which was a memorial, what day he was reconciled to the Pope and Church of Rome, and in what university he took his scapula, and such and such degrees; it being brought to the Governor he kept it, and sent the Governor of the Massachusetts word of his taking; who sent for him. So the Governor sent him and these notes to the Governor there who took it very thankfully; but after he got for England he showed his malice, but God prevented him.[254]

See the Governor's letter on the other side.

Sir: It hath pleased God to bring Sir Christopher Gardiner safe to us, with those that came with him. And howsoever I never intended, any hard measure to him, but to respect, and use him according to his quality; yet I let him know your care of him, and that he shall speed the better for your mediation. It was a special providence of God to bring those notes of his to our hands; I desire that you will please to speak to all that are privy to them, not to discover them to anyone, for that may frustrate the means of any further use to be made of them. The good Lord, our God who hath always ordered things for the good of His poor churches here direct us in this aright, and dispose it to a good issue. I am sorry we put you to so much trouble about this gentleman, especially at this time of great employment, but I knew not how to avoid it. I must again entreat you, to let me know what charge, and trouble any of your people have been at about him, that it may be recompensed. So with the true affection of a friend, desiring all

---

[254] Thomas Morton, in his *New English Canaan*, reported how he saw it: "Sir Christopher Gardiner . . . came into those parts, intending discovery. But the Separatists love not those good parts, when they proceed from a carnal man (as they call every good Protestant) in short time had found the means to pick a quarrel wit him . . . . So that when they find any man like to prove an enemy to their church, and state, . . . [t]he first precept in their politics is to defame the man at whom they aim, and then he is a holy Israelite in their opinions who can spread that fame broadest, like butter upon a loaf, no matter how thin . . . and then this man (who they have thus depraved) is a spotted unclean leper: he must out, lest he pollute the land . . . And thus they dealt with Sir Christopher: and plotted all the ways, and means they could, to overthrow his undertakings in those parts. They take occasion (some of them) to come to his house when he was gone up into the country: and (finding he was from home) so went to work, that they left him neither house, nor habitation, nor servant, nor anything to help him, if he should return . . . So they fired the place, and carried away the persons and goods."

happiness to yourself, and yours, and to all my worthy friends with you (whom I love in the Lord) I commend you to His grace, and good providence, and rest

Your most assured friend,
John Winthrop

Boston, May 5, 1631

By occasion hereof I will take a little liberty to declare what fell out by this man's means and malice, complying with others. And though I doubt not but it will be more fully done by my honored friends, whom it did more directly concern, and have more particular knowledge of the matter, yet I will here give a hint of the same; and God's providence in preventing the hurt that might have come by the same. The intelligence I had by a letter from my much honored and beloved friend Mr. John Winthrop, Governor of the Massachusetts.

Sir: Upon a petition exhibited by Sir Christopher Gardiner, Sir Ferdinando Gorges, Captain Mason, etc., against you and us, the cause was heard before the Lords of the Privy Council, and after reported to the King. The success whereof makes it evident to all, that the Lord hath care of His people here. The passages are admirable, and too long to write (I heartily wish an opportunity to impart them unto you being many sheets of paper). But conclusion was (against all men's expectation) an order for our encouragement; and much blame, and disgrace upon the adversaries; which calls for much thankfulness from us all. Which we purpose (the Lord willing) to express in a day of thanksgiving, to our merciful God (I doubt not but you will consider, if it be not fit for you to join in it) who as He hath humbled us by His late correction, so He hath lifted us up by an abundant rejoicing, in our deliverance out of so desperate a danger; so as that which our enemies built their hopes upon to ruin us by, He hath mercifully disposed to our great advantage. As I shall further acquaint you, when occasion shall serve.

The copy of the order follows.

At the Court at Whitehall, the 19 January 1632

Lord Privy Seal	Lord Cottington
Earl of Dorset	Mr. Treasurer
Lord Viscount Falkland	Mr. Vice Chamberlain
Lord Bishop of London	Mr. Secretary Coke
Mr. Secretary Windebank	

Whereas His Majesty hath lately been informed of great distraction and much disorder in that plantation in the parts of America called New England, which if they be true, and suffered, to run on would tend to the great dishonor of this kingdom, and utter ruin of that plantation. For prevention whereof, and for the orderly settling of government, according to the intention of those patents, which have been granted by His Majesty and from his late Royal Father King James. It hath pleased His Majesty that the Lords, and others of his most Honorable Privy Council, should take the same into consideration. Their Lordships in the first place thought fit, to make a Committee of this Board, to take examination of the matters informed. Which committees having called divers of the principal adventurers in that plantation; and heard those that are complainants against them. Most of the things informed being denied, and resting to be proved by parties that must be called from that place, which required a long expense of time. And at present their Lordships finding the adventurers were upon dispatch of men, victuals, and merchandise for that place. All which would be at a stand if the adventurers should have discouragement, or take suspicion that the State here had no good opinion of that plantation. Their Lordships not laying the fault, or fancies (if any be) of some particular men upon the General Government, or principal adventurers (which in due time is further to be inquired into) have thought fit in the meantime to declare, that the appearances were so fair, and hopes so great that the Country would prove both beneficial to this Kingdom, and profitable to the particular adventurers, as that the adventurers had cause to go on cheerfully with their undertakings; and rest assured if things were carried, as was pretended when the patents were granted, and accordingly as by the patents it is appointed, His Majesty would not only maintain the liberties and privileges heretofore granted, but supply anything further that might tend to the good government, prosperity and comfort of his people there of that place, etc.

William Trumball

Mr. Allerton returning for England little regarded his bond of a 1000£ to perform covenants; for whereas he was bound by the same, to bring the ship to London, and to pay 30£ per month for her hire, he did neither of both, for he carried her to Bristol again, from whence he intended to set her out again, and so did the 3 time into these parts (as after will appear) and though she had been 10 months upon the former voyage, at 30£ per month, yet he never paid penny for hire. It should seem he knew well enough how to deal with Mr. Sherley. And Mr. Sherley though he would needs tie her, and her account upon the general, yet he would dispose of her as himself pleased; for though Mr. Winslow had in their names protested against the receiving her on that account, or if ever they should hope to prevail in such a thing, yet never to suffer Mr. Allerton to have any more to do in her, yet he the last year let her wholly unto him and enjoined them to send all their supply in her to their prejudice, as is before noted, and now though he broke his bonds, kept no covenant, paid no hire, nor was ever like to keep covenants, yet now he goes and sells him all, both ship, and all her accounts, from first to last (and in effect he might as well have given him the same) and not only this, but he doth as good as provide a sanctuary for him, for he gives him one year's time to prepare, his account, and then to give up the same to them here; and then another year for him to make payment of what should he due upon that account. And in the meantime writes earnestly to them not to interrupt or hinder him from his business, or stay him about clearing accounts, etc. So as he in the meantime gathers up all moneys due for freight, and any other debts belonging either to her or the *Friendship's* accounts, as his own particular; and after sells ship and ordnance, fish, and what he had raised in Spain according to the first design, in effect; and who had, or what became of the money, he best knows. In the meantime their hands were bound, and could do nothing but look on, till he had made all away into other men's hands, (save a few cattle, and a little land and some small matters he had here at Plymouth) and so in the end removed (as he had already his person) so all his from hence. This will better appear by Mr. Sherley's letter.

Sir: These few lines are further to give you to understand, that seeing you, and we, that never differed yet, but about the *White Angel*, which somewhat troubleth us, as I perceive it doth you. And now Mr. Allerton being here, we have had some conference with him about her and find him very willing to give you, and us all content, that possibly he can, though he burthen himself. He is content to take the *White Angel* wholly on himself, notwithstanding he met with pirates near the coast of Ireland, which took away his best sails, and other provisions from her; so as verily if we should now sell her, she would yield but a small price, besides her ordnance. And to set her forth again with fresh money we would not, she being now at Bristol. Wherefore we thought it best, both for you and us, Mr. Allerton being willing to take her, to accept of his bond of two thousand pounds, to give you a true, and perfect account and take the whole charge, of the *White Angel*, wholly to himself from the first to the last. The account he is to make, and perfect within 12 months from the date of this letter; and then to pay you at 6 and 6 months after, whatsoever shall be due unto you, and us, upon the foot of that account. And verily, notwithstanding all the disasters he hath had, I am persuaded he hath enough, to pay all men here, and there. Only they must have patience till he can gather in what is due to him there. I do not write this slightly but upon some ground of what I have seen (and perhaps you know not of), under the hands and seal of some, etc. I rest

Your assured friend
James Sherley

December 6, 1632.

But here's not a word of the breach of former bonds and covenants, or payment of the ship's hire; this is passed by, as if no such thing had been, besides what bonds, or obligements soever they had of him, there never came any to the hands or sight of the partners here. And for this that Mr. Sherley seems to intimate (as a secret) of his ability under the hands and seals of some, it was but a trick; having gathered up an account of what was owing from such base fellows as he had made traders for him, and other debts, and then got Mr. Mayhew[255], and some others to affirm under their hand and seal, that they had seen such accounts that were due to him.

Mr. Hatherley came over again this year, but upon his own occasions; and began to make preparation to plant, and dwell in the country; he with his former dealings had wound in, what money he had in the partnership, into his own hands, and so gave off all partnership (except in name) as was found in the issue of things; neither did he meddle, or take any care about the same. Only he was troubled about his engagement about the *Friendship,* as will after appear, and now partly about that account, in some reckonings between Mr. Allerton and him, and some debts that Mr. Allerton otherwise owed him upon dealing between them in particular, he drew up an account of above 2000£ and would fain have engaged the partners here with it, because Mr. Allerton had been their agent. But they told him, they had been fooled long enough with such things, and showed him that it no way belonged to them; but told him he must look to make good his engagement for the *Friendship,* which caused some trouble between Mr. Allerton and him.

Mr. William Peirce did the like, Mr. Allerton being wound into his debt also, upon particular dealings; as if they had been bound to make good all men's debts; but they easily shook off these things, but Mr. Allerton hereby ran into much trouble and vexation, as well as he had troubled others, for Mr. Denison sued him for the money he had disbursed for the 6 part, of the *White Angel,* and recovered the same with damages.

Though the partners were thus plunged into great engagements, and oppressed with unjust debts, yet the Lord prospered their trading, that they made yearly large returns, and had soon wound themselves out of all; if yet they had otherwise been well dealt withal as will more appear hereafter.

Also the people of the plantation began to grow in their outward estates, by reason of the flowing of many people into the country especially into the Bay of the Massachusetts; by which means corn, and cattle rose to a great price, by which many were much enriched, and commodities grew plentiful; and yet in other regards this benefit, turned to their hurt; and this accession of strength, to their weakness. For now as their stocks increased, and the increase vendible; there was no longer any holding them together, but now

---

[255] Probably Thomas Mayhew (1593-1682) who came to New England in 1632 as a steward for Matthew Craddock.

they must of necessity go to their great lots; they could not otherwise keep their cattle, and having oxen grown, they must have land for plowing, and tillage. And no man now thought he could live, except he had cattle and a great deal of ground to keep them; all striving to increase their stocks. By which means they were scattered all over the Bay quickly, and the town in which they lived compactly till now was left very thin, and in a short time almost desolate. And if this had been all, it had been less, though too much; but the church must also be divided, and those that had lived so long together in Christian and comfortable fellowship; must now part, and suffer many divisions: first those that lived on their lots on the other side of the Bay (called Duxbury[256]) they could not long bring their wives, and children to the public worship, and church meetings here, but with such burthen; as growing to some competent number, they sued to be dismissed and become a body of themselves; and so they were dismissed (about this time) though very unwillingly. But to touch this sad matter, and handle things together that fell out afterward; to prevent any further scattering from this place, and weakening of the same: it was thought best to give out some good farms, to special persons, that would promise to live at Plymouth, and likely to be helpful to the church or commonwealth, and so tie the lands to Plymouth as farms for the same; and there they might keep their cattle, and tillage by some servants and retain their dwellings here. And so some special lands were granted at a place general called Green's Harbor[257] where no allotments had been in the former division, a place very well meadowed, and fit to keep and rear cattle good store. But alas this remedy proved worse than the disease; for within a few years those that had thus got footing there; rent themselves away, partly by force, and partly wearing the rest with importunity, and pleas of necessity, so as they must either suffer them, to go, or live in continual opposition, and contention. And other still, as they conceived themselves straitened or to want accommodation, broke away under one pretence or other, thinking their own conceived necessity, and the example of others, a warrant sufficient for them. And this I fear will be the ruin of New England; at least of the

---

[256] The Plymouth Colony Records indicate that in 1632, John Alden, Myles Standish, Jonathan Brewster and Thomas Prence were at least partially residing in Duxbury. Duxbury did not become formally recognized as a town until 7 June 1637.

[257] Green's Harbor later became the town of Marshfield.

churches of God there and will provoke the Lord's displeasure, against them.[258]

This year Mr. William Peirce came into the country, and brought goods and passengers in a ship called the *Lion*[259]; which belonged chiefly to Mr. Sherley, and the rest of the London partners, (but these here had nothing to do with her). In this ship, (besides beaver which they had sent home before) they sent upward of 800$^£$ in her, and some otter skins. And also the copies of Mr. Allerton's accounts, desiring that they would also peruse and examine them; and rectify such things as they should find amiss in them; and the rather because they were better acquainted with the goods bought there, and the disbursements made, than they could be here; yea a great part were done by themselves, though Mr. Allerton brought in the account, and sundry things seemed to them obscure and had need of clearing; also they sent a book of exceptions against his accounts in such things as they could manifest, and doubted not but they might add more thereunto. And also showed them how much Mr. Allerton was debtor to the account; and desired seeing they had now put the ship *White Angel*, and all wholly into his power, and tied their hands here, that they could not call him to account for anything, till the time was expired which they had given him, and by that time other men would get their debts of him, (as some had done already by suing him) and he would make all away here quickly out of their reach. And therefore prayed them to look to things and get payment of him there, as it was all the reason they should, seeing they kept all the bonds, and covenants they made with him in their own hands; and here they could do nothing by the course they had taken, nor had anything to show if they should go about it. But it pleased God this ship being first to go to Virginia before she went home, was cast away on that coast, not far from Virginia, and their beaver was all lost (which was the first loss they sustained in that kind). But Mr. Peirce, and the men saved their lives, and also their

---

[258] Bradford bemoans the departure of men from Plymouth in his poem "A Word to Plymouth": "Oh poor Plymouth, how dost thou moan, / Thy children all are form thee gone, / And left thou art in widow's state, / Poor, helpless, sad, and desolate. / Some thou hast had, it is well known, / That sought thy good before their own, / But times are changed; those days are gone, / And therefore thou art left alone. / To make others rich thyself art poor, / They are increased out of thy store, / But growing rich they thee forsake / And leave thee poor and desolate."

[259] The *Lion* arrived on 16 September 1632 with 123 passengers, fifty of which were children.

letters, and got into Virginia and so safely home, and the accounts were now sent from hence again to them. And thus much of the passages of this year.

A part of Mr. Peirce his letter from Virginia
It was dated in December 25, 1632 and came to their
hand the 7 of April before they had anything
from England.

Dear friends, etc. The bruit of this fatal stroke, that the Lord hath brought both on me, and you all, will come to your ears, before this cometh to your hands (it is like) and therefore I shall not need to enlarge the particulars, etc. My whole estate (for the most part) is taken away; and so yours in a great measure by this, and your former losses[260]. It is time to look about us; before the wrath of the Lord break forth to utter destruction. The good Lord give us all grace to search our hearts and try our ways, and turn unto the Lord, and humble ourselves under His mighty hand, and seek atonement, etc. Dear friends you may know that all your beaver, and the books of your accounts, are swallowed up in the sea; your letters remain with me, and shall be delivered if God bring me home. But what should I more say, have we lost our outward estates? Yet a happy loss if our souls may gain, there is yet more in the Lord Jehovah, than ever we had yet in the world. Oh that our foolish hearts, could yet be weaned from the things here below, which are vanity and vexation of spirit; and yet we fools catch after shadows, that fly away, and are gone in a moment, etc. Thus with my continual remembrance of you in my poor desires to the throne of grace, beseeching God to renew His love, and favor towards you all, in and through the Lord Jesus Christ, both in spiritual, and temporal good things, as may be most to the glory and praise of His name, and your everlasting good. So I rest.

Your afflicted brother in Christ,
William Peirce

Virginia, December 25, 1632

---

[260] He means by Mr. Allerton and the French. (Bradford).

By the first return this year, they had letters from Mr. Sherley of Mr. Allerton's further ill success; and the loss by Mr. Peirce, with many sad complaints; but little hope of anything to be got of Mr. Allerton, or how their accounts might be either eased, or any way rectified by them there. But now saw plainly that the burthen of all would be cast on their backs. The special passages of his letters I shall here insert, as shall be pertinent to these things; for though I am weary of this tedious and uncomfortable subject, yet for the clearing of the truth, I am compelled to be more large in the opening of these matters; upon which so much trouble hath ensued, and so many hard censures have passed on both sides. I would not be partial to either, but deliver the truth in all, and as near as I can, in their own words and passages; and so leave it to the impartial judgment, of any that shall come to read, or view these things. His letters are as follows, dated June 24, 1633.

Loving friends, my last[261] was sent in the *Mary and John*, by Mr. William Collier, etc. I then certified you of the great, and uncomfortable, and unseasonable loss, you, and we had, in the loss of Mr. Peirce his ship the *Lion*; but the Lord's holy name be blessed, who gives, and takes as it pleaseth Him, His will be done, Amen. I then related unto you, that fearful accident, or rather judgment, the Lord pleased to lay on London Bridge (by fire) and therein gave you a touch of my great loss, the Lord I hope will give me patience to bear it, and faith to trust in Him, and not in these slippery, and uncertain things of this world.

I hope Mr. Allerton is near upon safe with you by this; but he had many disasters here before he could get away; yet the last was a heavy one. His ship, going out of the harbor at Bristol, by stormy weather was so far

---

[261] March 22. (Bradford).

driven on the shore, as it cost him above 100£ before she could be got off again. Verily his case was so lamentable, as I could not but afford him some help therein (and so did some mere strangers to him). Besides your goods were in her, and if he had not been supported, he must have broke off his voyage and so loss could not have been avoided on all sides. When he first bought her, I think he had made a saving match, if he had then sunk her, and never set her forth. I hope he sees the Lord's hand against him, and will leave off these voyages; I think we did well in parting with her. She would have been but a clog to the account from time, to time, and now though we shall not get much by way of satisfaction, yet we shall lose no more. And now as before I have write, I pray you finish all the accounts and reckonings with him there; for here he hath nothing, but many debts, that he stands engaged to many men for. Besides, here is not a man that will spend a day, or scarce an hour about the accounts, but myself, and that business will require more time, and help than I can afford. I shall not need to say any more, I hope you will do that which shall be best, and just; to which add mercy, and consider his intent, though he failed in many particulars, which now cannot be helped, etc.

Tomorrow or next day at furthest we are to pay 300£ and Mr. Beauchamp is out of the town, yet the business I must do; oh the grief, and trouble that man, Mr. Allerton, hath brought upon you, and us; I cannot forget it, and to think on it draws many a sigh from my heart, and tears from my eyes; and now the Lord hath visited me with another great loss, yet I can undergo it with more patience. But this I have foolishly pulled upon myself, etc.

And in another he hath this passage:

By Mr. Allerton's fair propositions and large promises I have overrun myself; verily at this time grief hinders me to write, and tears will not suffer me to see; wherefore as you love those, that ever loved you, and that plantation, think upon us. Oh what shall I say of that man, who hath abused your trust, and wronged our loves; but now to complain is too late, neither can I complain of your backwardness; for I am persuaded it lies as heavy on your hearts, as it doth on our purses, or credits. And had the Lord sent Mr. Peirce safe home, we had eased both you, and us, of some of those debts; the Lord I hope will give us patience to bear these crosses. And that great God, whose care, and providence is everywhere, and specially over all those that desire truly to fear, and serve Him; direct, guide, prosper, and bless you so, as that you may be able (as I persuade myself you are willing) to discharge, and take off this great and heavy burthen which now lies upon me for your sakes. And I hope in the end for the good of you, and many thousands more, for had not you, and we joined, and continued together, New England might yet have been scarce known, I am persuaded; not so replenished, and inhabited with honest English people, as now it is. The Lord increase and bless them, etc. So with my continual prayers for you all, I rest

Your assured loving friend,
James Sherley

June 24, 1633

By this it appears when Mr. Sherley sold him the ship, and all her accounts; it was more for Mr. Allerton's advantage than theirs; and if they could get any there well, and good, for they were like to have nothing here. And what course was held to hinder them there, hath already been manifested. And though Mr. Sherley became more sensible of his own condition, by these losses, and thereby more sadly, and plainly, to complain of Mr. Allerton, yet no course was taken to help them here, but all left unto themselves; not so much as to examine and rectify the accounts, by which (it is like) some hundreds of pounds might have been taken off. But very probable it is the more they saw was taken off, the less might come unto themselves. But I leave these matters, and come to other things.

Mr. Roger Williams (a man godly and zealous, having many precious parts, but very unsettled in judgment) came over first to the Massachusetts, but upon some discontent left that place, and came hither, (where he was friendly entertained according to their poor ability) and exercised his gifts amongst them and after some time was admitted a member of the church. And his teaching well approved, for the benefit whereof I still bless God, and am thankful to him, even for his sharpest admonitions and reproofs so far as they agreed with truth. He this year began to fall into some strange opinions, and from opinion, to practice; which caused some controversy between the church, and him; and in the end some discontent on his part, by occasion whereof he left them something abruptly. Yet afterwards sued for his dismission to the church of Salem, which was granted, with some caution to them concerning him, and what care they ought to have of him. But he soon fell into more things there, both to their and the government's trouble, and disturbance. I shall not need to name particulars, they are too well known now to all, though for a time, the church here went under some hard censure by his occasion from some, that afterwards smarted themselves. But he is to be pitied and prayed for; and so I shall leave the matter, and desire the Lord to show him his errors, and reduce him into the way of truth, and give him a settled judgment, and constancy in the same; for I hope he belongs to the Lord, and that He will show him mercy. [262]

Having had formerly converse, and familiarity with the Dutch (as is before remembered) they seeing them seated here in a barren quarter, told them of a river called by them the Fresh River, but now is known by the name of Connecticut River, which they often commended unto them for a fine place both for plantation, and trade, and wished them to make use of it. But their hands being full otherwise, they let it pass. But afterwards there coming a company of banished Indians into these parts, that were driven out from thence by the potency of the Pequots, which usurped upon them, and drove them from thence; they often solicited them to go thither and they should have much trade, especially if they would keep a house there; and having now good store of commodities, and also need to look out where they could advantage themselves to help them out of their great engagements, they now began to send that way to discover the same, and trade with the natives; they found it to be a fine place but had no great store of trade, but the Indians excused the same in regard of the season, and fear the Indians were in of their enemies. So they tried divers times, not without profit, but saw the most certainty would be by keeping a house there, to receive the trade when it came down out of the inland. These Indians not seeing them

---

[262]   Nathaniel Morton in his *New England's Memorial* (Cambridge, 1669) reported: "In the year 1634, Mr. Roger Williams removed from Plymouth to Salem; he had lived about three years at Plymouth, where he was well accepted as an assistant in the ministry to Mr. Ralph Smith, then pastor of the church there, but by degrees venting of divers of his own singular opinions, and seeking to impose them upon others, he not finding such a concurrence as he expected, he desired his dismission to the church of Salem, which though some were unwilling to, yet through the prudent counsel of Mr. Brewster, the ruling elder there, fearing that his continuance amongst them might cause divisions, and there being many abler men in the Bay, they would better deal with him than themselves could, and foreseeing what he professed he feared concerning Mr. Williams, which afterwards came to pass, that he would run the same course of rigid separation and anabaptistry, which Mr. John Smith, the Sebaptist at Amsterdam had done; the church of Plymouth consented to his dismission, and such as did adhere to him were also dismissed, and removed with him, or not long after him, to Salem."

very forward to build there, solicited them of the Massachusetts in like sort (for their end was to be restored to their country again); but they in the Bay being but lately come, were not fit for the same, but some of their chief made a motion to join with the partners here, to trade jointly with them in that river, the which they willing to embrace, and so they should have built, and put in equal stock together; a time of meeting was appointed at the Massachusetts, and some of the chief here, were appointed to treat with them, and went accordingly, but they cast many fears, of danger, and loss and the like; which was perceived to be the main obstacles, though they alleged they were not provided of trading goods; but those here offered at present to put in sufficient for both, provided they would become engaged for the half, and prepare against the next year. They confessed more could not be offered, but thanked them, and told them they had no mind to it. They then answered, they hoped it would be no offense unto them, if themselves went on without them, if they saw it meet; they said there was no reason they should, and thus this treaty broke off, and those here took convenient time to make a beginning there, and were the first English that both discovered that place, and built in the same. Though they were little better than thrust out of it afterward as may appear.

But the Dutch (began now to repent) and hearing of their purpose, and preparation endeavored to prevent them; and got in a little before them, and made a slight fort, and planted 2 pieces of ordnance, threatening to stop their passage. But they having made a small frame of a house ready, and having a great new bark they stowed their frame in her hold, and boards to cover and finish it, having nails, and all other provisions fitting for their use (this they did the rather, that they might have a present defense against the Indians) who were much offended that they brought home and restored the right sachem of the place (called Natawanute) so as they were to encounter with a double danger in this attempt, both the Dutch and the Indians. When they came up the river, the Dutch demanded what they intended, and whither they would go; they answered up the river to trade (now their order was to go and seat above them); they bid them strike, and stay, or else they would shoot them, (and stood by their ordnance ready fitted). They answered they had commission from the Governor of Plymouth to go up the river to such a place, and if they did shoot, they must obey their order, and proceed; they would not molest them, but would go on. So they passed along, and though the Dutch threatened them hard, yet they shot not; coming to their place, they clapped up their house quickly and landed their provisions, and left the company appointed, and sent the bark home, and afterwards palisaded their house about, and fortified themselves better; the Dutch sent word home to the Manhattan what was done, and in process of time they sent a band of about 70 men in warlike manner with colors displayed, to assault them, but seeing them strengthened, and that it would cost blood, they came to parley, and returned in peace. And this was their entrance there; who deserved to have held it, and not by friends to have been thrust out as in a sort they were as will after appear. They did the Dutch no wrong, for they took not a foot of any land they bought, but went to the place above them and bought that tract of land which belonged to these Indians which they carried with them, and their friends, with whom the Dutch had nothing to do. But of these matters more in another place.

It pleased the Lord to visit them this year with an infectious fever of which many fell very sick and upward of 20 persons died, men and women besides children, and sundry of them of their ancient friends which had lived in Holland, as Thomas Blossom, Richard Masterson, with sundry others; and in the end (after he had much helped others) Samuel Fuller, who was their surgeon, and physician, and had been a great help and comfort unto them; as in his faculty, so otherwise being a deacon of the church, a man godly, and forward to do good, being much missed after his death. And he, and the rest of their brethren much lamented by them, and caused much sadness, and mourning amongst them; which caused them to humble themselves, and seek the Lord; and towards winter it pleased the Lord the sickness ceased. This disease also swept away many of the Indians from all the places near adjoining; and the spring before, especially all the month of May, there was such a quantity of a great sort of flies, like (for bigness) to wasps, or bumblebees, which came out of holes in the ground, and replenished all the woods, and ate the green things; and made such a constant yelling noise, as made all the woods ring of them, and ready to deaf the hearers; they have not by the English been heard, or seen before or since.[263] But the Indians told them that sickness would follow, and so it did in June, July, August, and the chief heat of summer.

It pleased the Lord to enable them this year, to send home a great quantity of beaver, besides paying all their charges, and debts at home, which good return did much encourage their friends in England. They sent in beaver 3366 weight, and much of it coat beaver, which yielded 20s per pound, and some of it above[264]. And of otter skins 346 sold also at a good price. And thus much of the affairs of this year.

---

[263] These were cicadas.

[264] The skin was sold at 14 and 15 the pound. (Bradford).

Mr. Sherley's letters were very brief, in answer of theirs this year. I will forbear to copy any part thereof; only name a head or 2 therein; first he desires they will take nothing ill in what he formerly write, professing his good affection towards them as before, etc. 2ly for Mr. Allerton's accounts, he is persuaded they must suffer and that in no small sums; and that they have cause enough to complain, but it was now too late. And that he had failed them there, those here and himself in his own aims. And that now having thus left them here, he feared God had or would leave him, and it would not be strange, but a wonder if he fell not into worse things, etc. 3ly he blesseth God, and is thankful to them for the good return made this year. This is the effect of his letters, other things being of more private nature.

I am now to enter upon one of the saddest things that befell them since they came: but before I begin it will be needful to premise such part of their patent as gives them right and privilege at Kennebec, as followeth:

The said Council hath further given, granted, bargained, sold, enfeoffed, allotted, assigned, and set over, and by these presents, do clearly and absolutely, give, grant, bargain, sell, alien, enfeoff, allot, assign and confirm unto the said William Bradford, his heirs, associates, and assigns, all that tract of land or part of New England in America aforesaid, which lieth within, or between, and extendeth itself, from the utmost limits of Cobbosseecontee, which adjoineth to the river of Kennebec, towards the western ocean, and a place called the Falls of Nequamkick in America, aforesaid; and the space of 15 English miles, on each side of the said river, commonly called Kennebec River, and all the said river called Kennebec, that lieth within the said limits and bounds eastward, westward, northward, and southward, last above mentioned; and all lands, grounds, soils, rivers, waters, fishing, etc. And by virtue of the authority to us derived by his said late Majesty's Letters patents to take, apprehend, seize, and

Silver drinking cup that belonged to William Bradford. It is about seven inches in height, and was handmade in London in 1634. It is jointly owned and exhibited by the Smithsonian's National Museum of American History and the Pilgrim Hall Museum. Photo courtesy of the Pilgrim Hall Museum, Plymouth, Massachusetts.

make prize of all such persons their ships and goods, as shall attempt to inhabit, or trade, with the savage people of that country within the several precincts, and limits of his, and their several plantations, etc.

Now it so fell out that one Hocking, belonging to the plantation of Piscataqua, went with a bark, and commodities to trade in that river; and would needs press into their limits, and not only so but would needs go up the river above their house (towards the falls of the river) and intercept the trade that should come to them. He that was chief of the place forbade them, and prayed him that he would not offer them that injury nor go about to infringe their liberties, (which had cost them so dear). But he answered he would go up and trade there in despite of them, and lie there as long as he pleased; the other told him he must then be forced to remove him from thence, or make seizure of him if he could. He bid him do his worst, and so went up, and anchored there. The other took a boat, and some men, and went up to him, when he saw his time; and again entreated him to depart, by what persuasion he could. But all in vain, he could get nothing of him but ill words. So he considered that now was the season for trade to come down, and if he should suffer him to lie, and take it from them, all their former charge would be lost, and they had better throw up all. So consulting with his men, (who were willing thereto), he resolved to put him from his anchors, and let him drive down the river with the stream; but commanded the men that none should shoot a shot upon any occasion except he commanded them. He spoke to him again, but all in vain; then he sent a couple in a canoe to cut his cable, the which one of them performs, but Hocking takes up a piece which he had laid ready, and as the bark sheered by the canoe he shot him close under her side, in the head (as I take it) so he fell down dead instantly. One of his fellows (which loved him well) could not hold, but with a musket shot Hocking, who fell down dead and never spoke word; this was the truth of the thing; the rest of the men carried home the vessel and the sad tidings of these things.[265]

---

[265] A legal deposition survives from this case, which is oddly found amongst the Plymouth Colony probate records; it is reprinted in Appendix I. A letter written by John Winthrop, dated 22 May 1634, states: "I shall now acquaint you with a sad accident which lately fell out between our neighbors of Plymouth and some of the Lord Saye his servants at Pascot . . . . The Lord's pinnace going with 3 men and a boy to trade at Kennebec were forbidden, and persisting in their purpose 2 of the magistrates of Plymouth, viz. John Alden and John Howland and about 9 more, came up to them in their pinnace and sent 3 men in a canoe to cut the cables of the . . . pinnace (her master one Hocking having given them provoking

Now the Lord Saye, and the Lord Brooke with some other great persons had a hand in this plantation; they write home to them, as much as they could to exasperate them in the matter; leaving out all the circumstances, as if he had been killed without any offense of his part, concealing that he had killed another first, and the just occasion, that he had given in offering such wrong; at which their Lordships were much offended till they were truly informed of the matter.

The bruit of this was quickly carried all about (and that in the worst manner) and came into the Bay to their neighbors there. Their own bark coming home, and bringing a true relation of the matter, sundry were sadly affected with the thing, as they had cause; it was not long before they had occasion to send their vessel into the Bay of the Massachusetts. But they were so prepossessed with this matter, and affected with the same, as they committed Mr. Alden to prison, who was in the bark, and had been at Kennebec (but was no actor in the business) but went to carry them supply; they dismissed the bark about her business, but kept him for some time; this was thought strange here, and they sent Captain Standish to give them true information, (together with their letters) and the best satisfaction they could, and to procure Mr. Alden's release. I shall recite a letter or 2 which will show the passages of these things, as followeth.

Good Sir:

I have received your letter, by Captain Standish, and am unfeignedly glad of God's mercy towards you in the recovery of your health, or some way thereto; for the business you write of I thought meet to answer a word or 2 to yourself, leaving the answer of your Governor's letter to our Court, to whom the same together with myself is directed. I conceive (till I hear new

---

speeches) and stood in their own pinnace with their pieces charged and ready to shoot: after they had cut one cable, Hocking came up, and asked them if they meant to cast away his vessel, etc., and swore withal that he would kill him that should come to cut the other cable, which while one was doing (for it was cut) Hocking shot one of them in the canoe dead, upon which one of the Plymouth men out of their pinnace shot at Hocking and killed him upon the place, whereupon another of Hocking's company coming up upon the deck one of the Plymouth men asked Howland if he should kill him also, but he forbade him saying he feared there had been too many killed already." *Proceedings of the Massachusetts Historical Society* 20:43-45.

matter to the contrary) that your patent may warrant your resistance of any English from trading at Kennebec; and that blood of Hocking, and the party he slew, will be required at his hands (yet do I with yourself and others sorrow for their deaths). I think likewise that your general letters will satisfy our Court, and make them cease from any further intermeddling in the matter. I have upon the same letter set Mr. Alden at liberty and his sureties, and yet lest I should seem to neglect the opinion of our Court and the frequent speeches of others, with us; I have bound Captain Standish to appear the 3 of June at our next Court to make affidavit for the copy of the patent, and to manifest the circumstances, of Hocking's provocations; both which will tend to the clearing of your innocency. If any unkindness hath been taken from what we have done, let it be further, and better considered of I pray you; and I hope the more you think of it, the less blame you will impute to us. At least you ought to be just in differencing them whose opinions concur with your own, from others who were opposites; and yet I may truly say, I have spoken with no man in the business who taxed you most, but they are such as have many ways heretofore declared their good affections towards your plantation. I further refer myself to the report of Captain Standish, and Mr. Alden; leaving you for this present to God's blessing, wishing unto you perfect recovery of health, and the long continuance of it. I desire to be lovingly remembered to Mr. Prence your Governor, Mr. Winslow, Mr. Brewster, whom I would see if I knew how. The Lord keep you all. Amen.

Your very loving friend in our Lord Jesus

Thomas Dudley

Newtown, the 22 of May 1634.

Another of his about these things
as followeth.

Sir:

I am right sorry for the news that Captain Standish, and other of your neighbors, and my beloved friends will bring now to Plymouth, wherein I suffer with you, by reason of my opinion, which differeth from others, who are godly, and wise amongst us here, the reverence of whose judgments, causeth me to suspect mine own ignorance; yet must I remain in it until I be convinced thereof. I thought not to have showed your letter written to me, but to have done my best to have reconciled differences in the best season, and manner I could; but Captain Standish requiring an answer thereof publicly in the Court, I was forced to produce it, and that made the breach so wide as he can tell you. I propounded to the Court, to answer Mr. Prence's letter (your Governor) but our Court said, it required no answer, itself being an answer to a former letter of ours. I pray you certify Mr. Prence so much, and others whom it concerneth, that no neglect or ill manners be imputed to me thereabout. The late letters I received from England wrought in me divers fears of some trials which are shortly like to fall upon us; and this unhappy contention between you, and us, and between you, and Piscataqua, will hasten them, if God with an extraordinary hand, do not help us. To reconcile this for the present will be very difficult, but time cooleth distempers; and a common danger to us both approaching, will necessitate our uniting again. I pray you therefore Sir set your wisdom and patience a work, and exhort others to the same, that things may not proceed from bad, to worse. So making our contentions like the bars of a palace, but that a way of peace may be kept open, whereat the God of peace may have entrance, in His own time. If you suffer wrong, it shall be your honor to bear it patiently; but I go far in needless putting you in mind of these things. God hath done great things for you, and I desire His blessings may be multiplied upon you more, and more. I will commit no more to writing; but commending myself to your prayers, do rest,

Your truly loving friend in our Lord Jesus,
Thomas Dudley

June 4, 1634

There was cause enough of these fears, which arise by the underworking of some enemies to the churches here, by which this commission following was procured from His Majesty.

Charles by the grace of God King of England, Scotland, France
and Ireland, Defender of the Faith, etc.

To the most Reverend father in Christ, our well beloved and faithful counselor William by divine Providence Archbishop of Canterbury, of all England Primate and Metropolitan; Thomas Lord

Coventry, Keeper of our Great Seal of England; the most Reverent father in Christ our well beloved and most faithful counselor Richard by divine Providence Archbishop of York, Primate and Metropolitan; our well beloved and most faithful cousins and counselors, Richard Earl of Portland, our High Treasurer of England; Henry Earl of Manchester, Keeper of our Privy Seal; Thomas Earl of Arundel, and Surrey, Earl Marshal of England; Edward Earl of Dorset, Chamberlain of our most dear consort, the Queen, and our beloved and faithful counselors, Francis Lord Cottington, Counselor and Undertreasurer of our Exchequer; Sir Thomas Edmonds knight, Treasurer of our household; Sir Henry Vane knight, comptroller of the same household; Sir John Cook knight, one of our Privy Secretaries, And Francis Windebank knight, another of our Privy Secretaries, greeting.

Whereas very many of our subjects, and of our late father's of beloved memory, our sovereign lord James, late King of England, by means of license royal, not only with desire of enlarging the territories of our empire, but chiefly out of a pious, and religious affection, and desire of propagating the gospel of our Lord Jesus Christ. With great industry and expenses have caused to be planted large colonies of the English nation, in divers parts of the world altogether unmanured; and void of inhabitants; or occupied of the barbarous people, that have no knowledge of divine worship. We being willing to provide a remedy for the tranquility and quietness of those people, and being very confident of your faith, and wisdom, justice and provident circumspection, have constituted you the aforesaid Archbishop of Canterbury, Lord Keeper of the Great Seal of England, the Archbishop of York, etc. And any 5 or more of you our Commissioners; and to you, and any 5 or more of you, we do give and commit power for the government, and safety of the said colonies, drawn, or which out of the English nation into those parts hereafter shall be drawn. to make laws, constitutions, and ordinances pertaining either to the public state of these colonies, or the private profit of them; and concerning the lands, goods, debts, and succession in those parts, and how they shall demean themselves, towards foreign princes, and their people, or how they shall bear themselves towards us, and our subjects, as well in any foreign parts whatsoever, or on the seas in those parts, or in their return sailing home, or which may pertain to the clergy government, or to the cure of souls among the people there living, and exercising trade in those parts; by designing out congruent portions arising in tithes, oblations, and other things there, according to your sound discretions, in political and civil causes; and by having the advice of 2 or 3 bishops, for the settling, making and ordering of the business, for the designing of necessary ecclesiastical, and clergy portions, which you shall cause to be called, and taken to you. And to make provision against the violation of those laws, constitutions, and ordinances, by imposing penalties, and mulcts, imprisonment if there be cause, and that the quality of the offense do require it, by deprivation of member, or life, to be inflicted. With power also (our assent being had) to remove, and displace the governors, or rulers of those colonies, for causes which to you shall seem lawful, and others in their stead to constitute, and require an account of their rule and government, and whom you shall find culpable, either by deprivation from their place, or by imposition of a mulct upon the goods of them in those parts to be lived, or banishment from those provinces in which they have been Governor or otherwise to cashier according to the quantity of the offense. And to constitute judges, and magistrates political, and civil, for civil causes, and under the power and form, which to you 5 or more of you shall seem expedient. And judges, and magistrates, and dignities, to causes ecclesiastical, and under the power, and form which to you 5 or more of you, with the bishops vicegerents (provided by the Archbishop of Canterbury for the time being) shall seem expedient; and to ordain courts, praetorian and tribunal, as well ecclesiastical, as civil, of judgments; to determine the forms, and manner of proceeding in the same; and of appealing from them in matters, and causes as well criminal, as civil, personal, real, and mixed and to their seats of justice, what may be equal and well ordered, and what crimes, faults, or excesses, of contracts, or injuries ought to belong to the ecclesiastical court, and what to the civil court and seat of justice.

Provided nevertheless that the laws, ordinances, and constitutions of this kind, shall not be put in execution, before our assent be had thereunto in writing under our signet, signed at least; and this assent being had, and the same publicly proclaimed in the provinces in which they are to be executed; we will and command that those laws, ordinances, and constitutions, more fully to obtain strength and be observed, and shall be inviolably, of all men whom they shall concern.

Notwithstanding, it shall be for you or any 5 or more of you (as is aforesaid) although those laws, constitutions, and ordinances shall be proclaimed with our royal assent, to change, revoke and abrogate them and other new ones, in form aforesaid, from time, to time frame and make as aforesaid; and to new evils arising, or new dangers to apply new remedies as is fitting, so often as to you it shall seem expedient. Furthermore you shall understand that we have constituted you, and every 5 or more of you, the aforesaid Archbishop of Canterbury; Thomas Lord Coventry, Keeper of the Great Seal of England; Richard Bishop of York, Richard Earl of Portland, Henry Earl of Manchester, Thomas Earl of Arundel and Surrey, Edward Earl of Dorset, Francis Lord Cottington, Sir Thomas Edmonds knight, Sir Henry Vane knight, Sir Francis Windebank knight, our Commissioners to hear and determine, according to your sound discretions all manner of complaints either against these colonies, or their rulers, or governors, at the instance of the parties grieved, or at their accusation brought concerning injuries from hence, or from thence, between them and their members to be moved, and to call the parties before you; and to the parties or to their procurators, from hence, or from thence being heard the full complement of justice to be exhibited. Giving unto you, or any 5 or more of you power, that if you shall find any of the colonies aforesaid, or any of the chief rulers upon the jurisdictions of others by unjust possession or usurpation, or one against another making grievance, or in rebellion against us, or withdrawing from our allegiance, or our commandments, not obeying, consultation first with us in that case had, to cause those colonies, or the rulers of them, for the causes aforesaid, or for other just causes, either to return to England, or to command them to other places designed, even as according to your sound discretions, it shall seem to stand with equity, and justice, or necessity. Moreover we do give unto you and any 5 or more of you power and special command over all the charters, letters patents, and rescripts Royal, of the regions, provinces, islands or lands in foreign parts, granted for rising colonies, to cause them to be brought before you. And the same being received, if anything surreptitiously, or unduly have been obtained, or that by the same privileges, liberties and prerogatives hurtful to us or to our crown or to foreign princes, have been prejudicially suffered, or granted; the same being better made known unto you, 5 or more of you, to command them according to the laws, and customs of England to be revoked, and to do such other things, which to the profit, and safeguard of the aforesaid colonies, and of our subjects resident in the same shall be necessary. And therefore we do command you that about the premises at days, and times, which for these things you shall make provision; that you be diligent in attendance, as it becometh you; giving in precept also, and firmly enjoining, we do give command to all, and singular chief rulers, of provinces into which the colonies aforesaid have been drawn, or shall be drawn, and concerning the colonies themselves, and concerning others, that have been interest therein, that they give attendance upon you, and be observant, and obedient, unto your warrants in those affairs, as often as, and even as in our name they shall be required, at their peril. In testimony whereof, we have caused these our letters to be made patent, witness ourself at Westminster the 28 day of April, in the tenth year of our reign.

By writ from the Privy Seal,
Willies

Anno Dom. 1634

By these things it appears what troubles rose hereupon, and how hard they were to be reconciled; for though they here were heartily sorry for what was fallen out, yet they conceived they were unjustly injured, and provoked, to what was done. And that their neighbors, (having no jurisdiction over them) did more than was meet, thus to imprison one of theirs, and bind them to their Court. But yet being assured of their Christian love; and persuaded what was done was out of godly zeal that religion might not suffer, nor sin any way covered, or borne with, especially the guilt of blood, of which all should be very conscientious in any whomsoever; they did endeavor to appease, and satisfy them the best they could; first by informing them the truth in all circumstances about the matter; 2ly in being willing to refer the case, to any indifferent, and equal hearing, and judgment of the thing here; and to answer it elsewhere, when they should be duly called thereunto; and further they craved Mr. Winthrop's, and other of the reverend magistrates there, their advice and direction herein. This did mollify their minds, and bring things to a good, and comfortable issue in the end.

For they had this advice given them by Mr. Winthrop, and others concurring with him; that from their Court they should write, to the neighbor plantations, and especially that of the Lords at Piscataqua; and theirs of the Massachusetts; to appoint some to give them meeting at some fit place; to consult and determine in this matter, so as the parties meeting might have full power to order and bind, etc. And that nothing be done to the infringing, or prejudice of the liberties of any place. And for the clearing of conscience, the law of God is, that the priest's lips must be consulted with. And therefore it was desired that the ministers, of every plantation, might be present to give their advice in point of conscience. Though this course seemed dangerous to some, yet they were so well assured of the justice of their cause, and the equity of their friends, as they put themselves upon it and appointed a time of which they gave notice to the several places a month beforehand, viz. Massachusetts, Salem, and Piscataqua or any other that they would give notice to, and desired them to produce any evidence they could in the case. The place for meeting was at Boston. But when the day and time came none appeared, but some of the magistrates and ministers of the Massachusetts, and their own; seeing none of Piscataqua or other places came (having been thus desired, and convenient time given them for that end), Mr. Winthrop and the rest said they could do no more, than they had done thus to request them; the blame must rest on them. So they fell into a fair debating of things themselves; and after all things had been fully opened and discussed, and the opinion of each one demanded, both magistrates, and ministers; though they all could have wished these things had never been, yet they could not but lay the blame, and guilt on Hocking's own head, and withal gave them such grave, and godly exhortations, and advice as they thought meet, both for the present, and future; which they also embraced with love, and thankfulness, promising to endeavor to follow the same. And thus was this matter ended, and their love and concord renewed; and also Mr. Winthrop, and Mr. Dudley write in their behalves, to the Lord Saye, and other gentlemen that were interested in that plantation, very effectually. With which together, with their own letters, and Mr. Winslow's further declaration of things unto them, they rested well satisfied.

This year (in the forepart of the same) they sent forth a bark to trade at the Dutch plantation; and they met there with one Captain Stone that had lived in Christopher's, one of the West Indies Islands, and now had been some time in Virginia, and came from thence into these parts. He kept company with the Dutch Governor. And I know not in what drunken fit, he got leave of the Governor to seize on their bark, when they were ready to come away, and had done their market, having to the value of 500$^£$ worth of goods aboard her, having no occasion at all, or any color of ground for such a thing, but having made the Governor drunk. So as he could scarce speak a right word, and when he urged him hereabout, he answered him, *Alst u beleeft*. So he got aboard (the chief of their men and merchant being ashore) and with some of his own men made the rest of theirs weigh anchor, set sail, and carry her away towards Virginia; but divers of the Dutch seamen, which had been often at Plymouth, and kindly entertained there, said one to another, shall we suffer our friends to be thus abused; and have their goods carried away before our faces, whilst our Governor is drunk; they vowed they would never suffer it, and so got a vessel, or 2 and pursued him, and brought him in again, and delivered them their bark, and goods again.

Afterwards Stone came into the Massachusetts; and they sent, and commenced suit against him for this fact; but by mediation of friends it was taken up, and the suit let fall. And in the company of some other gentlemen Stone came afterwards to Plymouth, and had friendly and civil entertainment amongst them, with the rest; but revenge boiled within his breast (though concealed) for some conceived, he had a purpose (at one time) to have stabbed the Governor and put his hand to his dagger for that end; but by God's providence, and the vigilance of some was prevented. He afterward returned to Virginia, in a pinnace with one Captain Norton; and some others, and I know not for what occasion, they would needs go up Connecticut River, and how they carried themselves I know not, but the Indians knocked him in the head as he lay in his cabin and had thrown the covering over his face (whether out of fear or desperation is uncertain). This was his end; they likewise killed all the rest, but Captain Norton defended himself a long time against them all in the cook room, till by accident the gunpowder took fire which (for readiness) he had set in an open thing before him, which did so burn and scald him, and blind his eyes, as he could make no longer resistance, but was slain also by them, though they much commended his valor; and having killed the men, they made a prey of what they had, and chaffered away some of their things, to the Dutch that lived there; but it was not long before a quarrel fell between the Dutch, and them; and they would have cut off their bark, but they slew the chief sachem, with the shot of a murderer.

Mr. Winslow was sent by them this year into England, partly to inform and satisfy the Lord Saye and others in the former matter. As also to make answer, and their just defense for the same, if anything should by any be prosecuted against them at Council table, or elsewhere; but this matter took end, without any further trouble, as is before noted. And partly to signify unto the partners in England, that the term of their trade with the company here was out; and therefore he was sent to finish the accounts with them. And to bring them notice how much debtor they should remain on that account, and that they might know what further course would be best to hold; but the issue of these things will appear in the next year's passages. They now sent over by him a great return, which was very acceptable unto them; which was in beaver 3738$^£$ weight, a great part of it being coat-beaver sold at 20s per pound[266]; and 234 otter skins, which altogether rise to a great sum of money.

I am now to relate some strange and remarkable passages; there was a company of people lived in the country, up above in the River of Connecticut; a great way from their trading house there; and were enemies to those Indians which lived about them, and of whom they stood in some fear (being a stout people). About a thousand of them had enclosed themselves in a fort, which they had strongly palisaded about; 3 or 4 Dutchmen, went up in the beginning of winter to live with them, to get their trade, and prevent them for bringing it to the English, or to fall into amity with them; but at spring to bring all down to their place. But their enterprise failed, for it pleased God, to visit these Indians with a great sickness, and such a mortality that of a 1000, above 900 and a half of them died, and many of them did rot above ground for want of burial, and the Dutchmen almost starved, before they could get away, for ice and snow; but about February they got with much difficulty to their trading house; whom they kindly relieved, being almost spent with

---

[266] And the skin at 14. (Bradford).

hunger, and cold; being thus refreshed by them divers days, they got to their own place, and the Dutch were very thankful for this kindness.

This spring also, those Indians that lived about their trading house there, fell sick of the small pox, and died most miserably; for a sorer disease cannot befall them, they fear it more than the plague; for usually they that have this disease, have them in abundance; and for want of bedding, and linen, and other helps, they fall into a lamentable condition as they lie on their hard mats, the pox breaking and mattering, and running one into another; their skin cleaving (by reason thereof) to the mats they lie on; when they turn them, a whole side will flay off, at once (as it were) and they will be all of a gore blood, most fearful to behold; and then being very sore, what with cold, and other distempers, they die like rotten sheep. The condition of this people was so lamentable, and they fell down so generally of this disease as they were (in the end) not able to help one another, no not to make a fire, nor to fetch a little water to drink, nor any to bury the dead; but would strive as long as they could, and when they could procure no other means to make fire, they would burn the wooden trays, and dishes they ate their meat in, and their very bows, and arrows; and some would crawl out on all fours to get a little water, and sometimes die by the way, and not be able to get in again. But those of the English house (though at first they were afraid of the infection) yet seeing their woeful, and sad condition, and hearing their pitiful cries, and lamentations; they had compassion of them, and daily fetched them, wood, and water, and made them fires, got them victuals, whilst they lived; and buried them when they died. For very few of them escaped, notwithstanding they did what they could for them; to the hazard of themselves. The chief sachem himself now died, and almost all his friends, and kindred. But by the marvelous goodness, and providence of God not one of the English, was so much as sick, or in the least measure tainted with this disease, though they daily did these offices for them, for many weeks together. And this mercy which they showed them, was kindly taken, and thankfully acknowledged of all the Indians, that knew or heard of the same. And their masters here, did much commend and reward them for the same.

Mr. Winslow was very welcome to them in England, and the more, in regard of the large return he brought with him, which came all safe to their hands, and was well sold. And he was borne in hand, (at least he so apprehended) that all accounts should be cleared before his return, and all former differences thereabout well settled. And so he writ over to them here, that he hoped to clear the accounts and bring them over with him; and that the account of the *White Angel* would be taken off, and all things fairly ended. But it came to pass that being occasioned to answer some complaints made against the country at Council Board; more chiefly concerning their neighbors in the Bay than themselves here, the which he did to good effect. And further prosecuting such things as might tend to the good of the whole, as well themselves, as others; about the wrongs, and encroachments that the French, and other strangers both had, and were like further to do unto them, if not prevented; he preferred this petition following to their Honors that were deputed Commissioners for the Plantations:

To the Right Honorable the Lords Commissioners
for the Plantations in America.

The Humble Petition of Edward Winslow,
on the behalf of the Plantations in New England.

Humbly sheweth unto your Lordships that whereas your petitioners, have planted themselves in New England under His Majesty's most gracious protection; now so it is right Honorables, that the French, and Dutch, do endeavor to divide the land between them; for which purpose the French have on the east side entered and seized upon one of our houses, and have

Portrait of Edward Winslow, painted in 1651. The original currently hangs in the Pilgrim Hall Museum, Plymouth, Massachusetts. Image reproduced from the 1912 Massachusetts Historical Society edition of Bradford's *History of Plimoth Plantation*.

carried away the goods, slew 2 of the men in another place, and took the rest prisoners with their goods. And the Dutch on the west have also made entry, upon Connecticut River, within the limits of His Majesty's letters patent; where they have raised a fort, and threaten to expel your petitioners thence, who are also planted upon the same river, maintaining possession for His Majesty to their great charge, and hazard both of lives, and goods.

In tender consideration hereof, your petitioners humbly pray that your Lordships will either procure their peace with those foreign states, or else to give special warrant unto your petitioners and the English Colonies, to right, and defend themselves against all foreign enemies. And your petitioners shall pray, etc.

This petition found good acceptation with most of them, and Mr. Winslow was heard sundry times by them, and appointed further to attend for an answer from their Lordships. Especially having upon conference with them, laid down a way, how this might be done without any either charge or trouble to the State: only by furnishing some of the chief of the country here with authority, who would undertake it at their own charge, and in such a way as should be without any public disturbance. But this crossed both Sir Ferdinando Gorges's, and Captain Mason's design, and the Archbishop of Canterbury's by them; for Sir Ferdinando Gorges (by the Archbishop's favor) was to have been sent over General Governor into the country, and to have had means from the State for that end; and was now upon dispatch and conclude of the business; and the Archbishop's purpose and intent was, by his means and some he should send with him, (to be furnished with Episcopal power) to disturb the peace of the churches here, and to overthrow their proceedings, and further growth, which was the thing he aimed at. But it so fell out (by God's providence) that though he in the end crossed this petition from taking any further effect in this kind; yet by this as a chief means, the plot, and whole business of his, and Sir Ferdinando's fell to the ground, and came to nothing. When Mr. Winslow should have had his suit granted (as indeed upon the point it was) and should have been confirmed, the Archbishop put a stop upon it, and Mr. Winslow thinking to get it freed, went to the Board again, but the Bishop, Sir Ferdinando and Captain Mason (had as it seems) procured Morton (of whom mention is made before, and his base carriage) to complain; to whose complaints Mr. Winslow made answer, to the good satisfaction of the Board, who checked Morton, and rebuked him sharply, and also blamed Sir Ferdinando Gorges, and Mason for countenancing him. But the Bishop had a further end and use of his presence, for he now began to question Mr. Winslow of many things, as of teaching in the church publicly, of which Morton accused him, and gave evidence that he had seen, and heard him do it; to which Mr. Winslow answered that some time (wanting a minister) he did exercise his gift to help the edification of his brethren, when they wanted better means, which was not often. Then about marriage, the which he also confessed that having been called to place of magistracy, he had sometimes married some. And further told their Lordships that marriage was a civil thing, and he found nowhere in the Word of God, that it was tied to ministry; again they were necessitated so to do having for a long time together at first no minister; besides it was no new thing for he had been so married himself in Holland by the magistrates in their Statt-house. But in the end (to be short) for these things the Bishop, by vehement importunity, got the Board (at last) to consent to his commitment; so he was committed to the Fleet, and lay there 17 weeks, or thereabout, before he could get to be released.[267] And this was the end of this petition, and this business; only the others design was also frustrated hereby, with other things concurring; which was no small blessing to the people here.

But the charge fell heavy on them here, not only in Mr. Winslow's expenses (which could not be small) but by the hindrance of their business both there, and here, by his personal employment. For though this was as much, or more, for others than for them here, and by them chiefly he was put on this business (for the plantation knew nothing of it, till they heard of his imprisonment) yet the whole charge lay on them. Now for their own business, whatsoever Mr. Sherley's mind was before, (or Mr. Winslow's apprehension of the same) he now declared himself plainly, that he would neither take off the *White Angel* from the account, nor give any further account, till he had received more into his hands, only a pretty good supply of goods were sent over; but of the most, no note of their prices, or so orderly an invoice as formerly, which Mr. Winslow said he could not help, because of his restraint. Only now Mr. Sherley and Mr. Beauchamp and Mr. Andrews sent over a letter of attorney, under their hands and seals, to recover what they could of Mr. Allerton for the *Angel's* account, but sent them neither, the bonds, nor covenants, or such other evidence, or accounts as they had about these matters. I shall here insert a few passages out of Mr. Sherley's letters about these things.

Your letter of the 22 July 1634 by your trusty, and our loving friend Mr. Winslow I have received; and your large parcel of beaver and otter skins (blessed

---

[267]   Edward Winslow's petition to the Lord's Council, written while he was in Fleet's Prison, is reprinted in Appendix 1.

be our God); both he, and it came safely to us and we have sold it in two parcels: the skin at 14s a pound and some at 16; the coat at 20s the pound. The accounts I have not sent you them this year, I will refer you to Mr. Winslow, to tell you the reason of it; yet be assured that none of you shall suffer, by the not having of them, if God spare me life. And whereas you say the 6 years are expired that the people put the trade into your and our hands for; for the discharge of that great debt which Mr. Allerton needlessly, and unadvisedly ran you and us into; yet it was promised it should continue till our disbursements, and engagements were satisfied. You conceive it is done; we feel, and know otherwise, etc. I doubt not but we shall lovingly agree, notwithstanding all that hath been written, on both sides, about the *White Angel.* We have now sent you a letter of attorney, thereby giving you power in our names (and to shadow it the more we say for our uses) to obtain what may be, of Mr. Allerton towards the satisfying of that great charge of the *White Angel*; and sure he hath bound himself (though at present I cannot find it) but he hath often affirmed (with great protestations) that neither you nor we should lose a penny by him, and I hope you shall find enough to discharge it; so as we shall have no more contesting about it. Yet notwithstanding, his unnatural, and unkind dealing with you; in the midst of justice, remember mercy, and do not all you may do, etc. Set us out of debt, and then let us reckon and reason together, etc. Mr. Winslow hath undergone an unkind imprisonment, but I am persuaded it will turn much to all your good, I leave him to relate particulars, etc.

Your loving friend,
James Sherley

London, Sept. 7, 1635

This year they sustained another great loss from the French; Monsieur de Alney coming into the harbor, of Penobscot; and having before got some of the chief that belonged to the house aboard his vessel; by subtlety coming upon them in their shallop, he got them to pilot him in; and after getting the rest into his power he took possession of the house in the name of the King of France. And partly by threatening, and otherwise, made Mr. Willet (their agent there) to approve of the sale of the goods there, unto him, of which he set the price himself in effect, and made an inventory thereof (yet leaving out sundry things). But made no payment for them; but told them in convenient time he would do it if they came for it. For the house and fortification etc. he would not allow, nor account anything, saying that they which build on another man's ground do forfeit the same. So thus turning them out of all, (with a great deal of compliment and many fine words) he let them have their shallop and some victuals to bring them home. Coming home and relating all the passages, they here were much troubled at it, having had this house robbed by the French once before, and lost then above 500ᶠ (as is before remembered) and now to lose house, and all, did much move them. So as they resolved to consult with their friends in the Bay, and if they approved of it (there being now many ships there) they intended to hire a ship of force and seek to beat out the French, and recover it again. Their course was well approved on (if themselves could bear the charge). So they hired a fair ship of above 300 tun well fitted with ordnance, and agreed with the master (one Girling) to this effect, that he and his company should deliver them the house, (after they had driven out, or surprised the French) and give them peaceable possession thereof, and of all such trading commodities as should there be found; (and give the French fair quarter, and usage if they would yield). In consideration whereof he was to have 700ᶠ of beaver, to be delivered him there when he had done the thing; but if he did not accomplish it, he was to lose his labor and have nothing. With him they also sent their own bark, and about 20 men, with Captain Standish, to aid him (if need were) and to order things if the house was regained; and then to pay him the beaver which they kept aboard their own bark. So they with their bark piloted him thither; and brought him safe into the harbor. But he was so rash, and heady, as he would take no advice; nor would suffer Captain Standish to have time to summon them, (who had commission and order so to do), neither would do it himself; the which it was like, if it had been done, and they come to a fair parley (seeing their force) they would have yielded. Neither would he have patience, to bring his ship where she might do execution; but began to shoot at distance like a madman, and did them no hurt at all; the which when those of the plantation saw, they were much grieved, and went to him, and told him he would do no good if he did not lay his ship better to pass (for she might lie within pistol shot of the house). At last when he saw his own folly he was persuaded, and laid her well, and bestowed a few shot to good purpose; but now when he was in a way to do some good, his powder was gone (for though he had pieces of ordnance) it did now appear he had but a barrel of powder, and a piece. So he could do no good but was fain to draw off again; by which means the enterprise was made frustrate; and the French encouraged; for all the while that he shot so unadvisedly, they lay close under a work of earth, and let him consume himself. He advised with the Captain how he might be supplied with powder, for he had not to carry him home; so he told him he would go to the next plantation, and do his endeavor to procure him some, and so did; but understanding by intelligence, that he intended to seize on the bark, and surprise the beaver; he sent him the powder and brought the bark, and beaver home;

but Girling never assaulted the place more (seeing himself disappointed) but went his way. And this was the end of this business.

Upon the ill success of this business, the Governor and Assistants here by their letters certified their friends in the Bay; how by this ship they had been abused and disappointed, and that the French partly had, and were now likely to fortify themselves more strongly; and likely to become ill neighbors to the English. Upon this they thus writ to them as followeth:

Worthy Sirs: Upon the reading of your letters, and consideration of the weightiness of the cause therein mentioned; the Court hath jointly expressed their willingness to assist you, with men and munition; for the accomplishing of your desires upon the French. But because here are none of yours that have authority to conclude of anything herein; nothing can be done by us for the present. We desire, therefore, that you would with all convenient speed, send some man of trust, furnished with instructions from yourselves; to make such agreement with us about this business, as may be useful for you, and equal for us. So in haste we commit you to God, and remain

Your assured loving friends,

John Haynes, Governor
Richard Bellingham, Deputy
John Winthrop
Thomas Dudley
John Humphry
William Coddington
William Pynchon
Atherton Hough
Increase Nowell
Richard Dumer
Simon Bradstreet

Newtown, October 9, 1635.

Upon the receipt of the above mentioned, they presently deputed 2 of theirs to treat with them, giving them full power to conclude, according to the instructions they gave them. Being to this purpose that if they would afford such assistance, as together with their own was like to effect the thing, and also bear a considerable part of the charge, they would go on; if not (they having lost so much already) should not be able, but must desist, and wait further opportunity, as God should give, to help themselves. But this came to nothing, for when it came to the issue, they would be at no charge; but sent them this letter and referred them more at large to their own messengers.

Sir:

Having, upon the consideration of your letter, with the message you sent, had some serious consultations, about the great importance, of your business with the French; we gave our answer to those whom you deputed to confer with us, about the voyage to Penobscot; we showed our willingness to help, but withal we declared our present condition, and in what state we were, for our ability to help; which we for our parts shall be willing to improve, to procure you sufficient supply of men, and munition. But for matter of moneys we have no authority at all to promise, and if we should, we should rather disappoint you than encourage you by that help, which we are not able to perform. We likewise thought it fit to take the help of other Eastern plantations; but those things we leave to your own wisdoms. And for other things we refer you to your own committees, who are able to relate all the passages more at large, we salute you, and wish you all good success in the Lord.

Your faithful and loving friend,
Richard Bellingham, Dep.
In the name of the rest of the committees

Boston, October 16, 1635

This thing did not only thus break off, but some of their merchants shortly after sent to trade with them, and furnished them both with provisions, and powder and shot; and so have continued to do till this day, as they have seen opportunity for their profit. So as in truth the English themselves, have been the chiefest supporters of these French; for besides these, the plantation at Pemaquid (which lies near unto them) doth not only supply them with what they want, but gives them continual intelligence of all things that pass among the English (especially some of them). So as it is no marvel though they still grow, and encroach more, and more upon the English, and fill the Indians, with guns, and munition. To the great danger of the English who lie open, and unfortified, living upon husbandry; and the other closed up in their forts, well fortified, and live upon trade, in good security. If these things be not looked to and remedy provided in time, it may easily be conjectured what they may come to. But I leave them.

This year, the 14 or 15 of August (being Saturday) was such a mighty storm of wind, and rain, as none living in these parts, either English, or Indians ever saw. Being like (for the time it continued) to those hurricanes, and typhoons that writers make mention of in the Indies; it began in the morning, a little before day, and grew not by degrees, but came with violence in the beginning, to the great amazement of many. It blew down sundry houses, and uncovered others; divers vessels were lost at sea, and many more in extreme danger; it caused the sea to swell (to the southward of this place) above 20 foot right up and down; and made many of the Indians to climb into trees for their safety; it took off the boarded roof of a house which belonged to this plantation at Manomet, and floated it to another place, the posts still standing in the ground. And if it had continued long without the shifting of the wind, it is like it would have drowned some part of the country. It blew down many hundred thousands of trees, turning up the stronger by the roots, and breaking the higher pine trees off in the middle; and the tall young oaks, and walnut trees of good bigness were wound like a withe, very strange, and fearful to behold. It began in the southeast and parted toward the south and east, and veered sundry ways, but the greatest force of it here was from the former quarters; it continued not (in the extremity) above 5 or 6 hours, but the violence began to abate; the signs, and marks of it will remain this 100 years in these parts where it was sorest. The moon suffered a great eclipse the 2 night after it.

Some of their neighbors in the Bay hearing of the fame of Connecticut River had a hankering mind after it, (as was before noted) and now understanding, that the Indians were swept away with the late great mortality, the fear of whom was an obstacle unto them before, which being now taken away, they began now to prosecute it with great eagerness. The greatest differences fell between those of Dorchester plantation, and them here; for they set their mind on that place which they had not only purchased of the Indians, but where they had built intending, only (if they could not remove them) that they should have but a small moiety left to the house, as to a single family. Whose doings and proceedings were conceived to be very injurious; to attempt not only to intrude themselves into the rights, and possessions of others, but in effect to thrust them out of all. Many were the letters, and passages that went between them hereabout, which would be too long here to relate.

I shall here first insert a few lines that was writ by their own agent from thence.

Sir, etc. The Massachusetts men are coming almost daily, some by water, and some by land, who are not yet determined where to settle, though some have a great mind to the place we are upon, and which was last bought; many of them look at that, which this river will not afford; except it be at this place which we have, namely to be a great town, and have commodious dwellings for many together. So as what they will do I cannot yet resolve you; for this place there is none of them say anything to me, but what I hear from their servants, (by whom I perceive their minds). I shall do what I can to withstand them. I hope they will hear reason, as that we were here first, and entered with much difficulty, and danger both in regard of the Dutch, and Indians, and bought the land (to your great charge, already disbursed) and have since held here a chargeable possession, and kept the Dutch from further encroaching, which would else long before this day have possessed all, and kept out all others, etc. I hope these and such like arguments will stop them. It was your will we should use their persons, and messengers kindly, and so we have done, and do daily, to your great charge; for the first company had well nigh starved, had it not been for this house, for want of victuals; I being forced to supply 12 men for 9 days together; and those which came last, I entertained the best we could; helping both them (and the other) with canoes, and guides; they got me to go with them to the Dutch, to see if I could procure, some of them to have quiet settling near them; but they did peremptorily withstand them. But this later company did not once speak thereof, etc. Also I gave their goods house room according to their earnest request, and Mr. Pynchon's[268] letter in their behalf (which I thought good to send you, here enclosed). And what trouble and charge I shall be further at I know not, (for they are coming daily), and I expect these back again from below, whither they are gone to view the country. All which trouble and charge we undergo for their occasion, may give us just cause (in the judgment of all wise and understanding men) to hold, and keep that we are settled upon. Thus with my duty remembered, etc. I rest

Yours to be commanded,

Jonathan Brewster[269]

---

[268]   William Pynchon (1590-1662), came to New England in 1630, settling in the Massachusetts Bay Colony and later was among the first wave of settlers to remove to Connecticut in 1636. He authored a pamphlet, *The Meritorius Price*, published in 1650, which made the book-burning lists in the Bay Colony, and authored several more after returning to England in 1652.

[269]   Jonathan Brewster (1593-1659) was the son of *Mayflower* passenger and Plymouth Colony Elder William Brewster. He himself came on the ship *Fortune* in 1621. In 1624 at Plymouth he married Lucretia Oldham, the sister of John Oldham, of the Oldham-Lyford scandals mentioned by Bradford under the year 1624.

Matianuck, July 6, 1635

Amongst the many agitations, that passed between them, I shall note a few out of their last letters, and for the present omit the rest (except upon other occasion I may have fitter opportunity).

After their thorough view of the place they began to pitch themselves upon their land and near their house, which occasioned much expostulation between them, some of which are such as follow:

Brethren, having lately sent 2 of our body unto you, to agitate, and bring to an issue some matters in difference between us about some lands at Connecticut, unto which you lay challenge, upon which God by His providence cast us, and as we conceive in a fair way of providence tendered it to us, as a meet place to receive our body, now upon removal.

We shall not need to answer all the passages of your large letter, etc. But whereas you say God in His providence cast you, etc., we told you before, and (upon this occasion) must now tell you still, that our mind is otherwise. And that you cast a rather partial, if not a covetous eye, upon that which is your neighbors, and not yours; and in so doing, your way could not be fair unto it. Look that you abuse not God's providence in such allegations.

Theirs

Now albeit we at first judged the place so free that we might with God's good leave take and use it, without just offense to any man. It being the Lord's waste, and for the present altogether void of inhabitants, that indeed minded the employment thereof, to the right ends for which land was created, Gen. 1:28. And for future intentions of any, and uncertain possibilities, of this; or that, to be done by any; we judging them (in such a case as ours especially) not meet to be equaled with present actions (such as ours was) much less worthy to be preferred before them; and therefore did we make some weak beginnings in that good work, in the place aforesaid.

Answer: Their answer was to this effect. That if it was the Lord's waste, it was themselves that found it so, and not they; and have since bought it of the right owners, and maintained a chargeable possession upon it all this while, as themselves could not but know. And because they could not presently remove themselves to it, because of present engagements, and other hindrances which lay at present, upon them; must it therefore be lawful for them, to go and take it from them? It was well known that they are upon a barren place, where they were by necessity cast; and neither they, nor theirs could long continue upon the same; and why should they (because they were more ready, and more able at present) go and deprive them, of that which they had (with charge and hazard) provided and intended to remove to, as soon as they could and were able?

They had another passage in their letter, they had rather have to do with the Lords in England, to whom (as they heard it reported) some of them should say, that they had rather give up their right to them (if they must part with it) than to the church of Dorchester, etc. And that they should be less fearful to offend the Lords, than they were them.

Answer: Their answer was; that whatsoever they had heard (more than was true) yet the case was not so with them; that they had need, to give away their rights and adventures, either to the Lords, or them? Yet if they might measure their fear of offense, by their practice, they had rather (in that point) they should deal with the Lords, who were better able to bear it, or help themselves, than they were.

But lest I should be tedious, I will forbear other things, and come to the conclusion that was made in the end. To make any forcible resistance was far from their thoughts (they had enough of that about Kennebec) and to live in continual contention, with their friends and brethren, would be uncomfortable, and too heavy a burthen to bear. Therefore for peace sake (though they conceived they suffered much in this thing) they thought it better to let them have it, upon as good terms as they could get. And so they fell to treaty. The first thing that (because they had made so many and long disputes about it) they would have them to grant, was that they had right to it, or else they would never treat about it. The which being acknowledged, and yielded unto by them, this was the conclusion they came unto in the end, after much ado. That they should retain their house, and have the 16 part, of all they had bought of the Indians, and the other should have all the rest of the land; leaving such a moiety to those of Newtown as they reserved for them. This 16 part was to be taken in two places, one towards the house, the other towards Newtown's proportion. Also they were to pay according to proportion, what had been disbursed to the Indians for the purchase; thus was the controversy ended, but the unkindness not so soon forgotten. They of Newtown dealt more fairly desiring only what they could conveniently spare from a competency reserved for a plantation, for themselves. Which made them the more careful to procure a moiety for them in this agreement, and distribution.

Amongst the other businesses that Mr. Winslow had to do in England, he had order from the church, to provide, and bring over, some able, and fit man for to be their minister. And accordingly he had procured a godly and worthy man, one Mr. Glover, but it pleased God when he was prepared for the voyage, he fell sick of a fever and died. Afterwards when he was ready to come away, he became acquainted with Mr. Norton, who was willing to come over, but would not engage himself to this place, otherwise than he should see occasion when he came here, and if he liked better elsewhere, to repay the charge laid out for him (which came to about 70$^£$) and to be at his liberty. He stayed about a year with them, after he came over, and was well liked of them, and much desired by them, but he was invited to Ipswich, where were many rich and able men, and sundry of his acquaintance, so he went to them, and is their minister. About half of the charge was repaid, and the rest he had for the pains he took amongst them.

In the former year (because they perceived by Mr. Winslow's later letters) that no accounts would be sent, they resolved to keep the beaver, and send no more till they had them, or came to some further agreement. At least they would forbear till Mr. Winslow came over, that by more full conference with him they might better understand what was meet to be done. But when he came though he brought no accounts, yet he persuaded them to send the beaver, and was confident upon the receipt of the beaver, and his letters, they should have accounts the next year, and though they thought his grounds but weak that gave him this hope, and made him so confident, yet by his importunity they yielded, and sent the same. There being a ship at the latter end of the year, by whom they sent 1150£ weight of beaver, and 200 otter skins, besides sundry small furs, as 55 minks, 2 black fox skins, etc. And this year in the spring came in a Dutchman who thought to have traded at the Dutch fort, but they would not suffer him. He having good store of trading goods came to this place, and tendered them to sell; of whom they bought a good quantity, they being very good, and fit for their turn, as Dutch roll, kettles, etc., which goods amounted to the value of 500£ for the payment of which they passed bills to Mr. Sherley in England; having before sent the forementioned parcel of beaver.

And now this year (by another ship) sent another good round parcel that might come to his hands, and be sold before, any of these bills should be due. The quantity of beaver now sent was 1809£ weight, and of otters 10 skins, and shortly after (the same year) was sent by another ship (Mr. Langrume master) in beaver 0719£ weight, and of otter skins 199 concerning which Mr. Sherley thus writes:

Your letters I have received, with 8 hogsheads of beaver by Ed. Wilkinson, master of the *Falcon*, blessed be God, for the safe coming of it.

I have also seen, and accepted 3 bills of exchange, etc. But I must now acquaint you; how the Lord's heavy hand is upon this kingdom in many places, but chiefly in this city, with His judgment of the plague; the last week's bill was 1200 and odd, I fear this will be more; and it is much feared it will be a winter sickness. By reason whereof it is incredible, the number of people that are gone into the country, and left the city; I am persuaded many more, than went out the last great sickness; so as here is no trading, carriers from most places put down; nor no receiving of any money, though long due. Mr. Hall owes us more than would pay these bills, but he, his wife, and all are in the country, 60 miles from London; I writ to him, he came up, but could not pay us. I am persuaded if I should offer to sell the beaver at 8s per pound, it would not yield money; but when the Lord shall please to cease His hand I hope we shall have better, and quicker markets, so it shall lie by. Before I accepted the bills, I acquainted Mr. Beauchamp, and Mr. Andrews with them, and how there could be no money made, nor received; and that it would be a great discredit to you, which never yet had any turned back, and a shame to us, having 1800$^£$ of beaver lying by us, and more owing than the bills come to, etc. But all was nothing, neither of them both will put to their finger to help; I offered to supply my 3 part, but they gave me their answer they neither would nor could, etc. However your bills shall be satisfied to the parties' good content; but I would not have thought they would have left either you, or me at this time, etc. You will, and may expect I should write more, and answer your letters, but I am not a day in the week at home at town, but carry my books, and all to Clapham; for here is the miserablest time, that I think hath been known, in many ages. I have known 3 great sicknesses, but none like this. And that which should be a means, to pacify the Lord, and help us; that is taken away, preaching put down in many places, not a sermon in Westminster on the Sabbath, nor in many towns about us; the Lord in mercy look upon us. In the beginning of the year was a great drought, and no rain for many weeks together, so as all was burnt up, hay at 5$^£$ a load, and now all rain, so as much summer corn, and later hay is spoiled. Thus the Lord sends judgment, after judgment, and yet we cannot see nor humble ourselves; and therefore may justly fear heavier judgments unless we speedily repent, and return unto Him, which the Lord give us grace to do if it be His blessed will. Thus desiring you to remember us in your prayers; I ever rest

Your loving friend,

James Sherley

Sept. 14, 1636

This was all the answer they had from Mr. Sherley, by which Mr. Winslow saw his hopes failed him. So they now resolved to send no more beaver in that way which they had done, till they came to some issue or other about these things: but now came over letters from Mr. Andrews, and Mr. Beauchamp, full of complaints; that they marveled that nothing was sent over, by which any of their moneys should be paid in; for it did appear by the account sent in anno 1631 that they were each of them out, about eleven hundred pounds apiece, and all this while had not received one penny towards the same. But now Mr. Sherley sought to draw more money from them, and was offended because they denied him. And blamed them here very much that all was sent to Mr. Sherley, and nothing to them. They marveled much at this, for they conceived, that much of their moneys had been paid in; and that yearly each of them had received a proportionable quantity out of the large returns sent home. For they had sent home since that account was received in anno 1631, (in which all, and more than all their debts, with that year's supply was charged upon them) these sums following:

Nov. 18, 1631	By Mr. Peirce	400$^£$ weight of beaver, and otters 20
July 13, 1632	By Mr. Griffin	1348$^£$ beaver, and otter 147
Anno 1633	By Mr. Graves	3366$^£$ beaver, and otter 346
Anno 1634	By Mr. Andrews	3738$^£$ beaver, and otter 234
Anno 1635	By Mr. Babb	1150$^£$ beaver, and otter 200
June 24, 1636	By Mr. Wilkinson	1809$^£$ beaver, and otter 10
1636	By Mr. Langrume	0719$^£$ beaver, and otter 199
		12150$^£$ [beaver], 1156 [otter]

All these sums were safely received, and well sold, as appears by letters; the coat beaver usually at 20s per pound, and some at 24s; the skin at 15s and sometimes 16; I do not remember any under 14. It may be the last year might be something lower, so also there were some small furs that are not reckoned in this account, and some black beaver at higher rates, to make up the defects. It was conceived that the former parcels of beaver came to little less than 10000$^£$ sterling, and the otter skins would pay all the charge, and they with other furs make up besides if anything wanted of the former sum. When the former account was passed all their debts (those of *White Angel* and *Friendship* included) came but to 4770$^£$. And they could not estimate that all the supplies, since sent them, and bills paid for them, could come to above 2000$^£$. So as they conceived their debts had been paid, with advantage or interest. But it may be objected, how comes it, that they could not as well exactly set down their receipts; as their returns, but thus estimate it. I answer 2 things were the cause of it; the first, and principal was, that the new accountant, which they in England would needs press upon them, did wholly fail them, and could never give them any account; but trusting to his memory, and loose papers, let things run into such confusion, that neither he, nor any with him could bring things to rights. But being often called upon, to perfect his accounts; he desired to have such a time, and such a time of leisure, and he would do it; in the interim he fell into a great sickness; and in conclusion it fell out he could make no account at all; his books were after a little good beginning left altogether unperfect; and his papers, some were lost, and others so confused, as he knew not what to make of them himself, when they came to be searched, and examined. This was not unknown to Mr. Sherley; and they came to smart for it to purpose (though it was not their fault) both thus in England, and also here, for they conceived they lost some hundreds of pounds, for goods trusted out in the place which were lost for want of clear accounts to call them in. Another reason of this mischief was, that after Mr. Winslow was sent into England to demand accounts, and to except against the *White Angel,* they never had any price sent with their goods, nor any certain invoice of them; but all things stood in confusion; and they were fain to guess at the prices of them.

They writ back to Mr. Andrews, and Mr. Beauchamp, and told them they marveled, they should write, they had sent nothing home since the last accounts, for they had sent a great deal; and it might rather be marveled how they could be able to send so much; besides defraying all charge at home, and what they had lost by the French and so much cast away at sea, when Mr. Peirce lost his ship on the coast of Virginia. What they had sent was to them all, and to themselves, as well as Mr. Sherley; and if they did not look after it, it was their own faults; they must refer them to Mr. Sherley, who had received it, to demand it of him. They also writ to Mr. Sherley to the same purpose, and what the others complaints were.

This year 2 shallops going to Connecticut with goods from the Massachusetts, of such as removed thither to plant, were in an easternly storm, cast away in coming into this harbor, in the night. The boat's men were lost, and the goods were driven all along the shore, and strewed up and down at high water mark. But the Governor caused them to be gathered up, and drawn together, and appointed some to take an inventory of them, and others to wash and dry, such things as had need thereof; by which means most of the goods were saved, and restored to the owners. Afterwards another boat of theirs (going thither likewise) was cast away near unto Manonscusset, and such goods as came ashore were preserved for them; such crosses they met with in their beginnings; which some imputed as a correction from God, for their intrusion, (to the wrong of others) into that place. But I dare not be bold with God's judgments in this kind.

In the year 1634 the Pequots (a stout and warlike people) who had made wars with sundry of their neighbors, and puffed up with many victories, grew now at variance with the Narragansetts (a great people bordering upon them there). These Narragansetts held correspondence, and terms of friendship with the English of the Massachusetts. Now the Pequots being conscious of the guilt of Captain Stone's death, whom they knew to be an Englishman, as also those that were with him; and being fallen out with the Dutch; lest they should have over many enemies at once, sought to make friendship with the English of the Massachusetts, and for that end sent both messengers, and gifts unto them. As appears by some letters sent from the Governor hither.

Dear and worthy Sir, etc. To let you know somewhat of our affairs; you may understand that the Pequots have sent some of theirs to us, to desire our friendship, and offered much wampum and beaver, etc. The first messengers, were dismissed without answer; with the next we had divers days conference; and taking the advice of some of our ministers, and seeking the Lord in it; we concluded a peace, and friendship with them, upon these conditions: that they should deliver up to us, those men who were guilty of Stone's death, etc. And if we desired to plant in Connecticut, they should give up their right to us, and so we would send to trade with them as our friends (which was the chief thing we aimed at, being now in war with the Dutch, and the rest of their neighbors). To this they readily agreed, and that we should mediate a peace, between them, and the Narragansetts, for which end they were content we should give the Narragansetts part of that present, they would bestow on us (for they stood so much on their honor as they would not be seen to give anything of themselves). As for Captain Stone, they told us there were but 2 left, of those who had any hand in his death; and that they killed him in a just quarrel, for (say they) he surprised 2 of our men, and bound them, to make them by force to show him the way up the river[270], and he with 2 other

---

[270]   There is little trust to be given to their relations in these things. (Bradford).

coming on shore, 9 Indians watched him, and when they were asleep in the night, they killed them, to deliver their own men, and some of them going afterwards to the pinnace, it was suddenly blown up. We are now preparing to send a pinnate unto them, etc.

In another of his, dated the 12 of the first month, he hath this:

Our pinnace is lately returned from the Pequots; they put off but little commodity; and found them a very false people, so as they mean to have no more to do with them. I have divers other things to write unto you, etc.

> Yours ever assured,
> John Winthrop

Boston, 12 of the 1 month 1634

After these things, and as I take this year, John Oldham (of whom much is spoken before) being now an inhabitant of the Massachusetts; went with a small vessel, and slenderly manned, a trading into these south parts, and upon a quarrel between him and the Indians was cut off by them (as hath been before noted) at an island called by the Indians Munisses, but since by the English Block Island. This, with the former, about the death of Stone, and the baffling of the Pequots with the English of the Massachusetts; moved them to set out some, to take revenge, and require satisfaction for these wrongs; but it was done so superficially (and without their acquainting those of Connecticut, and other neighbors with the same) as they did little good, but their neighbors had more hurt done. For some of the murderers of Oldham fled, to the Pequots, and though the English went to the Pequots, and had some parley with them; yet they did but delude them, and the English returned without doing anything to purpose, being frustrate of their opportunity by the others' deceit.

After the English were returned, the Pequots took their time, and opportunity to cut off some of the English as they passed in boats, and went on fowling, and assaulted them the next spring at their habitations, as will appear in its place; I do but touch these things, because I make no question, they will be more fully, and distinctly handled, by themselves, who had more exact knowledge of them, and whom they did more properly concern.

This year Mr. Smith laid down his place of ministry; partly by his own willingness, as thinking it too heavy a burthen; and partly at the desire, and by the persuasion of others. And the church sought out for some other, having often been disappointed in their hopes, and desires heretofore. And it pleased the Lord to send them, an able, and a godly man[271], and of a meek and humble spirit, sound in the truth; and every way unreproveable in his life, and conversation. Whom after some time of trial, they chose for their teacher; the fruits of whose labors they enjoyed many years with much comfort, in peace, and good agreement.

---

[271] Mr. John Reynor. (Bradford).

In the fore part of this year, the Pequots fell openly upon the English at Connecticut, in the lower parts of the river; and slew sundry of them (as they were at work in the fields) both men and women; to the great terror of the rest, and went away in great pride, and triumph; with many high threats. They also assaulted a fort[272] at the river's mouth, though strong and well defended; and though they did not there prevail, yet it struck them with much fear, and astonishment; to see their bold attempts, in the face of danger. Which made them in all places to stand upon their guard, and to prepare for resistance; and earnestly to solicit their friends and confederates in the Bay of Massachusetts, to send them speedy aid, for they looked for more forcible assaults. Mr. Vane, being then Governor, writ from their General Court to them here, to join with them in this war. To which they were cordially willing; but took opportunity to write to them about some former things, as well as present, considerable hereabout.[273] The which

---

[272]   Saybrook fort.

[273]   Edward Winslow, in a letter dated 22 May 1637, wrote to governor John Winthrop
of the Massachusetts Bay: "Capt. Underhill and company at the fort in health; he
hath violently taken a Pequot woman from the Dutch which was a sachem's wife,
and hath her prisoner; knows nothing of what we hear concerning Capt. Mason,
but only that he was expected down with ninety men. Mr. Gardiner it seems
much discourageth common men by extolling the valor of your adversaries,
preferring them before Spaniards . . . The Pequots follow their fishing and planting
as if they had no enemies. Their women of esteem and children are gone to Long
Island with a strong guard . . . The truth is if once they be routed we know their
courage will fail: ergo, fear not." Winslow's letters to Winthrop are reprinted in
Collections of the Massachusetts Historical Society 4th Series 6(1863):162-183.

will best appear in the Governor's answer, which he returned to the same, which I shall here insert.

Sir: The Lord having disposed, as that your letters to our late Governor is fallen to my lot to make answer unto; I could have wished I might have been at more freedom of time, and thoughts also, that I might have done it more to your, and my own satisfaction. But what shall be wanting now, may be supplied hereafter. For the matters which from yourself, and Council, were propounded, and objected to us; we thought not fit to make them so public as the cognizance of our General Court. But as they have been considered by those of our Council; this answer we think fit to return unto you.

(1) Whereas you signify your willingness to join with us, in this war against the Pequots, though you cannot engage yourselves, without the consent of your General Court; we acknowledge your good affection towards us (which we never had cause to doubt of) and are willing to attend your full resolution, when it may most seasonably be ripened. (2ly) Whereas you make this war, to be our people's; and not to concern yourselves, otherwise than by consequence, we do in part, consent to you therein; yet we suppose, that in case of peril, you will not stand upon such terms, as we hope, we should not do towards you; and withal we conceive, that you look at the Pequots, and all other Indians, as a common enemy, who though he may take occasion, of the beginning of his rage, from some one part of the English, yet if he prevail, will surely pursue his advantage, to the rooting out of the whole nation; therefore when we desired your help, we did it not without respect to your own safety, as ours. (3ly) Whereas you desire we should be engaged to aid you, upon all like occasions; we are persuaded, you do not doubt of it; yet as we now deal with you, as a free people, and at liberty, so as we cannot draw you into this war with us, otherwise than as reason may guide, and provoke you; so we desire we may be at the like freedom, when any occasion may call for help from us. And whereas it is objected to us, that we refused to aid you, against the French; we conceive the case was not alike; yet we cannot wholly excuse our failing in that matter.

(4ly) Whereas you object that we began the war, without your privity, and managed it contrary to your advice; the truth is, that our first intentions being only against Block Island, and the enterprise seeming of small difficulty, we did not so much, as consider of taking advice, or looking out for aid abroad. And when we had resolved upon the Pequots, we sent presently, or not long after to you about it; but the answer received, it was not seasonable for us to change our counsels, except we had seen, and weighed your grounds, which might have outweighed our own.

(5ly) For our people's trading at Kennebec, we assure you (to our knowledge) it hath not been by any allowance from us; and what we have provided in this, and like cases, at our last Court, Mr. Edward Winslow can certify you.

(6ly) And whereas you object to us that we should hold trade, and correspondency with the French your enemies; we answer you are misinformed, for besides some letters which hath passed between our late Governor and them, to which we were privy, we have neither sent, nor encouraged ours to trade with them, only one vessel, or two, for the better conveyance of our letters, had license from our Governor to sail thither[274].

Divers other things have been privately objected to us, by our worthy friend, whereunto he received some answer; but most of them concerning the apprehensions of particular discourtesies, or injuries from some particular persons amongst us; it concerns not us to give any other answer to them, than this: that if the offenders shall be brought forth, in a right way, we shall be ready to do justice as the case shall require. In the meantime, we desire you to rest assured, that such things are without our privity, and not a little grievous to us.

Now for the joining with us in this war (which indeed concerns us no otherwise than it may yourselves) viz. the relieving of our friends, and Christian brethren, who are now first in the danger. Though you may think us able to make it good without you, (as if the Lord please to be with us, we may) yet 3 things we offer to your consideration, which (we conceive) may have some weight with you. (First) that if we should sink under this burden, your opportunity of seasonable help would be lost in 3 respects: 1. You cannot recover us, or secure yourselves there, with 3 times the charge, and hazard which now ye may. 2ly. The sorrows, which we should lie under (if through your neglect) would much abate of the acceptableness of your help afterwards. 3ly, those of yours, who are now full of courage, and forwardness, would be much damped, and so less able to undergo so great a burden. The (2) thing is this, that it concerns us much to hasten this war to an end before the end of this summer; otherwise the news of it, will discourage, both your, and our friends from

---

[274] But by this means they did furnish them, and have still continued to do. (Bradford).

coming to us, next year, with what further hazard, and loss it may expose us unto, yourselves may judge.

The (3) thing is this, that if the Lord shall please to bless our endeavors, so as we end the war, or put it in a hopeful way without you; it may breed such ill thoughts in our people towards yours, as will be hard to entertain such opinion of your good will towards us, as were fit to be nourished among such neighbors, and brethren as we are. And what ill consequences may follow, on both sides, wise men may fear, and would rather prevent, than hope to redress. So with my hearty salutations to yourself, and all your council, and other our good friends with you, I rest

Yours most assured in the Lord,
John Winthrop

Boston, the 20 of the 3 month[275]
1637

In the meantime, the Pequots, especially in the winter before, sought to make peace with the Narragansetts, and used very pernicious arguments, to move them thereunto. As that the English were strangers, and began to overspread their country, and would deprive them thereof in time, if they were suffered to grow, and increase. And if the Narragansetts did assist the English, to subdue them; they did but make way for their own overthrow, for if they were rooted out; the English would soon take occasion to subjugate them. And if they would hearken to them, they should not need to fear the strength of the English, for they would not come to open battle with them; but fire their houses, kill their cattle, and lie in ambush for them as they went abroad upon their occasions; and all this they might easily do, without any or little danger to themselves. The which course being held, they well saw the English could not long subsist, but they would either be starved with hunger, or be forced to forsake the country; with many the like things; insomuch that the Narragansetts were once wavering and were half minded to have made peace with them, and joined against the English. But again when they considered, how much wrong they had received from the Pequots, and what an opportunity they now had by the help of the English to right themselves; revenge was so sweet unto them, as it prevailed above all the rest; so as they resolved to join with the English against them, and did.

---

[275]   The third month, by the Julian calendar in use at the time, was May, not March as it is on the Gregorian calendar in use today.

The Court here agreed forthwith to send 50 men at their own charge[276]; and with as much speed as possibly they could, got them armed, and had made them ready under sufficient leaders; and provided a bark to carry them provisions and tend upon them for all occasions; but when they were ready to march (with a supply from the Bay) they had word to stay, for the enemy was as good as vanquished, and there would be no need.

I shall not take upon me, exactly to describe their proceedings in these things, because I expect it will be fully done by themselves, who best know the carriage and circumstances of things; I shall therefore but touch them in general; from Connecticut (who were most sensible of the hurt sustained and the present danger) they set out a party of men, and another party met them from the Bay, at Narragansetts, who were to join with them; the Narragansetts were earnest to be gone, before the English were well rested, and refreshed, (especially some of them which came last). It should seem their desire was to come upon the enemy suddenly, and undiscovered. There was a bark of this place, newly put in there, which was come from Connecticut, who did encourage them, to lay hold of the Indians' forwardness, and to show as great forwardness as they, for it would encourage them, and expedition might prove to their great advantage. So they went on, and so ordered their march, as the Indians brought them, to a fort of the enemy's (in which most of their chief men were) before day; they approached the same with great silence, and surrounded it, both with English, and Indians, that they might not break out; and so assaulted them with great courage, shooting amongst them, and entered the fort with all speed, and those that first entered found sharp resistance, from the enemy who both shot at and grappled with them; others ran into their houses, and brought out fire, and set them on fire, which soon took in their mat; and standing close together, with the wind, all was quickly on a flame, and thereby more were burnt to death, than was otherwise slain. It burnt their bowstrings, and made them unserviceable; those that escaped the fire, were slain with the sword, some hewed to pieces, others run through with their rapiers; so as they were quickly dispatched and very few escaped. It was conceived they thus destroyed about 400 at this time. It was a fearful sight, to see them thus frying in the fire, and the streams of blood quenching the same, and horrible was the stink and scent thereof, but the victory seemed a sweet sacrifice, and they gave the praise thereof to God, who had

---

[276] The names of Plymouth's volunteers are found in the *Plymouth Colony Records* 1:60-61.

wrought so wonderfully for them; thus to enclose their enemies in their hands; and give them so speedy a victory over so proud, and insulting an enemy. The Narragansett Indians, all this while stood round about, but aloof of from all danger, and left the whole execution to the English; except it were the stopping of any that broke away. Insulting over their enemies in this their ruin, and misery, when they saw them dancing in the flames, calling them by a word in their own language, signifying, O brave Pequots, which they used familiarly among themselves in their own praise, in songs of triumph after their victories. After this service was thus happily accomplished, they marched to the waterside, where they met with some of their vessels, by which they had refreshing with victuals and other necessaries. But in their march the rest of the Pequots drew into a body, and accosted them, thinking to have some advantage against them by reason of a neck of land; but when they saw the English prepare for them, they kept aloof, so as they neither did hurt nor could receive any. After their refreshing, and repair together for further counsel and directions; they resolved to pursue their victory, and follow the war against the rest; but the Narragansett Indians most of them forsook them, and such of them as they had with them for guides, or otherwise, they found them very cold, and backward in the business, either out of envy, or that they saw the English would make more profit of the victory, than they were willing they should; or else deprive them of such advantage as themselves desired, by having them become tributaries unto them, or the like.

For the rest of this business I shall only relate the same, as it is in a letter which came from Mr. Winthrop to the Governor here. As followeth.

Worthy Sir: I received your loving letter, and am much provoked to express my affections towards you, but straitness of time forbids me. For my desire is to acquaint you, with the Lord's great mercies to wards us, in our prevailing against His, and our enemies; that you may rejoice, and praise His name with us. About 80 of our men having coasted along towards the Dutch Plantation (sometimes by water but most by land) met here, and there, with some Pequots, whom they slew or took prisoners. 2 sachems they took, and beheaded; and not hearing of Sassacus (the chief sachem) they gave a prisoner his life, to go and find him out. He went and brought them word where he was, but Sassacus suspecting him to be a spy, after he was gone fled away, with some 20 more, to the Mohawks; so our men missed of him. Yet dividing themselves, and ranging up, and down, as the providence of God guided them (for the Indians were all gone, save 3 or 4). And they knew not whither to guide them, or else would not; upon the 13 of this

John Winthrop, governor of the Massachusetts Bay Colony.

month, they light upon a great company of them viz. 80 strong men, and 200 women, and children, in a small Indian town, fast by a hideous swamp, which they all slipped into before our men could get to them. Our captains were not then come together, but there was Mr. Ludlow[277], and Captain Mason[278], with some 10 of their men, and Captain Patrick[279] with some 20 or more of his; who shooting at the Indians, Captain Trask[280] with 50 more came soon in at the noise; then they gave order to surround the swamp, it being about, a mile about. But Lieutenant Davenport[281], and some 12 more, not hearing that command, fell into the swamp among the Indians; the swamp was so thick with shrub wood, and so boggy withal, that some of them stuck fast, and received many shot. Lieutenant Davenport was dangerously wounded, about his armhole, and another shot in the head, so as fainting, they were in great danger to have been taken by the

---

[277]   Roger Ludlow (1590-c1666) came to New England in 1630 on the *Mary and John*, and took up residence at Dorchester, later moving to Windsor about 1635.

[278]   John Mason (c1605-1672) came to New England about 1632, taking up residence at Dorchester, and later moving to Windsor about 1635. A good number of his letters to John Winthrop can be found in the *Winthrop Papers*. He also authored *A Brief History of the Pequot War*, which was edited by Thomas Prince and first published in 1736.

[279]   Daniel Patrick (c1605-1643) came to New England in 1630, settling at Watertown. According to Winthrop, after the Pequot War he started to suspect the Bay Colony officials had discovered his extramarital affairs, and fearing it would be discovered he fled to Stamford to live near the Dutch; but there, in 1643, he got into a dispute with a Dutchman who accused him of treachery. After ill language and a spit in the face, Patrick turned to leave and was shot in the back of the head.

[280]   William Trask (1585-1666) came to New England in 1628, where he was joined later that year by John Endecott and took up residence in Salem.

[281]   Richard Davenport (c1606-1665), came to New England in 1628 with John Endecott, taking up residence in Salem. About 1642 he moved to Boston, where he lived for 13 years before being killed by lightning. Nathaniel Morton in his *New England's Memorial* (Cambridge, 1669), wrote: "This year [1665] it pleased God to cause a sad dispensation of his hand to pass before us, in reference to the sudden death of Captain Davenport, who, in the month of July, was slain, as he lay on his bed, with a blow of thunder and lightning."

Indians; but Sergeant Riggs[282], and Jeffery[283] and 2 or 3 more rescued them, and slew divers of the Indians, with their swords. After they were drawn out, the Indians desired parley; and were offered (by Thomas Stanton, our interpreter) that if they would come out, and yield themselves, they should have their lives all, that had not their hands in the English blood; whereupon the sachem of the place came forth, and an old man, or 2 and their wives, and children; and after that some other women, and children, and so they spoke 2 hours, till it was night; then Thomas Stanton was sent into them again, to call them forth; but they said, they would sell their lives there, and so shot at him so thick, as if he had not cried out, and been presently rescued, they had slain him. Then our men, cut off a place of the swamp, with their swords, and cooped the Indians into so narrow a compass, as they could easier kill them, through the thickets; so they continued all the night, standing about 12 foot one from another, and the Indians coming close up to our men, shot their arrows so thick, as they pierced their hat brims, and their sleeves and stockings, and other parts of their clothes, yet so miraculously, did the Lord preserve them, as not one of them, was wounded, save those 3 who rashly went into the swamp. When it was near day, it grew very dark, so as those of them, which were left, dropped away between our men, though they stood but 12 or 14 foot asunder; but were presently discovered, and some killed in the pursuit. Upon searching of the swamp, the next morning, they found 9 slain, and some they pulled up, whom the Indians had buried in the mire; so as they do think, that of all this company, not 20 did escape, for they after found some, who died in their flight, of their wounds received. The prisoners were divided, some to those of the river, and the rest to us; of these we send the male children to Bermuda[284], by Mr. William Peirce, and the women and maid children, are disposed about in the towns. There have been now slain, and taken in all about 700. The rest are dispersed, and the Indians in all quarters so terrified, as all their friends are afraid to receive them. 2 of the

---

[282] Edward Riggs (c1593-1672) came to New England in 1633. Over the next two years, three of his five children would die, as would his wife Elizabeth: perhaps from the sickness that was going around in 1633.

[283] Thomas Jeffrey came to New England about 1633, taking up residence in Dorchester; a couple of years after the Pequot War he took up residence in New Haven, where he died in 1661.

[284] But they were carried to the West Indies. (Bradford)

sachems of Long Island, came to Mr. Stoughton[285] and tendered themselves to be tributaries, under our protection. And 2 of the Nipmuc sachems have been with me to seek our friendship. Among the prisoners we have the wife and children of Mononotto, a woman of a very modest countenance, and behavior; it was by her mediation, that the 2 English maids, were spared from death, and were kindly used by her; so that I have taken charge of her; one of her first requests was, that the English would not abuse her body, and that her children might not be taken from her. Those which were wounded, were fetched off soon by John Gallup[286] who came with his shallop in a happy hour, to bring them victuals, and to carry their wounded men, to the pinnace where our chief surgeon was, with Mr. Wilson[287], being about 8 leagues off. Our people are all in health (the Lord be praised) and although they had marched in their arms, all the day, and had been in fight all the night, yet they professed, they found themselves so fresh as they could willingly have gone to such another business.

This is the substance of that which I received, though I am forced to omit many considerable circumstances. So being in much straitness of time (the ships being to depart within this 4 days, and in them, the Lord Lee, and Mr. Vane) I here break off, and with hearty salutes to, etc., I rest

Yours assured,
John Winthrop

The captain's report we have slain 13 sachems; but Sassacus and Mononotto, are yet living.

The 28 of the 5 month 1637

That I may make an end of this matter; this Sassacus (the Pequots' chief sachem) being fled to the Mohawks, they cut off his head, with

---

[285] Israel Stoughton (1602-1644) came to New England in 1632 and took up residence in Dorchester. Several letters of his to Governor Winthrop survive and can be found in the *Winthrop Papers*.

[286] John Gallop (c1593-1650) came to New England about 1630. His wife Christabell was apparently reluctant to make the voyage, staying behind with her children and taking a couple years of persuasion to get her to come over. He was owner of the boat upon which John Oldham was killed by the Pequot.

[287] Rev. John Wilson (c1591-1667) was educated at King's College, Cambridge and received his M.A. in 1613; he came to New England in 1630, making subsequent trips to England and back in 1632 and 1634. He became the pastor of the First Church of Boston in 1632. He lost a lottery between himself and John Eliot to see who would go with the soldiers against the Pequot in 1637.

some other of the chief of them, whether to satisfy the English, or rather the Narragansetts, (who as I have since heard, hired them to do it) or for their own advantage, I well know not; but thus this war took end. The rest of the Pequots were wholly driven from their place, and some of them submitted themselves to the Narragansetts, and lived under them; others of them betook themselves to the Mohegans, under Uncas their sachem, with the approbation of the English of Connecticut, under whose protection Uncas lived; and he, and his men had been faithful to them in this war, and done them very good service. But this did so vex the Narragansetts, that they had not the whole sway over them; as they have never ceased plotting, and contriving, how to bring them under; and because they cannot attain their ends, because of the English who have protected them, they have sought to raise a general conspiracy against the English; as will appear in another place.

They had now letters again out of England from Mr. Andrews, and Mr. Beauchamp, that Mr. Sherley neither had, nor would pay them any money, or give them any account; and so with much discontent, desired them here to send them some, much blaming them still, that they had sent all to Mr. Sherley, and none to themselves. Now though they might have justly referred them to their former answer, and insisted thereupon, and some wise men counseled them so to do; yet because they believed, that they were really out round sums of money (especially Mr. Andrews) and they had some in their hands, they resolved to send them what beaver they had[288].

Mr. Sherley's letters were to this purpose, that as they had left him in the payment of the former bills, so he had told them, he would leave them in this, and believe it, they should find it true? And he was as good as his word, for they could never get penny from him; nor bring him to any account, though Mr. Beauchamp sued him in the Chancery. But they all of them turned their complaints, against them here, where there was least cause, and who had suffered most unjustly; first from Mr. Allerton, and them; in being charged with so much of that, which they never had, nor drunk for; and now in paying all, and more than all (as they conceived). And yet still thus more demanded, and that with many heavy charges. They now discharged Mr. Sherley from his agency, and forbade him to buy, or send over any more goods for them; and pressed him to come to some end about these things.

---

[288]   But staid it till the next year. (Bradford).

Amongst other enormities that fell out amongst them; this year 3 men were (after due trial) executed for robbery, and murder, which they had committed; their names were these: Arthur Peach, Thomas Jackson, and Richard Stinnings; there was a 4 Daniel Cross who was also guilty, but he escaped away, and could not be found. This Arthur Peach was the chief of them and the ringleader of all the rest; he was a lusty, and a desperate young man, and had been one of the soldiers in the Pequot War; and had done as good service, as the most there, and one of the forwardest in any attempt. And being now out of means, and loath to work, and falling to idle courses, and company, he intended to go to the Dutch plantation; and had allured these 3 being other men's servants, and apprentices to go with him. But another cause there was also of his secret going away in this manner, he was not only run into debt but he had got a maid with child (which was not known till after his death) a man's servant in the town; and fear of punishment made him get away. The other 3 complotting with him, ran away from their masters in the night, and could not be heard of; for they went not the ordinary way, but shaped such a course as they thought to avoid the pursuit of any. But falling into the way that lieth between the Bay of Massachusetts, and the Narragansetts, and being disposed to rest themselves, struck fire and took tobacco, a little out of the way, by the wayside; at length there came a Narragansett Indian by, who had been in the Bay a-trading, and had both cloth and beads about him (they had met him the day before, and he was now returning). Peach called him to drink tobacco with them, and he came, and sat down with them; Peach, told the other, he would kill him, and take what he had from him, but they were something afraid. But he said, hang him rogue he had killed many of them; so they let him alone to do as he would. And when he saw his time, he took a rapier, and ran him through the body once, or twice, and took from him 5 fathom of wampum and 3 coats of cloth, and went their way, leaving him for dead. But he scrambled away, when they were gone, and made shift to get home, (but died within a few days after). By which means they were discovered; and by subtlety the Indians took them, for they desiring a canoe to set them over a water (not thinking their fact had been known), by the sachem's command they were carried to Aquidneck Island, and there accused of the murder; and were examined and committed upon it by the English there. The Indians sent for Mr. Williams, and made a grievous complaint; his friends, and kindred were ready to rise in arms, and provoke the rest thereunto, some conceiving they should now find the Pequots' words true; that the English would fall upon them. But Mr. Williams pacified them, and told them, they should see justice done upon the offenders; and went to the man, and took Mr. James a physician with him; the man told him who did it, and in what manner it was done; but the physician found his wounds mortal, and that he could not live, (as he after testified upon oath, before the jury in open court) and so he died shortly after, as both Mr. Williams, Mr. James, and some Indians testified in court. The Government in the Bay were acquainted with it, but referred it hither, because it was done in this jurisdiction[289]; but pressed by all means that justice might be done in it; or else the country must rise and see justice done; otherwise it would raise a war. Yet some of the rude, and ignorant sort murmured that any English should be put to death for the Indians. So at last they of the Island brought them hither, and being often examined, and the evidence produced, they all in the end freely confessed in effect, all that the Indian accused them of, and that they had done it, in the manner aforesaid; and so upon the forementioned evidence, were cast by the jury[290], and condemned, and executed for the same.[291] And some of the Narragansett

---

[289] And yet afterwards they laid claim to those parts in controversy about Seekonk (Bradford).

[290] The jury consisted of William Hatch, John Winslow, William Pontus, Edward Foster, Richard Derby, John Holmes, John Paybody, Richard Sillis, Humfrey Turner, Samuel Hinckley, Giles Rickett, and Gabriel Fallowell. *Plymouth Colony Records* 1:96.

[291] September 4. (Bradford). *Plymouth Colony Records* 1:96-97 notes: "Arthur Peach, Thomas Jackson, Richard Stinnings, and Daniel Cross were indicted for murdering and robbing by the highway. They killed and robbed one Penowanyanquis, an Indian, at Misquamsqueece, and took from him five fathom of wampum, and

Indians, and of the party's friends were present when it was done, which gave them, and all the country good satisfaction. But it was a matter of much sadness to them here, and was the 2 execution which they had since they came; being both for willful murder, as hath been before related. Thus much of this matter.

They received this year more letters from England full of renewed complaints: on the one side, that they could get no money nor account from Mr. Sherley; and he again that he was pressed thereto, saying he was to account with those here, and not with them, etc. So as was before resolved, if nothing came of their last letters, they would now send them what they could, as supposing when some good part was paid them, that Mr. Sherley, and they, would more easily agree about the remainder.

So they sent to Mr. Andrews, and Mr. Beauchamp by Mr. Joseph Young, in the *Mary and Anne* 1325$^£$ weight of beaver, divided between them; Mr. Beauchamp returned an account of his moiety that he made 400$^£$ sterling of it, freight, and all charges paid; but Mr. Andrews though he had the more and better part, yet he made not so much of his, through his own indiscretion; and yet turned the loss[292] upon them here, but without cause.

They sent them more by bills, and other payment, which was received, and acknowledged by them, in money[293], and the like, which was for cattle sold of Mr. Allerton's, and the price of a bark sold which belonged to the stock, and made over to them in money 434$^£$ sterling. The whole sum was 1234$^£$ sterling, save what Mr. Andrews lost in the beaver, which was otherwise made good. But yet this did not stay their clamors, as will appear hereafter more at large.

It pleased God in these times, so to bless the country with such access, and confluence of people into it; as it was thereby much enriched, and cattle of all kinds stood at a high rate for divers years together; kine were sold, at 20$^£$ and some at 25$^£$ apiece, yea sometimes at 28$^£$; a cow calf usually at 10$^£$. A milch goat at 3$^£$ and some at 4$^£$, and female kids at 30s and often at 40s apiece, by which means the ancient planters, which had any stock, began to

---

three coats of woolen cloth . . . . They [the jury] found the said Arthur Peach, Thomas Jackson, and Richard Stinnings guilty of the said felonious murdering and robbing of the said Penowanyauquis, . . . Daniel Crosse made an escape, and so had not his trial; but Peach, Jackson and Stinnings had sentence of death pronounced . . . to be hanged by the neck until their bodies were dead, which was executed upon them accordingly."

292   Being about 40$^£$ (Bradford).

293   And divided between them. (Bradford).

grow in their estates; corn also went at a round rate, viz. 6s a bushel, so as other trading began to be neglected; and the old partners (having now forbidden Mr. Sherley to send them any more goods) broke off their trade at Kennebec, (and as things stood) would follow it no longer. But some of them, (with other they joined with) being loath, it should be lost by discontinuance, agreed with the company for it; and gave them about the 6 part of their gains for it, with the first fruits of which they built a house for a prison; and the trade there hath been since continued, to the great benefit of the place; for some well foresaw that these high prices of corn, and cattle, would not long continue; and that then the commodities there raised would be much missed.

This year about the 1 or 2 of June, was a great, and fearful earthquake[294]; it was in this place heard, before it was felt; it came with a rumbling noise, or low murmur, like unto remote thunder. It came from the northward, and passed southward; as the noise approached nearer the earth began to shake, and came at length with that violence; as caused platters, dishes, and such like things, as stood upon shelves to clatter, and fall down. Yea persons were afraid of the houses themselves; it so fell out that at the same time, divers of the chief of this town were met together at one house, conferring with some of their friends, that were upon their removal from the place (as if the Lord would hereby show the signs of His displeasure, in their shaking a-pieces, and removals one from another). However it was very terrible for the time, and as the men were set talking in the house, some women, and others were without the doors, and the earth shook with that violence, as they could not stand without catching hold of the posts, and pales that stood next them; but the violence lasted not long. And about half an hour, or less, came another noise and shaking, but neither so loud nor strong as the former, but quickly passed over; and so it ceased. It was not only on the seacoast, but the Indians felt it within land; and some ships that were upon the coast were shaken by it. So powerful is the mighty hand of the Lord, as to make both the earth, and sea to shake, and the mountains to tremble before Him, when He pleases; and who can stay His hand?

It was observed, that the summers for divers years together after this earthquake; were not so hot, and seasonable, for the ripening of corn, and other fruits, as formerly; but more cold, and moist, and subject to early and untimely frosts, by which many times, much Indian corn came not to maturity; but whether this was any cause, I leave it to naturalists to judge.

---

[294] Several other primary sources mention this earthquake, and indicate the date was June 1.

These 2 years I join together, because in them fell not out many things more than the ordinary passages, of their common affairs, which are not needful to be touched.

Those of this plantation, having at sundry times granted lands for several townships, and amongst the rest to the inhabitants of Scituate, (some whereof issued from themselves). And also a large tract of land was given to their 4 London partners in that place, viz. Mr. Sherley, Mr. Beauchamp, Mr. Andrews, and Mr. Hatherley. At Mr. Hatherley's request and choice it was by him taken for himself and them in that place, (for the other 3 had invested him with power, and trust to choose for them). And this tract of land extended to their utmost limits that way; and bordered on their neighbors of the Massachusetts; who had some years after, seated a town (called Hingham) on their lands next to these parts. So as now there grew great difference between these 2 townships, about their bounds, and some meadow grounds that lay between them; they of Hingham presumed, to allot part of them to their people, and measure, and stake them out; the other pulled up their stakes, and threw them. So it grew to a controversy between the 2 governments, and many letters and passages were between them about it. And it hung some 2 years in suspense; the Court of Massachusetts appointed some to range their line, according to the bounds of their patent, and (as they went to work) they made it to take in all Scituate; and I know not how much more. Again on the other hand, according to the line of the patent of this place it would take in Hingham, and much more within their bounds.

In the end both Courts agreed to choose 2 commissioners of each side, and to give them full, and absolute power, to agree and settle the bounds between them; and what they should do in the case should stand irrevocably. One meeting they had at Hingham, but could not conclude; for their commissioners stood stiffly on a clause in their grant; that from Charles

River, or any branch or part thereof, they were to extend their limits, and three miles further to the southward; or from the most southward part of the Massachusetts Bay, and 3 mile further. But they chose to stand on the former terms, for they had found a small river, or brook rather, that a great way within land trended southward, and issued into some part of that river taken to be Charles River; and from the most southerly part of this, and three mile more southward of the same, they would run a line east to the sea, (about 20 mile), which will (say they) take in a part of Plymouth itself. Now it is to be known that though this patent, and plantation were much the ancienter, yet this enlargement of the same (in which Scituate stood) was granted after theirs; and so theirs were first to take place, before this enlargement. Now their answer was first that however according to their own plan, they could no way come upon any part of their ancient grant. 2ly they could never prove that to be a part of Charles River, for they knew not which was Charles River, but as the people of this place, which came first, imposed such a name upon that river, upon which since Charlestown is built, (supposing that was it, which Captain Smith in his map, so named). Now they that first named it, have best reason to know it, and to explain which is it; but they only took it to be Charles River, as far as it was by them navigated, and that was as far as a boat could go. But that every runlet or small brook, that should far within land, come into it, or mix their streams with it, and were by the natives called by other, and different names from it; should now by them be made Charles River, or parts of it they saw no reason for it. And gave instance in Humber, in Old England, which had the Trent, Ouse, and many others of lesser note fell into it, and yet were not counted parts of it; and many smaller rivers and brooks fell into the Trent, and Ouse, and no parts of them, but had names apart, and divisions and nominations of themselves. Again it was pleaded that they had no east line in their patent, but were to begin at the sea, and go west by a line, etc. At this meeting no conclusion was made, but things discussed, and well prepared for an issue. The next year the same commissioners had their power continued or renewed, and met at Scituate, and concluded the matter, as followeth.

The agreement of the bounds betwixt
Plymouth, and Massachusetts

Whereas there were two commissions granted by the 2 jurisdictions, the one of Massachusetts Government, granted unto John Endecott gent., and Israel Stoughton gent.; the other of New Plymouth Government to William

Bradford governor, and Edward Winslow gent.; and both these for the setting out, settling, and determining of the bounds, and limits of the lands between the said jurisdictions, whereby not only this present age, but the posterity to come may live peaceably and quietly in that behalf. And forasmuch as the said commissioners, on both sides have full power so to do, as appeareth by the records of both jurisdictions, we therefore the said commissioners above named, do hereby with one consent, and agreement conclude, determine, and by these presents declare, that all the marshes at Cohasset, that lie of the one side of the river next to Hingham, shall belong to the jurisdiction of Massachusetts Plantation. And all the marshes that lie on the other side of the river next to Scituate, shall belong to the jurisdiction of New Plymouth; excepting 60 acres of marsh at the mouth of the river, on Scituate side next to the sea; which we do hereby agree, conclude, and determine shall belong to the jurisdiction of the Massachusetts. And further we do hereby agree, determine and conclude, that the bounds of the limits between both the said jurisdictions, are as followeth; viz. from the mouth of the brook that runneth into Cohasset marshes (which we call by the name of Bound Brook) with a straight, and direct line, to the middle of a great pond, that lieth on the right hand, of the upper path, or common way, that leadeth between Weymouth, and Plymouth, close to the path as we go along, which was formerly named (and still we desire may be called) Accord Pond, lying about five or 6 miles from Weymouth southerly; and from thence with a straight line to the southernmost part of Charles River[295], and 3 miles southerly inward into the country according as is expressed in the patent granted by His Majesty to the Company of the Massachusetts Plantation provided always and never the less concluded, and determined by mutual agreement between the said commissioners, that if it fall out, that the said line from Accord Pond to the southernmost part of Charles River, and 3 miles southerly as is before expressed, straiten, or hinder any part of any plantation begun, by the Government of New Plymouth, or hereafter to be begun within 10 years after the date of these presents, that then notwithstanding the said line, it shall be lawful for the said Government of New Plymouth to assume on the northerly side of the said line, where it shall so entrench as aforesaid, so much land, as will make up the quantity of eight miles square, to belong to every such plantation begun, or to begun as aforesaid; which we agree, determine, and conclude to appertain, and belong to the said Government of New Plymouth. And whereas the said line, from the said brook which runneth into Cohasset saltmarsh (called by us Bound Brook,

---

[295] Which is Charles River may still be questioned. (Bradford).

and the pond called Accord Pond) lieth near the lands belonging to the townships of Scituate, and Hingham, we do therefore hereby determine, and conclude, that if any divisions already made, and recorded by either the said townships, do cross the said line, that then it shall stand and be of force according to the former intents and purposes of the said towns granting them (the marshes formerly agreed on excepted). And that no town in either jurisdiction shall hereafter exceed, but contain themselves within the said lines expressed. In witness whereof we the commissioners of both jurisdictions do by these presents indented, set our hands, and seals the ninth day of the 4 month in 16 year of our sovereign lord King Charles; and in the year of our Lord 1640.

> William Bradford Governor
> John Endecott
> Ed: Winslow
> Israel Stoughton

Whereas the patent was taken in the name of William Bradford (as in trust) and ran in these terms: to him, his heirs, and associates and assigns. And now the number of freemen being much increased, and divers townships established, and settled in several quarters of the government, as Plymouth, Duxbury, Scituate, Taunton, Sandwich, Yarmouth, Barnstable, Marshfield, and not long after Seekonk (called afterward at the desire of the inhabitants, Rehoboth) and Nauset; it was by the Court desired that William Bradford should make a surrender of the same into their hands. The which he willingly did, in this manner following.

Whereas William Bradford, and divers others the first instruments of God in the beginning of this great work of plantation, together with such as the all-ordering hand of God in His providence soon added unto them; have been at very great charges to procure the lands, privileges, and freedoms from all entanglements, as may appear by divers and sundry deeds, enlargements of grants, purchases, and payments of debts, etc.; by reason whereof the title, to the day of these presents, remaineth in the said William Bradford his heirs, associates, and assigns. Now for the better settling of the estate of the said lands (contained in the grant or patent) the said William Bradford, and those first instruments termed, and called in sundry orders upon public record the purchasers, or old comers, witness 2 in special, the one bearing date the 3 of March 1639, the other in December the 1, anno 1640, whereunto these presents have special relation, and agreement. And whereby they are distinguished from other the freemen, and inhabitants of the said corporation. Be it known unto all men therefore by these presents, that the said William Bradford for himself his heirs, together with the said purchasers, do only reserve unto themselves, their heirs, and assigns those 3 tracts of land, mentioned in the said resolution, order, and agreement bearing date the first of December 1640; viz. first from the bounds of Yarmouth, 3 miles to the eastward of Namskaket, and from sea, to sea, cross the neck of land. The 2 of a place called Acoughcus, which lieth in the bottom of the bay adjoining to the west side of Point Peril, and 2 miles to the western side of the said river, to another place called Acushnet River, which entereth at the western end of Nacata, and 2 miles to the eastward thereof, and to extend 8 miles up into the country. The 3 place from Sowamsett River, to Pawtucket River, (with Cawsumsett Neck), which is the chief habitation of the Indians, and reserved for them to dwell upon, extending into the land 8 miles through the whole breadth thereof. Together with such other small parcels of lands, as they or any of them are personally possessed of, or interested in, by virtue of any former titles or grant whatsoever. And the said William Bradford doth by the free, and full consent, approbation and agreement, of the said Old Planters, or purchasers, together with the liking, approbation, and acceptation of the other part of the said Corporation, surrender into the hands of the whole Court, consisting of the Freemen of this Corporation of New Plymouth, all that other right, and title, power, authority, privileges, immunities and freedoms granted in the said letters patents, by the said right Honorable Council for New England. Reserving his, and their personal right of freemen, together with the said Old Planters aforesaid, except the said lands before excepted, declaring the freemen of this Corporation, together with all such, as shall be legally admitted into the same, his associates. And the said William Bradford for him, his heirs, and assigns, do hereby further promise, and grant, to do and perform whatsoever further thing, or things, act, or acts, which in him lieth, which shall be needful, and expedient, for the better confirming, and establishing the said premises, as by counsel learned in the laws, shall be reasonably advised and devised, when he shall be thereunto required. In witness whereof, the said William Bradford hath in public Court surrendered the said letters patents actually into the hands, and power of the said Court, binding himself, his heirs, executors, administrators, and assigns to deliver up, whatsoever specialties are in his hands, that do or may concern the same.

In these 2 years they had sundry letters out of England to send one over to end the business and account with Mr. Sherley; who now professed he could not make up his accounts without the help of some from hence, especially Mr. Winslow's. They had serious thoughts of it; and the most part of the partners here thought it best to send; but they had formerly written such bitter, and threatening letters, as Mr. Winslow was neither willing to go, nor that any other of the partners should; for he was persuaded if any of them went, they should be arrested, and an action of such a sum laid upon them, as they should not procure bail, but must lie in prison, and then they would bring them to what they list; or otherwise they might be brought into trouble by the Archbishop's means, as the times then stood. But notwithstanding they were much inclined to send, and Captain Standish was willing to go; but they resolved, seeing they could not all agree in this thing, and that it was weighty, and the consequence might prove dangerous; to take Mr. Winthrop's advice in the thing, and the rather, because Mr. Andrews had by many letters acquainted him with the differences between them, and appointed him for his assign to receive his part of the debt. (And though they denied to pay him any as a debt, till the controversy was ended, yet they had deposited 110$^£$ in money in his hands for Mr. Andrews, to pay to him in part as soon as he would come to any agreement with the rest). But Mr. Winthrop was of Mr. Winslow's mind and dissuaded them from sending; so they broke off their resolution from sending; and returned this answer, that the times were dangerous as things stood with them, for they knew how Mr. Winslow had suffered formerly, and for a small matter was clapped up in the Fleet, and it was long before he could get out, to both his, and their great loss, and damage, and times were not better, but worse in that respect. Yet that their equal, and honest minds might appear to all men, they made them this tender; to refer the case to some gentlemen, and merchants in the Bay of the Massachusetts, such as they should choose, and were well known unto themselves (as they perceived there were many of their acquaintance and friends there, better known to them than the partners here). And let them be informed in the case by both sides, and have all the evidence that could be produced, in writing, or otherwise; and they would be bound to stand to their determination, and make good their award though it should cost them all they had in the world. But this did not please them, but they were offended at it, without any great reason for aught I know (seeing neither side could give in clear accounts); the partners here could not, by reason they (to their smart) were failed by the accountant they sent them, and Mr. Sherley pretended he could not also; save as they conceived it a disparagement to yield to their inferiors, in respect of the place, and other concurring circumstances; so this came to nothing; and afterward Mr. Sherley write that if Mr. Winslow would meet him in France, the Low Countries, or Scotland, let the place be known; and he come to him there. But in regard of the troubles that now began to arise in our own nation, and other reasons, this did not come to any effect. That which made them so desirous to bring things to an end; was partly to stop the clamors, and aspersions raised and cast upon them hereabout; though they conceived themselves to sustain the greatest wrong, and had most cause of complaint; and partly because they feared the fall of cattle, in which most part of their estates lay. And this was not a vain fear; for they fell indeed before they came to a conclusion; and that so suddenly, as a cow, that but a month before was worth 20$^£$ and would so have passed in any payment, fell now to 5$^£$ and would yield no more; and a goat that went at 3$^£$ or 50s, would now yield but 8 or 10s at most. All men feared a fall of cattle, but it was thought it would be by degrees, and not to be from the highest pitch, at once to the lowest as it did, which was greatly to the damage of many, and the undoing of some. Another reason was, they many of them grew aged, (and indeed a rare thing it was that so many partners should all live together so many years as these did) and some saw many changes were like to befall; so as they were loath to leave these entanglements upon their children, and posterity, who might be driven to remove places, as they had done; yea themselves might do it yet before they died. But this business must yet rest, the next year gave it more ripeness, though it rendered them less able to pay for the reasons aforesaid.

Mr. Sherley being weary of this controversy, and desirous of an end, (as well as themselves) write to Mr. John Atwood[296], and Mr. William Collier, 2 of the inhabitants of this place, and of his special acquaintance; and desired them to be a means to bring this business to an end; by advising, and counseling the partners here, by some way to bring it to a composition, by mutual agreement. And he write to themselves also to that end; as by his letter may appear, so much thereof as concerns the same I shall here relate.

Sir: My love remembered, etc. I have write so much concerning the ending of accounts betwixt us, as I profess I know not what more to write, etc. If you desire an end, as you seem to do; there is (as I conceive) but 2 ways; that is to perfect all accounts, from the first to the last, etc. Now if we find this difficult, and tedious, having not been so strict, and careful, as we should, and ought to have done; as for my own part I do confess I have been somewhat too remiss; and do verily think so are you, etc. I fear you can never make a perfect account of all your petty voyages, out, and home too and again, etc.[297] So then the second way must be, by biding, or compounding, and this way first, or last we must fall upon, etc. If we must war at law for it, do not you expect from me, neither will I from you, but to cleave the hair, and then I dare say the lawyers will be most gainers, etc. Thus let us set to the work, one way or other and end, that I may not always suffer in my name, and estate, and you are not free, nay the gospel suffers by your delaying and causeth the professors of it, to be hardly spoken of, that you being many, and

---

[296]   John Atwood arrived in Plymouth about 1636, and died there in 1644, leaving his estate to wife Ann.

[297]   This was but to pretend advantage, for it could not be done, neither did it need. (Bradford).

now able should combine and join together to oppress and burden me, etc. Fear not to make a fair, and reasonable offer, believe me I will never take any advantage to plead it against you, or to wrong you; or else let Mr. Winslow come over, and let him have such full power, and authority as we may end by compounding; or else the account so well, and fully made up, as we may end by reckoning. Now blessed be God the times be much changed here, I hope to see many of you return to your native country again, and have such freedom, and liberty as the Word of God prescribes. Our bishops were never so near a downfall as now, God hath miraculously confounded them, and turned all their popish, and Machiavellian plots, and projects on their own heads, etc. Thus you see what is fit to be done concerning our particular grievances, I pray you take it seriously into consideration, let each give way a little that we may meet, etc. Be you and all yours kindly saluted, etc. So I ever rest

Your loving friend,
James Sherley

Clapham, May 18, 1641

Being thus by this letter, and also by Mr. Atwood's, and Mr. Collier's mediation urged to bring things to an end, (and the continual clamors from the rest) and by none more urged than by their own desires. They took this course (because many scandals had been raised upon them) they appointed these 2 men before mentioned to meet on a certain day, and called some other friends on both sides, and Mr. Freeman, brother-in-law to Mr. Beauchamp: and having drawn up a collection of all the remains of the stock, in whatsoever it was, as housing, boats, bark and all implements belonging to the same, as they were used in the time of trade, were they better or worse, with the remains of all commodities, as beads, knives, hatchets, cloth, or anything else, as well the refuse as the more vendible, with all debts as well, those that were desperate as others more hopeful. And having spent divers days to bring this to pass, having the help of all books and papers, which either any of themselves had, or Josias Winslow who was their accountant. And they found the sum in all to arise (as the things were valued) to about 1400$^£$. And they all of them took a voluntary, but a solemn oath in the presence one of another, and of all their friends, the persons abovesaid that were now present; that this was all, that any of them knew of, or could remember; and Josias Winslow did the like for his part. But the truth is they wronged themselves much in the valuation; for they reckoned some cattle as they were taken of Mr. Allerton, as for instance a cow in the hands of one, cost 25$^£$ and so she was valued in this account, but when she came to be passed away in part of payment, after the agreement she would be accepted but at 4£ 15s. Also being tender of their oaths, they brought in all they knew owing to the stock, but they had not made the like diligent search what the stock might owe to any; so as many scattering debts fell upon afterwards more than now they knew of. Upon this they drew certain articles of agreement between Mr. Atwood, on Mr. Sherley's behalf, and themselves. The effect is as followeth.

Articles of agreement, made and concluded upon
the 15 day of October 1641

Imprimis: Whereas there was a partnership for divers years agreed upon between James Sherley, John Beauchamp, and Richard Andrews of London, merchants; and William Bradford, Edward Winslow, Thomas Prence, Myles Standish, William Brewster, John Alden, and John Howland, with Isaac Allerton, in a trade of beaver skins, and other furs arising in New England; the term of which said partnership being expired, and divers sums of money in goods adventured into New England by the said James Sherley, John Beauchamp, and Richard Andrews. And many large returns made from New England by the said William Bradford, Edward Winslow, etc. And difference arising about the charge of 2 ships the one called the *White Angel* of Bristol, and the other the *Friendship* of Barnstaple, and a voyage intended in her, etc., which said ships, and their voyages, the said William Bradford, Edward Winslow, etc. conceive do not at all appertain to their accounts of partnership.

And whereas the accounts of the said partnership, are found to be confused, and cannot orderly appear (through the default of Josias Winslow the book-keeper); And whereas the said W. B., etc. have received all their goods for the said trade, from the foresaid James Sherley, and have made most of their returns to him, by consent of the said John Beauchamp, and Richard Andrews; and whereas also the said James Sherley hath given power and authority, to Mr. John Atwood, with the advice, and consent of William Collier of Duxbury, for, and on his behalf to put such an absolute end to the said partnership, with all and every accounts, reckonings, dues, claims, demands whatsoever to the said James Sherley, John Beauchamp and Richard Andrews, from the said W. B., etc. for and concerning the said beaver trade, and also the charge the said 2 ships, and their voyages made or pretended whether just or unjust, from the world's beginning to this present, as also for the payment of a purchase of 1800£ made by Isaac Allerton for, and on the behalf of the said W. B., Ed. W., etc., and of the joint stock, shares, lands, and adventures, whatsoever in New England aforesaid, as appeareth by a deed bearing date the 6 of November 1627; and also for, and from such sum, and sums of money, or goods as are received by William Bradford, Thomas Prence, and Myles Standish for the recovery of dues, by accounts betwixt them the said James Sherley, John Beauchamp, and Richard Andrews, and Isaac Allerton, for the ship called the *White Angel*. Now the said John Atwood with advice and counsel of the said William Collier, having had much communication and spent divers days in agitation of all the said differences, and accounts with the said W. B., E. W., etc., and the said W. B., E. W. etc. have also with the said bookkeeper spent much time in collecting, and gathering together the remainder of the stock of partnership for the said trade, and whatsoever hath been received, or is due by the said attorneyship before expressed, and all, and all manner of goods, debts, and dues thereunto belonging, as well those debts that are weak, and doubtful, and desperate as those that are more secure, which in all do amount to the sum of 1400$^£$ or thereabout; and for more full satisfaction of the said James Sherley, John Beauchamp, and Richard Andrews, the said W. B. and all the rest of the abovesaid partners, together with Josias Winslow the bookkeeper have taken a voluntary oath that within the said sum of 1400$^£$ or thereabout, is contained whatsoever they know to the utmost of their remembrance.

In consideration of all which matters, and things before expressed, and to the end, that a full absolute, and final end may be now made, and all suits in law may be avoided, and love, and peace continued. It is therefore agreed, and concluded between the said John Atwood, with the advice, and consent of the said William Collier, for and on the behalf of the said James Sherley, to and with the said W. B. etc. in manner, and form following: viz. that the said John Atwood shall procure a sufficient release, and discharge under the hands, and seals of the said James Sherley, John Beauchamp, and Richard Andrews, to be delivered fair, and unconcealed to the said William Bradford, etc. at or before the last day of August next ensuing the date hereof; whereby the said William Bradford, etc., their heirs, executors, and administrators, and every of them shall be fully, and absolutely acquitted, and discharged of all actions, suits, reckonings, accounts, claims, and demands whatsoever concerning the general stock of beaver trade, payment of the said 1800$^£$ for the purchase, and all demands, reckonings, and accounts, just, or unjust, concerning the two ships, *White Angel*, and *Friendship* aforesaid, together with whatsoever hath been received by the said William Bradford, of the goods, or estate of Isaac Allerton, for the satisfaction of the accounts of the said ship called the *White Angel* by virtue of a letter of attorney to him, Thomas Prence and Myles Standish, directed from the said James Sherley, John Beauchamp and Richard Andrews, for that purpose as aforesaid.

It is also agreed, and concluded upon between the said parties to these presents, that the said W. B., E. W., etc. shall now be bound in 2400$^£$ for payment of 1200$^£$ in full satisfaction of all demands as aforesaid; to be paid in manner and form following, that is to say 400$^£$ within 2 months next after the receipt of the aforesaid releases, and discharges, one hundred and ten pounds whereof is already in the hands of John Winthrop Senior of Boston Esquire, by the means of Mr. Richard Andrews aforesaid; and 80$^£$ weight of beaver now deposited into the hands of the said John Atwood to be both in part of payment of the said 400$^£$ and the other 800$^£$ to be paid by 200$^£$ per annum to such assigns as shall be appointed, inhabiting either in Plymouth, or Massachusetts Bay, in such goods, and commodities, and at such rates, as the country shall afford, at the time of delivery, and payment; and in the meantime, the said bond of 2400$^£$ to be deposited into the hands of the said John Atwood. And it is agreed upon by, and between the said parties to these presents, that if the said John Atwood shall not or cannot procure such said releases, and discharges as aforesaid, from the said James Sherley, John Beauchamp, and Richard Andrews, at or before the last day of August next ensuing the date hereof, that then the said John Atwood shall at the said day precisely, redeliver, or cause to be delivered unto the said W. B., E. W., etc. their said bond of 2400$^£$, and the said 80$^£$ weight of beaver, or the due value thereof without any fraud, or further delay. And for performance of all, and singular the covenants, and agreements herein contained, and expressed, which on the one part and behalf of the said James Sherley are to be observed, and performed, shall become bound in the sum of 2400$^£$ unto them the said William Bradford, Edward Winslow, Thomas Prence, Myles Standish, William Brewster, John Alden, and John Howland. And it is lastly agreed upon between the said parties, that these presents shall be left in trust, to be kept for both parties, in the hands of Mr. John Rayner, teacher, of Plymouth. In witness whereof, all the said parties, have hereunto severally set their hands, the day, and year first above written.

John Atwood, William Bradford, Edward Winslow, etc.

In the presence of:

Edmond Freeman
William Thomas
William Paddy
Nathaniel Souther

The next year this long, and tedious business, came to some issue, as will then appear, though not to a final end, with all the parties, but thus much for the present.

I had forgotten to insert in its place, how the church here had invited, and sent for Mr. Charles Chauncy, a reverend, godly, and very learned man, intending upon trial, to choose him pastor of the church here, for the more comfortable performance of the ministry, with Mr. John Rayner, the teacher of the same[298]. But there fell out some difference about baptizing, he holding it ought only to be by dipping, and putting the whole body under water, and that sprinkling was unlawful. The church yielded that immersion, or dipping was lawful, but in this cold country, not so convenient. But they could not, nor durst not yield to him in this, that sprinkling (which all the churches of Christ do for the most part use at this day) was unlawful, and an human invention, as the same was pressed; but they were willing to yield to him as far as they could, and to the utmost; and were contented to suffer him to practice as he was persuaded, and when he came to minister that ordinance he might so do it, to any that did desire it in that way; provided he could peaceably suffer Mr. Rayner, and such as desired to have theirs, otherwise baptize by him, by sprinkling or pouring on of water upon them; so as there might be no disturbance in the church hereabout. But he said he could not yield thereunto. Upon which the church procured some other ministers to dispute the point with him publicly, as Mr. Ralph Partridge of Duxbury[299], who did it sundry times, very ably, and sufficiently; as also some other ministers within this government; but he was not satisfied so the church, sent to many other churches to crave their help, and advice in this matter, and with his will, and consent, sent them his arguments written under his own hand; they sent them to the church at Boston in the Bay of Massachusetts, to be communicated with other churches there; also they sent the same to the churches of Connecticut, and New Haven, with sundry others. And received very able, and sufficient answers, as they conceived, from them and their learned ministers, who all concluded against him. But himself was not satisfied therewith; their answers are too large here to relate; they conceived the church had done what was meet in the thing, so Mr. Chauncy, having been the most part of 3 years here removed himself to Scituate, where he

---

[298]   Mr. Chauncy came to them in the year 1638 and stayed till the latter part of this year 1641. (Bradford).

[299]   Ralph Partridge came to New England in 1636, and became the first minister for the town of Duxbury.

now remains a minister to the church there. Also about these times now that cattle, and other things began greatly to fall from their former rates, and persons began to fall into more straits; and many being already gone from them (as is noted before) both to Duxbury, Marshfield, and other places, and those of the chief sort, as Mr. Winslow, Captain Standish, Mr. Alden, and many other, and still some dropping away daily, and some at this time, and many more unsettled; it did greatly weaken the place. And by reason of the straitness, and barrenness of the place, it set the thoughts of many upon removal; as will appear more hereafter.

Marvelous it may be to see, and consider, how some kind of wickedness did grow, and break forth, here in a land, where the same was so much witnessed against, and so narrowly looked unto, and severely punished when it was known; as in no place more, or so much, that I have known, or heard of; insomuch that they have been somewhat censured, even by moderate and good men, for their severity in punishments. And yet all this could not suppress the breaking out of sundry notorious sins (as this year, besides other, gives us too many sad precedents, and instances) especially drunkenness, and uncleanness; not only incontinency, between persons unmarried, for which many both men and women have been punished sharply enough, but some married persons also. But that which is worse, even sodomy, and buggery (things fearful to name) have broke forth in this land, oftener than once. I say it may justly be marveled at; and cause us to fear, and tremble, at the consideration of our corrupt natures, which are so hardly bridled, subdued, and mortified; nay cannot by any other means, but the powerful work, and grace of God's Spirit. But (besides this) one reason may be, that the Devil may carry a greater spite, against the churches of Christ, and the gospel here; by how much the more they endeavor to preserve holiness, and purity amongst them; and strictly punisheth the contrary when it ariseth either in church or commonwealth; that he might cast a blemish, and stain upon them in the eyes of world, who use to be rash in judgment. I would rather think thus, than that Satan hath more power in these heathen lands, as some have thought, than in more Christian nations, especially over God's servants in them.

2. Another reason may be, that it may be in this case, as it is with waters when their streams are stopped, or dammed up; when they get passage they flow with more violence, and make more noise, and disturbance, than when

they are suffered to run quietly in their own channels; so wickedness being here more stopped by strict laws, and the same more nearly looked unto, so as it cannot run in a common road of liberty as it would, and is inclined, it searches everywhere and at last breaks out where it gets vent.

3. A third reason may be, here, (as I am verily persuaded) is not more evils in this kind, nor nothing near so many, by proportion as in other places; but they are here more discovered, and seen, and made public by due search, inquisition, and due punishment; for the churches look narrowly to their members, and the magistrates over all; more strictly than in other places. Besides here the people are but few in comparison, of other places, which are full, and populous, and lie hid, as it were in a wood, or thicket, and many horrible evils, by that means are never seen, nor known; whereas here, they are as it were brought into the light and set in the plain field, or rather on a hill, made conspicuous to the view of all.

But to proceed, there came a letter from the Governor in the Bay to them here, touching matters of the forementioned nature which because it may be useful I shall here relate it and the passages thereabout.

Sir: Having an opportunity to signify the desires of our General Court, in two things of special importance, I willingly take this occasion, to impart them to you, that you may impart them to the rest of your magistrates, and also to your Elders, for counsel; and give us your advice in them. The first is concerning heinous offenses in point of uncleanness; the particular cases, with the circumstances, and the questions thereupon you have here enclosed. The 2 thing is concerning the Islanders at Aquidneck, that seeing the chiefest of them, are gone from us, in offenses either to churches, or commonwealth, or both; others are dependents on them, and the best sort are such as close with them in all their rejections of us; neither is it only in faction that they are divided from us, but in very deed they rend themselves, from all the true churches of Christ, and many of them from all the powers of magistracy; we have had some experience hereof by some of their underworkers, or emissaries, who have lately come amongst us, and have made public defiance, against magistracy, ministry, churches, and church covenants, etc. as antichristian; secretly also sowing the seeds, of Familism and Anabaptistry, to the infection of some, and danger of others; so that we are not willing to join with them in any league, or confederacy at all; but rather that you would consider, and advise with us how we may avoid them, and keep ours from being infected by them. Another thing I should mention to you, for the maintenance of the trade of beaver; if there be not a company to order it in every jurisdiction, among the English, which companies should agree in general of their way in trade, I suppose that the trade will be overthrown, and the Indians will abuse us; for this cause we have lately put it into order amongst us, hoping of encouragement from you (as we have had) that we may continue the same. Thus not further to trouble you, I rest, with my loving remembrance to yourself, etc.

Your loving friend,
Richard Bellingham

Boston 28 (1) 1642.

The note enclosed follows on the other side[300].

Worthy and beloved sir:

Your letter (with the questions enclosed) I have communicated with our Assistants; and we have referred the answer of them, to such Reverend Elders as are amongst us; some of whose answers thereto, we have here sent you enclosed, under their own hands; from the rest we have not yet received any; our far distance, hath been the reason of this long delay; as also that they could not confer their counsels together.

For ourselves (you know our breedings, and abilities), we rather desire light from yourselves, and others, whom God hath better enabled; than to presume to give our judgments in cases so difficult, and of so high a nature. Yet under correction and submission to better judgments; we propose this one thing, to your prudent considerations. As it seems to us in the case even of willful murder, that though a man did smite, or wound another, with a full purpose, or desire to kill him (which is murder in a high degree before God) yet if he did not die, the magistrate was not to take away the other's life.[301] So by proportion in other gross, and foul sins, though high attempts, and near approaches, to the same be made, and such as in the sight and account of God, may be as ill, as the accomplishment of the foulest acts of that sin; yet we doubt whether it may be safe for the magistrate to proceed to death; we think upon the former grounds, rather he may not. As for instance in the case of adultery, (if it be admitted, that it is to be punished with death, which to some of us is not clear) if the body be not actually defiled, then death is not to be inflicted. So in sodomy, and bestiality, if there be not penetration,

---

[300] The leaf containing Bradford's note was missing from the manuscript prior to 1736, and is not known to now exist.

[301] Exodus 21:22. Deut. 19:11. Num. 35:16,18. (Bradford).

yet we confess foulness of circumstances, and frequency in the same; doth make us remain in the dark, and desire further light, from you, or any as God shall give.

As for the 2 thing, concerning the Islanders? We have no conversing with them, nor desire to have; further than necessity, or humanity may require.

As for trade? We have as far as we could, ever therein held an orderly course, and have been sorry to see the spoil thereof by others; and fear it will hardly be recovered. But in these, or any other things, which may concern the common good, we shall be willing to advise, and concur with you in what we may. Thus with my love remembered to yourself, and the rest of our worthy friends, your Assistants, I take leave, and rest

Your loving friend,
W.B.

Plymouth 17·3 month, 1642

Now follows the ministers' answers, and first
Mr. Rayner's

Question:

> What sodomitical acts are to be punished with death, and what very fact *(ipso facto)* is worthy of death, or if the fact itself be not capital, what circumstances concurring may make it capital?

Answer:

> In the judicial law (the morality whereof concerneth us) it is manifest that carnal knowledge of man, or lying with man, as with woman, *cum penetratione corporis,* was sodomy, to be punished with death; what else can be understood, by Leviticus 18:22 and 20:13 and Genesis 19:5. 2ly it seems also that this foul sin might be capital, though there was not *penetratio corporis,* but only *contactus,* and *fricatio usque ad effusionem seminis,* for these reasons:

1. Because it was sin to be punished with death, Leviticus 20:13 in the man who was lyen withal, as well as in him that lieth with him; now his sin is not mitigated where there is not penetration, nor augmented where it is; whereas it's charged upon the women, that they were guilty of this unnatural sin as well as men, Romans 1:26, 27, the same thing doth further appear.

2. Because of that proportion, betwixt this sin, and bestiality, wherein if a woman did stand before, or approach to a beast, for that end, to lie

down thereto (whether penetration was or not) it was capital, Leviticus 18:23 and 20:16.

3. Because something else might be equivalent to penetration where it had not been, viz. the forementioned acts with frequency, and long continuance with a high hand, utterly extinguishing all light of nature; besides full intention, and bold attempting of the foulest acts may seem to have been capital here, as well as coming presumptuously to slay with guile was capital. Exodus 21:14.

Yet it is not so manifest that the same acts were to be punished with death in some other sins of uncleanness, which yet by the law of God were capital crimes; besides other reasons:

1. Because sodomy, and also bestiality is more against the light of nature, than some other capital crimes of uncleanness, which reason is to be attended unto, as that which most of all made this sin capital

2. Because it might be committed with more secrecy, and less suspicion, and therefore needed the more to be restrained, and suppressed by the law

3. Because there was not the like reason and degree of sinning against family, and posterity in this sin as in some other capital sins of uncleanness.

2. Question

How far a magistrate, may extract a confession from a delinquent, to accuse himself of a capital crime, seeing *nemo tenetur prodere seipsum.*

Answer

A magistrate cannot without sin neglect diligent inquisition into the cause brought before him. Job 29:16; Proverbs 24:11,12 and 25:2. (2ly) if it be manifest that a capital crime is committed, and that common report, or probability, suspicion, or some complaint (or the like), be of this, or that person; a magistrate ought to require, and by all due means to procure, from the person (so far already bewrayed) a naked confession of the fact, as appears by that which is moral and of perpetual equity, both in the case of uncertain murder, Deuteronomy 21:1-9, and slander Deuteronomy 22:13-21, for though *nemo tenetur prodere seipsum,* yet by that which may be known to the magistrate, by the forenamed means he is bound thus to do, or else he may betray his country, and people to the heavy displeasure of God, Leviticus 18:24, 25, Joshua 22:18, Psalms 106:30. Such as are innocent to the sinful, base cruel lusts, of the profane, and such as are delinquents, and others with them, into the hands of the stronger temptations, and more boldness, and hardness of heart, to commit more and worse villainy, besides all the guilt, and hurt, he will bring upon himself. (3ly) to inflict some punishment merely for this reason to extract a confession of a capital crime is contrary to the nature of vindictive justice, which always hath respect to a known crime committed by the person punished; and it will therefore, for anything which can before be known, be the provoking, and forcing of wrath, as compared to the wringing of the nose, Proverbs 30:33 which is as well forbidden the fathers of the country, as of the family, Ephesians 6:4 as producing many sad, and dangerous effects. That an oath (*ex officio*) for such a purpose is no due means hath been abundantly proved by the godly learned, and is well known.

3. Question

In what cases of capital crimes one witness with other circumstances shall be sufficient to convince? Or is there no conviction without two witnesses?

Answer

In taking away the lie of man, one witness alone will not suffice; there must be two, or that which is *instar*, the texts are manifest, Numbers 35:30, Deuteronomy 17:6 and 19:15. 2ly there may be conviction by one witness, and something that hath the force of another, as the evidence of the fact done by such an one, and not another; unforced confession when there was no fear, or danger of suffering for the fact, handwritings acknowledged, and confessed.

John Reynor

Mr. Partridge his writing, in answer to the questions.

What is that sodomitical act which is to be punished with death?

Though I conceive probable that a voluntary effusion of seed *per modum concubitus* of man, with man, as of a man with woman, though *in concubitu* there be not *penetratio corporis*, is that sin which is forbidden, Leviticus 18:22, and adjudged to be punished with death, Leviticus 20:13 because though there be not *penetratio corporis*, yet there may be *similitudo concubitus muliebris*, which is that the law specifieth; yet I dare not be confident (1) because Genesis 19:5 the intended act of the Sodomites (who were the first noted masters of this unnatural art, of more than brutish filthiness) is expressed by carnal copulation of man with woman; bring them out unto us, that we may know them. (2ly) because it is observed among the nations where this unnatural uncleanness is committed, it is with penetration of the body. (3ly) because in the judicial proceedings of the judges in England, the indict so run (as I have been informed).

Question:

> How far may a magistrate extract a confession of a capital crime from a suspected and an accused person?

Answer:

> I conceive that a magistrate is bound by careful examination, of circumstances, and weighing of probabilities, to sift the accused; and by force of argument to draw him to an acknowledgment of the truth. But he may not extract a confession of a capital crime, from a suspected person by any violent means, whether it be by an oath imposed, or by any punishment inflicted, or threatened to be inflicted, for so he may draw forth an acknowledgment of a crime from a fearful innocent; if guilty he shall be compelled to be his own accuser, when no other can, which is against the rule of justice.

Question:

> In what cases of capital crimes, one witness with other circumstances, shall be sufficient to convict; or is there no conviction without two witnesses?

Answer:

> I conceive that in the case of capital crimes, there can be no safe proceedings unto judgment without two witnesses, as Numbers 35:30, Deuteronomy 19:15, except there can some evidence be produced as available, and firm to prove the fact, as a witness is, then one witness may suffice; for therein the end, and equity of the law is attained, but to proceed unto sentence of death upon presumptions, where probably there may *subesse falsum*, though there be the testimony of one witness, I suppose it cannot be a safe way; better for such a one to be held in safe custody for further trial, I conceive.

Ralph Partridge

The Answer of Mr. Charles Chauncy
An contactus et fricatio usque ad seminis effusionem
sine penetratione corporis sit sodomia
morte plectenda?

Question:

>The question is what sodomitical acts are to be punished with death, and what very fact committed *(ipso facto)* is worthy of death, or if the fact itself be not capital, what circumstances concurring may make it capital? The same question may be asked of rape, incest, bestiality, unnatural sins, presumptuous sins? These be the words of the first question.

Answer:

>The answer unto this I will lay down (as God shall direct by His Word and Spirit) in these following conclusions:

1. That the judicials of Moses, that are appendances to the moral law, and grounded on the law of nature, or the Decalogue, are immutable, and perpetual; which all orthodox divines acknowledge, see the authors following: Luther tome I Wittenberg: fol. 435 and fol. 7; Melancthon in *Locis Communibus loco de conjugio*; Calvin L. 4 *Institutio* C. 4 sect. 15; Junius *de Politiae Mosis* theses 29 and 30; Henry Bullinger *Decades* 3 sermo 8; Wolf. *Musculus Locis Communibus in 6 praecepti explicatione*; Bucer *de Regno Christi* L. 2 C. 17; Theo. Beza vol. 1 *de Haereticis Puniendis* fol. 154; Zanchi *in 3 praeceptum;* Ursinus part 4 *Explicatio Catecheticae;* John Piscator *in Aphorismis loco de Lege Dei,* aphor. 17. and more might be added, I forbear for brevity's sake to set down their very words; this being the constant, and general opinion of the best divines; I will rest in this as undoubtedly true, though much more might be said to confirm it.

2. That all the sins mentioned in the question were punished with death by the judicial law of Moses, as adultery, Leviticus 20:10, Deuteronomy 22:22, Ezekiel 16:38, John 8:5 which is to be understood not only of double adultery, when as both parties are married (as some conceive) but whosoever (besides her husband) lies with a married woman, whether the man be married, or not, as in the place Deuteronomy 22:22; or whosoever being a married man lieth with another woman (besides his wife) as Peter Martyr saith *Loci Communes* which in divers respects makes the sin worse, on the married man's part; for the Lord in this law hath respect as well to public honesty (the sin being so prejudicial, to the church, and state) as the private wrongs (saith Junius); so incest, is to be punished with death, Leviticus 20:11-22. Bestiality likewise, Leviticus 20:15, Exodus 22:19. Rapes in like manner, Deuteronomy 22:15[302].

---

[302] Bradford cites 22:15; Samuel Morison corrected this to Deuteronomy 22:25 in his edition of Bradford's *History*.

Sodomy in like sort, Leviticus 18:22 and 20:13. And all presumptuous sins, Numbers 15:30, 31.

3. That the punishment of these foul sins with death, is grounded on the law of nature, and is agreeable to the moral law. (1) because the reasons annexed show them to be perpetual, Deuteronomy 22:22: So shalt thou put away evil. Incest, bestiality, are called confusion, and wickedness. (2) Infamy to the whole human nature, Leviticus 22:12[303], Leviticus 18:22. Rapes are as murder, Deuteronomy 22:25. Sodomy is an abomination, Leviticus 22:22. No holier, and juster laws can be devised, by any man or angel, than have been by the Judge of all the world, the wisdom of the Father, by whom kings do reign, etc. (3) Because before the giving of the law, this punishment was anciently practiced, Genesis 26:11, 38:29, 39:20, and even by the heathen, by the very light of nature, as Peter Martyr shows. (4) Because the land is defiled by such sins, and spews out the inhabitants, Leviticus 18:24, 25, and that in regard of those nations, that were not acquainted with the law of Moses. (5) All the divines above specified consent in this, that the unclean acts punishable with death by the law of God are not only the gross acts of uncleanness, by way of carnal copulation but all the evident attempts thereof, which may appear by those several words, that are used by the Spirit of God expressing the sins to be punished with death; as the discovering of nakedness, Leviticus 18:20, which is *retegere pudenda*, as parts *per euphemismum* (saith Junius) or *detegere ad cubandum* (saith Willett) to uncover the shameful parts of the body (saith Ainsworth) which though it reaches to the gross acts, yet it is plain it doth comprehend the other foregoing immodest attempts, as *contactum, fricationem,* etc.

4. Likewise the phrase of lying with so often used, doth not only signify carnal copulation, but other obscure acts preceding the same, is implied in Paul's word αρσενοκοιται 1 Corinthians 6:9 and men lying with men, 1 Timothy 1:9, men defiling themselves with mankind; men burning with lust towards men, Romans 1.26 and Leviticus 8:22; sodomy, and sin going after strange flesh, Jude v. 7, 8; and lying with mankind, as with a woman, Leviticus 18:22. Abulentis says that it signifies *omnes modus quibus masculus masculo abutatur,* changing the natural use, into that which is against nature, Romans 1:26; *arrogare*

---

[303]   Bradford cites 22:12; Samuel Morison corrected this to Deuteronomy 22:13 in his edition of Bradford's *History.*

sibi cubare, as Junius well translates Leviticus 20:15 to give consent to lie withal, so approaching to a beast, and lying down thereto, Leviticus 20:16 *ob solum conatum* (saith Willett) or for going about to do it. Add to this a notable speech of Zepperus *de legibus* (who hath enough to end controversies of this nature, L. 1 he saith *in crimine adulterii volumas* (understanding manifest) *sine efectu subsecuto de jure attenditur;* and he proves it out of good laws, in these words, *Solicitatores alienarum nuptiarum itemque matrimoniorum interpellatores, et si effectu sceleris potiri non possunt, propter voluntatem tamen perniciosae libidinis, extra ordinem puniuntur. Nam gezerale est quidem afiectum sine effectu non puniri; sed contrarium observatur in atrocioribw, et horum similibus.*

5. In concluding punishments from the judicial law of Moses that is perpetual, we must often proceed by analogical proportion, and interpretation, *as a paribus similibus, minore ad majs,* etc.; for there will still fall out some cases, in every commonwealth, which are not in so many words extant in Holy Writ, yet the substance of the matter in every kind (I conceive under correction) may be drawn and concluded out of the Scripture by good consequence of an equivalent nature, as for example, there is no express law against destroying conception in the womb by potions, yet by analogy with Exodus 21:22, 23, we may reason that life, is to be given for life; again the question *an contactus et fricatio,* etc., and methinks that place Genesis 38:9 in the punishment of Onan's sin may give some clear light to it, it was (saith Pareus) *beluina crudelitas quam Deus pari loco cum parricidio habuit, nam semen corrumpere, quit fuit aliud quam hominem ex semine generandum occidere propterea juste a Deo occisus est.* Observe his words. And again, *Discamus quantopere Dew abominetur omlzem seminis genitalis abusum, illicitam effusionem, et corruptionem,* etc., very pertinent in this case. That also is considerable, Deuteronomy 25:11,12, God commanded that if any wife drew nigh to deliver her husband out of the hand of him that smiteth him, etc., her hand should be cut off; yet such a woman in that case, might say much for herself, that what she did was in trouble, and perplexity of her mind, and in her husband's defense; yet her hand must be cut off for such impurity (and this is moral, as I conceive) then we may reason from the less, to the greater, what grievous sin in the sight of God it is, by the instigation of burning lusts, set on fire of hell, to proceed to *contactum et fricationem ad emissionem seminis,* etc., and that *contra naturam,* or to attempt the gross acts of unnatural filthiness;

again if that unnatural lusts of men with men, or woman, with woman, or either with beasts, be to be punished with death than *a pari* natural lusts of men towards children under age are so to be punished.

6. *Circumstantiae variant uis e actiones* (saith the lawyers) and circumstances in these cases, cannot possibly be all reckoned up, but God hath given laws for those causes, and cases that are of greatest moment, by which others are to be judged of, as in the difference betwixt chance medley, and willful murder; so in the sins of uncleanness it is one thing to do an act of uncleanness, by sudden temptation, and another to lie in wait for it, yea to make a common practice of it; this mightily augments, and multiplies the sin; again some sins of this nature are simple, others compound, as that is simple adultery, or incest, or simple sodomy; but when there is a mixture of divers kinds of lust, as when adultery, and sodomy, and *perditio seminis* go together in the same act of uncleanness, this is capital double, and triple. Again when adultery or sodomy is committed by professors or church members, I fear it comes too near the sin of the priest's daughters, forbidden and commanded to be punished, Leviticus 21:9 besides the presumption of the sins of such. Again when uncleanness is committed with those whose chastity they are bound to preserve, this comes very near the incestuous copulation I fear; but I must hasten to the other questions.

2. Question

The second upon the point of examination, how far a magistrate may extract a confession from a delinquent to accuse himself in a capital crime, seeing *nemo tenetur prodere seipsum.*

Answer:

The words of the question may be understood of extracting a confession from a delinquent either by oath, or bodily torment; if it be meant of extracting by requiring an oath (*ex officio*, as some call it) and that in capital crimes, I fear it is not safe, nor warranted by God's Word, to extract a confession from a delinquent by an oath in matters of life and death, (1) because the practice in the Scriptures is otherwise, as in the case of Achan, Joshua 7:9: give I pray thee glory to the Lord God of Israel, and make a confession to him, and tell me how thou hast done; he did not compel him to swear; so when as Jonathan's life was endangered, 1 Samuel 14:43: Saul said unto Jonathan, tell me what thou hast done; he did not require an oath. And notable is that, Jeremiah 38:14. Jeremiah was charged by Zedekiah, who said I will ask thee a thing, hide it not from me, and Jeremiah said, if I declare it unto thee, wilt thou not surely put me to death; implying that in case of death he would have refused to answer him. (2). Reason shows it, and experience, Job 2:4: skin for skin, etc. It is to be feared that those words (whatsoever a man hath) will comprehend also the conscience of an oath, and the fear of God, and all care of religion, therefore for laying a snare before the guilty I think it ought not to be done. But now if the question be meant of inflicting bodily torments to extract a confession from a malefactor, I conceive that in matters of highest consequence, such as do concern the safety, or ruin of states, or countries, magistrates may proceed so far to bodily torments, as racks, hot irons, etc. to extract a confession, especially where presumptions are strong; but otherwise by no means. God sometimes hides a sinner till his wickedness is filled up.

Question 3.

In what cases of capital crimes, one witness with other circumstances shall be sufficient to convict, or is there no conviction without two witnesses?

Answer:

Deuteronomy 19:25. God hath given an express rule that in no case one witness shall arise in judgment, especially not in capital cases. God would not put our lives into the power of any one tongue. Besides by the examination of more witnesses agreeing, or disagreeing, any falsehood ordinarily may be discovered; but this is to be understood of our witness of another; but if a man witness against himself, his own testimony is sufficient, as in the case of the Amalekite, 2 Samuel 1:16; again when there are sure, and certain signs, and evidences, by circumstances, there needs no witness, in this case as in the business of Adonijah desiring Abishag the Shunamite to wife, that thereby he might make way for himself unto the kingdom, 1 Kings 2:23, 24. Again probably by many concurring circumstances, if probability may have the strength of a witness, something may be this way gathered, methinks, from Solomon's judging betwixt the true mother, and the harlot, 1 Kings 3:25. Lastly I see no cause why in weighty matters in defect of witnesses, and other proofs, we may not have recourse to a lot, as in the case of Achan, Joshua 7:16 which is a clearer way in such doubtful cases (it being solemnly, and religiously performed) than any other that I know, if it be made the last refuge, but all this under correction.

The Lord in mercy direct and prosper the desires of His servants that desire to walk before Him in truth, and righteousness in the administration of justice, and give them wisdom and largeness of heart.

Charles Chauncy

Besides the occasion before mentioned in these writings concerning the abuse of those 2 children; they had about the same time a case of buggery, fell out amongst them, which occasioned these questions, to which these answers have been made.

And after the time of the writing of these things, befell a very sad accident of the like foul nature in this government this very year, which I shall now relate. There was a youth whose name was Thomas Granger; he was servant to an honest man of Duxbury, being about 16 or 17 years of age (his father and mother lived at the same time, at Scituate.) He was this year detected of buggery, (and indicted for the same) with a mare, a cow, two goats, five sheep, 2 calves, and a turkey. Horrible it is to mention, but the truth of the history requires it. He was first discovered by one that accidentally saw his lewd practice towards the mare (I forbear particulars). Being upon it examined, and committed: in the end he not only confessed the fact with that beast at that time, but sundry times before; and at several times with all the rest of the forenamed in his indictment, and this his free confession was not only in private to the magistrates (though at first he strived to deny it) but to sundry both ministers, and others; and afterwards upon his indictment, to the whole court and jury; and confirmed it at his execution, and whereas some of the sheep could not so well be known by his description of them, others with them were brought before him, and he declared which were they, and which were not. And accordingly he was cast by the jury, and condemned, and after executed about the 8 of September 1642. A very sad spectacle it was, for first the mare, and then the cow, and the rest of the lesser cattle were killed before his face, according to the law, Leviticus 20:15; and then he himself was executed. The cattle were all cast into a great, and large pit that was digged of purpose for them, and no use made of any part of them.[304]

---

[304] *Plymouth Colony Records* 2:44: "Thomas Granger, late servant to Love Brewster, of Duxbury, was this court indicted for buggery with a mare, a cow, two goats, divers sheep, two calves, and a turkey, and was found guilty, and received the sentence of death by hanging until he was dead."

Upon the examination of this person, and also of a former that had made some sodomitical attempts upon another; it being demanded of them, how they came first to the knowledge and practice of such wickedness; the one confessed he had long used it in old England; and this youth last spoken of said he was taught it, by another that had heard of such things from some in England, when he was there, and they kept cattle together. By which it appears how one wicked person may infect many; and what care all ought to have what servants they bring into their families.

But it may be demanded how came it to pass, that so many wicked persons, and profane people, should so quickly come over into this land, and mix themselves amongst them? Seeing it was religious men that began the work, and they came for religion's sake? I confess this may be marveled at, at least in time to come, when the reasons thereof should not be known; and the more because here was so many hardships, and wants met withal. I shall therefore endeavor to give some answer hereunto.

1. And first according to that in the gospel, it is ever to be remembered, that where the Lord begins to sow good seed, there the envious man will endeavor to sow tares.

2. Men being to come over into a wilderness, in which much labor and service was to be done about building and planting, etc., such as wanted help in that respect, when they could not have such as they would, were glad to take such as they could; and so many untoward servants, sundry of them proved, that were thus brought over, both men, and women kind; who when their times were expired, became families of themselves, which gave increase hereunto.

3. Another, and a main reason hereof, was: that men finding so many godly disposed persons willing to come into these parts; some began to make a trade of it, to transport passengers, and their goods; and hired ships for that end; and then to make up their freight, and advance their profit, cared not who the persons were so they had money to pay them. And by this means the country became pestered with many unworthy persons, who being come over, crept into one place or other.

4. Again, the Lord's blessing usually following His people, as well in outward, as spiritual things (though afflictions be mixed withal) do make many to adhere to the People of God, as many followed Christ for the loaves' sake, John 6:26, and a mixed multitude came into the wilderness, with the People of God out of Egypt of old, Exodus 12.38. So also there were sent by their friends, some under hope that they

would be made better; others that they might be eased of such burdens, and they kept from shame at home, that would necessarily follow their dissolute courses. And thus by one means or other, in 20 years' time, it is a question whether the greater part be not grown the worser?

I am now come to the conclusion of that long and tedious business between the partners here, and them in England; the which I shall manifest by their own letters, as followeth; in such parts of them as are pertinent to the same.[305]

Mr. Atwood, my approved loving friend, your letter of the 18 of October last I have received, wherein I find you have taken a great deal of pains and care about that troublesome business, betwixt our Plymouth partners, and friends, and us here, and have deeply engaged yourself; for which compliments and words are no real satisfaction, etc. For the agreement you have made with Mr. Bradford, Mr. Winslow, and the rest of the partners there, considering how honestly, and justly, I am persuaded they have brought in an account of the remaining stock, for my own part, I am well satisfied, and so I think is Mr. Andrews; and I suppose will be Mr. Beauchamp. If most of it might accrue to him, to whom the least is due, etc. And now for peace sake, and to conclude as we began lovingly, and friendly, and to pass by all failings, of all. The conclude is accepted of; I say this agreement that you have made is condescended unto; and Mr. Andrews hath sent his release to Mr. Winthrop, with such directions as he conceives fit. And I have made bold to trouble you with mine, and we have both sealed in the presence of Mr. Weld, and Mr. Peters and some others and I have also sent you another for the partners there, to seal to me; for you must not deliver mine to them, except they seal, and deliver one to me; this is fit and equal, etc.

Yours to command in what I may or can,

James Sherley

June 14, 1642

His to the Partners as Followeth

Loving friends,

   Mr. Bradford, Mr. Winslow, Mr. Prence, Captain Standish, Mr. Brewster, Mr. Alden, and Mr. Howland, give me leave to join you all in

---

[305]   An additional Chancery Proceeding document in the case between Andrews, Beauchamp and Sherley is found in Appendix 1.

one letter, concerning the final end and conclude of that tedious, and troublesome business and I think I may truly say uncomfortable, and unprofitable to all, etc. It hath pleased God now to put us upon a way to cease all suits, and disquieting of our spirits, and to conclude with peace and love, as we began; I am contented to yield and make good what Mr. Atwood and you have agreed upon. And for that end have sent to my loving friend, Mr. Atwood, an absolute and general release unto you all, and if there want anything to make it more full, write it yourselves, and it shall be done, provided that all you either jointly, or severally, seal the like discharge to me, and for that end I have drawn one jointly, and sent it to Mr. Atwood, with that I have sealed to you; Mr. Andrews hath sealed an acquittance also, and sent it to Mr. Winthrop, with such directions as he conceived fit, and as I hear, hath given his debt, which he makes 544$^£$ unto the gentlemen of the Bay; indeed Mr. Weld, Mr. Peters and Mr. Hibbens, have taken a great deal of pains with Mr. Andrews, Mr. Beauchamp, and myself to bring us to agree, and to that end we have had many meetings and spent much time about it. But as they are very religious, and honest gentlemen, yet they had an end, that they drove at, and labored to accomplish (I mean not any private end, but for the general good of their patent). It had been very well you had sent one over. Mr. Andrews wished you might have one 3 part of the 1200$^£$ and the Bay 2 thirds; but then we 3 must have agreed together, which were a hard matter now. But Mr. Weld, Mr. Peters and Mr. Hibbens, and I have agreed, they giving you bond (so to compose with Mr. Beauchamp) as to procure his general release, and free you from all trouble and charge that he may put you to; which indeed is nothing, for I am persuaded Mr. Weld will in time gain him, to give them all that is due to him, which in some sort is granted already, for though his demands be great, yet Mr. Andrews hath taken some pains in it, and makes it appear to be less, than I think he will consent to give them for so good an use; so you need not fear, that for taking bond there to save you harmless, you be safe and well. Now our accord is that you must pay to the gentlemen of the Bay 900$^£$; they are to bear all charges that may any way arise, concerning the free, and absolute clearing of you, from us three. And you to have the other 300$^£$, etc.

Upon the receiving of my release from you, I will send you your bonds for the purchase money; I would have sent them now, but I would have Mr. Beauchamp release as well as I, because you are bound to him in them; now I know if a man be bound to 12 men, if one release it is, as if all released, and my discharge doth cut them off, wherefore doubt you not but you shall have them, and your commission, or anything else that is fit; now you know there is two years of the purchase money that I would not own, for I have formerly certified you that I would but pay 7 years, but now you are discharged of all, etc.

Your loving and kind friend in what I may or can,

James Sherley

June 14, 1642

The copy of his release is as
followeth

Whereas divers questions, differences, and demands have arisen, and depended between William Bradford, Edward Winslow, Thomas Prence, Myles Standish, William Brewster, John Alden, and John Howland, gentlemen, now or lately inhabitants, or resident at New Plymouth, in New England, on the one party; and James Sherley of London merchant and others on the other part, for and concerning a stock and partable trade of beaver and other commodities, and freighting of ships, as the *White Angel, Friendship* or others; and the goods of Isaac Allerton which were seized upon by virtue of a letter of attorney made by the said James Sherley, and John Beauchamp, and Richard Andrews, or any other matters concerning the said trade either here in Old England, or there in New England or elsewhere, all which differences are since by mediation of friends composed, compromised, and all the said parties agreed. Now know all men by these presents, that I the said James Sherley in performance of the said compromise and agreement, have remissed, released and quit-claimed, and do by these presents, remiss, release, and for me, mine heirs, executors, and administrators, and for every of us forever quit-claim, unto the said William Bradford, Edward Winslow, Thomas Prence, Myles Standish, William Brewster, John Alden, and John Howland, and every of them, their, and every of their heirs, executors, and administrators, all and all manner of actions, suits, debts, accounts, reckonings, commissions, bonds, bills, specialties, judgments, executions, claims, challenges, differences, and demands whatsoever with or against the said William Bradford, Edward Winslow, Thomas Prence, Myles Standish, William Brewster, John Alden, and John Howland or any of them, ever I had, now have or in time to come, can, shall, or may have, for any matter, cause, or thing whatsoever from the beginning of the world until the day of the date of these presents. In witness whereof I have hereunto put my hand and seal, given the second day of June 1642; and in the eighteenth year of the reign of our sovereign lord King Charles, etc.

James Sherley

Sealed and delivered in the presence of
    Thomas Weld
    Hugh Peters
    William Hibbens
    Arthur Tirrey, Scribe
    Thomas Sturges, his servant

Mr. Andrews his discharge was to the same effect; he was by agreement to have 500$^£$ of the money, the which he gave to them in the Bay; who brought his discharge and demanded the money; and they took in his release, and paid the money according to agreement, viz. one third of the 500$^£$ they paid down in hand and the rest in 4 equal payments, to be paid yearly, for which they gave their bonds, and whereas 44$^£$ was more demanded, they conceived they could take it off with Mr. Andrews, and therefore it was not in the bond. But Mr. Beauchamp would not part with any of his, but demanded 400$^£$ of the partners here, and sent a release to a friend to deliver it to them, upon the receipt of the money; but his release was not perfect, for he had left out some of the partners' names, with some other defects, and besides the other gave them to understand he had not near so much due. So no end was made with him till 4 years after, of which in its place. And in that regard that themselves did not agree, I shall insert some part of Mr. Andrews letter, by which he conceives the partners here were wronged, as followeth.

This letter of his was write to Mr. Edmund Freeman[306], brother-in-law to Mr. Beauchamp.

Mr. Freeman

My love remembered unto you, etc. I then certified the partners how I found Mr. Beauchamp and Mr. Sherley in their particular demands, which was according to men's principles, of getting what they could; although the one will not show any account, and the other a very unfair and unjust one. And both of them discouraged me from sending the partners my account, Mr. Beauchamp especially. Their reason I have cause to conceive was, that

---

[306] Edmund Freeman came to New England in 1635, settled in Lynn, and later was one of the first settlers of Sandwich.

although I do not, nor ever intended to wrong the partners, or the business; yet if I gave no account, I might be esteemed as guilty as they in some degree at least; and they might seem to be the more free from taxation in not delivering their accounts; etc. (who have both of them charged the account, with much interest they have paid forth and one of them would likewise for much interest he hath not paid forth as appeareth by his account), etc.

And seeing the partners have now made it appear that there is 1200£ remaining due between us all, and that it may appear by my account I have not charged the business, with any interest, but do forgive it unto the partners above 200£; if Mr. Sherley, and Mr. Beauchamp, who have between them wronged the business so many 100£ both in principal, and interest likewise, and have therein wronged me as well, and as much as any of the partners, yet if they will not make, and deliver fair and true accounts of the same, nor be content to take what by computation is more than can be justly due to either; that is to Mr. Beauchamp 150£ as by Mr. Allerton's account, and Mr. Sherley's account on oath in Chancery; and though there might be nothing due to Mr. Sherley, yet he requires 100£, etc. I conceive seeing the partners have delivered on their oaths the sum remaining in their hands, that they may justly detain the 650£ which may remain in their hands, after I am satisfied, until Mr. Sherley and Mr. Beauchamp, will be more fair, and just in their ending, etc. And as I intend, if the partners fairly end with me, in satisfying in part, and engaging themselves for the rest of my said 544£ to return back for the poor my part of the land at Scituate; so likewise I intend to relinquish my right, and interest in their dear patent, on which much of our money was laid forth, and also my right and interest in their cheap purchase, the which may have cost me first and last 350£. But I doubt whether other men have not charged or taken on account, what they have disbursed in the like case, which I have not charged, neither did I conceive any other durst so do; until I saw the account of the one, and heard the words of the other; the which gives me just cause to suspect both their accounts to be unfair[307]; for it seemeth they consulted one with another about some particulars therein; therefore I conceive the partners ought the rather to require just accounts from each of them, before they part with any money, to either of them, for merchants understand how to give an account; if they mean fairly they will not deny to give an account, for they

---

[307] This he means of the first adventures, all which were lost and hath before been shown; and what he here writes is probable at least. (Bradford).

keep memorials to help them to give exact accounts, in all particulars, and memorial cannot forget his charge, if the man will remember.

I desire not to wrong Mr. Beauchamp, or Mr. Sherley, nor may be silent in such apparent probabilities of their wronging the partners, and me likewise, either in denying to deliver or show any account; or in delivering one very unjust in some particulars, and very suspicious in many more; either of which, being from understanding merchants, cannot be from weakness, or simplicity, and therefore the more unfair. So commending you, and yours, and all the Lord's people unto the gracious protection, and blessing of the Lord, and rest your loving friend,

Richard Andrews

April 7, 1643

This letter was write the year after the agreement, as doth appear; and what his judgment was herein the contents doth manifest, and so I leave it, to the equal judgment of any to consider as they see cause. Only I shall add what Mr. Sherley further write in a letter of his, about the same time, and so leave this business. His is as followeth on the other side.

Loving friends, Mr. Bradford, Mr. Winslow, Captain Standish, Mr. Prence, and the rest of the partners with you; I shall write this general letter to you all, hoping it will be a good conclude of a general, but a costly, and tedious business I think to all, I am sure to me, etc.

I received from Mr. Winslow a letter of the 28 of September last, and so much as concerns the general business I shall answer in this, not knowing whether I shall have opportunity to write particular letters, etc. I expected more letters from you all, as some particular writes, but it seemeth no fit opportunity was offered. And now though the business for the main may stand, yet some particulars is altered, I say my former agreement with Mr. Weld, and Mr. Peters, before they could conclude, or get any grant of Mr. Andrews, they sought to have my release; and thereupon they sealed me a bond for a 110^f. So I sent my acquittance, for they said without mine there would be no end made (and there was good reason for it). Now they hoped, if they ended with me, to gain Mr. Andrews' part, as they did wholly to a pound (at which I should wonder, but that I observe some passages) and they also hoped to have gotten Mr. Beauchamp's part, and I did think he would have given it them; but if he did well understand himself, and that account he would give it, for his demands make a great sound; but it seemeth he would not part with it, supposing it too a great a sum, and that he might easily gain it from you[308] , once he would have given them 40$^£$ but now they say he will not do that, or rather I suppose they will not take it, for if they do, and have Mr. Andrews's, then they must pay me their bond of 110$^£$ 3 months hence. Now it will fall out far better for you, that they deal not with Mr. Beauchamp, and also for me, if you be as kind to me, as I have been and will be to you. And that thus, if you pay Mr. Andrews, or the Bay men by his order 544$^£$ which is his full demand; but if looked into perhaps might be less; the man is honest, and in my conscience would not wittingly do wrong, yet he may forget as well as other men, and Mr. Winslow may call to mind wherein he forgets, (but sometimes it is good to buy peace). The gentlemen of the Bay may abate 100$^£$, and so both sides have more right, and justice than if they exact all, etc. Now if you send me 150$^£$, then say Mr. Andrews' full sum, and this, it is near 700$^£$. Mr. Beauchamp he demands 400$^£$ and we all know that if a man demands money he must show wherefore, and make proof of his debt; which I know he can never make good proof of one hundred pound due unto him as principal money, so till he can, you have good reason to keep the 500$^£$ etc. This I protest I write not in malice against Mr. Beauchamp, for it is a real truth; you may partly see it by Mr. Andrews making up his account, and I think you are all persuaded, I can say more than Mr. Andrews, concerning that account, I wish I could make up my own as plain, and easily, but because of former discontents, I will be sparing till I be called, and you may enjoy the 500$^£$ quietly till he begin; for let him take his course here, or there, it shall be all one; I will do him no wrong; and if he have not one penny more, he is less loser than either Mr. Andrews, or I; this I conceive to be just, and honest; the having or not having of his release matters not, let him make such proof of his debt, as you cannot disprove, and according to your first agreement you will pay it, etc.

Your truly affectioned friend,
James Sherley

London, April 27, 1643

---

308 This was a mystery to them, for they heard nothing hereof from any side this last year, till now the conclusion was past and bonds given. (Bradford).

I am to begin this year, with that, which was a matter of great sadness, and mourning unto them all. About the 18 of April, died their Reverend Elder, and my dear, and loving friend Mr. William Brewster, a man that had done, and suffered much for the Lord Jesus, and the gospel's sake, and had bore his part in weal, and woe, with this poor persecuted church above 36 years in England, Holland, and in this wilderness, and done the Lord, and them faithful service in his place and calling; and notwithstanding the many troubles, and sorrows he passed through, the Lord upheld him to a great age; he was near fourscore years of age (if not all out) when he died. He had this blessing added by the Lord, to all the rest; to die in his bed in peace, amongst the midst of his friends, who mourned and wept over him; and ministered what help and comfort they could unto him, and he again re-comforted them, whilst he could. His sickness was not long, and till the last day thereof, he did not wholly keep his bed; his speech continued till somewhat more than half a day, and then failed him, and about 9 or 10 a clock that evening he died, without any pangs at all; a few hours before, he drew his breath short, and some few minutes before his last, he drew his breath long, as a man fallen into a sound sleep, without any pangs or gaspings, and so sweetly departed this life, unto a better.

I would now demand of any, what he was the worse, for any former sufferings? What do I say, worse; nay sure he was the better, and they now added to his honor. It is a manifest token (saith the Apostle, 2 Thessalonians 1:5, 6, 7) of the righteous judgment of God that ye may be counted worthy of the kingdom of God, for which ye also suffer; seeing it is a righteous thing with God, to recompense tribulation to them that trouble you: and to you who are troubled, rest with us, when the Lord Jesus shall be revealed from heaven, with his mighty angels. 1 Peter 4:14, If you be reproached for the

401

name of Christ, happy are ye, for the spirit of glory, and of God resteth upon you. What though he wanted the riches and pleasures of the world in his life? and pompous monuments at his funeral? Yet the memorial of the just shall be blessed, when the name of the wicked shall rot (with their marble monuments), Proverbs 10:7.

I should say something of his life, if to say a little were not worse, than to be silent. But I cannot wholly forbear (though happily more may be done hereafter). After he had attained some learning, viz. the knowledge of the Latin tongue, and some insight in the Greek, and spent some small time at Cambridge; and then being first seasoned with the seeds of grace, and virtue, he went to the Court, and served that religious and godly gentleman Mr. Davison divers years, when he was Secretary of State; who found him so discreet, and faithful, as he trusted him above all other that were about him, and only employed him in all matters of greatest trust and secrecy; he esteemed him rather as a son than a servant; and for his wisdom, and godliness, (in private) he would converse with him, more like a friend and familiar, than a master. He attended his master when he was sent in ambassage by the Queen into the Low Countries, in the (Earl of Leicester's time) as for other weighty affairs of State, so to receive possession of the cautionary towns, and in token and sign thereof the keys of Flushing being delivered to him, in Her Majesty's name, he kept them some time, and committed them to this his servant, who kept them under his pillow, on which he slept the first night. And at his return the States honored him with a gold chain, and his master committed it to him, and commanded him to wear it, when they arrived in England, as they rid through the country, till they came to the Court. He afterwards remained with him, till his troubles that he was put from his place, about the death of the Queen of Scots; and some good time after doing him many faithful offices of service in the tie of his troubles. Afterwards he went and lived in the country in good esteem amongst his friends, and the gentlemen of those parts, especially the godly and religious; he did much good in the country where he lived, in promoting and furthering religion, not only by his practice, and example, and provoking, and encouraging of others; but by procuring of good preachers to the places thereabout, and drawing on of others to assist, and help forward in such a work; he himself most commonly deepest in the charge, and sometimes above his ability. And in this state he continued many years, doing the best good he could, and walking according to the light he saw, till the Lord revealed further unto him. And in the end by the tyranny of the bishops against godly preachers, and people, in silencing the one, and persecuting the other; he and many more of those times, began to look further into things, and to see into the unlawfulness of their callings, and the burthen of many antichristian corruptions, which both he, and they endeavored to cast off[309]; as they also did.

After they were joined together in communion, he was a special stay, and help unto them; they ordinarily met at his house on the Lord's Day (which was a manor of the bishop's) and with great love he entertained them when they came, making provision for them to his great charge, and continued so to do, whilst they could stay in England. And when they were to remove out of the country he was one of the first in all adventures, and forwardest in any charge. He was the chief of those that were taken at Boston, and suffered the greatest loss; and of the seven that were kept longest in prison, and after bound over to the assizes. After he came into Holland he suffered much hardship, after he had spent the most of his means having a great charge, and many children; and in regard of his former breeding, and course of life, not so fit for many employments, as others were, especially such as were toilsome, and laborious. But yet he ever bore his condition with much cheerfulness, and contentation; towards the latter part of those 12 years spent in Holland, his outward condition was mended, and he lived well, and plentifully, for he fell into a way (by reason he had the Latin tongue) to teach many students, who had a desire to learn the English tongue, to teach them English, and by his method they quickly attained it with great facility, for he drew rules to learn it by, after the Latin manner. And many gentlemen, both Danes, and Germans resorted to him as they had time from other studies, some of them being great men's sons. He also had means to set up printing (by the help of some friends) and so had employment enough, and by reason of many books which would not be allowed to be printed in England, they might have had more than they could do. But now removing into this country all these things were laid aside again, and a new course of living must be framed unto; in which he was no way unwilling to take his part, and to bear his burthen with the rest, living many times without bread or corn, many months together, having many times nothing but fish, and often wanting that also; and drunk nothing but water for many years together, yea till within 5 or 6 years of his death; and yet he lived (by the blessing of God) in health till very old age.

And besides that he would labor with his hands in the fields as long as he was able, yet when the church had no other minister, he taught twice every Sabbath, and that both powerfully, and profitably, to the great contentment

---

[309]   As in the beginning of this treatise is to be seen. (Bradford).

of the hearers, and their comfortable edification; yea many were brought to God by his ministry. He did more in this behalf in a year than many that have their hundreds a year do in all their lives. For his personal abilities, he was qualified above many, he was wise, and discreet, and well spoken, having a grave and deliberate utterance, of a very cheerful spirit, very sociable, and pleasant, amongst his friends, of an humble and modest mind, of a peaceable disposition, undervaluing himself, and his own abilities, and sometime overvaluing others. Inoffensive, and innocent in his life and conversation, which gained him the love of those without, as well as those within; yet he would tell them plainly of their faults, and evils, both publicly, and privately, but in such a manner as usually was well taken from him. He was tenderhearted, and compassionate of such as were in misery, but especially of such as had been of good estate, and rank, and were fallen unto want and poverty, either for goodness, and religion's sake, or by the injury, and oppression of others; he would say of all men these deserved to be pitied most. And none did more offend, and displease him than such as would haughtily, and proudly carry, and lift up themselves, being risen from nothing, and having little else in them to commend them but a few fine clothes, or a little riches more than others. In teaching he was very moving and stirring of affections, also very plain and distinct in what he taught; by which means he became the more profitable to the hearers. He had a singular good gift in prayer, both public and private, in ripping up the heart, and conscience before God, in the humble confession of sin, and begging the mercies of God in Christ for the pardon of the same. He always thought it were better for ministers, to pray oftener, and divide their prayers than be long and tedious in the same (except upon solemn, and special occasions, as in days of humiliation, and the like). His reason was that the heart and spirits, of all, especially the weak, could hardly continue, and stand bent (as it were) so long towards God, as they ought to do in that duty without flagging and falling off. For the government of the church (which was most proper to his office) he was careful to preserve good order in the same; and to preserve purity, both in the doctrine, and communion of the same; and to suppress any error, or contention that might begin to rise up amongst them. And accordingly God gave good success to his endeavors herein all his days, and he saw the fruit of his labors in that behalf. But I must break off having only thus touched a few, as it were heads of things.

I cannot but here take occasion, not only to mention, but greatly to admire the marvelous providence of God! That notwithstanding the many changes, and hardships that these people went through, and the many enemies they had, and difficulties they met withal; that so many of them should live to very old age! It was not only this reverend man's condition (for one swallow makes no summer as they say) but many more of them did the like, some dying about, and before this time, and many still living; who attained to 60 years of age, and to 65; divers to 70 and above, and some near 80 as he did. It must needs be more than ordinary, and above natural reason that so it should be; for it is found in experience, that change of air, famine, or unwholesome food, much drinking of water, sorrows, and troubles, etc., all of them are enemies to health, causes of many diseases, consumers of natural vigor, and the bodies of men and shorteners of life. And yet of all these things they had a large part, and suffered deeply in the same; they went from England to Holland, where they found, both worse air, and diet, than that they came from; from thence (enduring a long imprisonment as it were in the ships at sea) into New England; and how it hath been with them here, hath already been shown; and what crosses, troubles, fears, wants and sorrows they had been liable unto is easy to conjecture; so as in some sort, they may say with the Apostle, 2 Corinthians 11:26, 27, they were in journeyings often, in perils of waters, in perils of robbers, in perils of their own nation, in perils among the heathen, in perils in the wilderness, in perils in the sea, in perils among false brethren; in weariness, and painfulness, in watching often, in hunger, and thirst, in fasting often, in cold and nakedness. What was it then that upheld them? It was God's visitation that preserved their spirits, Job 10:12, Thou hast given me life, and grace, and thy visitation hath preserved my spirit: he that upheld the Apostle upheld them, they were persecuted, but not forsaken, cast down, but perished not, 2 Corinthians 4:9. As unknown, and yet known; as dying, and behold we live; as chastened, and yet not killed, 2 Corinthians 6:9. God it seems, would have all men to behold, and observe such mercies, and works of His providence as these are towards His people; that they in like cases might be encouraged to depend upon God, in their trials, and also to bless His name when they see His goodness towards others. Man lives not by bread only, Deuteronomy 8:3. It is not by good and dainty fare, by peace, and rest, and heart's ease, in enjoying the contentments and good things of this world only, that preserves health, and prolongs life; God in such examples would have the world see, and behold that He can do it without them; and if the world will shut their eyes, and take no notice thereof, yet He would have His people, to see, and consider it. Daniel could be better liking with pulse, than others were with the king's dainties. Jacob though he went from one nation, to another people, and passed through famine, fears and many afflictions yet he lived till old age, and died sweetly, and rested in the Lord; as infinite others of God's servants have done; and still shall do (through God's goodness) notwithstanding all the malice of their enemies; when the branch of the wicked shall be cut off before his day, Job 15:32, and the bloody, and deceitful men shall not live half their days, Psalms 55:23.

By reason of the plottings of the Narragansetts (ever since the Pequots' War) the Indians were drawn into a general conspiracy against the English in all parts, as was in part discovered the year before; and now made more plain, and evident by many discoveries, and free confessions of sundry Indians (upon several occasions) from divers places, concurring in one. With such other concurring circumstances, as gave them sufficiently to understand the truth thereof. And to think of means how to prevent the same and secure themselves. Which made them enter into this more near union and confederation following.

Articles of Confederation between the Plantations under the government of the Massachusetts, the Plantations under the Government of New Plymouth, the Plantations under the Government of Connecticut, and the Government of New Haven, with the Plantations in combination therewith.

Whereas we all came into these parts of America, with one and the same end, and aim; namely to advance the kingdom of our Lord Jesus Christ, and to enjoy the Liberties of the Gospel, in purity with peace. And whereas in our settling (by a wise Providence of God) we are further dispersed upon the sea coasts, and rivers, than was at first intended, so that we cannot according to our desires, with conveniency communicate in one government, and jurisdiction. And whereas we live encompassed with people of several nations, and strange languages, which hereafter may prove injurious to us, and our posterity; and forasmuch as the natives have formerly committed sundry insolencies, and outrages upon several plantations of the English; and have of late combined themselves against us; and seeing by reason of those distractions in England (which they have heard of) and by which they know we are hindered, from that humble way of seeking advice, or reaping those comfortable fruits of protection, which at other times we might well expect; we therefore do conceive it our bounden duty, without delay to enter into a present consociation amongst ourselves for mutual help and strength in all our future concernments. That as in nation, and religion, so in other respects we be, and continue one according to the tenor, and true meaning of the ensuing articles.

1. Wherefore it is fully agreed, and concluded, by and between the parties or jurisdictions, above named, and they jointly, and severally do by

these presents agree and conclude, that they all be, and henceforth be called by the name of The United Colonies of New England.

2. The said United Colonies for themselves, and their posterities, do jointly and severally hereby enter into a firm, and perpetual league of friendship, and amity, for offense and defense, mutual advice, and succor upon all just occasions, both for preserving, and propagating the truth of the Gospel, and for their own mutual safety and welfare.

3. It is further agreed that the plantations, which at present are, or hereafter shall be settled with the limits of the Massachusetts, shall be forever under the Massachusetts, and shall have peculiar jurisdiction among themselves in all cases, as an entire body; and that Plymouth, Connecticut, and New Haven, shall each of them, have like peculiar jurisdiction, and government within their limits; and in reference to the plantations which already are settled, or shall hereafter be erected, or shall settle within their limits, respectively; provided that no other jurisdiction, shall hereafter be taken in as a distinct head, or member of this Confederation, nor shall any other plantation, or jurisdiction in present being, and not already in combination, or under the jurisdiction of any of these Confederates, be received by any of them; nor shall any two of the Confederates join in one jurisdiction without consent of the rest, which consent to be interpreted as is expressed in the sixth article ensuing.

4. It is by these Confederates agreed, that the charge of all just wars, whether offensive, or defensive, upon what part, or member of this Confederation soever they fall, shall both in men, provisions, and all other disbursements, be borne by all the parts of this Confederation, in different proportions, according to their different abilities, in manner following. Namely that the commissioners for each jurisdiction, from time, to time, as there shall be occasion, bring a true account, and number of all the males in every plantation, or any way belonging to or under their several jurisdictions, of what quality, or condition soever they be, from 16 years old to 60, being inhabitants there.[310] And that according to the different numbers, which from time to time, shall be found in each jurisdiction upon a true, and just account. The service of men, and all charges of the war be borne by the poll. Each jurisdiction, or plantation being left to their own just

---

[310] Plymouth Colony's list of all men able to bear arms in 1643 can be found in the *Plymouth Colony Records* 8:187-196.

course, and custom of rating themselves, and people according to their different estates, with due respects to their qualities, and exemptions amongst themselves, though the Confederates take no notice of any such privilege. And that according to their different charge of each jurisdiction, and plantation; the whole advantage of the war (if it please God to bless their endeavors), whether it be in lands, goods, or persons, shall be proportionably divided among the said Confederates.

5. It is further agreed, that if these jurisdictions or any plantation under, or in combination with them, be invaded by any enemy whomsoever, upon notice, and request of any 3 magistrates of that jurisdiction of invaded, the rest of the Confederates without any further meeting or expostulation, shall forthwith send aid to the Confederate in danger, but in different proportion; namely the Massachusetts an hundred men sufficiently armed, and provided for such a service, and journey, and each of the rest forty-five so armed, and provided, or any lesser number if less be required according to this proportion. But if such Confederate in danger may be supplied by their next Confederate, not exceeding the number hereby agreed, they may crave help there, and seek no further for the present; the charge to be borne, as in this article is expressed; and at the return to be victualed, and supplied with powder, and shot for their journey (if there be need) by that jurisdiction which employed, or sent for them. But none of the jurisdictions to exceed these numbers till by a meeting of the Commissioners for this Confederation, a greater aid appear necessary. And this proportion to continue till upon knowledge of greater numbers in each jurisdiction, which shall be brought to the next meeting, and some other proportion be ordered. But in such case of sending men for present aid, whether before, or after such order, or alteration, it is agreed that at the meeting of the Commissioners, for this Confederation, that the cause of such war or invasion be duly considered; and if it appear that the fault lay in the parties so invaded, that then that jurisdiction, or plantation make just satisfaction, both to the invaders whom they have injured, and bear all the charges of the war themselves, without requiring any allowance from the rest of the Confederates towards the same. And further that if any jurisdiction see any danger of any invasion approaching, and there be time for a meeting, that in such a case 3 magistrates, of that jurisdiction may summon a meeting, at such convenient place as themselves shall think

meet, to consider, and provide against the threatened danger; provided when they are met, they may remove to what place they please. Only whilst any of these four Confederates have but 3 magistrates, in their jurisdiction, their request, or summons, from any 2 of them shall be accounted of equal force with the 3 mentioned in both the clauses of this article, till there be an increase of magistrates there.

6. It is also agreed that for the managing, and concluding of all affairs proper, and concerning the whole Confederation, two Commissioners shall be chosen by, and out of each of these 4 jurisdictions, namely, 2 for the Massachusetts, 2 for Plymouth, 2 for Connecticut, and 2 for New Haven, being all in church fellowship with us, which shall bring full power from their several general courts, respectively, to hear, examine, weigh, and determine all affairs of war, or peace, leagues, aids, charges, and numbers of men for war, divisions of spoils, and whatsoever is gotten by conquest; receiving of more Confederates, or plantations into combination, with any of the Confederates, and all things of like nature, which are the proper concomitants, or consequences of such a Confederation, for amity, offense, and defense; not intermeddling with the government of any of the jurisdictions, which by the 3 article is preserved entirely to themselves. But if these 8 commissioners when they meet shall not all agree, yet it concluded that any 6 of the 8 agreeing, shall have power to settle, and determine the business in question. But if 6 do not agree, that then such propositions, with their reasons, so far as they have been debated be sent, and referred to the 4 general courts; viz. the Massachusetts, Plymouth, Connecticut, and New Haven; and if at all the said general courts, the business so referred be concluded, then to be prosecuted by the Confederates, and all their members. It was further agreed that these 8 commissioners shall meet once every year, besides extraordinary meetings (according to the fifth article) to consider, treat, and conclude of all affairs belonging to this confederation; which meeting shall ever be the first Thursday in September. And that the next meeting after the date of these presents, which shall be accounted the second meeting, shall be at Boston in the Massachusetts; the 3 at Hartford, the 4 at New Haven, the 5 at Plymouth, and so in course successively, if in the meantime, some middle place be not found out, and agreed on, which may be commodious for all the jurisdictions.

7. It is further agreed that at each meeting of these 8 commissioners, whether ordinary, or extraordinary, they all 6 of them agreeing as

before, may choose a president out of themselves, whose office, and work shall be to take care and direct for order, and a comely carrying on of all proceedings in the present meeting. But he shall be invested with no such power, or respect, as by which he shall hinder the propounding, or progress of any business or any way cast the scales otherwise, than in the precedent article is agreed.

8. It is also agreed that the Commissioners for this Confederation hereafter at their meetings, whether ordinary, or extraordinary, as they may have commission, or opportunity, do endeavor to frame and establish agreements, and orders in general cases, of a civil nature, wherein all the plantations are interested, for the preserving of peace amongst themselves, and preventing as much as may be all occasions of war, or difference with others; as about the free, and speedy passage of justice in every jurisdiction, to all the Confederates equally, as to their own not receiving those that remove from one plantation, to another without due certificate. How all the jurisdictions may carry towards the Indians, that they neither grow insolent, nor be injured without due satisfaction, lest war break in upon the Confederates through such miscarriages. It is also agreed that if any servant run away from his master into another of these confederated jurisdictions, that in such case, upon the certificate of one magistrate in the jurisdiction out of which the said servant fled, or upon other due proof, the said servant shall be delivered, either to his master, or any other that pursues and brings such certificate, or proof. And that upon the escape of any prisoner whatsoever, or fugitive for any criminal cause, whether breaking prison, or getting from the officer or otherwise escaping, upon the certificate of 2 magistrates of the jurisdiction out of which the escape is made that he was a prisoner, or such an offender at the time of the escape, the magistrates, or some of them of that jurisdiction where for the present the said prisoner or fugitive abideth, shall forthwith grant such a warrant as the case will bear, for the apprehending of any such person, and the delivering of him into the hands of the officer, or other person who pursues him; and if there be help required, for the safe returning of any such offender, then it shall be granted to him that craves the same, he paying the charges thereof.

9. And for that the justest wars may be of dangerous consequence, especially to the smaller plantations in these United Colonies, it is agreed that neither the Massachusetts, Plymouth, Connecticut, nor

New Haven, nor any members of any of them, shall at any time hereafter, begin, undertake, or engage themselves, or this Confederation, or any part thereof, in any war whatsoever (sudden exigents with the necessary consequents thereof excepted, which are also to be moderated as much as the case will permit) without the consent, and agreement of the forementioned 8 commissioners, or at the least 6 of them, as in the sixth article is provided. And that no charge be required of any of the Confederates, in case of a defensive war, till the said Commissioners have met, and approved the justice of the war, and have agreed upon the sum of money to be levied; which sum is then to be paid by the several Confederates in proportion to the fourth article.

10. That in extraordinary occasions, when meetings are summoned by three magistrates of any jurisdiction, or 2 as in the 5 article, if any of the Commissioners come not, due warning being given or sent, it is agreed that 4 of the Commissioners shall have power to direct a war which cannot be delayed, and to send for due proportions of men out of each jurisdiction, as well as 6 might do if all met; but not less than 6 shall determine the justice of the war, or allow the demands or bills of charges, or cause any levies to be made for the same.

11. It is further agreed that if any of the Confederates shall hereafter, break any of these present articles, or be any other ways injurious to any one of the other jurisdictions, such breach of agreement, or injury shall be duly considered, and ordered, by the Commissioners for the other jurisdictions, that both peace, and this present Confederation may be entirely preserved without violation.

12. Lastly this perpetual Confederation, and the several articles thereof being read, and seriously considered, both by the General Court for the Massachusetts, and by the Commissioners for Plymouth, Connecticut, and New Haven, were fully allowed, and confirmed by 3 of the forenamed confederates; namely the Massachusetts, Connecticut, and New Haven; only the Commissioners for Plymouth, having no commission to conclude, desired respite till they might advise with their General Court. Whereupon it was agreed, and concluded by the said Court of the Massachusetts, and the commissioners for the other two confederates, that if Plymouth consent, then the whole treaty as it stands in these present articles is, and shall continue firm, and stable without alteration. But if Plymouth come not in; yet the other three Confederates do by these presents

confirm the whole Confederation and the articles thereof. Only in September next, when the second meeting of the Commissioners is to be at Boston, new consideration may be taken of the 6 article which concerns number of Commissioners for meeting, and concluding the affairs of this Confederation to the satisfaction of the Court of the Massachusetts and the Commissioners for the other two Confederates; but the rest to stand unquestioned. In the testimony whereof, the General Court of the Massachusetts, by their Secretary, and the Commissioners for Connecticut, and New Haven have subscribed these present articles this 19 of the third month commonly called May, Anno Dom: 1643.

At a meeting of the Commissioners for the Confederation held at Boston the 7 of September: it appearing that the General Court of New Plymouth, and the several townships thereof, have read, and considered, and approved these Articles of Confederation; as appeareth by commission from their General Court bearing date the 29 of August 1643 to Mr. Edward Winslow, and Mr. William Collier, to ratify and confirm the same on their behalves; we therefore the Commissioners for the Massachusetts, Connecticut and New Haven do also for our several governments, subscribe unto them.

John Winthrop, Governor of the Massachusetts
Thomas Dudley　　　　　　Theophilus Eaton
George Fenwick　　　　　　Edward Hopkins
　　　　　　　　　　　　　Thomas Gregson

These were the articles of agreement in the union, and confederation which they now first entered into; and in this their first meeting held at Boston the day and year abovesaid, amongst other things they had this matter of great consequence to consider on. The Narragansetts after the subduing of the Pequots thought to have ruled over all the Indians about them. But the English, especially those of Connecticut, holding correspondency and friendship with Uncas, sachem of the Mohegan Indians which lived near them (as the Massachusetts had done with the Narragansetts) and he had been faithful to them in the Pequot War; they were engaged to support him in his just liberties, and were contented that such of the surviving Pequots as had submitted to him; should remain with him and quietly under his protection; this did much increase his power, and augment his greatness; which the Narragansetts could not endure to see. But Miantonomo, their chief sachem (an ambitious and politic man) sought privately, and by treachery (according to the Indian manner) to make him away, by hiring some to kill him; sometime they assayed to poison him, that not taking, then in the night time to knock him on the head in his house, or secretly to shoot him, and such like attempts. But none of these taking effect, he made open war, upon him, (though it was against the covenants, both between the English, and them, as also between themselves, and a plain breach of the same). He came suddenly upon him with 900 or 1000 men (never denouncing any war before). The other's power at that present was not about half so many; but it pleased God to give Uncas the victory, and he slew many of his men, and wounded many more; but the chief of all was, he took Miantonomo prisoner. And seeing he was a great man, and the Narragansetts a potent people, and would seek revenge; he would do nothing in the case without the advice of the English, so he (by the help and direction of those of Connecticut) kept him prisoner, till this meeting of the Commissioners. The Commissioners weighed the cause, and passages, as they were clearly represented and sufficiently evidenced betwixt Uncas, and Miantonomo; and the things being duly considered; the Commissioners apparently saw that Uncas could not be safe whilst Miantonomo lived; but either by secret treachery, or open force his life would be still in danger. Wherefore they thought he might justly put such a false, and bloodthirsty enemy to death; but in his own jurisdiction, not in the English plantations. And they advised in the manner of his death, all mercy and moderation should be showed, contrary to the practice of the Indians, who exercise tortures, and cruelty. And Uncas having hitherto showed himself a friend to the English, and in this craving their advice, if the Narragansett Indians, or others shall unjustly assault Uncas for this execution, upon notice and request the English promise to assist, and protect him, as far as they may against such violence.

This was the issue of this business. The reasons and passages hereof, are more at large to be seen in the acts and records of this meeting of the Commissioners. And Uncas followed this advice, and accordingly executed him, in a very fair manner, according as they advised, with due respect to his honor and greatness. But what followed on the Narragansetts' part will appear hereafter.

Many having left this place (as is before noted) by reason of the straitness and barrenness of the same and their finding of better accommodations elsewhere more suitable to their ends and minds; and sundry others still upon every occasion, desiring their dismissions; the church began seriously to think whether it were not better, jointly to remove to some other place than to be thus weakened, and as it were insensibly dissolved; many meetings, and much consultation was held hereabout, and divers were men's minds and opinions. Some were still for staying together in this place, alleging men might here live if they would be content with their condition; and that it was not for want or necessity so much that they removed as for the enriching of themselves, others were resolute upon removal and so signified that here they could not stay; but if the church did not remove they must. Insomuch as many were swayed rather than there should be a dissolution, to condescend to a removal, if a fit place could be found, that might more conveniently, and comfortably receive the whole, with such accession of others as might come to them for their better strength and subsistence; and some such like cautions, and limitations.

So as with the aforesaid provisos the greater part consented to a removal, to a place called Nauset which had been superficially viewed, and the good will of the purchasers (to whom it belonged) obtained with some addition thereto from the Court. But now they began to see their error, that they had given away, already, the best and most commodious places to others, and now wanted themselves; for this place was about 50 miles from hence, and at an outside of the country remote from all society; also that it would prove so strait, as it would not be competent to receive the whole body, much less be capable of any addition or increase; so as (at least in a short time) they should be worse there, than they are now here. The which with sundry other like considerations, and inconveniences, made them change their resolutions; but such as were before resolved upon removal, took advantage of this agreement, and went on notwithstanding; neither could the rest hinder them, they having made some beginning.[311] And thus was this poor church left, like an ancient mother, grown old and forsaken of her children, (though not in her affections) yet in regard of their bodily presence, and personal helpfulness; her ancient members being most of them worn away by death, and these of later time, being like children translated into other families, and she like a widow left only to trust in God. Thus she that had made many rich, became herself poor.

Some things handled and pacified
by the Commissioner this year.

Whereas by a wise providence of God, two of the jurisdictions in the western parts, viz. Connecticut, and New Haven have been lately exercised by sundry insolencies, and outrages from the Indians. As first an Englishman running from his master out of the Massachusetts, was murdered in the woods, in or near the limits of Connecticut jurisdiction, and about 6 weeks after, upon discovery by an Indian, the Indian sagamore in these parts promised to deliver the murderer to the English bound and having accordingly brought him within the sight of Uncaway, by their joint consent; as it is informed, he was there unbound, and left to shift for himself; whereupon 10 Englishmen forthwith coming to the place, being sent by Mr. Ludlow, at the Indians desire to receive the murderer; who seeing him escaped, laid hold of 8 of the Indians there present, amongst whom there was a sagamore or 2 and kept them in hold 2 days, till 4 sagamores engaged themselves within one month to deliver the prisoner. And about a week after this agreement, an Indian came presumptuously, and with guile in the daytime, and murderously assaulted an English woman in her house at Stamford, and by 3 wounds supposed mortal left her for dead, after he had robbed the house. By which passages the English were provoked, and called to a due consideration of their own safety; and the Indians generally in those parts arose in an hostile manner, refused to come to the English, to carry on treaties of peace, departed

---

[311] The town settled by these Plymouth defectors would later, in 1651, become formally named Eastham. Among those who removed were Thomas Prence, John Doane, Nicholas Snow, Josias Cooke, Richard Higgins, John Smalley and Edward Bangs.

from their wigwams, left their corn unweeded, and showed themselves tumultuously about some of the English plantations, and shot off pieces within hearing of the town, and some Indians came to the English and told them the Indians would fall upon them. So that most of the English thought it unsafe to travel in those parts by land, and some of the plantations were put upon strong watches, and ward night, and day and could not attend their private occasions, and yet distrusted their own strength for their defense; whereupon Hartford and New Haven were sent unto for aid, and saw cause both to send into the weaker parts of their own jurisdiction thus in danger, and New Haven for conveniency of situation, sent aid to Uncaway though belonging to Connecticut. Of all which passages they presently acquainted the Commissioners in the Bay, and had the allowance, and approbation from the General Court there, with directions neither to hasten war, nor to bear such insolencies too long. Which courses though chargeable to themselves, yet through God's blessing, they hope fruit is, and will be sweet, and wholesome to all the colonies; the murderers are since delivered to justice, the public peace preserved for the present, and probability it may be better secured for the future.

Thus this mischief was prevented, and the fear of a war hereby diverted; but now another broil was begun by the Narragansetts; though they unjustly had made war upon Uncas (as is before declared) and had the winter before this, earnestly pressed the Governor of the Massachusetts that they might still make war upon them to revenge the death of their sagamore which being taken prisoner was by them put to death (as before was noted) pretending that they had first received, and accepted his ransom, and then put him to death. But the Governor refused their presents, and told them, that it was themselves had done the wrong, and broken the conditions of peace; and he, nor the English neither, could nor would allow them to make any further war upon him; but if they did, must assist him, and oppose them; but if it did appear, upon good proof, that he had received a ransom for his life, before he put him to death; when the Commissioners met, they should have a fair hearing, and they would cause Uncas to return the same. But notwithstanding at the spring of the year they gathered a great power, and fell upon Uncas, and slew sundry of his men, and wounded more, and also had some loss themselves. Uncas called for aid from the English; they told him what the Narragansetts objected, he deny the same, they told him it must come to trial; and if he was innocent, if the Narragansetts would not desist, they would aid, and assist him. So at this meeting I they sent both to Uncas, and the Narragansetts, and required their sagamores to come or send to the Commissioners now met at Hartford, and they should have a fair and impartial hearing in all their grievances, and would endeavor that all wrongs should be rectified where they should be found; and they promised that they should safely come, and return without any danger or molestation; and sundry the like things, as appears more at large in the messenger's instructions. Upon which the Narragansetts sent one sagamore, and some other deputies with full power to do in the case as should be meet, Uncas came in person, accompanied with some chief about him. After the agitation of the business, the issue was this. The Commissioners declared to the Narragansett deputies as followeth:

1. That they did not find any proof of any ransom agreed on.
2. It appeared not that any wampum, had been paid as a ransom, or any part of a ransom, for Miantonomo's life.
3. That if they had in any measure proved their charge against Uncas, the Commissioners would have required him to have made answerable satisfaction.
4. That if hereafter they can make satisfying proof, the English will consider the same, and proceed accordingly.
5. The Commissioners did require that neither themselves, nor the Niantics make any war, or injurious assault upon Uncas or any of his company, until they make proof of the ransom charged, and that due satisfaction be denied, unless he first assault them.
6. That if they assault Uncas, the English are engaged to assist him.

Hereupon the Narragansett sachem advising with the other deputies engaged himself in the behalf of the Narragansetts, and Niantics that no hostile acts should be committed upon Uncas, or any of his, until after the next planting of corn; and that after that, before they begin any war, they will give 30 days warning to the Governor of the Massachusetts, or Connecticut.

The Commissioners approving of this offer, and taking their engagement under their hands, required Uncas, as he expected the continuance of the favor of the English, to observe the same terms of peace, with the Narragansetts, and theirs.

These foregoing conclusions were subscribed by the Commissioners, for the several jurisdictions, the 19 of September 1644.

Edward Hopkins, President
Simon Bradstreet
William Hathorne
Edward Winslow

John Browne
George Fenwick
Theophilus Eaton
Thomas Gregson

The forenamed Narragansetts deputies did further promise, that if contrary to this agreement, any of the Niantic Pequots should make any assault upon Uncas or any of his, they would deliver them up to the English to be punished according to their demerits; and that they would not use any means, to procure the Mohawks to come against Uncas during this truce. These were their names subscribed with their marks:

Weetowish   Chinnough
Pampiamett   Pummunish

The Commissioners this year were called to meet together at Boston, before their ordinary time; partly in regard of some differences fallen between the French and the Government of the Massachusetts; about their aiding of Monsieur La Tour, against Monsieur de Alney; and partly about the Indians, who had broken the former agreements about the peace concluded the last year. This meeting was held at Boston, the 28 of July.

Besides some underhand assaults made on both sides, the Narragansetts gathered a great power and fell upon Uncas, and slew many of his men, and wounded more, by reason that they far exceeded him in number and had got store of pieces, with which they did him most hurt. And as they did this without the knowledge, and consent of the English (contrary to former agreement) so they were resolved to prosecute the same notwithstanding anything the English said, or should do against them. So being encouraged by their late victory, and promise of assistance from the Mohawks (being a strong, warlike, and desperate people) they had already devoured Uncas, and his in their hopes, and surely they had done it indeed if the English had not timely set in for his aid. For those of Connecticut sent him 40 men who were a garrison to him till the Commissioners could meet and take further order.

Being thus met they forthwith sent 3 messengers viz. Sergeant John Davis, Benedict Arnold, and Francis Smith, with full and ample instructions, both to the Narragansetts, and Uncas, to require them that they should either come in person, or send sufficient men fully instructed to deal in the business. And if they refused, or delayed, to let them know (according to former agreements) that the English are engaged to assist against these hostile invasions, and that they have sent their men to defend Uncas and to know of the Narragansetts whether they will stand to the former peace, or they will assault the English also, that they may provide accordingly.

But the messengers returned not only with a slighting, but a threatening answer from the Narragansetts, (as will more appear hereafter). Also they brought a letter from Mr. Roger Williams, wherein he assures them, that the war would presently break forth, and the whole country would be all of a flame. And that the sachems of the Narragansetts had concluded a neutrality, with the English of Providence, and those of Aquidneck Island. Whereupon the Commissioners considering the great danger, and provocations offered; and the necessity we should put unto of making war with the Narragansetts; and being also careful in a matter of so great weight, and general concernment, to see the way cleared, and to give satisfaction to all the Colonies, did think fit to advise with such of the magistrates, and elders of the Massachusetts as were then at hand, and also with some of the chief military commanders there; who being assembled it was then agreed.

First that our engagement bound us to aid, and defend Uncas. 2. That this aid could not be intended only to defend him, and his fort, or habitation, but according to the common acceptation of such covenants, or engagements, considered with the grounds or occasion thereof; so to aid him as he might be preserved in his liberty and estate. 3ly that this aid must be speedy, lest he might be swallowed up in the meantime, and so come too late. 4ly. The justice of this war being cleared to ourselves, and the rest then present, it was thought meet that the case should be stated, and the reasons and grounds of the war declared and published. 5ly. That a day of humiliation should be appointed, which was the 5 day of the week following. 6ly. It was then also agreed by the Commissioners that the whole number of men to be raised in all the Colonies, should be 300; whereof from Massachusetts a 190, Plymouth 40, Connecticut 40, New Haven 30. And considering that Uncas was in present danger, 40 men of this number, were forthwith sent from the Massachusetts for his succor; and it was but need, for the other 40 from Connecticut had order to stay but a month, and their time being out they returned, and the Narragansetts hearing thereof, took the advantage, and came suddenly upon him, and gave him another blow, to his further loss, and were ready to do the like again; but these 40 men being arrived, they returned, and did nothing.

The declaration which they set forth I shall not transcribe it being very large, and put forth in print[312], to which I refer those that would see the same, in which all passages are laid open from the first. I shall only note their

---

[312] John Winthrop, *A Declaration of Former Passages and Proceedings Betwixt the English and the Narragansetts, with their Confederates* (Cambridge: Stephen Daye, 1645).

proud carriage, and answers to the 3 messengers sent from the Commissioners. They received them with scorn, and contempt; and told them they resolved to have no peace, without Uncas his head; also they gave this further answer; that it mattered not who began the war, they were resolved to follow it; and that the English should withdraw their garrison from Uncas, or they would procure the Mohawks against them, and withal gave them this threatening answer: that they would lay the English cattle on heaps as high as their houses, and that no Englishman should stir out of his door to piss, but he should be killed. And whereas they required guides to pass through their country to deliver their message to Uncas from the Commissioners, they denied them; but at length (in way of scorn) offered them an old Pequot woman; besides also they conceived themselves in danger, for whilst the interpreter was speaking with them about the answer he should return, 3 men came and stood behind him with their hatchets according to their murderous manner; but one of his fellows gave him notice of it, so they broke off and came away, with sundry such like affronts, which made those Indians they carried with them, to run away for fear, and leave them to go home as they could.

Thus whilst the Commissioners in care of the public peace sought to quench the fire kindled amongst the Indians, these children of strife, breathe out threatenings, provocations and war, against the English themselves. So that unless they should dishonor and provoke God, by violating a just engagement, and expose the Colonies to contempt, and danger from the barbarians; they cannot but exercise force, when no other means will prevail to reduce the Narragansetts, and their confederates, to a more just, and sober temper.

So as hereupon, they went on to hasten the preparations, according to the former agreement, and sent to Plymouth to send forth their 40 men with all speed to lie at Seekonk, lest any danger should befall it, before the rest were ready, it lying next the enemy; and there to stay, till the Massachusetts should join with them. Also Connecticut, and New Haven forces were to join together, and march with all speed, and the Indian confederates of those parts with them. All which was done accordingly, and the soldiers of this place were at Seekonk, the place of their rendezvous 8 or 10 days before the rest were ready; they were well armed all with snaphance pieces, and went under the command of Captain Standish; those from other places were led likewise by able commanders as Captain Mason for Connecticut, etc. And Major Gibbons was made general over the whole, with such commissions, and instructions as was meet.

Upon the sudden dispatch of these soldiers (the present necessity requiring it) the deputies of the Massachusetts Court (being now assembled immediately after the setting forth of their 40 men) made a question whether it was legally done, without their Commission. It was answered that howsoever it did properly belong to the authority of the several jurisdictions (after the war was agreed upon, by the Commissioners, and the number of men) to provide the men, and means to carry on the war; yet in this present case the proceeding of the Commissioners, and the commission given was as sufficient as if it had been done by the General Court.

1. First it was a case of such present and urgent necessity, as could not stay the calling of the Court, or Council.
2. In the articles of confederation, power is given to the Commissioners, to consult, order, and determine all affairs of war, etc. And the word *determine* comprehends all acts of authority belonging thereunto.
3. The Commissioners are the judges of the necessity of the expedition.
4. The General Court have made their own Commissioners, their sole counsel for these affairs.
5. These counsels could not have had their due effect except they had power to proceed in this case, as they have done; which were to make the Commissioners' power and the main end of the Confederation, to be frustrate, and that merely for observing a ceremony.
6. The Commissioners having sole power to manage the war for number of men, for time, place, etc., they only know their own counsels and determinations, and therefore none can grant commission to act according to these but themselves.

All things being thus in readiness, and some of the soldiers gone forth, and the rest ready to march, the Commissioners thought it meet before any hostile act was performed, to cause a present to be returned, which had been sent to the Governor of the Massachusetts from the Narragansett sachems, but not by him received, but laid up to be accepted or refused as they should carry themselves, and observe the covenants. Therefore they violating the same, and standing out thus to a war, it was again returned by 2 messengers and an interpreter. And further to let know that their men already sent to Uncas (and other where sent forth) have hitherto had express order only to stand upon his, and their own defense, and not to attempt any invasion of the Narragansetts' country; and yet if they may have due reparation for what is past and good security for the future; it shall appear they are as desirous of peace, and shall be as tender of the Narragansetts' blood, as ever. If therefore Pessacus, Innemo with other sachems, will (without further delay) come along with you to Boston, the Commissioners do promise, and assure them, they shall have free liberty to come, and return without molestation or any just grievance from the English. But deputies will not now serve, nor may the preparations in hand be now stayed, or the directions given recalled, till the forementioned sagamores come, and some further order be taken. But if they will have nothing but war, the English are providing, and will proceed accordingly.

Pessacus, Mixanno, and Witowash, three principal sachems of the Narragansett Indians, and Aumsequen deputy for the Niantics, with a large train of men, within a few days after came to Boston.

And to omit all other circumstances, and debates, that passed between them, and the Commissioners, they came to this conclusion following.

It was agreed betwixt the Commissioners of the United Colonies, and the forementioned sagamores, and Niantic deputy; that the said Narragansett, and Niantic sagamores,

1. Should pay or cause to be paid at Boston, to the Massachusetts Commissioners the full sum of 2000 fathom of good white wampum, or a third part of black wampampeag, in 4 payments, namely 500 fathom within 20 days, 500 fathom within 4 months, 500 fathom, at, or before next planting time, and 500 fathom, within 2 years next after the date of these presents; which 2000 fathom the Commissioners accept for satisfaction of former charges expended.

2. The foresaid sagamores, and deputy, on the behalf of the Narragansett, and Niantic Indians hereby promise and covenant, that they upon demand, and proof satisfy, and restore unto Uncas, the Mohegan sagamore, all such captives, whether men, or women, or children; and all such canoes, as they, or any of their men have taken, or as many of their own canoes in the room of them full as good as they were, with full satisfaction for all such corn, as they or any of their men have spoiled or destroyed, of his, or his men's since last planting time; and the English Commissioners hereby promise that Uncas shall do the like.

3. Whereas there are sundry differences, and grievances betwixt Narragansett and Niantic Indians, and Uncas and his men (which in Uncas his absence, cannot now be determined) it is hereby agreed that Narragansett, and Niantic sagamores either come themselves, or send their deputies to the next meeting of the Commissioners

for the Colonies either at New Haven in September 1646 or sooner (upon convenient warning, if the said Commissioners do meet sooner) fully instructed to declare, and make due proof of their injuries, and to submit to the judgment of the Commissioners, in giving or receiving satisfaction; and the said Commissioners (not doubting but Uncas will either come himself, or send his deputies, in like manner furnished) promising to give a full hearing to both parties with equal justice, without any partial respects, according to their allegations and proofs.

4. The said Narragansett, and Niantic sagamores, and deputies do hereby promise and covenant to keep and maintain a firm and perpetual peace both with all the English United Colonies, and their successors; and with Uncas the Mohegan sachem and his men; with Woosamequin, Pomham, Socanoket, Cutshamakin, Shoanan, Passaconaway, and all other Indian sagamores, and their companies, who are in friendship with, or subject to any of the English; hereby engaging themselves, that they will not at any time hereafter, disturb the peace of the country, by any assaults, hostile attempts, invasions, or other injuries, to any of the United Colonies, or their successors; or to the aforesaid Indians; either in their persons, buildings, cattle, or goods, directly or indirectly, nor will they confederate with any other against them. And if they know of any Indians or others that conspire or intend hurt against the said English, or any Indians subject to, or in friendship with them, they will without delay, acquaint and give notice thereof to the English Commissioners or some of them. Or if any questions or differences shall at any time hereafter arise, or grow betwixt them and Uncas, or any Indians before mentioned; they will according to former engagements (which they hereby confirm and ratify) first acquaint the English, and crave their judgments, and advice therein; and will not attempt, or begin any war, or hostile invasion, till they have liberty and allowance from the Commissioners of the United Colonies so to do.

5. The said Narragansetts, and Niantic sagamores, and deputies do hereby promise that they will forthwith deliver, and restore all such Indian fugitives, or captives which have at any time fled from any of the English, and are now living, or abiding amongst them, or give due satisfaction for them to the Commissioners for the Massachusetts; and further that they will (without more delays) pay, or cause to be

paid, a yearly tribute a month before harvest, every year after this at Boston, to the English Colonies, for all such Pequots, as live amongst them, according to the former treaty, and agreement, made at Hartford 1638, namely one fathom of white wampum for every Pequot man, and half a fathom for each Pequot youth, and one hand length for each male child. And if Weequashcook refuse to pay this tribute for any Pequots with him, the Narragansett sagamores promise to assist the English against him. And they further covenant that they will resign, and yield up, the whole Pequot country, and every part of it to the English colonies, as due to them by conquest.

6. The said Narragansett and Niantic sagamores, and deputy, do hereby promise, and covenant that within 14 days they will bring and deliver to the Massachusetts Commissioners on the behalf of the colonies, four of their children viz. Pessacus his eldest son, the son Tassaquanawit brother to Pessacus, Awashawe his son, and Ewangsos' son, a Niantic to be kept (as hostages, and pledges) by the English, till both the forementioned 2000 fathom of wampum be paid at the times appointed, and the differences betwixt themselves and Uncas be heard, and ordered, and till these articles be underwritten at Boston, by Ianemo, and Wipetock. And further they hereby promise, and covenant, that if at any time hereafter any of the said children shall make escape, or be conveyed away from the English, before the premises be fully accomplished; they will either bring back and deliver to the Massachusetts Commissioners, the same children, or if they be not to be found, such and so many other children, to be chosen by the Commissioners for the United Colonies, or their assigns, and that within 20 days after demand; and in the meantime, until the said 4 children be delivered as hostages, the Narragansett, and Niantic sagamores, and deputy, do freely, and of their own accord, leave with the Massachusetts Commissioners as pledges for present security 4 Indians, namely, Witowash, Pummash, Iawashoe, Waughwauio, who also freely consent, and offer themselves to stay as pledges, till the said children be brought, and delivered as abovesaid.

7. The Commissioners for the United Colonies do hereby promise, and agree, that at the charge of the United Colonies, the 4 Indians now left as pledges, shall be provided for, and that the 4 children to be brought, and delivered as hostages, shall be kept and maintained, at the same charge; that they will require Uncas, and his men, with all other Indian sagamores, before named to forbear all acts of hostility,

against the Narragansetts, and Niantic Indians for the future. And further all the promises being duly observed, and kept by the Narragansett, and Niantic Indians and their company, they will at the end of 2 years restore the said children delivered as hostages, and retain a firm peace with the Narragansetts and Niantic Indians, and their successors.

8. It is fully agreed by, and betwixt the said parties, that if any hostile attempt be made while this treaty is in hand, or before notice of this agreement (to stay further preparations and directions) can be given, such attempts, and the consequences thereof, shall on neither part be accounted, a violation of this treaty, nor a breach of the peace here made, and concluded.

9. The Narragansetts, and the Niantic sagamores, and deputy, hereby agree, and covenant to, and with the Commissioners of the United Colonies, that henceforth they will neither give, grant, sell or in any manner alienate any part of their country, nor any parcel of land therein, either to any of the English, or others without consent, or allowance of the Commissioners.

10. Lastly they promise that if any Pequot, or other be found, and discovered amongst them, who hath in time of peace murdered any of the English, he, or they shall be delivered, to just punishment. In witness whereof the parties above named, have interchangeably subscribed these presents, the day and year above written.

This treaty, and agreement betwixt the Commissioners of the United Colonies; of ye United Colonies, and ye sagamores, and deputy, of Narragansets, and Niantic yndeans; was made, and concluded, Benedict Arnold being interpretour, upon his oath, sergant Callicot, an yndean his man being presents; and Josias, e cutshamakin, too yndeans acquainted with ye English Language; assisting therin; who opened, e cleared the whole treaty, e every article to ye sagamores, and deputis there presents. And thus was ye warr at this time stayed, and prevented.

John Herbert   Winthrop *presidont*   Geo: Ffenwick
Tho.   pelham   Edwa: Hopkins
John   prence   Theoph: Eaton
   Browne   Steuen Goodyeare

pesecouß his mark
Meekesano his mark
Witowash his mark
Aumsequen his mark   the niantice deputy
Abdas his mark
punnaßh his mark
Cutshamakin his mark

This treaty, and agreement betwixt the Commissioners of the United Colonies, and the sagamores, and deputy, of Narragansetts, and Niantic Indians, was made, and concluded, Benedict Arnold being interpreter, upon his oath, Sergeant Collicott[313], and an Indian his man being present; and Josias, and Cutshamakin, two Indians acquainted with the English language, assisting therein; who opened, and cleared the whole treaty, and every article to the sagamores, and deputy there present. And thus was the war, at this time stayed, and prevented.

---

[313] Richard Collicott of Dorchester.

• *Anno Dom: 1646* •

About the middle of May this year came in 3 ships into this harbor (in warlike order). They were found to be men of war, the captain's name was Cromwell[314], who had taken sundry prizes from the Spaniards in the West Indies; he had a commission from the Earl of Warwick. He had aboard his vessels about 80 lusty men, (but very unruly) who after they came ashore, did so distemper themselves with drink as they became like madmen, and though some of them were punished, and imprisoned, yet could they hardly be restrained; yet in the end they became more moderate, and orderly. They continued here about a month, or 6 weeks, and then went to the Massachusetts, in which time they spent, and scattered a great deal of money among the people, and yet more sin (I fear) than money, notwithstanding all the care, and watchfulness that was used towards them, to prevent what might be.

In which time one sad accident fell out: a desperate fellow of the company, fell a-quarreling with some of his company; his captain commanded him to be quiet, and surcease his quarreling, but he would not, but reviled his captain with base language, and in the end half drew his rapier, and intended to run at his captain, but he closed with him, and wrested his rapier from him, and gave him a box on the ear, but he would not give over, but still assaulted his captain, whereupon he took the same rapier as it was in the scabbard, and gave him a blow with the hilt, but it lit on his head, and the small end of the bar of the rapier hilt pierced his skull, and he died a few days after. But the captain was cleared by a council of war. This fellow was so desperate quarreler, as the captain was fain many times to chain him under hatches from hurting his fellows, as the company did testify, and this was his end.

---

[314] Thomas Cromwell

This Captain Thomas Cromwell, set forth another voyage to the West Indies, from the Bay of the Massachusetts, well manned, and victualed, and was out 3 years, and took sundry prizes, and returned rich, unto the Massachusetts. And there died the same summer, having got a fall from his horse, in which fall, he fell on his rapier hilts, and so bruised his body, as he shortly after died thereof, with some other distempers, which brought him into a fever. Some observed that there might be something of the hand of God herein; that as the forenamed man, died of the blow he gave him with the rapier hilts; so his own death was occasioned by a like means.

This year Mr. Edward Winslow went into England, upon this occasion: some discontented persons, under the government of the Massachusetts, sought to trouble their peace and disturb (if not innovate their government) by laying many scandals upon them; and intended to prosecute against them in England, by petitioning and complaining to the Parliament. Also Samuel Gorton and his company made complaints against them.[315] So as they made choice of Mr. Winslow to be their agent, to make their defense, and gave him commission and instructions for that end. In which he so carried himself, as did well answer their ends, and cleared them from any blame, or dishonor, to the shame of their adversaries. But by reason of the great alterations in the State, he was detained longer than was expected; and afterwards fell into other employments there, so as he hath now been absent this 4 years; which hath been much to the weakening of this government; without whose consent, he took these employments upon him.[316]

Anno·1647· ⌣ ⌣ ⌣ ⌣ ⌣ And Anno·1648 }

---

[315] Edward Winslow devoted most of his book *Hypocrisy Unmasked* (London, 1646) to the Samuel Gorton affair.

[316] Bradford made a chapter heading for 1647 and 1648 but never added any text to it. Several blank pages follow before he recorded "The names of those which came over first, in the year 1620."

The names of those which came over first, in the year 1620
and were (by the blessing of God) the first beginners, and
(in a sort) the foundation of all the plantations, and
colonies, in New England (and their families.)

8	Mr. John Carver. Katherine, his wife. Desire Minter; & 2 man-servants John Howland Roger Wilder William Latham, a boy. & a maid servant, & a child that was put to him called, Jasper More	2	Mr. Samuel Fuller; and a servant, called William Butten. His wife was behind & a child, which came afterwards.
6	Mr. William Brewster. Mary his wife, with 2 sons, whose names were Love, and Wrestling and a boy was put to him called Richard More; and another of his brothers the rest of his children were left behind & came over afterwards.	2	John Crackston and his son John Crackston.
		2	Captain Myles Standish and Rose, his wife
5	Mr. Edward Winslow Elizabeth his wife, & 2 men servants, called George Soule, and Elias Story; also a little girl was put to him called Ellen, the sister of Richard More.	4	Mr. Christopher Martin, and his wife; and 2 servants, Solomon Prower, and John Langmore
		5	Mr. William Mullins, and his wife; and 2 children Joseph, & Priscilla; and a servant Robert Carter.
2	William Bradford, and Dorothy his wife, having but one child, a son left behind, who came afterward.	6	Mr. William White, and Susanna his wife; and one son called Resolved, and one born a-shipboard called Peregrine; & 2 servants, named William Holbeck, & Edward Thompson
6	Mr. Isaac Allerton, and Mary his wife; with 3 children Bartholomew Remember, & Mary; and a servant boy, John Hooke.	8	Mr. Stephen Hopkins, & Elizabeth his wife; and 2 children, called Giles, and Constanta a daughter, both by a former wife. And 2 more by this wife, called Damaris, & Oceanus, the last was born at sea. And 2 servants, called Edward Doty, and Edward Leister.

1	Mr. Richard Warren, but his wife and children were left behind and came afterwards.	3	Francis Eaton, and Sarah his wife, and Samuel their son, a young child.
4	John Billington, and Ellen his wife: and 2 sons, John, & Francis.	10	Moses Fletcher John Goodman Thomas Williams Degory Priest Edmond Margesson Peter Brown Richard Britteridge Richard Clarke Richard Gardinar Gilbert Winslow
4	Edward Tilley, and Ann his wife; and 2 children that were their cousins: Henry Sampson, and Humility Cooper.		
3	John Tilley, and his wife; and Elizabeth their daughter.		
2	Francis Cooke, and his son John; But his wife, & other children came afterwards.	1	John Alden was hired for a cooper, at Southampton where the ship victualed; and being a hopeful young man was much desired, but left to his own liking to go, or stay when he came here, but he stayed, and married here.
2	Thomas Rogers, and Joseph his son; his other children came afterwards.		
2	Thomas Tinker, and his wife, and a son.	2	John Allerton, and Thomas English were both hired, the later to go Mr. of a shallop here, and the other was reputed as one of the company, but was to go back (being a seaman) for the help of others behind. But they both died here, before the ship departed.
2	John Rigsdale, and Alice his wife.		
3	James Chilton, and his wife, and Mary their daughter; they had an other daughter that was married came afterward.	2	There were also other 2 seamen hired to stay a year here in the country, William Trevore; and one Ely; but when their time was out they both returned.
3	Edward Fuller, and his wife; and Samuel their son.		
3	John Turner, and 2 sons; he had a daughter came some years after to Salem, where she is now living.		

There being about a hundred souls came over in this first ship; and began this work, which God of His goodness hath hitherto blessed; let his holy name have praise.

And seeing it hath pleased Him to give me to see 30 years completed, since these beginnings. And that the great works of his providence are to be observed. I have thought it not unworthy my pains, to take a view of the decreasings, and increasings of these persons, and such changes as hath passed over them, & theirs, in this thirty years. It may be of some use to such as come after; but however I shall rest in my own benefit.

4

2

4

I will therefore take them in order as they lie.

2

Mr. Carver and his wife, died the first year, he in the spring, she in the summer; also his man Roger, and the little boy Jasper, died before either of them, of the common infection. Desire Minter, returned to her friend & proved not very well, and died in England. His servant boy Latham after more than 20 years stay in the country went into England; and from thence to the Bahama Islands in the West Indies; and there with some others was starved for want of food. His maid servant married, and died a year or two after here in this place. His servant John Howland married the daughter of John Tilley, Elizabeth, and they are both now living; and have 10 children now all living and their eldest daughter hath 4 children

8

4

And their 2 daughter, one, all living and other of their children marriageable so 15 are come of them.

8

15

Mr. Brewster lived to very old age; about 80 years he was when he died, having lived some 23 or 24 years here in the country & though his wife died long before, yet she died aged. His son Wrestling died a young man unmarried; his son Love, lived till this year 1650, and died, & left 4 children, now living. His daughters which came over after him, are dead but have left sundry children alive; his eldest son is still living, and hath 9 or 10 children, one married who hath a child, or 2. Richard More, his brother died the first winter; but he is married, and hath 4 or 5 children, all living.

Mr. Ed. Winslow, his wife died the first winter; and he married with the widow of Mr. White, and hath 2 children living by her marriageable, besides sundry that are dead. One of his servants died, as also the little girl soon after the ships arrival. But his man George Soule is still living, and hath 8 children.

William Bradford, his wife died soon after their arrival; and he married again; and hath 4 children, 3 whereof are married.

Mr. Allerton his wife died with the first, and his servant John Hooke. His son Bartle is married in England but I know not how many children he hath. His daughter Remember is married at Salem & hath 3 or 4 children living. And his daughter Mary is married here, & hath 4 children. Himself married again with the daughter of Mr. Brewster, & hath one son living by her but she is long since dead. And he is married again, and hath left this place long ago. So I account his increase to be 8 besides his sons in England.

2

Mr. Fuller, his servant died at sea; and
after his wife came over, he had two
children by her; which are living and
grown up to years. But he died some 15
years ago.

0

John Crackston died in the first
mortality; and about some 5 or 6 years
after his son died, having lost himself in
the woods, his feet became frozen, which
put him into a fever, of which he died.

4

Captain Standish his wife died in
the first sickness; and he married
again, and hath 4 sons living,
and some are dead.

Mr. Martin, he, and all his, died
in the first infection; not long
after the arrival.

15

Mr. Mullins, and his wife, his
son, & his servant died the first
winter. Only his daughter Priscilla
survived, and married with John
Alden, who are both living, and
have 11 children. And their eldest
daughter is married & hath five
children.

7

Mr. White, and his 2 servants died
soon after their landing. His wife married
with Mr. Winslow (as is before noted)
His 2 sons are married, and Resolved
hath 5 children; Peregrine two, all living.
So their increase are 7.

3

Mr. Hopkins, and his wife are now
both dead; but they lived above 20
years in this place, and had one
son, and 4 daughters born here.
Their son became a seaman, and died at
Barbados, one daughter died here and
2 are married, one of

4

them hath 2 children, & one is yet
to marry. So their increase, which
still survive, are 5. But his son Giles
is married, and hath 4 hildren.

12

His daughter Constanta, is also
married and hath 12 children all of
them living, and one of them
married.

4

Mr. Richard Warren lived some 4
or 5 years, and had his wife come
over to him, by whom he had 2
sons before died; and one of them
is married, and hath 2 children
So his increase is 4 but he had
5 daughters more come over
with his wife, who are all married;
& living & have many children.

8

John Billington after he had been
here 10 years, was executed, for
killing a man; and his eldest
son died before him; but his
2 son is alive, and married, &
hath 8 children.

7

Edward Tilley, and his wife both
died soon after their arrival; and
the girl Humility their cousin, was
sent for into England, and
died there. But the youth Henry
Sampson, is still living, and is
married, & hath 7 children.

John Tilley, and his wife both
died, a little after they came
ashore; and their daughter
Elizabeth married with John
Howland and hath issue as is before
noted.

---

8   Francis Cooke is still living, a
very old man, and hath seen
his children's children have
children: after his wife came over,
(with other of his children) he
hath 3 still living by her, all
married, and have 5 children
so their increase is 8. And his
son John which came over
4   with him, is married, and hath
4 children living.

---

6   Thomas Rogers died in the first sickness
but his son Joseph is still living, and is
married, and hath 6 children. The rest of
Thomas
Rogers came over, & are married, & have
many children.

Thomas Tinker, and his wife, and son, all
died in the first sickness.

And so did John Rigsdale, and his wife.

---

10   James Chilton, and his wife also died in
the first infection. But their daughter
Mary is still living
and hath 9 children; and one daughter is
married, & hath a child; so their increase
is 10.

---

4   Edward Fuller, and his wife died soon
after they came ashore; but their son
Samuel is living, &
married, and hath 4 children or more.

John Turner, and his 2 sons all died in
the first sickness. But he hath a
daughter still living at Salem, well
married, and approved of.

---

4   Francis Eaton, his first wife died in the
general sickness; and he married again,
& his 2 wife died, & he married the 3
and had by her 3 children; one of them
is married, & hath a child; the other are
living, but one of them is an idiot. He
1   died about 16 years ago. His son
Samuel, who came over a sucking child is
also married, & hath a child.

Moses Fletcher
Thomas Williams
Degory Priest
John Goodman
Edmond Margesson
Richard Britteridge
Richard Clarke
  All these died soon after their arrival in
the general sickness that befell. But
Degory Priest had his wife & children
sent hither afterwards, she being Mr.
Allerton's sister. But the rest left no
posterity here.

Richard Gardinar, became a seaman,
and died in England, or at sea. Gilbert
Winslow after divers years abode here,
returned into England and died there.

---

6   Peter Brown married twice; by his first
wife he had 2 children, who are living,
& both of them married; and the one
of them hath 2 children
by his second wife, he had 2 more; he
died about 16 years since.

Thomas English; and John Allerton
died in the general sickness.
John Alden married with Priscilla,
Mr. Mullins his daughter, and had issue
by her as is before related.

Edward Doty, & Edward Leister,
the servants of Mr. Hopkins: Leister after
he was at liberty, went to Virginia, &
there died; but Edward Doty by a second
wife hath 7 children and both he and
they are living.

Of these 100 persons which came
first over, in this first ship together,
the greater half died in the general
mortality; and most of them in 2
or three months time. And for
those which survived though some
were ancient & past procreation; &
others left the place and country;
yet of those few remaining are sprung
up above 160 persons; in this 30
years. And are now living in this
present year 1650. Besides many of
their children which are dead, and
come not within this account.
And of the old stock (of one, &
other) there are yet living this present
year 1650 near 30 persons.
Let the Lord have the praise; who is the
High Preserver of men.

A
RELATION OR

Journal of the beginning and proceedings of the
English Plantation settled at Plymouth in NEW
ENGLAND, by certain English Adventurers both
Merchants and others.

With their difficult passage, their safe arrival, their
joyful building of, and comfortable planting themselves
in the now well defended town
of NEW PLYMOUTH.

AS ALSO A RELATION OF FOUR
several discoveries since made by some of the
same English Planters there resident.

I. In a journey to Pokanoket the habitation of the Indian's greatest King
Massasoit: as also their message, the answer and entertainment they
had of him.
II. In a voyage made by ten of them to the Kingdom of Nauset, to seek
a boy that had lost himself in the woods: with such accidents as befell
them in that voyage.
III. In their journey to the Kingdom of Nemasket, in defense of their
greatest King Massasoit, against the Narragansetts, and to revenge
the supposed death of their interpreter Tisquantum.
IV. Their voyage to the Massachusetts, and their entertainment there.

With an answer to all such objections as are any way made
against the lawfulness of English plantations
in those parts.

LONDON,
Printed for John Bellamie, and are to be sold at his shop at the two
Greyhounds in Cornhill near the Royal Exchange, 1622.

To the Reader.

Courteous reader, be entreated to make a favorable construction of my forwardness, in publishing these ensuing discourses, the desire of carrying the Gospel of Christ, into those foreign parts, amongst those people that as yet have had no knowledge, nor taste of God, as also to procure unto themselves and others a quiet and comfortable habitation: where amongst other things the inducements (unto these undertakers of the then hopeful, and now experimentally known good enterprise for plantation, in New England, to set afoot and prosecute the same and though it fared with them, as it is common to the most actions of this nature, that the first attempts prove difficult, as the sequel more at large expresseth, yet it hath pleased God, even beyond our expectation in so short a time, to give hope of letting some of them see (though some he hath taken out of this vale of tears) some grounds of hope, of the accomplishment of both those ends by them, at first propounded.

And as myself then much desired, and shortly hope to effect, if the Lord will, the putting to of my shoulder in this hopeful business, and in the meantime, these relations coming to my hand from my both known and faithful friends, on whose writings I do much rely, I thought it not amiss to make them more general, hoping of a cheerful proceeding, both of adventurers and planters, entreating that the example of the honorable Virginia and Bermuda Companies, encountering with so many disasters, and that for divers years together, with an unwearied resolution, the good effects whereof are now eminent, may prevail as a spur of preparation also touching this no less hopeful country though yet an infant, the extent and commodities whereof are as yet not fully known, after time will unfold more: such as desire to take knowledge of things, may inform themselves by this ensuing treatise, and if they please also by such as have been there a first and second time, my hearty prayer to God is that the event of this and all other honorable and honest undertakings, may be for the furtherance of the Kingdom of Christ, the enlarging of the bounds of our Sovereign

Lord King James, and the good and profit of those, who either by purse, or person, or both, are agents in the same, so I take leave and rest

Thy friend, G. Mourt. [317]

---

[317] Generally identified as George Morton, who came to Plymouth on the ship *Anne* in 1623, and whose son Nathaniel Morton was the author of *New England's Memorial* (Cambridge, 1669).

CERTAIN USEFUL ADVERTISEMENTS SENT
in a Letter written by a discreet friend unto the Planters in New England, at their first setting sail from Southampton, who earnestly desireth the prosperity of that their new Plantation.

* *
*

Loving and Christian friends, I do heartily and in the Lord salute you all, as being they with whom I am present in my best affection, and most earnest longings after you, though I be constrained for awhile to be bodily absent from you, I say constrained, God knowing how willingly and much rather than otherwise I would have borne my part with you in this first brunt, were I not by strong necessity held back for the present. Make account of me in the meanwhile, as of a man divided in myself with great pain, and as (natural bonds set aside) having my better part with you. And though I doubt not but in your godly wisdoms you both foresee and resolve upon that which concerneth your present state and condition both severally and jointly, yet have I thought but my duty to add some further spur of provocation unto them who run already, if not because you need it, yet because I owe it in love and duty.

And first, as we are daily to renew our repentance with our God, special for our sins known, and general for our unknown trespasses; so doth the Lord call us in a singular manner upon occasions of such difficulty and danger as lieth upon you, to a both more narrow search and careful reformation of our ways in His sight, lest He calling to remembrance our sins forgotten by us or unrepented of, take advantage against us, and in judgment leave us for the same to be swallowed up in one danger or other; whereas on the contrary, sin being taken away by earnest repentance and the pardon thereof from the Lord, sealed up unto a man's conscience by His Spirit, great shall be his security and peace in all dangers, sweet his comforts in all distresses, with happy deliverance from all evil, whether in life or in death.

Now next after this heavenly peace with God and our own consciences, we are carefully to provide for peace with all men what in us lieth, especially with our associates, and for that end watchfulness must be had, that we neither at all in ourselves do give, no nor easily take offense being given by others. Woe be unto the world for offenses, for though it be necessary (considering the malice of Satan and man's corruption) that offenses come, yet woe unto the man or woman either by whom the offense cometh, saith Christ, Math. 18:7. And if offenses in the unseasonable use of things in themselves indifferent, be more to the feared than death itself, as the Apostle teacheth, 1 Cor. 9:15, how much more in things simply evil, in which neither honor of God nor love of man is thought worthy to be regarded.

Neither yet is it sufficient that we keep ourselves by the grace of God from giving offense, except withal we be armed against the taking of them when they be given by others. For how unperfect and lame is the work of grace in that person who wants charity to cover a multitude of offenses, as the Scriptures speak. Neither are you to be exhorted to this grace only upon the common grounds of Christianity, which are, that persons ready to take offense, either want charity to cover offenses, or wisdom duly to weigh human frailty; or lastly are gross, though close hypocrites, as Christ our Lord teacheth, Math. 7:1,2,3, as indeed in mine own experience, few or none have been found which sooner give offense, than such as easily take it; neither have they ever proved sound and profitable members in societies, which have nourished in themselves that touchy humor. But besides these, there are divers special motives provoking you above others to great care and conscience this way: as first, you are many of you strangers, as to the persons, so to the infirmities one of another, and so stand in need of more watchfulness this way, lest when such things fall out in men and women as you suspected not, you be inordinately affected with them; which doth require at your hands much wisdom and charity for the covering and preventing of incident offenses that way. And lastly your intended course of civil community will minister continual occasion of offense, and will be as fuel for that fire, except you diligently quench it with brotherly forbearance. And if taking of offense causelessly or easily at men's doings be so carefully to be avoided, how much more heed is to be taken that we take not offense at God Himself, which yet we certainly do so oft as we do murmur at His providence in our crosses, or bear impatiently such afflictions as wherewith He pleaseth to visit us. Store we up therefore patience against that evil day, without which we take offense at the Lord Himself in His holy and just works.

A fourth thing there is carefully to be provided for, to wit, that with your common employments you join common affections truly bent upon the general good, avoiding as a deadly plague of your both common and special comfort all retiredness of mind for proper advantage, and all singularly affected any manner of way; let every man repress in himself and the whole body in each person, as so many rebels against the common good, all private respects of men's selves, not sorting with the general conveniency. And as men are careful not to have a new house shaken with any violence before it be well settled and the parts firmly knit: so be you, I beseech you brethren, much more careful, that the house of God which you are and are to be, be not shaken with unnecessary novelties or other oppositions at the first settling thereof.

Lastly, whereas you are to become a body politic, using amongst yourselves civil government, and are not furnished with any persons of special eminency above the rest, to be chosen by you into office of government: let your wisdom and godliness appear, not only in choosing such persons as do entirely love, and will diligently promote the common good, but also in yielding unto them all due honor and obedience in their lawful administrations; not beholding in them the ordinariness of their persons, but God's ordinance for your good; not being like unto the foolish multitude, who more honor the gay coat, than either the virtuous mind of the man, or glorious ordinance of the Lord. But you know better things, and that the image of the Lord's power and authority which the Magistrate beareth, is honorable, in how mean persons soever. And this duty you both may the more willingly, and ought the more conscionably to perform, because you are at least for the present to have only them for your ordinary governors, which yourselves shall make choice of for that work.

Sundry other things of importance I could put you in mind of, and of those before mentioned in more words, but I will not so far wrong your godly minds, as to think you heedless of these things, there being also divers among you so well able to admonish both themselves and others of what concerneth them. These few things therefore, and the same in few words I do earnestly commend unto your care and conscience, joining therewith my daily incessant prayers unto the Lord, that He who hath made the heavens and the earth, the sea and all rivers of waters, and whose providence is over all His works, especially over all His dear children for good, would so guide and guard you in your ways, as inwardly by His Spirit, so outwardly by the hand of His power, as that both you and we also, for and with you, may have after matter of praising His name all the days of your and our lives. Fare you well in Him in whom you trust, and in whom I rest.

An unfeigned well-willer of your happy success in this hopeful voyage,

J.R.[318]

---

[318] John Robinson, the Pilgrims' pastor, who remained behind in Leiden, Holland. This letter is printed in numerous other places, including Bradford's *Of Plymouth Plantation.*

To His Much Respected Friend, Mr. J. P.[320]

Good Friend:

As we cannot but account it an extraordinary blessing of God in directing our course for these parts, after we came out of our native country, for that we had the happiness to be possessed of the comforts we receive by the benefit of one of the most pleasant, most healthful, and most fruitful parts of the world: so must we acknowledge the same blessing to be multiplied upon our whole company, for that we obtained the honor to receive allowance and approbation of our free possession, and enjoying thereof under the authority of those thrice honored persons, the President and Council for the affairs of New England, by whose bounty and grace, in that behalf, all of us are tied to dedicate our best service unto them, as those under His Majesty, that we owe it unto: whose noble endeavors in these their actions the God of heaven and earth multiply to his glory and their own eternal comforts.

As for this poor relation, I pray you to accept it, as being writ by the several actors themselves, after their plain and rude manner; therefore doubt nothing of the truth thereof: if it be defective in anything, it is their ignorance, that are better acquainted with planting than writing. If it satisfy those that are well affected to the business, it is all I care for. Sure I am the place we are in, and the hopes that are apparent, cannot but suffice any that will not desire more than enough, neither is there want of aught among us but company to enjoy the blessings so plentifully bestowed upon the inhabitants that are here. While I was a writing this, I had almost forgot, that I had but the recommendation of the relation itself, to your further consideration, and therefore I will end without saying more, save that I shall always rest

From PLYMOUTH in
> New England
> Yours in the way of friendship, R. G.[321]

---

[320] John Pierce, a large investor in, and the treasurer of, the Pilgrims' joint-stock company.

[321] *Mayflower* passenger Richard Gardinar is the only person known to have been at Plymouth with these initials. This may be a typographical error for "R.C.," Robert Cushman, a more probable person to have authored the letter.

A RELATION OR JOURNAL OF THE PROCEEDINGS OF THE
Plantation settled at Plymouth in New ENGLAND.

Wednesday the sixth of September, the wind coming east northeast, a fine small gale, we loosed from Plymouth, having been kindly entertained and courteously used by divers friends there dwelling, and after many difficulties in boisterous storms, at length by God's providence upon the ninth of November following, by break of the day we espied land which we deemed to be Cape Cod, and so afterward it proved.[322] And the appearance of it much comforted us, especially, seeing so goodly a land, and wooded to the brink of the sea, it caused us to rejoice together, and praise God that had given us once again to see land. And thus we made our course south southwest, purposing to go to a river[323] ten leagues[324] to the south of the Cape, but at night the wind being contrary, we put round again for the bay of Cape Cod: and upon the 11 of November, we came to an anchor in the bay[325], which is a good harbor and pleasant bay, circled round, except in the entrance, which is about four miles over from land to land, compassed about to the very sea with oaks, pines, juniper, sassafras, and other sweet wood; it is a harbor wherein 1000 sail of ships may safely ride, there we relieved ourselves with wood and water, and refreshed our people, while our shallop was fitted to coast the bay, to

---

[322] They had access to Captain John Smith's maps of New England, and several of the crew had been to the Cape Cod area.

[323] The Hudson River in modern-day New York was the Pilgrims' originally intended destination.

[324] 1 league = 3 miles

[325] Provincetown Harbor

search for an habitation: there was the greatest store of fowl that ever we saw.

And every day we saw whales playing hard by us, of which in that place, if we had instruments and means to take them, we might have made a very rich return, which to our great grief we wanted. Our master and his mate[326], and others experienced in fishing, professed, we might have made three or four thousand pounds worth of oil; they preferred it before Greenland whale-fishing, and purpose the next winter to fish for whale here; for cod we assayed, but found none, there is good store no doubt in their season. Neither got we any fish all the time we lay there, but some few little ones on the shore. We found great mussels, and very fat and full of sea pearl, but we could not eat them, for they made us all sick that did eat, as well sailors as passengers; they caused to cast and scour[327], but they were soon well again. The bay is so round and circling, that before we could come to anchor, we went round all the points of the compass. We could not come near the shore by three quarters of an English mile, because of shallow water, which was a great prejudice to us, for our people going on shore were forced to wade a bow shot or two in going a-land, which caused many to get colds and coughs, for it was many times freezing cold weather.

This day before we came to harbor, observing some not well affected to unity and concord, but gave some appearance of faction, it was thought good there should be an association and agreement, that we should combine together in one body, and to submit to such government and governors, as we should by common consent agree to make and choose, and set our hands to this that follows word for word.

In the name of God, Amen. We whose names are underwritten, the loyal subjects of our dread sovereign Lord King James, by the grace of God of Great Britain, France, and Ireland King, Defender of the Faith, etc.

Having undertaken for the glory of God, and advancement of the Christian faith, and honor of our King and Country, a voyage to plant the first colony

---

[326] Christopher Jones was master of the *Mayflower*, and John Clark and Robert Coppin are variously referred to as master's mates. There is no evidence that Jones or his mates had any first-hand experience with whaling. The previous ten years, Jones had been running trading voyages to France, primarily carrying cargos of wine.

[327] Vomit and have diarrhea

in the northern parts of Virginia, do by these presents solemnly and mutually in the presence of God and one of another, covenant, and combine ourselves together into a civil body politic, for our better ordering and preservation, and furtherance of the ends aforesaid; and by virtue hereof to enact, constitute, and frame such just and equal laws, ordinances, acts, constitutions, offices from time to time, as shall be thought most meet and convenient for the general good of the colony: unto which we promise all due submission and obedience. In witness whereof we have hereunder subscribed our names Cape Cod 11 of November, in the year of the reign of our sovereign Lord King James, of England, France, and Ireland 18 and of Scotland 54. Anno Domini 1620.[328]

The same day so soon as we could we set ashore 15 or 16 men, well armed, with some to fetch wood, for we had none left; as also to see what the land was, and what inhabitants they could meet with, they found it to be a small neck of land; on this side where we lay is the bay, and the further side the sea; the ground or earth, sand hills, much like the downs in Holland, but much better; the crust of the earth a spit's depth, excellent black earth; all wooded with oaks, pines, sassafras, juniper, birch, holly, vines, some ash, walnut; the wood for the most part open and without underwood, fit either to go or ride in: at night our people returned, but found not any person, nor habitation, and laded their boat with juniper[329], which smelled very sweet and strong, and of which we burnt the most part of the time we lay there.

Monday the 13 of November, we unshipped our shallop and drew her on land, to mend and repair her, having been forced to cut her down in bestowing her betwixt the decks, and she was much opened with the people's

---

[328] This is the so-called "Mayflower Compact," and is found in many other places including Bradford's *Of Plymouth Plantation*, and Nathaniel Morton's *New England's Memorial* (Cambridge, 1669). Morton is the first to add the names of the signers.

[329] Rambart Dodoens, in his *New Herball, or Historie of Plants* (London, 1586, page 893-894), says: "Juniper or the berries thereof burned, driveth away all venomous beasts, and all infection and corruption of the air: wherefore it is good to be burned in a plague time, in such places where as the air is infected." At least two *Mayflower* passengers, William Brewster and Myles Standish, owned this book. See image page opposite.

❧ *The vertues.*

The fruit or berries of Juniper is good for the stomack, lungs, liuer, and kidneies: it cureth the old cough, the gripings and windinesse of the bellie, and prouoketh vrine to be boiled in wine or honied water and dronken.

Also it is good for people that be bruised or squat by falling, to be taken in the aforesaid maner.

The iuice of the leaues doth withstand all venome, especially of vipers and serpents: it is good to drinke the same, and to lay it outwardly vpon the wounds. The fruit is good for the same purpose to be taken in what sort soeuer ye list.

Juniper or the berries thereof burned, driueth away all venomous beasts, and all infection and corruption of the aire: wherefore it is good to be burned in a plague time, in such places where as the aire is infected.

The rinde or barke of Juniper burned, healeth the naughtie scurffe, and fretting scabs, to be mingled with water & laid therto.

The gum of Juniper is good for them whose stomacks and bowels are cumbred with cold flemes: it expelleth all sorts of wormes, and staieth the inordinate course of womens flowers.

The perfume of Vernix is good for the braine, drieth vp the superfluous humors of the head, and stoppeth the falling downe of reume or humors from the same.

This gum tempered with oile of roses helpeth the rifts, cones or chappings of the hands and féete.

Except on the Juniper tree, showing the tree's medicinal "virtues," from Rambart Dodoens's *New Herbal, Or History of Plants* (London, 1586). Several *Mayflower* passengers owned copies of this book including Elder William Brewster and Captain Myles Standish.

lying in her, which kept us long there, for it was 16 or 17 days before the carpenter had finished her; our people went on shore to refresh themselves, and our women to wash, as they had great need; but whilst we lay thus still, hoping our shallop would be ready in five or six days at the furthest, but our carpenter made slow work of it, so that some of our people impatient of delay, desired for our better furtherance to travel by land into the country, which was not without appearance of danger, not having the shallop with them, nor means to carry provision, but on their backs, to see whether it might be fit for us to seat in or no, and the rather because as we sailed into the harbor, there seemed to be a river opening itself into the main land; the willingness of the persons was liked, but the thing itself, in regard of the danger was rather permitted than approved, and so with cautions, directions, and instructions, sixteen men were set out with every man his musket, sword, and corslet, under the conduct of Captain Myles Standish, unto whom was adjoined for counsel and advice, William Bradford, Stephen Hopkins, and Edward Tilley.

Wednesday the 15 of November, they were set ashore, and when they had ordered themselves in the order of a single file, and marched about the space of a mile, by the sea they espied five or six people, with a dog, coming towards them, who were savages, who when they saw them ran into the wood and whistled the dog after them, etc. First, they supposed them to be Master Jones, the master and some of his men, for they were ashore, and knew of their coming, but after they knew them to be Indians they marched after them into the woods, lest other of the Indians should lie in ambush; but when the Indians saw our men following them, they ran away with might and main and our men turned out of the wood after them, for it was the way they intended to go, but they could not come near them. They followed them that night about ten miles by the trace of their footings, and saw how they had come the same way they went, and at a turning perceived how they ran up an hill, to see whether they followed them. At length night came upon them, and they were constrained to take up their lodging, so they set forth three sentinels, and the rest, some kindled a fire, and others fetched wood, and there held our rendezvous that night. In the morning so soon as we could see the trace, we proceeded on our journey, and had the track until we had compassed the head of a long creek, and there they took into another wood, and we after them, supposing to find some of their dwellings, but we marched through boughs and bushes, and under hills and valleys, which tore our very armor in pieces, and yet could meet with none of them, nor their houses, nor find any fresh water, which we greatly desired, and stood in need of, for we brought

English pikeman's armor. Woodcut from Gervase Markham's
A School for Young Soldiers (London, 1615).

neither beer nor water with us, and our victuals was only biscuit and Holland cheese, and a little bottle of aquavitae, so as we were sore athirst. About ten o'clock we came into a deep valley, full of brush, wood-gaile, and long grass, through which we found little paths or tracks, and there we saw a deer, and found springs of fresh water, of which we were heartily glad, and sat us down and drunk our first New England water with as much delight as ever we drunk drink in all our lives. When we had refreshed ourselves, we directed our course full south, that we might come to the shore, which within a short while after we did, and there made a fire, that they in the ship might see where we were (as we had direction) and so marched on towards this supposed river; and as we went in another valley, we found a fine clear pond of fresh water, being about a musket shot broad, and twice as long; there grew also many small vines, and fowl and deer haunted there; there grew much sassafras: from thence we went on and found much plain ground, about fifty acres, fit for the plow, and some signs where the Indians had formerly planted their corn; after this, some thought it best for nearness of the river to go down and travel on the sea sands, by which means some of our men were tired, and lagged behind, so we stayed and gathered them up, and struck into the land again; where we found a little path to certain heaps of sand, one whereof was covered with old mats, and had a wooden thing like a mortar whelmed on the top of it, and an earthen pot laid in a little hole at the end thereof; we musing what it might be, digged and found a bow, and, as we thought, arrows, but they were rotten; we supposed there were many other things, but because we deemed them graves, we put in the bow again and made it up as it was, and left the rest untouched, because we thought it would be odious unto them to ransack their sepulchers. We went on further and found new stubble, of which they had gotten corn this year, and many walnut trees full of nuts, and great store of strawberries, and some vines; passing thus a field or two, which were not great, we came to another, which had also been new gotten, and there we found where an house had been, and four or five old planks laid together; also we found a great kettle, which had been some ship's kettle and brought out of Europe; there was also an heap of sand, made like the former, but it was newly done, we might see how they had paddled it with their hands, which we digged up, and in it we found a little old basket full of fair Indian corn, and digged further and found a fine great new basket full of very fair corn of this year, with some 36 goodly ears of corn, some yellow, and some red, and others mixed with blue, which was a very goodly sight: the basket was round, and narrow at the top, it held about three or four bushels, which was as much as two of us could lift up from the ground, and was very handsomely and cunningly made[330]; but whilst we were busy about these things, we set our men sentinel in a round ring, all but two or three which digged up the corn. We were in suspense, what to do with it, and the kettle, and at length after much consultation, we concluded to take the kettle, and as much of the corn as we could carry away with us; and when our shallop came, if we could find any of the people, and come to parley with them, we would give them the kettle again, and satisfy them for their corn, so we took all the ears and put a good deal of the loose corn in the kettle for two men to bring away on a staff; besides, they that could put any into their pockets filled the same; the rest we buried again, for we were so laden with armor that we could carry no more. Not far from this place we found the remainder of an old fort, or palisade, which as we conceived had been made by some Christians, this was also hard by that place which we thought had been a river, unto which we went and found it so to be, dividing itself into two arms by an high bank, standing right by the cut or mouth which came from the sea, that which was next unto us was the less, the other arm was more than twice as big, and not unlike to be an harbor for ships; but whether it be a fresh river, or only an indraught of the sea, we had no time to discover; for we had commandment to be out but two days. Here also we saw two canoes, the one on the one side, the other on the other side, we could not believe it was a canoe, till we came near it, so we returned leaving the further discovery hereof to our shallop, and came that night back again to the fresh water pond, and there we made our rendezvous that night, making a great fire, and a barricade to windward of us, and kept good watch with three

---

[330] The Indians stored their corn and seed in the ground. Thomas Morton, in his *New English Canaan* (Amsterdam, 1637) noted: "Their barns are holes made in the earth, that will hold a hogshead of corn apiece in them. In these (when their corn is out of the husk and well dried) they lay their store in great baskets (which they make of spark) with mats under, about the sides and on the top: and putting it into the place made for it, they cover it with earth: and in this manner it is preserved from destruction or putrefaction, to be used in case of necessity, and not else." The corn was a variety of New England flint. John Winthrop in a letter, noted that the corn was normally white or straw color, but that there were also "very many other colors, as red, yellow, blue, olive colors, and greenish and some very black and some of intermediate degrees of such colors, also many sorts of mixed colors and speckled or striped, and these various colored ears often in the same field and some grains that are of divers colors in the same ear."

sentinels all night, every one standing when his turn came, while five or six inches of match was burning.[331] It proved a very rainy night. In the morning we took our kettle and sunk it in the pond, and trimmed our muskets, for few of them would go off because of the wet, and so coasted the wood again to come home, in which we were shrewdly puzzled, and lost our way, as we wandered we came to a tree, where a young sprit was bowed down over a bow, and some acorns strewed underneath; Stephen Hopkins said, it had been to catch some deer[332], so as we were looking at it, William Bradford being in the rear, when he came looked also upon it, and as he went about, it gave a sudden jerk up, and he was immediately caught by the leg; it was a very pretty device, made with a rope of their own making, and having a noose as artificially made, as any roper in England can make, and as like ours as can be, which we brought away with us. In the end we got out of the wood, and were fallen about a mile too high above the creek, where we saw three bucks, but we had rather have had one of them. We also did spring three couple of partridges; and as we came along by the creek, we saw great flocks of wild geese and ducks, but they were very fearful of us. So we marched some while in the woods, some while on the sands, and other while in the water up to the knees, till at length we came near the ship, and then we shot off our pieces, and the long boat came to fetch us; Master Jones, and Master Carver being on the shore, with many of our people, came to meet us. And thus we came both weary and welcome home, and delivered in our corn into the store, to be kept for seed, for we knew not how to come by any, and therefore were very glad, purposing so soon as we could meet with any inhabitants of that place, to make them large satisfaction. This was our first discovery, whilst our shallop was in repairing; our people did make things as fitting as they could, and time would, in seeking out wood, and helving of tools, and sawing of timber to build a new shallop, but the discommodiousness of the harbor did

---

[331] The Pilgrims had matchlock muskets, which required a lighted match to ignite and fire the weapon.

[332] Stephen Hopkins was the only *Mayflower* passenger who had been to America previously, and had experience with the Indians. He was a passenger on the *Sea Venture*, which was bound for Virginia but shipwrecked in a hurricane on Bermuda in 1609; the marooned passengers eventually rebuilt two ships and escaped off the islands and arrived at the Jamestown Colony in Virginia. One of Hopkins' fellow castaways, John Rolfe, later married Pocahontas.

A cast iron cooking pot believed to have been owned by *Mayflower* passenger and
Plymouth militia captain Myles Standish.
Photo courtesy of the Pilgrim Hall Museum, Plymouth, Massachusetts.

much hinder us for we could neither go to, nor come from the shore, but at high water, which was much to our hindrance and hurt, for oftentimes they waded to the middle of the thigh, and oft to the knees, to go and come from land; some did it necessarily, and some for their own pleasure, but it brought to the most, if not to all, coughs and colds, the weather proving suddenly cold and stormy, which afterwards turned to scurvy, whereof many died.

When our shallop was fit indeed, before she was fully fitted, for there was two days' work after bestowed on her, there was appointed some 24 men of our own, and armed, then to go and make a more full discovery of the rivers before mentioned. Master Jones was desirous to go with us, and took such of his sailors as he thought useful for us, so as we were in all about 34 men; we made Master Jones our leader, for we thought it best herein to gratify his kindness and forwardness. When we were set forth, it proved rough weather and cross winds, so as we were constrained, some in the shallop, and others in the long boat, to row to the nearest shore the wind would suffer them to go unto, and then to wade out above the knees; the wind was so strong as the shallop could not keep the water, but was forced to harbor there that night, but we marched six or seven miles further, and appointed the shallop to come to us as soon as they could. It blowed and did snow all that day and night, and froze withal; some of our people that are dead took the original of their death here. The next day about 11 o'clock our shallop came to us, and we shipped ourselves, and the wind being good, we sailed to the river we formerly discovered, which we named, Cold Harbor[333], to which when we came we found it not navigable for ships, yet we thought it might be a good harbor for boats, for it flows there 12 foot at high water. We landed our men between the two creeks, and marched some four or five miles by the greater of them[334], and the shallop followed us; at length night grew on, and our men were tired with marching up and down the steep hills, and deep valleys, which lay half a foot thick with snow: Master Jones wearied with marching, was desirous we should take up our lodging, though some of us would have marched further, so we made there our rendezvous for that night, under a few pine trees, and as it fell out, we got three fat geese and six ducks to our supper, which we ate with soldiers' stomachs, for we had eaten little all that day; our resolution was next morning to go up to the head of this river, for we supposed it would prove fresh water, but in the morning our resolution held not, because

---

[333] Now called Pamet Harbor.

[334] Pamet River.

many liked not the hilliness of the soil, and badness of the harbor, so we turned towards the other creek[335], that we might go over and look for the rest of the corn that we left behind when we were here before; when we came to the creek, we saw the canoe lie on the dry ground, and a flock of geese in the river, at which one made a shot, and killed a couple of them, and we launched the canoe and fetched them, and when we had done, she carried us over by seven or eight at once. This done, we marched to the place where we had the corn formerly, which place we called Corn-hill[336]; and digged and found the rest, of which we were very glad: we also digged in a place a little further off, and found a bottle of oil; we went to another place, which we had seen before, and digged, and found more corn, viz. two or three baskets full of Indian wheat[337], and a bag of beans, with a good many of fair wheat ears; whilst some of us were digging up this, some others found another heap of corn, which they digged up also, so as we had in all about ten bushels, which will serve us sufficiently for seed. And sure it was God's good providence that we found this corn, for else we know not how we should have done, for we knew not how we should find, or meet with any of the Indians, except it be to do us a mischief. Also we had never in all likelihood seen a grain of it, if we had not made our first journey; for the ground was now covered with snow, and so hard frozen, that we were fain with our cutlasses and short swords, to hew and carve the ground a foot deep, and then wrest it up with levers, for we had forgot to bring other tools; whilst we were in this employment, foul weather being towards, Master Jones was earnest to go aboard, but sundry of us desired to make further discovery, and to find out the Indians' habitations, so we sent home with him our weakest people, and some that were sick, and all the corn, and 18 of us stayed still, and lodged there that night, and desired that the shallop might return to us next day, and bring us some mattocks and spades with them.

The next morning we followed certain beaten paths and tracks of the Indians into the woods, supposing they would have led us into some town, or houses; after we had gone a while, we light upon a very broad beaten path, well nigh two feet broad then we lighted all our matches and prepared ourselves, concluding we were near their dwellings, but in the end we found it to be only a path made to drive deer in, when the Indians hunt, as

---

[335]   Little Pamet River

[336]   The hill, just north of Pamet Harbor, with an elevation of about 100 feet, still carries the name Corn Hill.

[337]   Indian wheat was just another term for Indian corn.

we supposed; when we had marched five or six miles into the woods, and could find no signs of any people, we returned again another way, and as we came into the plain ground, we found a place like a grave, but it was much bigger and longer than any we had yet seen. It was also covered with boards, so as we mused what it should be, and resolved to dig it up, where we found, first a mat, and under that a fair bow, and there another mat, and under that a board about three quarters long, finely carved and painted, with three tines, or broaches, on the top, like a crown; also between the mats we found bowls, trays, dishes, and such like trinkets; at length we came to a fair new mat, and under that two bundles, the one bigger, the other less, we opened the greater and found in it a great quantity of fine and perfect red powder, and in it the bones and skull of a man.[338] The skull had fine yellow hair still on it, and some of the flesh unconsumed; there was bound up with it a knife, a packneedle, and two or three old iron things. It was bound up in a sailor's canvas cassock, and a pair of cloth breeches; the red powder was a kind of embalmment, and yielded a strong, but no offensive smell; it was as fine as any flour. We opened the less bundle likewise, and found of the same powder in it, and the bones and head of a little child, about the legs, and other parts of it was bound strings, and bracelets of fine white beads; there was also by it a little bow, about three quarters long, and some other odd knacks; we brought sundry of the prettiest things away with us, and covered the corpse up again. After this, we digged in sundry like places, but found no more corn, nor anything else but graves[339]:

---

[338]   Roger Williams in his *Key Into the Language of America*, printed in 1643, describes the burial practices of the Indians of New England: "When they come to the grave, they lay the dead by the grave's mouth, and then all sit down and lament, that I have seen tears run down the cheeks of stoutest Captains, as well as little children in abundance: and after the dead is laid in grave, and sometimes (in some parts) some goods cast in with them, they have then a second great lamentation, and upon the grave is spread the mat that the party died on, the dish he ate in; and sometimes a fair coat of skin hung upon the next tree to the grave, which none will touch, but suffer it there to rot with the dead."

[339]   One of Thomas Morton's complaints against the Pilgrims was their lack of respect towards non-Christian burials (*New English Canaan*, Amsterdam 1637). He reports on an incident in which those of Plymouth desecrated another Indian gravesite in the Massachusetts Bay: "The Planters of Plymouth, at their last being in those parts [the Massachusetts], having defaced the monument of the dead at

there was variety of opinions amongst us about the embalmed person; some thought it was an Indian lord and king: others said, the Indians have all black hair, and never any was seen with brown or yellow hair; some thought, it was a Christian of some special note, which had died amongst them, and they thus buried him to honor him; others thought, they had killed him, and did it in triumph over him. Whilst we were thus ranging and searching, two of the sailors, which were newly come on the shore, by chance espied two houses, which had been lately dwelt in, but the people were gone. They having their pieces, and hearing nobody entered the houses, and took out some things, and durst not stay but came again and told us; so some seven or eight of us went with them, and found how we had gone within a slight shot of them before. The houses[340] were made with long young sapling trees, bended and both ends stuck into the ground; they were made round, like unto an arbor, and covered down to the ground with thick and well wrought mats, and the door was not over a yard high, made of a mat to open; the chimney was a wide open hole in the top, for which they had a mat to cover it close when they pleased; one might stand and go upright in them, in the midst of them were four little trunches

---

Passonagessit (by taking away the hearse cloth which was two great bearskins sowed together at full length, and propped up over the grave of Chuatawback's mother,) the sachem of those territories, being enraged at the same, stirred up his men in his behalf, to take revenge."

[340] Thomas Morton describes Indian houses in his *New English Canaan* (Amsterdam, 1637): "The natives of New England are accustomed to build them houses, much like the wild Irish, they gather poles in the woods and put the great end of them in the ground, placing them in form of a circle or circumference, and bending the tops of them in form of an arch, they bind them together with the bark of walnut trees, which is wondrous tough, so that they make the same round on the top. For the smoke of their fire, to ascend and pass through, these they cover with mats, some made of reeds and some of long flags, or sedge finely sowed together with needles made of the splinter bones of a crane's leg, and with threads made of their Indian hemp, which there groweth naturally, leaving several places for doors, which are covered with mats, which may be rolled up, and let down again at their pleasure, making use of several doors according as the wind fits. The fire is always made in the middest of the house . . . their lodging is made in three places of the house about the fire; they lie upon planks commonly about a foot or 18 inches above the ground raised upon rails that are borne up upon forks; they

knocked into the ground, and small sticks laid over, on which they hung their pots, and what they had to seethe[341]; round about the fire they lay on mats, which are their beds. The houses were double matted, for as they were matted without, so were they within, with newer and fairer mats. In the houses we found wooden bowls, trays and dishes, earthen pots, handbaskets made of crab shells, wrought together; also an English pail or bucket, it wanted a bail, but it had two iron ears: there was also baskets of sundry sorts, bigger and some lesser, finer and some coarser: some were curiously wrought with black and white in pretty works, and sundry other of their household stuff: we found also two or three deer's heads, one whereof had been newly killed, for it was still fresh; there was also a company of deer's feet stuck up in the houses, harts' horns, and eagles' claws, and sundry such like things there was: also two or three baskets full of parched acorns, pieces of fish, and a piece of a broiled herring. We found also a little silk grass, and a little tobacco seed, with some other seeds which we knew not; without was sundry bundles of flags, and sedge, bulrushes, and other stuff to make mats; there was thrust into a hollow tree, two or three pieces of venison, but we thought it fitter for the dogs than for us: some of the best things we took away with us, and left the houses standing still as they were, so it growing towards night, and the tide almost spent, we hasted with our things down to the shallop, and got aboard that night, intending to have brought some beads, and other things to have left in the houses, in sign of peace, and that we meant to truck with them, but it was not done, by means of our hasty coming away from Cape Cod, but so soon as we can meet conveniently with them, we will give them full satisfaction. Thus much of our second discovery.

Having thus discovered this place, it was controversial amongst us, what to do touching our abode and settling there; some thought it best for many reasons, to abide there.

As first, that there was a convenient harbor for boats, though not for ships.

Secondly, good corn ground ready to our hands, as we saw by experience in the goodly corn it yielded, which would again agree with the ground, and be natural seed for the same.

---

lay mats under them, and coats of deerskin, otters, beavers, raccoons and of bear's hides, all which they have dressed and converted into good leather with the hair on for their coverings, and in this manner they lie as warm as they desire in the night . . ."

[341] boil

Thirdly, Cape Cod was like to be a place of good fishing, for we saw daily great whales of the best kind for oil and bone, come close aboard our ship, and in fair weather swim and play about us; there was once one when the sun shone warm, came and lay above water, as if she had been dead, for a good while together, within half a musket shot of the ship, at which two were prepared to shoot, to see whether she would stir or no, he that gave fire first, his musket flew in pieces, both stock and barrel, yet thanks be to God, neither he nor any man else was hurt with it, though many were thereabout. But when the whale saw her time she gave a snuff and away.

Fourthly, the place was likely to be healthful, secure, and defensible.

But the last and especial reason was, that now the heart of winter and unseasonable weather was come upon us, so that we could not go upon coasting and discovery, without danger of losing men and boat, upon which would follow the overthrow of all, especially considering what variable winds and sudden storms do there arise. Also cold and wet lodging had so tainted our people, for scarce any of us were free from vehement coughs, as if they should continue long in that estate, it would endanger the lives of many, and breed diseases and infection amongst us. Again, we had yet some beer, butter, flesh, and other such victuals left, which would quickly be all gone, and then we should have nothing to comfort us in the great labor and toil we were like to undergo at the first; it was also conceived, whilst we had competent victuals, that the ship would stay with us, but when that grew low, they would be gone, and let us shift as we could.

Others again, urged greatly the going to Anguum, or Angoum, a place twenty leagues off to the northwards, which they had heard to be an excellent harbor for ships; better ground, and better fishing. Secondly for anything we knew, there might be hard by us a far better seat, and it should be a great hindrance to seat where we should remove again. Thirdly, the water was but in ponds, and it was thought there would be none in the summer, or very little. Fourthly, the water there must be fetched up a steep hill: but to omit many reasons and replies used hereabouts; it was in the end concluded, to make some discovery within the bay, but in no case so far as Angoum: besides, Robert Coppin[342] our pilot, made relation of a great navigable river and good harbor in the other headland of this bay, almost right over against Cape Cod, being in a right line, not much above eight leagues distant, in

---

[342] Little is known of Robert Coppin, other than the fact he had been to New England on a previous voyage. He is perhaps the Robert Coppin who had a small investment in the Virginia Company of London in 1609.

which he had been once: and because that one of the wild men with whom they had some trucking, stole a harping iron from them, they called it Thievish Harbor. And beyond that place they were enjoined not to go, whereupon, a company was chosen to go out upon a third discovery: whilst some were employed in this discovery, it pleased God that Mistress White[343] was brought a-bed of a son, which was called Peregrine.

The fifth day, we through God's mercy escaped a great danger by the foolishness of a boy, one of Francis[344] Billington's sons, who in his father's absence, had got gunpowder, and had shot off a piece or two, and made squibs, and there being a fowling-piece charged in his father's cabin, shot her off in the cabin, there being a little barrel of powder half full, scattered in and about the cabin, the fire being within four foot of the bed between the decks, and many flints and iron things about the cabin, and many people about the fire, and yet by God's mercy no harm done.

Wednesday the sixth of December[345], it was resolved our discoverers should set forth, for the day before was too foul weather, and so they did, though it was well o'er the day ere all things could be ready: so ten of our men were appointed who were of themselves willing to undertake it, to wit, Captain Standish, Master Carver, William Bradford, Edward Winslow, John Tilley, Edward Tilley, John Howland, and three of London[346], Richard Warren,

---

[343] Susanna White, wife of William White. Peregrine is a word that means foreign, wandering, or migrating. Peregrine lived until 1704, long enough to have an obituary published in a Boston-area newspaper, the *Boston Newsletter*, on 31 July 1704.

[344] Francis Billington was actually the son; the father's name was John Billington.

[345] On December 4, Edward Thompson became the first passenger to sicken and die after the *Mayflower*'s arrival. Seven-year-old Jasper More died December 6. Mrs. Dorothy Bradford fell overboard and drowned on December 7. And James Chilton died December 8. This was the first wave of passengers to die during the "First Winter," before the Pilgrims had even decided where to settle.

[346] This statement has been misinterpreted on occasion to suggest these three men were born in London. In fact, Richard Warren was from co. Hertford, and Stephen Hopkins was baptized in Upper Clatford, and later lived at Winchester and Hursley, Hampshire. These men may have lived in London a short time before the voyage, or the "of London" designation may simply be a reference to the fact they boarded the *Mayflower* in London, rather than at Southampton where most of the Leiden congregation boarded.

The cradle of Peregrine White, son of William and Susanna White.
It is made out of willow (wicker), with oak rockers.
Photo courtesy of the Pilgrim Hall Museum, Plymouth, Massachusetts.

Stephen Hopkins and Edward Doty, and two of our seamen, John Allerton and Thomas English; of the ship's company there went two of the master's mates, Master Clark[347] and Master Coppin, the master gunner, and three sailors. The narration of which discovery follows, penned by one of the company.[348]

Wednesday the sixth of December we set out, being very cold and hard weather; we were a long while after we launched from the ship, before we could get clear of a sandy point, which lay within less than a furlong of the same. In which time, two were very sick, and Edward Tilley had like to have sounded with cold; the gunner also was sick unto death, (but hope of trucking made him to go) and so remained all that day, and the next night; at length we got clear of the sandy point, and got up our sails, and within an hour or two we got under the weather shore, and then had smoother water and better sailing, but it was very cold, for the water froze on our clothes, and made them many times like coats of iron: we sailed six or seven leagues by the shore, but saw neither river nor creek, at length we met with a tongue of land, being flat off from the shore, with a sandy point, we bore up to gain the point, and found there a fair income or road, of a bay[349], being a league over at the narrowest, and some two or three in length, but we made right over the land before us, and left the discovery of this income till the next day: as we drew near to the shore, we espied some ten or twelve Indians, very busy about a black thing, what it was we could not tell, till afterwards they saw us, and ran to and fro, as if they had been carrying something away, we landed a league or two from them, and had

---

[347] John Clark (c1575-1623). He had made several trips to Virginia, and in 1611 was captured by the Spanish. He was interrogated in Havana, then transferred and interrogated again in Madrid. He was released from captivity in 1616, and made another voyage to Virginia in 1618, before joining the *Mayflower*'s crew for the 1620 voyage. Transcripts of the depositions he gave while in Spanish custody can be found in Irene A. Wright, "Documents: Spanish Policy towards Virginia," *American Historical Review* 25(April 1920):448-479. He went to Virginia in 1623 with the intention of settling there, but died shortly after arrival.

[348] This work was written by multiple authors, having been compiled together apparently by George Morton. Edward Winslow authored the later segments of this work, but the authors of earliest chapters, including this one, remain anonymous.

[349] Welfleet Harbor.

much ado to put ashore anywhere, it lay so full of flat sands, when we came to shore, we made us a barricade, and got firewood, and set out our sentinels, and betook us to our lodging, such as it was; we saw the smoke of the fire which the savages made that night, about four or five miles from us, in the morning we divided our company, some eight in the shallop, and the rest on the shore went to discover this place, but we found it only to be a bay, without either river or creek coming into it, yet we deemed it to be as good an harbor as Cape Cod, for they that sounded it, found a ship might ride in five fathom[350] water, we on the land found it to be a level soil, but none of the fruitfullest; we saw two becks of fresh water, which were the first running streams that we saw in the country, but one might stride over them: we found also a great fish, called a grampus dead on the sands, they in the shallop found two of them also in the bottom of the bay, dead in like sort, they were cast up at high water, and could not get off for the frost and ice; they were some five or six paces long, and about two inches thick of fat, and fleshed like a swine, they would have yielded a great deal of oil, if there had been time and means to have taken it, so we finding nothing for our turn, both we and our shallop returned. We then directed our course along the sea sands, to the place where we first saw the Indians, when we were there, we saw it was also a grampus which they were cutting up, they cut it into long rands or pieces, about an ell long[351], and two handful broad, we found here and there a piece scattered by the way, as it seemed, for haste: this place the most were minded we should call, the Grampus Bay, because we found so many of them there: we followed the track of the Indians' bare feet a good way on the sands, at length we saw where they struck into the woods by the side of a pond, as we went to view the place, one said, he thought he saw an Indian house among the trees, so went up to see: and here we and the shallop lost sight one of another till night, it being now about nine or ten o'clock, so we light on a path, but saw no house, and followed a great way into the woods, at length we found where corn had been set, but not that year, anon we found a great burying place, one part whereof was encompassed with a large palisade, like a churchyard, with young spires four or five yards long, set as close one by another as they could two or three feet in the ground, within it was full of graves, some bigger, and some less, some were also paled about, and others had like an Indian house made over them, but not matted: those graves

---

[350] 1 fathom = 6 feet

[351] 1 English ell = 45 inches.

were more sumptuous than those at Corn-hill, yet we digged none of them up, but only viewed them, and went our way; without the palisade were graves also, but not so costly: from this place we went and found more corn ground, but not of this year. As we ranged we light on four or five Indian houses, which had been lately dwelt in, but they were uncovered, and had no mats about them, else they were like those we found at Corn-hill, but had not been so lately dwelt in, there was nothing left but two or three pieces of old mats, a little sedge, also a little further we found two baskets full of parched acorns hid in the ground, which we supposed had been corn when we began to dig the same, we cast earth thereon again and went our way. All this while we saw no people, we went ranging up and down till the sun began to draw low, and then we hasted out of the woods, that we might come to our shallop, which when we were out of the woods, we espied a great way off, and called them to come unto us, the which they did as soon as they could, for it was not yet high water, they were exceeding glad to see us, (for they feared because they had not seen us in so long a time) thinking we would have kept by the shore side, so being both weary and faint, for we had eaten nothing all that day, we fell to making our rendezvous and get firewood, which always cost us a great deal of labor, by that time we had done, and our shallop come to us, it was within night, and we fed upon such victuals as we had, and betook us to our rest, after we had set out our watch. About midnight we heard a great and hideous cry, and our sentinels called, *Arm, Arm*. So we bestirred ourselves and shot off a couple of muskets, and noise ceased; we concluded, that it was a company of wolves or foxes, for one told us, he had heard such a noise in Newfoundland. About five o'clock in the morning we began to be stirring, and two or three which doubted whether their pieces would go off or no made trial of them, and shot them off, but thought nothing at all, after prayer we prepared ourselves for breakfast, and for a journey, and it being now the twilight in the morning, it was thought meet to carry the things down to the shallop: some said, it was not best to carry the armor down, others said, they would be readier, two or three said, they would not carry theirs, till they went themselves, but mistrusting nothing at all: as it fell out, the water not being high enough, they laid the things down upon the shore, and came up to breakfast. Anon, all upon a sudden, we heard a great and strange cry, which we knew to be the same voices, though they varied their notes, one of our company being abroad came running in and cried, *They are men, Indians, Indians*; and withal, their arrows came flying amongst us, our men ran out with all speed to recover their arms, as by the good providence of

God they did. In the meantime, Captain Myles Standish, having a snaphance[352] ready, made a shot, and after him another, after they two had shot, other two of us were ready, but he wished us not to shoot, till we could take aim, for we knew not what need we should have, and there were four only of us, which had their arms there ready, and stood before the open side of our barricade, which was first assaulted, they thought it best to defend it, lest the enemy should take it and our stuff, and so have the more vantage against us, our care was no less for the shallop, but we hoped all the rest would defend it; we called unto them to know how it was with them, and they answered, Well, Well every one, and be of good courage: we heard three of their pieces go off, and the rest called for a firebrand to light their matches, one took a log out of the fire on his shoulder and went and carried it unto them, which was thought did not a little discourage our enemies. The cry of our enemies was dreadful, especially, when our men ran out to recover their arms, their note was after this manner, *Woath woach ha ha hach woach*: our men were no sooner come to their arms, but the enemy was ready to assault them.

There was a lusty man and no whit less valiant, who was thought to be their captain, stood behind a tree within half a musket shot of us, and there let his arrows fly at us; he was seen to shoot three arrows, which were all avoided, for he at whom the first arrow was aimed, saw it, and stooped down and it flew over him, the rest were avoided also: he stood three shots of a musket, at length one took as he said full aim at him, after which he gave an extraordinary cry and away they went all, we followed them about a quarter of a mile, but we left six to keep our shallop, for we were careful about our business: then we shouted all together two several times, and shot off a couple of muskets and so returned: this we did that they might see we were not afraid of them nor discouraged. Thus it pleased God to vanquish our enemies and give us deliverance, by their noise we could not guess that they were less than thirty or forty, though some thought that they were many more yet in the dark of the morning, we could not so well discern them among the trees, as they could see us by our fireside, we took up 18 of their arrows which we have sent to England by Master Jones, some whereof were headed with brass, others with harts' horn, and others with eagles' claws many more no doubt were shot, for these we found were almost covered with leaves: yet by the especial providence of God, none of them either hit or hurt us, though many came close by us, and on every

---

[352] A flintlock musket that did not require a burning match.

side of us, and some coats which hung up in our barricade, were shot through and through. So after we had given God thanks for our deliverance, we took our shallop and went on our journey, and called this place, *The First Encounter*[353], from thence we intended to have sailed to the aforesaid Thievish Harbor, if we found no convenient harbor by the way, having the wind good, we sailed all that day along the coast about 15 leagues, but saw neither river nor creek to put into, after we had sailed an hour or two, it began to snow and rain, and to be bad weather; about the midst of the afternoon, the wind increased and the seas began to be very rough, and the hinges of the rudder broke, so that we could steer no longer with it, but two men with much ado were fain to serve with a couple of oars, the seas were grown so great, that we were much troubled and in great danger, and night grew on: anon Master Coppin bade us be of good cheer he saw the harbor, as we drew near, the gale being stiff, and we bearing great sail to get in, split our mast in 3 pieces, and were like to have cast away our shallop, yet by God's mercy recovering ourselves, we had the flood with us, and struck into the harbor.

Now he that thought that had been the place was deceived, it being a place where not any of us had been before, and coming into the harbor, he that was our pilot did bear up northward, which if we had continued we had been cast away, yet still the Lord kept us, and we bare up for an island before us, and recovering of that island, being compassed about with many rocks, and dark night growing upon us, it pleased the Divine providence that we fell upon a place of sandy ground, where our shallop did ride safe and secure all that night, and coming upon a strange island kept our watch all night in the rain upon that island[354]: and in the morning we marched about it, and found no inhabitants at all, and here we made our rendezvous all that day, being Saturday, 10 of December, on the Sabbath day we rested, and on Monday we sounded the harbor, and found it a very good harbor for our shipping, we marched also into the land, and found divers cornfields, and little running brooks, a place very good for situation, so we returned to our ship again with good news to the rest of our people, which did much comfort their hearts.

On the fifteenth day, we weighed anchor, to go to the place we had discovered, and coming within two leagues of the land, we could not fetch the harbor, but were fain to put room again towards Cape Cod, our course

---

[353] Near modern-day Eastham.

[354] The island was named Clark's Island, after pilot John Clark, and it still bears this name today.

lying west; and the wind was at northwest, but it pleased God that the next day being Saturday the 16 day, the wind came fair, and we put to sea again, and came safely into a safe harbor; and within half an hour the wind changed, so as if we had been letted but a little, we had gone back to Cape Cod. This harbor[355] is a bay greater than Cape Cod, compassed with a goodly land, and in the bay, 2 fine islands uninhabited, wherein are nothing but wood, oaks, pines, walnut, beech, sassafras, vines, and other trees which we know not; this bay is a most hopeful place, innumerable store of fowl, and excellent good, and cannot but be of fish in their season: skote, cod, turbot, and herring, we have tasted of, abundance of mussels the greatest and best that ever we saw; crabs, and lobsters, in their time infinite, it is in fashion like a sickle or fish-hook.

Monday the 13 day[356], we went a-land, manned with the master of the ship, and 3 or 4 of the sailors, we marched along the coast in the woods, some 7 or 8 mile, but saw not an Indian nor an Indian house, only we found where formerly, had been some inhabitants, and where they had planted their corn: we found not any navigable river, but 4 or 5 small running brooks of very sweet fresh water, that all run into the sea: the land for the crust of the earth is a spit's depth, excellent black mould and fat in some places, 2 or 3 great oaks but not very thick, pines, walnuts, beech, ash, birch, hazel, holly, asp, sassafras, in abundance, and vines everywhere, cherry trees, plum trees, and many other which we know not; many kinds of herbs, we found here in winter, as strawberry leaves innumerable, sorrel, yarrow, carvel, brooklime, liverwort, watercresses, great store of leeks, and onions, and an excellent strong kind of flax, and hemp; here is sand, gravel, and excellent clay no better in the world, excellent for pots, and will wash like soap, and great store of stone, though somewhat soft, and the best water that ever we drunk, and the brooks now begin to be full of fish; that night many being weary with marching, we went aboard again.

The next morning being Tuesday the 19 of December, we went again to discover further; some went on land, and some in the shallop, the land we found as the former day we did, and we found a creek, and went up three English miles, a very pleasant river at full sea, a bark of thirty tons may go up, but at low water scarce our shallop could pass: this place we had a great liking to plant in, but that it was so far from our fishing our principal profit, and so encompassed with woods, that we should be in much danger of the

---

[355] Plymouth Harbor.

[356] This is a typographical error in the original; the correct date is Monday the 18th.

savages, and our number being so little, and so much ground to clear, so as we thought good to quit and clear that place, till we were of more strength; some of us having a good mind for safety to plant in the greater isle, we crossed the bay which is there five or six miles over, and found the isle about a mile and a half, or two miles about, all wooded, and no fresh water but 2 or 3 pits, that we doubted of fresh water in summer, and so full of wood, as we could hardly clear so much as to serve us for corn, besides we judged it cold for our corn, and some part very rocky, yet divers thought of it as a place defensible, and of great security.

That night we returned again a-shipboard, with resolution the next morning to settle on some of those places, so in the morning, after we had called on God for direction, we came to this resolution, to go presently ashore again, and to take a better view of two places, which we thought most fitting for us, for we could not now take time for further search or consideration, our victuals being much spent, especially, our beer, and it being now the 19 of December. After our landing and viewing of the places, so well as we could we came to a conclusion, by most voices, to set on the mainland, on the first place, on a high ground, where there is a great deal of land cleared, and hath been planted with corn three or four years ago, and there is a very sweet brook runs under the hill side, and many delicate springs of as good water as can be drunk, and where we may harbor our shallops and boats exceeding well, and in this brook much good fish in their seasons: on the further side of the river also much corn ground cleared, in one field is a great hill, on which we point to make a platform, and plant our ordnance, which will command all round about, from thence we may see into the bay, and far into the sea, and we may see thence Cape Cod: our greatest labor will be fetching of our wood, which is half a quarter of an English mile, but there is enough so far off; what people inhabit here we yet know not, for as yet we have seen none, so there we made our rendezvous, and a place for some of our people about twenty, resolving in the morning to come all ashore, and to build houses, but the next morning being Thursday the 21 of December[357], it was stormy and wet, that we could not go ashore, and those that remained there all night could do nothing, but were wet, not having daylight enough to make them a sufficient court of guard, to keep them dry. All that night it blew and rained extremely; it was so tempestuous, that the shallop could not

---

[357]   Richard Britteridge died this day, the first passenger to die after the *Mayflower* had anchored in Plymouth Harbor.

Town Brook in Plymouth.

Plymouth Rock is the rock that, by tradition, was used by the *Mayflower* passengers to step ashore at Plymouth. The rock cracked and broke in 1774 during an attempt to move it, and the date "1620" was carved into it in 1880 when the two halves were re-united.

go on land so soon as was meet, for they had no victuals on land. About 11 o'clock the shallop went off with much ado with provision, but could not return it blew so strong, and was such foul weather, that we were forced to let fall our anchor, and ride with three anchors an head.

Friday the 22 the storm still continued, that we could not get a-land, nor they come to us aboard: this morning goodwife Allerton[358] was delivered of a son, but dead born.

Saturday the 23 so many of us as could, went on shore, felled and carried timber, to provide themselves stuff for building.

Sunday the 24[359] our people on shore heard a cry of some savages (as they thought) which caused an alarm, and to stand on their guard, expecting an assault, but all was quiet.

Monday the 25 day, we went on shore, some to fell timber, some to saw, some to rive, and some to carry, so no man rested all that day, but towards night some as they were at work, heard a noise of some Indians, which caused us all to go to our muskets, but we heard no further. So we came aboard again, and left some twenty to keep the court of guard; that night we had a sore storm of wind and rain.

Monday the 25 being Christmas day, we began to drink water aboard, but at night the master caused us to have some beer, and so on board we had divers times now and then some beer, but on shore none at all.

Tuesday the 26 it was foul weather, that we could not go ashore.

Wednesday the 27 we went to work again.

Thursday the 28 of December, so many as could went to work on the hill, where we purposed to build our platform for our ordnance, and which doth command all the plain, and the bay, and from whence we may see far into the sea, and might be easier impaled, having two rows of houses and a fair street. So in the afternoon we went to measure out the grounds, and first, we took notice of how many families they were, willing all single men that had no wives to join with some family, as they thought fit, that so we might build fewer houses, which was done, and we reduced them to 19 families; to greater families we allotted larger plots, to every person half a pole in breadth, and three in length[360], and so lots were cast where every man should lie, which was done, and staked out; we thought this proportion

---

[358]   Mary (Norris) Allerton, who came on the *Mayflower* with husband Isaac and children Bartholomew, Remember, and Mary.

[359]   Solomon Prower died this day, the last person to die in December.

[360]   1 pole = 16.5 feet

A beer tankard believed to have been owned by *Mayflower* passenger Peter Browne.
It is about 10 inches tall, and made of oak staves and birch hoops.
Photo courtesy of the Pilgrim Hall Museum, Plymouth, Massachusetts.

was large enough at the first, for houses and gardens, to impale them round, considering the weakness of our people, many of them growing ill with colds, for our former discoveries in frost and storms, and the wading at Cape Cod had brought much weakness amongst us, which increased so every day more and more, and after was the cause of many of their deaths.

Friday and Saturday, we fitted ourselves for our labor, but our people on shore were much troubled and discouraged with rain and wet that day, being very stormy and cold; we saw great smokes of fire made by the Indians about six or seven miles from us as we conjectured.

Monday the first of January[361], we went betimes to work, we were much hindered in lying so far off from the land, and fain to go as the tide served, that we lost much time, for our ship drew so much water, that she lay a mile and almost a half off, though a ship of seventy or eighty ton at high water may come to the shore.

Wednesday the third of January, some of our people being abroad, to get and gather thatch, they saw great fires of the Indians, and were at their cornfields, yet saw none of the savages, nor had seen any of them since we came to this bay.

Thursday the fourth of January, Captain Myles Standish with four or five more, went to see if they could meet with any of the savages in that place where the fires were made, they went to some of their houses, but not lately inhabited, yet could they not meet with any; as they came home, they shot at an eagle and killed her, which was excellent meat; it was hardly to be discerned from mutton.

Friday the fifth of January, one of the sailors found alive upon the shore an herring, which the master had to his supper, which put us in hope of fish, but as yet we had got but one cod; we wanted small hooks.

Saturday the sixth of January, Master Martin[362] was very sick, and to our judgment, no hope of life, so Master Carver was sent for to come aboard to speak with him about his accounts, who came the next morning.

Monday the eighth day of January, was a very fair day, and we went betimes to work, Master Jones sent the shallop as he had formerly done, to see where fish could be got, they had a great storm at sea, and were in some danger, at night they returned with three great seals, and an excellent good cod, which did assure us that we should have plenty of fish shortly.

---

[361] Degory Priest died this day, the first of eight Pilgrims to die in January.

[362] Christopher Martin. He died two days later on January 8.

This day, Francis Billington, having the week before seen from the top of a tree on an high hill a great sea as he thought, went with one of the master's mates to see it, they went three miles, and then came to a great water, divided into two great lakes, the bigger of them five or six miles in circuit, and in it an isle of a cable[363] length square, the other three miles in compass; in their estimation they are fine fresh water, full of fish, and fowl; a brook issues from it, it will be an excellent help for us in time. They found seven or eight Indian houses, but not lately inhabited, when they saw the houses they were in some fear, for they were but two persons and one piece.[364]

Tuesday the 9 of January, was a reasonable fair day, and we went to labor that day in the building of our town, in two rows of houses for more safety: we divided by lot the plot of ground whereon to build our town: after the proportion formerly allotted, we agreed that every man should build his own house, thinking by that course, men would make more haste than working in common: the common house, in which for the first, we made our rendezvous, being near finished wanted only covering, it being about 20 foot square, some should make mortar, and some gather thatch, so that in four days half of it was thatched, frost and foul weather hindered us much, this time of the year seldom could we work half the week.

Thursday the eleventh, William Bradford being at work, (for it was a fair day) was vehemently taken with a grief and pain, and so shot to his huckle-bone; it was doubted that he would have instantly died, he got cold in the former discoveries, especially the last, and felt some pain in his ankles by times, but he grew a little better towards night and in time though God's mercy in the use of means recovered.

Friday the 12 we went to work, but about noon, it began to rain, that it forced us to give over work.

This day, two of our people put us in great sorrow and care, there was 4 sent to gather and cut thatch in the morning, and two of them, John Goodman and Peter Browne, having cut thatch all the forenoon, went to a further place, and willed the other two, to bind up that which was cut and to follow them; so they did, being about a mile and a half from our plantation: but when the two came after, they could not find them, nor hear anything of them at all, though they hallowed and shouted as loud as they could, so

---

[363] 1 cable = 608 feet
[364] The pond spotted by Francis Billington is still known as "Billington's Sea."

they returned to the company and told them of it: whereupon Master Leaver[365] and three or four more went to seek them, but could hear nothing of them, so they returning, sent more, but that night they could hear nothing at all of them: the next day they armed 10 or 12 men out, verily thinking the Indians had surprised them, they went seeking 7 or 8 miles, but could neither see nor hear anything at all, so they returned with much discomfort to us all. These two that were missed, at dinner time took their meat in their hands, and would go walk and refresh themselves, so going a little off they find a lake of water, and having a great mastiff bitch with them and a spaniel; by the water side they found a great deer, the dogs chased him, and they followed so far as they lost themselves, and could not find the way back, they wandered all that afternoon being wet, and at night it did freeze and snow, they were slenderly appareled and had no weapons but each one his sickle, nor any victuals, they ranged up and down and could find none of the savages' habitations; when it drew to night they were much perplexed, for they could find neither harbor nor meat, but in frost and snow, were forced to make the earth their bed, and the element their covering, and another thing did very much terrify them, they heard as they thought two lions roaring exceedingly for a long time together, and a third, that they thought was very near them, so not knowing what to do, they resolved to climb up into a tree as their safest refuge, though that would prove an intolerable cold lodging; so they stood at the tree's root, that when the lions came they might take their opportunity of climbing up, the bitch they were fain to hold by the neck, for she would have been gone to the lion; but it pleased God so to dispose, that the wild beasts came not: so they walked up and down under the tree all night, it was an extreme cold night, so soon as it was light they traveled again, passing by many lakes and brooks and woods, and in one place where the savages had burnt the space of 5 miles in length, which is a fine champaign country, and even. In the afternoon, it pleased God from an high hill they discovered the two isles in the bay, and so that night got to the plantation, being ready to faint with travel and want of victuals, and almost famished with cold, John Goodman was fain to have his shoes cut off his feet they were so swelled with cold, and it was a long

---

[365] Some have speculated this was a typographical error for Master Carver; however it seems more likely it is the name of one of the *Mayflower*'s crew: Carver is listed later in the paragraph as being sick in bed. There is a Thomas Leaver who is referred to on occasion in the records of the Virginia Company.

English spaniel, or "water dog." This woodcut is from Gervase Markham's very rare book, *The Whole Art of Fowling on Water and Land* (London, 1621), published just a year after the Pilgrims' voyage. The book was dedicated to Sir Edwin Sandys of the Virginia Company.

while after ere he was able to go; those on the shore were much comforted at their return, but they on shipboard were grieved at deeming them lost; but the next day being the 14 of January, in the morning about six of the clock the wind being very great, they on shipboard spied their great new rendezvous on fire, which was to them a new discomfort, fearing because of the supposed loss of men, that the savages had fired them, neither could they presently go to them for want of water[366], but after 3 quarters of an hour they went, as they had purposed the day before to keep the Sabbath on shore, because now there was the greater number of people. At their landing they heard good tidings of the return of the 2 men, and that the house was fired occasionally by a spark that flew into the thatch, which instantly burnt it all up, but the roof stood and little hurt; the most loss was Master Carver's and William Bradford's, who then lay sick in bed, and if they had not risen with good speed, had been blown up with powder: but through God's mercy they had no harm, the house was as full of beds as they could lie one by another, and their muskets charged, but blessed be God there was no harm done.

Monday the 15 day, it rained much all day, that they on shipboard could not go on shore, nor they on shore do any labor but were all wet.

Tuesday, Wednesday, Thursday, were very fair sunshiny days, as if it had been in April, and our people so many as were in health wrought cheerfully.

The 19 day, we resolved to make a shed, to put our common provision in, of which some were already set on shore, but at noon it rained, that we could not work. This day in the evening, John Goodman went abroad to use his lame feet, that were pitifully ill with the cold he had got, having a little spaniel with him, a little way from the plantation, two great wolves ran after the dog, the dog ran to him and betwixt his legs for succor, he had nothing in his hand but took up a stick, and threw at one of them and hit him, and they presently ran both away, but came again, he got a pale board in his hand, and they sat both on their tails, grinning at him, a good while, and went their way, and left him.

Saturday 20 we made up our shed for our common goods.

Sunday the 21 we kept our meeting on land.

Monday the 22 was a fair day, we wrought on our houses, and in the afternoon carried up our hogsheads of meal to our common storehouse.

The rest of the week we followed our business likewise.

Monday the 29[367] in the morning cold frost and sleet, but after reasonable fair; both the longboat and the shallop brought our common goods on shore.

---

[366]   i.e. the tide was not high enough.

[367]   Rose, the wife of Captain Myles Standish, died this day.

Tuesday and Wednesday 30 and 31 of January, cold frosty weather and sleet, that we could not work: in the morning the master and others saw two savages, that had been on the island near our ship, what they came for we could not tell, they were going so far back again before they were descried, that we could not speak with them.

Sunday the 4 of February, was very wet and rainy, with the greatest gusts of wind that ever we had since we came forth, that though we rid in a very good harbor, yet we were in danger, because our ship was light, the goods taken out, and she unballasted; and it caused much daubing of our houses to fall down.

Friday the 9 still the cold weather continued, that we could do little work. That afternoon our little house for our sick people was set on fire by a spark that kindled in the roof, but no great harm was done. That evening the master going ashore, killed five geese, which he friendly distributed among the sick people; he found also a good deer killed, the savages had cut off the horns, and a wolf was eating of him, how he came there we could not conceive.

Friday the 16 day, was a fair day, but the northerly wind continued, which continued the frost, this day after noon one of our people being a-fowling, and having taken a stand by a creek side in the reeds, about a mile and a half from our plantation, there came by him twelve Indians, marching towards our plantation, and in the woods he heard the noise of many more, he lay close till they were passed, and then with what speed he could he went home and gave the alarm, so the people abroad in the woods returned and armed themselves, but saw none of them, only toward the evening they made a great fire, about the place where they were first discovered: Captain Myles Standish, and Francis Cooke, being at work in the woods, coming home, left their tools behind them, but before they returned, their tools were taken away by the savages. This coming of the savages gave us occasion to keep more strict watch, and to make our pieces and furniture ready, which by the moisture and rain were out of temper.

Saturday the 17 day, in the morning we called a meeting for the establishing of military orders amongst ourselves, and we chose Myles Standish our captain, and gave him authority of command in affairs: and as we were in consultation hereabouts, two savages presented themselves upon the top of an hill, over against our plantation, about a quarter of a mile and less, and made signs unto us to come unto them; we likewise made signs unto them to come to us, whereupon we armed ourselves, and stood ready, and sent two over the brook towards them, to wit, Captain Standish and Stephen Hopkins, who went towards them, only one of them had a musket, which they laid down on the ground in their sight, in sign of peace, and to parley with them, but the savages would not tarry their coming: a noise of a great many more was heard behind the hill, but no more came in sight. This caused us to plant our great ordinances in places most convenient.

Wednesday the 21 of February[368], the master came on shore with many of his sailors, and brought with him one of the great pieces, called a minion[369], and helped us to draw it up the hill, with another piece that lay on shore, and mounted them, and a saller, and two bases; he brought with him a very fat goose to eat with us, and we had a fat crane, and a mallard, and a dried neat's tongue, and so we were kindly and friendly together.

Saturday the third of March, the wind was south, the morning misty, but towards noon warm and fair weather; the birds sang in the woods most pleasantly; at one of the clock it thundered, which was the first we heard in that country; it was strong and great claps, but short, but after an hour it rained very sadly till midnight.

Wednesday the seventh of March, the wind was full east, cold, but fair, that day Master Carver with five others went to the great ponds, which seem to be excellent fishing places; all the way they went they found it exceedingly beaten and haunted with deer, but they saw none; amongst other fowl, they saw one a milk-white fowl, with a very black head: this day some garden seeds were sown.

Friday the 16 a fair warm day towards; this morning we determined to conclude of the military orders, which we had begun to consider of before, but were interrupted by the savages, as we mentioned formerly; and whilst we were busied hereabout, we were interrupted again, for there presented himself a savage, which caused an alarm, he very boldly came all alone and along the houses straight to the rendezvous, where we intercepted him, not suffering him to go in, as undoubtedly he would, out of his boldness, he saluted us in English, and bade us welcome, for he had learned some broken English amongst the Englishmen that came to fish at Mohegan, and knew by

---

[368] Four *Mayflower* passengers, including William White and William Mullins, died on February 21, making this day the deadliest of the "First Winter." Mrs. Mary Allerton died four days later, on February 25. In all, seventeen Pilgrims died in the month of February, making it also the deadliest month of the First Winter.

[369] For more information on the muskets and cannons used by the Pilgrims, see Harold L. Peterson, *Arms and Armor of the Pilgrims* (Plymouth: Plimoth Plantation, 1957).

name the most of the captains, commanders, and masters, that usually come, he was a man free in speech, so far as he could express his mind, and of a seemly carriage, we questioned him of many things, he was the first savage we could meet withal; he said he was not of these parts, but of Mohegan, and one of the sagamores or lords thereof, and had been 8 months in these parts, it lying hence a day's sail with a great wind, and five days by land; he discoursed of the whole country, and of every province, and of their sagamores, and their number of men, and strength; the wind beginning to rise a little, we cast a horseman's coat about him, for he was stark naked, only a leather about his waist, with a fringe about a span[370] long, or little more; he had a bow and 2 arrows, the one headed, and the other unheaded; he was a tall straight man, the hair of his head black, long behind, only short before, none on his face at all; he asked some beer, but we gave him strong water, and biscuit, and butter, and cheese, and pudding, and a piece of mallard, all which he liked well, and had been acquainted with such amongst the English; he told us the place where we now live, is called Patuxet, and that about four years ago, all the inhabitants died of an extraordinary plague, and there is neither man, woman, nor child remaining, as indeed we have found none, so as there is none to hinder our possession, or to lay claim unto it; all the afternoon we spent in communication with him, we would gladly have been rid of him at night, but he was not willing to go this night, then we thought to carry him on shipboard, wherewith he was well content, and went into the shallop, but the wind was high and water scant, that it could not return back: we lodged him that night at Stephen Hopkins' house, and watched him; the next day he went away back to the Massasoits, from whence he said he came, who are our next bordering neighbors: they are sixty strong, as he saith: the Nausets are as near southeast of them, and are a hundred strong, and those were they of whom our people were encountered, as we before related. They are much incensed and provoked against the English, and about eight months ago slew three Englishmen, and two more hardly escaped by flight to Mohegan; they were Sir Ferdinando Gorges his men, as this savage told us, as he did likewise of the huggery, that is, fight, that our discoverers had with the Nausets, and of our tools that were taken out of the woods, which we willed him should be brought again, otherwise, we would right ourselves. These people are ill affected towards the English, by reason of one Hunt[371], a master of a ship, who deceived the people, and got them under

---

[370] 1 span = 9 inches
[371] The captain was Thomas Hunt, and the events described occurred in 1614.

color of trucking with them, twenty out of this very place where we inhabit, and seven men from Nauset, and carried them away, and sold them for slaves, like a wretched man (for 20 pound a man) that cares not what mischief he doth for his profit.

Saturday in the morning we dismissed the savage, and gave him a knife, a bracelet, and a ring; he promised within a night or two to come again, and to bring with him some of the Massasoits our neighbors, with such beavers' skins as they had to truck with us.

Saturday and Sunday reasonable fair days. On this day came again the savage, and brought with him five other tall proper men, they had every man a deer's skin on him, and the principal of them had a wild cat's skin, or such like on the one arm; they had most of them long hosen up to their groins, close made; and above their groins to their waist another leather, they were altogether like the Irish-trousers; they are of complexion like our English gypsies, no hair or very little on their faces, on their heads long hair to their shoulders, only cut before some trussed up before with a feather, broad-wise, like a fan, another a fox tail hanging out: these left (according to our charge given him before) their bows and arrows a quarter of a mile from our town, we gave them entertainment as we thought was fitting them, they did eat liberally of our English victuals, they made semblance unto us of friendship and amity; they song and danced after their manner like antics; they brought with them in a thing like a bow-case (which the principal of them had about his waist) a little of their corn pounded to powder, which put to a little water, they eat; he had a little tobacco in a bag, but none of them drunk but when he listed, some of them had their faces painted black, from the forehead to the chin, four or five fingers broad; others after other fashions, as they liked; they brought three or four skins, but we would not truck with them at all that day, but wished them to bring more, and we would truck for all, which they promised within a night or two, and would leave these behind them, though we were not willing they should, and they brought us all our tools again which were taken in the woods, in our men's absence, so because of the day we dismissed them so soon as we could. But Samoset our first acquaintance, either was sick, or feigned himself so, and would not go with them, and stayed with us till Wednesday morning: then we sent him to them, to know the reason they came not according to their words, and we gave him an hat, a pair of stockings and shoes, a shirt, and a piece of cloth to tie about his waist.

The Sabbath day, when we sent them from us, we gave every one of them some trifles, especially the principal of them, we carried them along with our arms to the place where they left their bows and arrows, whereat they were amazed, and two of them began to slink away, but that the other called them, when they took their arrows, we bade them farewell, and they were glad, and so with many thanks given us they departed, with promise they would come again.

Monday and Tuesday proved fair days, we digged our grounds, and sowed our garden seeds.

Wednesday a fine warm day, we sent away Samoset.

That day we had again a meeting, to conclude of laws and orders for ourselves, and to confirm those military orders that were formerly propounded and twice broken off by the savages' coming, but so we were again the third time, for after we had been an hour together, on the top of the hill over against us two or three savages presented themselves, that made semblance of daring us, as we thought, so Captain Standish with another, with their muskets went over to them, with two of the master's mates that follow them without arms, having two muskets with them, they whetted and rubbed their arrows and strings, and made show of defiance, but when our men drew near them, they ran away. Thus were we again interrupted by them; this day with much ado we got our carpenter that had been long sick of the scurvy, to fit our shallop, to fetch all from aboard.

Thursday, the 22 of March, was a very fair warm day. About noon we met again about our public business, but we had scarce been an hour together, but Samoset came again, and Squanto, the only native of Patuxet, where we now inhabit, who was one of the twenty captives that by Hunt were carried away, and had been in England, and dwelt in Cornhill with Master John Slaney a merchant, and could speak a little English, with three others, and they brought with them some few skins to truck, and some red herrings newly taken and dried, but not salted, and signified unto us, that their great sagamore Massasoit was hard by, with Quadequina his brother, and all their men. They could not well express in English what they would, but after an hour the King came to the top of a hill over against us, and had in his train sixty men, that we could well behold them, and they us: we were not willing to send our governor to them, and they unwilling to come to us, so Squanto went again unto him, who brought word that we should send one to parley with him, which we did, which was Edward Winslow[372], to know his mind, and to signify the mind and will of our governor, which was to have trading

---

[372] Edward Winslow's wife Elizabeth died two days after these events occurred, on March 24. In all, thirteen *Mayflower* passengers died in the month of March.

and peace with him. We sent to the king a pair of knives, and a copper chain, with a jewel at it. To Quadequina we sent likewise a knife and a jewel to hang in his ear, and withal a pot of strong water, a good quantity of biscuit, and some butter, which were all willingly accepted: our messenger made a speech unto him, that King James saluted him with words of love and peace, and did accept of him as his friend and ally, and that our governor desired to see him and to truck with him, and to confirm a peace with him, as his next neighbor: he liked well of the speech and heard it attentively, though the interpreters did not well express it; after he had eaten and drunk himself, and given the rest to his company, he looked upon our messenger's sword and armor which he had on, with intimation of his desire to buy it, but on the other side, our messenger showed his unwillingness to part with it: in the end he left him in the custody of Quadequina his brother, and came over the brook, and some twenty men following him, leaving all their bows and arrows behind them. We kept six or seven as hostages for our messenger; Captain Standish and Master Williamson[373] met the king at the brook, with half a dozen musketeers, they saluted him and he them, so one going over, the one on the one side, and the other on the other, conducted him to an house then in building, where we placed a green rug[374], and three or four cushions, then instantly came our governor with drum and trumpet after him, and some few musketeers. After salutations, our governor kissing his hand, the king kissed him, and so they sat down. The governor called for some strong water, and drunk to him, and he drunk a great draught that made him sweat all the while after, he called for a little fresh meat, which the king did eat willingly, and did give his followers. Then they treated of peace, which was;

1. That neither he nor any of his should injure or do hurt to any of our people.
2. And if any of his did hurt to any of ours, he should send the offender, that we might punish him.

---

[373] Master Williamson may have been a member of the *Mayflower*'s crew, or else may have been a pseudonym for William Brewster, who at the time was a fugitive from English authorities.

[374] Jeremy D. Bangs has suggested the green rug was "probably a Leiden 'laken'— a thick wool cloth usually dyed green." For further information, see *Pilgrim Edward Winslow: New England's First International Diplomat* (Boston: NEHGS, 2004), p. 23.

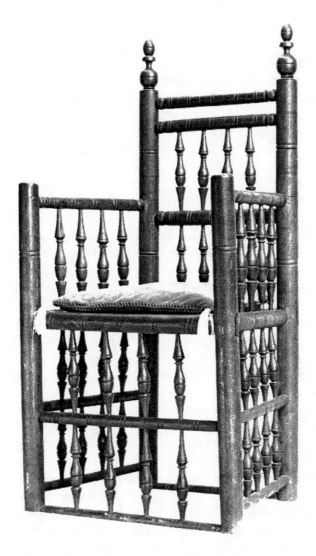

A chair that originally belonged to William Bradford. It was used as early as 1769 for Old Colony Club ceremonies, and President Warren G. Harding sat in it while presiding over tercentenary ceremonies in 1921. It was donated to the Pilgrim Hall Museum in 1953. Photo courtesy of the Pilgrim Hall Museum, Plymouth, Massachusetts.

3. That if any of our tools were taken away when our people are at work, he should cause them to be restored, and if ours did any harm to any of his, we would do the like to them.

4. If any did unjustly war against him, we would aid him; if any did war against us, he should aid us.

5. He should send to his neighbor confederates, to certify them of this, that they might not wrong us, but might be likewise comprised in the conditions of peace.

6. That when their men came to us, they should leave their bows and arrows behind them, as we should do our pieces when we came to them.

Lastly, that doing thus, King James would esteem of him as his friend and ally: all which the king seemed to like well, and it was applauded of his followers; all the while he sat by the governor he trembled for fear: in his person he is a very lusty man, in his best years, an able body, grave of countenance, and spare of speech: in his attire little or nothing differing from the rest of his followers, only in a great chain of white bone beads about his neck, and at it behind his neck, hangs a little bag of tobacco, which he drank and gave us to drink[375]; his face was painted with a sad red like murrey, and oiled both head and face, that he looked greasily: all his followers likewise, were in their faces, in part or in whole painted, some black, some red, some yellow, and some white, some with crosses, and other antic works, some had skins on them, and some naked, all strong, tall, all men in appearance: so after all was done, the governor conducted him to the brook, and there they embraced each other and he departed: we diligently keeping our hostages, we expected our messenger's coming, but anon word was brought us, that Quadequina was coming, and our messenger was stayed till his return, who presently came and a troop with him, so likewise we entertained him, and conveyed him to the place prepared; he was very fearful of our pieces, and made signs of dislike, that they should be carried away, whereupon commandment was given they should be laid away. He was a very proper tall young man, of a very modest and seemly countenance, and he did kindly like of our entertainment, so we conveyed him likewise as we did the king, but divers of their people stayed still, when he was returned, then they dismissed our messenger. Two of his people would have stayed all night, but we would not suffer it: one thing I forgot, the king had in his bosom hanging in a

---

[375] This is an archaic usage of the word drank, meaning "smoked."

string, a great long knife, he marveled much at our trumpet, and some of his men would sound it as well as they could, Samoset and Squanto, they stayed all night with us, and the king and all his men lay all night in the woods, not above half an English mile from us, and all their wives and women with them, they said that within 8 or 9 days they would come and set corn on the other side of the brook, and dwell there all summer, which is hard by us: that night we kept good watch, but there was no appearance of danger; the next morning divers of their people came over to us, hoping to get some victuals as we imagined, some of them told us the king would have some of us come see him; Captain Standish and Isaac Allerton went venturously, who were welcomed of him after their manner: he gave them three or four groundnuts, and some tobacco. We cannot yet conceive, but that he is willing to have peace with us, for they have seen our people sometimes alone two or three in the woods at work and fowling, when as they offered them no harm as they might easily have done, and especially because he hath a potent adversary the Narragansetts, that are at war with him, against whom he thinks we may be some strength to him, for our pieces are terrible unto them; this morning they stayed till ten or eleven of the clock, and our governor bid them send the king's kettle, and filled it full of peas, which pleased them well, and so they went their way.

Friday was a very fair day, Samoset and Squanto still remained with us, Squanto went at noon to fish for eels, at night he came home with as many as he could well lift in one hand, which our people were glad of, they were fat and sweet, he trod them out with his feet, and so caught them with his hands without any other instrument.

This day we proceeded on with our common business, from which we had been so often hindered by the savages' coming, and concluded both of military orders, and of some laws and orders as we thought behooveful for our present estate, and condition, and did likewise choose our governor for this year, which was Master John Carver a man well approved amongst us.

A
JOURNEY TO POKANOKET
The Habitation of the Great King
MASSASOIT.
As also our Message, the
Answer and entertainment
we had of
HIM.

It seemed good to the company for many considerations to send some amongst them to Massasoit, the greatest commander amongst the savages, bordering about us; partly to know where to find them, if occasion served, as also to see their strength, discover the country, prevent abuses in their disorderly coming unto us, make satisfaction for some conceived injuries to be done on our parts, and to continue the league of peace and friendship between them and us. For these, and the like ends, it pleased the governor to make choice of Stephen Hopkins, and Edward Winslow to go unto him, and having a fit opportunity, by reason of a savage, called Tisquantum (that could speak English) coming unto us; with all expedition provided a horseman's coat, of red cotton, and laced with a slight lace, for a present, that both they and their message might be the more acceptable amongst them. The message was as followeth; that forasmuch as his subjects came often and without fear, upon all occasions amongst us, so we were now come unto him, and in witness of the love and good will the English bear unto him, the governor hath sent him a coat, desiring that the peace and amity that was between them and us might be continued, not that we feared them, but because we intended not to injure any, desiring to live peaceably: and as with all men, so especially with them our nearest neighbors. But whereas his people came very often, and very many together unto us, bringing for the most part their wives and children with them, they were welcome; yet we being but strangers as yet at Patuxet, alias New Plymouth, and not knowing how our corn might prosper, we could no longer give them such entertainment as we had done, and as we desired still to do: yet if he would be pleased to come himself, or any special friend of his desired to see us, coming from him they should be welcome; and to the end we might know them from others, our governor had sent him a copper chain, desiring if any messenger should come from him to us, we might know him by bringing it with him, and hearken and give credit to his message accordingly. Also requesting him that such as have skins, should bring them to us, and that he would hinder the multitude from oppressing us with them. And whereas at our first arrival at Pamet (called by us Cape Cod) we found there corn buried in the ground, and finding no inhabitants but some graves of dead new buried, took the corn, resolving if ever we could hear of any that had right thereunto, to make satisfaction to the full for it, yet since we understand the owners thereof were fled for fear of us, our desire was either to pay them with the like quantity of corn, English meal, or any other commodities we had to pleasure them withal; requesting him that some one of his men might signify so much unto them, and we would content him for his pains. And last of all, our governor requested one favor of him, which was, that he would exchange some of their corn for seed with us, that we might make trial which best agreed with the soil where we live.

With these presents and message we set forward the tenth June, about 9 o'clock in the morning[376] , our guide resolving that night to rest at Nemasket[377] , a town under Massasoit, and conceived by us to be very near, because the inhabitants flocked so thick upon every slight occasion amongst us: but we found it to be some fifteen English miles. On the way we found some ten or

---

[376] The month of June for this travel is suspect, for numerous reasons; this expedition likely took place in April. First, June 10 was a Sabbath and the Pilgrims would not have sent out an expedition on Sunday. Second, Winslow later notes at Nemasket that they had abundance of shad spawning in the river, and shad spawn in April, not June. Winslow also mentions asking to trade for corn seed, but by June it would be too late in the season to plant. Additionally, the next voyage made by Plymouth men (to Nauset) set off on Monday, June 11, and it is unlikely Plymouth would have sent off so many men on several different expeditions simultaneously, given their weak state of defense. For more information, see Maurice Robbins, "The Path to Pokanoket: Winslow and Hopkins visit the Great Chief" (Massachusetts Archaeological Society, n.d.)

[377] An Indian village near modern-day Middleboro.

twelve men, women and children, which had pestered us, till we were weary
of them, perceiving that (as the manner of them all is) where victual is easiest
to be got, there they live, especially in the summer: by reason whereof our
bay affording many lobsters, they resort every spring tide thither: and now
returned with us to Nemasket. Thither we came about 3 o'clock after noon,
the inhabitants entertaining us with joy, in the best manner they could, giving
us a kind of bread called by them *maizium*, and the spawn of shads, which
then they got in abundance, insomuch as they gave us spoons to eat them,
with these they boiled musty acorns, but of the shads we ate heartily. After
this they desired one of our men to shoot a crow, complaining what damage
they sustained in their corn by them, who shooting some fourscore off and
killing, they much admired it, as other shots on other occasions. After this
Tisquantum told us we should hardly in one day reach Pokanoket, moving us
to go some 8 miles further, where we should find more store and better
victuals than there: being willing to hasten our journey we went, and came
thither at sunsetting, where we found many of the Namascheucks (they so
calling the men of Nemasket) fishing upon a weir which they had made on a
river which belonged to them, where they caught abundance of bass. These
welcomed us also, gave us of their fish, and we them of our victuals, not
doubting but we should have enough where ere we came. There we lodged in
the open fields: for houses they had none, though they spent the most of the
summer there. The head of this river is reported to be not far from the place
of our abode, upon it are, and have been many towns, it being a good length.
The ground is very good on both sides, it being for the most part cleared:
thousands of men have lived there, which died in a great plague not long
since: and pity it was and is to see, so many goodly fields, and so well seated,
without men to dress and manure the same. Upon this river dwelleth
Massasoit: it cometh into the sea at the Narragansett Bay, where the Frenchmen
so much use. A ship may go many miles up it, as the savages report, and a
shallop to the head of it: but so far as we saw, we are sure a shallop may.

But to return to our journey. The next morning we broke our fast, took
our leave and departed, being then accompanied with some six savages,
having gone about six miles by the river side[378], at a known shoal place, it
being low water, they spake to us to put off our breeches, for we must wade
through. Here let me not forget the valor and courage of some of the savages,
on the opposite side of the river, for there were remaining alive only 2 men,

---

[378] Taunton River.

both aged, especially the one being above threescore; these two espying a company of men entering the river, ran very swiftly and low in the grass to meet us at the bank, where with shrill voices and great courage standing charged upon us with their bows, they demanded what we were, supposing us to be enemies, and thinking to take advantage on us in the water: but seeing we were friends, they welcomed us with such food as they had, and we bestowed a small bracelet of beads on them. Thus far we are sure the tide ebbs and flows.

Having here again refreshed ourselves we proceeded in our journey, the weather being very hot for travel, yet the country so well watered that a man could scarce be dry, but he should have a spring at hand to cool his thirst, beside small rivers in abundance: but the savages will not willingly drink, but at a springhead. When we came to any small brook where no bridge was, two of them desired to carry us through of their own accords, also fearing we were or would be weary, offered to carry our pieces, also if we would lay off any of our clothes, we should have them carried: and as the one of them had found more special kindness from one of the messengers, and the other savage from the other so they showed their thankfulness accordingly in affording us all help, and furtherance in the journey.

As we passed along, we observed that there were few places by the river, but had been inhabited, by reason whereof, much ground was clear, save of weeds which grew higher than our heads. There is much good timber both oak, walnut tree, fir, beech, and exceeding great chestnut trees. The country in respect of the lying of it, is both champaign and hilly, like many places in England. In some places it is very rocky both above ground and in it: and though the country be wild and overgrown with woods, yet the trees stand not thick, but a man may well ride a horse amongst them.

Passing on at length, one of the company an Indian espied a man, and told the rest of it, we asked them if they feared any, they told us that if they were Narragansett, men they would not trust them, whereat, we called for our pieces and bid them not to fear; for though they were twenty, we two alone would not care for them: but they hailing him, he proved a friend, and had only two women with him: their baskets were empty, but they fetched water in their bottles, so that we drank with them and departed. After we met another man with other two women, which had been at rendezvous by the salt water, and their baskets were full of roasted crab fishes, and other dried shell fish, of which they gave us, and we ate and drank with them: and gave each of the women a string of beads, and departed.

After we came to a town of Massasoit's, where we ate oysters and other fish. From thence we went to Pokanoket[379], but Massasoit was not at home, there we stayed, he being sent for: when news was brought of his coming, our guide Tisquantum requested that at our meeting, we would discharge our pieces, but one of us going about to charge his piece, the women and children through fear to see him take up his piece, ran away, and could not be pacified, till he laid it down again, who afterward were better informed by our interpreter.

Massasoit being come, we discharged our pieces, and saluted him, who after their manner kindly welcomed us, and took us into his house, and set us down by him, where having delivered our foresaid message, and presents, and having put the coat on his back, and the chain about his neck, he was not a little proud to behold himself, and his men also to see their king so bravely attired.

For answer to our message, he told us we were welcome, and he would gladly continue that peace and friendship which was between him and us: and for his men they should no more pester us as they had done: also, that he would send to Pamet, and would help us with corn for seed, according to our request.

This being done, his men gathered near to him, to whom he turned himself, and made a great speech; they sometimes interposing, and as it were, confirming and applauding him in that he said. The meaning whereof was (as far as we could learn) thus; Was not he Massasoit, commander of the country about them? Was not such a town his and the people of it? And should they not bring their skins unto us? To which they answered, they were his and would be at peace with us, and bring their skins to us. After this manner, he named at least thirty places, and their answer was as aforesaid to every one: so that as it was delightful, it was tedious unto us.

This being ended, he lighted tobacco for us, and fell to discoursing of England, and of the King's Majesty, marveling that he would live without a wife. Also he talked of the Frenchmen, bidding us not to suffer them to come to Narragansett, for it was King James his country, and he also was King James his man. Late it grew, but victuals he offered none; for indeed he had not any, being he came so newly home. So we desired to go to rest: he laid us on the bed with himself and his wife, they at the one end and we at the other, it being only planks laid a foot from the ground, and a thin mat upon them.

---

[379] Pokanoket, home of Massasoit, was in the vicinity of modern-day Warren and Barrington, Rhode Island.

Two more of his chief men, for want of room pressed by and upon us; so that we were worse weary of our lodging than of our journey.

The next day being Thursday, many of their sachems, or petty governors came to see us, and many of their men also. There they went to their manner of games for skins and knives. There we challenged them to shoot with them for skins: but they durst not: only they desired to see one of us shoot at a mark, who shooting with hail-shot, they wondered to see the mark so full of holes. About one o'clock, Massasoit brought two fishes that he had shot, they were like bream but three times so big, and better meat. These being boiled there were at least forty looked for share in them, the most ate of them: this meal only we had in two nights and a day, and had not one of us bought a partridge, we had taken our journey fasting: very importunate he was to have us stay with them longer: but we desired to keep the Sabbath at home: and feared we should either be light-headed for want of sleep, for what with bad lodging, the savages' barbarous singing, (for they use to sing themselves asleep) lice and fleas within doors, and mosquitoes without, we could hardly sleep all the time of our being there; we much fearing, that if we should stay any longer, we should not be able to recover home for want of strength. So that on the Friday morning before sunrising, we took our leave and departed, Massasoit being both grieved and ashamed, that he could no better entertain us: and retaining Tisquantum to send from place to place to procure truck for us: and appointing another, called Tokamahamon in his place, whom we had found faithful before and after upon all occasions.

At this town of Massasoit's, where we before ate, we were again refreshed with a little fish; and bought about a handful of meal of their parched corn, which was very precious at that time of the year, and a small string of dried shell-fish, as big as oysters. The latter we gave to the six savages that accompanied us, keeping the meal for ourselves, when we drank we ate each a spoonful of it with a pipe of tobacco, instead of other victuals; and of this also we could not but give them so long as it lasted. Five miles they led us to a house out of the way in hope of victuals: but we found nobody there, and so were but worse able to return home. That night we reached to the weir where we lay before, but the Namascheucks were returned: so that we had no hope of anything there. One of the savages had shot a shad in the water, and a small squirrel as big as a rat, called a neuxis, the one half of either he gave us, and after went to the weir to fish. From hence we wrote to Plymouth, and sent Tokamahamon before to Nemasket, willing him from thence to send another, that he might meet us with food at Nemasket. Two men now only remained with us, and it pleased God to give them good store of fish, so that we were well refreshed. After supper we went to rest, and they to fishing again: more they got and fell to eating afresh, and retained sufficient ready roast for all our breakfasts. About two o'clock in the morning, arose a great storm of wind, rain, lightning, and thunder, in such violent manner, that we could not keep in our fire; and had the savages not roasted fish when we were asleep, we had set forward fasting: for the rain still continued with great violence, even the whole day through, till we came within two miles of home.

Being wet and weary, at length we came to Nemasket, there we refreshed ourselves, giving gifts to all such as had showed us any kindness. Amongst others one of the six that came with us from Pokanoket, having before this on the way unkindly forsaken us, marveled we gave him nothing, and told us what he had done for us; we also told him of some discourtesies he offered us, whereby he deserved nothing, yet we gave him a small trifle: whereupon he offered us tobacco: but the house being full of people, we told them he stole some by the way, and if it were of that we would not take it: for we would not receive that which was stolen upon any terms; if we did, our God would be angry with us, and destroy us. This abashed him, and gave the rest great content: but at our departure he would needs carry him on his back through a river, whom he had formerly in some sort abused. Fain they would have had us to lodge there all night: and wondered we would set forth again in such weather: but God be praised, we came safe home that night, though wet, weary, and surbated.

A
VOYAGE MADE BY TEN
of our Men to the Kingdom of
NAUSET, to seek a Boy that had
lost himself in the WOODS;
With such Accidents as
befell us in that
VOYAGE.

The 11th of June we set forth, the weather being very fair: but ere we had been long at sea, there arose a storm of wind and rain, with much lightning and thunder, insomuch that a spout arose not far from us: but God be praised, it dured not long, and we put in that night for harbor at a place, called Cummaquid, where we had some hope to find the boy. Two savages were in the boat with us, the one was Tisquantum our interpreter, the other Tokamahamon, a special friend. It being night before we came in, we anchored in the middest of the bay, where we were dry at a low water. In the morning we espied savages seeking lobsters, and sent our two interpreters to speak with them, the channel being between them; where they told them what we were, and for what we were come, willing them not at all to fear us, for we would not hurt them. Their answer was, that the boy was well, but he was at Nauset; yet since we were there they desired us to come ashore and eat with them: which as soon as our boat floated we did: and went six ashore, having four pledges for them in the boat. They brought us to their sachem or governor, whom they call Iyanough, a man not exceeding twenty-six years of age, but very personable, gentle, courteous, and fair conditioned, indeed not like the savage, save for his attire; his entertainment was answerable to his parts, and his cheer plentiful and various.

One thing was very grievous unto us at this place; there was an old woman, whom we judged to be no less than an hundred years old, which came to see us because she never saw English, yet could not behold us without breaking forth into great passion, weeping and crying excessively. We demanding the reason of it, they told us, she had three sons, who when Master Hunt was in these parts went aboard his ship to trade with him, and he carried them captives into Spain (for Tisquantum at that time was carried away also) by which means she was deprived of the comfort of her children in her old age. We told them we were sorry that, any Englishman should give them that offense, that Hunt was a bad man, and that all the English that heard of it condemned him for the same: but for us we would not offer them any such injury, though it would gain us all the skins in the country. So we gave her some small trifles, which somewhat appeased her.

After dinner we took boat for Nauset, Iyanough and two of his men accompanying us. Ere we came to Nauset, the day and tide were almost spent, insomuch as we could not go in with our shallop: but the sachem or governor of Cummaquid went ashore and his men with him, we also sent, Tisquantum to tell Aspinet the sachem of Nauset wherefore we came.[380] The savages here came very thick amongst us, and were earnest with us to bring in our boat. But we neither well could, nor yet desired to do it, because we

---

[380]   Iyanough and Aspinet, though courteous and friendly towards the Plymouth colonists in these early encounters, would a few years later be drawn into a conspiracy led by Pecksuot and Wituwamat of the Massachusetts Indians, to expel all the English from New England (including those at Plymouth), in retaliation for wrongs done to them by the English colonists at Wessagussett in the Massachusetts Bay. The conspiracy was discovered and violently quelshed by the English at Plymouth and Wessagussett. Edward Winslow reports that in 1623, "Concerning those other people that intended to join with the Massachusetts against us, though we never went against any of them, yet this sudden and unexpected execution, together with the just judgment of God upon their guilty consciences, hath so terrified and amazed them, as in like manner they forsook their houses, running to and fro like men distracted, living in swamps and other desert places, and so brought manifold diseases amongst themselves, whereof very many are dead, as Canacum the Sachem of Manomet, Aspinet the Sachem of Nauset, and Iyanhough, Sachem of Mattachiest. This Sachem in his life, in the midst of these distractions, said the God of the English was offended with them, and would destroy them in his anger, and certainly it is strange to hear how many of late have, and still daily die amongst them."

had least cause to trust them, being they only had formerly made an assault upon us in the same place, in time of our winter discovery for habitation. And indeed it was no marvel they did so, for: howsoever through snow or otherwise we saw no houses, yet we were in the midst of them.

When our boat was aground they came very thick, but we stood therein upon our guard, not suffering any to enter except two: the one being of Manamoyick, and one of those, whose corn we had formerly found, we promised him restitution, and desired him either to come to Patuxet for satisfaction, or else we would bring them so much corn again, he promised to come, we used him very kindly for the present. Some few skins we got there but not many.

After sunset, Aspinet came with a great train, and brought the boy with him, one bearing him through the water: he had not less than an hundred with him, the half whereof came to the shallop side unarmed with him, the other stood aloof with their bows and arrows. There he delivered us the boy, behung with beads, and made peace with us, we bestowing a knife on him, and likewise on another that first entertained the boy and brought him thither. So they departed from us.

Here we understood, that the Narragansetts had spoiled some of Massasoit's men, and taken him. This struck some fear in us, because the colony was so weakly guarded, the strength thereof being abroad: but we set forth with resolution to make the best haste home we could; yet the wind being contrary, having scarce any fresh water left, and at least 16 leagues home, we put in again for the shore. There we met again with Iyanough the sachem of Cummaquid, and the most of his town, both men, women and children with him. He being still willing to gratify us, took a runlet and led our men in the dark a great way for water, but could find none good: yet brought such as there was on his neck with him. In the meantime the women joined hand in hand, singing and dancing before the shallop, the men also showing all the kindness they could, Iyanough himself taking a bracelet from about his neck, and hanging it upon one of us.

Again we set out, but to small purpose: for we got but little homeward; our water also was very brackish, and not to be drunk.

The next morning, Iyanough espied us again and ran after us; we being resolved to go to Cummaquid again to water, took him into the shallop, whose entertainment was not inferior unto the former.

The soil at Nauset and here is alike, even and sandy, not so good for corn as where we are; ships may safely ride in either harbor. In the summer, they abound with fish. Being now watered, we put forth again, and by God's providence, came safely home that night.

A
JOURNEY TO THE
Kingdom of NEMASKET
in defense of the Great King
MASSASOIT against the
Narragansetts, and to revenge
the supposed Death
of our Interpreter
Tisquantum.

At our return from Nauset, we found it true, that Massasoit was put from his country by the Narragansetts. Word also was brought unto us, that Corbitant a petty sachem or governor under Massasoit (whom they ever feared to be too conversant with the Narragansetts) was at Nemasket, who sought to draw the hearts of Massasoit's subjects from him, speaking also disdainfully of us, storming at the peace between Nauset, Cummaquid, and us, and at Tisquantum the worker of it; also at Tokamahamon, and one Hobomok (two Indians, or Lemes, one of which he would treacherously have murdered a little before, being a special and trusty man of Massasoit's). Tokamahamon went to him, but the other two would not; yet put their lives in their hands, privately went to see if they could hear of their king, and lodging at Nemasket were discovered to Corbitant, who set a guard to beset the house and took Tisquantum (for he had said, if he were dead, the English had lost their tongue). Hobomok seeing that Tisquantum was taken, and Corbitant held a knife at his breast, being a strong and stout man, brake from them and came to New Plymouth, full of fear and sorrow for Tisquantum, whom he thought to be slain.

Upon this news the company assembled together, and resolved on the morrow to send ten men armed to Nemasket and Hobomok for their guide, to revenge the supposed death of Tisquantum on Corbitant our bitter enemy, and to retain Nepeof, another sachem or governor, who was of this confederacy, till we heard, what was become of our friend Massasoit.

On the morrow we set out ten men armed, who took their journey as aforesaid, but the day proved very wet. When we supposed we were within three or four miles of Nemasket, we went out of the way and stayed there till night, because we would not be discovered. There we consulted what to do, and thinking best to beset the house at midnight, each was appointed his task by the captain, all men encouraging one another, to the utmost of their power.

By night our guide lost his way, which much discouraged our men, being we were wet, and weary of our arms: but one of our men having been before at Nemasket brought us into the way again.

Before we came to the town we sat down and ate such as our knapsack afforded, that being done, we threw them aside, and all such things as might hinder us, and so went on and beset the house, according to our last resolution. Those that entered, demanded if Corbitant were not there: but fear had bereft the savages of speech. We charged them not to stir, for if Corbitant were not there, we would not meddle with them; if he were, we came principally for him, to be avenged on him for the supposed death of Tisquantum, and other matters: but howsoever we would not at all hurt their women, or children. Notwithstanding some of them pressed out at a private door and escaped, but with some wounds: at length perceiving our principal ends, they told us Corbitant was returned with all his train, and that Tisquantum was yet living, and in the town offering some tobacco, other such as they had to eat. In this hurley burley we discharged two pieces at random, which much terrified all the inhabitants, except Tisquantum and Tokamahamon, who though they knew not our end in coming, yet assured them of our honesty, that we would not hurt them. Those boys that were in the house seeing our care of women, often cried, *Neen squaes*, that is to say, I am a woman: the women also hanging upon Hobomok, calling him *towam*, that is, friend. But to be short, we kept them we had, and made them make a fire that we might see to search the house. In the meantime, Hobomok got on the top of the house, and called Tisquantum and Tokamahamon, which came unto us accompanied with others, some armed and others naked. Those that had bows and arrows we took them away, promising them again when it was day. The house we took for our better safeguard: but released those we had taken, manifesting whom we came for and wherefore.

On the next morning we marched into the middest of the town, and went to the house of Tisquantum to breakfast. Thither came all whose hearts were upright towards us, but all Corbitant's faction were fled away. There in the middest of them we manifested again our intendment, assuring them, that although Corbitant[381] had now escaped us, yet there was no place should secure him and his from us if he continued his threatening us, and provoking others against us, who had kindly entertained him, and never intended evil towards him till he now so justly deserved it. Moreover, if Massasoit did not return in safety from Narragansett, or if hereafter he should make any insurrection against him, or offer violence to Tisquantum, Hobomok, or any of Massasoit's subjects, we would revenge it upon him, to the overthrow of him and his. As for those were wounded, we were sorry for it, though themselves procured it in not staying in the house at our command: yet if they would return home with us, our surgeon should heal them.

---

[381] Edward Winslow would pay a more cordial visit to Corbitant a few years later, on a voyage described in his book, *Good News from New England* (London, 1624): "That night through the earnest request of Corbitant, who till now remained at Sowams or Pokanoket, we lodged with him at Mattapuyst. By the way I had much conference with him; so likewise at his house, he being a notable politician, yet full of merry jests and squibs, and never better pleased than when the like are returned again upon him . . . . [B]eing at his house he demanded further, how we durst being but two come so far into the country? I answered, where was true love there was no fear, and my heart was so upright towards them that for mine own part I was fearless to come amongst them. But, said he, if your love be such, and it brings forth such fruits, how cometh it to pass, that when we come to Patuxet, you stand upon your guard, with the mouths of your pieces presented towards us? Whereunto I answered, it was the most honorable and respective entertainment we could give them; it being an order amongst us so to receive our best respected friends: and as it was used on the land, so the ships observed it also at sea, which Hobomok knew, and had seen observed. But shaking the head he answered, that he liked not such salutations. Further, observing us to crave a blessing on our meat before we did eat, and after to give thanks for the same, he asked us what was the meaning of that ordinary custom? Hereupon I took occasion to tell them of God's works of creation, and preservation, of his laws and ordinances, especially of the ten commandments, all which they harkened unto with great attention, and liked well of: only the seventh commandment they excepted against, thinking there were many inconveniences in it, that a man should be tied to one woman: about which we reasoned a good time."

At this offer, one man and a woman that were wounded went home with us, Tisquantum and many other known friends accompanying us, and offering all help that might be by carriage of anything we had to ease us. So that by God's good providence we safely returned home the morrow night after we set forth.

A
RELATION OF OUR
Voyage to the MASSACHUSETTS,
And what happened there.

It seemed good to the company in general, that though the Massachusetts had often threatened us (as we were informed) yet we should go amongst them, partly to see the country, partly to make peace with them, and partly to procure their truck.

For these ends the governors chose ten men, fit for the purpose, and sent Tisquantum, and two other savages to bring us to speech with the people, and interpret for us.

We set out about midnight, the tide then serving for us; we supposing it to be nearer than it is, thought to be there the next morning betimes: but it proved well near twenty leagues from New Plymouth.

We came into the bottom of the bay, but being late we anchored and lay in the shallop, not having seen any of the people. The next morning we put in for the shore. There we found many lobsters that had been gathered together by the savages, which we made ready under a cliff. The captain set two sentinels behind the cliff to the landward to secure the shallop, and taking a guide with him, and four of our company, went to seek the inhabitants, where they met a woman coming for her lobsters, they told her of them, and contented her for them. She told them where the people were; Tisquantum went to them, the rest returned, having direction which way to bring the shallop to them.

The sachem, or governor of this place, is called Obbatinewat, and though he lives in the bottom of the Massachusetts Bay, yet he is under Massasoit. He used us very kindly; he told us, he durst not then remain in any settled place, for fear of the Tarrantines. Also the Squaw Sachem, or Massachusetts' queen, was an enemy to him.

We told him of divers sachems that had acknowledged themselves to be King James his men, and if he also would submit himself, we would be his safeguard from his enemies: which he did, and went along with us to bring us to the Squaw Sachem: again we crossed the bay which is very large, and hath at least fifty islands in it: but the certain number is not known to the inhabitants. Night it was before we came to that side of the bay where his people were. On shore the savages went but found nobody. That night also we rid at anchor aboard the shallop.

On the morrow we went ashore, all but two men, and marched in arms up in the country. Having gone three miles, we came to a place where corn had been newly gathered, a house pulled down, and the people gone. A mile from hence, Nanepashemet their king in his lifetime had lived. His house was not like others, but a scaffold was largely built, with poles and planks some six foot from ground, and the house upon that, being situated on the top of a hill.

Not far from hence in a bottom, we came to a fort built by their deceased king, the manner thus; there were poles some thirty or forty foot long, stuck in the ground as thick as they could be set one by another, and with these they enclosed a ring some forty or fifty foot over. A trench breast high was digged on each side; one way there was to go into it with a bridge; in the midst of this palisade stood the frame of an house wherein being dead he lay buried.

About a mile from hence, we came to such another, but seated on the top of an hill: here Nanepashemet was killed, none dwelling in it since the time of his death. At this place we stayed, and sent two savages to look the inhabitants, and to inform them of our ends in coming, that they might not be fearful of us: within a mile of this place they found the women of the place together, with their corn on heaps, whither we supposed them to be fled for fear of us, and the more, because in divers places they had newly pulled down their houses, and for haste in one place had left some of their corn covered with a mat, and nobody with it.

With much fear they entertained us at first, but seeing our gentle carriage towards them, they took heart and entertained us in the best manner they could, boiling cod and such other things as they had for us. At length with much sending for came one of their men, shaking and trembling for fear. But when he saw we intended them no hurt, but came to truck, he promised us his skins also. Of him we inquired for their queen, but it seemed she was far from thence, at least we could not see her.

Here Tisquantum would have had us rifle the savage women, and taken their skins, and all such things as might be serviceable for us; for (said he) they are a bad people, and have oft threatened you: but our answer was; were they never so bad, we would not wrong them, or give them any just occasion against us: for their words we little weighed them, but if they once attempted anything against us, then we would deal far worse than he desired.

Having well spent the day, we returned to the shallop, almost all the women accompanying us, to truck, who sold their coats from their backs, and tied boughs about them, but with great shamefacedness (for indeed they are more modest than some of our English women are) we promised them to come again to them, and they us, to keep their skins.

Within this bay, the savages say, there are two rivers; the one whereof we saw, having a fair entrance, but we had no time to discover it. Better harbors for shipping cannot be than here are. At the entrance of the bay are many rocks; and in all likelihood very good fishing ground. Many, yea, most of the islands have been inhabited, some being cleared from end to end, but the people are all dead, or removed.

Our victual growing scarce, the wind coming fair, and having a light moon, we set out at evening, and through the goodness of God, came safely home before noon the day following.

A
LETTER SENT FROM
New England to a friend in these parts,
setting forth a brief and true Declaration
of the worth of that Plantation;
As also certain useful Directions
for such as intend a VOYAGE
into those Parts.

Loving, and old Friend; although I received no letter from you by this ship[382], yet forasmuch as I know you expect the performance of my promise, which was, to write unto you truly and faithfully of all things. I have therefore at this time sent unto you accordingly. Referring you for further satisfaction to our more large relations.[383] You shall understand, that in this little time, that a few of us have been here, we have built seven dwelling-houses, and four for the use of the plantation, and have made preparation for divers others. We set the last spring some twenty acres of Indian corn, and sowed some six acres of barley and peas, and according to the manner of the Indians, we manured our ground with herrings or rather shads, which we have in great abundance, and take with great ease at our doors. Our corn did prove well, and God be praised, we had a good increase of Indian corn, and our barley indifferent good, but our peas not worth the gathering, for we feared they were too late sown, they came up very well, and blossomed, but the sun parched them in the blossom; our harvest being

---

[382]   The *Fortune*.

[383]   A large portion of the relations written by governor William Bradford were taken by pirates on the *Fortune*'s return home.

gotten in[384], our governor sent four men on fowling, that so we might after a more special manner rejoice together, after we had gathered the fruit of our labors; they four in one day killed as much fowl, as with a little help beside, served the company almost a week, at which time amongst other recreations, we exercised our arms, many of the Indians coming amongst us, and among the rest their greatest King Massasoit, with some ninety men, whom for three days we entertained and feasted, and they went out and killed five deer, which they brought to the plantation and bestowed on our governor, and upon the captain, and others. And although it be not always so plentiful, as it was at this time with us, yet by the goodness of God, we are so far from want, that we often wish you partakers of our plenty. We have found the Indians very faithful in their covenant of peace with us; very loving and ready to pleasure us: we often go to them, and they come to us; some of us have been fifty miles by land in the country with them; the occasions and relations whereof you shall understand by our general and more full declaration of such things as are worth the noting, yea, it hath pleased God so to possess the Indians with a fear of us, and love unto us, that not only the greatest king amongst them called Massasoit, but also all the princes and peoples round about us, have either made suit unto us, or been glad of any occasion to make peace with us, so that seven of them at once have sent their messengers to us to that end, yea, an Fle[385] at sea, which we never saw hath also together with the former yielded willingly to be under the protection, and subjects to our sovereign Lord King James, so that there is now great peace amongst the Indians themselves, which was not formerly, neither would have been but for us; and we for our parts walk as peaceably and safely in the wood, as in the highways in England, we entertain them familiarly in our houses, and they as friendly bestowing their venison on us. They are a people without any religion, or knowledge of any God[386], yet very trusty, quick

---

[384] This begins the only detailed account of the Pilgrims' "Thanksgiving." Bradford contributes a few additional details in his *Of Plymouth Plantation*, where he mentions the ubiquitous wild turkeys.

[385] It is unknown what this means.

[386] Winslow takes back, and corrects, this statement in his 1624 publication *Good News from New England*: "And first, whereas myself and others, in former letters (which came to the press against my will and knowledge) wrote, that the Indians about us are a people without any religion, or knowledge of any God, therein I erred, though we could then gather no better. For as they conceive of many divine powers, so of one whom they call Kiehtan, to be the principal and maker of all the

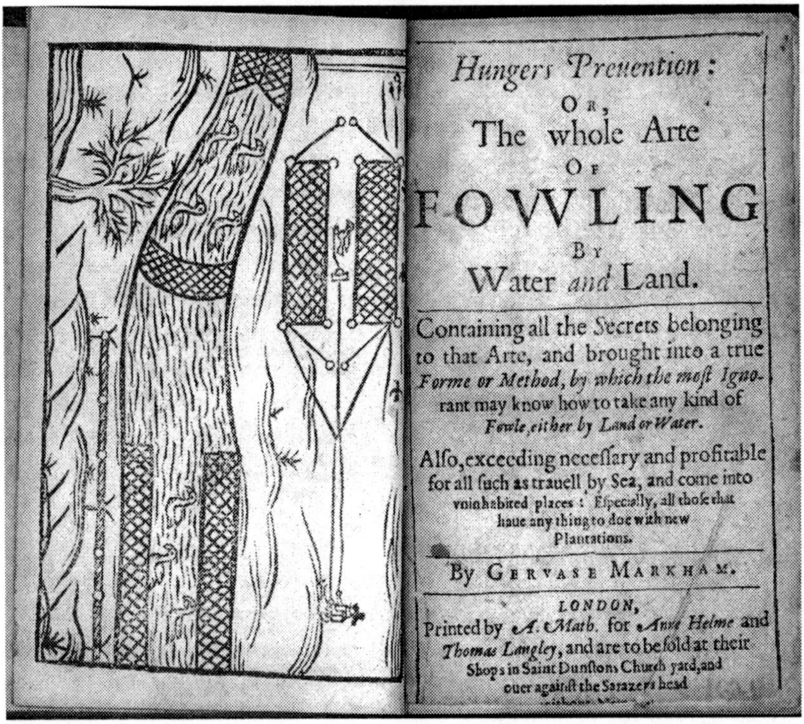

Hungers Preuention:
OR,
The whole Arte
OF
FOWLING
BY
Water *and* Land.

Containing all the Secrets belonging to that Arte, and brought into a true *Forme or Method, by which the moſt Ignorant* may know how to take any kind of *Fowle, either by Land or Water.*

Alſo, exceeding neceſſary and profitable for all ſuch as trauell by Sea, and come into vninhabited places: Eſpecially, all thoſe that haue any thing to doe with new Plantations.

By GERVASE MARKHAM.

LONDON,
Printed by *A. Math.* for *Anne Helme* and *Thomas Langley*, and are to be ſold at their Shops in Saint Dunſtons Church yard, and ouer againſt the Sarazens head

Title page and woodcut from Gervase Markham's *Hungers Prevention: Or, The Whole Art of Fowling by Water and Land* (London, 1621). The woodcut depicts a man hunting fowl using various netting techniques.

of apprehension, ripe-witted, just, the men and women go naked, only a skin about their middles; for the temper of the air, here it agreeth well with that in England, and if there be any difference at all, this is somewhat hotter in summer, some think it to be colder in winter, but I cannot out of experience so say; the air is very clear and not foggy, as hath been reported. I never in my life remember a more seasonable year, than we have here enjoyed: and if we have once but kine, horses, and sheep, I make no question, but men might live as contented here as in any part of the world. For fish and fowl, we have great abundance, fresh cod in the summer is but coarse meat with us, our bay is full of lobsters all the summer, and affordeth variety of other fish; in September we can take a hogshead of eels in a night, with small labor, and can dig them out of their beds, all the winter we have mussels and othus at our doors: oysters we have none near, but we can have them brought by the Indians when we will; all the springtime the earth sendeth forth naturally very good salad herbs: here are grapes, white and red, and very sweet and strong also. Strawberries, gooseberries, raspas, etc. Plums of three sorts, with black and red, being almost as good as a damson: abundance of roses, white, red, and damask: single, but very sweet indeed; the country wanteth only industrious men to employ, for it would grieve your hearts (if as I) you had seen so many miles together by goodly rivers uninhabited, and withal to consider those parts of the world wherein you live, to be even greatly burdened with

---

rest, and to be made by none. He (they say) created the heavens, earth, sea, and all creatures contained therein. Also that he made one man and one woman, of whom they and we and all mankind came: but how they became so far dispersed that know they not. At first they say, there was no Sachem or King, but Kiehtan, who dwelleth above in the Heavens, whither all good men go when they die, to see their friends, and have their fill of all things. This his habitation lieth far westward in the heavens, they say; thither the bad men go also, and knock at his door, but he bids them Quatchet, that is to say, 'Walk abroad,' for there is no place for such; so that they wander in restless want and penury." Roger Williams, in his *Key into the Language of America* (London, 1643), noted "[T]hey have it from their fathers, that Kautantowit made oen man and woman of stone, which disliking, he broke them into pieces, and made another man and woman of a tree, which were the fountains of all mankind . . . They believe that the souls of men and women go to the Southwest, their great and good men and women to Kautantowit his house, where they have hopes (as the Turks have of carnal joys): murderers, thieves and liars, their souls (say they) wander restless abroad."

abundance of people. These things I thought good to let you understand, being the truth of things as near as I could experimentally take knowledge of, and that you might on our behalf give God thanks who hath dealt so favorably with us.

Our supply of men from you came the ninth of November 1621, putting in at Cape Cod, some eight or ten leagues from us, the Indians that dwell thereabout were they who were owners of the corn which we found in caves, for which we have given them full content, and are in great league with them, they sent us word there was a ship near unto them, but thought it to be a Frenchman, and indeed for ourselves, we expected not a friend so soon. But when we perceived that she made for our bay, the governor commanded a great piece to be shot off, to call home such as were abroad at work; whereupon every man, yea, boy that could handle a gun were ready, with full resolution, that if she were an enemy, we would stand in our just defense, not fearing them, but God provided better for us than we supposed; these came all in health unto us, not any being sick by the way (otherwise than seasickness) and so continue at this time, by the blessing of God, the goodwife Ford was delivered of a son the first night she landed, and both of them are very well. When it pleaseth God, we are settled and fitted for the fishing business, and other trading, I doubt not but by the blessing of God, the gain will give content to all; in the mean time, that we have gotten we have sent by this ship, and though it be not much, yet it will witness for us, that we have not been idle, considering the smallness of our number all this summer. We hope the merchants will accept of it, and be encouraged to furnish us with things needful for further employment, which will also encourage us to put forth ourselves to the uttermost. Now because I expect your coming unto us with other of our friends, whose company we much desire, I thought good to advertise you of a few things needful; be careful to have a very good bread-room to put your biscuits in, let your cask for beer and water be iron-bound for the first tire if not more; let not your meat be dry-salted, none can better do it than the sailors; let your meal be so hard trod in your cask that you shall need an adz or hatchet to work it out with: trust not too much on us for corn at this time, for by reason of this last company that came, depending wholly upon us, we shall have little enough till harvest; be careful to come by some of your meal to spend by the way, it will much refresh you, build your cabins as open as you can, and bring good store of clothes, and bedding with you; bring every man a musket or fowling-piece, let your piece be long in the barrel, and fear not the weight of it, for most of our shooting is from stands; bring juice of lemons, and take it fasting, it is of good use; for hot waters, aniseed water is the best, but use it sparingly: if you bring anything for comfort in the country, butter or sallet oil, or both is very good; our Indian corn even the coarsest, maketh as pleasant meat as rice, therefore spare that unless to spend by the way; bring paper, and linseed oil for your windows, with cotton yarn for your lamps; let your shot be most for big fowls, and bring store of powder and shot: I forbear further to write for the present, hoping to see you by the next return, so I take my leave, commending you to the Lord for a safe conduct unto us. Resting in Him

Plymouth in New England
this 11 of December 1621.

Your loving Friend
E. W.[387]

---

[387]   Edward Winslow

Reasons and considerations touching the lawfulness of removing out of England into the parts of America.

Forasmuch as many exceptions are daily made against the going into, and inhabiting of foreign desert places, to the hindrances of plantations abroad, and the increase of distractions at home: it is not amiss that some which have been ear witnesses of the exceptions made, and are either agents or abettors of such removals and plantations, do seek to give content to the world, in all things that possibly they can.

And although the most of the opposites are such as either dream of raising their fortunes here, to that then which there is nothing more unlike, or such as affecting their home-born country so vehemently, as that they had rather with all their friends beg, yea starve in it, than undergo a little difficulty in seeking abroad; yet are there some who out of doubt in tenderness of conscience, and fear to offend God by running before they be called, are straitened and do straiten others, from going to foreign plantations.

For whose cause especially, I have been drawn out of my good affection to them, to publish some reasons that might give them content and satisfaction, and also stay and stop the willful and witty cavalier: and herein I trust I shall not be blamed of any godly wise, though through my slender judgment I should miss the mark, and not strike the nail on the head, considering it is the first attempt that hath been made (that I know of) to defend those enterprises. Reason would therefore, that if any man of deeper reach and better judgment see further or otherwise, that he rather instruct me, then deride me.

And being studious for brevity, we must first consider, that whereas God of old did call and summon our fathers by predictions, dreams, visions, and certain illuminations to go from their countries, places and habitations, to reside and dwell here or there, and to wander up and down from city to city, and land to land, according to his will and pleasure. Now there is no such calling to be expected for any matter whatsoever, neither must any so much as imagine that there will now be any such thing. God did once so train up his people, but now he doth not, but speaks in another manner, and so we must apply ourselves to God's present dealing, and not to his wonted dealing: and as the miracle of giving manna ceased, when the fruits of the land became plenty, so God having such a plentiful storehouse of directions in his holy word, there must not now any extraordinary revelations be expected.[388]

But now the ordinary examples and precepts of the Scriptures reasonably and rightly understood and applied, must be the voice and word, that must call us, press us, and direct us in every action.[389]

Neither is there any land or possession now, like unto the possession which the Jews had in Canaan, being legally holy and appropriated unto a holy people the seed of Abraham, in which they dwelt securely, and had their days prolonged, it being by an immediate voice said, that he (the Lord) gave it them as a land of rest after their weary travels, and a type of eternal rest in heaven, but now there is no land of that sanctimony, no land so appropriated; none typical: much less any that can be said to be given to God to any nation as was Canaan, which they and their seed must dwell in, till God sendeth upon them sword or captivity: but now we are all in all places strangers and pilgrims, travelers and sojourners, most properly, having no dwelling but in this earthen tabernacle; our dwelling is but a wandering, and our abiding but as a fleeting, and in a word our home is nowhere, but in the heavens: in that house not made with hands, whose maker and builder is God, and to which all ascend that love the coming of our Lord Jesus.[390]

Though then, there may be reasons to persuade a man to live in this or that land, yet there cannot be the same reasons which the Jews had, but now as natural, civil and religious bands tie men, so they must be bound, and as good reasons for things terran and heavenly appear, so they must be led. And so here falleth in our question, how a man that is here born and bred and hath lived some years, may remove himself into another country.

I answer, a man must not respect only to live, and do good to himself, but he should see where he can live to do most good to others: for as one saith, *He whose living is but for himself, it is time he were dead.* Some men there are who of necessity must here live, as being tied to duties either to

---

[388] Cautions. *Gen.* 12:1,2 & 35:1; *Mat.* 2:19; *Psal.* 105:13; *Heb.* 1:1,2; *Josh.* 5:12. (Robert Cushman).

[389] *Gen.* 17:8 (Robert Cushman).

[390] 1 *Cor.* 5:1,2,3. So were the Jews, but yet their temporal blessings and inheritances were more large than ours. (Robert Cushman).

Church, Commonwealth, household, kindred, etc. but others, and that many, who do no good in none of those nor can do none, as being not able, or not in favor, or as wanting opportunity, and live as outcasts: nobodies, eye sores, eating but for themselves, teaching but themselves, and doing good to none, either in soul or body, and so pass over days, years, and months, yea so live and so die. Now such should lift up their eyes and see whether there be not some other place and country to which they may go to do good and have use towards others of that knowledge, wisdom, humanity, reason, strength, skill, faculty, etc. which God hath given them for service of others and his own glory.

But not to pass the bounds of modesty so far as to name any, though I confess I know many, who sit here still with their talent in a napkin, having notable endowments both of body and mind, and might do great good if they were in some places, which here do none, nor can do none, and yet through fleshly fear, niceness, straightness of heart, etc. sit still and look on, and will not hazard a dram of health, nor a day of pleasure, nor an hour of rest to further the knowledge and salvation of the sons of Adam in that new world, where a drop of the knowledge of Christ is most precious, which is here not set by.[391] Now what shall we say to such a profession of Christ, to which is joined no more denial of a man's self? But some will say, what right have I to go live in the heathens' country?

Letting pass the ancient discoveries, contracts and agreements which our Englishmen have long since made in those parts, together with the acknowledgement of the histories and chronicles of other nations, who profess the land of America from the Cape de Florida unto the Bay of Canada (which is south and north 300 leagues and upwards; and east and west, further than yet hath been discovered) is proper to the King of England, yet letting that pass, lest I be thought to meddle further than it concerns me, or further than I have discerning: I will mention such things as are within my reach, knowledge, sight and practice, since I have travailed in their affairs.

And first seeing we daily pray for the conversion of the heathens, we must consider whether there be not some ordinary means, and course for us to take to convert them, or whether prayer for them be only referred to God's extraordinary work from heaven. Now it seemeth unto me that we ought also to endeavor and use the means to convert them, and the means cannot be used unless we go to them or they come to us: to us they cannot come, our land is full: to them we may go, their land is empty.

---

[391] Luk. 19:20 (Robert Cushman).

This then is a sufficient reason to prove our going thither to live, lawful their land is spacious and void, and there are few and do but run over the grass, as do also the foxes and wild beasts: they are not industrious, neither have art, science, skill or faculty to use either the land or the commodities of it, but all spoils, rots, and is marred for want of manuring, gathering, ordering, etc. As the ancient patriarchs therefore removed from straighter places into more roomy, where the land lay idle and waste, and none used it, though there dwelt inhabitants by them, as Gen. 13:6,11,12, and 34:21 and 41:20, so it is lawful now to take a land which none useth, and make use of it.

And as it is a common land or unused, and undressed country; so we have it by common consent, composition and agreement, which agreement is double[392]: first the imperial governor Massasoit, whose circuits in likelihood are larger than England and Scotland, hath acknowledged the King's Majesty of England to be his master and commander, and that once in my hearing, yea and in writing, under his hand to CaptainStandish, both he and many other kings which are under him, as Pamet, Nauset, Cummaquid, Narragansett, Nemasket, etc. with divers others that dwell about the bays of Patuxet, and Massachusetts: neither hath this been accomplished by threats and blows, or shaking of sword, and sound of trumpet, for as our faculty that way is small, and our strength less: so our warring with them is after another manner, namely by friendly usage, love, peace, honest and just carriages, good counsel, etc. that so we and they may not only live in peace in that land, and they yield subjection to an earthly prince, but that as voluntaries they may be persuaded at length to embrace the Prince of Peace Christ Jesus, and rest in peace with him forever.[393]

Secondly, this composition is also more particular and applicatory, as touching ourselves there inhabiting: the emperor by a joint consent, hath promised and appointed us to live at peace, where we will in all his dominions, taking what place we will, and as much land as we will, and bringing as many people as we will, and that for these two causes. First because we are the servants of James King of England, whose the land (as he confesseth) is, 2 because he hath found us just, honest, kind and peaceable, and so loves our company; yea and that in these things there is no dissimulation on his part, nor fear of breach (except our security engender in them some unthought of treachery, or our uncivility provoke them to

---

[392] This is to be considered as respecting New England, and the territories about the plantation. (Robert Cushman).

[393] Psal. 110:3 & 48:3 (Robert Cushman).

anger) is most plain in other relations, which show that the things they did were more out of love than out of fear.

It being then first a vast and empty chaos: secondly acknowledged the right of our sovereign King: Thirdly, by a peaceable composition in part possessed of divers of his loving subjects, I see not who can doubt or call in question the lawfulness of inhabiting or dwelling there, but that it may be as lawful for such as are not tied upon some special occasion here, to live there as well as here, yea, and as the enterprise is weighty and difficult, so the honor is more worthy, to plant a rude wilderness, to enlarge the honor and fame of our dread Sovereign, but chiefly to display the efficacy and power of the Gospel both in zealous preaching, professing, and wise walking under it, before the faces of these poor blind infidels.

As for such as object the tediousness of the voyage thither, the danger of pirates' robbery, of the savages' treachery, etc., these are but lions in the way, and it were well for such men if they were in heaven, for who can show them a place in this world where inequity shall not compass them at the heels, and where they shall have a day without grief, or a lease of life for a moment; and who can tell by God, what dangers may lie at our doors, even in our native country, or what plots may be abroad, or when God will cause our sun to go down at noon days, and in the midst of our peace and security, lay upon us some lasting scourge for our so long neglect and contempt of the most glorious Gospel.[394]

But we have here great peace, plenty of the Gospel, and many sweet delights and variety of comforts.

True indeed, and far be it from us to deny and diminish the least of these mercies, but have we rendered unto God thankful obedience for this long peace, whilst other peoples have been at wars? Have we not rather murmured, repined, and fallen at jars amongst ourselves, whilst our peace hath lasted with foreign power[395]? Was there ever more suits in law, more envy, contempt, and reproach then nowadays? Abraham and Lot departed asunder when there fell a breach betwixt them, which was occasioned by the straightness of the land: and surely I am persuaded, that howsoever the frailties of men are principal in all contentions, yet the straightness of the place is such, as each man is fain to pluck his means as it were out of his neighbor's throat, there is such pressing and oppressing in town and country, about farms, trades, traffic, etc. so as a man can hardly any where set up a trade but he shall pull down two of his neighbors.

---

[394]   *Prov.* 22:13; *Psal.* 49:5; *Mat* 6:34; *Amos* 8:9 (Robert Cushman).
[395]   2 *Chro.* 32:25; *Gen.* 13:9,10 (Robert Cushman).

The towns abound with young tradesmen, and the hospitals are full of the ancient, the country is replenished with new farmers, and the almshouses are filled with old laborers, many there are who get their living with bearing burdens, but more are fain to burden the land with their whole bodies: multitudes get their means of life by prating, and so do numbers more by begging. Neither come these straits upon men always through intemperancy, ill husbandry, indiscretion, etc. as some think, but even the most wise, sober, and discreet men, go often to the wall, when they have done their best, wherein as God's providence swayeth all, so it is easy to see, that the straightness of the place having in it so many straight hearts, cannot but produce such effects more and more, so as every indifferent minded man should be ready to say with Father Abraham, *Take thou the right hand, and I will take the left*: Let us not thus oppress, straighten, and afflict one another, but seeing there is a spacious land, the way to which is through the sea, we will end this difference in a day.

That I speak nothing about the bitter contention that hath been about religion, by writing, disputing, and inveighing earnestly one against another, the heat of which zeal if it were turned against the rude barbarism of the heathens, it might do more good in a day, than it hath done here in many years. Neither of the little love to the Gospel, and profit which is made by the preachers in most places, which might easily drive the zealous to the heathens who no doubt if they had but a drop of that knowledge which here flieth about the streets, would be filled with exceeding great joy and gladness, as that they would even pluck the kingdom of heaven by violence, and take it as it were by force.

The greatest let that is yet behind is the sweet fellowship of friends, and the satiety of bodily delights.

But can there be two nearer friends almost than Abraham and Lot, or than Paul and Barnabas, and yet upon as little occasions as we have here, they departed asunder, two of them being Patriarchs of the Church of old; the other the apostles of the Church which is new, and their covenants were such as it seemeth might bind as much as any covenant between men at this day, and yet to avoid greater inconveniences they departed asunder.

Neither must men take so much thought for the flesh, as not to be pleased except they can pamper their bodies with variety of dainties. Nature is content with little, and health is much endangered, by mixtures upon the stomach: the delights of the palate do often inflame the vital parts: as the tongue setteth a fire the whole body. Secondly, varieties here are not common at all, but many good men are glad to snap at a crust.[396] The rent taker lives on sweet morsels, but the rent payer eats a dry crust often with watery eyes: and it is nothing to say what some one of a hundred hath, but what the bulk, body and commonalty hath, which I warrant you is short enough.

And they also which now live so sweetly, hardly will their children attain to that privilege, but some circumventor or other will outstrip them, and make them sit in the dust, to which men are brought in one age, but cannot get out of it again in 7 generations.

To conclude, without all partiality, the present consumption which groweth upon us here, whilst the land groaneth under so many close-fisted and unmerciful men, being compared with the easiness, plainness and plentifulness in living in those remote places, may quickly persuade any man to a liking of this course, and to practice a removal, which being done by honest, godly and industrious men, they shall there be right heartily welcome, but for other of dissolute and profane life, their rooms are better than their companies; for if here where the Gospel hath been so long and plentifully taught, they are yet frequent in such vices as the heathen would shame to speak of, what will they be when there is less restraint in word and deed? My only suit to all men is, that whether they live there or here, they would learn to use this world as they used it not, keeping faith and a good conscience, both with God and men, that when the day of account shall come, they may come forth as good and fruitful servants, and freely be received, and enter into the joy of their Master.

---

[396] *James* 3:6. (Robert Cushman).

Appendix 1

Supplementary Documents

Seven Articles in Respect of Going to Virginia, 1618

Seven articles which the Church of Leiden sent to the Council of England to be considered of in respect of their judgment occasioned about their going to Virginia, anno. 1618.

1. To the confession of faith published in the name of the Church of England and to every article thereof we do with the Reformed Churches where we live and also elsewhere assent wholly.
2. As we do acknowledge the doctrine of faith there taught so do we the fruits and effects of the same doctrine to the begetting of saving faith in thousands in the land (conformists and reformists) as they are called with whom also as with our brethren we do desire to keep spiritual communion in peace and will practice in our parts all lawful things.
3. The King's Majesty we acknowledge for Supreme Governor in his Dominion in all causes and over all persons, and that none may decline or appeal from his authority or judgment in any cause whatsoever, but that in all things obedience is due unto him, either active, if the thing commanded be not against God's word, or passive if it be, except pardon can be obtained.
4. We judge it lawful for His Majesty to appoint bishops, civil overseers, or officers in authority under him, in the several provinces, dioces, congregations or parishes to oversee the Churches and govern them civilly according to the laws of the land, unto which they are in all things to give an account and by them to be ordered according to godliness.
5. The authority of the present bishops in the land we do acknowledge so far forth as the same is indeed derived from His Majesty unto them and as they proceed in his name, whom we will also therein honor in all things and him in them.

6. We believe that no synod, classes, convocation or assembly of ecclesiastical officers hath any power or authority at all but as the same by the magistrates given unto them.

7. Lastly, we desire to give unto all superiors due honor to preserve the unity of the spirit with all that fear God, to have peace with all men what in us lieth and wherein we err to be instructed by any. Subscribed by

John Robinson, and William Brewster

Pierce Patent of 1621

This indenture made the first day of June 1621. And in the years of the reign of our sovereign Lord James by the grace of God, King of England, Scotland, France and Ireland, defender of the faith, etc. That is to say of England, France and Ireland the Nineteenth and of Scotland the four and fiftieth. Between the President and Council of New England of the one party, and John Peirce, citizen and clothworker of London and his Associates of the other party.

Witnesseth that whereas the said John Peirce and his Associates have already transported and undertaken to transport at their cost and charges themselves and divers persons into New England and there to erect and build a town and settle divers inhabitants for the advancement of the general plantation of that Country of New England; now the said President and Council in consideration thereof and for the furtherance of the said plantation and encouragement of the said Undertakers have agreed to grant, assign, allot and appoint to the said John Peirce and his associates and every of them his and their heirs and assigns one hundred acres of ground for every person so to be transported besides divers other privileges, liberties and commodities hereafter mentioned. And to that intent they have granted, allotted, assigned and confirmed, and by these presents do grant, allot, assign and confirm unto the said John Peirce and his Associates his and their heirs and assigns and the heirs and assigns of every of them severally and respectively one hundred several acres of ground in New England for every person so transported or to be transported, if the said John Peirce or his Associates continue there three whole years either at one or several times or die in the mean season after he or they are shipped with intent there to inhabit. The same land to be taken and chosen by them their deputies or assigns in any place or places wheresoever not already inhabited by any English and where no English person or persons are already placed or settled or have by order of the said President and Council made choice of, nor within ten miles of the same, unless it be the opposite side of some great or navigable river to the former particular plantation, together with the one half of the river or rivers,

The Pierce Patent of 1621, the document that formalized the Pilgrims' authority to
establish and govern a colony at Plymouth. Photo courtesy of the Pilgrim Hall
Museum, Plymouth, Massachusetts, where the original is on display.

that is to say to the middest thereof, as shall adjoin to such lands as they shall make choice of together with all such liberties, privileges, profits, and commodities as the said land and rivers which they shall make choice of shall yield together with free liberty to fish in and upon the Coast of New England and in all havens, ports and creeks thereunto belonging, and that no person or persons whatsoever shall take any benefit or liberty of or to any of the grounds or the one half of the rivers aforesaid, excepting the free use of highways by land and navigable rivers, but that the said undertakers and planters their heirs and assigns shall have the sole right and use of the said grounds and the one half of the said rivers with all their profits and appurtenances. And forasmuch as the said John Peirce and his associates intend to have undertaken to build churches, schools, hospitals, town houses, bridges and such like works of charity, as also for the maintaining of magistrates and other inferior officers; in regard whereof and to the end that the said John Peirce and his Associates his and their heirs and assigns may have wherewithal to bear and support such like charges. Therefore the said President and Council aforesaid to grant unto the said Undertakers their heirs and assigns fifteen-hundred acres of land more over and above the aforesaid proportion of one hundred the person for every undertaker and planter to be employed upon such public uses and the said Undertakers and Planters shall think fit. And they do further grant unto the said John Peirce and his Associates their heirs and assigns, that for every person that they or any of them shall transport at their own proper costs and charges into New England either unto the Lands hereby granted or adjoining to them within seven years after the feast of St. John Baptist next coming if the said person transported continue there three whole years either at one or several times or die in the mean season after he is shipped with intent there to inhabit that the said person or persons that shall so at his or their own charges transport any other shall have granted and allowed to him and them and his and their heirs respectively for every person so transported or dyeing after he is shipped one hundred acres of land, and also that every person or persons who by contract and agreement to be had and made with the said Undertakers shall at his and their own charge transport him and themselves or any other and settle and plant themselves in New England within the said seven years for three years space as aforesaid or die in the meantime shall have granted and allowed unto every person so transporting or transported and their heirs and assigns respectively the like number of one hundred acres of land as aforesaid the same to be by him and them or their heirs and assigns chosen in any entire place together and adjoining to the aforesaid lands and not straglingly not before the type of such choice made possessed or inhabited by any English Company or within ten miles of the same, except it be on the opposite side of some great navigable river as aforesaid yielding and paying unto the said President and Council for every hundred acres so obtained and possessed by the said John Peirce and his said Associates and by those said other persons and their heirs and assigns who by contract as aforesaid shall at their own charges transport themselves or others the yearly rent of two shillings at the feast of St. Michael the Archangel to the hand of the rent-gatherer of the said President and Council and their successors forever, the first payment to begin after the expiration of the first seven years next after the date hereof; and further it shall be lawful to and for the said John Peirce and his Associates and such as contract with them as aforesaid their tenants and servants upon dislike of or in the Country to return for England or elsewhere with all their goods and chattels at their will and pleasure without let or disturbance of any paying all debts that justly shall be demanded; and likewise it shall be lawful and is granted to and for the said John Peirce and his Associates and Planters their heirs and assigns their tenants and servants and such as they or any of them shall contract with as aforesaid and send and employ for the said plantation to go and return trade traffic, import or transport their goods and merchandize at their will and pleasure into England or elsewhere paying only such duties to the King's moiety his heirs and successors as the President and Council of New England do pay without any other taxes, impositions, burdens or restraints whatsoever upon them to be imposed (the rent hereby reserved being only excepted); and it shall be lawful for the said Undertakers and Planters, their heirs and successors freely to truck, trade and traffic with the savages in New England or neighboring thereabouts at their wills and pleasures without let or disturbance. As also to have liberty to hunt, hawk, fish or fowl in any place or places not now or hereafter by the English inhabited. And the said President and Council do covenant and promise to and with the said John Peirce and his Associates and others contracted with as aforesaid his and their heirs and assigns, that upon lawful survey to be had and made at the charge of the said Undertakers and Planters and lawful information given of the bounds, meets, and quantity of land so as aforesaid to be by them chosen and possessed they the said President and Council upon surrender of this present grant and indenture and upon reasonable request to be made by the said Undertakers and Planters their heirs and assigns within seven years now next coming, shall and will by their deed indented and under their common seal grant, enfeoff and confirm all and every the said lands so set out and bounded as aforesaid to the firm all and every the said lands so set out and bounded as aforesaid to the said John Peirce and his Associates and such as contract with them their heirs and assigns in as large and beneficial manner as the same are in these presents granted or intended to be granted to all intents and purposes with all and every particular privilege and freedom, reservation and condition with all dependences herein specified and granted; and shall also at any time within the said term of seven years upon request unto the said President and Council made, grant unto them the said John Peirce and his Associates, Undertakers and Planters their heirs and assigns, letters and grantees of incorporation by some usual and fit name and title with liberty to them and their successors from time to time to make orders, laws, ordinances and constitutions for the rule government, ordering and directing of all persons to be transported and settled upon the lands hereby granted, intended to be granted or hereafter to be granted and of the said lands and profits thereby arising. And in the meantime until such grant made, it shall be lawful for the said John Peirce, his Associates, Undertakers, and Planters their heirs and assigns by consent of the greater part of them to establish such laws and ordinances as are for their better government, and the same by such officer or officers as they shall by most voices elect and choose to put in execution; and lastly the said President and Council do grant and agree to and with the said John Peirce and his Associates and others contracted with and employed as aforesaid their heirs and assigns, that when they have planted the lands hereby to them assigned and appointed, that then it shall be lawful for them with the privity and allowance of the President and Council as aforesaid to make choice of and to enter into and have an addition of fifty acres more for every person transported into New England with like reservations, conditions and privileges as are above granted to be had and chosen in such place or places where no English shall be then settled or inhabiting or have made choice of and the same entered into a book of acts at the time of such choice so to be made or within ten miles of the same, excepting on the opposite side of some great navigable river as aforesaid. And that it shall and may be lawful for the said John Peirce and his Associates their heirs and assigns from time to time and at all times hereafter for their several defense and safety to encounter, expulse, repel and resist by force of arms as well by sea as by land and by all ways and means whatsoever all such person or persons as without the especial license of the said President or Council and their successors or the greater part of them shall attempt to inhabit within the several precincts and limits of their said Plantation, or shall enterprise or attempt at any time hereafter destruction, invasion, detriment or annoyance to the said Plantation. And the said John Peirce and his associates and their heirs and assigns do covenant and promise to and with the said President and Council and their successors, that they the said John Peirce and his Associates from time to time during the said seven years shall make a true certificate to the said President and Council and their successors from the chief officers and the places respectively of every person transported and landed in New England or shipped as aforesaid to be entered by the Secretary of the said President and Council into a Register book for that purpose to be kept; and the said John Peirce and his Associates jointly and severally for them their heirs and assigns do covenant, promise and grant to and with the said President and Council and their successors, that the persons transported to this their particular Plantation shall apply themselves and their labors in a large and competent manner to the planting, setting, making and procuring of good and staple commodities in and upon the said land hereby granted unto them as corn and silkgrass, hemp, flax, pitch and tar, sopeashes and potashes, iron, clapboard and other the like materials.

In witness whereof the said President and Council have to the one part of this present indenture set their seals; and to the other part hereof the said John Peirce in the name of himself and his said Associates have set to his seal given the day and years first above written.

Lenox Hamilton Warwick Sheffield Ferd: Gorges

Deposition Relating to the Pirating of the ship *Fortune*.[397]

Sheweth

That a ship belonging to them, named the *Fortune*, of the burden of between 40 and 50 tons or thereabouts, being upon their way homeward, and near the English coast, some eight leagues off Use, called by the Frenchmen Ile d'Yeu, was, the 19th of January last, assailed and taken by a French Man of War, the Captain whereof was called Fontenau de Pennart de Britagne: and carried to the Isle of Use.

That Fontenau presented the ship, and company thereof, being 13 persons, as prisoners to Monsieur le Marquis de Cera, Governor of the Isle. Who although upon examination and sight of their Commission, he found that they were neither pirates, nor assistants to Rochelle[398], and acknowledged there was no breach between England and France: yet said, he would make prize of them, to give content to his Captains and servitors.

That thereupon Monsieur de Cera kept Thomas Barton, master of the ship, seven days, close prisoner in his Castle; and the rest of the company under guard: and commanded his soldiers to pillage them; who left them not so much as a kettle to boil their meat in, nor a can to drink in.

That Monsieur de Cera took away of the goods of the Adventurers, in beaver skins and other commodities, to the value of £400, at the least.

That he took away of the owners, a new sheet-cable, an anchor, two murderers with their chambers, eight calivers with bandileers, a flag, ensign, powder, shot, ropes, lines, and other instruments, to the value of £50.

That he suffered his solders to pillage the company, that they took away all their apparel; not leaving some of them a hat to their heads, nor a shoe to their feet, to the damage of £50 at least.

That he sent for all their letters; opened and kept what he pleased: especially, though he was much entreated to the contrary, a letter written by

---

[397] Public Records Office, State Papers Colonial, Volume 5, Number 112.

[398] i.e. helping the French Huguenots.

the Governor of our Colony in New England, containing a general Relation of all matters there.

That when any ship, English or Dutch, came into the road; he caused our company to be stowed under the hatches. And having detained them thirteen days; and fed them with lights, livers, and entrails: because he suffered his soldiers to eat all their good victuals, at length, he sent them aboard a little lean flesh, a hogshead of small wine, some little bread and vinegar, to victual them home. But withal propounded them, to testify, under their hands, that he had taken from them but two hogsheads of fox skins; else, he said, they should not have liberty.

Howbeit, by the kindness of a young Gentleman, pitying their distress, who only amongst the French could speak English, they were discharged; giving, under their hands, that the Marquis of Cera had taken from them two hogsheads of beaver skins, and some other small matters.

Letter of William Bradford and Isaac Allerton 8 September 1623

Beloved and kind friends.

We have received your letters both by the *Anne* and the *James*, which are both safely arrived here, thanks be to God, the *Anne* about the later end of July, and the *James* a fortnight after, and by them a large and liberal supply, for which together with your loving and honest letters we give you hearty thanks, being very sorry to hear of your losses and crosses, and how you have been turmoiled thereabout. If God had seen it good we should have been right glad it had come sooner, both for our good and your profit; for we have both been in a languishing state; and also fain to put away our furs at a small value to help us to some necessaries, without which notwithstanding we should have done full ill, yea indeed could have not subsisted; so as we have little or nothing to send you, for which we are not a little sorry; but if you knew how necessarily we were constrained to it, and how unwillingly we did it, we suppose you cannot at all blame us for it; we put away as much at one time and other of beaver as, if they had been saved together and sold at the best hand, would have yielded 3 or 4 hundred pounds; and yet those are nothing to those we have lost for want of means to gather them when the time was, which I fear will scarce ever be again, seeing the Dutch on one side and the French on the other side and the fishermen and other plantations between both have, and do furnish the savages, not with toys and trifles, but with good and substantial commodities, as kettles, hatches, and clothes of all sorts; yea the French do store them with Biscay shallops fitted both with sails and oars, with which they can either row or sail as well as we; as also with pieces, powder and shot for fowling and other services; (we are informed that there are at this present a 100 men with 8 shallops coming from the eastward, to rob and spoil their neighbors westwards); also I know upon my own knowledge many of the Indians to be as well furnished with good kettles, both strong and of a large size, as many farmers in England; yet notwithstanding we shall not neglect to use the best means we can with the pinnace and means we now have, both for trading or any other employment the best we can for both your and our advantage; but we are sorry that she is manned with so rude a crew of sailors; we hope the master is an honest man; and we find the captain to be a loving and courteous gentleman; yet they could not both of them rule them, so as we were fain to alter their conditions and agree with them for wages as well as we could; and this we did not only by the captain, and masters, together with Mr. Pierce's advice, but we saw we were of necessity constrained thereunto to prevent further mischief, which we saw would unavoidably ensue; for besides the endangering of the ship, they would obey no command, at least without continual murmuring, alleging that they were cousined and deceived and should sail and work for nothing, the which they would be hanged rather than they would do, as also that they would not fish, or do any such thing; they said they were fitted out for a taker, and were told that they might take any ship whatsoever that was not too strong for them, as far as the West Indies, and no other employment would they follow; but we doubt not now to have them at a better pass, and hope to raise some benefit by her employment; she is now to go to the southward; we have sent to the Indians, and they promise us we shall have both corn and skins; at her return we think to send her northward, both to fish and truck, if it please God to bless them.

We have sent unto you (with these our letters) one of our honest friends, Edward Winslow by name, who can give you better and more large information of the state of all things than we can possibly do by our letters; unto whom we refer you in all particulars; and also we have given him instruction to treat with you of all such things as concern our public good and mutual concord; expecting his return by the first fishing ships.

We have written to the Council for another patent for Cape Anne to wit for the westerside of it, which we know to be as good a harbor as any in this land, and it thought to be as good fishing place; and seeing fishing must be the chief, if not the only means to do us good; and it is like to be so fit a place, and lieth so near us; we think it very necessary to use all diligence to procure it; and therefore we have now written unto you and the Council again about it, lest our former letters should not be come, or not delivered, of which we have some suspicion; Mr. Weston hath written for it, and is desirous to get it before us; and the like doth Mr. Thompson; which is one special motive that hath moved us to send over this messenger forenamed; as also about that grand patent which we understand you got from Mr. Pierce, which if it be as we have it is by Mr. Thompson's relation, but to go by a right line from the Gurnet's nose due west into the land a certain way, and no further northward, it will strip us of the best part of the bay, which will be most commodious for us, and better then all the rest; therefore seeing now is the time to help these things we thought it were then necessary to send about the former patent for Cape Anne; we desire it may be procured with as ample privileges as it may, and not to be simply confined to that place, but in our liberty to take any other, if we like it better.

Mr. Pierce (for ought I hear) hath used our passengers well, and dealt very honestly with us; but we wanted a perfect bill of lading, to call for each parcel of our goods, which as you have occasion we pray you see to hereafter, for it is very requisite though you have to deal with honest men. We have agreed with him to lade him back for a 150 pounds, which you will think something much, but we could get him no cheaper; we did it the rather that he might come directly home, for the furtherance of our other affairs; as also for some other respects necessary and beneficial for us; we have laded him with clapboard, the best we could get, which we hope at least will quit the cost; for lengths they are not cut by the advice of the cooper and pipestaffmaker which you sent us; for thickness they are bigger than those which come from other places, which must accordingly be considered in the prices; the cooper of the ship saith they are worth 5 per 100 and I hear he means to buy some of them of you; of which I thought good to give you notice.

We have also sent you that small parcel of furs which we have left, besides those we put away formerly; if the ship had but come one month sooner, we had sent you a good many more, though since that conspiracy raised against us by the Indians, caused by Mr. Weston's people, and that execution we did at the Massachusetts, chiefly for the saving of their lives, we have been much endamaged in our trade, for there where we had most skins the Indians are run away from their habitations, and set no corn, so as we can by no means as yet come to speak with them. We have taken up of Mr. Pierce sundry provisions, the chief whereof is bread, and course cloth, and some other needful things withal; and with them he hath put upon us some other things less necessary, as beef etc. which we would not have had if we could have had the other without them; fear of want again before supply come to us, as also a little to encourage our people after their great disheartening hath made us presume to charge you herewith; a bill of the particulars we have here sent you; we hope the furs will defray it.

It is for certain that great profit is here raised by fishing; the ships have this year made great voyages, and were a great many of them; and if we could fall once into the right course about it, and be able to manage it, it would make good all; a good fishing place will be a great advantage for it, where the boats may go quickly in and out to sea at all times of the tide, and well stowed with fish near at hand, and convenient places to make it, and build stages in, and then it will not only serve for our own fishing, but after it be known once by experience to be a place well qualified for that purpose, benefit will be made of it by granting license to others to fish there. But about these things we refer you for further information to our messenger and Mr. Pierce, who is a man we perceive very skillful and diligent in his business, and a very honest man, whose employments may do us much good; and if you resolve, as we earnestly desire you may, of any course about fishing we think he is as fit an instrument as you can use.

It would be a principal stay and a comfortable help to the Colony if they had some cattle, in many respects, first it would much encourage them, and be in time a greater ease both for tillage of ground, and carriage of burden; 2ly, it will make victuals both more plentiful, and comfortable; 3ly, it will be a good benefit after some increase that they might be able to spare some to others that should have thoughts this way; especially goats are very useful for the first, and very fit for this place, for they will here thrive very well, are a hardy creature, and live at no charge, either winter or summer, their increase is great and milk very good, and need little looking to; also they are much more easily transported and with less difficulty and hazard, than other cattle; yet two of those which came last died by the way, but it was by some negligence.[399] For kine and other cattle it will be best when any comes that it be in the spring, and if they should come against the winter, they would go near to die; the Colony will never be in good estate till they have some.

As touching making of salt we have by accident had speech with one of the north country, who came with Mr. Reynolds (who put in here), and was his mate; he had speech with our smith about the making of salt pan, which doubts he cannot do it; also he saith if they go about it that have no skill they will quickly burn the pans and do no good, whereas if they be skillfully ordered they may last a long time. He thought we might have some from about Newcastle that would best fit our turn for that business we pray you provide for us here about as soon as you can, that we may do something to the purpose.

Mr. Weston's colony is dissolved (as you cannot but hear before this time). They had by their evil and deboist carriage so exasperated the Indians

---

[399] The ship *Anne* carried a few cattle to Plymouth in 1623 including a "great black cow," another black cow, and a "great white-back cow."

among them as they plotted their overthrow; and because they knew not how to effect it for fear we would revenge it upon them, they secretly instigated other peoples to conspire against us also, thinking to cut off our shallop abroad and then to assault us with their force at home. But their conspiracy and treachery was discovered unto us by Massasoit, (the occasion and further relation whereof our messenger can declare unto you at large, to whom we refer you). We went to rescue the lives of our countrymen, whom we thought (both by nature, and conscience) we were bound to deliver, as also to take vengeance of them for their villainy intended and determined against us, which never did them harm, waiting only for opportunity to execute the same. But by the good providence of God they were taken in their own snare, and their wickedness came upon their own part; we killed seven of the chief of them, and the head of one of them stands still on our fort for a terror unto others; they met our men in the field and shot at them, but thanks be to God not a man of them were hurt; neither could they hurt the Indians with their pieces, they did so shelter themselves behind great trees, only they broke the arm of a notable rogue as he was drawing his bow to shoot at Captain Standish, after which they came away. We gave the Captain order, if Mr. Weston's people would, that he should bring them to us and we would afford them the best succor we could, or if they chose rather to go to Mohegan, that then if he took any corn from the Indians, he should let them have to victual them thither (which accordingly was done, though ours had scarce enough to bring them home again). Yet for all this, and much more they cannot afford us a good word but reproach us behind our backs.

Touching our government you are mistaken if you think we admit women and children[400] to have to do in the same, for they are excluded, as both reason and nature teacheth they should be; neither do we admit any but as are above the age of 21 years, and they also but only in some weighty matters, when we think good; yet we like well of your course, and advice propounded unto us, and will as soon as we can with convenience bring it into practice, though it should be well it were so ordered in our patent.

Now whereas you think we have been too credulous in receiving insinuations against you, and too rash in complaining and censoring of you; as also that to particular men letters have been written not with that discretion

---

[400] It is unclear why some rumored that the Pilgrims admitted women into government. If Nathaniel Morton's list of "Mayflower Compact" signers is authentic, then there was at least one minor who signed: Gilbert Winslow had just turned 20 years old.

and deliberation which was meet, we answer what others have written we know not, neither could hinder; if there be anything otherwise then well let them bear their blame; only what we have written we best know, and can answer. And first we wished you would either roundly supply us, or else wholly forsake us, that we might know what to do; this you call a short and preemptory resolution, be it as it will, we were necessarily occasioned by our wants (and the discontents of many) thereunto. Yet it was never our purpose or once came into our minds to enter upon any course before we knew what you would do, upon an equal treaty of things, according to our former, as we conceived, bonds between us. And then if you should have left us we meant not to join with any other (as you it should seem conceived) but thought we could get ourselves food, and for clothes we intended to take the best course we could, and so to use the best means we could to subsist, or otherwise to return. Though indeed we think if you had left us we might have had others desirous to join with us. Also you may conceive some of us have had enough to do to hold things together amongst men of so many humors, under so many difficulties, and fears of many kinds; and if anything more hath been said or written to any by us, it hath been only to show that it might rather be marveled that we could at all subsist, then that we were in no better case having been so long without supply, and not at all for your disgrace. If necessary or passion have carried others further, your wisdoms will (I doubt not) bear with it. As for Captain Standish we leave him to answer for himself; but this we must say, he is as helpful an instrument as any we have, and as careful of the general good, an doth not well approve himself.

Indeed friends it doth us much good to read your honest letters. We perceive your honest minds, and how squarely you deal in all things, which giveth us much comfort, and howsoever things have been for time past, we doubt not for time to come but there shall be that good correspondence which is meet. And we shall labor what we can to be answerable to your kindness and cost.

For our friends in Holland we much desired their company, and have long expected the same; if we had had them in the stead of some others we are persuaded things would have been better than they are with us, for honest men will ever do their best endeavor, whilst others (though they be more able of body) will scarce by any means be brought to; but we know many of them to be better able, either for labor or counsel than ourselves; and indeed if they should not come to us, we would not stay here, if we might gain never so much wealth, but we are glad to take knowledge of what you would write touching them, and like well of your purpose not to make the general body bigger, save only to furnish them with useful members, for special faculties.

Touching those articles of agreement, we have taken ourselves bound by them unto you, and you unto us, being by Mr. Weston much pressed thereunto, we gave Mr. Cushman full commission to conclude and confirm the same with you. For anything further thereabout we refer you to our messenger; though in any bound made, or to be made between you and us, we take our friends at Leiden to be comprehended in the same, and as much interested as ourselves; and their consents to be accordingly had; for though we be come first to this place, yet they are as principal in the actions and they and we to be considered as one body.

We found the surgeon in the pinnace to be so proud and quarrelsome a man, and to use his terms in that sort, as the Captain and others durst not go to sea with him; being over ready to raise factions and mutiny in the ship; so as we were constrained to dismiss him, and hire Mr. Rogers in his room, Mr. Pierce being willing to release him, to do us a favor. He is to have 35s per month, whereof he desires his wife may have 16s a month, which we pray you may be accordingly performed.

About Hopkins and his men we are come to this issue. The men we retain in the general according to his resignation and equity of the thing. And about that reckoning of 20 odd pounds, we have brought it to this pass, he is to have 6$^£$ paid by you there, and the rest to be quit; it is for nails and such other things as we have had of his brother here for the company's use, and upon promise of payment by us, we desire you will accordingly do it.

For the tokens of your love and other charges you have been at with myself, befit you many thanks, (and so do they likewise) not knowing how to recompense your kindness. It is more than we have deserved at your hands.

Touching those which came to us in their particular, we have received them in as kindly manner as we could, according to our ability, and offered them as favorable terms as we could touching their footing with us. Yet they are sundry of them discouraged I know not whether by the country (of which they have no trial) or rather for want of those varieties which England affords, from which they are not yet weened, and being so delightful to nature cannot easily be forgotten without a former grounded resolution. But as they were welcome when they came, so shall they be when they go, if they think it is not for their good, though we are most glad of honest men's company; and loath to part from the same.

Thus again giving you hearty thanks for your loving affections and long hands extended unto us, we rest your loving friends to use,

William Bradford, Governor, Plymouth

Isaac Allerton, Assistant

September 8, 1623

Division of Land at Plymouth (1623)

The falls of their grounds which came first over in the *Mayflower* according as their lots were cast.

These lie on the south side of the brook to the baywards

Robert Cushman 1
Mr. William Brewster 6
William Bradford 3
Richard Gardinar 1
Francis Cooke 2
George Soule 1
Mr. Isaac Allerton 7
John Billington 3
Peter Brown 1
Samuel Fuller 2
Joseph Rogers 2

The number of acres to each one

These contain 29 acres

These lie on the south side of the brook to the woodward opposite the former.

John Howland 4
Stephen Hopkins 6
Edward 1
Edward 1
Gilbert Winslow 1
Samuel Fuller junior 3

These contain 16 acres besides Hobomok's ground which lieth between John Howland's and Hopkins'.

This 5 acres lieth behind the fort to the little pond.

William White 5

These lie on the north side of the town next adjoining to their gardens which came in the *Fortune*.

Edward Winslow 4
Richard Warren 2
John Goodman .... [damage]
John Crackston .... [damage]
John Alden .... [damage]
Mary Chilton .... [damage]
Capt. Myles Standish 2
Francis Eaton 4
Henry Sampson 1
Humility Cooper 1

The falls of their grounds which came in the *Fortune* according as their lots were cast 1623. This ship came Nov. 1621.

These lie to the sea, eastward		These lie beyond the first brook to the wood westward.	
William Hilton	1	William Wright &	
John Winslow	1	William Pitt	2
William Conner	1	Robert Hicks	1
John Adams	1	Thomas Prence	1
William Tench &		Stephen Deane	1
John Cannon	2	Moses Simonson &	
		Philip Delano	2
		Edward Bumpass	1
		Clement Briggs	1
These following lie beyond the 2 brook		James Steward	1
		William Palmer	2
		Jonathan Brewster	1
Hugh Stacey	1	Bennett Morgan	1
William Beale &		Thomas Flavell	
Thomas Cushman	2	& his son	2
Austin Nicholas	1	Thomas Morton	1
Widow Ford	4	William Bassett	2

15 acres	19 acres

The falls of their grounds which came over in the ship called the *Anne*,
according as their lots were cast. 1623.

	Acres		Acres
		These to the sea eastward.	
James Rande	1	Francis Sprague	3

These following lie beyond the brook to Strawberry Hill.

	Acres		Acres
Edmond Flood	1	Edward Burcher	2
Christopher Connant	1	John Jenny	5
Francis Cooke	4	Goodwife Flavell	1
		Manessah & John Faunce	2

These butt against the swamp and reed-pond

This goeth in with a corner by the pond.

	Acres		Acres
George Morton &		Alice Bradford	1
Experience Mitchell	8	Robert Hicks his	
Christian Penn	1	wife & children	4
Thomas Morton junior	1	Bridgett Fuller	1
William Hilton's wife		Ellen Newton	1
& 2 children	3	Patience & Fear Brewster,	
		with Robert Long	3
		William Heard	1
		Mrs. Standish	1

These following lie on the other side of the town towards the Eel River.

	Acres		Acres
Mary Buckett adjoining to		Robert Ratcliffe beyond the	
Joseph Rogers	1	swamp & stony ground	2
Mr. Oldham & those joined			
with him	10	These butt against Hobb's Hole	
Godbert Godbertson	6	Nicholas Snow	[damaged]
Anthony Annable	4	Anthony Dix	[damaged]
Thomas Tilden	3	Mr. Pierce's 2 servants	[damaged]
Richard Warren	5	Ralph Wallen	[damaged]
Bangs	4		

South side

North side

	Acres		Acres
Stephen Tracey three acres	3	Edward Holman 1 acre	1
Thomas Clarke one acre	1	Frances wife to William Palmer	1 acre
Robert Bartlett one acre	1	Joshua Pratt &	
		Phineas Pratt	2

The Patent for Cape Anne, 1623

This indenture made the first day of January Anno. Dom. 1623, and in the year of the reign of our Sovereign Lord James by the grace of God King of England, France and Ireland, Defender of the Faith, etc. the one and twentieth and of Scotland the seven and fiftieth, between the right honorable Edmond Lord Sheffield Knight of the most noble Order of the Garter on the one part and Robert Cushman and Edward Winslow for themselves, and their associates and planters at Plymouth in New England in America on the other part. Witnesseth that the said Lord Sheffield (as well in consideration that the said Robert and Edward and divers of their associates have already adventured themselves in person, and have likewise at their own proper costs and charges transported divers persons into New England aforesaid; and for that the said Robert and Edward and their associates also intend as well to transport more persons as also further to plant at Plymouth aforesaid, and in other places in New England aforesaid, as for the better advancement and furtherance of the said Planters, and encouragement of the said undertakers) hath given, granted, assigned, allotted, and appointed, and by these presents doth give, grant, assign, allot, and appoint unto the said Robert and Edward and their Associates as well, a certain tract of ground in New England aforesaid lying in forty-three degrees or thereabouts of northerly latitude and in a known place there commonly called Cape Anne, together with the free use and benefit as well of the Bay commonly called the Bay of Cape Anne, as also of the Islands within the said Bay; and free liberty, to fish, fowl, hawk, and hunt, truck, and trade in the lands thereabout, and in all other places in New England aforesaid; whereof the said Lord Sheffield is, or hath been possessed, or which have been allotted to him the said Lord Sheffield, or within his jurisdiction (not now being inhabited, or hereafter to be inhabited by any English) together also with five hundred acres of free land adjoining to the said Bay to be employed for public uses, as for the building of a town, schools, churches, hospitals, and for the maintenance of such ministers, officers, and magistrates, as by the said undertakers, and their associates are there already appointed, or which hereafter shall (with their good liking) reside, and inhabit there. And also thirty acres of land, over and beside the five hundred acres of land, before mentioned, to be allotted, and appointed for every particular person, young or old (being the Associates, or servants of the said undertakers or their successors) that shall come, and dwell at the aforesaid Cape Anne within seven years next after the date hereof, which thirty acres of land so appointed to every person as aforesaid, shall be taken as the same doth lie together upon the said Bay in one entire place, and not straggling in divers, or remote parcels not exceeding an English mile, and a half in length on the water's side of the said Bay, yielding and paying forever yearly unto the said Lord Sheffield, his heirs, successors rent gather, or assigns for every thirty acres so to be obtained, and possessed, by the said Robert and Edward their heirs, successors or associates, twelve pence of lawful English money at the Feast of St. Michael the Archangel, only (if it be lawfully demanded). The first payment thereof to begin immediately from and after the end and expiration of the first seven years next after the date hereof. And the said Lord Sheffield for himself, his heirs, successors, and assigns doth covenant, promise, and grant to and with the said Robert Cushman, and Edward Winslow their heirs, associates, and assigns, that they the said Robert, and Edward, and such other persons as shall plant, and contract with them, shall freely and quietly, have, hold, possess, and enjoy all such profits, rights, privileges, benefits, commodities, advantages, and preeminences, as shall hereafter by the labor, search, and diligence of the said Undertakers their Associates, servants, or assignees be obtained, found out, or made within the said tract of ground so granted unto them as aforesaid; reserving unto the said Lord Sheffield his heirs, successors, and assignees the one moiety of all such mines as shall be discovered, or found out at any time by the said Undertakers, or any their heirs, successors, or assigns upon the grounds aforesaid. And further that it shall and may be lawful to and for the said Robert Cushman, and Edward Winslow their heirs, associates, and assignees from time to time and at all times hereafter so soon as they or their assignees have taken possession, or entered into any of the said lands to forbid, repel, repulse and resist by force of arms all and every such persons as shall build, plant, or inhabit, or which shall offer, or make show to build, plant, or inhabit within the lands so as aforesaid granted, without the leave, and license of the said Robert, and Edward or their assigns. And the said Lord Sheffield doth further covenant, and grant that upon a lawful survey had, and taken of the aforesaid land, and good information given to the said Lord Sheffield his heirs, or assignees, of the meat, bounds, and quality of lands which the said Robert, and Edward their heirs, associates, or assigns shall take in and be by them their Associates, servants or assigns inhabited as aforesaid; he the said Lord Sheffield his heirs, assigns, at and upon the reasonable request of the said undertakers, or their associates, shall and will by good and sufficient assurance in the law grant, enfeoffe, confirm and allot unto the said Robert Cushman and Edward Winslow their associates, and assignees all and every the said lands so to be taken in within the space of seven years next after the date hereof in as large, ample, and beneficial manner, as the said Lord Sheffield his heirs, or assigns now have, or hereafter shall have the same lands, or any of them granted unto him, or them; for such rent, and under such covenants, and provisos, as herein are contained (*mutates mutandis*) and shall and will also at all times hereafter upon reasonable request made to him the said Lord Sheffield his heirs or assignes by the said Edward and Robert their heirs, associates, or assigns, or any of them grant, procure, and make good, lawful, and sufficient letters, or other grants of incorporation whereby the said Undertakers, and their associates shall have liberty and lawful authority from time to time to make and establish laws, ordinances, and constitutions for the ruling, ordering, and governing of such persons as now are resident, or which hereafter shall be planted, and inhabit there. And in the meantime until such grant be made it shall be lawful for the said Robert, and Edward their heirs, associates and assigns by consent of the greater part of them to establish such laws, provisions, and ordinances as are or shall by them thought most fit, and convenient for the government of the said plantation which shall be from time to time executed, and administered by such officer, or officers, as the said undertakers, or their associates or the most part of them shall erect, and make choice of provided always that the said laws, provisions and ordinances which are, or shall be agreed on, be not repugnant to the laws of England, or to the orders, and constitutions of the President and Council of New England, provided further that the said undertakers, their heirs and successors, to be their chief Lord, and to answer and do service unto his Lordship or his successors, at his, or their Court when upon his, or their own plantation. The same shall be established, and kept. In witness whereof the said parties to these present indentures interchangeably have put their hands and seals the day and years first abovewritten.

E. Sheffield

Sealed and delivered in the presence of
John Bulmer, Thomas Belwield, John Fowler

Division of Cattle at Plymouth (1627)

1. The first lot fell to Francis Cooke and his company joined to him, his wife Hester Cooke.
3. John Cooke
4. Jacob Cooke
5. Jane Cooke
6. Hester Cooke
7. Mary Cooke
8. Moses Simonson
9. Philip Delano
10. Experience Mitchell
11. John Faunce
12. Joshua Pratt
13. Phineas Pratt

To this lot fell the least of the 4 black heifers came in the *Jacob*, and two she goats.

2. The second lot fell to Mr. Isaac Allerton and his company joined to him his wife Fear Allerton.
3. Bartholomew Allerton
4. Remember Allerton
5. Mary Allerton
6. Sarah Allerton
7. Godbert Godbertson
8. Sarah Godbertson
9. Samuel Godbertson
10. Mary Priest
11. Sarah Priest
12. Edward Bumpass
13. John Crackston

To this lot fell the Great Black cow came in the *Anne* to which they must keep the lesser of the two steers, and two she goats.

3. The third lot fell to Capt. Standish and his company joined to him
2. his wife Barbara Standish
3. Charles Standish
4. Alexander Standish
5. John Standish
6. Edward Winslow
7. Susanna Winslow
8. Edward Winslow
9. John Winslow
10. Resolved White
11. Peregrine White
12. Abraham Pierce
13. Thomas Clarke

To this lot fell the Red Cow which belogeth to the poor of the Colony to which they must keep her calf of this year being a bull for the Company. Also to this lot came two she goats.

4. The fourth lot fell to John Howland and his company joined to him
2. his wife Elizabeth Howland
3. John Howland Junior
4. Desire Howland
5. William Wight
6. Thomas Morton Junior
7. John Alden
8. Priscilla Alden
9. Elizabeth Alden
10. Clement Briggs
11. Edward Doty
12. Edward Holman
13. John Alden

To this lot fell one of the 4 heifers came in the *Jacob* called Raghorn.

5. The fifth lot fell to Mr. William Brewster and his company joined to him.
2. Love Brewster
3. Wrestling Brewster
4. Richard More
5. Henry Sampson
6. Jonathan Brewster
7. Lucretia Brewster

To this lot fell one of the four heifers came in the *Jacob* called the Blind Heifer and 2 she goats.

8. William Brewster
9. Mary Brewster
10. Thomas Prence
11. Patience Prence
12. Rebecca Prence
13. Humility Cooper

6. The sixth lot fell to John Shaw and his company joined
1. to him
2. John Adams
3. Eleanor Adams
4. James Adams
5. John Winslow
6. Mary Winslow
7. William Bassett
8. Elizabeth Bassett
9. William Bassett Junior
10. Elizabeth Bassett Junior
11. Francis Sprague
12. Anna Sprague
13. Mercy Sprague

To this lot fell the lesser of the black cows came in the *Anne* which they must keep the biggest of the 2 steers. And to this lot was two she goats.

7. The seventh lot fell to Stephen Hopkins and his company joined to
2. him his wife Elizabeth Hopkins
3. Giles Hopkins
4. Caleb Hopkins
5. Deborah Hopkins
6. Nicholas Snow
7. Constance Snow
8. William Palmer
9. Frances Palmer
10. William Palmer Junior
11. John Billington Senior
12. Helen Billington
13. Francis Billington

To this lot fell a black weining calf to which was added the calf of this year to come of the black cow, which fell to John Shaw and his company, which proving a bull they were to keep it ungelt 5 years for common use and after to make their best of it. Nothing belongeth of these two, for the company of the first stock: but only half the increase.

To this lot there fell two she goats: which goats they possess on the like terms which others do their cattle.

8. The eighth lot fell to Samuel Fuller and his company joined to him his wife
2. Bridget Fuller
3. Samuel Fuller Junior
4. Peter Brown
5. Martha Brown
6. Mary Brown
7. John Ford
8. Martha Ford
9. Anthony Annable
10. Jane Annable
11. Sarah Annable
12. Hannah Annable
13. Thomas Morton Senior
13. Damaris Hopkins

To this lot fell a Red Heifer came of the cow which belongeth to the poor of the colony and so is of that consideration. (viz) these persons nominated, to have half increase, the other half, with the old stock, to remain for the use of the poor.
To this lot also two she goats.

9. The ninth lot fell to Richard Warren and his company joined with
2. him his wife Elizabeth Warren
3. Nathaniel Warren
4. Joseph Warren
5. Mary Warren
6. Anna Warren
7. Sarah Warren
8. Elizabeth Warren
9. Abigail Warren
10. John Billington
11. George Soule
12. Mary Soule
13. Zachariah Soule

To this lot fell one of the 4 black heifers that came in the *Jacob* called the Smooth-horned Heifer and two she goats.

10. The tenth lot fell to Francis Eaton and those joined with him his
2. wife Christian Eaton
3. Samuel Eaton
4. Rachel Eaton
5. Stephen Tracey
6. Triphosa Tracey

To this lot fell an heifer of the last year called the White-bellied Heifer and two she goats.

7. Sarah Tracey
8. Rebecca Tracey
9. Ralph Wallen
10. Joyce Wallen
11. Sarah Morton
12. ~~Edward Flood~~
12. Robert ~~Hilton~~ Bartlett
13. Thomas Prence

11. The eleventh lot fell to the Governor Mr. William Bradford and
2. those with him, to wit, his wife Alice Bradford and
3. William Bradford, junior   To this lot fell an heifer of the last year
4. Mercy Bradford   which was of the great white-back cow that
5. Joseph Rogers   was brought over in the *Anne*, and two she
6. Thomas Cushman   goats.
7. William Latham
8. Manasseh Kempton
9. Juliana Kempton
10. Nathaniel Morton
11. John Morton
12. Ephraim Morton
13. Patience Morton

12. The twelvth lot fell to John Jenny and his company joined to him,
2. his wife Sarah Jenny
3. Samuel Jenny   To this lot fell the great white-backed cow
4. Abigail Jenny   which was brought over with the first in the
5. Sarah Jenny   *Anne*, to which cow the keeping of the bull
6. Robert Hicks   was joined for these persons to provide for.
7. Margaret Hicks   Here also two she goats.
8. Samuel Hicks
9. Ephraim Hicks
10. Lydia Hicks
11. Phoebe Hicks
12. Stephen Deane
13. Edward Bangs

James Sherley's
Plymouth Company Accounts, 1628

1628.   The Company of Plymouth in New England are debtors as foll. viz.

To so much paid for Mr. Rogers' passage, 20s. his diet 11 weeks at 4s. 8d	3 11 4
Paid for Constant Souther's passage, 20s. and diet 11 weeks at 4s. 8d.	3 11 4
John Gibbs, for freight of beaver and other skins, 30s. charges at custom house,	1 13 0
To Mr. Elbridge for freight of 3 hogsheads,	3 0 0
For primage of the said 3 hogsheads,	10 0
For custom thereof at Bristowe,	8 0 0
To the boatswain, by Mr. Winslow's order,	2 5 0
For bringing the beaver from Bristowe,	1 15 0
Paid to Mr. Elbridge for 125£. Taken up at 50£. p.c. for 2 years,	137 10 0
Paid to John Pocock for 20£ taken up at 30£. P.c. for 2 years,	32 0 0
Paid to Edward Basse for 5£ taken up at 6s. p. £. for 2 years,	8 0 0
Paid to Timothy Hatherley for 10£ taken up at 6s. p. £. for two years,	16 0 0
Paid to Wm. Thomas for 10£. Taken up at 6s. p. £. for 2 years	16 0 0
Paid to Mr. Linge for 5£. At 6. p. £. for 2 years	8 0 0
Paid, being the first year's payment towards the purchase,	200 0 0
Paid to Mrs. Armstrong in full for her debt, which now belongeth to the Company,	2 0 0
To Mr. Viner about the patent, and spent thereabouts,	39 15 0
More since laid out by Mr. Hatherley, as in your account, for the patent,	7 0
To so much paid for custom and charges by Mr. Brand for the goods out of Mr. Wm. Peeters,	7 12 4
	541 10 0
So here you are indebted to the Company which I set here to balance,	118 6 11
	659 16 11

But now I find in your letter of the 7th and 12th of December, 1628, that you have laid out for the Company as followeth, besides what you know belongeth unto them, and that I have not taken out of the account betwixt you and me:

Paid for shoes and leather,	30 0 0
Paid for cloth,	40 0 0
Irish stockings and cloth of all sorts,	40 0 0
Pitch, tar, ropes and twine,	5 0 0
Knives, scissors, and the piece of rowle,	18 0 0
Rudge of divers sorts,	14 0 0
Lead, shot and powder	25 0 0
Hatchets, hoes, axes, scythes, reap-hooks, shovels, spades, saws, files, nails, iron pots, drugs and spices,	60 0 0
All these I find you put down, which amount to	232 0 0

Besides many other I imagine you omit, and the charge of your servants. So now I find the Company are in your debt (the 118:6:11 above being set off) the sum of   131 13 1

James Sherley.

1628.   The Company of Plymouth in New England are creditors for goods sent by them, and sold here, as foll.

Rec. out of the *Marmaduke*, by John Gibbs, 220 otters' and minks' and quash skins, sold at	78	12	0
Rec. out of the *White Angel*, by Christopher Burkett, 494 lb. 8 d. beaver, sold at 15s. 6d. amounts to	383	14	3
Rec. out of the *Pleasure*, Wm. Peeters master, 209 lb. 12 d. beaver, at 16s. 4d.	171	5	11
40 otters' skins sold together,	29	0	0
	200	5	11
Rebated, because they were exceeding wet, and doubtful some mistake in weight, the sum of	2	15	3
So they yielded, to be put to account,	197	10	8
	659	16	11
	James Sherley		

Memorandum. The Company stand indebted unto these several men following, for principal moneys borrowed of them, as foll.

To John Beauchamp, p. bond bearing date the 18th day of November, 1628, payable on the 25th of October, 1629, being principal money only,	160	0	0
To James Sherley, p. bond dated 18th of November, 1628, payable on the 25th day of October, 1629, being principal money only,	80	0	0
To Richard Andrews, p. bond dated the 18th of November, 1628, payable the 15th of October, 1629, being principal money,	40	0	0
	280	0	0

The Bradford Patent of 1629/1630

To all to whom these presents shall come greeting:

Whereas our late sovereign lord King James for the advancement of a colony and plantation in the country called or known by the name of New England in America, by his highness' letters patents under the great seal of England: bearing date at Westminster the third day of November in the eighteenth year of his highnesses' reign of England etc. did give, grant, and confirm unto the right honorable Lodowick late lord duke of Lenox, George late lord marques of Buckingham, James Marques Hamilton, Thomas Earl of Arundell, Robert Earl of Warwick and Ferdinando Gorges, knight, and divers others whose names are expressed in the said letters patents and their successors that they should bee one body politic and corporate perpetually consisting of forty persons, and that they should have perpetual succession and one common seal to serve for the said body and that they and their successors should be incorporated called and known by the name of the Council established at Plymouth in the county of Devon for the planting, ruling, ordering, and governing of New England in America, and also of his special grace certain knowledge and mere motion did give grant and confirm unto the said president and council and their successors forever under the reservations limitations and declarations in the said letters patents expressed, all that part and portion of the said country now called New England in America situate, lying and being in breadth from forty degrees of northerly latitude from the equinoctial line to forty eight degrees of the said northerly latitude inclusively, and in length of and in all the breadth aforesaid throughout the mainland from sea to sea, together also with all the former lands, soils, grounds, creeks, inlets, havens, ports, seas, rivers, islands, waters, fishings, mines and minerals, as well royal mines of gold and silver as other mines and minerals, precious stones, quarries and all and singular the commodities, jurisdictions, royalties, privileges, franchises, and preeminencies both within the said tract of lands upon the main, as also within the said islands and seas adjoining: to have, hold, possess and enjoy all and singular the foresaid continent, lands, territories, islands, hereditaments, and precincts, sea, waters, fishings with all and all manner their commodities, royalties, privileges, preeminencies, and profits that shall arise from thence, with all and singular their appurtenances and every part and parcel thereof unto the said council and their successors and assigns forever: to be holden of His Majesty, his heirs and successors as of his manor of East Greenwich in the county of Kent in free and common soccage and not in capite nor by knights service yielding and praying therefore to the said late King's Majesty, his heirs and successors the fifth part of the ore of gold and silver which from time to time and at all times from the date of the said letters patents shall be there gotten had and obtained for and in respect of all and all manner of duties demands and services whatsoever to be done made and paid unto his said late Majesty, his heirs and successors as in and by the said letters patents amongst sundry other privileges and matters therein contained more fully and at large it doth and may appear. Now know ye that the said council by virtue and authority of his said late Majesty's letters patents and for and in consideration that William Bradford and his associates have for these nine years lived in New England aforesaid and have there inhabited and planted a town called by the name of New Plymouth at their own proper costs and charges: And now seeing that by the special providence of God, and their extraordinary care and industry they have increased their plantation to near three hundred people, and are upon all occasions able to relieve any new planters or others His Majesty's subjects who may fall upon that coast; have given, granted, bargained, sold, enfeoffed, allotted, assigned and set over and by these presents do clearly and absolutely give, grant, bargain, sell, alien, enfeoffe, allot, assign, and confirm unto the said William Bradford, his heirs, associates and assigns all that part of New England in America aforesaid, and tract and tracts of land that lie within or between a certain rivulet or runlet there commonly called Cohasset alias Conahassett towards the north, and the river commonly called Narragansetts river towards the south; and the great western ocean towards the east, and between and within a straight line directly extending up into the mainland towards the west from the mouth of the said river called Narragansetts river to the utmost limits and bounds of a country or place in New England called Pokanoket alias Sowamsett westward, and another like straight line extending itself directly from the mouth of the said river called Cohasset alias Conahassett towards the west so far up into the mainland westwards as the utmost limits of the said place or country commonly called Pokanoket alias Sowamsett do extend, together with one half of the said river called Narragansetts and the said rivulet or runlet called Cohasset alias Conahassett and all lands, rivers, waters, havens, creeks, ports, fishings, fowlings, and all hereditiments, profits, commodities, and emoluments whatsoever situate, lying, and being or arising within or between the said limits and bounds or any of them. And for as much as they have no convenient place either of trading or fishing within their own precincts whereby (after so long travel and great pains,) so hopeful a plantation may subsist, as also that they may be encouraged the better to proceed in so pious a work which may especially tend to the propagation of religion and the great increase of trade to His Majesty's realms, and advancement of the public plantation, the said council have further given, granted, bargained, sold, enfeoffed, allotted, assigned and set over and by these presents do clearly and absolutely give, grant, bargain, sell, alien, enfeoffe, allot, assign and confirm unto the said William Bradford his heirs, associates, and assigns all that tract of land or part of New England in America aforesaid which lyeth within or between and extendeth itself from the utmost limits of Cobbosseecontee alias Comasee-Conte which adjoineth to the river of Kennebec alias Kenebekike towards the western ocean and a place called the falls at Mequamkike in America aforesaid, and the space of fifteen English miles on each side of the said river commonly called Kennebec river, and all the said river called Kennebec that lies within the said limits and bounds eastward, westward, northward, or southward last above mentioned, and all lands, grounds, soils, rivers, waters, fishings, hereditaints and profits whatsoever situate lying and being, arising, happening or accruing, or which shall arise, happen or accrue in or within the said limits and bounds or either of them together with free ingress, egress and regress with ships, boats, shallops, and other vessels from the sea commonly called the western ocean to the said river called Kennebec and from the said river to the said western ocean, together with all prerogatives, rights, royalties, jurisdictions, privileges, franchises, liberties, and immunities, and also marine liberty with the escheats and casualties thereof the Admiralty Jurisdiction excepted with all the interest right title claim and demand whatsoever which the said council and their successors now have or ought to have an claim or may have and acquire hereafter in or to any the said portions or tracts of land hereby mentioned to be granted, or any the premises in as free large ample and beneficial manner to all intents, constructions and purposes whatsoever as the said council by virtue of His Majesty's said letters patents may or can grant; to have an to hold the said tract and tracts of land and all and singular the premises above-mentioned to be granted with their and every of their appurtenances to the said William Bradford, his heirs, associates and assigns forever, to the only proper and absolute use and behoove of the said William Bradford, his heirs, associates and assigns forever; yielding and paying unto our said sovereign Lord the King, his heirs and successors forever one-fifth part of the ore of the mines of gold and silver and one other fifth part thereof to the president and council, which shall be had, possessed and obtained within the precincts aforesaid for all services and demands whatsoever. And the said council do further grant and agree to and with the said William Bradford, his heirs, associates and assigns, and every of them, his and their factors, agents, tenants and servants, and all such as he or they shall send and employ about his said particular plantation, shall and may from time to time freely and lawfully go and return, trade and traffic, as well with the English, as any of the natives within the precincts aforesaid, with liberty of fishing upon any part of the sea, coast and seashores of any the seas or islands adjacent and not being inhabited or otherwise disposed of by order of the said president and council: also to import, export and transport their goods and merchandize at their wills and pleasures paying only such duty to the king's Majesty, his heirs and successors as the said President and council do or ought to pay without any other taxes, impositions, burdens and restraints upon them to be imposed. And further the said council do grant and agree to and with the said William Bradford, his heirs, associates and assigns, that the persons transported by him or any of them shall not be taken away, employed or commanded either by the Governor for the time being of New England or by any other authority there, from the business and employment of the said William Bradford and his associates, his heirs and assigns; necessary defense of the country, preservation of the peace, suppressing of tumults within the lands, trials in matters of justice by appeal upon special occasion only excepted. Also it shall be lawful and free for the said William Bradford, his associates, his heirs and assigns at all times hereafter to incorporate by some usual or fit name and title, him or themselves or the people there inhabiting under him or them with liberty to them and their successors from time to time to frame, and make orders, ordinances and constitutions as well for the better government of their affairs here and the receiving or admitting any to his or their society, as also for the better government of his or their people and affaires in New England or of his and their people at sea in going thither, or returning from thence, and the same to put in execution or cause to be put in execution by such officers and ministers as he and they shall authorize and depute: provided that the said laws and orders be not repugnant to the laws of England, or the frame of government by the said president and council hereafter to be established. And further it shall be lawful and free for the said William Bradford, his heirs, associates and assigns to transport cattle of all kinds, also powder, shot, ordnance and munitions from time to time as shall be necessary for their strength and safety hereafter for their several defense; to encounter, expulse, repel and resist by force of arms as well by sea as by land, by all ways and means whatsoever. And by virtue of the authority to us derived by his said late Majesty's letters patents to take, apprehend, seize, and make prize of all such persons, their ships and goods as shall attempt to inhabit or trade with the savage people of that country within the several precincts and limits of his and their several plantations, or shall enterprise or attempt at any time destruction, invasion, detriment or annoyance to his and their said plantation; the one moiety of which goods so seized and taken it shall be lawful for the said William Bradford, his heirs, associates and assigns to take to their own use and behoove; the other moiety thereof to be delivered by the said William Bradford, his heirs, associates and assigns to such officer and officers as shall be appointed to receive the same for His Majesty's use. And the said council do hereby covenant and declare that it is their intent and meaning for the good of this plantation that the said William Bradford, his associates, his or their heirs or assigns shall have and enjoy whatsoever privilege or privileges of what kind soever, as are expressed or intended to be granted in and by his said late Majesty's letters patents, and that in as large and ample manner as the said council thereby now may or hereafter can grant, coining of money excepted. And the said council for them and their successors do covenant and grant to and with the said William Bradford, his heirs, associates and assigns by these presents, that they the said council shall at any time hereafter upon request at the only proper costs and charges of the said William Bradford, his heirs, associates and assigns do make, suffer, execute and willingly consent unto any further act or acts, conveyance or conveyances, assurance or assurances whatsoever, for the good and perfect investing, assuring, and conveying and sure making of all the aforesaid tract and tracts of lands, royalties, mines, minerals, woods, fishings and all and singular their appurtenances, unto the said William Bradford, his heirs, associates and assigns as by him or them or his or their heirs and assigns, or his or their council learned in the law shall be devised, advised and required. And lastly know ye that we the said council have made, constituted, deputed, authorized and appointed Captain Myles Standish, or in his absence Edward Winslow, John Howland and John Alden, or any of them to be our true and lawful attorney and attorneys jointly and severally in our name and steed to enter into the said tract and tracts of land and other the premises with their appurtenances, or into some part thereof in the name of the whole for us and in our names to take possession and seizing thereof, and after such possession and seizing thereof or of some part thereof in the name of the whole had and taken; then for us and in our names to deliver the full and peaceable possession and seizing of all and singular the said mentioned to be granted premises unto the said William Bradford, his heirs, associates and assigns or to his or their certain attorney or attorneys in that behalf ratifying, allowing and confirming all whatsoever our said attorney doe in or about the premises. In witness whereof, the said council established at Plymouth in the county of Devon for the planting, ruling, ordering and governing of New England in America have hereunto put their seal the thirteenth day of January in fifth year of the reign of our Sovereign Lord Charles by the grace of God, King of England, Scotland, France and Ireland, defender of the faith, etc.

Anno. Domi. 1629
    R. WARWICK.

Deposition on the killing of Moses Talbot by John Hocking in 1634, in a dispute over Kennebec River trading rights.

This deponent saith that upon the _____ day of April, John Hocking riding at anchor within our limits above the house; Mr. John Howland went up to him with our bark and charged the said Hocking to weight his anchors and depart; who answered he would not, with foul speeches, demanding why he spoke not to them that sent him forth: answer was made by John Howland that the last year a boat was sent having no other business to know whether it was their mind that he should thus wrong us in our trade, who returned answer they sent him not thither and therefore Mr. Howland told him that he would not now suffer him there to ride. John Hocking demanded what he would do whether he would shoot; Mr. Howland answered no but he would put him from thence. John Hocking said and swore he would not shoot but swore if we came aboard him he would send us.

Thus passing by him we came to an anchor something near his bark; Mr. Howland bid three of his men go cut his cable, whose names were John Irish, Thomas Savory and William Reinolds, who presently cut one but were put by the other by the strength of the stream. Mr. Howland seeing they could not well bring the canoe to the other cable called them aboard and bade Moses Talbot go with them who accordingly went very readily and brought the canoe to Hocking's cable; he being upon the deck came with a carbine and a pistol in his hand and presently presented his piece at Thomas Savory but the canoe with the tide was put near the bow of the bark which Hocking seeing presently put his piece almost to Moses Talbot's head, which Mr. Howland seeing called to him desiring him not to shoot his man but take himself for his mark saying his men did but that which he commanded them and therefore desired him not to hurt any of them; if any wrong was done it was himself that did it and therefore called again to him to take him for his mark saying he stood very fair; but Hocking would not hear nor look towards our bark but presently shooteth Moses in the head, and presently took up his pistol in his hand but the Lord stayed him from doing any further hurt by a shot from our bark; himself was presently struck dead being shot near the same place in the head where he had murderously shot Moses.

Petition of Edward Winslow to the Lord's Council, Written from Fleet Prison, London (1634)[401]

Your petitioner humbly beseecheth your Lordship's further to consider,
First. That whereas he confessed that he had both spoken by way of exhortation to the people and married, yet that it was in America and at such a time as necessity constrained them that were there not only to these but to many other things far differing from a settled commonwealth. And if he had been here would not have married nor should have needed to preach, as your Lordship's term it, but having no minister in 7 or 8 years at least, some of us must do both or else for want of the one, we might have lost the life and face of Christianity; and if the other which is marriage had been neglected all that time we might become more brutish than the heathen when as in doing it we did but follow the precedent of other reformed churches.

Second. That however we disliked many things in practice here in respect of church ceremony yet chose rather to leave the country than to be accounted troublers of it, and therefore went into Holland. And that from thence we procured a motion to be made to His Majesty of late and famous memory for liberty of conscience in America, under his gracious protection which His Majesty thinking very reasonable (as Sir Robert Naunton principal Secretary to the State in that time can testify) we cheerfully proceeded and afterwards procured a commission for the ordering of our body politic. And have so demeaned ourselves from that time to this and we can give a good account of our loyalty towards His Majesty and have showed loving respect and relief to others his subjects in their extremities.

Third. That we were so tender of His Majesty's honor as we would not enter into league with any of the natives that would not together with ourselves

---

[401]   Reprinted from *Proceedings of the Massachusetts Historical Society*, 5(1861):131-134.

acknowledge our Sovereign for their king as appeareth by a writing to that end, whereunto their known marks are prefixed.

Fourth. That however the main objection against us is that we are Brownists, Factious, Puritans, Schismatics, etc. If there be any position we hold contrary to the Word of God, contrary to the Royal honor of a king and due allegiance of a subject, then let His Majesty reject us and take all severe courses against us. But if we be found truly loyal we humbly entreat to be embraced and encouraged as subjects, and that we may still enjoy the gracious liberty granted by his Royal Father and hitherto enjoyed under His Majesty's happy government, who daily pray for His Majesty, his royal heirs and successors.

Fifth. That however we follow the discipline rather of other the reformed churches then this yet the accusation is false, that we require of those who join in church communion with us to censure the Church of England and her Bishops; all we require being to render by reason of that faith and hope they have in Christ which together with a good testimony of an honest life we admit them, not meddling further with the Church of England than as we are bound to pray for the good thereof.

Sixth. That the country of New England is fruitful where we live as well for English grain as Indian; the air temperate, agreeing with our bodies, the sea rich in fish, the havens commodious. The northern parts thereof for which we must content with the French, if this State enjoy them able to supply the navy of England with masts if need require. The Southern for which we contest with the Dutch being like to prove as serviceable for cordage by reason of the abundance of hemp and flax that groweth naturally; all which by our industry if His Majesty and the State be pleased to continue our liberty of conscience, to keep open the passage of such as will resort to us, and give us so free a commission for displanting French and Dutch as planting the places by us His Majesty's loyal subjects, your Honors shall soon see His Majesty's revenues of customs by reason of this Plantation enlarged many thousands per annum and this Kingdom supplied with many necessaries it wanteth, when as England shall only part with a part of her overcharged multitudes which she can better miss than bear and for which God hath plentifully provided in the other.

Seventh. Consider, I beseech your Lordships, what our adversaries that accuse us are, and you shall see them to be such as Morton who hath been twice sent hither as a delinquent, first for that he furnished the natives with pieces, powder and shot and taught them the use of them. Secondly by my

Lord Chief Justice Hide's warrant to answer to the murder of a person specified therein. Such like was Sir Christopher Gardiner, a knight of the Sepulcher and Jesuited gentleman as appeareth by a diary of his own under his hand which is extant in the country aforesaid. A third they offered the last year for testimony against us was one Dixie Bull who was out in piracy at the same time and after went to the French, etc. These and such like who are enemies to all goodness are the men that trouble and grieve the State with false accusations and cause them to be prejudiced against us the well-deserving subjects of his royal Majesty.

Eighth. Whereas they have formerly accused us unjustly with correspondency with the French and Dutch, themselves may justly be suspected who cannot do the French and Dutch better service than by going about to persuade the State here to deprive us of our liberty of conscience, granted as aforesaid, as also of our freedom of government, and set such a governor over us as will impose the same things upon us we went thither to avoid. And if your Lordships for want of due information, I speak with all submissive reverence, should send such a governor as between whom and the country there is personal distaste and difference, he might be more prejudicial to the plantations then the swords of French and Dutch which your petitioner humbly beseecheth your Lordships to consider.

Ninth. That we give a real testimony to our loyalty by the present possession we maintain by force at a great charge against the Dutch and the great losses we sustain by the French. In which cases I came to seek the pleasure of the State, being so tender of His Majesty's and your Lordship's displeasure, as we durst attempt no further design without your honorable approbation; yet assure myself Right Honorable the enemy durst not have attempted what is past nor threaten as at present and whereof I can inform, if it be desired, unless encouraged by some English.

Lastly. Consider I beseech your Honors that the same persons to whom as I conceive your Lordship's promised large commission for planting the country and displanting the French and Dutch, and which intend God permitting to use their best endeavor thereabout if your Lordships think meet to refer the ordering thereof to us that offer to bear the charge on those terms, do all now suffer by me their agent who cannot by reason of mine imprisonment provide a fit and seasonable supply for the Plantation or be assured any commission or encouragement but the contrary; when as the adversaries in the meantime have too great advantage against us, who by credible report intend to assault the Plantation this ensuing spring.

All which your petitioner humbly beseecheth your Lordships to take unto your honorable consideration, that a country so hopeful be not ruinated, His Majesty abused and his faithful subjects vexed and destroyed, and not only your petitioner but many thousands His Majesty's loyal subjects will be further bound to pray for a recompense of your honorable care.

Your Lordship's humble servant dejected by your displeasure,

Edward Winslow

Richard Andrews and John Beauchamp's Bill of Complaint, with James Sherley's Answer (1641)[402]

To the Right Honorable Sir Edward Littleton, knight Lord Keeper of the Great Seal of England.

In all humbleness complaining showeth unto your good lordship your daily orator Richard Andrews and John Beauchamp citizens and merchants of the city of London, that whereas in or about the year of our lord one thousand six hundred twenty five, twenty six and twenty seven there was a treaty and communication between your orators and one James Sherley citizen and goldsmith of the said city of London concerning their joining together to maintain a trade and adventure with the Governor and the rest of the partners of Plymouth Plantation in New England, the which proceeded so far as that it was at last fully concluded and agreed upon by and between themselves and the said James Sherley that they and each of them should adventure and put into stock to the purpose aforesaid the sum of eleven hundred pounds or thereabouts apiece and that the said James Sherley should receive and dispose thereof in and about the managing of the said trade and adventure and should be sole factor and agent in the said trade and adventure as well for your orators as himself in all respects concerning the same both for receipts of the said stocks here and laying out and dispose thereof as in the said business and for the receipts, sale and disposal of all goods, commodities and returns whatsoever in what kind soever the same repay the same unto your orator as aforesaid and that he may set forth whether he did not keep some notes, writings, books of accounts of and concerning his said dealings and proceedings and of the particulars of the several returns and quantities of beaver skins and other skins or goods which he had received as aforesaid

<hr />

[402] Public Records Office, Chancery Bills and Answers, Charles I. A39/51, 15 February 1640/1.

563

and that he may show forth and produce the same unaltered upon his oath and may . . . orators and either of them a just and true account of all his said dealings and proceedings aforesaid and may give and pay your orators and either of them their just and true shares and parts of the said adventure with damages since the same ought to have been paid and may make a full and perfect answer to all other and singular the aforesaid premises whereby your said orators may be received therein according . . . and that your orator may be relieved in the premises. May it therefore please your good lordship the premises considered to grant unto your orators His Majesty's most gracious writ of subpoena to be directed to the said Sherley commanding him thereby at a certain day and under a certain plain therein to be limited personally to be and appear before your good lordship in the high and honorable Court of Chancery then and there . . . premises and further and to stand to and abide such further order and direction therein as your lordship shall think most fit and convenient and your orators shall daily pray for your good health and . . .

Bowyer.

Jur. Xxx Martii 1641
      Ro: Riche

     The several answer of James Sherley defendant to the bill of complaint of Richard Andrews and John Beauchamp, complaintants.
     The said defendant saving to himself now and at all times hereafter all advantages and benefit of exceptions to the incertainty and insufficiency of the said complaintants bill for a full and perfect answer thereunto or to so much thereof as concerneth him this defendant to make answer unto. He saith that the said Richard Andrews (named for a complaintant in the said bill) liveth at Rotterdam in Holland. And saith that the said Richard Andrews before he went over to Rotterdam aforesaid told this defendant that the said complaintant John Beauchamp had spoken to him and said Andrews to join with him in suit against him, this defendant, but he the said Andrews refused and would not join with the said complaintant John Beauchamp. And therefore this defendant doth verily believe that if the said Richard Andrews knew that the other complaintant John Beauchamp did make him the said Andrews a party to this suit he the said Andrews would take it very ill there being no cause at all wherefore the said complaintants should put this defendant to the trouble and expense of a suit. For first this defendant absolutely denyeth that ever there was any such agreement made by, with or amongst the said

complaintants or either of them and him this defendant of putting in such a stock or adventure of £1100 a piece mentioned in the bill or any other sum whatsoever for the purpose in the bill mentioned for both they the said complaintants and also this defendant were at several times solicited and drawn into the adventure at the earnest persuasion of one Isaac Allerton, agent for the planters of Plymouth in New England mentioned in the bill. And for that end the said planters gave the said Allerton commission under their hands and seals and writ and gave letters of credit that what the said Allerton took up or procured they tied themselves to allow and make good and when the said Allerton had gotten in this defendant and the complaintants largely in adventure and in engagements the said Allerton told this defendant that the said complaintants that all would be lost if this defendant and the said complaintants did not enlarge their adventures by putting in greater sums of money. And this defendant denyeth that it was ever agreed or that he consented or undertook to be factor or agent for the complaintants in the said adventure or for any other but only for the said planters in their agent's absence. The said planters having their husband agent or factor here or sent one over from time to time as they had occasion who did or should have bought such goods as the said planters gave order for and usually the said planters gave their said agents commission under their hands and sometimes hands and seal of the town for that purpose to authorize him for their agent which the defendant never had. And for the receipts and sale of any of the goods the said planters they sent over their then agent Isaac Allerton who had the full power of buying, selling and receiving the same from the year 1626 to the year 1631 only they had the use of this defendant's house and warehouse and sometimes desired this defendant to receive and pay forth their moneys which he did for them of all which receipts and payments this defendant (by and with the help of the said Isaac Allerton the said planter's factor or agent) did make and deliver unto the said Isaac Allerton on their behalf a true and just account in writing and delivered a copy thereof unto one Edward Winslow a planter and at that time was also the general husband factor or agent for the said plantation in the room and place of the said Isaac Allerton. And in that account which this defendant thinketh beareth date the 16th of March 1631 it did appear that this defendant was really and truly out of purse the full sum of £1866, 3s, 4d. only he then accepted with proviso in case they were received by way of discount certain debts that were then owing to the said planters to the value of £675, 14s, 7d. which being deducted out of the aforesaid sum of £1866, 3s, 4d. there remains as debt due to this defendant the sum of £1190, 8s, 9d. And then upon the said account making this defendant gave unto the said complaintants a note of what he conceived either of them were out of purse which amounteth to the sum mentioned in the bill or thereabouts but before the making of such note this defendant showed to the complaintants a note of some particulars to have them rectify what they should find amiss concerning the said account which the said complaintants to this defendant's best remembrance did not do and this defendant denyeth that he received so much money of the said complaintant John Beauchamp for the said business and adventure as is mentioned in the bill but only the sum of £527, 4d. And further the said defendant denyeth that there was any agreement between him and the said complaintants or that he undertook to be factor or agent for the said complaintants or either of them as before is set forth but what he did was for the said planters and at their earnest request for he often desired the said planters and their agent by word of mouth and by letters to make choice of some other for it was too great a burden for him to undergo for that in the year 1633 this defendant sent to the said planters an abstract or brevet of the accounts betwixt the said planters and this defendant by which it appeared that this defendant was out of purse for the said planters £1200 and upwards more than his said adventure before the planter's commodities which they returned into England could be sold and the money got in for the same. And had it not been for the deep engagements of this defendant and the earnest request of the said complaintants he would have long ago left the said business. And this defendant denyeth that (to his knowledge or remembrance) he ever made any promise or agreement to and with the said complaintants for keeping any account for them for what he did was only for the said planters and to them he is ready to give an account of anything he hath received or done as he formerly did in the years 1623 and 1631: provided the said planters or their agents or some other deputed by them do make a just and particular account of the employment and proceed of the said adventures, for this defendant saith he conceiveth it is the said planter's part to render an account to them this defendant and the said complaintants and not the complaintants and this defendant to account one to another for it was always taken and conceived that the planters were on party and this defendant and the said complaintants the other. And this defendant further saith that what hath been received upon the account betwixt the planters and this defendant he this defendant cannot set down till the said planters or their agent and this defendant have conferred or compared their notes together and then he shall be ready and willing to show the said account or anything else that concerneth the said adventure to the said complaintants. And this defendant denyeth that he hath converted to his own use or sold away any of the goods or skins or any other commodities which he hath at any time received from the said planters but what he will bring to their account. And he further saith that he doth not remember that ever he sold any parcel of skins or other goods of any value since the making of his last account to the planters, but he acquainted the said complaintants or one of them with the sale thereof and desired his or their advise, and most commonly took the bills or bonds entered into for such goods in the names of the said complaintants and this defendant jointly and the said complaintants never seemed to dislike anything that this defendant did in the business. However there is but a debt of twelve pounds or thereabouts concerning the said account which this defendant thinketh to be desperate and for that there is a bond to be delivered to the said planters upon making up the said account. And this defendant is so ready and willing to come to an account with the said planters that he hath often writ unto the said planters and their agent factor or husband to come or send over that so all accounts might be made up and finished betwixt them. And further this defendant saith that he hath offered (as by copies of letters he can make appear) that if they desired it he would give them a meeting in any place in England, France or Holland that so all accounts concerning the said adventure might be settled for this defendant affirmeth that in making up both the said former accounts he had from time to time the help of the said planter's agent who for the most part did manning all the business here both in buying and selling. And they have delivered in this defendant several notes for commodities bought, in which other men had parts so as he cannot tell justly what to charge on their account without their assistance by reason whereof he keeps the notes, but hath not nor cannot book them. And likewise the beaver and other skins which they sent over other planters (some whereof had no share in the said adventure) had several parcels thereof delivered them some by their agent and some by letter so as this defendant cannot justly set forth what was received but by and with their help and assistance. And whereas the complaintants allege in their bill that he this defendant intendeth to deceive and defraud them of their dues he this defendant denyeth that he hath any such intention. Neither is it in his power so to do but in the said planters which he is persuaded they will not for he doth verily think and hope that when all accounts are drawn up and balanced betwixt the planters and this defendant that the said planters will be much in this defendant's debt as they were when both the former accounts were made up, and this defendant denyeth that he ever altered any notes or books of account as is most falsely pretended by the said bill whereby the complaintants might be any way wronged or damnified. And further this defendant confesseth that he hath and doth refuse to account with the said complaintants because as before is set forth he is not liable to give an account for anything received or done by him to any other but to the said planters, he having not received anything to enlarge the complaintants said adventure since the time of the making of the said last account which was in the said year 1631 from any other person or persons but from the said planters. And what is due unto the said complaintants or him this defendant the planters are to make good ratably as their several debts or adventures do arise. For if this defendant had any surplus of money as in the bill is surmised which he verily believeth he hath not (but that the said planters be much in his debts) he conceiveth he might not safely pay it to any person or persons without order and direction from the said planters. And the said defendant saith as before that upon the making up the account unto the said planters in the said year 1631 upon the changing of their agent or factor from Isaac Allerton to Edward Winslow which was in March 1631 he gave the said complaintants voluntarily and freely without any demand made by either of them a note out of the account which he delivered to the said planters or their agent of what he conceived the said planters owned either unto the said complaintants or to this defendant by reason of the said adventure, a true copy whereof he hath still to show; and the complaintant Beauchamp hath another comply also as this defendant verily believeth, whereby it appeareth that the said planters were debtors to the said complaintants and to this defendant and not this defendant a debtor to either of the said complaintants or to any of the planters so as under the favor of this honorable Court he conceives it very unconscionable and unjust for the said complaintants to require that of this defendant which in their own consciences they know he is not to be accountable for. For what sum or sums the complaintants did at any time lay forth or expend in and concerning the said adventure was for the said planters and not for this defendant as is falsely surmised in the said bill. And this defendant saith and confesseth that he and the complaintants John Beauchamp were bound in several bonds together to Mr. Hudson, Mr. Buttell, and Mr. Host for £600 but he doth not remember that he requested the complaintant Beauchamp to lay it down till moneys could be received in and concerning the said adventure, but this defendant paid the interest and some after in January 1631 he delivered unto the said complaintant three specialties of one Walter White amounting to the sum of £234. And this defendant saith that he and the said complaintant Beauchamp laid down £100 apiece to pay Derrick Host his debt but all thee . . . this defendant paid from time to time notwithstanding this defendant did then make it appear to the said complaintants and so the truth is that he this defendant was really out of purse for the said planters the sum of £480 and upwards because the years 1635 and 1636 were so sickly in and about London that this defendant could not sell the planters' commodities for their further satisfaction and delivered some in New England by their or one of their appointment and therefore this defendant hath done no wrong to the complaintant Beauchamp as is falsely suggested in the bill, but believeth he is fully satisfied the foresaid sums. And this defendant doth absolutely deny that ever he gave out in speeches that he had taken out his stock, debt or profit but wisheth he could truly have said so but now and as before in this his answer he saith that he doth verily believe that upon making up of the accounts it will appear that the said planters are still much in this defendants debt and more than they are indebted to either of the said complaintants by reason of the said planters' late sending and setting over goods unto the said complaintants towards satisfaction of their debts. And this defendant saith he doth verily believe the complaintant John Beauchamp did not deliver such sums of money toward the adventure as is specified in the said bill for that the said planters' agent Isaac Allerton did take some exceptions against the sum put in by the complaintant Beauchamp at or about the time that this defendant delivered up the account to the said Allerton in regard to the sum put in by the complaintant Beauchamp did appear to be but £777 or thereabouts. And this defendant saith that what skins, goods or commodities were sent over from New England into this Kingdom were sold and the proceeds returned back in divers other commodities which for the most part the said planters' agent bought or else towards payment of bills of exchange, debts and interest for the same; for the said complaintant Beauchamp and this defendant were engaged to several men for great sums besides their own adventure so as when this defendant made up the foresaid account in anno 1631 the said planters were indebted to several men above five thousand and nine hundred pounds which this defendant hath since endeavored to pay as much as in him lay so as what gains or profits hath been made must come from the said planters which what it is this defendant would as fain know as the complaintants but saith he doth not know nor indeed cannot know till the said planters and this defendant have met together or they have made up their account which when it comes to his hand he shall willingly show to the said complaintants. In the meantime he denyeth that he detained any part of the complaintant's share or profit in his this defendant's hands or custody to his knowledge as is surmised in the said bill of complaint. And further this defendant saith that he cannot find by any former account that ever the said complaintant Beauchamp paid in so much money as is specified in the said bill or note made by the said defendant for there . . . any agreement or contract made betwixt the said complaintants and him this defendant nor betwixt the said planters and the said complaintants and him this defendant what sum should be put into the adventure by them or either of them. But the adventure was voluntary and each of them might adventure more or less as they pleased, for the planters did not furnish any stock or adventure but the most part of the . . . defendant as he hath above expressed as the said planters at several times in their letters have acknowledged and what the complaintant Beauchamp is out of purse in and about the adventure this defendant cert . . . saith that the planters' agent Isaac Allerton sets down but £777, 4d. as this defendant hath to show of the said Allerton's writing as he verily believeth. And this defendant saith that in March 1630 he made . . . to Isaac Allerton, the planters' agent, he being then at Bristol and this defendant then desired the complaintant Beauchamp to give him a note how much he was out of purse for all did not come to the . . . as he could not make up the complaintant's account neither then nor now, and then the complaintant delivered this defendant a note in general that he was out concerning the said adventure £1086, 18s, 7d. and from that . . . hath this defendant ever since made up the said Beauchamp's debt or some adventured but how true that note which the complaintant Beauchamp so delivered to this defendant was this defendant knoweth not nor the several . . . but how much this defendant hath upon his own adventure he hath set down before and the books and former accounts will justify. A copy whereof was delivered to the said planters or their . . . thereof and for the returns and proceeds from the said planters it will appear when the accounts be made up betwixt the said planters and this defendant. And as for the converting of . . . he this defendant saith that when the planters' commodities were sold and money received for the same he might perhaps use some part thereof for his own occasions as he had often lent . . . great sums to supply their occasions and many times he lent to the complaintant Beauchamp some of the planters' money he having done often the like to them and sometimes . . . other friends which he is liable to make good to the said planters upon account without that that any other matter or thing in the said bill of complaint contained material . . . this defendant to answer unto and not herein sufficiently answered unto, confessed and avoided, traversed or denied is true, all which matters and things this defendant is ready to . . . honorable Court shall award. And humbly prayeth to be dismissed out of the same with his reasonable costs and charges in this behalf wrongfully and without cause.

Appendix II
The Mayflower *Passengers*

The *Mayflower* Passengers

JOHN ALDEN. Born about 1599, possibly from Harwich, co. Essex. *Mayflower*'s cooper. Married fellow *Mayflower* passenger Priscilla Mullins about 1623.

ISAAC ALLERTON. Born about 1586, possibly near Ipswich, co. Suffolk. Tailor, merchant. Brought wife Mary (Norris), and children Bartholomew, Remember, and Mary. Wife Mary died the first winter.

JOHN ALLERTON. Perhaps a relative of Isaac. Lived for a time in Leiden. Seaman. Died the first winter.

JOHN BILLINGTON. Born about 1580, probably near Cowbit or Spaulding, co. Lincolnshire. Husbandman, woodsman. Brought wife Eleanor and children John and Francis. Hanged for murder, 1630.

WILLIAM BRADFORD. Baptized 19 March 1589/90, Austerfield, Yorkshire. Husbandman in England, fustian weaver in Leiden, governor at Plymouth. Brought wife Dorothy (May). She accidentally fell off the *Mayflower* and drowned shortly after arrival.

WILLIAM BREWSTER. Born about 1565, near Scrooby, co. Nottingham. Student at Cambridge. Secretary to William Davison, the Secretary of State under Queen Elizabeth. Postmaster of Scrooby. Church Elder in Leiden and Plymouth. Brought wife Mary, and children Love and Wrestling.

RICHARD BRITTERIDGE. Age and origin unknown; perhaps from vicinity of Crowhurst, co. Sussex. Died the first winter, 21 December 1620.

PETER BROWNE. Baptized 26 January 1594/5, at Dorking, co. Surrey. Possibly a weaver.

WILLIAM BUTTEN. A "youth," servant to Dr. Samuel Fuller. Died on the *Mayflower's* voyage, three days before land was sighted.

ROBERT CARTER. Likely a teenager. Servant to William Mullins. Died the first winter.

JOHN CARVER. Age unknown, but apparently married by 1609. Deacon. First governor of Plymouth. Died April 1621 of apparent sunstroke. Brought wife Katherine (White).

JAMES CHILTON. Born about 1556, probably Canterbury, co. Kent. Brought wife (name unknown: some secondary sources published as early as 1841 call her Susanna), and daughter Mary. He and wife died the first winter.

RICHARD CLARKE. Age, origin and occupation unknown.

FRANCIS COOKE. Born about 1583, possibly near Norwich, co. Norfolk. Brought son John, leaving wife and other children to come over later. Woolcomber in Leiden, husbandman and surveyor at Plymouth.

HUMILITY COOPER. Born 1619. One-year old girl, came in the custody of aunt and uncle, Ann and Edward Tilley.

JOHN CRACKSTON. Born about 1570, likely near Stratford St. Mary, co. Suffolk, where he was married. Brought son John. Died the first winter.

EDWARD DOTY. Born about 1599. Came as a servant to Stephen Hopkins.

FRANCIS EATON. Baptized 11 September 1596, St. Thomas, Bristol, co. Gloucester. House carpenter. Brought wife Sarah, and suckling child Samuel. Wife Sarah died the first winter.

THOMAS ENGLISH. Age, origin and occupation unknown. Died the first winter.

MOSES FLETCHER. Born about 1565, probably near Canterbury, co. Kent. Died the first winter. Left behind children in Leiden.

EDWARD FULLER. Baptized 4 September 1575, Redenhall, co. Norfolk. Son of a butcher. Brother of Samuel Fuller. Brought wife (name unknown: some secondary sources as early as 1860 call her Ann), and son Samuel. Died the first winter.

SAMUEL FULLER. Baptized 20 January 1580, Redenhall, co. Norfolk. Son of a butcher. Deacon. Doctor at Plymouth.

RICHARD GARDINAR. Perhaps the man bp. 12 February 1582 at Harwich, co. Essex. Became a seaman and returned to England.

JOHN GOODMAN. Age, origin and occupation unknown. Perhaps from Everdon, Northamptonshire.

WILLIAM HOLBECK. Under 21 years at the time of the voyage. Came as a servant to William White. Died the first winter.

JOHN HOOKE. Born about 1607, likely near St. Peter Mancroft, Norwich, co. Norfolk. Apprenticed to Isaac Allerton. Died the first winter.

STEPHEN HOPKINS. Baptized 30 April 1581, Upper Clatford, co. Hampshire. Shopkeeper, minister's clerk. Brought wife Elizabeth (Fisher) and children Constance and Giles (by earlier wife Mary), and Damaris (by wife Elizabeth). Son Oceanus was born enroute. Previously had been shipwrecked on the Bermudas and then spent several years at Jamestown, Virignia.

JOHN HOWLAND. Born about 1599. Married *Mayflower* passenger Elizabeth Tilley in 1624. Came as servant to Gov. John Carver. Husbandman, fur trader.

JOHN LANGMORE. Under 21 years at the time of the voyage. Servant to Christopher Martin family. Died the first winter.

WILLIAM LATHAM. Born about 1609, perhaps from Eccleston by Chorley, co. Lancashire. Servant to Gov. John Carver family, and later the Gov. Bradford family. Wife Mary was executed for adultery, 1643. Returned to England, then went to the Bahamas where he died of starvation about 1647.

EDWARD LEISTER. Born about 1595-1599. Came as servant to Stephen Hopkins. Left Plymouth for Virginia about 1623.

EDMUND MARGESSON. Age and origin unknown, but was an adult, perhaps from Swinnington, co. Norfolk. Died the first winter.

CHRISTOPHER MARTIN. Born about 1580, from Great Burstead, Billericay, co. Essex. Merchant. Brought wife Mary (Prower) and step-son Solomon Prower.

DESIRE MINTER. A young girl, exact age unknown. Parents were from Norwich, co. Norfolk. After her father died, she was raised by John Carver.

ELLEN, JASPER, RICHARD and MARY MORE. The More children were all baptized at Shipton, co. Shropshire, England, in 1612, 1613, 1614, and 1616, respectively. They were placed in the custody of leading Plymouth men (Brewster, Winslow, Carver) following the bitter divorce of their parents that resulted in their father shipping them off to America. All but Richard died the first winter.

WILLIAM MULLINS. Born about 1572, likely at Dorking, co. Surrey. Shoe and boot dealer. Brought wife Alice, and children Priscilla and Joseph. All but Priscilla died the first winter.

DEGORY PRIEST. Born about 1579. Hatter. Married to Sarah Allerton, sister of Isaac Allerton, but left her and two children behind in Leiden. Died the first winter.

JOHN RIGSDALE. Age and origin unknown. Brought wife Alice. Possibly from St. Mary, Weston, Lincolnshire.

THOMAS ROGERS. Born about 1572, probably near Watford, co. Northampton. Left wife Alice and three children behind in Leiden, but brought son Joseph. Died the first winter.

HENRY SAMSON. Baptized 15 January 1603/4, Henlow, co. Bedford. Came in the custody of his uncle and aunt Edward and Ann Tilley.

GEORGE SOULE. Born about 1595-1599. Possibly from Tingrith, co. Bedford. Came as servant to Edward Winslow.

MYLES STANDISH. Born about 1584 or 1587, likely in Lancashire. Soldier and lieutenant in English army, militia captain at Plymouth. Brought wife Rose, who died the first winter.

ELIAS STORY. Under the age of 21. Servant to Edward Winslow. Died the first winter.

EDWARD THOMPSON. Under the age of 21. Servant in the William White family. Died the first winter.

EDWARD TILLEY. Baptized 27 May 1588, Henlow, co. Bedford. Brought wife Ann (Cooper). Brother of John Tilley. Both Edward and Ann died the first winter.

JOHN TILLEY. Baptized 19 December 1571, Henlow, co. Bedford. Brought wife Joan (Hurst) and daughter Elizabeth. Brother of Edward Tilley. John and Joan both died the first winter.

THOMAS TINKER. Age and origin unknown, but possibly from Thurne, co. Norfolk. Wood sawyer. Brought wife and son (names unknown.) All died the first winter.

WILLIAM TREVORE. Adult, origin unknown. Returned to England in 1621.

JOHN TURNER. Age, origin, and occupation unknown. Brought two sons (names unknown). All died the first winter.

RICHARD WARREN. Born about 1580, probably in co. Hertford. Merchant. Left wife and five daughters behind in England.

WILLIAM WHITE. Age, origin, and occupation unknown. Came with wife Susanna, and son Resolved. Son Peregrine was born onboard the ship after it had arrived. William died the first winter. Susanna remarried in May 1621 to Edward Winslow.

ROGER WILDER. Under 21 years of age. Servant to Gov. John Carver. Died the first winter.

THOMAS WILLIAMS. Baptized 12 August 1582, Great Yarmouth, co. Norfolk. Died the first winter.

EDWARD WINSLOW. Born 18 October 1595, Driotwich, co. Worcester. Printer. Governor at Plymouth. Brother of Gilbert Winslow. Brought wife Elizabeth (Barker). She died the first winter. Edward remarried in 1621 to Susanna, widow of William White.

GILBERT WINSLOW. Baptized 29 October 1600, St. Peters, Droitwich, co. Worcester. Brother of Edward Winslow.

Index

D

E

F

L

M

N

O

P

Pliny, 197
Plooij
  Daniel, 50
plum, 469, 508
Plymouth, 15, 21, 22, 72, 80, 86, 102,
    106, 115, 134, 135, 144, 145,
    161, 164, 170, 182, 225, 232,
    235, 236, 241, 244, 245, 247,
    249, 252, 259, 270, 277, 288,
    289, 295, 300, 307, 309, 316,
    322, 328, 340, 367, 369, 370,
    373, 377, 383, 394, 396, 406,
    407, 409, 410, 411, 412, 415,
    420, 421, 437, 440, 444, 445,
    446, 448, 458, 480, 489, 493,
    498, 502, 510, 534, 537, 541, 551
Plymouth Rock, 471
Pocahontas, 57, 454
Pocanocket, 134, 135
pockets, 453
Pocock
  John, 236
poem, 92, 186
poetry, 257
Point Care, 110
Pointon
  Daniel, 236
poison, 194, 413
Pokanoket, 134, 437, 489, 490, 492,
    494, 500, 552
politic, 84, 99, 127, 413, 443, 448,
    551, 559
political, 324
Polyander, 52
Pomham, 424
pond, 116, 368, 452, 461, 465, 480,
    538, 540
Pontus
  William, 363

pope, 68, 302
popery, 27, 36
popish, 30, 32, 33, 374
Portugal, 285, 297
Pory
  John, 109, 120, 163, 164
pot, 108, 145, 168, 452, 455, 460,
    469, 484, 549
potashes, 528
poultry, 188
powah, 136
pox, 107, 330
Pratt
  Joshua, 247, 540, 544
  Phineas, 128, 136, 167, 168, 247,
    540, 544
pray, 66, 146, 552, 570
prayer, 18, 45, 59, 64, 66, 73, 79, 91,
    100, 106, 119, 179, 216, 224,
    230, 278, 279, 314, 323, 345,
    404, 439, 443, 466, 513
prayerful, 22
preach, 211, 213, 345, 515, 559
preacher, 32, 35, 37, 38, 52, 97, 191,
    196, 402, 516
predestination, 51
prelate, 36
prelate-like, 32
Prence
  Patience, 546
  Rebecca, 546
  Thomas, 22, 247, 309, 322, 323,
    375, 376, 377, 394, 396, 399,
    415, 538, 546, 548
pretty, 141, 149, 161, 182, 189, 256,
    334, 454, 460
Price
  David, 57
pride, 27, 33, 209, 246, 351

Q

R

Rande
    James, 540
random, 499
ransom, 416, 417
rape, 387, 388
rapier, 302, 355, 363, 428, 429
rascal, 202
Rasieres
    Isaac de, 173, 243, 254
raspberries, 508
rat, 85, 493
Ratcliffe
    Robert, 540
rebellion, 32, 204, 326
rebels, 99, 202, 215, 443
recantation, 221
red, 452, 458, 483, 486, 488, 508
reed-pond, 540
Reformed Churches, 21, 67, 221, 521
regiment, 30, 105
Rehoboth, 369
Reinolds
    William, 557
religion, 33, 35, 36, 40, 60, 140, 193,
        327, 391, 393, 402, 404, 406,
        506, 516, 553
rent, 72, 309, 517, 526, 542
rent-gatherer, 526
repugnant, 543, 554
Revell
    John, 236
revenge, 134, 136, 142, 168, 328,
        349, 354, 413, 416, 437, 498,
        500, 535
Reynolds
    William, 87, 101, 159, 534
Reynor
    John, 350, 385
rice, 510

Rickett
    Giles, 363
rigging, 214
Riggs
    Edward, 359
Rigsdale
    Alice, 431
    John, 125, 431, 434, 576
    Mrs. Alice, 576
Ring
    Mary, 106
    William, 102, 106
ringleader, 362
riotous, 258
river, 91, 100, 115, 178, 227, 243,
        253, 300, 302, 315, 316, 318,
        320, 333, 340, 348, 351, 359,
        367, 368, 370, 406, 443, 446,
        450, 452, 456, 461, 464, 468,
        469, 470, 490, 491, 494, 504,
        508, 523, 551
rivulet, 552
road, 381, 464, 482, 530
Roanoke, 57, 59
roaring, 109, 476
roast, 494
roasted, 491, 494
Robinson
    John, 38, 41, 47, 48, 49, 52, 53,
        54, 55, 63, 65, 66, 67, 69, 71,
        75, 78, 81, 83, 96, 100, 104,
        140, 146, 164, 194, 196, 197,
        202, 207, 221, 228, 229, 230,
        444, 522
Rochelle, 529
rock, 189, 302, 468, 504
Rogers
    Joseph, 431, 434, 538, 540, 548,
        576

T

W

Y

Z

Printed in the United States
67553LVS00001B/1-3